WH TO FINU BIRDS IN AUSTRALIA

What they said about *Where to Find Birds in Australia...*

'This is exactly the kind of guide that Australian and overseas visitors need. It contains a mass of accurate, first-hand information, compressed into usable form, and would make an ideal companion to my *Field Guide to the Birds of Australia.'*
Graham Pizzey

'I would recommend *Where to Find Birds in Australia* to anyone who is at all interested in Australian wild life... with the warning that, once started, it is very difficult to put aside'
Virginia Morrison, *The Bird Observer*

'It is a useful, practical book which fills a glaring hole in the Australian ornithological literature'
Scott O' Keefe, *Sunbird*

'... he has that wonderful ability to write a diary / travelogue that is far from boring. It is, in fact, a comprehensive and reliable traveller's guide to the birdlife of Australia'
Barry Larkman, Society for Growing Australian Plants

'The glove-box size, the wealth of information and its easy-to-read style all support Peter Slater's contention that this book is a classic in the making'
South Australian National Parks Association

'... this book is a must for any birder in Australia, resident or visitor'
P. Latham, Ornithological Society of New Zealand

JOHN BRANSBURY

WHERE TO FIND BIRDS IN AUSTRALIA

Waymark

First published in 1987 by Century Hutchinson Australia
Reprinted in 1992 by Waymark Publishing Australia
Reprinted with Author's Note in 2000

Editor: Margaret Barrett
Designed by Derrick I. Stone Design
Cartography by Greg Dunnett
Current cover design by Quick Brown Dog Productions

Original typesetting by Setrite Typesetters Ltd, Hong Kong
Typesetting, layout and colour separation for this reprint
by Graphics '91 Pte. Ltd, Singapore
Printed by Kyodo Printing Co. Ltd, Singapore

National Library of Australia
Cataloguing-in-Publication Data
Bransbury, John
    Where to find birds in Australia

    Bibliography.
    Includes index.
    ISBN 0 646 12677 6

    1. Bird watching - Australia. 2. Birds - Australia
      - Geographical distribution. I. Title

    598.0723494

Waymark Publishing is an imprint of
7th Wave Creative Publishing
Northiam, East Sussex, TN31 6PW, U.K.

Contents

Preface

This book is essentially a guide for travellers, and it should enable you to find your way to many of the best bird-watching sites in Australia. Though not a book of identification, it is portable enough to be used in the field in conjunction with Graham Pizzey's *A Field Guide to the Birds of Australia,* or *The Slater Field Guide to Australian Birds*, or another of the bird identification books currently available.

The format is quite straightforward; each state or territory has its own chapter, and each chapter is divided into sections dealing with different regions. There are fifty-three sections in all. Eight cover the capital cities, while the remainder feature regions such as the Victorian Mallee, the Snowy Mountains, Cairns and the Atherton Tableland, Tasmania's South-West, the Flinders Ranges, the Kimberley, and Alice Springs and the MacDonnell Ranges. In all but the capital city sections sites are grouped where possible to form holiday units, providing the visitor with a wide range of habitats and birds.

For the most part, the bird names used in this book are those recommended by the Royal Australasian Ornithologists Union ('Recommended English Names for Australian Birds', supplement to Emu, 77, 1978, pp. 245-307). The keen-eyed reader will notice that I have not mentioned introduced species like House Sparrow and Common Starling anywhere in the text. The only reason for this is that I personally would not travel any distance to see such birds, and I have assumed that most bird-watchers feel the same way. Where appropriate I have given an indication of a bird's seasonal status in a particular area; bear in mind, however, that the movements of quite a number of Australian birds are somewhat erratic - don't be surprised if every now and then you find a species in winter in an area where I have indicated it occurs in summer, or vice versa.

In general I have tried to avoid lengthy bird lists, mentioning only those species that I consider you have a reasonable chance of seeing. But there are exceptions. Some areas are so rich in birds that I had difficulty deciding which species to leave out; after all, what you or I might regard as commonplace another observer might consider really special. And there are places where I have listed rare or seldom-seen species, especially waders and seabirds, because I feel it is helpful if you know what has been recorded at a particular spot; then at least you can consult your field guide and be on the lookout for something unusual.

Lastly, if you are new to bird-watching and this is the first bird book that you have acquired, I suggest that you buy at least one of the two field guides mentioned earlier as well as one or more of the other general titles listed under Further Reading at the end of this book. In addition, Rosemary Balmford's *Learning about Australian Birds* (Collins, Sydney, 1980), J. D. Macdonald's *Australian Birds - a popular guide to bird life* (revised edn, Reed Books, Sydney, 1985), and Ian Rowley's *Bird Life* (Collins, Sydney, 1975) all contain a great deal of useful information for beginners - and indeed for experienced observers wishing to broaden their horizons.

Hints for beginners

- Bird-watching is a relatively inexpensive hobby: all you really need to start with is a field guide and a moderately priced pair or two of binoculars: 8 x 30 for looking at bush birds, and perhaps also a more powerful pair, say 10 x 50, for watching waterfowl, waders, seabirds and other groups of species that can be difficult to approach closely.

- To begin with you may have difficulty identifying similar-looking species, even with the aid of binoculars. Start by becoming thoroughly acquainted with all the birds that frequent your neighbourhood; when you look carefully you will be amazed just how many species there are in your local area.

- Learn to judge size accurately – is the bird small like a thorn-bill, medium-sized like a wattlebird, or large like a raven? Look closely at the bird's essential features and note the colour, length and shape of its bill, the colour and size of its eye, the colour and length of its legs, and the length and shape of its tail. Study its plumage and look for distinctive markings such as eyebrows, wingbars and breastbands. Remember that most birds, even closely related species, differ in some way.

- Make a habit of carrying your field guide and a notebook with you when out birding, and get to know the main bird groups so that you can turn quickly to the section of your field guide that deals with the type of bird you are looking at. If in doubt take notes and make rough sketches.

- It helps if you know the sort of habitat a bird prefers and, since most birds spend a good deal of time feeding, where it obtains its food. Try to become familiar, too, with bird calls (some bird-watching societies, the Bird Observers Club for example, sell a wide range of cassettes featuring them).

- If you are planning a trip to a different part of your state, or to another state, don't wait until you reach your destination before reading up on the birds you are likely to encounter. If you know in advance what to look for, you have a much better chance of seeing new birds as you travel from place to place.

- Every so often you will come across a bird that doesn't exactly match any of the illustrations in your field guide, or one that appears to be far outside its known range. Before claiming a new record for Australia or your state, remember that no book can illustrate every conceivable plumage form - there are simply too many variables. For instance, if it's a migratory wader or oceanic seabird you are looking at, the bird's strange appearance may merely be the result of worn plumage (most of the wader species found in Australia breed in the northern hemisphere and fly great distances to reach our shores). Or the bird may simply be a female, juvenile, or even an aberrant form of a species that is quite usual in the area.

- Last but by no means least, do consider joining one or more of the bird-watching clubs mentioned in this book. You will meet lots of like-minded people, and benefit greatly from the experience of others.

Author's Note

Sooner or later guides like this one show their age. Thus, when weighing up the pros and cons of reprinting this book, its usefulness 13 years after it was first published had to be my first consideration. In the end I decided that another reprint was worthwhile.

Needless to say, when using this book you should keep in mind that some of the bird information it contains might now be out of date. For example, the numbers of some species may have declined since the late 1980s, in which case these birds may be more difficult to find. On the other hand, successful conservation programmes may have resulted in some scarce species becoming more plentiful in recent years, thus these birds may be easier to locate than I suggest. All in all, however, many of the birds mentioned in this book probably occur in much the same numbers, and in more or less the same places, as they did 10 or 15 years ago.

As regards the site information, a great many of the localities included in this book are reserves of one sort or another; in theory these sites should be protected from degradation. In a few places reserves may have been damaged by development, but for the most part they will have been improved - in the eyes of the majority of visitors that is - with better access, better facilities, more rangers, and more information such as bird lists. Bush fires are an ever-present threat to many of Australia's reserves, and while most people accept that fires play an important part in shaping Australia's environment, it is still a sad experience to arrive at a national park only to find a once beautiful forest reduced to blackened, smouldering stumps. Fires can occur at any time, of course, even within weeks or months of a book like this being published - if you are planning a trip to some far-off reserve, it would pay to check its condition in advance.

If you visit the sites mentioned in this guide that are not protected, you can expect some changes to have taken place. In particular, sites in and around the capital cities may have gone completely (e.g. wetlands may have been filled in) or been reduced in size and importance.

Finally, birdwatching is now a very popular pastime in many parts of the world so that today there is a huge range of binoculars and telescopes for the birder to choose from, as well as a wealth of bird identification books. Since this book first appeared, several more field guides have been published in Australia - these are listed below.

Good birding.
J.B. September 2000

Some more useful books

The Slater Field Guide to Australian Birds. Revised edn. 1993

The Graham Pizzey & Frank Knight Field Guide to the Birds of Australia. 1997

Field Guide to the Birds of Australia. Ken Simpson & Nicolas Day. 6th edn. 1999

Field Guide to Australian Birds. Michael Morcombe. 2000

Acknowledgements

Over the past three years or so a great many people have helped me in a variety of ways. For their kindness, assistance and advice I thank Margaret Blakers, Walter Boles, Sandra Beaumont, Dawn Magarry, John Crowhurst, Roger Pink, Leo Joseph, Lena Dunkley, Mark Bonnin, John and Kathy Truran, Chris and Diana Harte, Shapelle McNee, Doug Watkins, Graeme Folley, Ron Johnstone, Nick Dymond, Ron Van Delft, John McKean, Keith Thomas, Andrew Isles, Brett Lane, Jack Bourne, Richard Phillips, Brian Clark, Leigh Ahern, Rex Ellis, Dick Cooper, Mike Newman, Eric Bull, Lois Padgham, Martine Timmins, John, Maria, Joanne and Kathy Nikas, Edie, and my parents. Special thanks go to Roger Jaensch, Field Officer, Royal Australasian Ornithologists Union, Perth, who gave me a large amount of material for the Western Australian chapter. I am sure there are some people whose names I have forgotten - if you helped me in any way you have my sincere gratitude.

I managed to get to most of the places mentioned in this book, but there were some, notably Christmas Island and the Cocos (Keeling) Islands, that for one reason or another I could not reach. My accounts of these islands are therefore based largely on information supplied by Tony Stokes, Government Conservator, Christmas Island. I am greatly indebted to him for giving me so much useful material; any errors or omissions, however, are entirely my responsibility.

I am very grateful for the assistance given by the staff of the following government departments and organisations: the Australian National Parks and Wildlife Service; the Victorian National Parks Service; the National Parks and Wildlife Services of New South Wales, Queensland, Tasmania and South Australia; the Western Australian Department of Conservation and Land Management; the Australian Capital Territory Parks and Conservation Service; the Conservation Commission of the Northern Territory; the various museums around Australia, particularly the Queensland Museum, the Western Australian Museum and the Queen Victoria Museum, Launceston, Tasmania; the State Library of South Australia, especially the periodicals section and the map room; the Lord

Howe Island Board; the Christmas Island Services Corporation; the Cocos (Keeling) Islands Administration; and the various state government tourist bureaux and travel centres. Thanks are also due to the doctors, nurses and staff of the Maryborough Base Hospital for looking after me so well following a slight mishap I suffered in North Queensland.

I particularly wish to record my deep gratitude to the committee of the South Australian Ornithological Association for allowing me unrestricted use of the association's extensive library. Societies such as the SAOA do much to advance our understanding of Australian birds and to protect them; if you have not already done so, I urge you to join your local bird club. I also freely acknowledge my debt to the authors of the numerous papers, articles and notes published by Australia's ornithological societies, and of the wealth of books and other publications housed in their libraries.

Finally, I would especially like to thank Elizabeth Douglas who, as Editorial Director of Century Hutchinson, gave me the opportunity to write this book and who encouraged me at every stage; and Margaret Barrett, my editor, who has been involved with the book right from the beginning and whose keen, experienced eye has saved me from many a slip.

This book is dedicated to all who are working to conserve Australia's wild places.

Introduction

While planning this book I had only one main aim in mind – to produce an up-to-date, easy-to-follow guide featuring as many of the best bird-watching sites in Australia as possible, a guide giving details of where to go to look for birds, how to get to the places mentioned, where to stay, the ideal time of year for a visit, and of course what species you can expect to see once you arrive at your destination. It is basically a book for those who find bird-watching an absorbing pastime because it can be enjoyed just about anywhere, and can lead them to new and exciting places.

If you are contemplating a birding trip, whether it be a half-day excursion to your local park or a lengthy journey to one of the more remote corners of the continent, I hope that you will be encouraged by what I have written, and that the information provided will be of use. By way of an appetiser, so to speak, here are a few notes taken from the diaries I kept while travelling around Australia collecting the material that forms the basis of this book.

9 February 1984. Mt Field National Park, Tasmania: Started raining heavily just as I finished packing away the tent. Drove to Maydena, then on to the South West National Park where I found a delightful camping spot on the edge of a patch of forest, at the end of Scotts Peak Road. Managed to get the tent erected and tea cooked between downpours, but the rain continued on and off all night.

10 February 1984. Huon River camping ground, South West National Park, Tasmania: Day began dry but very overcast. Just finished breakfast before it started to rain in earnest; remainder of day cold, dark and wet. Even so I set out mid-morning back along Scotts Peak Road to search for the elusive Ground Parrot, which to my surprise I found on my first attempt while walking through an area of swampy buttongrass. A long-tailed, medium-sized parrot, the bird flew fast and low over the buttongrass for a short distance before dropping back into the dense cover. Managed to flush it three times in all, then it disappeared into a particularly thick patch of vegetation. A day to remember – despite the miserable conditions.

23 June 1984. Waterfall Creek Nature Park, Northern Territory: A warm to hot day – not a cloud in the sky. After an overnight stay at the Yellow Water camping area in Kakadu National Park, where the birds were outnumbered only by mosquitoes, moved on to Waterfall Creek and made camp a short distance from a patch of luxuriant monsoon forest adjoining a clear, deep waterhole. Enjoyed a refreshing dip late in the afternoon, then scrambled to the top of the escarpment overlooking our campsite. There to greet me was a party of White-throated Grasswrens! What luck. I had scarcely regained my breath when the birds, five of them, came scurrying over the boulders to within a few metres of where I was standing. And what handsome creatures they are − so richly coloured and somewhat larger than I had expected. Fascinated by their activities, I stood and watched the birds for ten minutes or more before they moved on.

24 June 1984. Waterfall Creek Nature Park, Northern Territory: Rose early and took Edie to the top of the escarpment to show her the grasswrens. But they were nowhere to be seen, and after an hour or so we returned to camp and spent the remainder of the morning birding in and around the monsoon forest. Here we found plenty of interesting species, among them a delightful Emerald Dove, a lone Rainbow Pitta, and a charming White-browed Robin. We also found plenty of evidence of human activity. It is indeed a great pity that some thoughtless people, by leaving behind litter and other signs of their presence, spoil such places as Waterfall Creek not only for other campers, but more importantly for the many birds that make their homes there.

26 August 1984. O'Reilly's, Lamington National Park, Queensland: Awoke to a bright, sunny day. After breakfast walked for several hours along the Border Track, which commences near the guest house and passes through magnificent stands of subtropical rainforest as well as areas of temperate rainforest dominated by Antarctic beech. Returned to camp for lunch, then spent the afternoon − and two rolls of film − photographing the three or four male Regent Bowerbirds that frequent the camping ground. Resplendent in black and gold, the bowerbirds are highly photogenic but difficult to capture on film, not because they hide in the forest like the Wonga Pigeons, but because in their eagerness to see what you have to offer by way of food they often approach too near to allow accurate focusing. And a picture of a bowerbird perched on the picnic table examining the leftovers of my lunch isn't exactly what I want!

26 April 1985. Lord Howe Island: Unfortunately it has been raining virtually non-stop since I arrived here four days ago. Today the sun shone brightly, however, and I made the most of it and cycled down past the aerodrome to the southern part of the island. Along the track that skirts the lower slopes of Mt Lidgbird I had little difficulty finding the Lord Howe Island Woodhen. One of the islanders had told me that if I called out as I walked along the track, the woodhens would almost certainly emerge from the forest to investigate the cause of the disturbance. Though somewhat sceptical I did as I was told; sure enough a woodhen appeared right on cue and, while I hurriedly got the camera ready, proceeded to peck at my binoculars, which were lying at my feet.

A short while later I had a similar experience, this time with a seabird − a Providence Petrel. I had read that early in the breeding season the petrels can be called down to land by shouting loudly, so I climbed a little way up Mt Lidgbird and yelled at the top of my voice. At first the birds, which were present in large numbers wheeling and calling overhead, took no notice, but after a few minutes one or two circled close to me. Then, to my astonishment, one landed a few metres from where I was standing and fluttered towards me. I could have reached out and touched it; only at such close range can you appreciate what a beautiful bird the Providence Petrel is, with its soft, dove-like face and bright, gentle eyes. I didn't repeat the exercise, fearing that the petrels might injure themselves − after all they are oceanic creatures, built for flying not walking.

28 April 1985. Lord Howe Island: Another fine sunny day, though regrettably my last on this wonderful island. In the early evening I walked to Malabar, north of where I am staying, and sat for an hour or so at the top of the sheer coastal cliffs overlooking Sugarloaf Passage. Red-tailed Tropicbirds glided to and fro along the edge of the cliff, and there were a number of Masked Boobies sitting (on nests?) on an island just offshore. I sat there until sunset when the waters of the ocean far below turned gold, providing a fitting end to a brief but most memorable stay on what must surely be one of the loveliest islands in the world.

31 May 1985. Porongurup National Park, Western Australia: Left Albany early in the morning and drove to the Tree in the Rock picnic area, Porongurup National Park. Enjoyed a pleasant three-hour walk to Nancy Peak via Hayward Peak, then returned to Tree in the Rock for a well-earned 'cuppa'. There were several White-breasted Robins flitting about in the forest surrounding the picnic ground, but the Rufous Treecreepers that the ranger had told us to look out for were nowhere to be seen. We decided to try the Bolganup Dam picnic area, a short distance back along the entrance road. Here we had no difficulty finding the birds; there were two or three foraging on the ground, and a couple doing what treecreepers are supposed to do − creeping mouse-like up the trunks of trees. Obtained some good photographs before a rather noisy group of picnickers arrived and the treecreepers retreated into the forest.

14 August 1986. The Chalet, Mt Buffalo National Park, Victoria:
Since we arrived here the days have been warm and sunny, the

nights cold and clear. But last night it snowed heavily, and this morning the view from the guest house is very different — the distant mountains which only yesterday stood out sharply beneath a deep blue sky are almost completely shrouded in cloud, and everywhere the countryside is white not green. These are the alps that we came to see. Having donned our warmest winter gear we set out briskly along the track to Wilkinsons Lookout, not far from The Chalet. Given the chilly conditions we certainly didn't expect to see any birds. But we were wrong — en route to the lookout we were treated to good views of a Superb Lyrebird as it raked about in the snow beside the track, and a little further on we were surprised and delighted to find a pair of Pilotbirds busily feeding in an area that had somehow escaped the night's wintery blast.

Chapter

1

Victoria

Useful addresses

Royal Australasian Ornithologists Union
21 Gladstone Street
Moonee Ponds, Vic. 3039

Bird Observers Club
PO Box 185
Nunawading, Vic. 3131
(The BOC has a shop at 183 Springvale Road, Nunawading.)

Victorian Ornithological Research Group
c/- Curator of Birds, Museum of Victoria
71 Victoria Crescent
Abbotsford, Vic. 3067

Australasian Wader Studies Group
Secretary, 34 Centre Road
Vermont, Vic. 3133

Geelong Field Naturalists Club
PO Box 1047
Geelong, Vic. 3220

Sunraysia Bird Observers Club
PO Box 1722
Mildura, Vic. 3500

Victorian National Parks Service
240 Victoria Parade
East Melbourne, Vic. 3002

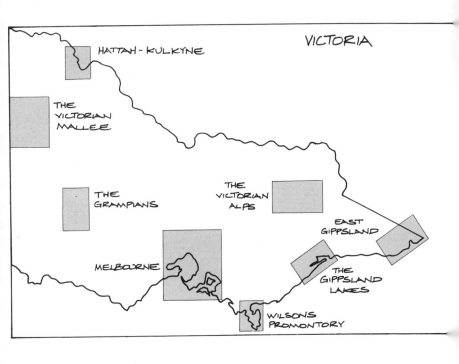

Key to Maps

Public land		Marsh	
Areas of water		Major road or highway	
▲ Mountain peak		Minor road	
Mountain range or plateau		Foot track	
COBAR● Place name		National park boundary	
✗ Camping area		State boundary	
Lighthouse		River or creek	

MELBOURNE

Victoria's large and cosmopolitan capital lies on the northern shores of Port Phillip Bay, near the mouth of the Yarra River. The suburbs extend around much of the bay, from Altona to the Mornington Peninsula, and sprawl to the Dandenong Ranges in the east. Though the northern boundaries have moved out more slowly, it is only twenty minutes drive from the northernmost suburbs to the slopes of the Great Dividing Range.

Melburnians have on their doorstep a wonderful array of bird-watching areas: suburban parks and gardens, luxuriant eucalypt forests, dry woodlands, rivers, lakes, marshes, coastal mudflats and offshore islands. The great diversity of habitats supports an equal diversity of birds, and over three hundred species have been recorded in the region. Melbourne is unique among Australian capitals in having two world-famous avian tourist attractions — the lyrebirds at Sherbrooke Forest and the penguins on Phillip Island.

The city has a wide range of accommodation that includes international-class hotels, motels and guest houses. During the Melbourne Cup season in early November, and the Moomba Festival in early March, rooms may be difficult to find. There are a number of conveniently situated caravan parks at Dandenong, Seaford and Werribee South, all 32 km from the city, and others at Beaconsfield, Carrum Downs, Frankston, Lilydale, Monbulk, Narre Warren and Moorooduc. For those on a tight budget — old as well as young — there are youth hostels at 500 Abbotsford Street and 76 Chapman Street, North Melbourne; for further information contact the Youth Hostels Association at 122 Flinders Street, Melbourne.

From Tullamarine Airport there are frequent services to all parts of the world, as well as daily flights to all the major cities within Australia. Rental cars are readily available.

Melbourne is a lively and interesting city, well known for its wide range of restaurants. It has some fine colonial properties, including Como in South Yarra and Rippon Lea in Elsternwick. The Old Melbourne Gaol in Russell Street is also well worth seeing. The Victorian Arts Centre, in St Kilda Road, houses the National Gallery of Victoria, the Melbourne Concert Hall, the

Performing Arts Museum and a theatre complex.

The following are some of the best places to go bird-watching near the capital; consult a Melbourne street guide for precise directions.

Royal Botanic Gardens

These beautifully landscaped gardens occupy 36 ha on the banks of the Yarra River, just 2 km from the city centre. Considered to be among the finest in the southern hemisphere, they have extensive lawns and three lakes, with over twelve thousand plants from throughout the world providing a colourful display all year round.

While introduced birds abound, the gardens are also quite good for native species, the lakes attracting a variety of common waterbirds including Australasian Grebe, Great, Little Black and Little Pied Cormorant, White-faced Heron, Black Swan, Pacific Black Duck, Maned Duck, Dusky Moorhen, Purple Swamphen, Eurasian Coot and Silver Gull. Occasionally, rarer species such as Hardhead and Buff-banded Rail turn up, and Rufous Night Heron can sometimes be found roosting during the day in the dense vegetation along the western edge of the ornamental lake. In summer Sacred Kingfisher is a possibility.

The Australian native section in the southern part of the gardens is a good place to look for honeyeaters, including Red and Little Wattlebird, White-plumed Honeyeater and Eastern Spine-bill; Welcome Swallow, Willie Wagtail, Superb Fairy-wren, Silvereye, Australian Magpie-lark, Australian Magpie and Little Raven occur throughout the area. There are usually a few White-browed Scrubwrens in the fern gully.

From the city centre it is a very pleasant walk to the gardens along the banks of the river, and there are regular bus and tram services. An information leaflet is available from boxes at each of the entrance gates, and a brochure describing the common birds of the gardens can be purchased from the kiosk. In summer, opening times are 7 a.m. until sunset during the week, and 8.30 a.m. until sunset on weekends and public holidays. The gardens open half an hour later during winter. Most of the paths are wide and sealed, and wheelchairs are available at the kiosk.

Melbourne Zoo (Great Flight Aviary)

Although zoos may not be good places for bird-watching in the usual sense, many now have walk-through aviaries that provide opportunities, especially for beginners and overseas visitors, to see many native birds in relatively natural surroundings.

The Great Flight Aviary in Melbourne Zoo was opened in 1980 and is divided into three sections – rainforest, wetland and

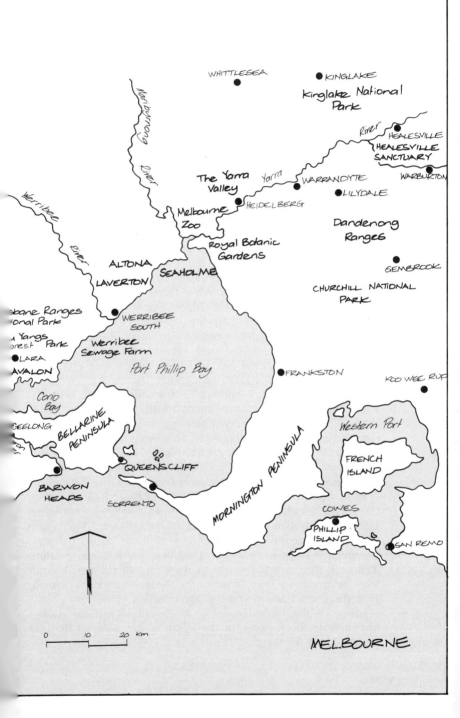

scrubland. It houses well over one hundred species and the suspended walkways enable visitors to come face to face with many of our most interesting, and often most elusive, birds.

As well as the aviary, the zoo has many attractions including native and exotic animals, nocturnal enclosures and a restaurant. A very full and enjoyable day could be spent here; the zoo lies a few kilometres north of the city centre, in Royal Park, and a number 55 tram stops right outside the entrance. The Royal Park railway station is also very close: catch trains on the Gowrie or Upfield line.

The Yarra Valley

The parklands, gardens, golf courses and strips of native bush along the Yarra River, east of Melbourne, form a green corridor that extends right into the heart of the city. Although much of the vegetation is exotic, especially in the inner suburban area, some good patches of native bush exist further out − at, for instance, Jumping Creek Reserve in the Warrandyte State Park.

An astonishing 178 species are listed for the valley. Many are only rarely recorded, of course, but a wide variety can usually be observed readily enough: Australasian Grebe, Great, Little Black and Little Pied Cormorant, White-faced Heron, Cattle Egret (winter), Sacred Ibis, Pacific Black Duck, Dusky Moorhen, Eurasian Coot, Masked Lapwing, Latham's Snipe (summer), Silver Gull, Galah, Sulphur-crested Cockatoo, Eastern Rosella, Red-rumped Parrot, Pallid and Fan-tailed Cuckoo (spring−summer), White-throated Needletail (summer, especially during unsettled weather), Sacred Kingfisher (summer), Welcome Swallow, Fairy Martin (summer), Black-faced Cuckoo-shrike, Flame Robin (winter), Grey Shrike-thrush, Grey Fantail, Willie Wagtail, Clamorous Reed-Warbler (summer), Little Grassbird, Superb Fairy-wren, White-browed Scrubwren, Brown Thornbill, Red Wattlebird, Noisy Miner, White-plumed Honeyeater, Spotted Pardalote, Silvereye, Red-browed Firetail, Australian Magpie-lark, Grey Butcherbird, Australian Magpie and Little Raven.

More rarely, Rufous Night Heron, Yellow-billed Spoonbill, Grey Teal, Black-shouldered Kite, Brown Goshawk, Australian Hobby, Australian Kestrel, Black-fronted Plover, Gang-gang Cockatoo (autumn−winter), Shining Bronze-Cuckoo (spring−summer), Tawny Frogmouth, Laughing Kookaburra, Eastern Yellow Robin, Crested Shrike-tit, Golden and Rufous Whistler (the latter usually only in summer), Yellow-rumped Thornbill, Bell Miner and Eastern Spinebill are recorded.

Many of the birds listed can be found in suitable habitat anywhere in the region, but the following are some of the best places to look for them.

Yarra Bend Park, Kew: Lies about 4 km north-east of the city centre via Studley Park Road and Yarra Boulevard. There are picnic facilities and toilets and the entire area is quite good for birds, although at weekends it may be crowded and noisy.

Wilson Reserve and Chelsworth Park, Ivanhoe: Lie about 9 km north-east of the city centre via Heidelberg Road or Burke Road, and The Boulevard. The two reserves occupy about 29 ha on the floodplain north of the Yarra and offer some of the best bird-watching in the area. There are no facilities in Wilson Reserve but the adjacent Chelsworth Park has toilets and electric barbecues.

Warringal Parklands and Banyule Flats Reserve, Heidelberg: Are situated about 12 km north-east of the city centre and can be reached via Lower Heidelberg Road, Burgundy Street, Beverley Road, Buckingham Drive, Banyule Road and Somerset Drive. The Warringal Parklands consist chiefly of open, grassy sports areas, but the small swamp there is worth a visit. The adjacent Banyule Flats Reserve has a fine wetland billabong, and with a bird list exceeding 150 species it offers the best bird-watching in the Heidelberg area. There are toilets and barbecues in Warringal Park.

Warrandyte State Park: Lies about 24 km north-east of the city centre and consists of three separate reserves with a combined area of 385 ha. The reserves are: Pound Bend, via Warrandyte Road and Pound Road; Black Flat, via Warrandyte Road and Tills Drive; and Jumping Creek Reserve, via Warrandyte Road and Jumping Creek Road.

All three reserves have visitor facilities – those at Pound Bend are suitable for the disabled – and there are canoe ramps at Pound Bend and Sandy Bay (Jumping Creek).

A number of walking tracks have been constructed in the park, including a 2.5 km nature trail at Black Flat and a track for the disabled at Pound Bend. The walk to Blue Tongue Bend, in Jumping Creek Reserve, is especially good for birds – Common Bronzewing, Eastern Rosella, Bell and Noisy Miner are plentiful here. Exploring the river by canoe would be an excellent way of seeing the birdlife; camping is not permitted, but there is a youth hostel at Warrandyte, and others – off the Yarra – at Emerald and Warburton.

The Dandenong Ranges

Although Melbourne's suburbs are gradually creeping east to-wards Lilydale and Belgrave, the Dandenongs have retained much of their original charm and character and both residents and visitors alike will find this a superb area for bird-watching. The semi-rural landscape is dotted with small farms, market gardens and plant nurseries, interspersed with art and craft shops, tea rooms and restaurants catering for the constant stream of visitors.

Throughout the ranges there are state forests, national parks, crown land reserves, water supply reserves and parks and gardens, and many pleasant days could be spent exploring the region. Visitors with only a little time to spare should be sure to see the following spots.

Sherbrooke Forest Park: Lies about 40 km east of Melbourne via Belgrave and Kallista. It is perhaps the most famous and scenic reserve in the Dandenongs, and bird-watchers from all over the world make a pilgrimage to the forest in the hope of seeing a Superb Lyrebird. The vegetation is predominantly mountain ash, which forms a spectacular forest rising to between 55 m and 65 m above a dense understorey of blackwood, silver wattle, sassafras, musk daisy-bush and hazel pomaderris. A profusion of ferns, including soft and rough tree ferns, kangaroo and mother shield ferns and many smaller ground ferns, complete the superb scene.

The forest resounds with bird calls, and the fantastic mimicry of the lyrebird is most frequently heard in autumn when males commence their famous displays in preparation for the winter breeding season. Contrary to popular belief lyrebirds are usually very shy, and bird-watchers who come to Sherbrooke expecting to see them at close range may be disappointed. Probably the best place to look for them is Clematis Avenue, which is a five-minute walk from the Kallista picnic area via the Tree Fern track. The avenue is quite wide and the lyrebirds' characteristic scratchings may be seen all along it. The best time to look is in the early morning or late afternoon. A multitude of familiar bird sounds − kookaburra, whistler, thornbill, all originating from the same place − usually mean that a lyrebird is close by. Lyrebirds are by no means confined to the ground and males often sing from a perch, sometimes quite high up.

After a kilometre or so Clematis Avenue joins the Firebreak Track, which leads to the O'Donohue picnic area (a good spot to photograph Crimson Rosella and Laughing Kookaburra, as both are exceedingly tame here) and Sherbrooke Falls. From the falls another good walking track follows Sherbrooke Creek for a time and leads back to the O'Donohue picnic ground and Sherbrooke Road. This track is usually very good for birds and, although the vegetation is dense in places, the creek is in full view at several points. On hot summer evenings many birds, including normally elusive species such as Eastern Whipbird, come freely to the water's edge to drink and bathe.

Apart from lyrebirds the forest holds a host of interesting species including Brown Goshawk, Brush Bronzewing, Yellow-tailed Black-Cockatoo, Gang-gang Cockatoo (autumn−winter), Sulphur-crested Cockatoo, Brush and Fan-tailed Cuckoo (spring−

summer), Shining Bronze-Cuckoo (spring–summer), Sooty Owl, White's Thrush, several robins including Rose (summer) and Pink, Olive Whistler, Satin Flycatcher (summer), Rufous Fantail (common breeding summer visitor), Eastern Whipbird, Pilotbird (quite common in forest gullies where it sometimes associates with lyrebirds), Large-billed Scrubwren, White-throated and, more rarely, Red-browed Treecreeper, honeyeaters (Yellow-faced, White-eared, White-naped and Crescent), Eastern Spinebill, Red-browed Firetail and Pied Currawong. The gorgeous Australian King-Parrot occasionally visits the area, usually in winter.

There are a number of pleasant picnic grounds in the forest and many good walking tracks, including a specially constructed path suitable for wheelchairs. Camping is not allowed but there is a caravan park nearby at Belgrave and a motel in idyllic surroundings opposite the park's main entrance in Sherbrooke Road. After finding a lyrebird, visitors might like to celebrate over a Devonshire tea in the Kallista tea rooms. The Forests Commission office at Kallista has a wealth of useful information, including bird and plant lists for Sherbrooke and other reserves in the Dandenongs.

Ferntree Gully National Park: Another delightful bird-watching spot close to the city, this 450 ha park lies 36 km east of Melbourne via the Burwood Highway (route 26) and Upper Ferntree Gully. The main entrance is on the Mount Dandenong Tourist Road, within easy walking distance of the Upper Ferntree Gully railway station.

Within the park are two distinct types of vegetation. On the sheltered southern slopes the tall, dense forest is dominated by manna gum and blackwood, with gully communities characterised by soft and rough tree ferns, epiphytic ferns, ground ferns and mosses. On the northern and western slopes the open eucalypt forest consists of narrow-leaved peppermint, messmate stringy-bark and long-leaved box, with a generally sparse understorey where many of the park's 150 flower species, including a wide variety of orchids, can be found in spring and summer.

Many of the birds occurring nearby at Sherbrooke can be seen in the park. Interestingly, Powerful Owls bred at Ferntree Gully in 1982, and other breeding species of note include Fan-tailed Cuckoo, Horsfield's Bronze-Cuckoo, Rose, Pink and Eastern Yellow Robin, Golden Whistler, Satin Flycatcher, Rufous Fantail, Eastern Whipbird, White-throated Treecreeper, Crescent Honeyeater, Eastern Spinebill and Red-browed Firetail.

For those with little time to spare, the Living Bush Nature Trail, which starts just inside the main entrance, provides a glimpse of this marvellous reserve; during the summer both Satin Flycatcher and Rufous Fantail can be seen along the track. The park is very popular – about 370 000 people visit it annually – and bird-watchers will find an early morning walk during the week more rewarding than a weekend visit. There are picnic facilities, electric barbecues, toilets and a kiosk near the main entrance, and another picnic area to the north at One Tree Hill. Numerous walking tracks criss-cross the park, making this one of the best places near Melbourne for bird-watching. Camping is not permitted.

Yellingbo State Nature Reserve: This fragmented 300 ha reserve lies about 50 km east of Melbourne and is accessible from the north via Lilydale, the Warburton Highway, Seville and Woori Yallock, or from the south via the Burwood Highway, Belgrave, Macclesfield and Cockatoo. The reserve is unique in that it protects narrow strips of vegetation, primarily manna and swamp gum, along several creeks where the Helmeted Honeyeater occurs. This honeyeater, Victoria's bird emblem and the state's only endemic, is considered to be a subspecies of the Yellow-tufted Honeyeater. Its population is estimated to be fewer than two hundred individuals, but its whereabouts are widely known and obviously bird-watchers will want to see one. However, it should be remembered that this is an endangered bird and bird-watchers should not pursue it relentlessly, nor leave the established tracks during the breeding season (September to February). The honey-eater is quite large, about Willie Wagtail size, boldly marked and exuberant, and it often associates with the Bell Miners that are very common in the area. The following are known haunts of the honeyeater.

Sheepstation Creek: Lies between Woori Yallock and Yelling-bo and is reached via Sheepstation Creek Road, about 2 km north of Yellingbo. About 500 m along the road there is a clearing on the left and from here it is possible to walk in behind the reserve and along the creek.

Yellingbo: Is accessible via Seville, Woori Yallock or Cockatoo. Just west of the township there is a bridge over Woori Yallock Creek on the Seville road, and this is the best place to look for the honeyeater. During the breeding season the birds form loose colonies, and on hot days they forage high in the canopy and may be difficult to locate. An early morning or late afternoon visit in summer would therefore be best. In winter, as far as is known, the honeyeaters disperse over a wider area.

The surrounding countryside is very good for birds, and even if the honeyeater is not found you can expect to see at least some of the following: Black-shouldered Kite, Wedge-tailed Eagle, Brown Falcon, Australian Kestrel, Common Bronzewing, Yellow-tailed Black-Cockatoo, Sulphur-crested Cockatoo, Swift Parrot (autumn–winter), Azure Kingfisher (rarely), Eastern Yellow Robin, Crested Shrike-tit, Superb Fairy-wren, White-browed Scrubwren, Striated Thornbill, Varied Sittella, White-throated Treecreeper, Bell

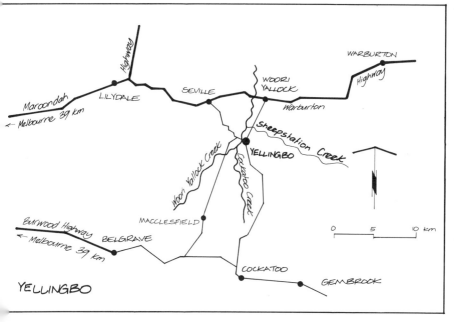

YELLINGBO

Miner, White-naped Honeyeater, Spotted Pardalote, Red-browed and (rarely) Beautiful Firetail, Dusky Woodswallow and Grey Butcherbird. The rare Southern Emu-wren is a possibility.

There are caravan parks at Lilydale, Warburton and Monbulk.

Churchill National Park

This small park lies on the southern slopes of the Lysterfield Hills, 32 km east of Melbourne via Stud Road and Bergins Road, or via Heatherton Road and Power Road. The park entrance is in Churchill Park Drive. At first glance this 193 ha reserve does not look very promising – State Electricity Commission transmission lines dominate the scene – but it is one of the few remaining areas of bushland close to the city and holds a surprising variety of birds (about a hundred species), including Brown Goshawk, Australian Hobby, Musk and Purple-crowned Lorikeet (when the eucalypts are flowering), Pallid and Fan-tailed Cuckoo (spring–summer), Horsfield's Bronze-Cuckoo (spring-summer), Sacred Kingfisher (summer), Black-faced Cuckoo-shrike, Flame (winter), Scarlet and Eastern Yellow Robin, Golden and Rufous Whistler (the latter in summer), Grey Shrike-thrush, Grey Fantail, Superb Fairy-wren, White-browed Scrubwren, Brown, Yellow-rumped and Striated Thornbill, Mistletoebird, Spotted and Striated Pardalote, Silvereye, Red-browed Firetail, Dusky Woodswallow, Grey Butcherbird, Australian Magpie and Little Raven.

Honeyeaters are usually well represented, with Red Wattlebird, Yellow-faced, White-eared, White-plumed, White-naped and New Holland Honeyeater all occurring regularly. Noisy Miners are plentiful, and the small colony of Bell Miners is of particular interest; the birds' melodious bell-like calls can be heard round the main picnic area, just inside the park entrance.

The best times to visit the reserve are spring and early summer when the wildflowers, including twelve species of orchids, are at their best. In summer it can be hot and dry and the flies are a real menace, so carry insect repellent. Those able to linger until dusk may be lucky enough to see the handsome Gang-gang Cockatoo settling in for the night. Camping is not permitted.

Seaholme, Altona, Laverton, Werribee and Avalon

The beaches, mudflats, marshes, lakes and saltworks along the northern shores of Port Phillip Bay, west of Melbourne, hold large numbers of waders and other waterbirds and are well worth exploring. Although some of the best bird-watching spots, namely Werribee Sewage Farm, Laverton Saltworks and the government explosives reserve at Point Wilson, are not open to the public, there are many accessible areas along the coast and visits to the following are recommended.

Seaholme: Lies about 12 km south-west of Melbourne, and the entire foreshore between Point Cook and Point Gellibrand is worth investigating — especially the area between the Altona Yacht Club and the mouth of Kororoit Creek. Unfortunately this stretch of the foreshore is now threatened with redevelopment, but for the time being at least the wide tidal mudflats are favoured by waders such as Pied and (rarely) Sooty Oystercatcher, Masked Lapwing, Red-capped Plover, Greenshank, Sharp-tailed and Curlew Sandpiper, and Red-necked Stint. Lesser Golden Plover and Eastern Curlew are usually present in small numbers during summer, and rarities such as Large Sand Plover turn up from time to time.

Some of the other waterbirds regularly recorded are Australian Pelican, cormorants, White-faced Heron, Great Egret, ibis, spoonbills, Pacific and (rarely) Kelp Gull, and Common (summer), Fairy and Crested Tern. Summer is the best time for migratory waders; remember to check tide times in advance.

Cherry Lake, Altona: This large freshwater lake is 11 km southwest of Melbourne via Millers Road, Kororoit Creek Road and Civic Parade. There are picnic facilities and toilets south of the lake off Millers Road. Despite the rather uninspiring industrial surroundings, the lake and adjacent area, especially Kororoit Creek to the north-east and the swamps to the south-west, are well worth looking over for waterbirds. These include Hoary-headed and Australasian Grebe, cormorants, Pacific Heron, Great Egret, ibis, spoonbills, waterfowl such as Black Swan, Australian Shelduck, Pacific Black Duck, Grey and Chestnut Teal and Musk Duck, Dusky Moorhen, Purple Swamphen, Eurasian Coot, waders such as Masked Lapwing, Black-fronted Plover and Black-winged Stilt, and gulls and terns.

Some very interesting species have been recorded from the area and the experienced observer can hope to see at least a few of the following: Little Egret, Little and Australasian Bittern, Buff-banded Rail, Baillon's and Spotless Crake, Red-kneed Dotterel, Wood Sandpiper, Latham's Snipe, Black-tailed Godwit, Pectoral, Cox's and Broad-billed Sandpiper, Long-toed Stint, Ruff, and Red-necked and Wilson's Phalarope. In summer, Whiskered and occasionally White-winged Terns are present.

Laverton Saltworks: Lie about 20 km south-west of Melbourne via the Princes Freeway and Aviation (Point Cook) Road. The main entrance to the saltworks is about 3 km south of the freeway. Saltworks are always excellent places for waders, and these are no exception. Unfortunately the owners of such places are increasingly less willing to allow anyone, even bird-watchers, onto their properties because of vandalism and other problems. The best way to get into the saltworks is to join a recognised group such as the Bird Observers Club of Victoria (the address is at the beginning of this chapter). The BOC runs regular excursions to the saltfields and those unfamiliar with waders will benefit from joining such a group. Otherwise visiting bird-watchers should telephone the manager in advance and seek permission to enter.

Needless to say, the area has an impressive bird list: many of the rarities listed for Cherry Lake have turned up at Laverton. Some of the other interesting species which have been seen here are Blue-billed Duck, Black-tailed Native-hen, Oriental Plover, Banded Stilt, Red-necked Avocet, Marsh and Terek Sandpiper, and Great Knot.

If permission to enter the saltworks is refused, try the Point Cook Metropolitan Park about 2 km further along Aviation Road. It has several shallow lakes, and the beach holds good numbers of Lesser Golden Plover in summer and Double-banded Plover in winter. Interestingly, Brown Quail have been recently sighted in the area, and in early 1984 a Buff-breasted Sandpiper was present in the park.

Werribee Sewage Farm: Lies about 45 km south-west of Melbourne via the Princes Freeway. Both the sewage farm and the explosives reserve nearby at Point Wilson are prohibited areas that, like the saltworks at Laverton, are more readily opened up to organisations such as the BOC than to individuals. However, it is still possible to explore the surrounding area without entering any of the restricted zones.

The sewage farm holds a multitude of waterbirds including grebes, cormorants, egrets, ibis, spoonbills, waterfowl, rails, crakes, waders, gulls and terns. Lake Borrie is an important roosting site for Sacred and Straw-necked Ibis, and at times ducks occur in large numbers: early in 1981 there were 200+ Freckled Duck, 2000 Australasian Shoveler, 50 000 Pink-eared Duck, 600+ Blue-billed Duck and 150+ Musk Duck. The area has a long list of rarities including Intermediate Egret, Australasian Bittern, Glossy Ibis, Plumed Whistling-Duck, Northern Shoveler, Lewin's Rail, Spotless Crake, Brolga, Painted Snipe, Little Curlew, Wood, Terek, Pectoral, Cox's and Broad-billed Sandpiper, Black-tailed Godwit, Little and Long-toed Stint, Ruff, Red-necked Phalarope and Oriental Pratincole.

To the south of Werribee, near Point Wilson, lies The Spit State Nature Reserve (300 ha). This well-known wader spot has also produced some outstanding rarities: Mongolian and Large Sand Plover, Asian Dowitcher, White-rumped and Buff-breasted Sandpiper, and Ruff. The Spit can be reached by driving about 5 km along the Point Wilson road, turning left at the gates marked 'Sanctuary' and following the unsealed track that leads to a boat ramp. From here the coast can be explored in either direction and The Spit lies about 2–3 km from the boat ramp, towards Geelong. If possible join a group of wader enthusiasts who know the area and what to look for.

Waterbirds are not the only attraction at Werribee. The sur-rounding area holds a good variety of land birds: raptors such as Black-shouldered and (rarely) Letter-winged Kite, Black Kite, Whistling Kite, Wedge-tailed and Little Eagle, Spotted and Marsh Harrier, Black Falcon, Brown Falcon and Australian Kestrel are recorded from time to time, and Point Wilson is a major wintering ground of the very rare Orange-bellied Parrot.

Avalon: Lies on the northern shores of Corio Bay, about 70 km south-west of Melbourne, and can be easily reached via the Princes Highway. Although not as well known as some of the other spots along the coast, the beach and adjacent area attract a fair variety of waterbirds, including waders. The saltworks there are also worth visiting (a Buff-breasted Sandpiper was seen at the saltworks in January 1986).

The entire coast between Geelong and Melbourne is rich in birdlife (in 1981 approximately 38 000 waders − about 30 per cent of the Victorian wader population − were recorded along the western shores of Port Phillip Bay), and bird-watchers travelling to Melbourne from the west should allow time for a stop here. The You Yangs lie just to the north and a visit there for bush birds, including the Speckled Warbler, should find a place on the itinerary. There are two caravan parks at Werribee South, and plenty of accommodation at Geelong, which has many caravan parks and a youth hostel.

You Yangs Forest Park

This 2000 ha park lies a few kilometres north of the Princes Highway, about 22 km from Geelong via Lara and about 60 km from Melbourne via Little River. Flinders Peak (350 m), the highest point in the You Yangs, dominates the Werribee Plains and is a familiar sight to motorists travelling to Melbourne from Geelong.

The park includes an 800 ha eucalypt plantation, an art gallery and many pleasant picnic sites, and there are a number of good walking tracks − for instance a two-hour walk round Flinders Peak that offers fine views across the surrounding plains. Over much of the area the vegetation is predominantly dry, open woodland with red ironbark, red stringybark, yellow gum, river red gum, she-oak and wattle; in spring and early summer wildflowers are abundant and include many species of orchids. On the slopes of the range there are massive granite boulders and frequent outcrops.

The You Yangs are exceedingly rich in birdlife; a list giving details of the two hundred species recorded in the region can be obtained from the Forests Commission in Geelong, or from the resident ranger. Naturally the list includes many infrequent sightings, but even those unable to spend much time in the park should see many of the following: Common Bronzewing, Sulphur-crested Cockatoo, Eastern Rosella, Red-rumped Parrot, Pallid and Fantailed Cuckoo (spring−summer), Horsfield's and Shining Bronze-Cuckoo (spring−summer), Laughing Kookaburra, Sacred Kingfisher (spring−summer), Tree and Fairy Martin (spring−summer), Black-faced Cuckoo-shrike, robins − including Flame (winter), Scarlet, Hooded and Eastern Yellow − Jacky Winter, Crested Shrike-tit, Golden Whistler (winter), Rufous Whistler (spring−summer), Grey Shrike-thrush, Satin Flycatcher (spring−summer), Restless Flycatcher, Grey Fantail, Brown Songlark (summer), Superb Fairy-wren, thornbills − including Brown, Buff-rumped, Yellow-rumped, Yellow and Striated − Varied Sittella, White-throated and Brown Treecreeper, honeyeaters − including Red Wattlebird, Noisy Miner, Yellow-faced, White-plumed, Brown-headed, White-naped and New Holland Honeyeater and Eastern Spinebill − Mistletoebird, Spotted and Striated Pardalote, Silver-eye, Red-browed and Diamond Firetail, White-winged Chough, Dusky Woodswallow, Australian Magpie and Little Raven.

Perhaps the most interesting species occurring in the park is the Speckled Warbler. Indeed this is one of the few places west of Melbourne where the diligent observer can be virtually assured of a sighting of this fine little bird. The warbler favours open wood-land with a sparse understorey and scattered rocks, and the habitat in the park meets all these requirements. A good spot to look for it is round the Big Rock picnic area. The warbler is not usually shy and its merry song is quite characteristic; its strongly speckled breast readily distinguishes it from the thornbills with which it often associates. Big Rock is also a haunt of the rather rare Black-eared Cuckoo, which visits the park in spring.

There are many other interesting birds to be found in the You Yangs, including raptors such as Black-shouldered Kite, Brown Goshawk, Australian Hobby, Brown Falcon and Australian Kestrel. Nocturnal birds include Southern Boobook, Barn Owl, Tawny Frogmouth and Australian Owlet-nightjar. When in flower, the extensive eucalypt plantations attract a wealth of nectar-feeding species including Musk, Purple-crowned and Little Lorikeet, Swift Parrot (occasionally, and only in autumn and winter), and some of the rarer honeyeaters such as Yellow-tufted, Fuscous, Black-chinned and Painted.

Undoubtedly this is one of the finest bird spots near Melbourne. The birding is good at any time of the year and even in late summer, when it can be hot and dusty, there are still the Rainbow Bee-eaters to delight the eye. Camping is not permitted. Unfortunately about 90 per cent of the park was burnt in early 1985, and it will be some time before the vegetation fully recovers.

Brisbane Ranges National Park

Probably few bird-watchers outside Victoria have heard of the Brisbane Ranges, but this fascinating region about 30 km north of Geelong is rich in history, animals, plants and birds. Over four hundred species of wildflowers are found in the ranges, including the Brisbane Ranges grevillea, which is confined to the area, and many species of orchids such as nodding and dwarf greenhoods. Birds abound, and close to 170 species have been recorded; the strikingly beautiful Yellow-tufted Honeyeater (closely related to the Helmeted Honeyeater) is fairly common in the park. There are many other interesting birds such as Powerful Owl, White-throated Nightjar (rarely reported west of Melbourne, but there are breeding records from the Brisbane Ranges), Rainbow Bee-eater, Satin Flycatcher, Rufous Fantail, Spotted Quail-thrush, Speckled Warbler and Olive-backed Oriole. Mammals include grey kangaroo, wallabies, possums, gliders and koalas; the koala population is steadily increasing, in fact, and these endearing creatures are now quite widespread in the park.

The thin, generally infertile soils have saved the area from being developed for agriculture, but extensive tracts were once cleared for firewood and to provide pit props for the gold-mining industry

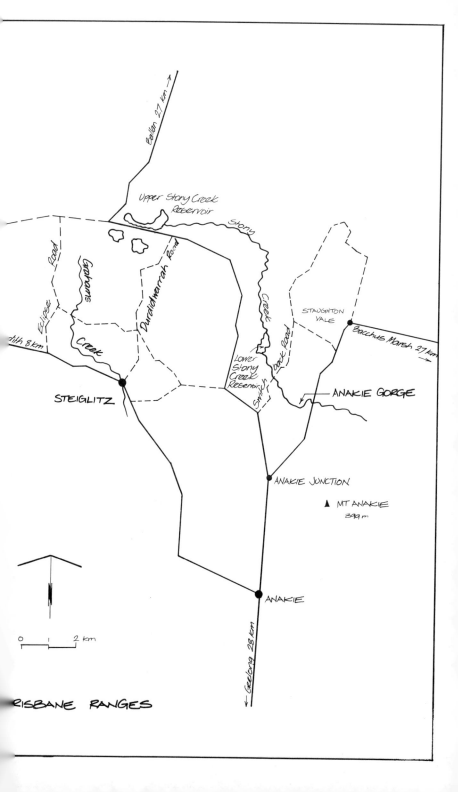

that flourished nearby at Steiglitz in the nineteenth century. The township is now a historic park.

Many of the creeks hold water all year round, attracting an abundance of small birds. The entire region, including the water catchment reserves, is well worth thorough exploration – the following spots being particularly good.

Durdidwarrah Road, south of the Upper Stony Creek Reservoir: The juxtaposition of reservoirs, dams, cleared land and open and dense forest makes this a very favourable area for birds. Near the park boundary on Durdidwarrah Road there are numerous tracks through the open forest and a walk here should produce many of the following: Common Bronzewing, Southern Boobook, Tawny Frogmouth, Australian Owlet-nightjar, Sacred Kingfisher (summer), White-winged Triller (summer), Scarlet Robin, Jacky Winter, Crested Shrike-tit, Satin Flycatcher (spring–summer), Restless Flycatcher, Brown, Buff-rumped, Yellow-rumped and Striated Thornbill, Varied Sittella, White-throated and Brown Treecreeper, honeyeaters – including Yellow-tufted – Mistletoebird, pardalotes, Diamond Firetail, Olive-backed Oriole (summer), White-winged Chough, Dusky and, more rarely, White-browed Woodswallow, and Grey Currawong. In summer, Rainbow Bee-eaters can often be found here.

Anakie Gorge: Lies just west of the Anakie Junction to Staughton Vale road, on the south-eastern boundary of the park. Stony Creek flows through the gorge and beside the creek there is a good walking track connecting the picnic ground at Anakie Gorge with another on Switchback Road (the Lower Stony Creek picnic ground). The return walk takes about one and a half hours, with excellent birding en route. Near the Lower Stony Creek picnic ground there are a number of large gums growing in the creek bed and this is the best place in the park for Yellow-tufted Honeyeater. There are nearly always a few pairs here.

From Anakie Gorge picnic ground, with its fireplaces and toilets (and usually koalas) another walking track leads to Nelsons Lookout. Spotted Quail-thrush has been sighted here, and Peregrine Falcons are known to nest locally.

Grahams Creek: Lies on the south-western edge of the park, just north of Steiglitz. Bush camping is permitted here but you should contact the ranger at Anakie first. The creek usually has some water in it all year round and attracts many bush birds. At night, Australian Owlet-nightjars buzz the campfires while koalas grunt in the trees overhead. It is a delightful spot and the surrounding hills are worth exploring for White-throated Nightjar and Spotted Quail-thrush.

The park is about 80 km west of Melbourne. A very full and interesting weekend could be spent here, with wonderful bird-watching and the bonus of seeing some fine old buildings nearby at Steiglitz, especially the historic courthouse. This spot is highly recommended.

Bellarine Peninsula

The Bellarine Peninsula lies to the south-west of Melbourne via the Princes Highway and Geelong. Stretching east from Anglesea to Portarlington and Queenscliff, it is bisected by the Barwon River, which feeds the extensive Lake Connewarre wetland between Geelong and Barwon Heads. Most of the vegetation in the region has been cleared, and the beaches attract many thousands of holiday-makers from Melbourne and Geelong during the summer months. Nevertheless the peninsula is exceedingly rich in birdlife — nearly three hundred species have been recorded — and there are many excellent spots for waders, seabirds and other water-birds, as well as some good remnants of scrub along the south coast. The following places are especially recommended.

Queenscliff: This popular resort lies at the south-eastern tip of the peninsula, about 30 km from Geelong; it is a very good area indeed for waders. Swan Island and the Mud Islands State Nature Reserve are the main wader localities, but the shores of Swan Bay to the north are also well worth a visit. To reach Swan Island, drive to the end of Bridge Street and take the causeway. The area is an army training ground and strictly speaking entry is prohibited, but there are a golf course and yacht club on Swan Island, and bird-watchers from Melbourne regularly visit to study and band

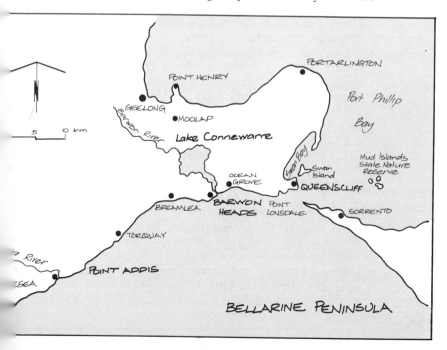

waders. Ask the guard at the gate for permission to enter, explaining that the purpose of the visit is bird-watching, and there should be no problem as long as a few simple rules are obeyed.

The area adjacent to the yacht club is usually the best place for waders. Pied Oystercatcher, Masked Lapwing, Red-capped Plover, Greenshank, Sharp-tailed Sandpiper, Red-necked Stint and Curlew Sandpiper all occur regularly, and Grey, Lesser Golden and Mongolian Plover, Ruddy Turnstone, Eastern Curlew, Whimbrel, Black-tailed and Bar-tailed Godwit, and Red and Great Knot are present less frequently. At high tide some of the rarer species congregate in good numbers near the yacht club, with flocks of 100 Grey Plover, 80 Ruddy Turnstone, 40 Eastern Curlew, 100 Bar-tailed Godwit and 40 Great Knot recorded on occasions. Swan Island is a well-known haunt of the rather rare Grey-tailed Tattler, and about thirty can often be found in summer on or near the causeway leading to the yacht club. (Do not leave vehicles parked on the causeway or you will obstruct traffic; in any case the tattlers are best viewed from inside the car and are likely to move away if pursued too hard.)

The best time for migratory waders is December to February, and at low tide many of the birds disperse over a wide area: remember to check tide times in advance. The entrance gates close at about 7 p.m. in summer and inquiries should be made on arrival. Other waterbirds occurring in good numbers include Australian Pelican, cormorants, Black-faced Shag, herons, egrets, ibis, waterfowl, gulls and terns. Swan Island is a well-known wintering ground of the Orange-bellied Parrot, and Double-banded Plover – a visitor from New Zealand – also turns up in winter, with 280+ recorded in July 1982.

Like other good wader spots the area has produced some notable rarities, including an Asian Dowitcher in 1975 and a Ringed Plover in 1981. There is a small but thriving Australasian Gannet colony on Wedge Light, off Queenscliff. Forty birds were present in 1980, and in 1980–81 they were joined by a solitary Cape Gannet (an African species), which was still there in 1982–83.

The Mud Islands lie at the entrance to Port Phillip Bay, about 10 km offshore, and can be reached by boat from Queenscliff. The three low islets, which are usually joined at low tide, are excellent for waders and seabirds and are a stronghold in the region for Grey, Lesser Golden, Mongolian and Large Sand Plover, Ruddy Turnstone, Eastern Curlew, Whimbrel, Black-tailed and Bar-tailed Godwit, Grey-tailed Tattler, Red and Great Knot, and Common and Little Tern. All the waders occurring nearby at Swan Island can be seen here, and some outstanding rarities including Little Curlew, Terek, Pectoral and Broad-billed Sandpiper, have turned up. Little Penguin, White-faced Storm-Petrel and Caspian, Fairy and Crested Tern all breed on the islands.

Permission to land on this reserve should be obtained from the Victorian National Parks Service in Melbourne.

Barwon Heads: Lies on the south coast of the peninsula, about 15 km west of Queenscliff. In winter, especially during bad weather, the Bluff at Barwon Heads is a very good place for pelagics — that is, seabirds. These include Wandering, Royal (rarely), Black-browed, Yellow-nosed and Shy Albatross, Cape, Great-winged and (rarely) Kerguelen Petrel, Slender-billed and Fairly Prion, and Fluttering Shearwater.

At the western end of the beach, towards Breamlea, there is an area of exposed lava known as Black Rocks. The sewer outlet from Geelong enters the sea at this point and it is a very good spot for Giant-Petrels. Good numbers of Southern Giant-Petrel, and a few Northern, can usually be seen here between June and September. The beach holds a few Hooded Plover and, in summer, Sanderling.

Point Addis: Lies on the south coast, roughly midway between Torquay and Anglesea. A sealed road leads to a carpark on the edge of the cliffs, an excellent spot for seabirds in winter. Indeed it is one of the few places where you can sit in the comfort of a warm car and watch while the fierce winter gales blow in all kinds of seabirds: a place to share with a disabled friend, perhaps.

From the point there are sweeping views along the coast, and the well-vegetated surrounding area holds a good variety of bush birds. These include the Rufous Bristlebird, which is close to the eastern limit of its range here, and the Southern Emu-wren. The cliffs may still hold a few pairs of Peregrine Falcon.

Lake Connewarre: This vast wetland, its stretches of open water fringed with reedbeds and numerous shallow lakes and marshes, lies between Geelong and Barwon Heads. It is readily accessible and the southern section can be viewed from the Barwon Heads to Torquay road. Power-boats under 3 h.p. are permitted on the lake and obviously this would be an excellent way of getting around.

There is an abundance of waterbirds: cormorants, herons, egrets (including at times the rare Intermediate Egret), Little and Australasian Bittern, ibis (Sacred and Straw-necked breed, and Glossy is seen occasionally), spoonbills, waterfowl (including at times the very rare Freckled Duck), Buff-banded and Lewin's Rail, Baillon's, Australian and Spotless Crake, Black-tailed Native-hen, Dusky Moorhen, Purple Swamphen, Eurasian Coot, Brolga (rarely), waders (including Black-winged Stilt, Latham's Snipe, Sharp-tailed Sandpiper, Red-necked Stint and Curlew Sandpiper, with Painted Snipe, Black-tailed Godwit, Marsh and Pectoral Sandpiper, Little and Long-toed Stint and Red-necked Phalarope turning up occasionally), gulls, and Whiskered and White-winged (the latter rarely, and only in summer) Tern.

The peninsula is ornithologically very exciting and the ideal location for a bird-watching holiday. There is ample accommodation, including caravan parks in nearly every town and a youth hostel at Portarlington, but at peak periods it can be very crowded. Other spots worth visiting include the Geelong Saltworks at Moolap (very good for waders — a Lesser Yellowlegs, the first Australian record of this species, was seen there in early 1983), Point Henry, Ocean Grove Nature Reserve, Anglesea River and Point Lonsdale.

Healesville Sanctuary

This open-air zoo, established in 1921 by Sir Colin Mackenzie, lies about 60 km north-east of Melbourne via Lilydale. It is one of the finest zoos of its type in Australia and attracts visitors from all over the world. Within the grounds there are many bird exhibits including wetland and woodland species, raptors, cockatoos and parrots, lyrebirds, brolgas, emus, cassowaries and nocturnal birds. The ibis rookery is of particular interest and visitors can see (and smell) at close range these gregarious creatures going about their domestic duties. Bell Miners and a host of other wild birds frequent the zoo and surrounding area, and the walk-through lyrebird aviary houses a variety of pigeons and doves.

Apart from birds there are kangaroos, wallabies, platypus, wombats, dingoes, reptiles, Tasmanian devils — indeed, almost every native animal. The sanctuary is open daily from 9 a.m. to 5.30 p.m. throughout the year, and there are picnic facilities, a bookstore, a restaurant, and facilities for the handicapped within the grounds. A day here is highly recommended, especially for overseas visitors.

Kinglake National Park

Victorians are justifiably proud of their national parks and this fine 11 270 ha reserve offers some of the best walking and birdwatching near the capital. Situated on the southern slopes of the Great Dividing Range, the park consists of three sections centred on the township of Kinglake, about 65 km north-east of Melbourne.
The Jehosaphat Gully section: Lies to the south-east of Kinglake and is reached via the Yarra Glen to Yea road. There is an attractive picnic area in a cool gully where the tall wet forest is characterised by mountain ash, grey gum, hazel pomaderris, blackwood, and tree and ground ferns. Thirty-seven species of ferns and three hundred and thirty species of wildflowers are found in the park, and Gunn's orchid (one of thirty-two varieties occurring at Kinglake) is quite common in Jehosaphat Gully.

From the picnic area numerous tracks wind through the forest and there are walks ranging from an easy hour or so to a full day. In addition to common species such as Crimson Rosella, Eastern Yellow Robin, Golden Whistler, Grey Fantail, White-browed Scrubwren and White-throated Treecreeper, visitors can expect to see at least some of the following: Brush Bronzewing, Gang-gang Cockatoo (autumn–winter), Brush Cuckoo (summer), Superb Lyrebird (most often heard in autumn and winter), White's Thrush, Rose (summer) and Pink Robin, Olive Whistler, Rufous Fantail (summer), Eastern Whipbird, Large-billed Scrubwren and Red-browed Treecreeper. Grey Goshawk and Powerful Owl are possibilities.

The Masons Falls section: Lies south of the road from Kinglake to Kinglake West and is accessible from the west via Whittlesea or from the east via Yarra Glen. It is the most popular part of the reserve and there are picnic facilities at Masons Falls and Mt Sugarloaf. The 45 m falls are the highest near Melbourne and the bird-watching there is quite good.

On the higher slopes the vegetation is predominantly dry sclerophyll forest with narrow-leaved peppermint and messmate stringybark, while in the vicinity of Running Creek, along the western boundary of the park, the tall, dense forest consists of mountain ash, grey gum, blackwood and tree ferns. The varied vegetation supports an equally varied birdlife, and this must be one of the few places in Victoria where Superb Lyrebird, Rufous Fantail and Spotted Quail-thrush occur almost side by side.

There are several walking tracks in this section, including a short walk to Masons Falls, but for good all-round birding the following route is suggested. From just north of the park office, which is near the main entrance, turn left on to the Wallaby Track (signposted). This track descends steeply through dry forest into a gully where it connects with the Mt Sugarloaf to Masons Falls track. At the junction turn left, towards Mt Sugarloaf, and follow the track along Running Creek and through tall, wet forest. There is a marked change in the birdlife as the track descends, and at 'Ferny Nook' and 'The Tryst' (both signposted) look for Superb Lyrebird, Pilotbird and Rufous Fantail.

After an hour or so the track ascends steeply through dry forest once again. Along this stretch keep your eyes open for Spotted Quail-thrush, especially where the forest floor catches the full afternoon sun. This secretive species is well camouflaged and difficult to locate, but on quiet days it comes out on the track and when approached calls characteristically with a thin, high-pitched whistle. The birds are usually in pairs and prefer open forest with plenty of leaf and stick litter.

The track emerges on the Mt Sugarloaf road, about 2 km south of the park office. It is quite a strenuous walk, requiring three hours or more if the birding is good. Since in summer it can get quite hot, carry water; you will also need insect repellent − it is no fun standing motionless listening for lyrebirds while mosquitoes drink their fill.

The Andrews Hill section: Lies to the north-east of Kinglake via Eucalyptus Road, or the Yarra Glen to Yea road. This is the least developed section of the park, although it has a number of walking tracks including a 5.5 km walk to Andrews Hill (661 m), the highest point in the park.

The drive from Whittlesea to Yarra Glen via Kinglake is very pleasant; the main road winds through attractive farmland and cool forests, offering frequent views over the rolling countryside. In summer, especially ahead of a storm, White-throated Needle-tails can often be seen hawking over the fields. Camping is not permitted in the reserve but there are caravan parks at Lilydale, Healesville and Yea. A visit at any time of the year will be rewarding, although spring and early summer are the best times for wildflowers.

Mornington Peninsula

This popular holiday area, to the east of Port Phillip Bay, is about 45 km south-east of Melbourne via the Nepean Highway and Frankston. Like the Bellarine Peninsula, it can be very crowded during the summer months; it does not have such a wide range of good bird-watching spots, but there are a number of places worth visiting.

Coolart: This fine historic property is classified by the National Trust and lies on the east coast, near Somers. It is about 80 km from Melbourne via Balnarring. Under the direction of well-known naturalist Graham Pizzey, the property has been developed as a nature reserve. There are walking tracks and bird hides including the Minsmere hide which overlooks a lagoon where up to five hundred pairs of Sacred Ibis breed from August to January. Coolart is one of the few reserves of its type in Australia and bird watchers, especially the disabled and beginners, will find a day here most rewarding.

Within the grounds there are examples of many different habitats, including farmland, wetland and woodland, and over 150 bird species have been recorded. The house and grounds are open on Sunday and Tuesday to Thursday from 11 a.m. to 5 p.m.

Nepean State Park: This fragmented reserve of about 1000 ha protects remnants of the original vegetation around Arthurs Seat and along Main and Lightwood Creeks in an area known as Greens Bush. Arthurs Seat is about 75 km from Melbourne, and Greens Bush lies a few kilometres to the south.

A feature of the park is Seawinds, a historic 34 ha property with a formal garden surrounded by natural bush and farmland. Waterfall Gully, which lies just south of Seawinds, is worth visiting for walks and birds. Seawinds and Waterfall Gully can be reached from Arthurs Seat via Purves Road, and Greens Bush via the Rosebud to Flinders road and Patterson Road. Greens Bush is the best spot for bird-watching and camping is permitted, but you should contact the ranger at Seawinds beforehand.

Cape Schanck Coastal Park: This long, narrow reserve protects about 30 km of the Bass Strait coastline between London Bridge, near Portsea, and Cape Schanck. It is possible to walk the entire length of the coast via the Peninsula Coastal Walk, and en route there are some superb beaches, fine coastal scenery and a good variety of birds. Cape Schanck is a well-known seabird spot and in winter especially a variety of pelagics can be seen: Wandering, Royal, Black-browed, Yellow-nosed and Shy Albatross, Southern and Northern Giant-Petrel, Great-winged and Kerguelen Petrel, Hutton's Shearwater and Arctic Tern are just some of the species that have been recorded here.

There is a nature trail at Bushrangers Bay and picnic grounds at Sorrento Back Beach and Cape Schanck; both have facilities for the disabled. Camping is not permitted in the park but the peninsula has a good deal of accommodation, with caravan parks at Rye, Rosebud, Sorrento and Portsea.

The Sorrento—Rosebud area is a haunt of the Common Tern, which visits Australia during the summer months, and a good place for Arctic and Pomarine Jaeger. Those wishing to see the jaegers should take the ferry from Portsea (or Sorrento) to Queenscliff during summer; up to fifty Arctic Jaegers have been recorded during a single crossing.

Other spots worth visiting on the Mornington Peninsula include Seaford Swamp for waterbirds including rails, crakes and waders; Langwarrin Reserve near Frankston for bush birds; Devilbend Reservoir at Moorooduc South for waterbirds (especially at the shallow end); and Mt Eliza, where there is a Bell Miner colony.

French Island

This 17 000 ha island lies to the east of the Mornington Peninsula in Western Port Bay. Over 40 per cent of the island is now a state park and there are some extensive areas of heathland (which hold Tawny-crowned Honeyeater and other interesting species), as well as mangroves, numerous swamps and lagoons, and about 1200 ha of saltmarshes and mudflats. Many species of waterbirds breed on the island: Short-tailed Shearwater, Pied, Little Black and Little Pied Cormorant, White-faced Heron, Sacred and Straw-necked Ibis, Royal Spoonbill, Black Swan, Australian Shelduck, Chestnut Teal, Blue-billed Duck, Pied Oystercatcher, Masked

Lapwing, and Caspian and Fairy Tern. There are cormorant, ibis and spoonbill colonies at Clump Lagoon and Heifer Swamp, and the magnificent White-bellied Sea-Eagle also breeds locally.

Western Port Bay supports fair numbers of waders — about 9000, 7 per cent of the Victorian wader population, were counted in 1981 — and at high tide many birds roost on French Island, for instance at Tortoise Head and Duck Splash. Lesser Golden Plover, Eastern Curlew, Grey-tailed Tattler, Greenshank, Bar-tailed Godwit, Red Knot, Red-necked Stint, Sharp-tailed and Curlew Sandpiper are usually quite plentiful in summer, while Mongolian and Large Sand Plover, Ruddy Turnstone, Whimbrel, Common, Terek and Pectoral Sandpiper, Latham's Snipe, Black-tailed Godwit and Great Knot turn up in smaller numbers. In winter, Double-banded Plovers visit the region from New Zealand.

Some notable rarities have been seen on the island — for instance King Quail at Heifer Swamp in 1981 and at Duck Splash in 1984 — and recent sightings of interest include Australasian Bittern, Lewin's Rail, Australian Crake, and Blue-winged and Orange-bellied Parrot. The best birding spots are Duck Splash, Bullock Swamp, Mt Wellington, Heifer Swamp, Clump Lagoon and Tortoise Head (a good place to look for Large Sand Plover).

With a bird list exceeding two hundred species, this is clearly an excellent place for a relaxed bird-watching weekend or holiday. Camping is allowed, but you should contact the resident ranger in advance. As an alternative to camping, a lodge on the island caters for a limited number of guests. There are regular ferry services from Stony Point on Mornington Peninsula, and less frequent services from Cowes on Phillip Island. Bicycles are the main mode of transport and can be hired locally.

Phillip Island

Phillip Island is about 130 km south-east of Melbourne via Koo Wee Rup and San Remo. The island is internationally famous for its penguins, and the nightly parade at Summerland Beach is worth seeing despite the inevitable razzmatazz. Phillip Island is overrun with holiday-makers during the summer months and bird-watchers will find a visit at other times more rewarding. Apart from the penguins, the island has ornithological attractions that include about half a million pairs of Short-tailed Shearwaters, which breed along the south coast during summer.

There is ample accommodation on the island, including several caravan parks and a youth hostel at Cowes, and in addition to birds the island has some superb beaches and several interesting historic properties. The following spots are worth visiting.

Churchill Island: Lies near San Remo and is managed by the National Parks Service. Although the bird-watching is not especial-

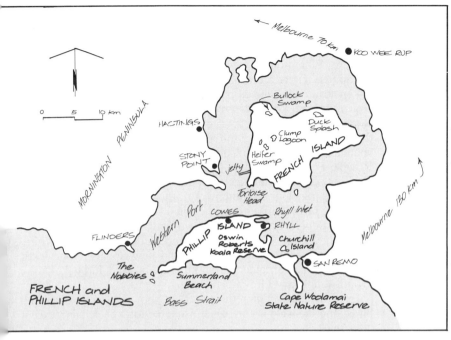

FRENCH and PHILLIP ISLANDS

ly good, there are a few waterbirds and the dwarf mangroves are particularly interesting. The main attraction is the historic Amess homestead, which is open several days a week.

Cape Woolamai State Nature Reserve (308 ha): Is situated on the south coast and has a superb beach, Short-tailed Shearwater colonies containing an estimated 356 000 nest burrows, and a good walking track system. It is a good spot for seabirds in winter and the beach usually holds a few Hooded Plover and Pied Oyster-catcher.

Summerland Penguin Parade: Lies near the south-west tip of the island and is claimed to be Australia's third-largest tourist attraction (after the Great Barrier Reef and Ayers Rock). It draws coach-loads of overseas visitors during the summer months. The penguins are most numerous between October and January, but there are always some at any time of the year. The beach is floodlit, and as a bonus a few shearwaters usually put in an appearance. Take a pullover because even in summer it can be quite chilly.

The Nobbies: Many people go to The Nobbies, at the western tip of the island, to watch the sunset, and then they visit Summerland for the parade. It would be an excellent place in winter for seabirds, and in summer there are usually a few penguins and seals to be seen. Several pairs of Kelp Gull breed on Seal Rocks, just offshore, and are worth looking out for.

Conservation Hill, Rhyll: Is to be found just north of the Cowes to Rhyll road. From the carpark there is a walking track to Rhyll Inlet and in summer this is a good spot for waders, including Pied Oystercatcher, Masked Lapwing, Lesser Golden Plover, Eastern Curlew, Whimbrel, Greenshank, Red-necked Stint and Curlew Sandpiper. There are usually Cape Barren and Magpie Geese in the enclosure near the carpark.

Oswin Roberts Koala Reserve: Lying between Cowes and San Remo, it is best reached via Harbison Road. From the carpark there are walking tracks through the reserve and the area has an abundance of bush birds: Common and Brush Bronzewing, Eastern Rosella, Fan-tailed Cuckoo (spring−summer), Horsfield's Bronze-Cuckoo (spring−summer), Southern Boobook, Black-faced Cuckoo-shrike (spring−summer), Eastern Yellow Robin, Golden Whistler, Grey Shrike-thrush, Satin Flycatcher (summer), Grey Fantail, Superb Fairy-wren, Brown and Yellow-rumped Thornbill, honeyeaters − such as Red and Little Wattlebird, White-eared, White-plumed, White-naped and New Holland Honeyeater − Spotted and Striated Pardalote, Red-browed Firetail, Dusky Woodswallow and Grey Currawong.

Even in late summer this excellent spot is usually alive with birds, and the wide firebreaks are suitable for wheelchairs (except after rain).

THE GRAMPIANS

The Grampians rise abruptly from the plains south of the main Melbourne to Adelaide highway, between Ararat and Horsham. The area is one of Victoria's most scenic and popular tourist spots, and consists of three main ranges: Mt William, to the east, which includes the region's highest point (1167 m); the long central Serra Range; and the Victoria Range to the west. The main tourist centre is Halls Gap, which is located in a beautiful setting between Mt Difficult and Mt William, with Lake Lonsdale and Lake Fyans a little to the north-east and the damp Victoria Valley to the south-west. Zumsteins, another popular tourist spot, is 22 km west of Halls Gap, close to the Wartook Reservoir.

On 1 July 1984 the Grampians became Victoria's largest national park (167 000 ha). Up until 1984 much of the area was state forest and the Forests Commission had already established over 1000 km of roads, 100 km of walking tracks and numerous picnic and bush-camping sites, many with water and toilet facilities. The vegetation is predominantly dry sclerophyll forest, with open woodland on the lower slopes and swamps and heathland in the valleys. In spring the profusion of wildflowers and flowering shrubs is one of the region's chief attractions. Incredibly, there are over nine hundred different native plants, including nearly one

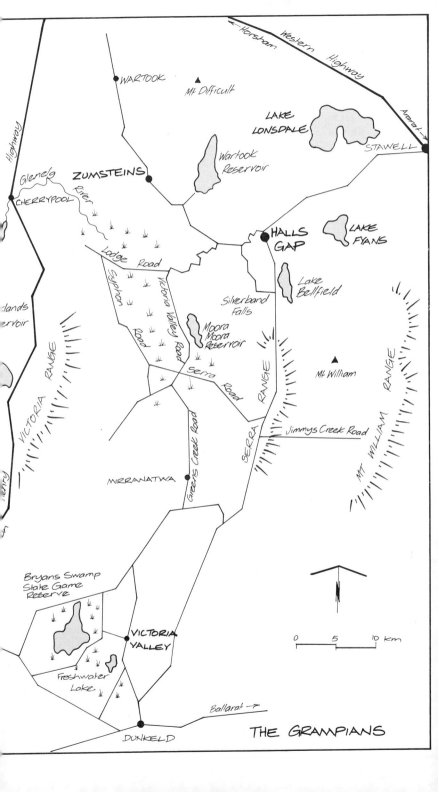

hundred species of orchid. The rare spectral duck-orchid is found only in the Grampians, and Victoria's floral emblem, the common heath, blooms all year round. Although the best time for wild-flowers is between August and November, there is something to see at any time of the year.

One of Australia's best known and most popular animals, the koala, is quite common and can be readily seen in and around Halls Gap. It has a surprisingly crude voice and its pig-like snorts can be heard at night all over the caravan park, much to the amazement of the campers. Kangaroos and wallabies are wide-spread, and the best place to see them is the viewing area near Zumsteins where they regularly congregate in the late afternoon to receive handouts from the tourists. Other animals include gliders, possums, potoroos, echidnas and short-nosed bandicoots, and there are platypus in some of the permanent creeks.

Over two hundred species of birds occur in the region but, as dry sclerophyll forest forms the main habitat, the variety is not as great as one might expect and the birdlife consists chiefly of forest-dwelling species. Much of the area is densely vegetated, making access difficult, and the best places for birds are along the roads and tracks, round the margins of the many picnic and camping grounds, and in centres such as Halls Gap and Zumsteins. The open woodland on the lower slopes is generally easier to penetrate than the thick forest at higher elevations, and is as a result better for bird-watching. Away from the ranges there are several lakes surrounded by open forest and these areas are also rewarding. For the keen bird-watcher, the region has some special birds including Spotted Quail-thrush and Speckled Warbler. Although both are rare and difficult to locate, they are certainly worth pursuing.

The following areas are recommended and generally offer the best bird-watching.

Halls Gap

This is the main centre and it has stores, restaurants, petrol (not readily available elsewhere), motels, caravan parks and other accommodation including a youth hostel. It is advisable to book motel accommodation in advance during school holidays, especially at Easter, and during the wildflower season. At peak times the main caravan park in Halls Gap can be very crowded and noisy and there are alternative parks at Lake Bellfield, just to the south, and on the Stawell road. Zumsteins is perhaps a more desirable base, although it has only a caravan park and kiosk. There are also many bush-camping sites within the park, and these are usually much quieter than the caravan parks. The Victorian National Parks Service office at Halls Gap provides detailed camping information.

The most conspicuous birds around Halls Gap include Crimson Rosella and several cockatoos — the Long-billed Corella, the Gang-gang and the Sulphur-crested. The attractive Gang-gang (only males have the distinctive red head plumes) is quite common and often roosts in the tall trees near the caravan park. In the evening the 'squeaky-door' calls of Gang-gangs announce their arrival.

Other birds commonly seen at Halls Gap include Common Bronzewing, Red-rumped Parrot, Fan-tailed Cuckoo (spring–summer), Horsfield's and Shining Bronze-Cuckoo (spring–summer), Laughing Kookaburra, Sacred Kingfisher (summer), Welcome Swallow, Tree Martin, Eastern Yellow Robin, Grey Shrike-thrush, Grey Fantail, Superb Fairy-wren, White-browed Scrubwren, Brown and Yellow-rumped Thornbill, White-throated Treecreeper, Red Wattlebird, White-plumed, White-naped and New Holland Honeyeater, Eastern Spinebill, Spotted Pardalote, Australian Magpie-lark, Dusky Woodswallow, Australian Magpie, Pied Currawong and Australian Raven.

The flowering eucalypts attract a variety of nectar-feeding birds including Rainbow, Musk and Little Lorikeet, and a few pairs of Peregrine Falcon frequent the adjacent cliffs. Wedge-tailed Eagles sometimes soar above the ranges, and White-bellied Sea-Eagles occasionally visit lakes in the region where they have been known to breed. Two nocturnal species, Southern Boobook and Tawny Frogmouth, are quite plentiful (although rarely seen); the owl's characteristic 'more-pork more-pork' call is frequently heard at night in the forest behind the main caravan park. (Incidentally, the Tawny Frogmouth has been given the name 'mopoke' in the mistaken belief that it makes this call.)

Numerous excellent walking tracks commence close to Halls Gap, including Wonderland Turntable, Chatauqua Peak, Bullaces Glen and Clematis Falls, and many of the birds mentioned can be seen along any of these tracks. Lake Bellfield lies a little to the south, but it has no emergent vegetation and usually holds few birds, although the fishing is said to be good. The road from Halls Gap to Dunkeld skirts the lake's western shores and about 8 km south of Halls Gap it crosses Dairy Creek at the Silverband Falls turn-off. There is a good walking track that follows the creek through a sheltered gully, where the wet forest is characterised by tall, sturdy eucalypts and tree ferns and the vegetation is quite different from that of the dry sclerophyll forest elsewhere in the region.

Dairy Creek is a very good bird spot and a pleasant place for an evening walk after a hot day. Eastern Yellow Robin, Golden Whistler, White-browed Scrubwren and Red-browed Firetail are especially numerous, and White's Thrush is a real possibility. It is also one of the few places in the Grampians where the delightful Rufous Fantail regularly appears during the summer months. Grey Fantails are plentiful here too, but you should take care not to overlook their more colourful relative. Koalas abound in the tall trees and in spring this is a good spot for the lovely greenhood orchid; be prepared to watch the ground as well as the trees here.

Halls Gap to Zumsteins (22 km) is a very pleasant drive with fine forest scenery en route. Several lookouts include the Boroka Lookout, one of Victoria's best-known viewing points. It offers sweeping views over Halls Gap and the ranges to the plains beyond.

Zumsteins

There is a small caravan park here, attractively laid out on the banks of a crystal-clear creek. The road from Halls Gap is unsuitable for caravans and those towing vans should approach Zumsteins from the west via Wartook. Since there is a kiosk for basic provisions but no other facilities or accommodation, it is considerably quieter than Halls Gap. The kangaroo-viewing area lies just west of the caravan park and to the east there is an easy twenty-minute walk along the creek to Broken Falls. Gang-gang Cockatoo, Crimson Rosella, Eastern Yellow Robin, Grey Fantail, Superb Fairy-wren, White-browed Scrubwren, White-throated Treecreeper and Red-browed Firetail can be seen near the creek, and Laughing Kookaburra and Pied Currawong frequent the camping area.

Just west of Zumsteins, on the road to Wartook, there is an extensive area of open woodland. Here the grassy understorey makes walking relatively easy and the open nature of the forest allows the observer to see many more birds than is generally possible elsewhere in the ranges. Emus are quite common here, and other species include Brown Goshawk, Painted Button-quail, Eastern Rosella, Pallid Cuckoo and Horsfield's Bronze-Cuckoo (spring–summer), Australian Owlet-nightjar, Sacred Kingfisher (summer), Black-faced and (rarely) White-bellied Cuckoo-shrike, Scarlet Robin, Jacky Winter, Crested Shrike-tit, Rufous Whistler, Restless Flycatcher, White-browed Babbler, Speckled Warbler (rarely), Weebill, Brown, Buff-rumped, Yellow-rumped, Yellow and Striated Thornbill, Varied Sittella, White-throated Tree-creeper, Yellow-faced, Black-chinned (rarely), Brown-headed and White-naped Honeyeater, Spotted and Striated Pardalote, Diamond Firetail, White-winged Chough, Dusky Woodswallow and Pied Currawong.

Many of the trees are heavily infested with mistletoe and when the plants bear fruit this is a good place for Mistletoebird and, very rarely, Painted Honeyeater. The strikingly beautiful Yellow-tufted

Honeyeater is also recorded on occasions.

Cherrypool is situated on the Glenelg River about 30 km west of Zumsteins — ideal for a day trip. There is a nice picnic area on the banks of the river, which is quite good for waterbirds, and substantial patches of open forest lie adjacent to the Rocklands Reservoir close by. A good way to reach Cherrypool from Zumsteins is via the Asses Ears Road to Glenisla Cross, and from there to the Henty Highway. There is an extensive Aboriginal art site just south of Glenisla Cross; it can be reached via Red Rock Road or from the Henty Highway via Billywing Road.

Wartook Reservoir lies a little to the north-east of Zumsteins and has a pleasant picnic area and a boat ramp, although the lake attracts few birds. The Mt Difficult road skirts the lake's shores and the adjacent forest is worth exploring.

Victoria Valley

This extensive area of woodland and swamp heathland lies south-west of Halls Gap, between the Serra and Victoria Ranges. Victoria Valley Road, which joins the Halls Gap to Zumsteins road about 8.5 km west of Halls Gap, is the main route through the valley and, although unsealed, is quite good under normal conditions. The woodlands consist of yellow box, peppermint and river red gum, with dense stands of melaleuca, wattle and banksia. The valley holds a good variety of birds, and Emus and kangaroos are frequently encountered along the road.

The Glenelg River flows through the valley and near it there are some extensive swampy heaths with sedge, beard-heath, sprengelia and grass trees. A particularly good patch occurs between Victoria Valley Road and Syphon Road, and it is easily reached via Serra Road. This is a good place to look for Southern Emu-wren, Chestnut-rumped Hylacola and, perhaps, the very rare King Quail. The quail has been recorded previously in the Grampians — in 1980 a pair were seen in the Grasstree Creek area south of Lake Bellfield — but there are few other places in Victoria (or indeed in southern Australia) where the bird has been sighted in recent times.

The northern section of the valley is worthy of a full day's exploration, but for those wishing to see the entire region in one day it is possible to drive south to Dunkeld via Greens Creek Road and Mirranatwa, and to return to Halls Gap on the main tourist road via Jimmys Creek. In the southern section, two spots are well worth a visit. Bryans Swamp State Game Reserve (648 ha) lies about 8 km south-west of the tiny township of Victoria Valley (actually just a loose collection of houses and some tennis courts). Because the swamp has few stretches of open water, waterfowl are scarce; it holds mainly cormorants, Sacred and Straw-necked Ibis, Black Swan, Purple Swamphen, Whiskered Tern and possibly Australasian Bittern. Whistling Kite and Marsh Harrier are quite plentiful, and the surrounding open country holds Long-billed Corella and Sulphur-crested Cockatoo, with Yellow-tailed Black-Cockatoo usually present wherever introduced pines occur.

Between Victoria Valley township and Dunkeld, at the Bundol Road junction, there is a picnic reserve beside Freshwater Lake (signposted). The lake is more open than Bryans Swamp and is easily viewed from the road. It usually holds plenty of waterbirds including Australian Shelduck, Pacific Black Duck, Grey Teal, Purple Swamphen and Eurasian Coot. The small swamp opposite is good for White-faced and occasionally Pacific Heron, egrets, ibis, Yellow-billed Spoonbill and Masked Lapwing.

The Victoria Valley, with its woodlands, and swampy heaths reminiscent of Tasmania's south-west, has much to offer the bird-watcher; the round trip from Halls Gap and back will require a full day. Remember that there is no petrol other than at Halls Gap and Dunkeld, and many of the roads and so-called townships are difficult to locate, so carry a good map as well as spare fuel. If time permits, a stop at the Jimmys Creek picnic ground, roughly midway between Dunkeld and Halls Gap, could produce something of interest. Powerful Owls were recorded there in 1982.

Lake Fyans and Lake Lonsdale

These lakes lie approximately north-east of Halls Gap and are part of the Victorian rural water supply system. Lake Fyans (526 ha) is the smaller of the two but is the better for bird-watching. It can easily be reached from Halls Gap via the Stawell road. A caravan park, boat club and picnic area are situated on the lake's eastern shore, but since power-boats are allowed on some parts of the lake it is best avoided at busy times. Opposite the caravan park there is an excellent swamp that usually holds masses of waterbirds such as cormorants, Pacific and White-faced Heron, egrets, ibis, spoonbills, Black Swan, Australian Shelduck, Pacific Black Duck, Grey Teal, Purple Swamphen, Eurasian Coot, Masked Lapwing and Black-winged Stilt.

On the southern edge of the lake there is an extensive area of open woodland that favours birds including Peaceful Dove, Eastern Rosella, Red-rumped Parrot, Sacred Kingfisher (summer), White-winged Triller (summer), Hooded Robin, Brown Treecreeper, Noisy Miner and White-plumed Honeyeater. On rare occasions both Blue-faced and Fuscous Honeyeater are recorded.

The lake has little emergent vegetation and holds few birds, but the margins are quite swampy in places, especially along the southern shores, and Black-fronted Plover and, in summer,

Latham's Snipe can be found here. Red-kneed Dotterel turns up from time to time.

Lake Lonsdale lies to the north and is best reached via the Stawell to Ledcourt road, which skirts its northern shores. Although at 2620 ha it is substantially larger than Lake Fyans, it has no emergent vegetation and its sandy shores are generally unattractive to birds. Nevertheless there are some good forested areas north of the lake and the sandy beaches make this an ideal place for swimming. There are no facilities but many visitors camp at a spot appropriately called Sandbar.

THE VICTORIAN MALLEE

Since European settlement, vast tracts of mallee in north-western Victoria have been cleared for cereal production and pastoral use. Today, Wyperfeld and Little Desert National Parks are virtually islands in a generally bare landscape, although fortunately they are substantial islands. Wyperfeld (100 000 ha) is one of the largest national parks in Victoria, and Little Desert (35 300 ha) one of the state's most valuable reserves. Further west, along the South Australian border between Kaniva and Pinnaroo, an extensive area of mallee and heathland has survived almost untouched and is now protected in the Big Desert Wilderness Park (113 500 ha).

Average rainfall in the region is about 300–400 mm per annum, but the amount varies considerably from year to year and the semi-arid environment is a delicate and complex one. A large group of plants and animals have adapted to the harsh conditions and, despite its seemingly lifeless appearance, the region supports abundant birdlife including many typical mallee species. These include the Malleefowl, Red-lored Whistler, Chestnut Quailthrush, Rufous-crowned Emu-wren, Striated Grasswren and Shy Hylacola. The Western Whipbird, now very rare in Victoria, possibly maintains a tenuous foothold in the Big Desert but it has not been reliably reported from there since 1969.

Wyperfeld National Park

This important reserve lies about 45 km north-west of Hopetoun and may be approached from the south via the Henty Highway and Yaapeet, or from the north via Ouyen. Despite its isolation, Wyperfeld is very well organised and has a splendid camping area with shelter huts, picnic facilities and toilets. There are no powered sites or showers, but water is provided for drinking and washing. The park has an exceedingly good information centre that houses displays covering the main points of interest, and there are two nature walks, a self-guided nature drive and longer bush walks. Slide talks and other activities are arranged from time to time, and detailed plant, mammal and bird lists are available from the information centre.

The vegetation at Wyperfeld can be broadly divided into three main communities: the riverine woodlands along Outlet Creek (the only watercourse in the park), dominated by river red gum and black box; the mallee scrublands to the east and north-west of Outlet Creek, dominated by mallee eucalypts with extensive patches of porcupine grass (*Triodia irritans*, called spinifex outside of Victoria); and the heathlands to the west and south-west dominated by banksia, she-oak and tea-tree. In spring and early summer, depending on winter rainfall, the park is usually blanketed with everlastings, orchids and other wildflowers, while a colourful array of flowering shrubs such as beard-heath, mintbush, honey-myrtle, heath-myrtle and grevillea further enliven the scene.

Western grey kangaroos are a common sight, but many of the other mammals are nocturnal and seldom seen. The birdlife is prolific: 224 species are listed for the park, although this figure includes quite a large number of waterbirds that only turn up when the area is flooded, usually once every twenty or thirty years. Many others are only occasionally recorded and a few, such as Red-lored Whistler, Chestnut Quail-thrush, Rufous-crowned Emu-wren, Striated Grasswren and Shy Hylacola, are secretive or elusive species that will take a good deal of searching out. Bird-watchers should try to arrange a visit to the park in winter, when it is possible to take longer walks and there is more hope of finding the special birds. At other times visitors should at least cover the two nature walks, and visit the mallee adjacent to Eastern Look-out where Malleefowl and Chestnut Quail-thrush are virtual certainties.

The park entrance is 18 km from Yaapeet and along the road there are several sandy embankments where White-backed Swallows breed. Round the camping area, 10 km inside the park, there is usually a good variety of birds including Emu, Brown Falcon, Australian Kestrel, Peaceful Dove, Galah, Sulphur-crested Cockatoo, Mallee Ringneck, Red-rumped Parrot, Southern Boo-book, Rainbow Bee-eater (summer), Welcome Swallow, Tree Martin, Richard's Pipit, Black-faced Cuckoo-shrike, Willie Wag-tail, Inland and Yellow-rumped Thornbill, Southern Whiteface, Red Wattlebird, Spiny-cheeked, Singing and White-plumed Honey-eater, Yellow-throated Miner, Striated Pardalote, Dusky Wood-swallow, Grey Butcherbird, Australian Magpie and Australian Raven. Small flocks of Pink Cockatoos, one of the region's special birds and surely Australia's most beautiful cockatoo, frequently fly over the camping ground, adding to the din created by the more numerous and noisy Sulphur-crested Cockatoos.

Lake Brambruk nature walk (6 km return) starts just east of the camping ground and on a hot day can be completed before breakfast. The track crosses several sand-dunes where there are

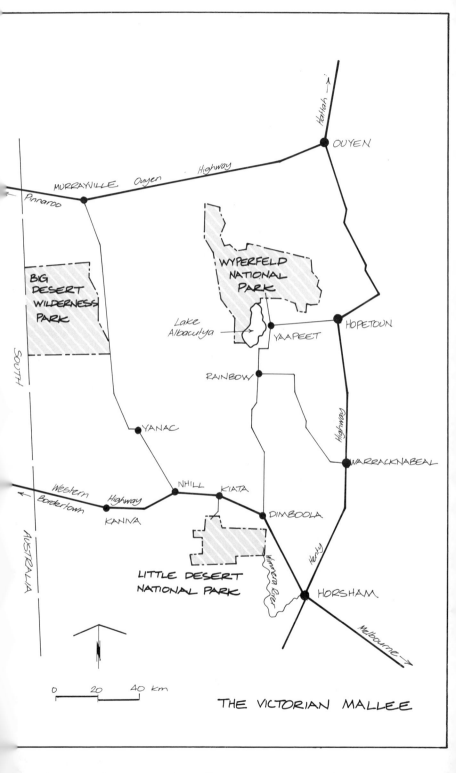

THE VICTORIAN MALLEE

patches of mallee, and between the dunes the flats are covered with heath and porcupine grass. Red-capped Robin and the exquisite Splendid Fairy-wren can be seen here, and Redthroats are quite plentiful in the heathy areas. This splendid songster can often be seen delivering its lovely canary-like notes from the top of a bush. The track continues to Lake Brambruk, which is usually dry, and the riverine woodland there is alive with parrots, honey-eaters and other birds.

The Eastern Lookout nature drive follows a 15 km circular route and passes through some of the best and most accessible mallee in the park. Along the way parrots are plentiful — among them Pink and Sulphur-crested Cockatoo, Mallee Ringneck, Red-rumped, Mulga and Regent Parrot, Blue Bonnet and, more rarely, Little Corella, Cockatiel and Budgerigar.

From the lookout there are sweeping views over the surrounding mallee, which holds Malleefowl, Chestnut Quail-thrush, Striated Grasswren and a host of other interesting species. Two good tracks (the Dattuck and Lowan tracks) provide easy access to the mallee and the lookout is a useful landmark. Nevertheless it is easy to get lost in this sort of country, so take great care. Adjacent to the Dattuck track there are some extensive patches of porcupine grass worth looking over for Striated Grasswren and Shy Hylacola, and Chestnut Quail-thrush is quite common in areas with plenty of stick litter. The well-camouflaged quail-thrush is very difficult to locate in the mallee and a good place to search for it is along the Lowan track, about 2 km south of the lookout. An early morning or late afternoon visit will be best. Watch for it running on or near the track and listen for its thin, high-pitched whistle.

To the left of the nature drive, about 500 m south of the Dattuck track, there is a narrow path leading to an active Mallee-fowl mound. A screen has been constructed to enable observers to watch the birds at work; approach quietly in case others are already there. Malleefowls are quite common at Wyperfeld and more than one hundred working mounds have been located in the park.

Other birds occurring in this area include Common Bronzewing, Purple-crowned Lorikeet, Horsfield's Bronze-Cuckoo (spring—summer), Australian Owlet-nightjar, Spotted Nightjar, Southern Scrub-robin, Hooded Robin, Jacky Winter, Crested Bellbird, Restless Flycatcher, White-browed Babbler, Weebill, Chestnut-rumped Thornbill, Striped, White-eared, Purple-gaped (especially when the mallees are in flower), Yellow-plumed, Brown-headed and White-fronted Honeyeater, Yellow-rumped Pardalote, White-winged Chough and Grey Currawong.

In addition to the Lake Brambruk track and the nature drive, bird-watchers should visit the open woodland and heathland to

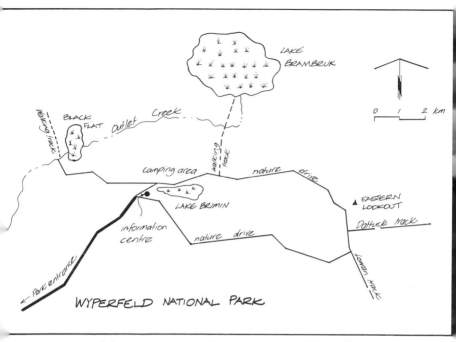

the west of the camping area, in the vicinity of Black Flat. The 6 km (return) Tyakil nature walk starts from the carpark at Black Flat and there are a number of birds in this area that are less likely to be seen in the mallee. Brown Treecreepers are very common in the woodlands; White-browed Treecreepers are worth looking for, particularly where there are cypress pines; and Tawny-crowned Honeyeaters occur in the heathlands.

'Peaceful' is the most frequent comment in the visitors book at Wyperfeld, and that just about sums up this wonderful park. The birdlife is not spectacular − there are no lakes teeming with waterbirds − but those who appreciate the subtle beauty of the mallee will not be disappointed. Visitors who do not wish to camp in the park will find caravan parks and motels at Rainbow and Hopetoun.

Little Desert National Park

Desert is an unflattering misnomer for what is, in fact, one of the richest wildflower areas in Victoria. In spring, if winter rains have been good, the park is carpeted with orchids and everlastings and a profusion of flowering shrubs add to the colourful scene. The varied vegetation supports an equally diverse avifauna and over two hundred species of birds have been recorded in the reserve. Many of the birds occurring further north at Wyperfeld can be seen here, including Malleefowl, many parrots, Southern Scrub-robin, Gilbert's Whistler, Splendid and Variegated Fairy-wren, Shy Hylacola, Calamanthus, and Purple-gaped, Yellow-plumed, White-fronted and Tawny-crowned Honeyeater.

Little Desert lies about 60 km north-west of Horsham via the Western Highway and Kiata. South of Kiata there are a splendid camping area, picnic facilities and walking tracks, and another picnic ground is located near the Wimmera River, south of Dimboola. There are several caravan parks and motels at Dimboola and Nhill, including the Little Desert Lodge (Nhill), which organises four-wheel-drive tours of the park.

Big Desert Wilderness Park

This huge area of trackless mallee heathland lies about 60 km to the west of Wyperfeld and stretches across the border into South Australia, where it is known as the Ninety Mile Desert. Despite a lack of surface water the region is not a desert, although early pastoralists regarded it as such. It is fortunate that they did, for the unique flora and fauna have survived virtually untouched and are now protected for future generations by the creation of the Big Desert Wilderness Park and several conservation parks in South Australia.

Big Desert is accessible from the south via the Western Highway and Nhill, or from the north via the Ouyen Highway and Murrayville. The unsealed road from Yanac to Murrayville passes close to its eastern boundary, but there are no facilities for visitors and this is not the place for a family holiday. Bush camping is permitted within the reserve (contact the ranger at Horsham first), and those with bushwalking skills will find this the ideal place for long-distance hiking. All supplies, including water, must be carried in.

Many of the birds occurring at Wyperfeld can be found here, and Big Desert is the only place in Victoria where the Western Whipbird may possibly still be found. The whipbird is more likely to be seen in South Australia, for instance at Comet Bore in Ngarkat Conservation Park. (Comet Bore is situated on the Bordertown to Pinnaroo road, about 8 km north of Bunns Bore. It is a very good spot for birds, including such sought-after species as Red-lored Whistler, Rufous-crowned Emu-wren, Striated Grass-wren, Calamanthus and Slender-billed Thornbill.)

HATTAH-KULKYNE

The Murray River flows some 2600 km from its source in the Snowy Mountains before entering the sea near Goolwa on the South Australian coast. It is Australia's principal river, one of the great waterways of the world, yet sadly there is only one national park on the Murray between Albury-Wodonga and the coast, a distance of 2300 km or so.

Hattah-Kulkyne National Park, with an area of 48 000 ha, is one of the largest reserves in Victoria. It features a series of billabongs and lakes on the Murray River floodplain south of Mildura. Fed by the Murray and Chalka Creek, the tranquil lakes — Hattah, Tullamook, Bulla, Marramook, Arawak, Nip Nip and many more — are surrounded by towering river red gums, while the intervening flats support open woodlands dominated by black box. Much of Hattah-Kulkyne, however, consists of sandy, semi-arid country (rainfall in the far north-west of Victoria averages about 250 mm per annum), and away from the lakes there are large tracts of low mallee with an understorey of porcupine grass (*Triodia*).

Following good floods, the Chalka Creek lake system attracts large numbers of waterfowl, as well as herons, egrets, spoonbills and a host of other waterbirds. When the lakes are full, Hattah-Kulkyne is a bird-watcher's paradise. Well over two hundred species of birds have been recorded in the park, and the juxtaposition of three well-defined habitats — wetland, open woodland and mallee — enables visitors to see a wide variety of birds in a relatively short time. Indeed, even inexperienced observers should have little difficulty finding at least fifty species in a day or two.

In 1980 a further 1550 ha immediately east of Hattah-Kulkyne National Park were declared a reserve. This area, known as the Murray-Kulkyne Park, was set aside to preserve the river red gum and black box woodlands along the Murray River, and to provide opportunities for a wide range of outdoor activities including camping, boating and fishing.

Hattah-Kulkyne National Park

There are two formal camping areas in this splendid national park — one on the shores of Lake Hattah, the other at Lake Mournpoul some 5 km to the north. While both areas have toilets and fireplaces, there are no showers. Since drinking water may be scarce, especially in summer, visitors should bring their own supplies. Caravans are allowed, but power is not available and the nearest caravan parks are at Ouyen (about 35 km to the south) and Mildura (about 70 km to the north).

To reach Lake Hattah, turn off the Calder Highway at Hattah township and follow the Murray Valley Highway towards Swan Hill. The main entrance to the park is about 4 km east of Hattah township. About 1.5 km along the entrance road there is a visitors centre housing displays covering the fauna and flora of the region. Park information, including bird and plant lists, can be obtained here. Those wishing to camp away from Lakes Hattah and

Mournpoul should contact the ranger before setting out. There is no kiosk in the park, but petrol and basic food supplies are available at Hattah township.

Lake Hattah, with its majestic river red gums, makes an ideal base for the bird-watcher. From the camping ground you can walk to the mallee areas along the Calder Highway, which forms the western boundary of the park. To the east, a wide walking track takes you through open woodland along the northern shores of Lakes Bulla, Brockie, Tullamook and Nip Nip.

For many visitors the lakes are the most attractive feature of the park. They occasionally dry up completely, therefore those travelling to Hattah in the hope of seeing large numbers of waterbirds should contact the ranger in advance and inquire about conditions. In early 1985, following several years of floods, the entire lake system was full, attracting a wealth of waterbirds: Great Crested, Hoary-headed and Australasian Grebe, Australian Pelican, Darter, Great, Little Black and Little Pied Cormorant, Pacific and White-faced Heron, Great Egret, Rufous Night Heron, Sacred and Straw-necked Ibis, Royal and Yellow-billed Spoonbill, Black Swan, Australian Shelduck, Pacific Black, Maned and Musk Duck, Grey Teal, Chestnut Teal, Australasian Shoveler, Pink-eared Duck, Hardhead, Black-tailed Native-hen, Purple Swamphen, Eurasian Coot, Red-kneed Dotterel, Black-fronted Plover and Black-winged Stilt.

Many of the species listed can be seen in the vicinity of Lake Hattah, especially in the early morning and late afternoon. A short distance east of the camping ground there is an embankment separating Lake Hattah from Little Lake Hattah. This is a particularly good spot for cormorants, herons, egrets, ibis and spoonbills; several species can usually be found feeding side by side near the regulator between the two lakes. With luck you may see a Rufous Night Heron here.

Other birds occurring in and around the camping area include Whistling Kite, Peaceful Dove, Common Bronzewing, Crested Pigeon, Galah, Sulphur-crested Cockatoo, Yellow Rosella, Red-rumped Parrot, Laughing Kookaburra, Noisy Miner, Spiny-cheeked and White-plumed Honeyeater, Striated Pardalote and White-winged Chough. Two sought-after species — Pink Cockatoo and Regent Parrot — are quite common in the park, often visiting Lake Hattah towards dusk.

For those wishing to explore the area to the east of Lake Hattah, the walk to Lake Nip Nip is highly recommended. To get to the lake, walk across the embankment and follow the track along the northern shores of Lakes Bulla, Brockie and Tullamook. Lake Nip Nip is about 5 km from the camping ground. Late in the day large numbers of kangaroos and Emus gather at the lakes to

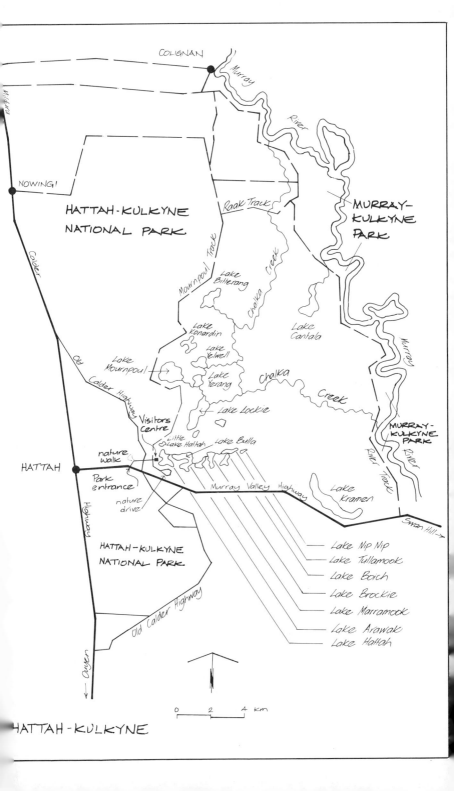

HATTAH - KULKYNE

drink, while small groups of beautiful Regent Parrots speed overhead, their harsh 'currak-currak' calls forewarning of their approach. If you are fortunate the parrots may alight nearby in a river red gum, the afternoon sun highlighting their rich, golden plumage.

Extensive tracts of mallee, much of which is in pristine condition, exist in the south-western section of Hattah-Kulkyne; however, the area to the north of the Murray Valley Highway is probably the best place to go bird-watching. Here the Murray Valley Highway, the Calder Highway and the Old Calder Highway form a convenient triangle within which there is little chance of becoming lost. The mallee, at its best in winter and spring, holds a host of interesting birds including Malleefowl, Mallee Ringneck, Crested Bellbird, Splendid and Variegated Fairy-wren, Chestnut-rumped Thornbill, Striped, White-eared, Yellow-plumed, Brown-headed and White-fronted Honeyeater, and Yellow-rumped Pardalote. Those prepared for some hard work may be rewarded with sightings of elusive species such as Southern Scrub-robin, Gilbert's Whistler, Chestnut Quail-thrush, Rufous-crowned Emu-wren, Striated Grasswren and Shy Hylacola.

Although many of Hattah-Kulkyne's birds can be found in the southern section of the park, it is worth taking a trip to the area north of Lake Mournpoul. Here there are remnants of the buloke and cypress pine woodlands that once covered the sandhills between the mallee and the floodplain. (In the late 1800s and early 1900s, when the land was used extensively for grazing, many trees were cut down for fence posts, while others were felled to provide stock feed in times of drought.)

Access to the northern section of the park can be gained via the Mournpoul Track. If you have time, drive around Lake Mournpoul and continue on to the Raak Track, then head east towards the Murray and south to the Murray Valley Highway via the River Track. This is a rather long trip (70 km or so), but well worthwhile because it takes you through a variety of habitats. En route you should see many of the following birds: Emu, Brown Goshawk, Wedge-tailed and Little Eagle, Australian Hobby, Brown Falcon, Australian Kestrel, Peaceful Dove, Crested Pigeon, Pink Cockatoo, Yellow Rosella (along the Murray), Mulga Parrot, Pallid (spring—summer) and Black-eared Cuckoo, Spotted Nightjar, Red-backed Kingfisher, Rainbow Bee-eater (summer), White-backed Swallow, Ground Cuckoo-shrike (rather rare), White-winged Triller (summer), Red-capped and Hooded Robin, Jacky Winter, Rufous Whistler, Restless Flycatcher, White-browed and Chestnut-crowned Babbler, Rufous Songlark (spring—summer), Brown Songlark, Yellow-rumped Thornbill, Southern Whiteface, White-browed (rare) and Brown Treecreeper, Spiny-cheeked and (along the Murray) Blue-faced Honeyeater, Little Friarbird (summer), Yellow-throated Miner, White-fronted Chat, Mistletoebird, Masked Woodswallow, White-browed Woodswallow (summer) and Grey Butcherbird.

The Mournpoul, Raak and River Tracks are well formed but rather sandy in places; ask the ranger about the condition of the tracks before setting out. Allow a full day for the trip and pack a picnic — along the Murray there are numerous shady spots where you can stop for lunch.

Hattah-Kulkyne, with its lovely tree-lined lakes and varied birdlife, is the perfect place for a short holiday. Winter and spring are the best seasons to visit the park; in summer it is often hot and dusty. For those not wishing to stay long in the park there is a short, circular nature walk through the mallee just inside the park entrance, and a 6 km nature drive commencing at the visitors centre.

Murray-Kulkyne Park
This small reserve adjoins Hattah-Kulkyne National Park, providing access to the west bank of the Murray River. It can be reached from the national park via the Mournpoul and Raak Tracks; from the Calder Highway via Colignan; and from the Murray Valley Highway via the River Track. Picnic tables and fireplaces are provided at intervals along the Murray, and camping is permitted at a number of sites on the banks of the river.

Murray-Kulkyne is an excellent place to go fishing, swimming, canoeing and of course bird-watching.

THE VICTORIAN ALPS
Victoria, with its remarkable diversity of habitats, has much to offer the bird-watcher. It is the smallest mainland state, yet the rugged mountains, turbulent rivers and tall wet sclerophyll forests of the north-east contrast dramatically with the rolling sand-dunes, dry watercourses and low mallee scrub in the north-west. These totally different environments are less than ten hours drive apart; on a summer's day, with a little luck and careful planning, you could be watching a Malleefowl at Wyperfeld National Park in the morning, and stalking a Superb Lyrebird on the slopes of Mt Buffalo before nightfall.

The Victorian Alps form part of a great crescent of high country stretching from the New South Wales border, in the north-east, to Lake Eildon in the south-west. Much of this magnificent region is virtually inaccessible, but the thriving towns of Bright and Mt Beauty can be reached readily enough via Wangaratta and the Ovens Highway.

Bright is probably the best place to stay. Mt Buffalo National Park (31 000 ha), one of the oldest and most scenic reserves in

Victoria, lies a short distance west of the town, while to the east is the incomparable Bogong National Park (81 000 ha). Proclaimed in 1981, Bogong protects a large area of alpine habitat and includes the state's highest peak — Mt Bogong (1986 m).

Bright

This attractive holiday resort lies in the heart of some of the finest walking country in Victoria. It has a wealth of accommodation including motels, hotels, guest houses, holiday units and at least six caravan parks. As might be expected, the town is packed with visitors during holiday periods and it would be wise to book accommodation well in advance, especially at Christmas and Easter.

Unfortunately a good deal of the original vegetation in the Bright district has been cleared, and the introduced pine plantations covering many of the surrounding hills are typically poor in birdlife. Nevertheless an assortment of common species can be seen in and around the town — Australian Kestrel, Galah, Crimson and Eastern Rosella, Laughing Kookaburra, Black-faced Cuckoo-shrike, Grey Shrike-thrush, Grey Fantail, Superb Fairy-wren, Brown and Yellow-rumped Thornbill, White-throated Tree-creeper, Red Wattlebird, Spotted and Striated Pardalote, Red-browed Firetail and Pied Currawong.

If you enjoy walking in lovely surroundings there are many kilometres of marked tracks in the vicinity of Bright (a map can be obtained from the Forests Commission office in Bakers Gully Road). A number of these — the Canyon Walk, the Golf Course Walk, the Valley View Walk and the Huggins Lookout Walk for example — can be completed in under two hours; those wishing to venture further afield, however, should try the Clear Spot Lookout Walk. Commencing some 2 km south of the town centre on Bakers Gully Road, this track climbs steadily through pine forests to a lookout offering panoramic views. You can see many of Victoria's highest mountains from the lookout on a fine day — Mt Buller, Mt Cobbler, Mt Hotham, Mt Feathertop, Mt Bogong, The Twins and The Horn.

Mt Buffalo National Park

This well-known and much-loved national park lies about 12 km west of Bright via the Ovens Highway and Porepunkah. Camping is permitted between November and May at a delightful site on the shores of Lake Catani, where toilets, hot-water showers and laundry facilities are provided. There are no powered sites (and no washing machines). Bookings are essential during the Christmas and Easter holidays; write to the ranger, Mt Buffalo National Park, Vic. 3745, enclosing a stamped, addressed envelope.

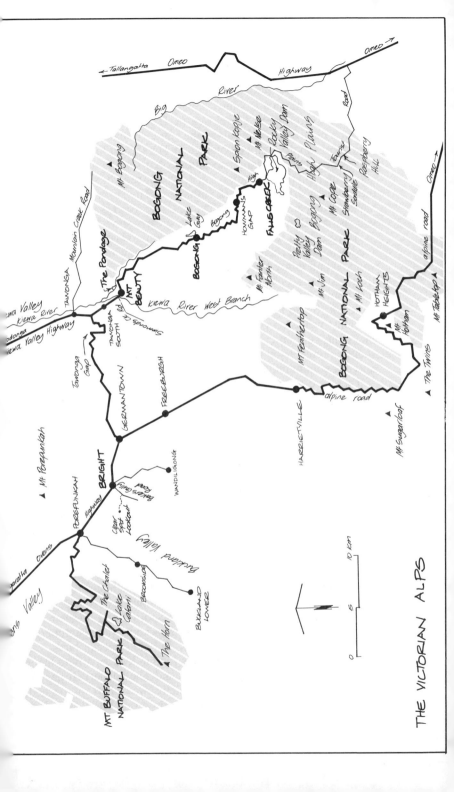

THE VICTORIAN ALPS

If you do not wish to camp, accommodation is available at The Chalet, a beautiful old guest house some 20 km from the park entrance. (During the snow season, usually June to September, accommodation is also provided at the Tatra Inn high on the Mt Buffalo Plateau.) Rooms can be booked at any branch of the Victorian Government Travel Centre. Day visitors will find picnic sites at a number of places along the entrance road, and meals and basic food supplies can be obtained at The Chalet kiosk.

A wide variety of plant associations occurs in the national park, and changes in the vegetation can be clearly seen by simply driving the 35 km or so from the park entrance to The Horn (1720 m), the highest point in the reserve. The entrance road is sealed, but if you visit Mt Buffalo in winter you must carry snow chains.

As you climb to The Horn, the following vegetation types are readily apparent (before reaching the plateau, wind down your car window and enjoy the fresh fragrance of the forest − alpine ash trees exude a delightful aroma reminiscent of camphor). Dry sclerophyll forest and open woodland, dominated by red stringy-bark and broad-leaved peppermint, cover the lower slopes and foothills; wet sclerophyll forest, consisting mainly of candlebark, mountain gum and alpine ash, occurs at higher elevations and in sheltered gullies; and snow gum woodland, grassland, heathland and bog communities dominate the plateau.

There are about 140 km of walking tracks at Mt Buffalo and you could easily spend two or three days exploring the park on foot. Those with less time to spare, however, will find the following walks provide an interesting introduction to the flora and fauna of the reserve.

Eurobin Falls: This short (1.5 km) but somewhat strenuous walk is about 2 km from the park entrance. The track climbs to Ladies Bath Falls, then continues on to Eurobin Falls.

The surrounding forest is usually alive with birds including Gang-gang Cockatoo, Australian King-Parrot, Crimson Rosella, Fan-tailed Cuckoo (chiefly spring−summer), Shining Bronze-Cuckoo (spring−summer), White's Thrush, Scarlet and Eastern Yellow Robin, Crested Shrike-tit, Golden Whistler, Satin Fly-catcher (summer), Rufous Fantail (summer), Eastern Whipbird, White-browed Scrubwren, Striated Thornbill, White-throated and Red-browed Treecreeper, Yellow-faced, Brown-headed and White-naped Honeyeater, Eastern Spinebill, Spotted and Striated Pardalote, Red-browed Firetail and Olive-backed Oriole (summer).

The Superb Lyrebird, one of Mt Buffalo's special birds, can usually be found near Eurobin Falls (and indeed anywhere along the road between the park entrance and The Chalet). It has the rather frustrating habit of slipping quietly away when approached, but if you tread carefully you may surprise one busily scratching

The Great Flight Aviary at the Melbourne Zoo, Victoria

Blue-faced Honeyeater – just one of the many birds to be seen in the Great Flight Aviary, Melbourne Zoo, Victoria

One of Victoria's best-known viewing points – Boroka Lookout, Grampians National Park

Early morning at Lake Hattah, Hattah-Kulkyne National Park, north-west Victoria

Crystal Brook drops into The Gorge a short distance from The Chalet at Mt Buffalo National Park, north-east Victoria

Snow gums in winter, Mt Buffalo Plateau, north-east Victoria

Crimson Rosellas are common around The Chalet at Mt Buffalo National Park

From the summit of Mt Oberon in Wilsons Promontory National Park, south-east Victoria, there are magnificent views over Tidal River, the site of the reserve's main camping area

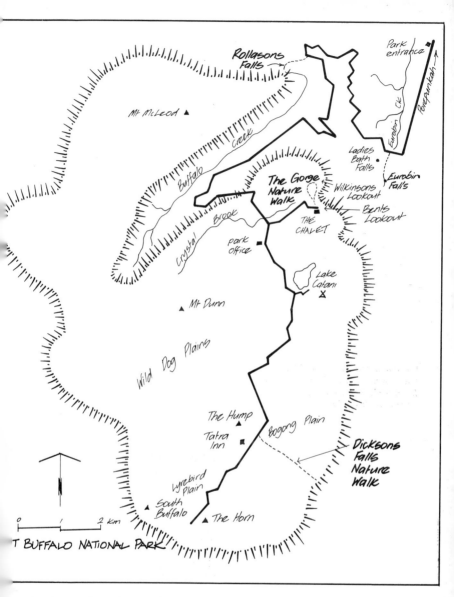

the forest floor in search of food. And you may be fortunate enough to spot a Pilotbird – a small, plump ground-dweller with a penetrating 'guinea-a-week' call – following in the lyrebird's footsteps. The two species are said to live in close association, the Pilotbird taking insects and other invertebrates from soil raked over by the lyrebird.

Rollasons Falls: This 4 km walk commences at a small picnic ground some 8 km from the park entrance. Towards the end of the track there is a T-junction; the path to the left leads to the upper falls, while the one to the right takes you to the lower falls.

The tall wet forest in this section of the park holds a good variety of birds, and many of the species already listed can be seen here. If you are reasonably fit, walk along the road from Eurobin Falls to the Rollasons Falls picnic area, bird-watching en route (it would be best to get to the park early in the day, before the traffic becomes heavy).

The Gorge Nature Walk: This 2 km circular walk begins at the Crystal Brook footbridge, a short distance from the Bents Lookout carpark (opposite The Chalet). The track leads to several lookouts including Wilkinsons Lookout, situated at the top of a sheer 250 m cliff-face. The views are truly breathtaking but birds are rather scarce, although you should see a few of the park's common species: Laughing Kookaburra, Flame Robin, Grey Shrike-thrush, Superb Fairy-wren, White-browed Scrubwren, Brown Thornbill, White-throated Treecreeper, Red Wattlebird, White-eared Honeyeater, Silvereye and Pied Currawong.

If you do not see a Superb Lyrebird between the park entrance and The Chalet, try looking in the forest near Bents Lookout — a tame lyrebird has taken up residence there, much to the delight of picnickers.

Dicksons Falls Nature Walk: South of The Chalet, the entrance road runs across the Mt Buffalo Plateau where the alpine ash forests give way to snow gum woodlands. In winter much of the plateau is covered by a deep blanket of snow; after the thaw a profusion of wildflowers — royal bluebells, mountain violets, orange everlastings, snow daisies, alpine marsh marigolds, Gunn's alpine buttercups — add a riot of colour to the wonderful alpine landscape.

The Dicksons Falls Nature Walk (4 km) commences near the Tatra Inn, about 30 km from the park entrance, and leads to the edge of the plateau. At this altitude birds are not particularly plentiful; in summer, however, the woodlands hold a number of interesting species such as Olive Whistler and Crescent Honeyeater, and it is worth searching boggy areas for Latham's Snipe. Other more common birds occurring on the plateau include Australian Kestrel, Richard's Pipit, Flame Robin, Grey Shrikethrush, Grey Fantail, White-browed Scrubwren, Silvereye and Grey Currawong.

Dicksons Falls is an ideal spot for a quiet stroll at the end of a warm summer's day. As the sun sets, wombats can be seen emerging from their burrows to feed near the track, while deep in the snow gums Grey Shrike-thrushes pour forth their rich, melodious notes.

Mt Buffalo is certainly a splendid national park. In winter the snow-covered plateau provides excellent downhill and cross-country skiing; in summer, visitors can enjoy a wide range of outdoor activities such as fishing, swimming, canoeing, rock-climbing and bushwalking. A walking track guide, detailed bird and plant lists, and many other useful publications can be obtained from the park office just south of the turn-off to The Chalet.

Mt Beauty

This pleasant country town is situated in the lovely Kiewa Valley at the foot of Mt Bogong. It has ample accommodation — hotels, holiday units, a guest house (the Mt Beauty Chalet) and a caravan park — and for those not wishing to stay at Bright it makes an excellent alternative base.

There are a number of good birding spots near the town itself and along the road to Falls Creek, which lies some 30 km to the south-east.

The Pondage: Is a large expanse of water about 1 km from the town centre via Lakeside Avenue. It usually holds a fair variety of waterbirds: Australasian Grebe, Great and Little Pied Cormorant, White-faced Heron, Great Egret, Black Swan, Pacific Black and Musk Duck, Grey Teal, Hardhead, Dusky Moorhen, Purple Swamphen and Eurasian Coot.

Picnic facilities are provided at the lake.

Simmonds Creek Road: Runs south from the Kiewa Valley Highway, providing ready access to a patch of tall eucalypt forest along Simmonds Creek. To reach the forest, turn off the highway near the West Kiewa River bridge and follow Simmonds Creek Road for about 4 km. From here the road is unsealed and narrow, but it carries little traffic and is therefore a good place for a walk.

Some of the birds you can expect to see here are Yellow-tailed Black-Cockatoo, Gang-gang Cockatoo, Australian King-Parrot, Brush Cuckoo (summer), White's Thrush, Eastern Yellow Robin, Olive Whistler, Satin Flycatcher (summer), Rufous Fantail (summer), Eastern Whipbird, White-throated and Red-browed Treecreeper, Noisy Friarbird (chiefly summer), Regent Honeyeater (rare, but certainly one to look out for), Yellow-faced, Fuscous and White-naped Honeyeater, Eastern Spinebill, Red-browed Firetail and Olive-backed Oriole (summer).

Tawonga Gap (895 m): Is on the Bright road, about 9 km north-west of Mt Beauty. From the picnic area at the gap there are magnificent views over the Kiewa Valley to Mt Bogong. Opposite the picnic ground a narrow track leads to a State Electricity Commission lookout; a walk here may prove fruitful, with Spotted Quail-thrush a distinct possibility.

Bogong: Situated in picturesque surroundings overlooking Lake Guy, Bogong is about 16 km south-east of Mt Beauty on the road to Falls Creek. It is the perfect place to stop for lunch (there is a picnic ground near the lake) or afternoon tea.

In summer there are usually a few waterbirds on Lake Guy, and the adjacent ornamental gardens, while not perhaps the best habitat for native birds, may produce something of interest – in April 1985 a small flock of Satin Bowerbirds was seen foraging near the tea rooms.

Howmans Gap (1250 m):   There is a picnic area here, some 26 km from Mt Beauty and 4 km from Falls Creek. State Electricity Commission tracks provide access to the surrounding forest; if the main road is not too busy, the walk from Howmans Gap to Falls Creek should be rewarding.

Falls Creek: This popular ski resort is located at 1500 m on the northern edge of the Bogong High Plains. There is of course no shortage of accommodation, including many guest houses that are open throughout the year. The resort does not, however, have a caravan park, and the nearest camping area is at Raspberry Hill in Bogong National Park.

During the snow season Falls Creek offers some of the finest skiing in Australia. In the warmer months, the resort could serve as a base for exploring the magnificent alpine country of the nearby Bogong National Park.

Bogong National Park

Stretching from Mt Bogong in the north to Mt Tabletop in the south, and from Big River in the east to Mt Hotham in the west, this fine national park contains most of the highest peaks in Victoria. The wet sclerophyll forests covering the slopes of the mountains give way to snow gum woodlands at about 1500 m. On the Bogong High Plains, which lie in the centre of the reserve south of Falls Creek, alpine grasslands and heaths are interspersed with numerous boggy swamps.

The park supports a rich and varied flora and more than three hundred species of plants have been recorded, including over forty that are endangered. Many small mammals, such as the rare mountain pygmy possum (thought to be extinct in the region until rediscovered at Mt Hotham in 1966), and nearly 150 species of birds occur in the reserve.

Bogong is largely undeveloped and much of it is inaccessible. Along the high plains road, however, between Falls Creek and the Omeo Highway, picnic grounds have been provided at the Rocky Valley Dam and Strawberry Saddle, and there is a small camping area with toilets and fireplaces at Raspberry Hill. Bush camping is permitted throughout the park, but walkers should be well prepared since weather conditions may change rapidly – with snowfalls occurring at any time of the year.

Alpine grasslands and heaths are poor in birdlife and, ornithologically at least, the high plains are not very exciting. Nevertheless the superb countryside south of Falls Creek is well worth seeing, and in summer this section of the park is readily accessible via Mt Beauty.

There are a number of walking tracks near the Rocky Valley Dam (a guide to Bogong's walks can be obtained from the park office on the Kiewa Valley Highway just north of Mt Beauty), and you should see a few of the following birds in this area: Emu, White-faced Heron, Maned Duck, Australian Kestrel, Latham's Snipe, Common Bronzewing, Yellow-tailed Black-Cockatoo, Gang-gang Cockatoo, Crimson Rosella, Richard's Pipit, Flame Robin, Olive Whistler, Grey Shrike-thrush, White-browed Scrubwren, Red Wattlebird, Crescent Honeyeater, Silvereye, Pied and Grey Currawong.

For those wishing to see more of this wonderful park, access to the northern section can be gained via Tawonga and Mountain Creek Road, while the western section can be reached via Harrietville and Hotham Heights.

WILSONS PROMONTORY

This beautiful area once formed part of a land bridge connecting Tasmania with the rest of Australia, but when the sea level rose and reopened Bass Strait the promontory became an island. Since then a sand-bank known as the Yanakie Isthmus has formed, and Wilsons Promontory is now the southernmost point of the Australian mainland.

Affectionately known as 'The Prom', this splendid national park of 49 000 ha lies about 230 km south-east of Melbourne and is one of the best known and most popular reserves in Victoria. The massive granite formations rise to 754 m at Mt La Trobe, the region's highest point, and the combination of superb coastal scenery and fine forest walks makes it an ideal place for holidays.

Tidal River, on the west coast about 32 km from the park entrance, has five hundred campsites (many are suitable for caravans but there is no power), a store, a post office, take-away food and petrol. For those not wishing to camp there are flats, lodges and motor huts. Advance bookings for campsites and accommodation are essential at Christmas, Easter and other holiday times, and it would be wise to check the availability of accommodation at any time of year. Write to the ranger, Wilsons Promontory National Park, Tidal River, via Foster, Vic. 3960, enclosing a stamped, addressed envelope. The main camping area is very crowded during the summer months, particularly at weekends, and a weekday visit would be rather more pleasant. Away from Tidal River, camping areas are available only for walkers;

permits must be obtained in advance.

The region has a varied and interesting flora with over seven hundred plant species, including the lilly-pilly, which is usually associated with subtropical and tropical rainforests. Coast and saw banksias are widespread and their flowers are an important food source for many nectar-feeding birds. Mammals include grey kangaroos, wallabies, wombats, possums and koalas.

Over 250 bird species have been recorded, and the promontory is one of the few places on the Australian mainland where the rare Ground Parrot occurs in fair numbers (it is still quite plentiful in south-western Tasmania). Visitors have the opportunity of seeing seabirds, waterfowl, waders and bush birds in a comparatively small area, and for bird-watching purposes four main habitats can be identified: Corner and Shallow Inlets, which lie east and west of the Yanakie Isthmus and consist of extensive tidal mudflats fringed with saltmarshes and mangroves; the grasslands, heathlands and swamps of the isthmus, which extend southwards to Darby River; the promontory proper, with its densely vegetated peaks and wet gullies containing remnants of rainforest; and the coastal zone, including the sandy beaches and offshore islands.

Corner and Shallow Inlets

Corner Inlet lies to the east of the isthmus and covers an area of approximately 52 000 ha. At low tide the exposed mudflats support a wealth of waders: in February 1983 about 46 000 birds comprising at least twenty-one species were recorded. Many waders occur in large numbers — 873 Pied Oystercatchers, 240 Sooty Oystercatchers, 851 Grey Plovers, 20 338 Red-necked Stints and 9068 Curlew Sandpipers were counted in 1983. Other species to be seen in good numbers include Mongolian Plover, Greenshank, Bartailed Godwit (about 7000 regularly visit the region in summer) and Red Knot. Corner and Shallow Inlets between them hold the largest numbers of Eastern Curlew yet discovered in Australia (about 2300 were present in 1983), and small populations of Masked Lapwing, Large Sand Plover, Ruddy Turnstone, Whimbrel, Great Knot, Sharp-tailed Sandpiper and Sanderling are also recorded. Double-banded Plovers visit the region in large numbers (1460 in July 1982) during winter.

Caspian, Fairy and Crested Terns breed, and Corner Inlet supports a large waterfowl population, particularly of Chestnut Teal. Access to Corner Inlet is somewhat limited, although the southern shores can be reached on foot via the Millers Landing track, and the western shores are accessible by car via Red Bluff and Foley Roads, just south of Yanakie. Access to the northern shores can be gained from a number of places including Foster Beach, Port Franklin and Barrys Beach. At low tide the mudflats

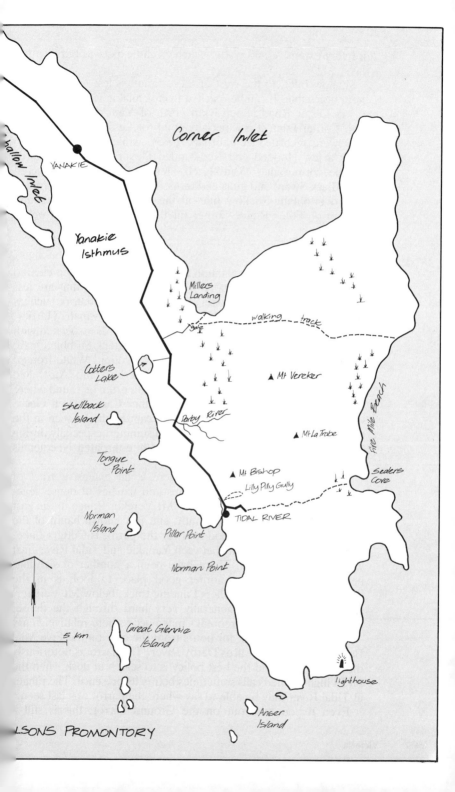

are very extensive and wader-watchers can expect to put in a full day.

Shallow Inlet, to the west of the isthmus, is less extensive and more accessible. It can be reached from Yanakie via Millar Road, or via Lester Road about 3 km north of Yanakie. More sandy than Corner Inlet, it is especially good for Lesser Golden Plover (303 were recorded in February 1983), while the ocean beach holds a few Hooded and Red-capped Plover. Other waterbirds include cormorants, White-faced Heron, Great Egret, Sacred Ibis, Black Swan, and gulls and terns. There is a pleasant caravan park overlooking Shallow Inlet at the end of Lester Road, and another on Foley Road, Corner Inlet. Both parks have powered sites.

Yanakie Isthmus

Much of the original vegetation on the isthmus has been cleared and the open habitat supports a number of species that are less likely to be found elsewhere. These include predators such as Black-shouldered Kite, Wedge-tailed Eagle, Marsh Harrier, Brown Falcon and Australian Kestrel. Other birds associated with the grasslands include Emu, Cattle Egret (winter), Stubble Quail, Galah, Sulphur-crested Cockatoo, Richard's Pipit, White-fronted Chat, Dusky Woodswallow, Grey Butcherbird and Australian Magpie. Yellow-tailed Black-Cockatoos can often be found where there are introduced pines, and in summer Cape Barren Geese visit the area to graze on pasture; they can usually be seen in the fields adjacent to Shallow Inlet. Also in summer, especially during unsettled weather, large numbers of White-throated Needletails hawk over the surrounding farmland.

To the south of the isthmus there is an extensive tract of heathland interspersed with swamps and patches of dense vegetation. This area is bounded by the Mt Vereker Range to the east and the Darby River to the south, and is a known haunt of the rare Ground Parrot. A good spot for the parrot is Cotters Lake, which lies roughly midway between Yanakie and Tidal River, just west of the main road. There have been a number of sightings here in recent years. Another good place to look is in the heathland south of the Millers Landing track, below Mt Vereker. Although the going is generally very hard through the dense, waist-high vegetation, firebreaks make access here relatively easy — it is possible to walk for hours from the gate on the Five Mile Beach track south towards Darby River. The parrot is notoriously difficult to flush and the best policy is to search at dusk when the bird's high-pitched calls sometimes betray its presence. The ranger at Tidal River may be able to say where the parrot was last seen.

Even if you miss out on the Ground Parrot, this is still a

wonderful area for walking, and other typical heathland birds, including Southern Emu-wren, Chestnut-rumped Hylacola, Calamanthus and Tawny-crowned Honeyeater, are there to reward the diligent searcher. Golden-headed Cisticola are also present in small numbers.

Darby River and the adjacent wetlands hold a variety of waterbirds, chiefly waterfowl such as Black Swan and Chestnut Teal, and the area is worth looking over for more elusive species including Brown Quail, Buff-banded and Lewin's Rail, Baillon's and Australian Crake, and possibly Australasian Bittern. Clamorous Reed-Warbler (summer) and Little Grassbird are sometimes seen round the margins.

The Promontory

In 1951 about 75 per cent of the park was burnt out, and as a result much of the vegetation is now very dense and virtually impenetrable. The best bird-watching areas are along the roads and tracks, and round Tidal River and the other camping and picnic grounds. Although Tidal River is often crowded and noisy, there are many fine walks to remote parts of the promontory; even at peak periods it is surprisingly quiet away from the main camping area.

The Lilly Pilly Gully nature track (5 km) is a short but pleasant walk that provides an excellent introduction to the region. The track passes through examples of heathland and dry and wet sclerophyll forest, and in the gully there is a patch of luxuriant rainforest dominated by lilly-pilly, swamp gum and blackwood and containing massed stands of beautiful tree ferns. The varied vegetation supports an equally diverse avifauna and there are probably few comparable areas in Victoria where such sought-after species as White's Thrush, Rose Robin (summer), Rufous Fantail (summer), Eastern Whipbird, Olive Whistler and Beautiful Firetail can be seen in under three hours.

The circular walking track leaves a carpark just north of Tidal River and for the first kilometre or so crosses a patch of heath where Beautiful Firetail and honeyeaters, including Red and Little Wattlebird, and Crescent and New Holland Honeyeater, are usually quite plentiful. The sclerophyll forest nearby on the slopes of Mt Bishop supports a good variety of birds including Brush Bronzewing, Gang-gang Cockatoo, Crimson Rosella, Pallid, Brush and Fan-tailed Cuckoo (spring–summer), Horsfield's and Shining Bronze-Cuckoo (spring–summer), Southern Boobook, Laughing Kookaburra, Black-faced Cuckoo-shrike, Flame, Scarlet and Eastern Yellow Robin, Crested Shrike-tit, Golden Whistler, Grey Shrike-thrush, Satin Flycatcher (summer), Grey Fantail, Superb Fairy-wren, White-browed Scrubwren, Brown and Striated Thornbill, Varied Sittella, White-throated and (rarely) Red-browed Treecreeper, Yellow-faced, White-eared, Brown-headed and White-naped Honeyeater, Eastern Spinebill, Spotted Pardalote, Silvereye, Grey Currawong and Forest Raven.

In the wetter, taller forest the delightful Rufous Fantail is quite common during the summer months, and the rainforest holds White's Thrush, Rose Robin and Olive Whistler. There is a small picnic area near Lilly Pilly Gully, and from here it is possible to return to the carpark along the upper slopes of Mt Bishop. The track ascends steeply from the picnic area along the edge of a deep gully where Eastern Whipbird can be seen. Although usually difficult to locate, the whipbird occasionally shows itself while running up a fallen limb and uttering its characteristic chuckling or whipcrack call.

The track levels out, and just past the Bishop Peak turn-off there is a lookout offering fine views over Tidal River. The surrounding forest is usually alive with small birds and the treetops are at eye-level for a change. The track is well graded, with only one short steep section. Koalas can be seen in the tall trees along the way, and wallabies frequent the picnic area. Allow three hours for this enjoyable walk, or more if the birding is good. Although sandy in places, the track is quite level for the first kilometre or so and would be a pleasant place to take a disabled friend.

There are many other fine walks on the promontory, ranging from 1 km to 27 km; the day walk to Sealers Cove is especially recommended. The track winds through wet forest and rainforest and en route there is outstanding forest scenery with masses of ferns. White's Thrush, Rose Robin, Olive Whistler and Rufous Fantail should be seen along the way, and near Sealers Cove Pilotbird is a possibility. The secluded beach at the cove is an ideal spot for lunch.

The Coastal Zone

The superb beaches of Wilsons Promontory are a feature of the national park but they generally hold few birds except Pied and Sooty Oystercatcher, Hooded and Red-capped Plover, and gulls and terns. Black-faced Shags frequent the rocky areas, and in summer Arctic Jaegers can occasionally be seen patrolling the offshore waters. Australasian Gannets are quite plentiful at any time of the year, and White-bellied Sea-Eagles can sometimes be seen circling majestically over the bays.

During the winter months the promontory is a good place to look for pelagics: Tongue, Pillar and Norman Points are all good viewing spots. Many of the offshore islands support seabird colonies where Little Penguins, Fairy Prions, Common Diving-Petrels, Short-tailed Shearwaters and Silver and Pacific Gulls breed. A permit to land on the islands must be obtained from the National

Parks Service at Tidal River.

Ornithologically Wilsons Promontory is an outstanding area and its relative isolation adds to its charm. The best times to visit are spring and autumn, when the cooler temperatures discourage some of the crowds.

THE GIPPSLAND LAKES

Situated to the east of Wilsons Promontory, the Gippsland Lakes are a group of coastal lagoons protected from the sea by a long finger of sand called Ninety Mile Beach. The four main lakes — King, Victoria, Wellington and Reeve — were virtually land-locked until 1889 when a channel was cut through Ninety Mile Beach at Lakes Entrance to provide access for ocean-going ships. Since then the salinity of the water has increased, particularly in Lake King and Lake Victoria, and today only the western portion of Lake Wellington remains fresh.

Gippsland is one of the most densely populated parts of rural Australia and much of the original vegetation has been cleared for housing and agriculture. Nevertheless the region's avifauna is by no means impoverished. Indeed, during a survey carried out between August 1977 and December 1978, 319 species of birds were recorded in the Gippsland Lakes catchment area, of which more than ninety were waterbirds.

Known as the Victorian Riviera, Gippsland's beaches and waterways attract many thousands of holiday-makers during the summer months. Not surprisingly there is no shortage of accommodation, which includes motels, hotels and caravan parks in Bairnsdale, Sale and Lakes Entrance. There is a youth hostel in Bairnsdale for those travelling on a tight budget.

If you want a really relaxing holiday away from the crowds, hire a cabin-cruiser in Metung and explore the lakes at your own pace. For details contact your nearest Victorian Government Travel Centre. Alternatively, stay a few nights at the Royal Australasian Ornithologists Union's bird observatory on Rotamah Island, south of Paynesville. Here you can get inexpensive accommodation while enjoying the company of fellow birders. A wide range of courses covering such topics as birds for beginners, natural history photography, sound recording and bird study projects are held at the observatory throughout the year. Further details can be obtained from the RAOU (the address is at the beginning of this chapter).

There are three main reserves in the Gippsland Lakes region: The Lakes National Park (2380 ha); the Gippsland Lakes Coastal Park (15 500 ha); and Glenaladale National Park (183 ha). The two larger parks protect a section of the coast west of Lakes Entrance and include areas of eucalypt and banksia woodland,

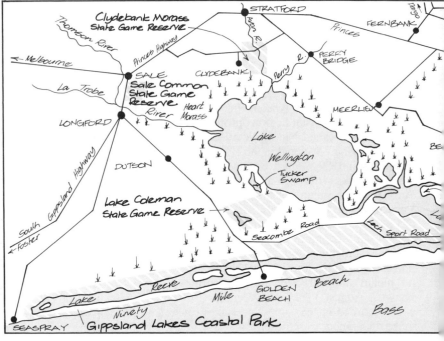

numerous low-lying swamps, and stretches of Ninety Mile Beach. Within Glenaladale National Park, which lies to the north-west of Bairnsdale, areas of dry sclerophyll forest growing on the more exposed slopes and ridges contrast markedly with patches of rainforest in the sheltered gullies. Glenaladale is of considerable interest to the bird-watcher because it is one of the few places in Victoria where Black-faced Monarchs breed.

In addition to these reserves there are many places worth visiting for birds, including Lake Tyers Forest Park, and Ewing Morass, Sale Common, Lake Coleman, Clydebank Morass and Macleod Morass State Game Reserves.

The Lakes National Park

Access to this reserve, which embraces the Spermwhale Head Peninsula and Rotamah Island, can be gained via Sale, Longford and Loch Sport. You can also reach the park by boat from Paynesville. Those wishing to visit the RAOU bird observatory on Rotamah Island should telephone the warden and arrange to be collected from Trapper Point on the Spermwhale Head Peninsula. At the entrance to the reserve, just east of Loch Sport township, there is a ranger's office where you can obtain camping permits, maps, brochures and a detailed bird list.

Camping is permitted at Point Wilson, about 12 km east of the

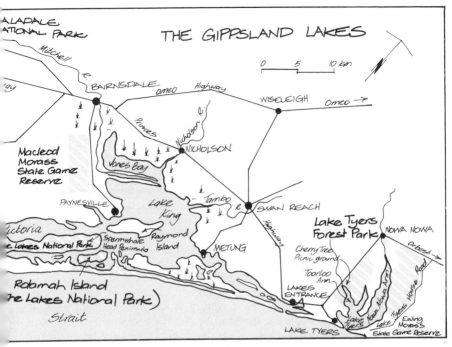

THE GIPPSLAND LAKES

park entrance. The camping area has toilets and picnic facilities
but no showers. During summer the reserve is very popular and
since there are only about ten campsites it would be wise to book
in advance. Write to the ranger, The Lakes National Park, Loch
Sport, Vic. 3851. Tracks within the park are sandy and unsuitable
for caravans, but there is a caravan park in Loch Sport. Day
visitors will find picnic facilities at Emu Bight, Cherry Tree,
Trouser Point, and several spots on the shores of Lake Reeve.

The vegetation on Spermwhale Head Peninsula consists mainly
of eucalypt and banksia woodland with an understorey of bracken.
In winter and spring the park is ablaze with wildflowers and
flowering shrubs including nearly forty varieties of orchid, and
heathland species such as golden grevillea, common fringe-myrtle
and ribbed thryptomene. Along the shores of Lake Victoria and
Lake Reeve, and around many of the peninsula's swamps, there
are dense stands of swamp paperbark.

There are more than 170 species of birds on the park's list.
Waterbirds are well represented (over fifty species), but forest-
dwellers, particularly honeyeaters, are also plentiful. Needless to
say the peninsula is good for waterfowl, waders and seabirds, and
many of the following can be seen quite readily: Great Crested
Grebe (at times in large numbers on Lake Victoria), Hoary-
headed Grebe, Australian Pelican, Great, Little Black and Little

Pied Cormorant, White-faced Heron, Great and (rather rare) Little Egret, Rufous Night Heron (rather rare), Sacred and Straw-necked Ibis, Royal and Yellow-billed Spoonbill (mostly in autumn), Black Swan, Australian Shelduck, Pacific Black and Musk Duck, Grey Teal, Chestnut Teal (especially plentiful), Australasian Shoveler, Lewin's Rail (seldom seen, but possibly more common than records suggest), Eurasian Coot, Pied Oystercatcher (can often be found at Point Wilson), Masked Lapwing, Silver and Pacific Gull, and Caspian and Crested Tern. In spring and summer, migratory waders — Eastern Curlew, Common, Sharp-tailed and Curlew Sandpiper, Greenshank, Latham's Snipe, Bar-tailed Godwit and Red-necked Stint — turn up in small numbers.

One of the best places to look for waterbirds (and to photograph them) is on the spit adjacent to the jetty at Point Wilson. It is a particularly good spot for terns, especially during stormy weather, and in summer at least three species, Whiskered, Common and Little, can often be found there. Bird hides have been constructed on the edge of Cygnet Swamp and at Lake Killarney; both places may be completely dry in late summer, however.

The park has quite an extensive network of walking tracks, including the Lake Reeve Nature Walk, the Dolomite track, the Lake Victoria track, the Murphy Hill track and the Lake Killarney track. Although these walks are short (they vary in length from 0.8 km to 3.5 km), they provide opportunities for nature study and introduce visitors to the flora and fauna of the park.

The Dolomite track is particularly rewarding. It commences at the Dolomite picnic area, near the ranger's office, and heads north around the edge of Dolomite Swamp to Pelican Point on the shores of Lake Victoria. The walk takes you through a variety of vegetation types — tea-tree thickets, stands of paperbarks and areas of eucalypt-banksia woodland — and along the way you should see many of the park's bush birds: Pallid and Fan-tailed Cuckoo (chiefly spring–summer), Horsfield's Bronze-Cuckoo (spring–summer), Black-faced Cuckoo-shrike (rarely in winter), White's Thrush (favours dense tea-tree thickets), Scarlet and Eastern Yellow Robin, Golden Whistler, Rufous Whistler (rarely in winter), Grey Shrike-thrush, Satin Flycatcher (summer), Grey Fantail, Eastern Whipbird (frequents areas of dense scrub), Superb Fairy-wren, White-browed Scrubwren, Brown and Striated Thornbill, White-throated Treecreeper, Red and Little Wattle-bird, Noisy Miner, Yellow-faced, White-eared, White-naped, Crescent and New Holland Honeyeater, Eastern Spinebill, Striated Pardalote, Silvereye, Red-browed Firetail, Dusky Woodswallow (spring–summer), Grey Butcherbird and Grey Currawong.

In addition to water and bush birds, the national park boasts an impressive list of predators. Raptor buffs can look forward to

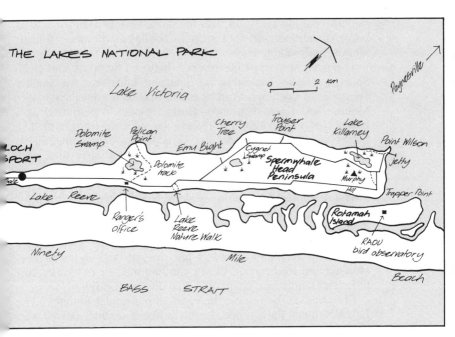

The Lakes National Park

seeing many of the following: Black-shouldered and Whistling Kite, Brown Goshawk, Collared Sparrowhawk, Wedge-tailed and Little Eagle, Marsh Harrier, Peregrine Falcon, Australian Hobby, Brown Falcon and Australian Kestrel. The White-bellied Sea-Eagle, arguably our most majestic bird of prey, breeds throughout the Gippsland Lakes region and is occasionally seen in the park.

Other species occurring in the reserve include Emu, Painted Button-quail, Brush Bronzewing, Yellow-tailed Black-Cockatoo, Rainbow, Musk and occasionally Little Lorikeet, Crimson and Eastern Rosella, Blue-winged Parrot (chiefly summer–autumn), Southern Boobook, Tawny Frogmouth, White-throated Needle-tail (a common summer visitor), Laughing Kookaburra, Sacred Kingfisher (mainly in summer), Welcome Swallow (spring–summer) and Tree Martin (spring–summer).

While many of the birds mentioned are quite common and can be found throughout much of south-eastern Victoria, rarity-hunters should not discount the possibility of seeing something notable in the park – in April 1985 two Channel-billed Cuckoos turned up on Rotamah Island.

Gippsland Lakes Coastal Park

This fragmented reserve covers sections of the Gippsland coast between Lakes Entrance and Seaspray, including a large area west of Loch Sport. The park was established to preserve tracts of the original coastal vegetation, and to enable visitors to enjoy a wide range of outdoor activities such as boating, swimming, fishing, hunting and walking.

The main section of the reserve, between Seaspray and Loch Sport, is readily accessible via Sale and Longford; the smaller areas east of Loch Sport can be reached by boat from Paynesville, Metung and Lakes Entrance. Bush camping is permitted at a number of sites within the reserve (contact the ranger at The Lakes National Park for details). Basic facilities, including toilets, are provided in some areas but campers must carry their own water supplies. For those wanting power and hot water there are caravan parks in Seaspray and Loch Sport.

The ocean-facing sand-dunes along Ninety Mile Beach are for the most part sparsely vegetated and attract few birds. Behind the dunes, where conditions are less severe, there are dense tea-tree thickets and stands of coast banksia. The beach itself is predominantly steep and narrow; a few pairs of Pied Oystercatcher, Hooded and Red-capped Plover can be found there, while Australasian Gannets are commonly seen diving offshore.

Elsewhere in the reserve the vegetation is similar to that of The Lakes National Park — open eucalypt woodland interspersed with banksias and coast tea-tree. As might be expected, many of the birds already mentioned can be found in the park.

Glenaladale National Park

Located on the Mitchell River, north-west of Bairnsdale, this picturesque national park has much to offer the bird-watcher. Despite its small size (183 ha), the reserve has an impressive bird list totalling nearly 140 species. Some of the more interesting birds that have been recorded there are Wonga Pigeon, Australian King-Parrot, White-throated Nightjar, Azure Kingfisher, Superb Lyrebird, Rose Robin, Pink Robin, Black-faced Monarch, Rufous Fantail, Brown Gerygone, Lewin's Honeyeater and Satin Bowerbird.

The best known feature of the park is the Den of Nargun, a small cavern situated in the bed of Woolshed Creek about 1 km west of the Mitchell River. According to Aboriginal legend the cavern was inhabited by the fierce 'Nargun', a mysterious rock-like creature that lured young Aboriginals into his den and ate them.

In Woolshed Creek gorge, and in some of the deeper side gullies, patches of warm temperate rainforest thrive in the moist conditions. Here kanookas, lilly-pillies and pittosporums, hung with thick woody vines, provide cover for a wealth of ferns, mosses and orchids. This is ideal habitat for the Black-faced Monarch, a species seldom seen further west in Victoria. Perhaps the most attractive bird on the park's list, the monarch is a regular summer visitor to Glenaladale; in early 1984 a pair successfully raised young in the rainforest near the Den of Nargun. If you walk along Woolshed Creek towards the Mitchell River you may find several other rainforest-dwellers – Rose Robin, Brown Gerygone and Satin Bowerbird.

Away from the sheltered gullies the vegetation changes abruptly to dry sclerophyll forest dominated by Victorian blue gum, mountain grey gum, yellow box, red box and kurrajong. In 1965 a severe fire swept through the park, destroying much of the forest on the higher slopes. The vegetation has largely recovered, however, and visitors can expect to see a wide variety of bush birds including many of the following: Common Bronzewing, Scarlet and Eastern Yellow Robin, Jacky Winter, Crested Shrike-tit, Golden Whistler, Rufous Whistler (spring–summer), Grey Shrike-thrush, Grey Fantail, Spotted Quail-thrush, Superb Fairy-wren, White-browed Scrubwren, Brown, Buff-rumped and Striated Thornbill, Varied Sittella, White-throated Treecreeper, Red Wattle-bird, Yellow-faced, Brown-headed and White-naped Honeyeater, Eastern Spinebill, Spotted and Striated Pardalote, Silvereye, Red-browed and Diamond Firetail, Olive-backed Oriole (summer) and White-winged Chough.

Glenaladale National Park is about 40 km from Bairnsdale via Lindenow and Walpa, and about 65 km from Sale via Fernbank. At the end of the entrance road (Waller Road) there is a picnic area with toilets; camping is not permitted. From the picnic ground, walking tracks lead to the Den of Nargun and to the Mitchell River. These walks can be completed in an hour or so. Those wishing to spend a full day in the park should follow the Mitchell River to Billy Goat Bend and The Amphitheatre – Eastern Whipbirds are plentiful in the dense scrub near the start of the Billy Goat Bend track.

Lake Tyers Forest Park

Lake Tyers Forest Park is a Forests Commission reserve lying to the east of Lakes Entrance. It covers an area of 5300 ha and protects remnants of the original vegetation around Lake Tyers, including isolated pockets of rainforest.

The main section of the park, west of Nowa Nowa Arm, is readily accessible via the Princes Highway. Here there are many kilometres of forest roads, walking tracks, and picnic sites at Blackfellows Arm, Caligurnie Bay, Long Point, Crystal Bay, Burnt Bridge and Cherry Tree. The eastern section can be reached via Lake Tyers House Road, which leaves the Princes Highway about 7 km east of Nowa Nowa. Access to this part of the reserve is rather limited; there are, however, picnic grounds on Nowa Nowa Arm near the end of Lake Tyers House Road. Camping is not permitted in the park.

Lake Tyers is an excellent place to go bird-watching and visitors could easily spend several days exploring the area. Some of the more interesting birds that have been recorded in the vicinity of the lake include Rufous Night Heron, Australasian Bittern, Blue-billed Duck, Buff-banded Rail, Wonga Pigeon, Brush Cuckoo (summer), Powerful and Sooty Owl, White-throated Nightjar, Azure Kingfisher, Rose Robin (summer), Olive Whistler, Rufous Fantail (summer), Brown Gerygone, and Lewin's and Scarlet Honeyeater.

For those with little time to spare, a walk along the upper reaches of Toorloo Arm is highly recommended. Commence your walk at the Cherry Tree picnic ground (just off the Princes Highway about 12 km north-east of Lakes Entrance) and head south to Burnt Bridge, a distance of 1.5 km or so. Lewin's Honeyeaters are quite common in this area, and the sharp-eyed observer may catch a glimpse of an Azure Kingfisher perched in the trees bordering Toorloo Arm. This avian gem is seldom found far from water; it is a true kingfisher, diving beneath the surface to catch its prey. The kingfisher is often overlooked since it has a habit of sitting motionless for long periods; but eventually a loud plop tells you one is fishing nearby.

Lake Tyers itself is sheltered and peaceful — the perfect spot to go boating (there is a boat ramp at Lake Tyers township) or canoeing. The entrance to the lake is usually sealed by a sand-bar, enabling the more adventurous to walk along the coast from Lake Tyers township to Ewing Morass State Game Reserve — a good place for Brown Quail, rails, crakes, Little Grassbird, Southern Emu-wren, Chestnut-rumped Hylacola, Calamanthus and Beautiful Firetail.

Gippsland Lakes state game reserves

The lakes, swamps and morasses extending from Sale eastwards to Lakes Entrance regularly support an estimated 40 000 to 50 000 waterfowl, and hold good numbers of other waterbirds including cormorants, herons, egrets and waders. Many of the region's game reserves are readily accessible, but visitors are not allowed to camp and there are no facilities other than a few walking tracks. Since shooting is permitted in these reserves they are best avoided during the duck-hunting season, usually March to May.

Sale Common State Game Reserve: Is on the South Gippsland Highway opposite the Thomson River Caravan Park, about 2 km from the town centre. Much of the area can be seen from the highway; for better views climb over the main gate and follow the wide track through the reserve.

Waterbirds — cormorants, herons, egrets, spoonbills and ducks — are usually present in good numbers, and at least one pair of Whistling Kites breeds in the reserve. Part of the reserve is well timbered and holds quite a variety of bush birds. Golden-headed Cisticolas are common.

Lake Coleman State Game Reserve: Lies to the south-east of Sale, just off the Dutson to Loch Sport road. Access can be gained via Lake Coleman Road. Between Lake Coleman and Lake Wellington there are numerous lagoons, swamps and morasses worth exploring, but in places the vegetation is extremely dense — be prepared for some hard work!

Notable species recorded in the area include Australasian Bittern, Glossy Ibis, Freckled Duck, Buff-banded Rail and White-winged Tern. Tucker Swamp, on the shores of Lake Wellington, is an important breeding ground for Pied Cormorants.

Clydebank Morass State Game Reserve: Is on the Avon River, between Perry Bridge and Clydebank, and is readily accessible via the Stratford to Meerlieu road. It is a good place for waterbirds — cormorants, herons, egrets, waterfowl, and possibly rails and crakes. Masked Lapwing and Black-fronted Plover can usually be found here, while other species include Marsh Harrier, Golden-headed Cisticola and White-fronted Chat.

Macleod Morass State Game Reserve: Situated to the south of Bairnsdale, this important wildlife refuge can be reached via the Bairnsdale to Paynesville road. The morass, the Mitchell River and Jones Bay provide some of the best birding in the Gippsland Lakes region. Great Crested, Hoary-headed and Australasian Grebe, Australian Pelican, Great Egret, Sacred and Straw-necked Ibis (both species breed in the reserve), Royal and Yellow-billed Spoonbill, Black Swan, Australian Shelduck, Chestnut Teal, Australasian Shoveler, Maned Duck, Marsh Harrier, Purple Swamphen, Eurasian Coot, Black-winged Stilt and Caspian Tern are some of the birds you can expect. Occasionally rarities such as Darter, Glossy Ibis and Blue-billed Duck turn up.

Undoubtedly the Gippsland Lakes region is one of the best places in Victoria for a bird-watching holiday. Even around major tourist centres such as Lakes Entrance birds are plentiful and easy to observe. And you should not leave without taking a cruise on the lakes; during the summer holiday season commercial operators in Lakes Entrance offer half-day and full-day trips to Metung and Paynesville.

EAST GIPPSLAND

Croajingolong National Park
For many years Victorian conservationists endeavoured to have

the entire coast between Sydenham Inlet and the New South Wales border declared a national park. In 1979 their efforts were rewarded when Mallacoota Inlet, Wingan Inlet and Captain James Cook National Parks were enlarged and amalgamated to form Croajingolong (86 000 ha), one of the state's most impressive reserves.

Protecting nearly 100 km of wild, unspoiled coastline, Croajingolong contains a rich diversity of habitats — vast tracts of open eucalypt forest, large areas of coastal heath, patches of banksia woodland and pockets of warm temperate rainforest. It is one of the best places to go bird-watching in Victoria — about 250 species have been recorded there — and the heathlands in particular hold a number of rare and interesting birds: Ground Parrot, Southern Emu-wren, Eastern Bristlebird, Chestnut-rumped Hylacola, Calamanthus, Tawny-crowned Honeyeater and Beautiful Firetail.

Access to much of the reserve is somewhat difficult, but the following spots can be reached quite easily from the Princes Highway, which runs more or less parallel to the park's northern boundary. The Thurra River and Wingan Inlet camping grounds are very popular, and sites must be booked in advance for the Christmas and Easter holidays. Write to the ranger, Croajingolong National Park, PO Box 60, Cann River, Vic. 3889, enclosing a stamped, addressed envelope. Bookings are not accepted at other times of the year; however it would be wise to call at the park office (at Cann River township) to inquire about the availability of sites, since the camping grounds are almost 40 km from the highway — a long way to drive if you are going to find them full.

Thurra River camping ground: Is located to the south-east of Cann River township, near the mouth of the Thurra River. It has toilets and fireplaces, but there are no showers. Caravans are permitted, although the unsealed road leading to the camping area is narrow and steep in places and may become impassable after heavy rain.

This section of the park features long sandy beaches, backed by low hills covered with tall eucalypt forest and heath. In March 1983 about 70 per cent of Croajingolong was burnt in the disastrous bushfires that devastated many of the East Gippsland forests. The vegetation has recovered remarkably well, but the effects of the fires are still readily apparent, especially in the area south of Cann River township.

Wingan Inlet camping ground: Can be reached via West Wingan Road, which leaves the Princes Highway about 17 km east of Cann River township. The entrance road is unsealed and the last 10 km or so are rough, narrow and winding, making this route unsuitable for caravans. Situated in superb surroundings on the western shores of Wingan Inlet, the camping area has been rebuilt

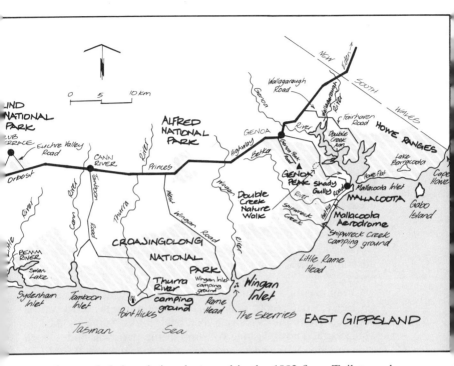

and extended since being destroyed in the 1983 fires. Toilets and fireplaces are provided, but there are no showers.

From the camping ground a walking track leads southwards along the edge of the inlet to the ocean beach, passing through a variety of vegetation types including patches of swamp paperbark and thickets of coast tea-tree. Some of the birds you can expect to see between the camping ground and the beach are Rainbow Lorikeet (especially when the eucalypts are in flower), Crimson Rosella, Fan-tailed Cuckoo (chiefly spring–summer), Laughing Kookaburra, Black-faced Cuckoo-shrike (rarely in winter), Eastern Yellow Robin, Crested Shrike-tit, Golden Whistler, Grey Shrike-thrush, Grey Fantail, Eastern Whipbird, Superb Fairy-wren, White-browed Scrubwren, Brown and Striated Thornbill, White-throated Treecreeper, Red and Little Wattlebird, Lewin's, Yellow-faced, Crescent and New Holland Honeyeater, Eastern Spinebill, Spotted and Striated Pardalote, Silvereye, Red-browed Firetail and Pied Currawong.

Wingan Inlet – a broad expanse of sheltered water that is best explored by boat or canoe – usually holds an assortment of waterbirds such as Hoary-headed Grebe, Australian Pelican, Great, Little Black and Little Pied Cormorant, White-faced Heron, Great Egret, Royal Spoonbill, Black Swan, Pacific Black Duck,

Grey Teal, Chestnut Teal, Silver Gull, Caspian and Crested Tern.

Those who enjoy beach and coast walking will find that Croajingolong has much to offer. The beaches do not attract large numbers of birds, but a few species — Pied and Sooty Oystercatcher, Hooded and Red-capped Plover — can be found readily enough in the vicinity of the inlet, while Australasian Gannets and an occasional White-bellied Sea-Eagle can be seen patrolling the coast. Little Penguins, Silver Gulls and Crested Terns breed on The Skerries, a group of three small islets lying 100 m offshore from the mouth of the Wingan River.

Having explored the area around Wingan Inlet, it is worth spending some time bird-watching along West Wingan Road. Spotted Quail-thrush and a number of other interesting species occur in the forests between the inlet and the Princes Highway.

Mallacoota: Is a very popular holiday spot on the western shores of Mallacoota Inlet. The township, about 25 km south-east of Genoa via a good sealed road, has a wealth of accommodation including motels, holiday units, a youth hostel and five caravan parks.

Croajingolong National Park can be reached from Mallacoota via Betka Road; more detailed information about access can be obtained from the Victorian National Parks Service office in Mallacoota. Those wishing to camp in the park will find a small camping area with toilets and fireplaces near the mouth of Shipwreck Creek, about 15 km south-west of the township. The track leading to Shipwreck Creek is narrow and steep and therefore unsuitable for caravans.

Although it is usually very crowded at holiday times, Mallacoota is an excellent place for birds and there are many areas nearby worth visiting.

Shady Gully: Is on the Genoa road, 1 km north-west of the town centre. The tall wet sclerophyll forest here holds quite a variety of birds: Wonga Pigeon, Australian King-Parrot, Brush Cuckoo (summer), Shining Bronze-Cuckoo (spring—summer), Cicadabird (summer), Rose Robin (rarely in winter), Pink and Eastern Yellow Robin, Crested Shrike-tit, Black-faced Monarch (summer), Leaden Flycatcher (summer), Rufous Fantail (summer), Brown Gerygone, Red-browed Treecreeper, Lewin's, White-naped and possibly Scarlet Honeyeater, Red-browed Firetail and Satin Bowerbird.

Double Creek Nature Walk: Commences about 8 km north-west of Mallacoota on the road to Genoa. It is a short (1 km) circular trail leading through a patch of rainforest (part of Croajingolong National Park) where you may find Superb Lyrebird, White's Thrush, Rufous Fantail (summer), Pilotbird and Lewin's Honeyeater. Large-billed Scrubwren is a possibility here.

If you have time, walk across the road and follow the track along Double Creek Arm − a likely place for Azure Kingfisher.

Mallacoota Aerodrome: Lies about 5 km south-west of the township and can be easily reached via Betka Road. En route a stop at the Betka River bridge should produce a few waterbirds. However, it is the coastal woodlands and heathlands stretching from the aerodrome to beyond Little Rame Head that make this such an interesting area. Well known to Victorian bird-watchers, the heathlands hold a number of sought-after species including Southern Emu-wren (quite plentiful, but best pursued on a still day when there is no wind to carry away the bird's thin trill), Chestnut-rumped Hylacola, Calamanthus and Tawny-crowned Honeyeater. You should have little difficulty finding these birds in the heath just south of the aerodrome. Ground Parrots are also occasionally seen in this area, but you will have a better chance of finding this extremely elusive species if you methodically search the heathlands between Shipwreck Creek and Little Rame Head. Although Ground Parrots are now generally rare on the Australian mainland, they remain quite common in suitable habitat within Croajingolong National Park.

If you are not fortunate enough to find a Ground Parrot, the trip to Shipwreck Creek should nevertheless prove rewarding. The open woodlands in the vicinity of the creek offer excellent birding, and you should see many of the following species: Brown Goshawk, Collared Sparrowhawk, Australian Hobby, Painted Button-quail, Common Bronzewing, Yellow-tailed Black-Cockatoo, Rainbow, Musk and Little Lorikeet, Turquoise Parrot (seldom recorded, but one worth searching for), Pallid and Fan-tailed Cuckoo (chiefly spring−summer), Horsfield's Bronze-Cuckoo (spring−summer), Tawny Frogmouth, Sacred Kingfisher (mainly in summer), Scarlet Robin, Jacky Winter, Golden Whistler, Rufous Whistler (rarely in winter), Satin Flycatcher (summer), White-throated Gerygone (summer), Brown and Striated Thornbill, Varied Sittella, White-throated Treecreeper, Red and Little Wattlebird, Regent Honeyeater (rare), Yellow-faced, Brown-headed, White-naped, Crescent and New Holland Honeyeater, Mistletoebird, Spotted and Striated Pardalote, Red-browed Firetail, Olive-backed Oriole (summer), Dusky Woodswallow (chiefly spring−summer) and Grey Butcherbird.

Genoa Peak: Is about 35 km north-west of Mallacoota via Genoa and the Princes Highway. Picnic facilities are provided near the carpark at the end of Genoa Peak Road, and a walking track leads to the top of the peak from where there are magnificent views of Mallacoota Inlet. The surrounding forest holds many interesting birds − Glossy Black-Cockatoos are often to be found feeding in casuarinas on the slopes below the peak.

Howe Ranges: Lie to the east of Mallacoota Inlet, adjacent to the New South Wales border. The entire area is densely forested and worthy of thorough exploration. To get there, take the road from Mallacoota to Genoa, head east along the Princes Highway and turn off after about 8 km at Wallagaraugh Road. En route it is worth spending a little time birding in and around Genoa. The Genoa River flats usually hold something of interest — Cattle Egret for instance.

About 6 km along Wallagaraugh Road there is a junction (a good spot for Bell Miners); turn left here and follow Fairhaven Road until you reach the boundary of Croajingolong National Park (signposted). Fairhaven Road takes you to the eastern side of Mallacoota Inlet and into the Howe Ranges. It is well signposted and suitable for conventional vehicles, but many other tracks in the area are poorly marked and may become impassable after rain. Before setting out, call at the Victorian National Parks Service office at Mallacoota where you can obtain more detailed information about access to this remote section of the park.

The Howe Ranges are exceedingly rich in birdlife (pack a picnic lunch and spend a full day there), and you can expect to see a wide variety of species including such highlights as Brush Bronzewing, Wonga Pigeon, Gang-gang Cockatoo, Australian King-Parrot, Powerful Owl, Sooty Owl, White-throated Nightjar, Azure Kingfisher, Superb Lyrebird, White-bellied Cuckoo-shrike, Cicadabird, White's Thrush, Rose Robin, Pink Robin, Olive Whistler, Black-faced Monarch, Rufous Fantail, Spotted Quail-thrush, Pilotbird, Large-billed Scrubwren, Brown Gerygone, Red-browed Tree-creeper, Yellow-tufted Honeyeater and Scarlet Honeyeater.

The more adventurous may care to visit the Howe Flat — Lake Barracoota area, where there is a possibility of finding the rare Eastern Bristlebird.

Lind and Alfred National Parks

It would take at least a week to explore Croajingolong thoroughly, since it is by far the most extensive national park in East Gippsland; indeed, it is one of the largest reserves in Victoria. There are, however, two smaller parks in the region, Lind and Alfred, that can be easily reached from the Princes Highway. Both are worth seeing, although unfortunately Alfred National Park was almost totally burnt out during the 1983 fires and it will be many years before its splendid rainforests recover.

Lind National Park (1166 ha): Lies just north of the Princes Highway, about 53 km east of Orbost and about 20 km west of Cann River. To reach the park, leave the highway on the road to Club Terrace; the reserve entrance is on the right about 3.5 km from the turn-off.

Within the park there are two distinct types of vegetation. Warm temperate rainforest, characterised by lilly-pilly, kanooka and blackwood, with a profusion of tree and ground ferns, occurs along Euchre Creek. Away from the creek, which flows through the centre of the park, the open eucalypt forest is dominated by silvertop ash.

Lind is quite rich in birdlife. Superb Lyrebird and Olive Whistler are two notable species that can be seen while walking along Euchre Valley Road (the only route through the park), and Spotted Quail-thrush occur in the more open forest near Club Terrace township.

Camping is not permitted in the reserve. There is a picnic area on Euchre Valley Road about 2 km from Club Terrace, and a 4 km walking track leading from the picnic ground to the Princes Highway.

Alfred National Park (2300 ha): Straddles the Princes Highway, about 18 km east of Cann River and about 25 km west of Genoa. Camping is not permitted, and walking tracks in the reserve have been closed due to fire damage. If you wish to visit the park, call at the Victorian National Parks Service office at Cann River or Mallacoota for up-to-date information about access.

New South Wales

Useful addresses

Australian Bird Study Association
PO Box A313
Sydney South, NSW 2000

New South Wales Field Ornithologists Club
Box C436, PO Clarence Street
Sydney, NSW 2000

Cumberland Bird Observers Club
Secretary, 1 Balmoral Road
Kellyville, NSW 2153

Illawarra Bird Observers Club
Secretary, PO Box 56
Fairy Meadow, NSW 2519

Hunter Bird Observers Club
Secretary, PO Box 24
New Lambton, NSW 2305

New South Wales National Parks and Wildlife Service
189 Kent Street
Sydney, NSW 2000

Key to Maps

▨	Public land
▨	Areas of water
▲	Mountain peak
⌁	Mountain range or plateau
COBAR ●	Place name
✕	Camping area
⌁	Lighthouse
⌁ ⌁ ⌁	Marsh
▬▬▬	Major road or highway
───	Minor road
------	Foot track
··—··—	National park boundary
·───	State boundary
∿	River or creek

SYDNEY

In 1788 Captain Arthur Phillip sailed into Port Jackson with fewer than 1500 settlers and established Australia's first European colony at Sydney Cove. Today that first settlement has become a flourishing modern city with a population of over three million. Built around one of the finest natural harbours in the world, Sydney is Australia's largest and, many would say, most colourful capital. On summer afternoons, when all of Sydney seems to be out on the harbour, the billowing spinnakers of thousands of yachts transform the sparkling blue waters of Port Jackson into a collage of red, gold and green. And with its numerous delightful coves, inlets and beaches, and of course its bridge and opera house, the harbour is every bit as beautiful from the air as it is from the water. For overseas visitors arriving by plane it provides a fitting and memorable introduction to Australia.

From the main business district, on the southern shores of Port Jackson, the city's suburbs extend north along the coast to Palm Beach, south to beyond Cronulla, and west to the foothills of the Blue Mountains. Despite its size, however, Sydney has a great deal to offer the bird-watcher. It is almost entirely surrounded by reserves and there are no fewer than twelve national parks close to the city — Sydney Harbour National Park to the east; Royal and Heathcote National Parks to the south; Ku-ring-gai Chase, Marramarra, Dharug, Brisbane Water and Bouddi National Parks to the north; and Blue Mountains, Kanangra Boyd, Wollemi and Thirlmere Lakes National Parks to the west. In addition there are a number of parks and gardens, state recreation areas and state forests in and around the city, as well as some notable waterbird spots such as those in the vicinity of Kurnell on the southern shores of Botany Bay.

The region's avifauna is prolific. More than half of Australia's birds — some four hundred species — have been recorded in the Sydney area, and a wide variety can be found within 50 km or so of the city centre. At Royal National Park, for example, less than 40 km south of Sydney, well over two hundred species have been observed, including such sought-after birds as Grey Goshawk, Peregrine Falcon, Topknot and Wonga Pigeon, Powerful Owl,

Superb Lyrebird, Black-faced Monarch, Southern Emu-wren, Pilotbird, Origma (this species, better known as the Rock Warbler, is the state's only endemic), Yellow-throated Scrubwren, Chestnut-rumped Hylacola, Red-browed Treecreeper, Beautiful Firetail and Green Catbird.

Sydney has a wealth of accommodation that includes international-class hotels, motels and guest houses. There are two youth hostels within walking distance of the city centre — one on the corner of Ross Street and St Johns Road, Forest Lodge, the other at 262 Glebe Point Road, Glebe. There are also youth hostels at 407 Marrickville Road, Dulwich Hill (about 7 km south-west of the city centre), Pittwater (about 30 km north of the city centre, near the boundary of Ku-ring-gai Chase National Park) and Garie Beach (about 50 km south of Sydney in Royal National Park). The Youth Hostels Association's head office is at 355 Kent Street, Sydney. There are caravan parks at Rockdale, Woronora, Bass Hill, North Ryde, Narrabeen, Dural and Berowra, but many have only a limited number of tourist sites and most do not allow tents. (The camping area at Bonnie Vale in Royal National Park is one of the few places close to Sydney where you are permitted to pitch a tent.) From Kingsford-Smith Airport there are direct flights to most of the world's major cities, and rental cars are readily available.

Sydney is Australia's oldest capital and has many places of historical interest — Cadman's Cottage (the city's oldest dwelling), Captain Cook's Landing Place and the fort on Bare Island are among the best known. Other places worth visiting include The Rocks area just west of Circular Quay, Paddington near Centennial Park, and Vaucluse House in the attractive bayside suburb of Vaucluse.

The following are some of the best birding areas near Sydney. Most should be easy to locate with the aid of a street directory, and many are accessible by public transport.

Royal Botanic Gardens

Sydney's Royal Botanic Gardens, the oldest public gardens in Australia, are situated just east of the city centre within a stone's throw of the harbour bridge, Circular Quay and the opera house. They cover an area of 30 ha and are open daily from 8 a.m. until sunset. Admission is free, and wheelchairs are available on request.

The gardens feature large expanses of lawn interspersed with flower-beds and palm groves, several lakes, a succulent garden containing many species of succulent plants from throughout the world, a pyramid glasshouse featuring numerous orchids, ferns and palms, and areas of native Australian vegetation. A kiosk,

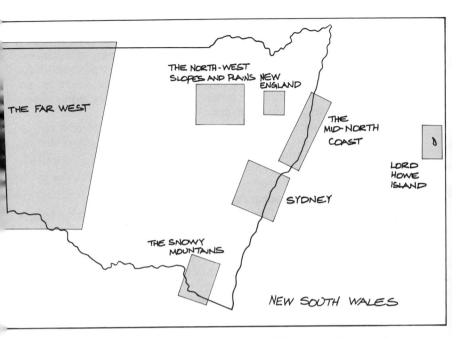

The map shows regions of New South Wales: THE FAR WEST, THE NORTH-WEST SLOPES AND PLAINS, NEW ENGLAND, THE MID-NORTH COAST, LORD HOWE ISLAND, SYDNEY, THE SNOWY MOUNTAINS, NEW SOUTH WALES.

restaurant and visitors centre are situated within the gardens, and there are a number of self-guided walks – the rainforest walk is particularly enjoyable. Leaflets describing points of interest along these walks can be obtained from the visitors centre.

Although introduced birds abound, the gardens hold a variety of common native species and you should have little difficulty finding many of the following: Little Pied Cormorant, White-faced Heron, Sacred Ibis, Black Swan, Pacific Black and Maned Duck, Chestnut Teal, Dusky Moorhen, Silver Gull, Crested Tern, Galah, Sulphur-crested Cockatoo, Rainbow Lorikeet, Eastern Rosella, Tawny Frogmouth (breeds regularly in the gardens), Laughing Kookaburra, Sacred Kingfisher (spring–summer), Welcome Swallow, Tree Martin, Black-faced Cuckoo-shrike, Eastern Yellow Robin, Willie Wagtail, Superb Fairy-wren, Yellow Thornbill, Noisy Miner, White-plumed and New Holland Honey-eater, Eastern Spinebill, Silvereye, Figbird (a common breeding resident), Australian Magpie-lark and Pied Currawong.

A useful booklet featuring many of the hundred or so birds that have been recorded in the Royal Botanic Gardens can be purchased from the visitors centre.

Taronga Zoological Park

No visitor should leave Sydney without taking a ferry trip across the harbour to Taronga Zoo. From the water you get an uninterrupted view of the city framed by the harbour bridge and the opera house, while the zoo has many interesting exhibits including a platypus house, a nocturnal house, a koala house, an aquarium, and a walk-through rainforest aviary where Australian and New Guinea birds can be seen in natural surroundings. There are an information centre and a restaurant within the zoo's grounds, and wheelchairs are available on request.

Open daily between 9 a.m. and 5 p.m., Taronga Zoo can be reached by car (it is about 10 km north-east of the city centre via the harbour bridge), bus, or by ferry from Number Five Wharf, Circular Quay (the crossing takes about fifteen minutes).

Sydney Harbour National Park

Although Sydney Harbour National Park is not one of the largest reserves near Sydney, its value is immeasurable since it protects much of the remaining natural vegetation around the shores of Port Jackson, east of the harbour bridge. At present the fragmented reserve has a total area of only 388 ha, but further sections of the harbour's foreshore may be added to the park in future years. The following are some of the main places of interest.

Ashton Park: Is adjacent to Taronga Zoo, just a few minutes walk from the Taronga Park ferry jetty. This section of the national park has toilets with facilities for the disabled, picnic areas, and over 4 km of well-graded walking tracks; it features three small sandy beaches and a patch of bushland (about 45 ha) where a variety of common birds can be found.

Dobroyd Head: Situated about 15 km north-east of the city centre, between North Harbour and Middle Harbour, this part of the reserve protects an area of coastal heathland and dry sclerophyll forest. It can be reached via the harbour bridge, Military Road and Spit Road, and is an ideal place to go bushwalking, fishing, swimming and sightseeing. There are toilets at Reef Beach and Tania Park (off Dobroyd Scenic Drive), and walking tracks leading to Reef Beach and Crater Cove.

North Head: Accessible via Military Road, Spit Road and Manly Road, or via the Sydney to Manly ferry, this very popular scenic spot is about 20 km north-east of the city centre. The attractions here include several secluded beaches, extensive areas of bushland, and a number of lookouts offering panoramic views northwards along the coast and southwards across the entrance to Port Jackson.

North Head is one of the best places near Sydney for seabirds. During the winter months, especially when the weather is really bad, a wide variety of oceanic species may be seen in the vicinity of the head. These include Wandering, Black-browed, Yellow-nosed and Shy Albatross, Southern and, more rarely, Northern

Sydney's Taronga Zoo boasts a fine bird collection − this is a male Darter

The Three Sisters, in the Blue Mountains west of Sydney, New South Wales, are seen − and photographed − by many thousands of visitors each year

Galahs wait for handouts from the tourists outside the information centre at Echo Point in the Blue Mountains, New South Wales

A section of the Snowy Mountains, seen from the track leading from Charlotte Pass to the summit of Mt Kosciusko, Kosciusko National Park, New South Wales

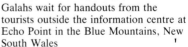

Wallis Lake, on the mid-north coast of New South Wales south of Forster

Point Lookout, New England National Park, New South Wales

Satin Bowerbirds are quite common in the rainforests of coastal New South Wales — this is a female

Situated in the far west of New South Wales, Kinchega National Park has much to offer the waterbird enthusiast

Dominated by jagged pinnacles, barren spires and rocky domes, the Warrumbungles in north-central New South Wales attract bushwalkers and rock climbers from all over Australia

Idyllic Lord Howe Island — the perfect place for a peaceful, relaxing holiday

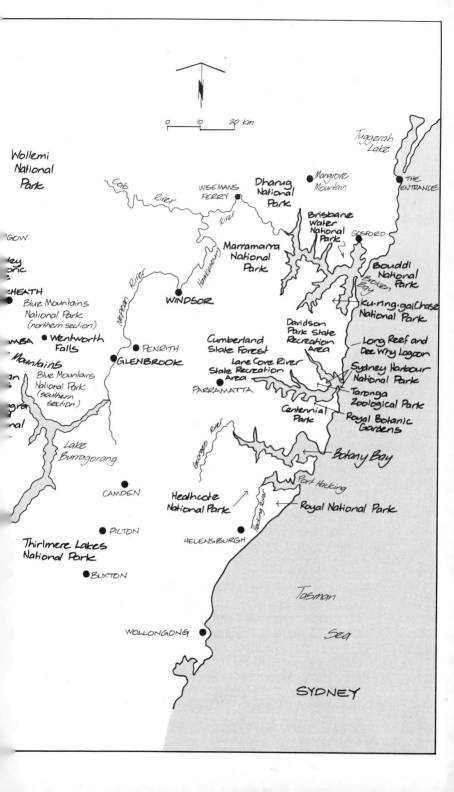

Giant-Petrel, Cape, Great-winged and Providence Petrel, Fairy Prion, Fluttering and Hutton's Shearwater, Wilson's Storm-Petrel Australasian Gannet and Great Skua.

With the aid of a pair of powerful binoculars, preferably 10× or 12×, you should be able to identify, from North Head, at least a few of the birds mentioned. If you want to see species such as albatrosses at close range, however, it would pay to join the New South Wales Field Ornithologists Club (the address is at the beginning of this chapter). From time to time the FOC organises boat trips to the edge of the continental shelf, east of Sydney. Albatrosses are sometimes recorded in large numbers during these excursions – as many as forty to fifty Black-browed and twenty to thirty Yellow-nosed have been seen during a single trip – while rare seabirds such as Royal and Grey-headed Albatross, White-headed, Herald, Mottled, White-necked and Black Petrel, Buller's and Audubon's Shearwater, South Polar Skua and Arctic Tern are observed on odd occasions.

South Head: Another good seabird spot, South Head is about 15 km north-east of the city centre via New South Head Road. There are toilets at Camp Cove Beach, and a walking track leading from the beach to Hornby Lighthouse (built in 1858) at South Head. Dotted with old fortifications, this historic area is ideal for sight seeing, fishing and swimming.

Nielsen Park: Situated 2 or 3 km south-west of South Head and accessible by car or bus, this section of Sydney Harbour National Park features a beach with a shark-proof net, picnic areas, walking tracks, and historic Greycliffe House – an impressive sandstone building once owned by explorer and statesman W. C. Wentworth. The property has been extensively restored and is now the national park headquarters and visitors centre.

Centennial Park

Only 5 km or so south-east of Sydney via Oxford Street or Anzac Parade, Centennial Park covers an area of about 202 ha and is easily reached by public transport. Although the park consists chiefly of open grassy areas and features many exotic trees and shrubs, it also has some substantial patches of native vegetation and is therefore a good place for bush birds. More importantly though its lakes – there are about ten in the park – attract many waterbirds, especially common species such as Australasian Grebe, Australian Pelican, Great, Little Black and Little Pied Cormorant (Little Black and Little Pied Cormorants breed regularly in small numbers), White-faced Heron, Great Egret, Sacred Ibis, Black Swan, Pacific Black and Musk Duck, Grey Teal, Hardhead, Dusky Moorhen, Purple Swamphen, Eurasian Coot and Masked Lapwing.

More rarely, interesting birds such as Hoary-headed Grebe, Darter, Pacific Heron, Little and Intermediate Egret, Royal Spoonbill, Chestnut Teal, Buff-banded Rail, Baillon's Crake, Red-kneed Dotterel, Black-fronted Plover, Black-winged Stilt and Latham's Snipe (summer) are recorded, while every now and then something really special turns up — Little Bittern for example.

As might be expected, the land birds that occur at Centennial Park are essentially the same as those of the nearby Royal Botanic Gardens. However, a number of species that are rarely found in the botanic gardens are seen rather more frequently at Centennial Park: Crested Pigeon, Red-rumped Parrot, Horsfield's Bronze-Cuckoo (mainly spring–summer), Common Koel (spring–summer), Jacky Winter, Rufous Whistler (spring–summer), Black-faced Monarch (spring–summer), Rufous Fantail (spring–summer), Yellow-rumped Thornbill and Red-browed Firetail. In addition, Clamorous Reed-Warbler (spring–summer), Little Grassbird and Golden-headed Cisticola inhabit the reedy margins of the lakes.

Over 150 species (including introductions) have been recorded in Centennial Park, and clearly you could spend a most productive day here. A visit during the week will be best; it is one of the most popular parks near Sydney and attracts large crowds at weekends. There are picnic facilities, toilets and a kiosk in the park, and many of the paths are sealed and suitable for wheelchairs. The gates are open from sunrise to sunset throughout the year.

Botany Bay

At first glance Botany Bay does not appear to have any areas likely to attract birds or bird-watchers. Kingsford-Smith Airport dominates its northern shore; Sydney's southern suburbs extend from the airport around the bay to La Perouse in the east and to Sans Souci in the south; and the Kurnell Peninsula, though less urbanised, is the site of several large industrial complexes and oil refineries. But despite this, and despite the inevitable pollution and reclamation schemes, the bay has many attractions — particularly if you are a wader enthusiast. The entire area is worth exploring, especially in summer, although the following spots are generally regarded as the most productive.

General Holmes Drive: Skirts the bay's north-western shores, south of the airport, but is normally very busy and there are few places where you can stop. You can, however, park on Foreshore Road, which runs from General Holmes Drive eastwards towards La Perouse, and walk back along the edge of Botany Bay as far as the airport's main runway.

In summer, at low tide, the sand and mud flats between the

runway and Foreshore Road usually hold a variety of migratory waders, including Lesser Golden Plover, Bar-tailed Godwit, Sharp-tailed and Curlew Sandpiper and Red-necked Stint. In winter Double-banded Plovers can often be found here, while Red-capped Plovers are usually present throughout the year. Other species worth looking for during the summer months are Common and Little Tern. (Little Terns once bred in quite large numbers on sand-bars and shingle beaches around Botany Bay, but this delightful small seabird is now restricted to a few sites, most of which are man-made.)

While you are in the vicinity of the airport visits to the following spots may also prove fruitful: the mouth of Cooks River, just west of the airport's main runway; Engine Pond and Mill Pond, both of which are situated a few hundred metres east of the intersection of General Holmes Drive and Foreshore Road (the ponds are fenced off, but they can be viewed quite easily from General Holmes Drive); and the Eastlakes Golf Course, which lies about 2 km north of Foreshore Road via Botany Road and Wentworth Avenue.

Although the northern shores of Botany Bay do not as a rule attract large numbers of waterbirds, there are always some species to be found here and the area has produced a number of outstanding rarities in recent years. These include a Baird's Sandpiper in 1976, a Buller's Albatross in 1977, a Ringed Plover in 1980 and a Franklin's Gull in 1981.

Woolooware Bay: Is situated about 20 km south of Sydney via the Princes Highway and Rocky Point Road. Another area much favoured by waterbirds, the shores of Woolooware Bay usually support fair numbers of waders during summer, including Grey (rather rare), Lesser Golden and (rather rare) Mongolian Plover, Ruddy Turnstone, Eastern Curlew, Whimbrel, Grey-tailed Tattler, Greenshank, Black-tailed (rather rare) and Bar-tailed Godwit, Red and (rather rare) Great Knot, Terek (rather rare), Sharp-tailed and Curlew Sandpiper, and Red-necked Stint. Non-migratory waders such as Pied Oystercatcher and Red-capped Plover, as well as a variety of common waterbirds — Australian Pelican, Pied and other cormorants, White-faced Heron, Sacred Ibis, Black Swan and Crested Tern — can usually be found here at any time of the year.

Unfortunately access to much of Woolooware Bay is somewhat difficult, but you can reach its western shores by car via Atkinson Street, Shell Point, and its southern shores via Captain Cook Drive. The best way to explore the area, however, is by boat — there is a boat ramp just to the north at Taren Point.

Having found at least a few of the species mentioned, birders may care to visit the swamps south of the bay (opposite Cronulla

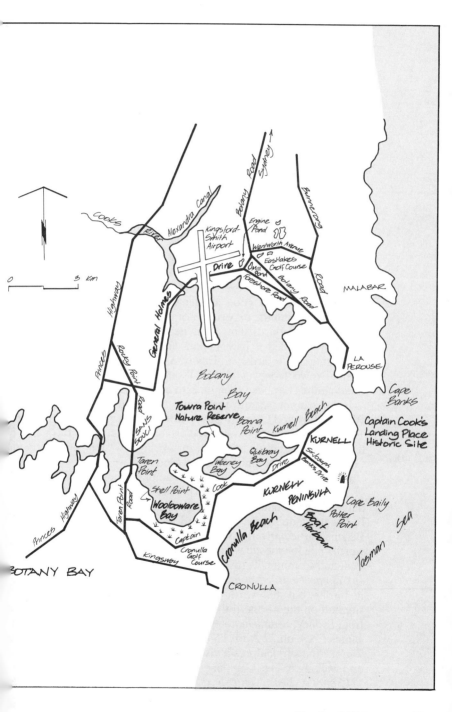

Golf Course). This area is readily accessible from Captain Cook Drive. In recent years many interesting birds have been sighted here – Little and Australasian Bittern, Australian and Spotless Crake, Painted Snipe, Red-kneed Dotterel and Pectoral Sandpiper are perhaps the most notable.

Kurnell Peninsula: Lies to the south of Botany Bay, about 25 km from Sydney via Rocky Point Road, Taren Point Road and Captain Cook Drive. Although the peninsula is dominated by a large oil refinery and many of its swamps have been filled in, the area still has a number of excellent bird-watching spots much frequented by Sydney's birding fraternity. The following are among the most favoured localities.

Towra Point Nature Reserve: Is situated to the north of Cronulla. The reserve can be reached on foot from Captain Cook Drive, but you will have to walk across private property to get there and permission must be obtained in advance from the owner. The only sure way of gaining entry is to join a recognised group such as the New South Wales Field Ornithologists Club. The FOC organises regular excursions to Towra Point during summer; if you are not very good at identifying waders you will benefit enormously from the experience of the club's tour leaders.

All the waterbirds that occur nearby at Woolooware Bay are regularly recorded at Towra Point, and the area holds a number of interesting land birds – Tawny Grassbird, Variegated Fairy-wren, Brown Honeyeater and White-fronted Chat for example. Calamanthus has been seen on rare occasions.

If you cannot get into the nature reserve try the area between Weeney Bay and Quibray Bay, a little to the east of Towra Point. Though littered with old car bodies and other rubbish this part of the Kurnell Peninsula attracts a sprinkling of waders, among them Grey-tailed Tattler and Bar-tailed Godwit.

Kurnell: There are still a few swamps remaining in the vicinity of Kurnell, near the tip of the peninsula. If you search the area diligently you could turn up something of interest – a Wood or Pectoral Sandpiper perhaps. And at high tide a visit to Kurnell Beach, particularly the western end (Bonna Point), may prove worthwhile for roosting waders as well as for seabirds such as Kelp Gull and Common Tern.

Captain Cook's Landing Place Historic Site: Is not famed for its birdlife but well worth a visit all the same. The 354 ha reserve, situated on the northern tip of the Kurnell Peninsula some 35 km from Sydney, commemorates the first Australian landing of Captain James Cook on 29 April 1770. Open daily between 7.30 a.m. and 7 p.m., the site features a visitors centre, a museum, picnic areas and walking tracks. Camping is not permitted.

Cronulla Beach and Boat Harbour: Are situated on the

southern side of the Kurnell Peninsula and can be reached from Captain Cook Drive via Sir Joseph Banks Drive. At the end of Sir Joseph Banks Drive there is a parking area; from here tracks lead eastwards to the Cape Baily lighthouse, and southwards to Potter Point, Boat Harbour and Cronulla Beach.

This part of the peninsula is very exposed and is therefore a good place for seabirds. Species to look for include albatrosses, petrels, prions and shearwaters in winter, and Arctic, Pomarine and, more rarely, Long-tailed Jaeger in summer. Crested Terns can usually be found here at any time of the year, while White-fronted may be present in winter, and Common and Little in summer.

Seabirds are not the only attraction — the rocky areas adjacent to Boat Harbour are favoured by Eastern Reef Egret and Sooty Oystercatcher, while migratory waders such as Lesser Golden, Mongolian and (rarely) Large Sand Plover, Ruddy Turnstone, Eastern Curlew and (rarely) Sanderling occur on the beaches nearby.

Royal National Park

Situated on the coast just 36 km south of Sydney, Royal National Park covers an area of 15 014 ha and stretches from Port Hacking in the north to beyond Lilyvale in the south. Dedicated in 1879, it is the oldest national park in Australia and the second oldest in the world. (Yellowstone National Park, in the USA, is the world's oldest — established in 1872). The reserve consists mainly of a heath-covered sandstone plateau and is dominated by dense, low-growing vegetation interspersed with patches of mallee and areas of banksia woodland. Between July and October, the park's colourful wildflower displays are a great attraction.

Although heathland forms the main habitat, Royal National Park has four other major plant communities: subtropical rain-forest characterised by turpentine, coachwood, sassafras, lilly-pilly, cabbage tree palm, tree ferns and vines occurs along the Hacking River, which flows through the centre of the reserve; wet sclerophyll forest dominated by blackbutt and Sydney blue gum is found on the sheltered slopes of many of the park's gullies; eucalypt woodland consisting chiefly of bloodwood, snappy gum and black ash covers the more exposed slopes and ridges; and patches of mangroves grow around the shores of Port Hacking.

The park headquarters and visitors centre are situated on Farnell Avenue, about 1 km east of the Princes Highway near Royal National Park railway station. Information (including a walking track guide and a comprehensive bird list) and camping permits can be obtained from the visitors centre. There are picnic grounds, most of which have barbecues and toilets, at Audley,

Bonnie Vale, Wattamolla, Garie Beach and elsewhere, and a camping ground with basic facilities at Bonnie Vale, on the shores of Port Hacking. Bush camping is permitted throughout the reserve, but not within 1 km of any road or picnic area. The park has many excellent walking tracks, ranging from a short (1 km or so) historical walk commencing at the visitors centre to a 26 km coastal walk from Port Hacking Point to Otford Lookout.

Despite its close proximity to Sydney and its popularity − it probably receives more visitors than any other national park in New South Wales − Royal remains relatively unspoilt and there are many peaceful spots ideal for bird-watching. A large number of the two hundred or so species recorded in the reserve can be found along the roads and tracks, and around the picnic grounds. The following are common and should be quite easy to find: Yellow-tailed Black-Cockatoo, Sulphur-crested Cockatoo, Rainbow and Little Lorikeet (especially when the eucalypts are in flower), Crimson and Eastern Rosella, Fan-tailed Cuckoo, Common Koel (spring−summer), Laughing Kookaburra, Sacred Kingfisher (spring−summer), Dollarbird (spring−summer), Black-faced Cuckoo-shrike, Eastern Yellow Robin, Golden Whistler, Rufous Whistler (spring−summer), Grey Shrike-thrush, Grey Fantail, Eastern Whipbird, White-browed Scrubwren, Brown and Striated Thornbill, White-throated Treecreeper, Red and Little Wattlebird, Noisy Friarbird, Yellow-faced, White-eared, White-naped and New Holland Honeyeater, Eastern Spinebill, Mistletoebird, Spotted Pardalote, Silvereye, Red-browed Firetail, Grey Butcherbird and Pied Currawong.

You could spend many days exploring Royal National Park, but if you have only a little time to spare − or simply want to search for some of the reserve's special birds − the following spots are highly recommended.

Audley: Is situated on the Hacking River, about 1 km south-east of the visitors centre. There is a kiosk together with several pleasant picnic grounds here, and with a small boat or canoe (they can be hired locally) you could explore the river north and south of the Audley causeway.

Lady Carrington Drive: Follows the Hacking River for a distance of 10 km or so and takes you through some of the best areas of wet sclerophyll forest and rainforest in the park. It commences at Audley and runs southwards to Sir Bertram Stevens Drive. The one-way road is usually closed to traffic at weekends and is therefore an ideal place for a quiet walk or cycle ride. Though unsealed, it is reasonably level and suitable for wheelchairs.

Some of the birds you can expect to see along Lady Carrington Drive are Wonga Pigeon, Australian King-Parrot, Brush Cuckoo (spring−summer), Azure Kingfisher, Superb Lyrebird, Rose

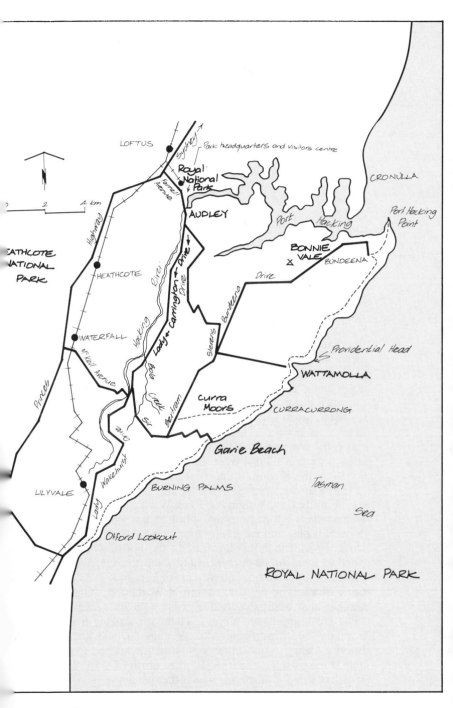

LOFTUS

Park headquarters and visitors centre

CRONULLA

Royal National Park

AUDLEY

Port Hacking

Port Hacking Point

HEATHCOTE NATIONAL PARK

HEATHCOTE

BONNIE VALE

BUNDEENA

Drive

WATERFALL

Providential Head

WATTAMOLLA

Curra Moors

CURRACURRONG

Garie Beach

LILYVALE

BURNING PALMS

Tasman

Sea

Otford Lookout

ROYAL NATIONAL PARK

Robin, Crested Shrike-tit, Leaden Flycatcher (spring–summer), Rufous Fantail (spring–summer), Yellow-throated Scrubwren, Brown Gerygone, Lewin's Honeyeater and Satin Bowerbird. Less often seen, but certainly worth looking for, are Grey Goshawk, Australian Hobby, Topknot Pigeon, Brown Cuckoo-Dove, Emerald Dove, Powerful Owl, Cicadabird (spring–summer), White's Thrush, Black-faced Monarch (spring–summer), Pilotbird, Large-billed Scrubwren, Red-browed Treecreeper, Scarlet Honeyeater and Green Catbird.

If you have time, a walk along the entire length of Lady Carrington Drive should prove most rewarding. If you simply want to look for rainforest birds, however, walk northwards from the southern entrance (on Sir Bertram Stevens Drive) about 1 km to Bola Creek, where there is a good patch of rainforest.

Curra Moors: The extensive coastal heathlands of Royal National Park hold a host of sought-after species – Southern Emu-wren, Chestnut-rumped Hylacola, Tawny-crowned Honeyeater and Beautiful Firetail for example. Perhaps the best place to look for these birds is Curra Moors, a large expanse of low heath between Wattamolla and Garie Beach.

To reach this section of the park drive south from Audley along Sir Bertram Stevens Drive. About 5 km south of the turn-off to Wattamolla (1 km or so north of the Garie Beach road) there is a picnic area on the left-hand side of the road. From here a well-marked walking track leads eastwards to Curracurrong, then north along the coast to Wattamolla. For the first kilometre or so the track passes through dense coastal woodland, then crosses a stretch of heath where Southern Emu-wrens are quite plentiful – though as always a little difficult to find. If you are feeling energetic continue along the track to Curracurrong, where several large waterfalls plunge over the magnificent sandstone cliffs that dominate this section of the coast. Sandstone areas in the vicinity of Curracurrong are well worth looking over for one of the park's special birds – the Origma or Rock Warbler.

Wattamolla: Is on the coast about 15 km from Audley. It is a popular fishing and swimming spot, and has a picnic ground and a kiosk. Providential Head, a little to the north, would be a good place to look for seabirds in winter, and the sea cliffs along this stretch of the coast hold a few pairs of Peregrine Falcon.

Garie Beach: Some 11 km south of Wattamolla, Garie Beach is another area well patronised by swimmers and fishermen. It too has a kiosk and picnic ground. There are walking tracks leading from the beach northwards to Wattamolla, and southwards to Burning Palms (a pocket of coastal rainforest) and Otford Lookout. During winter, the headland just north of Garie Beach is an excellent spot for albatrosses and other pelagics.

Bonnie Vale: Is situated on the southern shores of Port Hacking, some 20 km east of Audley via Bundeena Drive. Many bush birds can be found around the camping ground and picnic area, but the main attraction is Port Hacking with its mangroves and mudflats. In summer a variety of migratory waders can often be found here, while waterbirds such as cormorants, herons, egrets, ibis, spoonbills, waterfowl, gulls and terns are usually present throughout the year. Mangrove areas are worth exploring for Striated Heron, Black Bittern (rarely) and Brown Honeyeater.

With its wide range of habitats — heaths, forests, swamps, rivers and coastal cliffs — Royal National Park is undoubtedly one of the best birding areas near Sydney, and in New South Wales for that matter. The Field Ornithologists Club runs regular excursions to the park and it is not uncommon for its members to record over seventy species during a single visit.

Heathcote National Park

Heathcote is a 2251 ha reserve situated to the west of Royal National Park, about 32 km south of Sydney. It consists mainly of low sandstone ridges cut by deep gullies, and contains a wide diversity of sandstone flora with vegetation ranging from dry eucalypt woodland to low, dense heathland.

Although it is much smaller than Royal National Park, Heathcote is an excellent place to go bird-watching since it has no roads and there are few facilities for visitors. As a result the reserve is usually very peaceful. Bush camping is allowed in most areas (there is no formal camping ground), but you must obtain a permit in advance from the visitors centre at Royal National Park. Access can be gained from the north via Heathcote Road, from the east via the Princes Highway, and from the south via Woronora Dam Road. There are two picnic areas near the end of Woronora Dam Road, and numerous walking tracks running through the reserve from north to south and from east to west.

Some of the more interesting birds recorded at Heathcote are Glossy Black-Cockatoo, White-throated Nightjar (summer), Spotted Quail-thrush, Variegated Fairy-wren, Origma, and White-cheeked and Tawny-crowned Honeyeater. Late winter and early spring are the best seasons to visit the park; at this time of year the birds are most active, and there is a profusion of wildflowers — the gymea lily with its large, rich red flowers on spikes up to 4 m tall is particularly delightful.

Lane Cove River and Davidson Park State Recreation Areas

These two popular reserves, to the north of Sydney, offer city-dwellers the opportunity to enjoy a wide range of outdoor activities, including bushwalking, picnicking, fishing, boating and, of course, bird-watching. Davidson Park (1215 ha) is the larger of the two, but Lane Cove River (327 ha) is the best place to go birding — more than 150 species have been observed there.

Lane Cover River State Recreation Area: Is a long, narrow reserve stretching from Delhi Road, Chatswood West, to beyond Lane Cove Road, Macquarie Park. It lies about 15 km north-west of the city centre via the harbour bridge, the Pacific Highway and Fullers Road. The main picnic ground is located near Fullers Bridge, just inside the reserve's southern boundary, but there are numerous smaller (and usually quieter) picnic areas off Riverside Drive, which runs through the park along the west bank of the Lane Cove River. There are a visitors centre and kiosk in the reserve, and boats and canoes are available for hire. Camping is not permitted.

Some of the waterbirds you can expect to find here are Australasian Grebe, Great, Pied, Little Black and Little Pied Cormorant, White-faced Heron, Great Egret, Black Swan, Pacific Black and Maned Duck, Grey Teal, Chestnut Teal, Dusky Moorhen and Eurasian Coot, while bush birds include Sulphur-crested Cockatoo, Rainbow Lorikeet, Pallid (spring–summer) and Fan-tailed Cuckoo, Common Koel (spring–summer), Laughing Kookaburra, Sacred Kingfisher (spring–summer), Dollarbird (spring–summer), Crested Shrike-tit, Golden and (spring–summer) Rufous Whistler, Eastern Whipbird, White-throated Gerygone (spring–summer), Brown, Buff-rumped, Yellow-rumped, Yellow and Striated Thornbill, White-throated Treecreeper, Red Wattlebird, Noisy Miner, Lewin's, Yellow-faced, White-plumed and White-naped Honeyeater, Eastern Spinebill, Spotted Pardalote, Silvereye, Red-browed Firetail, Olive-backed Oriole (spring–summer), Figbird and Pied Currawong.

On occasions more interesting species are recorded, among them Darter, Rufous Night Heron, Peregrine Falcon, Topknot Pigeon, Brown Cuckoo-Dove, Australian King-Parrot, Channel-billed Cuckoo (spring–summer), Powerful Owl, Azure Kingfisher, Rose Robin, Black-faced Monarch (spring–summer), Rufous Fantail (spring–summer) and Scarlet Honeyeater.

Although many of the common birds listed can be found closer to Sydney's centre — at Centennial Park for example — Lane Cove River has much to offer the city's northern residents. It is, however, enormously popular; over a million people visit the reserve each year. Clearly an early morning or late afternoon excursion during the week will be best!

Davidson Park State Recreation Area: Bounded by the Pacific Highway, Mona Vale Road, Forest Way and Warringah Road, this reserve is bisected by Middle Harbour and features steep, heavily wooded slopes, gorges and valleys. Unlike Lane Cove

River it has few facilities; the only picnic ground is located near Roseville Bridge at the southern end of the park, about 15 km north of Sydney via the harbour bridge, the Warringah Freeway and Eastern Valley Way. Amenities within the picnic area include toilets, barbecues and a kiosk, and there is a boat ramp nearby. Access to the central and northern sections of the reserve can be gained at many points (consult a Sydney street directory for details), but the only major walking track is the one leading from Hunter Avenue, St Ives, eastwards to Middle Harbour.

Most of the common bush birds that occur nearby at Lane Cove River can be seen at Davidson Park, with honeyeaters being especially plentiful during late winter and spring. Red and Little Wattlebird, Noisy Friarbird, Noisy Miner, Yellow-faced, White-eared, Yellow-tufted, Brown-headed, White-naped, New Holland and White-cheeked Honeyeater and Eastern Spinebill are the main species to look for.

Long Reef and Dee Why Lagoon

Though perhaps not as well known as some of the waterbird spots around Botany Bay, Long Reef and Dee Why Lagoon are well worth visiting nonetheless. Situated on the coast about 22 km north-east of Sydney, both are readily accessible via the harbour bridge, Military Road, Sydney Road and Pittwater Road.

Long Reef: Lies just to the east of Pittwater Road, adjacent to the Long Reef Golf Course. In summer, at low tide, the reef attracts a fair variety of waders, chiefly those species frequently recorded in the Sydney area — Lesser Golden Plover, Ruddy Turnstone, Whimbrel, Grey-tailed Tattler, Sharp-tailed and Curlew Sandpiper and Red-necked Stint — but also on occasions rarer birds such as Grey, Mongolian and Large Sand Plover, Wandering Tattler, and Red and Great Knot. In winter a few Double-banded Plovers can nearly always be found here, while resident species include Pied and Sooty Oystercatcher (the latter sometimes in quite large numbers).

Seabirds are another attraction at Long Reef. Albatrosses, petrels, Great Skua and White-fronted Tern are recorded during the winter months; Little Penguin, shearwaters, Australasian Gannet, gulls and Crested Tern can usually be found throughout the year; and Arctic and Pomarine Jaeger and Common Tern are species to watch for in summer. Long-tailed Jaeger and Arctic Tern feature among the rarities listed for the area.

Dee Why Lagoon: Is situated less than a kilometre south of Long Reef and can be reached on foot from Pittwater Road or from Long Reef via the golf course. The lagoon holds a number of waterbirds that you are unlikely to find at the reef (egrets, ibis, spoonbills and waterfowl for example), and Golden-headed Cisticolas are plentiful in the dense vegetation around its margins. Notable species such as Intermediate Egret, Lewin's Rail and Ruff turn up from time to time.

Cumberland State Forest

An oasis in Sydney's northern suburbs, Cumberland State Forest is yet another good birding spot within half an hour's drive of the city centre. The forest is dominated by trees such as smooth-barked apple (*Angophora costata*), blackbutt and Sydney blue gum, but in sheltered gullies there are patches of rainforest containing a wide variety of plants: hoop pine, rose maple, corkwood, tallowwood, bonewood, native plum, black bean, native frangipani, turpentine and black booyong.

Not surprisingly, the state forest is much frequented by Sydney bird-watchers. Grey Goshawk, Scaly-breasted and Musk Lorikeet, Australian King-Parrot, Powerful Owl, Tawny Frogmouth, White-bellied Cuckoo-shrike, Cicadabird (spring−summer), White's Thrush, Rose Robin, Black-faced Monarch (spring−summer), Rufous Fantail (spring−summer), Brown Gerygone, Bell Miner, Yellow-tufted Honeyeater and Satin Bowerbird are just a few of the many notable species regularly recorded there.

The state forest has excellent facilities, including an information centre and a short 'senses' nature trail where a rope has been installed to assist blind walkers. Markers along the nature trail have a braille text describing some of the features of the surrounding forest. The main entrance is on Castle Hill Road, about 30 km north-west of the city centre via the Pacific Highway, Epping Road and Beecroft Road. The forest is open daily between 9 a.m. and 4.30 p.m.

The northern parks

Sydney's northern residents are very fortunate in that they have five splendid national parks virtually on their doorstep. Thanks largely to the foresight of early conservationists, the bays and inlets to the north of the city are fringed by a chain of reserves − Ku-ring-gai Chase, Marramarra, Dharug, Brisbane Water and Bouddi. All are readily accessible via the Pacific Highway, and most have at least some facilities for visitors.

Ku-ring-gai Chase National Park (14 591 ha): With its extensive system of deep waterways and many kilometres of walking tracks, this is by far the most popular of Sydney's northern reserves. During the summer months, many thousands of city-dwellers flock there at weekends to enjoy a wide range of outdoor activities − fishing, boating, bushwalking, picnicking and sightseeing.

Ku-ring-gai Chase is situated less than 30 km from the city centre, and can be reached by car, train or bus. The park's excellent visitors centre is located at Kalkari, about 3 km east of the Pacific Highway via Ku-ring-gai Chase Road. It is open daily from 9 a.m. to 4.30 p.m. and houses displays covering the flora, fauna and history of the region. A wealth of information, including a walking track guide and a bird list, can be obtained from the visitors centre, and there is a short circular nature trail nearby. There is also a specially designed 'senses' trail where blind and handicapped visitors can learn a little about Sydney's natural environment. The wide, level track is paved and suitable for wheelchairs.

There are picnic areas at Kalkari, Bobbin Head, Apple Tree Bay, Illawong Bay, Akuna Bay, West Head and several other sites; kiosks at Bobbin Head, Apple Tree Bay, Akuna Bay and Cottage Point; and boat ramps at Apple Tree Bay and Akuna Bay. Boats can be hired at Bobbin Head, Cottage Point and Akuna Bay. Camping is permitted at The Basin, a delightful spot on the shores of Pittwater. The camping ground, which has toilets and fireplaces, can only be reached on foot (from West Head Road) or by boat. Bush camping is not allowed.

Like most parks in the Sydney region, Ku-ring-gai Chase consists mainly of rugged Hawkesbury sandstone country. Typically heathland and open eucalypt woodland predominate, though there are patches of tall, wet forest in many of the gullies as well as areas of mangroves lining the upper reaches of the park's numerous bays and inlets. As might be expected, the avifauna of Ku-ring-gai Chase is essentially the same as that of Royal National Park, although fewer species have been recorded − about 160.

Many birds can be found along the park's walking tracks, most of which start from West Head Road between Terrey Hills and West Head. There are enough tracks in this part of the reserve to satisfy even the most energetic walker: the Elvina track (2.5 km), the Waratah track (4 km), the Salvation Loop track (2 km), the Bairne track (4 km), the America track (1 km), the Basin track (3 km), the Headland Loop track (5 km) − and many more.

Birds you can expect to see in the vicinity of West Head include Brown Goshawk, Collared Sparrowhawk, White-bellied Sea-Eagle, Brown Quail, Painted Button-quail, Common Bronzewing, Rainbow Lorikeet, Eastern Rosella, Horsfield's and Shining Bronze-Cuckoo (spring−summer), White-throated Nightjar (spring−summer), Superb Lyrebird, Spotted Quail-thrush, Variegated Fairy-wren, Southern Emu-wren, Origma (can usually be found near the lookout at West Head, but only during the week when there are few people about), Chestnut-rumped Hylacola, White-throated Gerygone (spring−summer), and White-cheeked and Tawny-crowned Honeyeater.

The shores of Pittwater, Broken Bay and the lower reaches of the Hawkesbury River hold a wide variety of waterbirds, including Striated Heron where patches of mangroves occur. Lion Island Nature Reserve, in Broken Bay 2 km or so north of West Head, supports small breeding colonies of Little Penguin, and Wedge-tailed and Sooty Shearwater. If you wish to visit the island you must obtain a permit from the New South Wales National Parks and Wildlife Service in Sydney.

Marramarra National Park (11 539 ha): Lies to the north-west of Ku-ring-gai Chase, south of the Hawkesbury River. Since it is undeveloped, Marramarra attracts few visitors and is therefore an ideal place to go bushwalking and bird-watching. Bush camping is allowed − permits and details can be obtained from the New South Wales National Parks and Wildlife Service regional office at Bobbin Head in Ku-ring-gai Chase National Park.

Although low open forest constitutes the main habitat at Marramarra there are some fine stands of mangroves fringing the Hawkesbury River, which forms the park's northern boundary. Waterbirds such as Striated Heron can be found in the reserve, while bush birds of interest include Wonga Pigeon and Glossy Black-Cockatoo.

The park is situated about 40 km north of Sydney and can be reached from the Pacific Highway via Galston Road and Old Northern Road. From the latter several tracks provide ready access to the reserve, the main one being Canoelands Ridge Road, north of Glenorie. The best time to visit Marramarra is late winter and early spring; it is usually hot, dry and dusty during summer.

Dharug National Park (14 785 ha): Stretching northwards from the Hawkesbury River between Wisemans Ferry and Spencer, this rugged sandstone wilderness is accessible from the south via the Pacific Highway, Old Northern Road and Wisemans Ferry, or from the north via Mangrove Mountain and Spencer. Though largely undeveloped, the park has quite good facilities for visitors. The ranger's office and main picnic area are located at Hazel Dell, about 5 km east of Wisemans Ferry, and there is a small camping ground (tents only) with toilets and fireplaces nearby at Mill Creek. Bush camping is allowed at Ten Mile Hollow, in the northern section of the reserve. This area is accessible only on foot, or by four-wheel-drive vehicle via Old Great North Road. Camping permits should be obtained in advance from the ranger.

Dharug supports a wide range of vegetation types, including fine stands of casuarina, woodlands of grey gum and narrow-leaved apple, and patches of rainforest dominated by lilly-pilly, sassafras and coachwood. Birds such as Brown Cuckoo-Dove, Wonga Pigeon, Brush Cuckoo (spring−summer), Cicadabird (spring−summer), Rufous Fantail (spring−summer), Large-billed

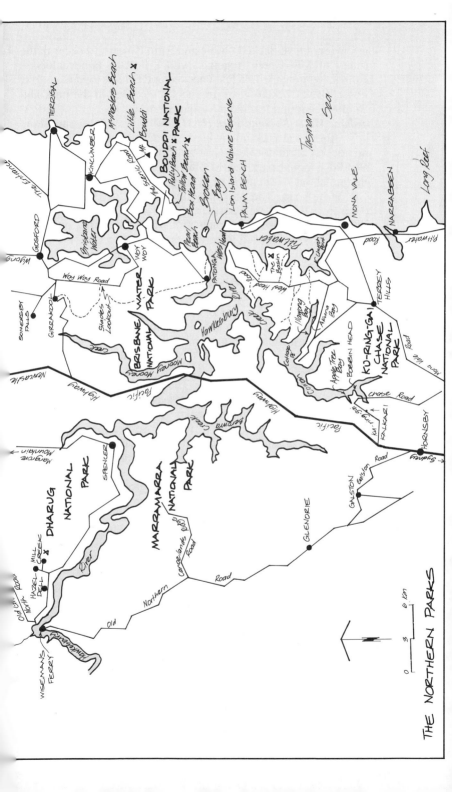

THE NORTHERN PARKS

Scrubwren, Olive-backed Oriole and Satin Bowerbird occur in the vicinity of Mill Creek, together with a host of honeyeaters – Lewin's, White-naped, White-cheeked and Scarlet to name a few. Glossy Black-Cockatoos are frequently recorded in the park and can often be found feeding in casuarina groves.

Brisbane Water National Park (11 317 ha): Waterfalls, sandstone cliffs, Aboriginal rock engravings, wonderful wildflower displays and pockets of rainforest are just some of the many attractions this splendid national park has to offer. It is situated to the east of Dharug, about 70 km north of Sydney via the Pacific Highway and Woy Woy Road. The park headquarters are at Gosford, some 10 km from the reserve's northern boundary.

There is no formal camping ground in the park, but bush camping may be allowed in certain areas; contact the park headquarters for further information. Picnic facilities are provided at Somersby Falls, Girrakool, Staples Lookout, Pearl Beach and Patonga, and there are walking tracks leading from some of the picnic grounds to nearby lookout points. For those with more time to spare there are a number of longer walks leading through the heart of the reserve to the shores of the Hawkesbury River, as well as a 6.5 km circular nature trail in the vicinity of the Girrakool picnic area. A walking track guide can be obtained from the park headquarters.

Bouddi National Park (1160 ha): The smallest and most easterly of the region's parks, Bouddi protects a narrow strip of magnificent coastline stretching from McMasters Beach in the north to Box Head in the south. The reserve features several beautiful sandy beaches, high coastal cliffs and extensive heathlands, and is not difficult to reach from Gosford (about 80 km north of Sydney) via The Scenic Road. This road runs more or less parallel with the park's western boundary. There are picnic grounds at Little Beach (accessible on foot from the end of Graham Drive), Mt Bouddi, Putty Beach and Tallow Beach. All have toilets and barbecues. Tent camping is permitted at Little Beach, Putty Beach and Tallow Beach, but permits must be obtained in advance from the New South Wales National Parks and Wildlife Service at 168 Mann Street, Gosford (postal address PO Box 1393, Gosford South, NSW 2250 – remember to enclose a stamped, addressed envelope when applying). For those not wishing to camp there are motels, hotels and caravan parks at Gosford.

Despite its small size Bouddi holds a fair variety of birds, including sought-after species such as White-bellied Sea-Eagle and Southern Emu-wren. The best time to visit the park is late winter through to early summer; between August and November in particular the heathlands are alive with wildflowers – and honeyeaters.

Windsor

Over the past ten or fifteen years the marshes, swamps and lagoons in the Windsor district have produced a remarkable number of rare and interesting birds, among them Little and Australasian Bittern, Black-necked Stork, Freckled Duck, Painted Snipe, Little Curlew, Wood, Pectoral and White-rumped Sandpiper, Ruff and Oriental Pratincole. Species such as these only turn up now and then, of course, but the area always repays a visit because it holds an excellent variety of both water and bush birds throughout the year. Windsor is situated about 60 km north-west of Sydney via Parramatta, and has several motels and a caravan park.

The following are some of the best known birding spots; most are on private property, however, and you should obtain permission from local land-owners before venturing too far. Alternatively, join the New South Wales Field Ornithologists Club — the FOC has permission to enter many properties in the region.

Bakers Lagoon: Is about 7 km north-west of Windsor via Cornwallis Road. One of the largest lagoons in the district, it lies just south of the Hawkesbury River and can be viewed from Cornwallis Road or from Cupitts Lane. Depending on conditions elsewhere in the state, it usually holds a wide variety of waterbirds — grebes, cormorants, herons, egrets, bitterns, ibis, spoonbills, waterfowl, rails, crakes and waders.

Notable rarities recorded at Bakers Lagoon in recent years include Buff-breasted Sandpiper, Ruff, White-winged Tern, Yellow Wagtail and Star Finch (the finches have been seen on a number of occasions, but are probably aviary escapees). Interesting raptors such as Black Kite, Spotted Harrier and Black Falcon appear from time to time.

Pughs Lagoon: Lies a few kilometres south-west of Bakers Lagoon via Cornwallis Road, Cornwells Lane and Onus Lane. It is best viewed from Old Kurrajong Road and, like Bakers Lagoon, often supports a wide range of waterbirds. A visit to the Hawkesbury River, a little to the north, may also prove worthwhile.

McGraths Hill: About 1 km south-east of Windsor, the sewage treatment works and adjacent swamps at McGraths Hill can be approached from Windsor Road or from Mulgrave Road (opposite Windsor High School). The area is much favoured by Sydney bird-watchers — it usually supports a wealth of waterbirds including grebes, Darter, cormorants, herons, Great and Little Egret, Glossy (sometimes in quite large numbers), Sacred and Straw-necked Ibis, Royal and Yellow-billed Spoonbill, Plumed Whistling-Duck, Australian Shelduck, Pacific Black, Pink-eared and Maned Duck, Grey Teal, Chestnut Teal, Australasian Shoveler, Hardhead, Red-kneed Dotterel, Black-fronted Plover, Black-winged Stilt and Whiskered Tern. In summer a few species of migratory wader are often present.

An impressive array of rare and sought-after birds have been recorded in the McGraths Hill area: Black-necked Stork, Freckled Duck, Buff-banded Rail, Australian and Spotless Crake, Painted Snipe, Little Curlew, Wood, Marsh and Pectoral Sandpiper, Black-tailed Godwit, Long-toed Stint, Ruff, Gull-billed Tern and Barn Swallow are perhaps the most notable.

The agricultural lands surrounding the sewage works are worth looking over for Banded Lapwing, Rufous Songlark, Brown Songlark (both songlarks occur mainly in summer), Double-barred Finch and Chestnut-breasted Mannikin, as well as for raptors such as Black-shouldered and Whistling Kite, Little Eagle, Spotted and Marsh Harrier, Black and Peregrine Falcon, and Australian Hobby.

Bushells Lagoon: Is situated about 6 km north of Windsor via Putty Road and Freemans Reach Road. A large lagoon, it can be viewed from Gorricks Lane to the west and from Argyle Reach Road to the east. Most of the birds already mentioned have been recorded at Bushells, and it too has produced a string of interesting species – Great Crested Grebe, Cattle Egret, Glossy Ibis, Red-chested Button-quail, Baillon's Crake, Red-necked Avocet and Buff-breasted Sandpiper for example.

Pitt Town Lagoon: Lies about 6 km north-east of Windsor via Windsor Road and Pitt Town Road. Church Street (in the centre of Pitt Town) provides ready access to this well-known birding spot: Cattle Egret, Glossy Ibis, Plumed Whistling-Duck, Australian Shelduck, Pink-eared Duck, Greenshank (summer) and Double-banded Plover (winter) are just a few of the many species you can expect to find. Most of the rarities listed for McGraths Hill have been recorded at Pitt Town Lagoon, while other recent sightings of note include Intermediate Egret, Mongolian Plover and White-rumped Sandpiper (a bird seen at Pitt Town in October 1977 was the first record of this species for New South Wales).

Longneck Lagoon: Another good waterbird locality, Longneck Lagoon is about 10 km north-east of Windsor via Pitt Town Road and Cattai Road. Its northern section can be viewed with ease from Cattai Road, while its southern shores can be reached via Dural Road and Whitmore Road.

Longneck Lagoon Field Studies Centre occupies part of the lagoon's eastern shores and is open Monday to Friday between 9 a.m. and 4 p.m. (closed during school holidays). The centre, accessible via Whitmore Road and Greenfield Place, is an excellent place for bush birds – ask the warden for permission to walk through its grounds.

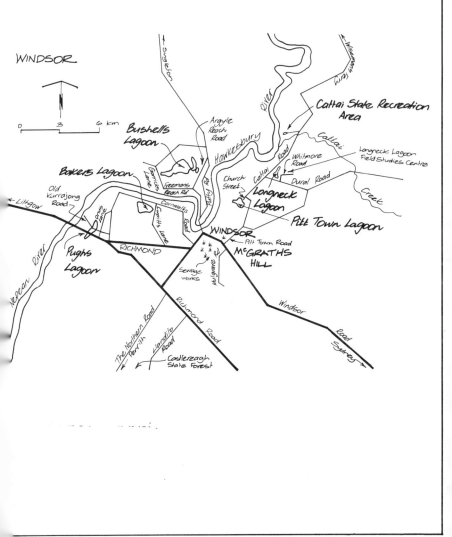

WINDSOR

0   3   6 km

Singleton

Bushells Lagoon

Bakers Lagoon

Old Kurrajong Road

Lithgow

Pughs Lagoon

RICHMOND

Argyle Reach Road

Freemans Reach Rd

Cornwallis Lane

Cupitt's Lane

Davis Lane

Granite Lane

Hawkesbury River

Rd Fitts

Church Street

Cornwallis Road

Nepean River

Sewage Works

The Northern Road Penrith

Llandilo Road

Castlereagh State Forest

Richmond Road

Wilgaro Rd

WINDSOR

Pitt Town Road

McGRATHS HILL

Windsor

Road Sydney

Cattai State Recreation Area

Wisemans Ferry

Cattai Road

Cattai

Whitmore Road

Dural Road

Longneck Lagoon

Pitt Town Lagoon

Longneck Lagoon Field Studies Centre

Cattai Creek

Cattai State Recreation Area (224 ha): Is situated on the banks of the Hawkesbury River, about 12 km north-east of Windsor via Pitt Town Road and Cattai Road. Formerly known as Caddie Park, the reserve features a beautiful sandstone homestead built by convicts in 1821, numerous shady picnic areas and a children's playground. Boats and canoes are available for hire — a most pleasant way to explore the Hawkesbury River. Camping is not permitted.

Needless to say you could spend a very full and enjoyable day birding in the Windsor area. Those with the time to venture further afield may care to head north along the Hawkesbury River to Wisemans Ferry, or south along the Nepean River to Penrith. And Castlereagh State Forest, about 12 km south-west of Windsor between The Northern Road and Llandilo Road, is worth visiting for bush birds normally associated with inland New South Wales.

The Blue Mountains

You have only to drive for a few hours west of Sydney to reach one of Australia's most spectacular wilderness areas, a vast tract of rugged sandstone country that in many respects has changed little since European settlers first set foot on the continent two centuries ago. Long famous for their beauty and grandeur, the Blue Mountains possess some of the finest scenery in New South Wales — majestic canyons sheltering pockets of rainforest, waterfalls plunging over yellow and orange-tinted sandstone cliffs, heathlands dotted with wildflowers in springtime, and wide expanses of virgin eucalypt forest. This superb region, much loved by bushwalkers, provides artists and photographers with endless inspiration and attracts many thousands of visitors each year.

The region contains three of the state's largest national parks — Blue Mountains (215 955 ha), Kanangra Boyd (68 276 ha) and Wollemi (485 221 ha) — but much of the area is accessible only on foot. If you are not an experienced bushwalker, or if you have limited time, you can see a little of what the Blue Mountains have to offer by visiting the places mentioned. All can be reached quite readily by car from the Great Western Highway, and bus tour operators based in Sydney include many of the better known places of interest on their itineraries. There is also a regular train service from the city to Katoomba, a small town with ample accommodation situated in the heart of the mountains. From Katoomba railway station you can either walk or catch a bus to several well-known lookouts, including Echo Point, which overlooks one of Australia's most famous landmarks — The Three Sisters.

Glenbrook: Is situated on the northern boundary of the south-eastern section of Blue Mountains National Park, about 65 km west of Sydney via Penrith. There is a visitors centre together with several picnic and camping grounds (caravans are not permitted) just south of Glenbrook, as well as walking tracks leading to Glenbrook Gorge, the Nepean River, Red Hands Cave, Euroka Clearing and other places of interest. Many of the bush birds − including the Origma − listed for reserves closer to Sydney can be found in this part of Blue Mountains National Park; a detailed list can be obtained from the visitors centre.

Wentworth Falls: This small township, 867 m above sea level, offers motel and guest house accommodation and is situated on the Great Western Highway about 99 km from Sydney. There are picnic grounds, walking tracks and several lookouts in the vicinity of the township; its celebrated 275 m waterfall is at the end of Falls Road, about 2 km south of the highway.

Katoomba: Located 1017 m above sea level and 105 km west of Sydney, Katoomba has numerous fine old guest houses as well as motels, hotels, a youth hostel and two caravan parks. It makes an excellent base from which to explore what is arguably the most attractive part of the Blue Mountains.

There is an information centre at Echo Point, about 3 km south of the Great Western Highway via Lurline Street and Echo Point Road. Many useful publications, including maps and walking track guides, can be obtained from the centre. The lookout at Echo Point offers unforgettable views over the deeply dissected Jamison Valley, and walking tracks lead from the point eastwards to the Giant Stairway and westwards to Orphan Rock. There are also many longer walks commencing at Echo Point, but since most involve a good deal of climbing you will need to be fit and well prepared. If you are not feeling particularly energetic try the track to Katoomba Cascades. This 2 km walk is reasonably level and can be completed in half an hour or so. Along the way you should see at least a few exciting birds − Gang-gang Cockatoo and Australian King-Parrot for example.

Blackheath: About 10 km north of Katoomba via the Great Western Highway, Blackheath is the highest township in the Blue Mountains − 1065 m above sea level. It has motel accommodation and a caravan park, and is the gateway to the northern section of Blue Mountains National Park, which lies just a few kilometres to the east. The park headquarters are located at 65 Leichhardt Street, Blackheath. Picnic facilities are provided at Evans Lookout, Govetts Leap, Anvil Rock, Victoria Falls and Pierces Pass, and there is a small camping area (tents only) with toilets and fireplaces at Perrys Lookdown at the end of Hat Hill Road.

There are numerous walking tracks in the Blackheath area − Evans Lookout to Govetts Leap (2 km), Evans Lookout to Beauchamp Falls (1.5 km), Govetts Leap to Pulpit Rock (2.5

km), and Govetts Leap to Popes Glen (3 km) are among the less strenuous. If you are reasonably fit the Grand Canyon Walk, though very steep in places, is well worth the effort. It commences at Neates Glen on Evans Lookout Road, zigzags down a cliff-face to the Grand Canyon, then runs along a series of sandstone ledges with Greaves Creek rushing through a narrow chasm far below. After 2 km or so, just before Beauchamp Falls, the track heads northwards and climbs steeply to Evans Lookout. Along the way there are pockets of lush rainforest, masses of delicate ferns, moss-covered logs and beautiful silvery waterfalls, making this one of the most pleasant walks in the Blue Mountains. Birds to look out for en route include Crimson Rosella, Superb Lyrebird, Eastern Yellow Robin, Eastern Whipbird and Pilotbird, all of which are quite common in the area.

Hartley Historic Site (10 ha):   Hartley is an early-Australian village in a picturesque rural setting about 27 km north-west of Katoomba via the Great Western Highway. The village has many well-preserved historic buildings, including a court house (1837), post office (1839), St Bernards Catholic Church (1842), and St Johns Church of England (1859). St Bernards Presbytery now houses a visitors centre, and there is a museum in the court house. Both buildings are open from 10 a.m. until 5 p.m. every day except Wednesday.

Jenolan Caves: Glistening helictites, stalactites and stalagmites, exquisite grottos, colourful caverns and placid underground pools are just a few of the many features that have made Jenolan the most famous limestone cave system in New South Wales. Since they were first opened to the public over a hundred years ago, the caves have been seen by more than three million people. Today nine caves are open for inspection; guided tours are conducted daily throughout the year.

Situated about 80 km south-west of Katoomba, Jenolan can be reached via the Great Western Highway and Hartley. The road from Hartley to the caves is sealed. Accommodation can be obtained at Caves House, a rambling four-storey hotel built in the early 1900s. It is a most impressive building − a tourist attraction in itself − located in delightful surroundings a few hundred metres from the main caves.

Not all the attractions at Jenolan are underground. The caves form part of a 2500 ha reserve and there are walking tracks − long and short, steep and level − leading to interesting features such as the Devils Coachhouse, the Grand Arch, Carlotta Arch and Blue Lake. And there are birds of course − including the Origma. In fact Jenolan is probably the only place in the state where you can be virtually assured of seeing this species. About the size of a White-browed Scrubwren, the Origma is grey-brown above, rich rufous below, and on occasions utters a spirited twittering call reminiscent of a Welcome Swallow. It can usually be found without difficulty in the vicinity of the Grand Arch, and along the track that follows the Jenolan River past Blue Lake.

Kanangra Boyd National Park: Lies to the south of Jenolan Caves and is accessible via Kanangra Walls Road. It can be reached by conventional vehicle but the access road is unsealed, narrow and very steep in places and is therefore unsuitable for caravans. Picnic facilities are provided at Kanangra Walls, about 35 km from Jenolan, and there is a small camping ground with toilets and fireplaces at Boyd Crossing some 25 km from the caves. Bush camping is permitted in most parts of the reserve; for further information contact the New South Wales National Parks and Wildlife Service at Blackheath.

Kanangra Boyd probably has no birds that cannot be found more easily elsewhere in the Blue Mountains. Nevertheless it contains magnificent scenery − deep valleys, massive rock walls and numerous crystal-clear streams and waterfalls − and has much to offer the hardy bushwalker. There are well-used walking tracks leading from the access road to many places of interest, including Tuglow Caves, the Kowmung River, Colong Caves and Mt Thurat.

Wollemi National Park: The most extensive wilderness area remaining in New South Wales, Wollemi is the state's second-largest national park. It offers spectacular unspoilt wilderness scenery and contains the magnificent Colo River Gorge, as well as a number of basalt-capped peaks rising to over 1200 m. The reserve adjoins the northern section of Blue Mountains National Park and can be approached from the south via the Lithgow to Windsor road (Bells Line of Road), or from the east via the Windsor to Singleton road. There are no roads running through the park and no facilities for visitors. If you wish to camp or walk in Wollemi you should contact the New South Wales National Parks and Wildlife Service in Sydney or Blackheath beforehand.

Thirlmere Lakes National Park

Five interconnected freshwater lakes are the dominant feature of this small but significant national park. The reserve has an area of only 630 ha, yet it is of considerable scientific importance in a region where very few wetlands remain undisturbed. The long shallow lakes, which lie in a sandstone valley, are fringed by extensive reedbeds and other emergent vegetation. As a result they attract many waterbirds − Great Crested Grebe, Darter, Australasian Bittern, Lewin's Rail and Azure Kingfisher are some of the species you may be fortunate enough to find there.

In addition to waterbirds the park supports quite a variety of bush birds. In the eucalypt forest surrounding the lakes you should have little difficulty locating many of the following: Peaceful Dove, Yellow-tailed Black-Cockatoo, Sulphur-crested Cockatoo, Horsfield's Bronze-Cuckoo (spring–summer), Common Koel (spring–summer), Southern Boobook, Cicadabird (spring–summer), Scarlet Robin (especially in winter), Jacky Winter, Leaden Flycatcher (spring–summer), Spotted Quail-thrush, Variegated Fairy-wren, Origma (quite plentiful near sandstone cliffs), Chestnut-rumped Hylacola, White-throated Gerygone (spring–summer), Varied Sittella, Red-browed Treecreeper, Yellow-tufted and Fuscous Honeyeater, and Olive-backed Oriole. Two sought-after finches, Beautiful and Diamond Firetail, are well worth searching for.

The reserve is situated about 100 km south-west of Sydney via the Hume Highway and Picton. From Picton take the road to Thirlmere township, continue on towards Buxton and turn right at Slades Road (about 2 km south of Thirlmere). Slades Road leads to the eastern shore of the largest lake – the site of a picnic area and boat ramp. Camping is not permitted, but there are a motel and caravan park at Camden about 30 km to the north.

THE SNOWY MOUNTAINS

Immortalised by A. B. Paterson, one of Australia's most celebrated poets, the Snowy Mountains lie in the densely populated south-eastern corner of the continent and form part of the great crescent of high country that stretches across the New South Wales – Victorian border between Canberra and Melbourne. Sometimes described as the roof of Australia, the region contains our highest peaks, among them Carruthers Peak (2145 m), Ramshead (2191 m), Mt Twynam (2196 m), Mt Townsend (2210 m) and the highest – Mt Kosciusko (2228 m). These are the mountains made famous in 'Banjo' Paterson's 'The Man from Snowy River': anyone who has walked from Charlotte Pass along the track that crosses the Snowy River – little more than a stream at this point – then climbs through glorious alpine countryside to the summit of Mt Kosciusko will find that classic ballad especially meaningful.

The earliest visitors to the high country were the Aboriginals who came during summer from as far afield as the Omeo district in Victoria to feast on bogong moths. Unlike the Aboriginals, who have left few reminders of their activities, Europeans have had a considerable impact on the environment. For over one hundred years, from the early 1800s until the mid-1900s, graziers from the neighbouring lowlands drove their sheep and cattle to Kosciusko's verdant alpine slopes each summer to feed on fresh young plants uncovered by the melting snow. This practice led to soil erosion and was opposed by conservationists and, perhaps ironically,

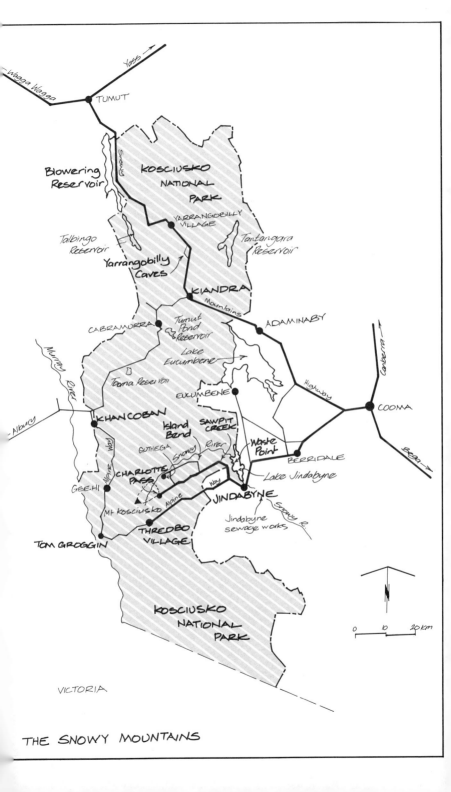

THE SNOWY MOUNTAINS

dam-builders. The graziers' snow leases were eventually withdrawn in the 1960s. Evidence of a different kind of human activity can be seen at Kiandra, in the northern section of Kosciusko National Park. In the mid-1800s, when the discovery of gold along the creeks attracted thousands of hopeful diggers to the mountains, Kiandra was the scene of one of Australia's most hectic and short-lived gold rushes.

Today, with increasing numbers of tourists visiting the region for winter sports, ski lifts and imitation alpine chalets, rather than sluicing races and miners' huts, are in demand. And in summer hordes of people, instead of mobs of cattle and sheep, trample the fragile alpine countryside around the summit of Mt Kosciusko.

Kosciusko National Park

With an area of 646 059 ha, Kosciusko is the largest national park in New South Wales and one of the most important reserves in Australia. Stretching from the Victorian border in the south to beyond the Blowering Reservoir in the north, it encompasses much of the Snowy Mountains and includes all the state's major snowfields. On average, snow covers about 100 000 ha of the park each winter. During summer the park's alpine areas are ablaze with masses of wildflowers − snow daisies, everlastings, buttercups, bluebells, eyebrights, billy buttons and others. Below about 1800 m, the treeless herbfields and heathlands of the alpine zone give way to snow gum woodlands interspersed with expanses of snow grass, which in turn are replaced by wet and dry sclerophyll forests at lower elevations.

Although at a glance Kosciusko's bird list looks impressive (over 200 species have been recorded in the park), bear in mind that the reserve is vast and that a significant part of it lies above 1500 m. Many birds on the list visit the higher ground only in summer. In addition, at least forty species listed for the area are waterbirds that only turn up occasionally (the region's lakes and reservoirs, though extensive, are generally deep and steep-sided; as a result they are unattractive to waterbirds such as waders and dabbling ducks). Nevertheless quite a variety of interesting species can be found in the park, including some that are keenly sought-after: Grey Goshawk, Peregrine Falcon, Wonga Pigeon, Glossy Black-Cockatoo, Gang-gang Cockatoo (common, particularly during summer when it can be seen even at the highest elevations − around the summit of Mt Kosciusko for example), Little Lorikeet, Australian King-Parrot, Powerful and Masked Owl, White-throated Nightjar (summer), Azure Kingfisher, Superb Lyrebird, White's Thrush, Rose (summer) and Pink Robin, Olive Whistler (common during summer in the Thredbo area), Satin Flycatcher (summer), Rufous Fantail (summer), Spotted Quail-

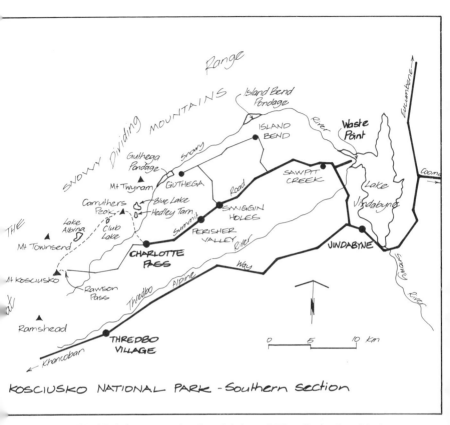

KOSCIUSKO NATIONAL PARK - Southern Section

thrush, Pilotbird (common in the vicinity of Thredbo), Speckled Warbler, Red-browed Treecreeper, Crescent Honeyeater (quite common on the higher ground in summer), Diamond Firetail and Satin Bowerbird.

Other species of interest, many of which are more plentiful than the birds already listed, include Black-shouldered Kite, Brown Goshawk, Wedge-tailed Eagle, Yellow-tailed Black-Cockatoo, Sulphur-crested Cockatoo, Crimson Rosella, Brush and Fan-tailed Cuckoo (summer), Shining Bronze-Cuckoo (summer), White-throated Needletail (sometimes seen in large numbers during summer), Flame and Eastern Yellow Robin, Crested Shrike-tit, Eastern Whipbird, White-eared, Yellow-tufted and Fuscous Honeyeater, Eastern Spinebill and Olive-backed Oriole (summer).

Because Kosciusko is such a large park it will take you a week or more to explore it thoroughly. The best time to tour the area is of course during the summer months (November to March); in winter (May to September) some of the region's roads, including the Alpine Way linking Jindabyne with Khancoban, may be blocked by snow. The following route will take you to most of the main places of interest and to many of the best birding localities.

Jindabyne: This small township is situated on the shores of Lake Jindabyne, about 8 km from Kosciusko's south-eastern boundary. It has a shopping centre, petrol outlets, motels, numerous holiday apartments and two caravan parks.

Lake Jindabyne is a popular fishing and boating spot, and its shallow sections attract small numbers of waterbirds. A visit to the Jindabyne sewage works (a few kilometres south-east of the township near the southern end of Lake Jindabyne − ask locally for precise directions) may also prove rewarding.

Sawpit Creek: Is about 5 km inside the national park boundary, just south of the road from Jindabyne to Charlotte Pass. The reserve's visitors centre is located here; it houses displays covering the history, flora and fauna of the region, and you can obtain a bird list and other information from the ranger.

Kosciusko's main camping ground is situated about 500 m from the visitors centre. Hot-water showers and powered sites are provided, and there are a number of cabins available for rental: bookings can be made at any New South Wales Government Travel Centre. Bookings for campsites are not taken.

Waste Point: Lies on the north-western shores of Lake Jindabyne, about 5 km east of Sawpit Creek, and is readily accessible by road. You could launch a boat here and explore the lake, which in late summer is usually quite shallow at this point, and the open woodland just west of Waste Point is worth a visit for bush birds such as Fuscous Honeyeater.

Island Bend: You can camp here at a lovely spot overlooking the Snowy River. Toilets and fireplaces are provided, but there are no other facilities. The camping ground is about 15 km from Sawpit Creek via the road to Guthega.

Charlotte Pass: Is about 27 km south-west of Sawpit Creek via Summit Road. Accessible only in summer, the pass is the gateway to Kosciusko's superb alpine countryside. From the carpark at the end of Summit Road a walking track leads to the top of Mt Kosciusko, a distance of 11 km or so. Undoubtedly the most scenic walk in the reserve, the track crosses the Snowy River valley, climbs steeply to Carruthers Peak, then follows a line of ridges − the highest in the Snowy Mountains − in a south-westerly direction before terminating at Rawson Pass near the summit of Mt Kosciusko.

Although this is a strenuous walk, the rewards are great indeed for it offers breathtaking views over alpine slopes dotted with glacial lakes − Hedley Tarn, Blue Lake, Club Lake and Lake Albina. If you feel unable to tackle this rather demanding walk, Summit Road continues as a track (closed to vehicles) beyond

Charlotte Pass and provides a more direct and easier route of about 8 km to the summit of Mt Kosciusko. There is also a short boardwalk leading from the Charlotte Pass carpark to a lookout offering fine views over the Snowy River valley.

Thredbo Village: Readily accessible via the Alpine Way, this well-known ski resort is about 35 km south-west of Jindabyne. It has shops, petrol stations, ample accommodation (summer and winter), a youth hostel and a caravan park with powered sites.

Thredbo makes a good base for the bird-watcher since there are a number of reasonably level walking tracks in the area. You can also take the chair lift to the lower slopes of Mt Kosciusko, then walk from the terminus to the top of the mountain.

Tom Groggin: Cars towing caravans or trailers are not permitted to travel along the Alpine Way beyond Thredbo, but those with tents will find Tom Groggin a delightful spot to camp. Situated on the banks of the Murray River (not a wide, deep waterway, merely a creek here), some 55 km south-west of Jindabyne, the informal camping area has no facilities but is usually very peaceful.

Khancoban: Is a small township with a motel and caravan park on the western boundary of Kosciusko National Park, about 110 km from Jindabyne. From Khancoban you can either head west to Albury, or north-east through the northern section of the national park via the very scenic road to Cabramurra and Kiandra.

Kiandra: This deserted gold-mining town was home to more than ten thousand diggers during the gold rush of 1859−60. Evidence of the feverish activity that once took place here − dams, water races, heaps of spoil, open cut mines − can still be seen in and around the historic township, which is situated on the Snowy Mountains Highway, about 90 km from Khancoban.

Yarrangobilly Caves: Are situated within Kosciusko National Park, about 20 km north of Kiandra and about 75 km south-east of Tumut. Part of the extensive limestone cave system, long famous for the variety and beauty of its calcite formations, is open to the public. Ranger-guided tours are available; details can be obtained from the visitors centre, which is located a few kilometres west of the Snowy Mountains Highway (the caves are well signposted).

There are picnic grounds, a thermal pool and several walking tracks near the caves. Camping is not permitted, but a small informal camping area is provided at Yarrangobilly Village, about 10 km to the north via the Snowy Mountains Highway.

Blowering Reservoir: Is on the north-western boundary of Kosciusko National Park, some 15 km south of Tumut. Camping and picnic grounds are located at intervals along the Snowy Mountains Highway, which skirts the reservoir's eastern shores, and boat ramps are provided at several points.

THE MID-NORTH COAST

To the north of Sydney, between the heavily industrialised city of Newcastle and the popular resort town of Coffs Harbour, there are long stretches of beautiful sandy beaches separated by rocky headlands and backed by numerous peaceful lakes and waterways. This is undoubtedly one of the most attractive parts of Australia's east coast, an area of diverse landscapes with much to offer the bird-watcher. The Pacific Highway provides ready access to the region's three splendid national parks — Myall Lakes, Crowdy Bay and Hat Head — as well as to a number of state forests and state recreation areas. And all along the coast there are beach resorts with ample accommodation, making this an ideal place for a holiday.

Myall Lakes National Park

With an area of 31 116 ha, Myall Lakes National Park is by far the largest reserve on the New South Wales coast north of Newcastle. It stretches from Port Stephens in the south to beyond Sugarloaf Point in the north, and is dominated by a huge natural lake system that covers almost a third of the park. The vegetation is varied: banksia woodlands, and dry sclerophyll forests consisting chiefly of blackbutt and smooth-barked apple (*Angophora costata* — some fine examples of this beautiful tree can be seen in the park), occur on the extensive sand-dunes that separate the lakes from the sea; wet and dry heaths cover much of the low-lying area between the dunes and the lake system; dense stands of paperbark and swamp mahogany grow around the shores of the lakes and in adjacent swamps; and patches of rainforest occur at Mungo Brush and Seal Rocks.

Access to the southern section of Myall Lakes National Park can be gained via Tea Gardens and Hawks Nest. From here an unsealed road (suitable for conventional vehicles though sandy in places) runs right through the park to Seal Rocks. The central part of the reserve can be reached from Bulahdelah via the Bombah Point ferry, and the northern section via the Bungwahl to Seal Rocks road.

The park's main camping ground is situated at Mungo Brush, on the eastern shores of The Broadwater. It has only basic facilities — picnic tables, fireplaces and toilets — and bookings are not necessary. Bush camping is permitted in most areas of the reserve; details can be obtained from the ranger at Bombah Point. There is a privately owned caravan park (Legges Camp), with hot-water showers and powered sites, at Bombah Point. It is usually crowded during the summer months and you should book a site well in advance. Other caravan parks are located at Tea Gardens,

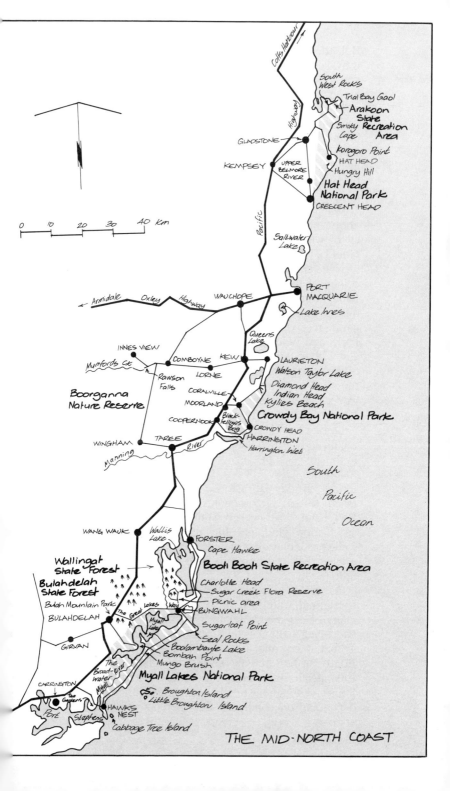

THE MID-NORTH COAST

Bulahdelah and Seal Rocks, while motel and hotel accommodation is available at Tea Gardens, Bulahdelah and Forster. The nearest youth hostels are at Carrington, on the northern shores of Port Stephens, and at Girvan some 20 km south-west of Bulahdelah.

The Myall Lakes district supports an immensely rich and varied avifauna. The three hundred or so species that have been recorded in the area can be broadly divided into five groups: seabirds; waders; waterbirds such as grebes, cormorants, herons, egrets, ibis, spoonbills and waterfowl; woodland, forest and heathland birds; and rainforest species. In addition there are, of course, a number of species that can be found virtually anywhere.

Seabirds include Little Penguin, Gould's Petrel, Wedge-tailed, Sooty and Short-tailed Shearwater and White-faced Storm-Petrel, all of which breed on islands in the vicinity of Port Stephens. Gould's Petrel is of particular interest since Cabbage Tree Island, near the entrance to Port Stephens, holds the only known breeding colony of this species in Australia. Access to Broughton, Little Broughton, Cabbage Tree and other islands off Port Stephens is difficult, except in calm weather. And most of the islands are nature reserves under the control of the New South Wales National Parks and Wildlife Service; you must therefore obtain a permit if you wish to visit them. Other seabirds occurring along this stretch of the coast, most of which can be found much more readily than those already mentioned, are Australasian Gannet (mainly winter), and Caspian, Common (summer), White-fronted (winter), Little and Crested Tern.

During summer quite a variety of migratory waders visit the region and a trip to the northern shores of Port Stephens, especially to the area east of Carrington, should produce at least a few of the following: Grey, Lesser Golden, Mongolian and Large Sand Plover, Ruddy Turnstone, Eastern Curlew, Whimbrel, Grey tailed Tattler, Greenshank, Black-tailed and Bar-tailed Godwit Red Knot, Red-necked Stint, and Marsh, Terek, Sharp-tailed and Curlew Sandpiper. In winter Double-banded Plovers turn up while resident waders include Pied and, more rarely, Sooty Oyster catcher, Masked Lapwing, Red-capped Plover and Black-winged Stilt.

As might be expected waterbirds such as cormorants, herons egrets and waterfowl are well represented at Myall Lakes. In many places the shores of The Broadwater, Boolambayte Lake and Myall Lake can be reached by vehicle or on foot; however a boat is essential if you wish to explore the area thoroughly Boats can be hired at Tea Gardens, houseboats are available a Bulahdelah, and canoes can be hired from the store at Bomba Point. Although the number of species present varies considerably depending on conditions elsewhere in the state, the lakes an adjacent swamps usually hold a fair assortment of waterbirds including Great Crested, Hoary-headed and Australasian Grebe, Australian Pelican, Darter, Great, Pied, Little Black and Little Pied Cormorant, Pacific and White-faced Heron, Great and, more rarely, Little and Intermediate Egret, Rufous Night Heron, Little, Black and Australasian Bittern (though uncommon, all three bitterns are certainly worth searching for), Black-necked Stork (one of the region's special birds, this stately species breeds regularly in Myall Lakes National Park), Glossy (rarely), Sacred and Straw-necked Ibis, Royal and, more rarely, Yellow-billed Spoonbill, Black Swan, Pacific Black, Maned and Musk Duck, Grey Teal, Chestnut Teal, Hardhead, Buff-banded Rail, Baillon's, Australian and Spotless Crake, Dusky Moorhen, Purple Swamphen, Eurasian Coot and Painted Snipe (rarely).

Because Myall Lakes National Park contains a wide variety of vegetation types it holds a large number of land birds, the extensive heathlands to the north-east of Bombah Point being favoured by species such as Pheasant Coucal, Tawny Grassbird, Variegated Fairy-wren, Southern Emu-wren, Little Wattlebird and White-cheeked and Tawny-crowned Honeyeater, and the neighbouring forested dunes and coastal woodlands attracting Bar-shouldered Dove, Scaly-breasted Lorikeet (especially when the eucalypts are in flower), Eastern Rosella, Jacky Winter, Rufous Whistler, Leaden Flycatcher (chiefly summer), White-throated Gerygone (mainly summer), White-throated Tree-creeper, Noisy Friarbird, Yellow-faced, White-naped and New Holland Honeyeater, Red-browed Firetail, Olive-backed Oriole (mainly summer), Dusky Woodswallow, Grey Butcherbird and Pied Currawong. Rainforest birds can be found at Mungo Brush, although the rainforest here is somewhat impoverished (there are fewer species of plants at Mungo Brush than there are in the rainforests a little to the north of the lakes − at Wallingat State Forest for example). The lush, palm-dominated forest is none-theless a splendid place for a short walk, and you could see some interesting birds − Black-faced Monarch (summer), Rufous Fan-tail (summer), Brown Gerygone, and Lewin's and Scarlet Honey-eater.

Bulahdelah and Wallingat State Forests

Bulahdelah and Wallingat State Forests are located between Bulahdelah and Forster, and can be reached via the Pacific Highway and The Great Lakes Way. Bulahdelah State Forest has a picnic area and many kilometres of forestry tracks, while Wallingat has picnic facilities, a well-signposted forest drive and a splendidly situated camping area. Both are excellent places to go birding.

Bulahdelah State Forest (9900 ha):   Access to the picnic ground at Bulah Mountain Park can be gained from the Pacific Highway at Bulahdelah. Toilets and fireplaces are provided (camping is not permitted), and there are numerous tracks leading into the adjacent wet sclerophyll forest. There are also many forestry roads running through the main part of the state forest which lies to the north of The Great Lakes Way, east of Bulahdelah township.

Wallingat State Forest (6500 ha):   Is readily accessible via The Great Lakes Way and Bungwahl. About 4 km north of Bungwahl there is a picnic ground with a shelter hut and fireplaces. A leaflet describing points of interest in the state forest can be obtained from a box near the shelter hut.

From the picnic area a forest drive leads through wet sclerophyll forest consisting of fine stands of blackbutt, flooded gum, tallowwood, Sydney blue gum, brush box and turpentine. Sugar Creek Flora Reserve, which lies within the state forest just north of the picnic area, is of special interest. Set aside for scientific study, it protects 82 ha of varied vegetation including pure stands of flooded gum, and patches of dense rainforest dominated by cabbage tree palms (*Livistona australis*). There is a short (2 km or so) circular walking track in the southern section of the reserve, commencing just east of the junction of Sugar Creek Road and Hotel Creek Road. A camping ground, with toilets, picnic tables and fireplaces, is located on the banks of the Wallingat River, some 5 km north-west of the picnic area via Link Road.

Wallingat State Forest holds many interesting birds, including a number that you are less likely to see in Myall Lakes National Park. Among these are Pacific Baza, Grey Goshawk, Australian Brush-turkey, Wompoo Fruit-Dove, Topknot, White-headed and Wonga Pigeon, Brown Cuckoo-Dove, Emerald Dove, Australian King-Parrot, Common Koel (summer), Channel-billed Cuckoo (summer), White's Thrush, Large-billed and Yellow-throated Scrubwren, Satin Bowerbird and Green Catbird (the bowerbird and catbird can usually be found quite readily in the dense forest adjacent to the picnic area).

Booti Booti State Recreation Area

Located 10 km south of Forster via The Great Lakes Way, this 1588 ha reserve encompasses the magnificent surfing beaches between Cape Hawke and Charlotte Head and is an ideal place to go boating, swimming, fishing and walking. Although crowded at times, particularly during the summer months, it has picnic and camping facilities that make it an excellent base from which to explore the placid waters of Wallis Lake and the rugged headlands at Cape Hawke and Charlotte Head.

Part of the eastern shore of Wallis Lake is included in the park

– a good spot for waterbirds such as grebes, Australian Pelican, cormorants, herons, egrets, ibis, spoonbills, waterfowl, waders and terns. Little Terns breed regularly in the Forster area during summer. Unfortunately, however, breeding populations of this delightful small tern are declining in New South Wales and Victoria owing to disturbance – albeit unintentional – from holiday-makers. The mangroves towards the northern end of Wallis Lake may be worth visiting for Striated Heron and Mangrove Gerygone (spring–summer).

Crowdy Bay National Park

Crowdy Bay National Park is situated on the coast east of the Pacific Highway, and is bounded by the Manning River in the south and by Watson Taylor Lake in the north. Covering an area of 7237 ha, it features a fine stretch of beach backed by banksia woodlands and low-lying, swampy heathlands.

The park is accessible from the south via Coopernook, Harrington and Crowdy Head; from the west via Moorland and Coralville; and from the north via Laurieton and Diamond Head. Though unsealed, all roads in the reserve are suitable for conventional vehicles except after heavy rain. Camping is permitted in the northern section of the park at Diamond Head, Indian Head and Kylies Beach. Toilets and fireplaces are provided, but there are no showers or powered sites and bookings are not taken. Diamond Head is usually crowded with fishermen during summer; the camping areas at Indian Head and Kylies Beach, however, attract fewer visitors. The nearest caravan parks are located at Harrington and Laurieton, and motel accommodation is available in Crowdy Head, Harrington and Laurieton. There is a youth hostel at Wauchope, some 40 km to the north.

About one hundred species of birds have been recorded in the park, the banksia woodlands and heaths attracting many honeyeaters. Little Wattlebird, Noisy Friarbird, Noisy Miner, Yellowfaced, White-cheeked and Tawny-crowned Honeyeater and Eastern Spinebill all occur in the Diamond Head and Kylies Beach area, where several walking tracks provide ready access to the heath-covered headland. Honeyeaters are particularly numerous in spring and early summer when many of the trees and shrubs are in flower. Other species regularly recorded near Diamond Head include White-bellied Sea-Eagle, Brown Quail, Bar-shouldered Dove, Scaly-breasted Lorikeet, Eastern Yellow Robin, Superb Fairy-wren, White-browed Scrubwren, Brown, Yellow and Striated Thornbill, Silvereye, Red-browed Firetail and Grey Butcherbird.

Although many of the birds that occur at Crowdy Bay (including most of those listed) can be found quite easily, the park holds a number of species that are usually much more difficult to locate — Black-necked Stork, King Quail, Red-backed Button-quail, Buff-banded and Lewin's Rail, Baillon's, Australian and Spotless Crake, Tawny Grassbird and Southern Emu-wren. Most of these birds inhabit the less accessible sections of the reserve, but those prepared to tramp through the dense, wet heaths between Kylies Beach and Harrington may be rewarded for their efforts. Black-fellows Bog, which can be reached via the Moorland to Crowdy Head road, would be a good place to begin searching. And while you are in this part of the park keep your eyes open for Eastern Grass Owl and Ground Parrot. The owl, a rare and elusive species, has been recorded at Harrington; the Ground Parrot on the other hand has not as yet been found in the area, but as the habitat at Crowdy Bay is apparently suitable for them a thorough search of the park may bring results. (If you are really keen to see a Ground Parrot, try Bundjalung and Broadwater National Parks on the coast north of Coffs Harbour. The parrots are said to be reasonably plentiful in the heathlands there.)

Boorganna Nature Reserve

This small (396 ha) reserve lies to the north-west of Crowdy Bay National Park, and can be reached from the Pacific Highway via Kew, Lorne and Comboyne. Protecting a remnant of rainforest along Mumfords Creek, which forms much of the reserve's northern boundary, it is an excellent place for birds such as Grey Goshawk, Australian Brush-turkey, Topknot, White-headed and Wonga Pigeon, Brown Cuckoo-Dove, Little Lorikeet, Australian King-Parrot, Brush Cuckoo (summer), Azure Kingfisher, Noisy Pitta, Superb Lyrebird, White's Thrush, Rose (mainly summer) and Pale-yellow Robin, Black-faced and Spectacled Monarch (both species are present only in summer), Logrunner, Eastern Whip-bird, Large-billed and Yellow-throated Scrubwren, Brown Gery-gone, Lewin's and Scarlet Honeyeater, Regent Bowerbird and Green Catbird.

The reserve has no facilities for visitors other than a shelter hut and a short (1 km) walking track. The walking track commences just south of the Comboyne to Innes View road, about 6.5 km west of Comboyne, and leads through the subtropical rainforest that covers the north-eastern section of the park to a lookout near Rawson Falls. Boorganna's rainforest communities are of particular interest because a number of trees, including the red carabeen, do not occur further south in the region.

A detailed bird list for Boorganna Nature Reserve, and information about other parks in the area, can be obtained from the New South Wales National Parks and Wildlife Service in Port Macquarie.

Hat Head National Park

The coastal strip between Crescent Head and South West Rocks, much of which is contained in Hat Head National Park (6219 ha), consists chiefly of wide sandy beaches, banksia woodlands, heaths and swamps. Thus the birds of Hat Head are essentially the same as those of Crowdy Bay National Park, less than 100 km to the south.

The park is accessible from the south via the road from Kempsey to Crescent Head and Upper Belmore River, and from the west via the road linking Kempsey, Gladstone and South West Rocks. Camping grounds with basic facilities (picnic tables, fireplaces and toilets) are located near Hungry Hill, just south of Hat Head township, and near Smoky Cape in the northern section of the park. Hungry Hill is perhaps the best place to camp; Smoky Cape is often crowded, especially in summer. Caravan parks with showers and powered sites are situated at Hat Head township and South West Rocks, and there are motels and holiday units in South West Rocks and Kempsey. There is a youth hostel at Coffs Harbour to the north.

Although for many visitors the beaches are undoubtedly the chief attraction at Hat Head − fishing and swimming are the main activities − the park supports a rich flora and fauna and is a good place for birds, particularly honeyeaters and other heathland species. There are walking tracks leading to Korogoro Point, east of Hat Head township, and to the beach in the vicinity of Smoky Cape.

Arakoon State Recreation Area

The ruins of historic Trial Bay Gaol, a penal institution built in the late 1800s, are the main feature of this 472 ha reserve situated to the north of Hat Head National Park, just east of South West Rocks. A museum has been established in the gaol and is well worth seeing; in addition Arakoon has two attractive beaches and several kilometres of walking tracks.

There is a camping ground with hot-water showers, toilets and barbecues, but it has no powered sites. Since the reserve is very popular − about 600 000 people visit it each year − you should book a site in advance: write to the manager, Arakoon State Recreation Area, PO Box 25, South West Rocks, NSW 2431, enclosing a stamped, addressed envelope.

NEW ENGLAND

In some respects New England is like the Atherton region of the far north of Queensland. Both places are rich in natural beauty, possessing spectacular mountain ranges, fast-flowing rivers, and deep fertile soils that once supported extensive tracts of rainforest

— tropical rainforest in the Atherton district, subtropical and temperate rainforest in New England. And like the Atherton region, where much of the original vegetation has been removed to make way for agriculture and to supply the needs of the timber industry, New England is prime farming and forestry country. As a result it too has been largely cleared; near Armidale only a few patches of rainforest remain, notably in Dorrigo and New England National Parks.

Despite the changes that have taken place since European settlement, however, New England is an excellent place for a bird-watching holiday. In addition to rainforests and cleared land the region contains a great variety of habitats, including wet and dry sclerophyll forests, open woodlands, heaths, swamps and lakes. The wide range of vegetation types supports an equally diverse avifauna; well over two hundred different birds occur in the Armidale–Dorrigo area alone, including such sought-after species as Pacific Baza, Grey Goshawk, Rose-crowned and Wompoo Fruit-Dove, Topknot, White-headed and Wonga Pigeon, Emerald Dove, Glossy Black-Cockatoo, Powerful and Sooty Owl, Noisy Pitta, Superb Lyrebird, Rufous Scrub-bird, Pale-yellow Robin, Black-faced and Spectacled Monarch, Logrunner, Spotted Quail-thrush, Yellow-throated Scrubwren, Speckled Warbler, Red-browed Treecreeper, Scarlet Honeyeater, Satin and Regent Bowerbird, Green Catbird and Paradise Riflebird.

Dorrigo National Park

In the late 1800s and early 1900s large areas of virgin subtropical rainforest on the Dorrigo Plateau were cleared for dairying. Today virtually all that remains of this wonderfully luxuriant habitat is contained in Dorrigo National Park, a 7819 ha reserve situated about 140 km east of Armidale. To reach the park take the road from Armidale to Dorrigo; the park headquarters are situated about 3 km south-east of Dorrigo township on the road to Bellingen. Camping is not permitted, but there are hotels, motels and caravan parks nearby in Dorrigo and Bellingen. Armidale, the region's main centre, is a picturesque university city with many historic buildings and plenty of accommodation, including a youth hostel. Other youth hostels are located at Coffs Harbour, to the east of Dorrigo, and at Wauchope to the south.

Dorrigo National Park has two delightfully situated picnic areas – The Glade and Never Never. The Never Never picnic area, deep within the park some 11 km from the Dorrigo–Bellingen road, has barbecues, toilets, water and a shelter hut (you may need to make use of the shelter hut – Dorrigo receives about 2500 mm of rain per annum and it can be wet at any time of the year). Never Never makes an excellent base from which to explore the

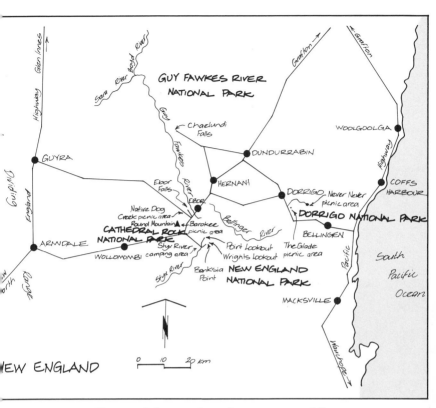

reserve's magnificent rainforests since there are many kilometres of well-graded walking tracks in this area: the Rosewood Creek track (5.5 km); the Blackbutt track (6.4 km); the Cedar Falls track (6.4 km); and the Casuarina Falls track (4.8 km).

Those with ample time will find all of these walks rewarding, but if you have only a few hours to spare the Rosewood Creek track is highly recommended. It provides ready access to an area of superb rainforest, and to Coachwood Falls on the eastern boundary of the park. Along the way beautiful trees such as red cedar, yellow carabeen, coachwood, Dorrigo plum, blackbutt and tallowwood tower above the rainforest floor. Many of the trees are festooned with epiphytic ferns and orchids, and birds are plentiful though often difficult to spot in the dim light. Even so you should see some interesting species, including Australian Brush-turkey, Rose-crowned and Wompoo Fruit-Dove, Topknot, White-headed and Wonga Pigeon (the Wonga Pigeon favours the forest margins and is often seen early in the day in the vicinity of the Never Never picnic area), Brown Cuckoo-Dove, Emerald Dove (also a bird of the forest edges), Australian King-Parrot,

Crimson Rosella, Brush Cuckoo (summer), Shining Bronze-Cuckoo (chiefly summer), Common Koel (summer), Sooty Owl (though uncommon, this nocturnal rainforest-dweller is worth searching for), Marbled Frogmouth (another nocturnal bird, this species has been recorded at Dorrigo but is apparently very rare in the district; it is more likely to be found further north, in the Border Ranges, Mt Warning and Nightcap National Parks for example), Noisy Pitta, Superb Lyrebird, Rufous Scrub-bird (if you cannot find this elusive species at Dorrigo, try New England National Park where it occurs in temperate rainforest in the vicinity of Point Lookout), White's Thrush, Rose (mainly summer), Eastern Yellow and Pale-yellow Robin, Black-faced and Spectacled Monarch (both these species are present only in summer), Rufous Fantail (summer), Logrunner, Eastern Whipbird, Large-billed and Yellow-throated Scrubwren, Brown Gerygone, Lewin's and Scarlet Honeyeater, Eastern Spinebill, Figbird, Spangled Drongo, Satin and Regent Bowerbird, Green Catbird and Paradise Riflebird.

Guy Fawkes River National Park

Guy Fawkes River National Park is a large (33 854 ha) reserve situated to the north of Ebor, a small township some 55 km west of Dorrigo and about 80 km east of Armidale. It contains a long section of the Guy Fawkes River — one of the few remaining wild rivers in New South Wales — which forms a boundary between the Dorrigo Plateau and the New England Tableland. The country surrounding the river is exceedingly rugged, and the vegetation ranges from open woodland on the higher slopes to rainforest in the sheltered gullies.

Access to the park is difficult; the only way to explore it is on foot. Bush camping is permitted throughout the area, and there is a small camping ground with barbecues, picnic tables and toilets at Chaelundi Falls, just inside the park's south-eastern boundary. If you wish to walk or camp in the reserve it would be wise to contact the ranger at Dorrigo National Park beforehand.

Those who do not have time to drive to Chaelundi Falls can see a little of what the area has to offer by visiting Ebor Falls, which lie outside the park near Ebor township. Here several lookouts provide breathtaking views over the southern section of the Guy Fawkes River valley. The falls are readily accessible via a good sealed road which leaves the Armidale–Dorrigo road about 1 km south of Ebor township.

Cathedral Rock National Park

One of the most interesting things about the New England district is the way the vegetation changes so abruptly as you travel from east to west. For the bird-watcher the juxtaposition of many different types of habitat is particularly attractive, for it provides an opportunity to see a wide variety of species within a short period of time. For example, you could if you wished spend the morning looking for rainforest birds at Dorrigo National Park, and in the afternoon visit Cathedral Rock National Park where an entirely different assemblage of birds occurs.

Cathedral Rock National Park covers an area of only 6500 ha, yet it contains dry sclerophyll forests, snow gum woodlands, heaths and swamps. Thus it is a very good place to go birding and, unlike nearby Guy Fawkes River National Park, it is readily accessible. Some of the more interesting birds you can expect to find here are Peregrine Falcon, Painted Button-quail, Latham's Snipe (summer), Glossy Black-Cockatoo, Little Lorikeet, White-throated Nightjar (summer), Flame and Scarlet Robin, Leaden Flycatcher (summer), Spotted Quail-thrush, Speckled Warbler, White-throated Gerygone (mainly summer), Buff-rumped Thorn-bill, Noisy Friarbird (mainly summer), Yellow-faced and White-eared Honeyeater, Diamond Firetail and Olive-backed Oriole (summer).

The park consists of three sections, the largest and most accessible of which lies to the north of Round Mountain (1608 m). In this part of the reserve camping is permitted at two sites — the Native Dog Creek picnic area, which is located 11 km from Ebor just south of the Ebor–Guyra road, and the Barokee picnic area, which is about 14 km from Ebor via the Round Mountain road. Both areas have barbecues, picnic tables and toilets. Walking tracks lead from the Native Dog Creek picnic area to Woolpack Rocks (2.5 km), and from the Barokee picnic area to Cathedral Rock (2 km). If you are short of time and energy the Warrigal Circuit track, commencing at the Native Dog Creek picnic area, is an easy 1 km walk that provides an interesting introduction to the park's flora and fauna. The reserve is about 80 km east of Armidale via the Armidale–Dorrigo road.

New England National Park

Situated about 85 km east of Armidale via the Armidale–Dorrigo road, New England National Park contains some of the finest mountain country in New South Wales. It covers 29 823 ha and includes part of the eastern edge of the New England Tableland, from which heavily forested slopes drop steeply to the Bellinger River valley more than 1200 m below. The great range of altitude, topography and soil types gives rise to many different plant communities. Snow gum woodlands, open sclerophyll forests and temperate rainforests clothe the cool, high western section of the reserve, while wet sclerophyll forests and subtropical rainforests cover the warm, low eastern part.

Needless to say the park supports a rich avifauna, but those who visit the reserve in the hope of seeing birds such as the Wompoo Fruit-Dove and Noisy Pitta may be disappointed. Although these species are found in the park, the subtropical rainforests in which they occur are largely inaccessible and can only be reached by descending the rugged escarpment. On the other hand, areas of temperate rainforest are relatively easy to get to, especially in the vicinity of Point Lookout. From here walking tracks lead southwards along the edge of the escarpment to Banksia Point and Wrights Lookout, providing access to a variety of vegetation types including patches of temperate rainforest. Along these tracks — they are well marked but very steep in places — you have a reasonable chance of seeing one of the region's special birds, the Rufous Scrub-bird, as well as a number of other species such as Superb Lyrebird, White's Thrush, Rose Robin (summer), Rufous Fantail (summer) and Red-browed Treecreeper.

There are several picnic areas and a camping ground (tents only) in the park. Those with caravans can make use of the Styx River camping area, which is located just off the Point Lookout road about 2 km outside the park boundary. Toilets and barbecues are provided at both campsites, and there is a cold-water shower in the tent area. There is also a small chalet, with room for up to six people, and a two-bedroom cabin in the reserve. Accommodation can be booked up to six months in advance; write to the New South Wales National Parks and Wildlife Service, PO Box 170, Dorrigo, NSW 2453, enclosing a stamped, addressed envelope. Information, including walking track guides and a bird list, can be obtained from the resident ranger at Banksia Point.

THE NORTH-WEST SLOPES AND PLAINS

In northern New South Wales, between the densely forested highlands of the Great Dividing Range and the sparsely vegetated inland plains, there is a belt of transitional country often described as the place where east meets west. Here plants and animals typical of Australia's dry interior can be found together with those normally associated with the wet east coast. This is not one of the most spectacular parts of the state — the countryside is rather unimpressive compared with that of the New England district to the east — but the region is undulating and picturesque and certainly not monotonous. Indeed there are some very scenic spots, notably Warrumbungle and Mt Kaputar National Parks. Both are excellent places to go camping, walking and bird-watching.

Warrumbungle National Park, west of Coonabarabran, is one of the best known reserves in New South Wales. It supports a rich and varied avifauna that includes birds such as Turquoise Parrot,

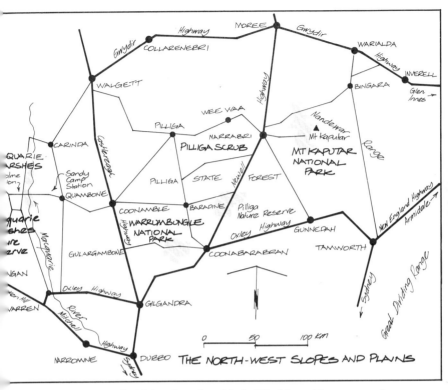

The North-West Slopes and Plains

Chestnut-rumped Hylacola, Speckled Warbler, Regent and Yellow-tufted Honeyeater, and Plum-headed Finch. Mt Kaputar National Park, in the Nandewar Range east of Narrabri, contains a wide range of habitats and is a good place for Red-winged Parrot, Spotted Quail-thrush, Diamond Firetail and a host of other interesting species. In addition to these national parks there are many splendid birding localities north of the Oxley Highway between Tamworth and Warren, among them Pilliga Scrub and the Macquarie Marshes.

Warrumbungle National Park

Dominating the landscape between Coonabarabran and Gilgandra, the eroded volcanic peaks of Warrumbungle National Park attract bushwalkers and rock climbers from all over Australia. Throughout the 19 651 ha reserve jagged pinnacles, barren spires and rocky domes tower above the surrounding lightly wooded countryside. The Breadknife, an isolated, vertical wall of rock some 90 m high but only a few metres thick, is one of the park's most impressive features.

To reach the reserve turn off the Oxley Highway at Coonabarabran. The park headquarters are located about 35 km west of the town, just north of the John Renshaw Parkway, which runs through the centre of the reserve. Warrumbungle National Park has very good facilities for visitors, including an excellent walking track system, numerous picnic areas and four camping grounds — Camp Blackman, Camp Pincham, Camp Wambelong and Camp Burbie (Camp Burbie is accessible only by four-wheel-drive vehicle). Camp Blackman has powered sites, hot-water showers and laundry facilities; it is, however, a very popular spot and can be crowded and noisy at times, particularly during school holidays. The other camping grounds have only fireplaces and toilets, but they attract fewer visitors and are therefore usually more peaceful. Since there is no kiosk in the park you should take along adequate food supplies, and if you intend going there in summer it would be wise to carry drinking water. Camping permits and information, including a walking track guide and a comprehensive bird list, can be obtained from the park headquarters. For those not wishing to camp in the reserve there are motels, hotels, caravan parks and a youth hostel in Coonabarabran.

Like the avifauna, the flora of Warrumbungle National Park is diverse and interesting. The park supports a number of plants typical of the arid western plains, as well as species usually associated with the higher rainfall areas of the New England district. The vegetation ranges from open forest, dominated by rough-barked apple (*Angophora floribunda*) and white box, at lower elevations, to dry woodland consisting chiefly of white gum, narrow-leaved ironbark and cypress pine on the upper slopes and exposed ridges. Low heathland covers much of the higher ground, and there are patches of spinifex (*Triodia*) on the west-facing summit of Mt Exmouth. In spring (late August to November), especially in the sandstone areas, there is a profusion of wild-flowers including donkey and greenhood orchids and many species of wattle. Animals such as grey kangaroos, wallaroos, red-necked wallabies and koalas are quite plentiful in the park, and can usually be found without difficulty around the picnic and camping areas. The brush-tailed rock wallaby, once fairly common in the area but now close to extinction, inhabits some of the isolated peaks and outcrops.

Warrumbungle National Park is famous for its fine network of walking tracks. These range from a short, easy nature trail (1 km) to longer, more strenuous half-day and full-day walks such as the Split Rock Circuit (4.6 km) and the Breadknife — Grand High Tops Circuit (14.5 km). The Split Rock Circuit, which commences near the junction of the John Renshaw Parkway and the Camp Burbie road, is highly recommended since it provides an intro-duction to the park's landforms, flora and fauna. Having broken

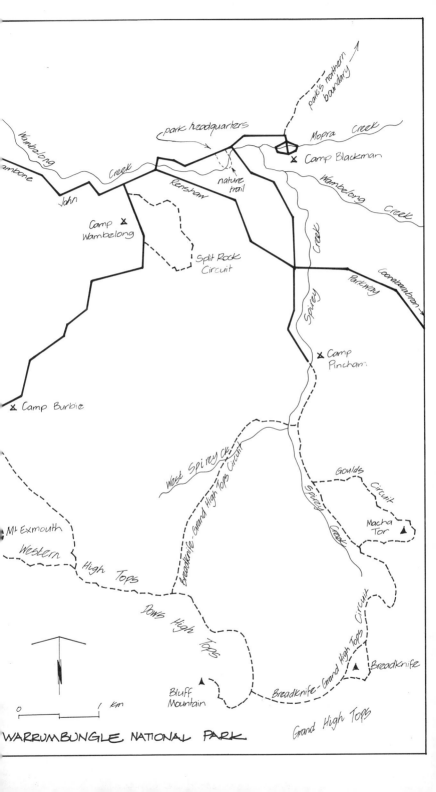

WARRUMBUNGLE NATIONAL PARK

in your walking boots on this track — it is very steep in places, as are most of the more worthwhile walks in the Warrumbungles — pack a picnic lunch and spend a day exploring the Grand High Tops area. For many visitors the Breadknife — Grand High Tops Circuit is the ultimate walk in the reserve, for it provides breathtaking views over virtually the entire park. You may be exhausted by the time you arrive back at camp, but you will not be disappointed.

Given the steepness of most of the walking tracks, it is perhaps fortunate that many of the 180 species of birds recorded in the park can be found in the vicinity of the picnic and camping grounds, and along the roads that run through the reserve. Some of the more common species are Emu (this well-known flightless bird can usually be found early in the day feeding in the open grassy area just north of Camp Blackman, along with large numbers of kangaroos), Peaceful Dove, Common Bronzewing, Galah, Sulphur-crested Cockatoo, Little Lorikeet (plentiful along Spirey Creek, south of Camp Pincham, when the eucalypts are in flower), Red-winged and Red-rumped Parrot, Crimson and Eastern Rosella, Pallid (spring—summer) and Fan-tailed Cuckoo, Horsfield's and Shining Bronze-Cuckoo (spring—summer), Laughing Kookaburra, Sacred Kingfisher (spring—summer), Rainbow Bee-eater (spring—summer), White-backed Swallow, Tree and (spring—summer) Fairy Martin, Richard's Pipit, Black-faced Cuckoo-shrike, White-winged Triller (spring—summer), Hooded and Eastern Yellow Robin, Jacky Winter, Crested Shrike-tit, Golden Whistler (mainly winter), Rufous Whistler (chiefly summer), Grey Shrike-thrush, Restless Flycatcher, Grey Fantail, Superb and Variegated Fairy-wren, White-browed Scrubwren, Speckled Warbler (this attractive ground-feeding species can be found on lightly timbered, rocky hillsides throughout the park), Weebill, Western and White-throated Gerygone (both species are worth looking for, particularly during the summer months), Buff-rumped, Yellow-rumped, Yellow and Striated Thornbill, Varied Sittella, White-throated and Brown Treecreeper, Noisy Friarbird, Noisy Miner, Spiny-cheeked, Striped, Yellow-faced, White-eared, Yellow-tufted (this delightful honeyeater is plentiful in some parts of the reserve — along Spirey Creek for example), Fuscous, White-plumed, Brown-headed and White-naped Honeyeater, Mistletoebird, Spotted and Striated Pardalote, Red-browed and Diamond Firetail, Double-barred Finch, Olive-backed Oriole (spring—summer), White-winged Chough, Dusky Woodswallow, Grey and Pied Butcherbird and Pied Currawong.

Most of the species listed, as well as raptors such as Black-shouldered Kite, Brown Goshawk, Wedge-tailed and Little Eagle, Brown Falcon and Australian Kestrel, should be quite easy to locate, but four of the park's special birds — Turquoise Parrot, Chestnut-rumped Hylacola, Regent Honeyeater and Plum-headed Finch — will be more difficult to find.

For Turquoise Parrot, try the area north of Camp Blackman where there is a wide, level track leading towards the park's northern boundary. The parrot can sometimes be found early in the morning and late in the afternoon feeding on the open grassy hillside to the right of the track. The Turquoise Parrot is small — not much larger than a Budgerigar — and although brightly coloured it is easily overlooked, especially while feeding on the ground. It usually occurs in flocks of five or six, however, and when disturbed the parrots often fly to nearby trees advertising their presence with high-pitched tinkling flight-calls.

To have the best chance of finding a Chestnut-rumped Hylacola you should search the park's heathlands, although the bird is occasionally seen in the undergrowth bordering Spirey Creek. The nomadic Regent Honeyeater visits the area from time to time; in 1976–77 it was recorded along Spirey Creek near Camp Pincham, and along Mopra Creek near Camp Blackman. Another rare visitor, the Plum-headed Finch, favours creekside vegetation, particularly patches of long grass where it can sometimes be found in company with the more common Double-barred Finch.

Mt Kaputar National Park

With an area of 36 817 ha, Mt Kaputar National Park covers much of the scenic Nandewar Range and includes a number of peaks rising to over 1300 m. Mt Kaputar itself, the highest point in the reserve, is 1508 m above sea level and, in marked contrast to the dry, dusty plains west of Narrabri, may be blanketed with snow during the winter months. Needless to say the park supports a wide variety of vegetation types, ranging from snow gum woodland on the higher ground to dry sclerophyll forest lower down. Small patches of wet sclerophyll forest occur in several of the valleys.

The national park is about 55 km east of Narrabri via an unsealed road that is steep and narrow in places. Caravans are not permitted in the reserve, but there are caravan parks, motels and hotels at Narrabri. Camping grounds are provided at two sites along the entrance road — Bark Hut and Dawsons Spring. Both have hot-water showers, toilets and fireplaces. There is no kiosk in the park, and in summer drinking water may be in short supply. A walking track guide, a bird list and other information can be obtained from the ranger at Dawsons Spring, or from the New South Wales National Parks and Wildlife Service at Narrabri.

Like Warrumbungle National Park, Mt Kaputar has many excellent walking tracks. These include the Dawsons Spring nature trail, an easy 1.5 km walk through areas of heath and snow gum woodland; the Mt Coryah track, a more strenuous 4 km walk to the summit of Mt Coryah (1405 m); and the Yulludunida Crater track, a steep but rewarding 4 km climb to one of the park's most spectacular features — a high, circular rocky ridge formed by erosion. There are also a number of longer walks; bushwalkers are permitted to camp in most parts of the reserve but should notify the ranger before setting out.

More than 150 species of birds have been recorded at Mt Kaputar and, since dry sclerophyll forest forms the main habitat, bush birds are well represented. These include Painted Button-quail, Bar-shouldered Dove, Musk and Little Lorikeet, Red-winged Parrot, Crimson, Eastern and, more rarely, Pale-headed Rosella, Pallid (spring—summer) and Fan-tailed Cuckoo, Tawny Frogmouth, Dollarbird (spring—summer), White-bellied Cuckoo-shrike, White-winged Triller (spring—summer), Scarlet and Eastern Yellow Robin, Crested Shrike-tit, Leaden Flycatcher (spring—summer), Spotted Quail-thrush, Grey-crowned and White-browed Babbler, White-throated Gerygone (spring—summer), Varied Sittella, White-throated and Brown Tree-creeper, Red Wattlebird, Noisy and (spring—summer) Little Friarbird, Yellow-faced, White-eared, Yellow-tufted, Fuscous, Black-chinned, Brown and Painted Honeyeater (though rather rare, the Painted Honeyeater is a definite possibility during summer, especially in areas where the trees are heavily infested with mistletoe), Eastern Spinebill, Diamond Firetail, Double-barred Finch and Apostlebird.

You should be able to find many of the species listed along the park's walking tracks or, if you do not wish to walk far, by simply stopping at intervals along the entrance road. Although birds are generally scarce on the higher ground, a visit to the Mt Kaputar summit area might prove worthwhile — Grey Goshawk and Peregrine Falcon are occasionally seen there, and Chestnut-rumped Hylacolas are said to be common in the heathlands.

Pilliga Scrub

'Scrub' is a most unimpressive name for what is in fact a rich mosaic of forests containing a large variety of trees, among them Pilliga box, white box, yellow box, narrow-leaved ironbark, cypress pine, belah and brigalow. The 'scrub' covers an area of about 800 000 ha, of which about 400 000 ha is managed by the New South Wales Forestry Commission and approximately 100 000 ha by the National Parks and Wildlife Service. The remaining 300 000 ha has not been developed for agriculture because of the low fertility of the sandy soil.

Pilliga State Forest forms a triangle between Pilliga township,

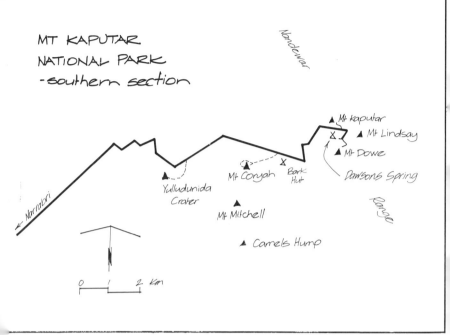

MT KAPUTAR
NATIONAL PARK
-southern section

Nandewar

▲ Mt Kaputar
X
▲ Mt Lindsay
▲ Mt Dowe
Dawsons Spring

← Narrabri

Yulludunida
Crater

Mt Coryah

Bark
Hut
X

Range

▲ Mt Mitchell

▲ Camels Hump

0   1   2 Km

Narrabri and Coonabarabran, and can be reached most easily via the Newell Highway. From the highway a number of forestry tracks lead westwards to the road linking Coonabarabran with Pilliga township, providing access to a number of picnic grounds. A guide (with a map) to the forest drives of Pilliga State Forest can be obtained from the Forestry Commission's office on the corner of Darling and Lachlan Streets, Baradine. Camping is not permitted, and since there is a real possibility of becoming lost in the area you should not stray too far from the main tracks.

Pilliga Nature Reserve adjoins the state forest and is readily accessible via the Newell Highway. It has no facilities for visitors; further information can be obtained from the National Parks and Wildlife Service in Coonabarabran.

Clearly you could spend many days exploring this vast area. Some of the more interesting birds that have been recorded are Malleefowl (an isolated population), Bush Thick-knee, Glossy Black-Cockatoo (especially in areas dominated by casuarinas), Turquoise Parrot (quite common in suitable habitat throughout the area), Red-capped Robin, Spotted Quail-thrush, Speckled Warbler, Western Gerygone (mainly summer), Chestnut-rumped Thornbill, and Striped, Blue-faced and Black-chinned Honey-eater.

Macquarie Marshes

One of the most important wetland areas in New South Wales, the Macquarie Marshes support large breeding populations of waterbirds including significant colonies of cormorants, herons, Cattle, Great, Little and Intermediate Egret, Rufous Night Heron, Glossy, Sacred and Straw-necked Ibis, and Royal and Yellow-billed Spoonbill. In addition many uncommon waterbirds are regularly reported from the area — Little and Australasian Bittern, Black-necked Stork, Wandering and Plumed Whistling-Duck, Freckled and Blue-billed Duck, Brolga and Painted Snipe are among the most notable.

Part of the wetland to the west of Quambone, a small township about 90 km north of Warren, is protected by the Macquarie Marshes Nature Reserve. Access to the reserve can be gained from Quambone via the road linking Sandy Camp Station with Fairholme Station. This road runs through the southern section of the reserve, but the best birding area lies some distance to the north and you will have to walk across private property to reach it. Those approaching the area from the east should call at the National Parks and Wildlife Service office in Coonabarabran — the ranger there will advise you how to get into the reserve.

Waterbirds are not the only attraction in the Macquarie Marshes area; the surrounding plains, though stripped of much of their vegetation by sheep and cattle, hold a host of dry-country species such as Australian Pratincole, Cockatiel, Blue Bonnet, Black-eared Cuckoo, Ground Cuckoo-shrike, Grey-crowned Babbler, White-winged Fairy-wren and Crimson Chat. The area is also reputed to be a favoured haunt of the Plum-headed Finch.

THE FAR WEST

Although the far west of New South Wales is mainly flat and superficially uninteresting, the region has in fact a great deal to offer the observant visitor. Indeed, if you have a taste for outback travel, and are adventurous and well prepared, you could spend at least a month exploring this part of the state. Much of the country is arid or semi-arid — Broken Hill, for instance, receives on average less than 250 mm of rain per annum — yet a surprising variety of animals and plants thrive in the harsh environment. In addition the area contains many fascinating landforms, such as the famous Walls of China in Mungo National Park, as well as a wealth of immensely rich Aboriginal and archaeological sites. Those interested in anthropology should be sure to include Mootwingee and Mungo National Parks on their itineraries since these reserves hold numerous Aboriginal relics — campsites, stone arrangements, burial grounds, middens, and rock engravings, stencils and paintings.

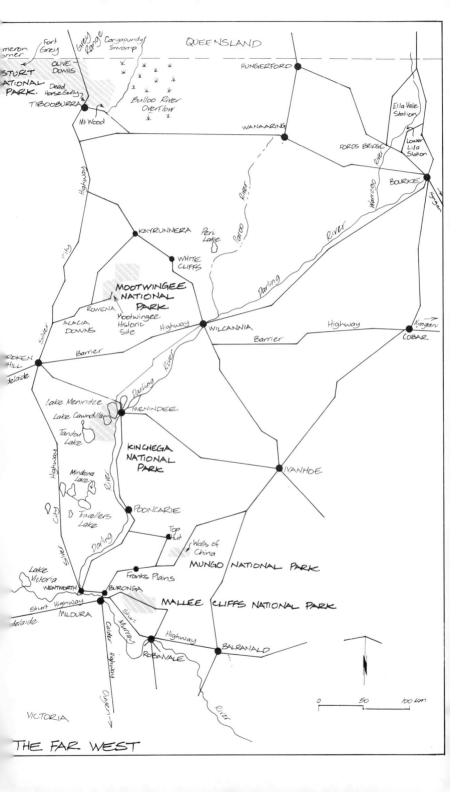

Bird-watchers, especially those who live on or east of the Great Dividing Range, will find the western plains particularly interesting. Kinchega National Park is easy to get to and an excellent place for waterbirds and dry-country birds; Sturt National Park, though rather remote, is well worth visiting for Grey Falcon and a number of other predominantly inland species; the Bulloo River Overflow, north-east of Tibooburra, is one of only six or seven localities in Australia where the Grey Grasswren has been recorded; and Mallee Cliffs National Park, at the southern end of the region near Mildura, contains mallee habitat where birds such as the Mallee-fowl occur.

Kinchega National Park

Covering an area of 44 182 ha, Kinchega National Park lies on the west bank of the Darling River about 112 km south-east of Broken Hill. There is a good sealed road from Broken Hill to Menindee township on the north-eastern boundary of the park, but all other roads in the area are unsealed and may become impassable after rain. The park headquarters are located near Lake Emu, 16 km from the main entrance at Menindee. Here you can obtain camping permits, leaflets describing the reserve's nature walk and historic drive, and plant, reptile, mammal and bird lists. Although there is no formal camping ground at Kinchega, visitors are allowed to camp at a number of sites along the Darling River where basic facilities are provided. Menindee township has hotel and motel accommodation, and there are two caravan parks nearby. The nearest youth hostel is at Broken Hill.

Proclaimed in 1967, Kinchega National Park was once part of Kinchega Station. This vast 405 000 ha property was established in the early 1850s and was one of the first pastoral settlements in the region. A visit to the old woolshed, which stands deserted near Lake Emu, is well worthwhile. A detailed brochure describing points of interest in the woolshed can be obtained from the park headquarters nearby.

Kinchega is dominated by two huge saucer-shaped lakes — Menindee and Cawndilla. The lakes cover more than half the reserve and are part of the overflow system of the Darling River, which forms the eastern boundary of the park. Not surprisingly, waterbirds feature prominently on the park's bird list. Some fifty or more species have been recorded, including many that are uncommon or rare: Great Crested Grebe, Darter, Little and Intermediate Egret, Rufous Night Heron, Australasian Bittern, Glossy Ibis, Magpie Goose, Freckled and Blue-billed Duck, Baillon's, Australian and Spotless Crake, Brolga, Red-kneed Dotterel, Banded Stilt, Red-necked Avocet and Gull-billed Tern. Other more usual species include Hoary-headed and Australasian

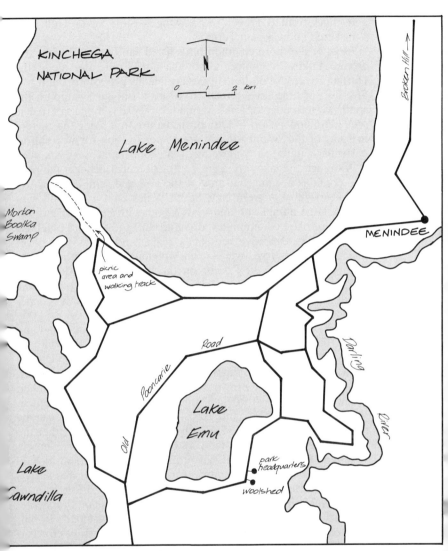

Grebe, Australian Pelican, Great, Pied, Little Black and Little
Pied Cormorant (large numbers of cormorants breed in the reserve
– in 1974 an estimated 40 000 Great and some 1000 Pied nested at
Lake Menindee), Pacific and White-faced Heron, Great Egret,
Sacred and Straw-necked Ibis, Royal and Yellow-billed Spoonbill,
Black Swan, Australian Shelduck, Pacific Black, Pink-eared,
Maned and Musk Duck, Grey Teal, Chestnut Teal, Australasian
Shoveler, Hardhead, Black-tailed Native-hen, Dusky Moorhen,
Purple Swamphen, Eurasian Coot, Masked Lapwing, Red-capped

and Black-fronted Plover, Black-winged Stilt, Silver Gull, and Whiskered and Caspian Tern.

Most of the more common birds listed can be found with ease around Lakes Menindee, Cawndilla and Emu, and along the Darling River. All of these places are readily accessible, but if you are short of time drive directly to Morton Boolka Swamp on the south-western edge of Lake Menindee. There is a pleasant picnic area here, and a short (4 km return) nature trail along the eastern margins of the swamp. It is a good spot to look for waterbirds, particularly in the early morning or late afternoon.

Although the lakes are a great attraction at Kinchega, the park also contains a significant area of the arid and semi-arid country characteristic of western New South Wales, and as a result supports a large number of land birds (about 140 species). There are two major plant communities: dry grassland and areas of bluebush dominate the extensive red sandy plains and dunes that cover much of the reserve, while open woodlands of river red gum, coolibah and black box occur on the floodplains bordering the Darling River. In addition stands of canegrass grow in some of the floodplain swamps, and there are patches of lignum in the deeper channels.

Some of the park's land birds − Black Kite, Wedge-tailed and Little Eagle, Crested Pigeon, Cockatiel, Pallid Cuckoo, Southern Boobook, Barn Owl, Australian Owlet-nightjar, Spotted Nightjar, Rainbow Bee-eater, White-backed Swallow, Rufous Whistler, Restless Flycatcher, Brown Songlark, Weebill, Spiny-cheeked Honeyeater, Yellow-throated Miner, Mistletoebird, Zebra Finch, White-winged Chough and Apostlebird for example − can be found almost anywhere. Many others, however, prefer either the sparsely vegetated sand plains and dunes or the more densely vegetated floodplains. Birds favouring the former habitat include Emu, Black-breasted Buzzard (rare, but recorded regularly), Spotted Harrier, Brown Falcon, Australian Kestrel, Little Button-quail, Australian Bustard (rather rare), Australian Pratincole, Richard's Pipit, Ground Cuckoo-shrike, Red-capped Robin, Crested Bellbird, Chirruping Wedgebill, Chestnut-crowned Babbler, Variegated and White-winged Fairy-wren, Chestnut-rumped Thornbill, Southern Whiteface, White-browed Tree-creeper, Black and Pied Honeyeater (though uncommon and nomadic these honeyeaters are worth searching for, especially when the emu-bushes are in flower), Crimson Chat, Orange Chat, and Masked, White-browed and Black-faced Woodswallow.

Species that are more likely to be found in the woodlands along the Darling River include Whistling Kite, Brown Goshawk, Collared Sparrowhawk, Black Falcon, Australian Hobby, Peaceful and, more rarely, Diamond Dove, Common Bronzewing,

Red-tailed Black-Cockatoo (rarely), Little Corella, Pink Cockatoo, Yellow Rosella, Mallee Ringneck, Red-rumped Parrot, Blue Bonnet, Tawny Frogmouth, Red-backed and Sacred Kingfisher, White-winged Triller, Jacky Winter, Crested Shrike-tit, Yellow-rumped Thornbill, Brown Treecreeper, Little Friarbird (mainly spring—summer), Singing and White-plumed Honeyeater, Striated Pardalote, White-breasted and Dusky Woodswallow, and Grey and Pied Butcherbird.

Mungo National Park

Mungo National Park does not compare with Kinchega for bird-watching. Nevertheless the 27 847 ha reserve is of considerable interest since it contains part of an ancient dry lake system that includes Lake Mungo, Australia's earliest known site of Aboriginal occupation. Scientific research carried out at Lake Mungo has established that Aboriginals lived in the area more than 35 000 years ago, making the park one of this country's, and indeed the world's, most important archaeological sites. The lakes, set in a vast saltbush plain, are surrounded by sand-dunes; the deeply eroded lunette (dune) known as the Walls of China stretches some 30 km or so along the eastern side of Lake Mungo.

The reserve is located about 110 km north-east of Mildura via Buronga and Franks Plains, and about 240 km south-east of Menindee via Pooncarie and Top Hut. You can reach Mungo by conventional vehicle, but all roads in the area are unsealed and may become impassable after rain. Carry adequate food, drinking water and petrol. The park has a visitors centre, picnic areas, and a small camping ground with barbecues, toilets and tank water. There are hotels, motels and caravan parks at Balranald, Robinvale and Mildura to the south, and at Ivanhoe to the north-east. For those not wishing to venture into the wilderness on their own, several commercial operators in Mildura offer coach tours of the park.

Mallee Cliffs National Park

Situated 30 km east of Mildura, this 57 969 ha park preserves relatively undisturbed tracts of mallee scrub and rosewood-belah woodland. These vegetation types, once widespread in north-western Victoria and south-western New South Wales, have been extensively cleared for agriculture, and Mallee Cliffs was primarily set aside to protect the region's distinctive mallee flora and fauna, particularly the Malleefowl, which is an endangered species in New South Wales.

Unfortunately the reserve was devastated by bushfires in the late 1970s and public access is still restricted. If you wish to visit the area contact the New South Wales National Parks and Wildlife Service, Shop 8, Buronga Shopping Centre, Buronga. There are no facilities for visitors in the park.

Mootwingee National Park

This 68 912 ha reserve encompasses a section of the rough, semi-arid ranges to the north-east of Broken Hill and includes the Aboriginal art galleries at Mootwingee Historic Site, which is located just inside the park's south-western boundary. The ranges – home to the rare yellow-footed rock wallaby – are cut by narrow gorges lined with river red gums, while the surrounding plains support a sparse covering of mulga. The area's birdlife, though not especially rich, includes many cockatoos and parrots. Little Corella, Pink Cockatoo, Budgerigar, Mallee Ringneck, Blue Bonnet, and Mulga and Bourke's Parrot are some of the species that you can expect to see.

At present there is no public access to the north-eastern section of Mootwingee National Park, but the south-western section (Mootwingee Historic Site) can be reached from Broken Hill via the Silver City Highway, Acacia Downs and Rowena. The reserve entrance is about 130 km from Broken Hill, all roads in the area are unsealed, and you should carry adequate food, drinking water and petrol. The park has a visitors centre, and a small camping ground with toilets and cold-water showers. It is not usually necessary to book a campsite in advance. If you are travelling to the park via Broken Hill, however, it would be wise to call at the New South Wales National Parks and Wildlife Service office at 32 Sulphide Street before setting out.

Sturt National Park

The eastern section of Sturt National Park, a vast 310 634 ha reserve in the north-western corner of New South Wales, consists chiefly of open, featureless gibber plains broken only by the flat-topped mesas (mountains) of the Grey Range. This 'jump-up country', as it is known locally, is the most prominent feature of the park; its western half, particularly in the vicinity of Cameron Corner, is dominated by a series of sandhills stretching endlessly to the horizon. It is a harsh place. In summer daytime temperatures frequently exceed 40 degrees C, sometimes reaching 50 degrees C. In winter the days are pleasant, but at night the temperature often falls below zero. Rainfall is low – less than 200 mm per annum.

Despite its isolation and the rather forbidding terrain, Sturt is a fascinating park. It holds a surprising variety of birds, including many raptors – Letter-winged Kite, Black-breasted Buzzard, Wedge-tailed and Little Eagle, Spotted Harrier, and Black, Peregrine and, outstandingly, Grey Falcon. Other species of interest, some of which you are unlikely to see at Kinchega, are

Australian Bustard, Inland Dotterel, Ground Cuckoo-shrike, Chirruping Wedgebill, Cinnamon Quail-thrush, Black and Pied Honeyeater, Crimson Chat, Orange Chat, Gibberbird, and Red-browed Pardalote. And, perhaps incongruously, the seasonal lakes in the Fort Grey basin, towards the western end of the park, at times attract fair numbers of waterbirds − 153 Freckled Ducks and 16 Blue-billed Ducks were seen there in early 1980.

Sturt National Park is about 350 km north of Broken Hill via the Silver City Highway and Tibooburra. The highway, though unsealed and rough in places, is suitable for conventional vehicles except after rain. You should call at the park headquarters on arrival at Tibooburra. Here you can obtain information and inquire about road conditions in the reserve. The park entrance is 1 km north of Tibooburra, and there are camping and picnic areas with basic facilities (toilets and fireplaces) at Dead Horse Gully, Mt Wood, Olive Downs and Fort Grey. Hotel accommodation is available at Tibooburra. The best time to visit Sturt is, of course, during the relatively cool winter months (May to September).

Having explored the far west of New South Wales, birders travelling east may care to spend a little time looking for two of the state's special birds − the Grey Grasswren and Hall's Babbler. The Grey Grasswren, though not confined to New South Wales, has a very limited range; so far as is known it occurs only at a few isolated localities in north-eastern South Australia and south-western Queensland, and in New South Wales it is restricted to the Bulloo River Overflow, north-east of Tibooburra. Similarly Hall's Babbler is not endemic in New South Wales, but although this inland species is widely distributed in western Queensland it has only a relatively small range across the border, occurring mainly in the area between the Bulloo River Overflow and the Warrego River, north of the road linking Tibooburra, Wanaaring and Bourke.

The best place to look for the Grey Grasswren, a secretive species that favours dense stands of canegrass and lignum − not the easiest habitat to penetrate − is reputed to be Caryapundy Swamp on the New South Wales − Queensland border, some 100 km north-east of Tibooburra. The ranger at Sturt National Park may be able to direct you to a less distant spot where the grasswrens have been seen recently. Those wishing to search for Hall's Babbler should travel east to Bourke, then north-west on the Hungerford road to Fords Bridge (about 70 km from Bourke). The babblers have been recorded in recent years in the vicinity of Lower Lila Station, about 30 km north-east of Fords Bridge, and along the road running north from Fords Bridge to Ella Vale Station. You may not, of course, be fortunate enough to find either the babbler or the grasswren. However, the road from

Tibooburra to Bourke is suitable for conventional vehicles (in dry weather), and it provides a far shorter route east than the Silver City and Barrier Highways.

LORD HOWE ISLAND

Situated in the South Pacific Ocean some 700 km north-east of Sydney, Lord Howe Island and the towering peak of Balls Pyramid nearby are the eroded remains of ancient volcanoes that erupted in the area many millions of years ago. Famous for its remarkable scenic beauty, Lord Howe contains a wide variety of landscapes yet is barely 12 km long and on average less than 2 km wide. Its southern half is dominated by two precipitous mountains, Mt Gower (875 m) and Mt Lidgbird (777 m), which form a superb backdrop to the island's lovely coral-fringed lagoon. There are several kilometres of beautiful sandy beaches, while the spectacular cliffs along the north coast are home to many thousands of nesting seabirds, including large numbers of Red-tailed Tropicbirds.

Although many of the island's three hundred or so inhabitants depend almost entirely on tourism for their livelihoods, Lord Howe is not at all commercialised. Most of the small, single-storey guest houses and apartments are tucked away in the dense palm forest that covers much of the low-lying, central part of the island. Tranquil, unspoilt, beautiful beyond belief, Lord Howe has everything a bird-watcher could wish for. It has been described as a naturalist's paradise, and with its fascinating flora (many of the plant species that occur there are found nowhere else in the world), extensive seabird colonies and fine network of walking tracks, it is the perfect place for a quiet, relaxing holiday.

You can get to Lord Howe by air from Sydney, Newcastle, Port Macquarie, Brisbane, Coolangatta and Norfolk Island. There are no camping grounds, but a holiday on the island need not cost a fortune. Seven nights at one of the less expensive guest houses, for example, will cost you about $1100 per person (meals provided), while a week in a self-contained unit will cost around $800 per person. These prices include your return airfare from Sydney and a boat trip to Lord Howe's superb coral reef, said to be the most southerly coral reef in the world. For further information contact your local travel agent, or call at any branch of the New South Wales Government Travel Centre.

Once on the island you can get by with very little money, simply because there are few places to spend it. (If you stay in a self-contained unit, however, you will have to buy food. Basic supplies can be purchased locally and prices are not unreasonable.) And since you can easily walk from one end of the island to the other in a day, you will not need to hire a car. In any case most visitors use bicycles; they are readily available and cheap to hire.

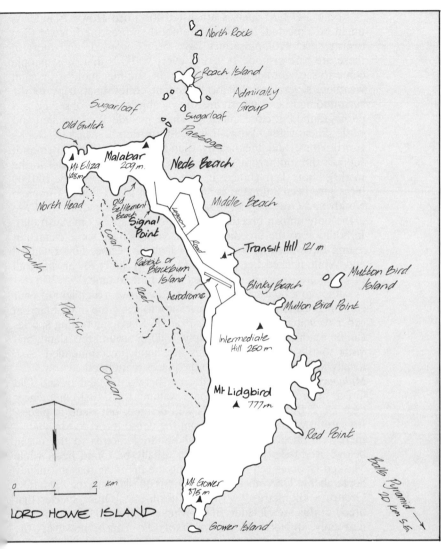

LORD HOWE ISLAND

The climate on Lord Howe is subtropical. The island receives about 1700 mm of rain per annum, and it can rain at any time of the year. In summer (December to March) the days are pleasant, averaging 25 degrees C. In winter, daytime temperatures are seldom less than 16 degrees C although the nights can be chilly — take along a book to read while warming yourself beside a roaring log fire. The island has two banks, a post office, a resident doctor, a bowling club and golf course, several inexpensive restaurants and a small but interesting museum.

About 140 bird species are listed for Lord Howe Island. As might be expected, land birds are poorly represented; fewer than twenty species of passerines have been recorded, and most of these are rare visitors. It is, however, seabirds that most people come to see, not land birds. During the summer months, in calm weather, several of the local residents offer boat trips to the surrounding islands where breeding seabirds can be observed and photographed at close quarters. These include Wedge-tailed and Little Shearwater, White-bellied Storm-Petrel, Masked Booby (Lord Howe and the nearby islands, including Balls Pyramid, support the southernmost breeding colonies of this species in the world), Sooty Tern (breeds in very large numbers — some 100 000 birds have been estimated to nest on Roach Island alone), Common Noddy and Grey Ternlet (apart from Norfolk Island, Lord Howe is the only known breeding location of this species in Australia). In addition to the breeding species, visitors have some chance of seeing birds such as Wandering Albatross, Cape, Great-winged and White-necked Petrel, Fairy Prion and Sooty Shearwater, all of which are recorded in the area from time to time.

Although a boat trip will undoubtedly prove a highlight of your stay on Lord Howe, it is not necessary to leave the main island in order to watch seabirds at close range. Many interesting species can be readily observed by simply walking around the island, and visits to the following localities are highly recommended. Ask locally for precise directions to the places mentioned.

Malabar: The superb coastal cliffs between Malabar and Old Gulch are readily accessible via a walking track that commences near Neds Beach. The track is well defined, but steep in places. Be careful when you emerge from the dense forest at Malabar — there is a sheer drop of several hundred metres to the ocean below. Red-tailed Tropicbirds can usually be found here, while Masked Boobies can be seen during the breeding season (mainly September to December) sitting on nests on islands in the Admiralty Group, a kilometre or so to the north-east. Other species that breed in this area include Black-winged Petrel (to date known to nest only at North Head, south of Old Gulch; however, the petrels are active and noisy during the day and can usually be seen between November and April flying about the headlands at the northern end of Lord Howe), Wedge-tailed Shearwater (September to April), Sooty Tern (chiefly September to February), Common Noddy (mainly September to March) and Grey Ternlet (breeds during summer in large numbers on the cliffs east of Old Gulch).

Neds Beach and Transit Hill: Are situated on the rugged eastern side of Lord Howe, and are readily accessible via well-marked walking tracks. From September to May many thousands of Flesh-footed Shearwaters nest in the palm forest south of Neds

Beach, while Blinky Beach near Transit Hill is a good place for Red-tailed Tropicbird and Masked Booby (the boobies breed at Mutton Bird Point at the southern end of Blinky Beach).

Signal Point: The Norfolk Island pines that line Lagoon Road, particularly in the vicinity of Signal Point, are a favoured haunt of the very beautiful White Tern. Described as the most ethereal of all seabirds, this small tropical tern is quite plentiful on the island between November and June.

Mt Lidgbird: The lower, western slopes of Mt Lidgbird can be reached via Lagoon Road and the aerodrome. The upper slopes of the mountain, and those of Mt Gower just to the south, support vast numbers of Providence Petrels; Lord Howe Island is the only known breeding station of this species in the world. In autumn and early winter the petrels make a spectacular sight as they wheel and dive overhead. If you want a really close view of the birds, call out to them at the top of your voice; surprising as it may seem the petrels respond to the shouts of humans and will fly towards you, even on occasion landing at your feet!

Although seabirds are without question the main reason why many bird-watchers travel to Lord Howe, the island has other ornithological attractions, notably the Lord Howe Island Woodhen. In the early 1970s the total population of this large, flightless, rather drab brown rail was estimated at fewer than thirty individuals, and the birds were virtually confined to a small area at the top of Mt Gower. It is still one of the rarest birds in the world, but thankfully measures to save it from almost certain extinction appear to have been successful. During the past five years or so the NSW National Parks and Wildlife Foundation has spent almost $270 000 on a captive-breeding programme, and the birds now number about 150.

Visitors to Lord Howe have an excellent chance of seeing the woodhens since it is no longer necessary to climb to the summit of Mt Gower in order to find them. The best place to look is along the track that skirts the lower slopes of Mt Lidgbird, south of the aerodrome. A number of captive-reared birds have been released here and have taken up residence in the dense palm forest. The woodhens are quite tame; if you go to the area early in the day when the birds are most active, and call loudly, they will almost certainly emerge from the forest to investigate the cause of the disturbance.

Having seen and perhaps photographed many of the island's seabirds and the woodhen, birders will find that Lord Howe has much to offer the wader enthusiast — and both the aerodrome and Old Settlement Beach are worth a visit. In summer Lesser Golden Plover, Ruddy Turnstone, Whimbrel and Bar-tailed Godwit occur in fair numbers, while Double-banded Plovers turn up in winter.

Occasionally rarer species are recorded — for example, in March 1985 two Little Curlews were seen at the aerodrome. And land birds though few in number are worth searching for, in particular the delightful Emerald Dove (quite plentiful in the forest surrounding the main settlement), Sacred Kingfisher, Lord Howe Golden Whistler (closely related to the Golden Whistler that occurs on the Australian mainland), Lord Howe Silvereye (a distinctive endemic form) and Lord Howe Pied Currawong (a subspecies of the form occurring in eastern Australia).

It would be difficult to find a more idyllic spot than Lord Howe Island. Late at night the only sounds are the eerie cries of shearwaters squabbling over nest sites, the rustling of palm leaves, and the crashing of waves on the coral reef. Even the most seasoned traveller will find a stay on this enchanting island an unforgettable experience.

At one time threatened with extinction, the Lord Howe Island Woodhen is now reasonably plentiful thanks to a successful captive-breeding programme

Providence Petrel — so far as is known, Lord Howe Island is the only place in the world where this species breeds

Gorgeous male Regent Bowerbirds are frequent visitors to the camping area at O'Reilly's, Lamington National Park, south-east Queensland

Lake Boomanjin on Fraser Island, Queensland. Fraser is the largest sand island in the world

Some of the most beautiful stands of rainforest in Australia occur at Eungella National Park, west of Mackay, Queensland

Pioneer Valley as seen from one of the many viewing points in Eungella National Park, Queensland

Shute Harbour, gateway to Queensland's wonderful Whitsunday Coast

Magpie Geese and other waterbirds at Townsville Town Common Environmental Park, North Queensland

Magnetic Island, off Townsville, North Queensland, is an excellent place to spend a day or so walking and birding

Bush Thick-knees, Townsville Town Common, North Queensland. Although it is known chiefly for its waterbirds, the environmental park also supports a wide range of bush birds

Dense fan palm forest near Mission Beach, North Queensland

Australian Capital Territory

Useful addresses

Canberra Ornithologists Group
PO Box 301
Civic Square, ACT 2608

Australasian Seabird Group
PO Box 65
Civic Square, ACT 2608

Field Naturalists Association of Canberra
GPO Box 249
Canberra, ACT 2601

Australian National Parks and Wildlife Service
217 Northbourne Avenue
Turner, ACT 2601

Australian Capital Territory Parks and Conservation Service
1st Floor North Building
London Circuit
Canberra, ACT 2600

Key to Maps

▨	Public land
▨	Areas of water
▲	Mountain peak
⛰	Mountain range or plateau
COBAR ●	Place name
✕	Camping area
🗼	Lighthouse
⥮⥮⥮	Marsh
▬▬▬	Major road or highway
─────	Minor road
------	Foot track
--—--	National park boundary
-─────	State boundary
⌇⌇	River or creek

CANBERRA

Canberra, federal capital of Australia and seat of the national government since 1927, is situated in the north-eastern corner of the Australian Capital Territory, on the western edge of the Great Dividing Range. Built around Lake Burley Griffin, a huge artificial

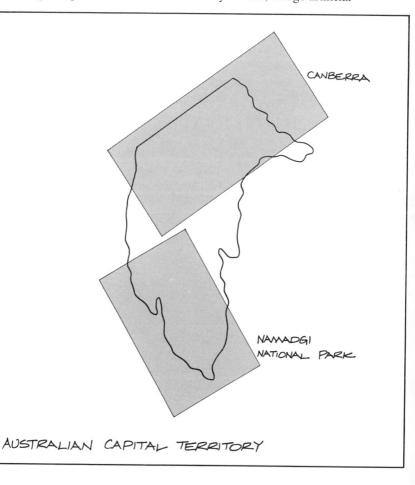

CANBERRA

NAMADGI
NATIONAL PARK

AUSTRALIAN CAPITAL TERRITORY

lake fed by the Molonglo River, the capital lies in a shallow basin ringed by low wooded hills and higher mountains. With a population of almost 220 000, it is Australia's largest inland city.

Canberra attracts some two million visitors annually, most of whom come to see the capital's wealth of public monuments and buildings: the National Gallery, the War Memorial, the National Library, Parliament House and the Royal Australian Mint, to name just a few. Needless to say the city has ample accommodation, including international-class hotels and numerous motels. For those travelling on a tight budget there is a youth hostel in Dryandra Street, O'Connor, and a number of private houses in and around the city offer inexpensive bed and breakfast accommodation. Caravan parks are located at O'Connor, Watson, Fyshwick, Queanbeyan and Cotter River. From Canberra Airport there are frequent flights to all the major cities within Australia, and rental cars are readily available.

About 260 species of birds have been recorded in the Canberra district, an impressive number by any standards. And it is not necessary to travel far in order to enjoy good birding — nearly 120 species have been observed in the Australian National Botanic Gardens, just a kilometre or two from the heart of the city.

Australian National Botanic Gardens

The Australian National Botanic Gardens cover an area of about 40 ha and are situated to the west of the city centre, on the lower slopes of Black Mountain. Set in a patch of dry sclerophyll forest, the gardens contain an extensive collection of Australian plants, most of which are arranged according to botanical family or genus. There are, for example, fine displays of banksias, acacias, cassias, casuarinas, grevilleas, correas and, of course, eucalypts. Since the flora is almost exclusively native, and because there is a year-round water supply (summers in Canberra are usually dry and hot), the gardens provide ideal conditions for a large number of bush birds throughout the year. Honeyeaters are especially plentiful during the colder months when many of the nectar-producing trees and shrubs are in flower.

Just inside the entrance to the gardens (off Clunies Ross Street) there is a kiosk together with an excellent information centre where you can obtain many useful publications, including walking track guides and a comprehensive bird list. There is also an area set aside for the disabled and elderly — the Banksia Centre. This section of the gardens has wide, sealed paths that provide easy access to a number of alcoves containing a variety of textured and scented native plants, some of which have been specially chosen to attract birds. Those wishing to visit the centre should telephone in advance and make a booking.

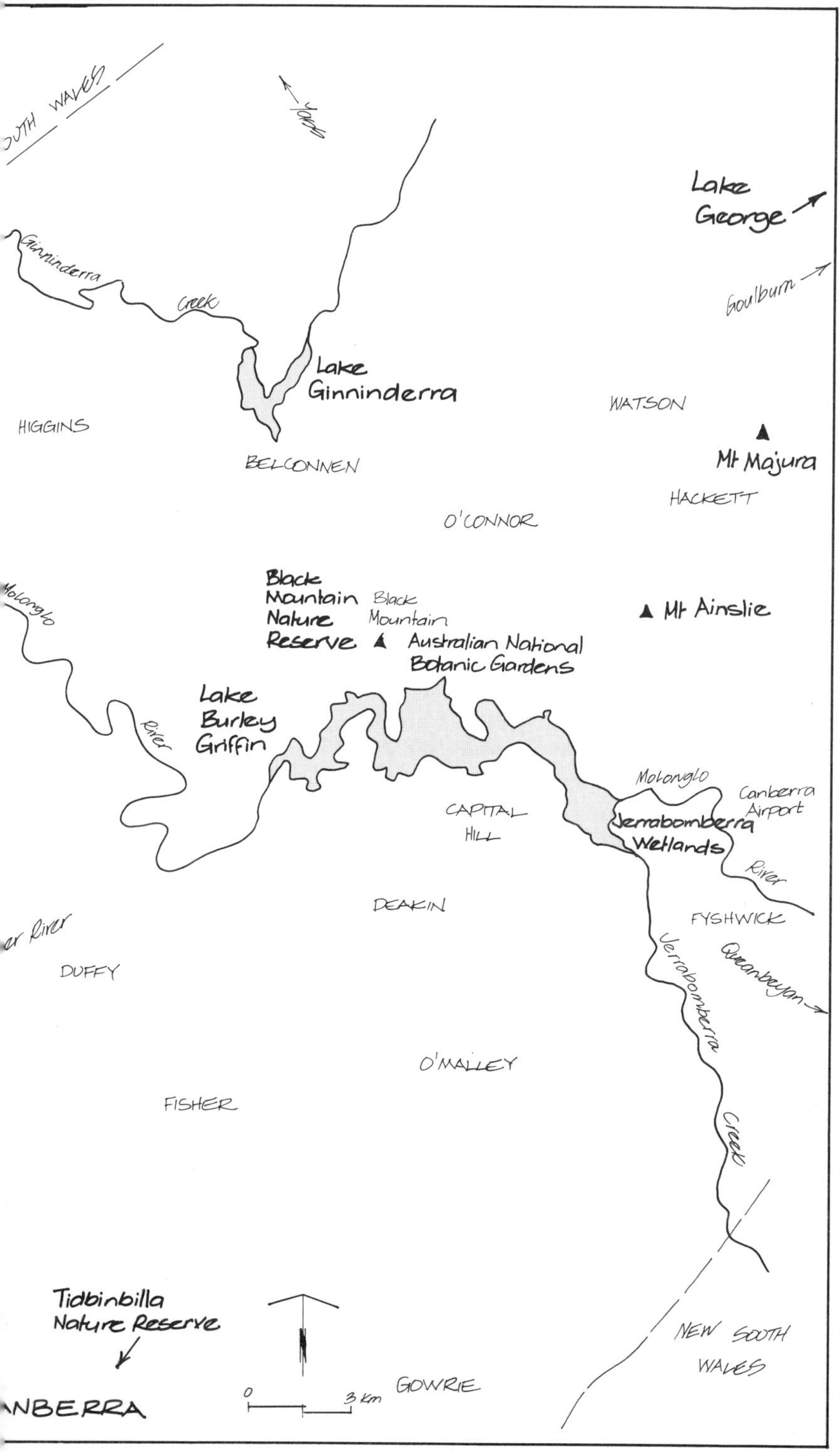

OUTH WALES
Yass
Lake George
Goulburn
Ginninderra Creek
Lake Ginninderra
WATSON
HIGGINS
BELCONNEN
Mt Majura
HACKETT
O'CONNOR
Molonglo
Black Mountain Nature Reserve
Black Mountain
Mt Ainslie
Australian National Botanic Gardens
Lake Burley Griffin
River
Molonglo
Canberra Airport
CAPITAL HILL
Jerrabomberra Wetlands
River
DEAKIN
FYSHWICK
er River
DUFFY
Jerrabomberra Creek
Queanbeyan
O'MALLEY
FISHER
Tidbinbilla Nature Reserve
NEW SOUTH WALES
N
0
3 km
GOWRIE
NBERRA

There are four walking tracks in the gardens: the White Arrow Walk (1.5 km), the Blue Arrow Walk (3 km), a 600 m nature trail, and a 1 km Aboriginal trail featuring an assortment of food-producing plants utilised by Aboriginals. Birders able to spend time exploring these tracks can expect to find many of the following species: Common Bronzewing, Gang-gang Cockatoo (chiefly winter), Crimson and Eastern Rosella, Fan-tailed Cuckoo (mainly spring—summer), Shining Bronze-Cuckoo (spring—summer), Tawny Frogmouth, Laughing Kookaburra, Black-faced Cuckoo-shrike, Flame (mainly autumn—winter), Scarlet and Eastern Yellow Robin, Golden Whistler (mostly winter), Rufous Whistler (chiefly summer), Grey Shrike-thrush, Leaden Flycatcher (spring—summer), Grey Fantail, Willie Wagtail, Superb Fairy-wren, White-browed Scrubwren, Speckled Warbler, Weebill, White-throated Gerygone (spring—summer), Brown, Buff-rumped, Yellow-rumped, Yellow and Striated Thornbill, Varied Sittella, White-throated Treecreeper, Red Wattlebird, Noisy Friarbird (spring—summer), Yellow-faced (chiefly spring—summer), White-eared (especially in winter), Fuscous (mainly winter—spring), White-plumed, Brown-headed, White-naped (chiefly spring—summer), Crescent (especially in winter) and New Holland Honeyeater, Eastern Spinebill, Spotted and Striated Pardalote, Silvereye, Red-browed Firetail, Double-barred Finch, Olive-backed Oriole (spring—summer), White-winged Chough, Australian Magpie-lark and Pied Currawong (especially in winter).

On odd occasions birds such as Brush Cuckoo (spring—summer), White-winged Triller (spring—summer), White's Thrush (winter), Western Gerygone (spring—summer), and Regent and Yellow-tufted Honeyeater turn up in the gardens. A visit to the rainforest gully during the spring and autumn months may produce a Rose Robin or Rufous Fantail, while in winter the delightful Pink Robin is a possibility.

The gardens are open daily between 9 a.m. and 5 p.m. Ranger-guided tours commence at the carpark every Sunday at 10 a.m. and 2 p.m.

Black Mountain Nature Reserve

Situated only 2 km or so west of Canberra's central business district, and bounded by Clunies Ross Street, Parkes Way, Caswell Drive and Belconnen Way, this reserve of about 520 ha is readily accessible on foot, by car or by public transport. Although the dry sclerophyll forest that covers much of the mountain has been partly cleared to make way for power lines, the reserve contains extensive stands of scribbly gum and red stringybark and is therefore quite good for bush birds. The area is rather uninviting during the dry summer months, however, and bird-watchers visiting Canberra between December and March will find the nearby botanic gardens more pleasant and productive.

The summit of Black Mountain, site of a Telecom communications tower housing viewing galleries, a revolving restaurant, an exhibition room and a theatrette, can be reached via Clunies Ross Street and Black Mountain Drive. From the summit, 813 m above sea level, there are magnificent views over the capital and Lake Burley Griffin. For those wishing to explore the mountain on foot there are walking tracks commencing at carparks on Caswell Drive and Belconnen Way. Camping is not permitted.

Mt Ainslie and Mt Majura

Rising a little to the east of Canberra's inner northern suburbs, Mt Ainslie and Mt Majura have been kept free of development in accordance with Walter Burley Griffin's original plan for the capital. Along with Black Mountain Nature Reserve they provide residents and visitors with the opportunity to enjoy a range of outdoor activities, including horse-riding, bushwalking and bird-watching.

Mt Ainslie (843 m) is the more accessible of the two; the lookout at its summit can be reached by car via Fairbairn Avenue and Mt Ainslie Drive, or on foot via a well-formed walking track that commences at a picnic ground off Treloar Crescent (behind the Australian War Memorial). The 4.5 km track passes through an area of grassland, then meanders gradually to the top of the mountain through open eucalypt forest dominated by scribbly gum and red stringybark. The climb takes about three hours at a leisurely pace and is not too strenuous.

Mt Majura (891 m) lies to the north-east of Mt Ainslie, two kilometres or so south of the Federal Highway. The road leading to its summit crosses private property, but walkers can reach the western slopes of the mountain via a track commencing at the end of Jukes Street, Hackett. The 4 km track, though steep in places, is well formed and can be completed in under three hours.

Birds recorded in the Mt Ainslie — Mt Majura area include Black-shouldered Kite, Brown Goshawk, Wedge-tailed Eagle, Brown Falcon, Australian Kestrel, Galah, Sulphur-crested Cockatoo, Red-rumped Parrot, Pallid Cuckoo (spring—summer), Horsfield's Bronze-Cuckoo (spring—summer), Southern Boobook, Sacred Kingfisher (spring—summer), Rainbow Bee-eater (spring—summer), Dollarbird (spring—summer), Richard's Pipit, Hooded Robin (rather rare, and mainly in winter), Noisy Miner, Mistletoebird (spring—summer), Diamond Firetail (rather rare), White-browed and Dusky Woodswallow (both species occur only in summer — the Dusky is the more common of the two), Grey Butcherbird and Grey Currawong.

Lake Burley Griffin and Lake Ginninderra

Like many man-made lakes, Lake Burley Griffin and Lake Ginninderra are generally rather deep and as a result do not attract a wide variety of waterbirds. Nevertheless both are worth visiting because they usually hold at least a few common species: Hoary-headed and Australasian Grebe, Great, Little Black and Little Pied Cormorant, White-faced Heron, Great Egret, Black Swan, Pacific Black, Maned and Musk Duck, Grey Teal, Dusky Moorhen, Purple Swamphen and Eurasian Coot. The parklands adjacent to the lakes are favoured by Masked Lapwing, while Clamorous Reed-Warbler (mainly summer) and Little Grassbird occur in swampy areas.

Other birds worth looking for include Great Crested Grebe, Australian Pelican, Darter, Pacific Heron, Little (mainly summer) and Intermediate Egret, Rufous Night Heron (chiefly summer), Little Bittern (summer), Glossy (mostly summer), Sacred and Straw-necked Ibis, Royal (mainly summer) and Yellow-billed Spoonbill, Australian Shelduck, Chestnut Teal, Australasian Shoveler, Hardhead, Buff-banded Rail (chiefly summer), Baillon's, Australian and Spotless Crake, Red-kneed Dotterel, Black-winged Stilt and Whiskered Tern. Some of the species mentioned turn up regularly, others very rarely.

Lake Ginninderra is situated about 8 km north-west of the city centre via Barry Drive, Belconnen Way, Haydon Drive and Ginninderra Drive. Access to both Lake Burley Griffin and Lake Ginninderra can be gained at many points, and there is a cycle track running virtually right around the former. Numerous picnic grounds, most of which have toilets and barbecues, are provided along the shores of the two lakes, and there are boat ramps at a number of places.

The best areas for waterbirds are said to be the Black Mountain Peninsula, Acacia Inlet and Warrina Inlet at the western end of Lake Burley Griffin, and the north-eastern arm of Lake Ginninderra (adjacent to Belconnen Naval Station). There are also some good spots for bush birds along the western edge of Lake Burley Griffin, although in many places the vegetation is predominantly exotic.

Jerrabomberra Wetlands

The Jerrabomberra Wetlands, Canberra's prime waterbird area, lie to the east of Lake Burley Griffin between the Molonglo River and Jerrabomberra Creek. Although the number and variety of birds to be seen vary considerably depending on conditions elsewhere in the region, the wetlands usually support quite an assortment of species — grebes, cormorants, herons, egrets, ibis, spoonbills and waterfowl. A few migratory waders — Greenshank,

Latham's Snipe, Sharp-tailed and Curlew Sandpiper, and Red-necked Stint – turn up in summer, and Double-banded Plovers are occasionally seen during winter. Resident waders such as Red-kneed Dotterel, and Red-capped and Black-fronted Plover, may be present throughout the year, while Cattle Egret, Marsh Harrier (summer), Brown Quail and White-fronted Chat are recorded from time to time. Over the years the area has produced a number of local rarities, including Pink-eared Duck, Lewin's Rail and Black-tailed Native-hen.

To get to this well-known birding locality travel along Parkes Way and Morshead Drive until you reach the Dairy Road turn-off, about 6 km south-east of the city centre. Some 2 km south of the turn-off there is a carpark on the right-hand side of Dairy Road; from here a short walking track leads to two bird-observation hides overlooking a shallow, reed-fringed lake. The lake usually holds at least a few waterbirds, and Golden-headed Cisticolas can often be found in the dense vegetation around its margins. If you are feeling energetic, it is possible to walk for some distance from the carpark westwards through the marshes that lie between Dairy Road and Lake Burley Griffin.

Having spent some time exploring the wetlands it may be worth your while driving a few hundred metres further south along Dairy Road to the entrance of the Canberra Sewage Works. The works are fenced off, but with a pair of powerful binoculars (or preferably a telescope) you can scan the ponds from outside the entrance gates.

Tidbinbilla Nature Reserve

In contrast to Black Mountain, Mt Ainslie and Mt Majura, the ranges to the south-west of Canberra support large stands of wet sclerophyll forest dominated by tall, sturdy eucalypts such as brown barrel, manna gum, mountain ash and mountain gum. Some excellent examples of this habitat can be found in Tidbinbilla Nature Reserve, a splendid 5515 ha park situated about 40 km from Canberra via the road to Cotter Dam.

Just inside the entrance to the reserve there is a visitors centre housing displays covering the history, flora and fauna of the region. Walking track guides, a detailed bird list and other information can be obtained from the centre. Camping is not permitted (the nearest camping ground is at Cotter River Reserve, about 17 km to the north), but picnic facilities are provided at several sites along the entrance road.

A few kilometres beyond the visitors centre are native fauna enclosures where kangaroos, wallabies and koalas can be observed in natural surroundings, as well as a wetland complex featuring a series of ponds specially designed so that the water level in each can be raised or lowered to suit the habitat requirements of various waterbirds. Observation hides, complete with binoculars, have been provided to enable visitors to watch and photograph Black-necked Storks, Magpie Geese and a number of other species that have been introduced to the reserve. Emus have also been introduced and are now flourishing; indeed, they have become something of a nuisance around the picnic areas.

Tidbinbilla has about 40 km of walking tracks. Some are short and easy, others long and somewhat strenuous. Most of the easier walks — the Cascades Nature Trail (1.6 km), the Lyrebird Nature Trail (2.7 km), the Mountain Creek Nature Trail (1.6 km) and the Red Hill Nature Trail (3.5 km) — commence at the carpark at the end of Mountain Creek Road, just past the koala enclosure. The nature trails provide good birding, and those with the time to explore them should be able to find at least some of the 120 species of birds regularly recorded in the reserve. These include Wonga Pigeon (quite plentiful in the brown barrel forest on the slopes of Red Hill), Yellow-tailed Black-Cockatoo, Gang-gang and Sulphur-crested Cockatoo, Crimson Rosella, Shining Bronze-Cuckoo (spring—summer), Powerful Owl (though said to be quite common at Tidbinbilla, this sought-after species is rather elusive and may not be easy to find), Tawny Frogmouth, Superb Lyrebird (common, although most often heard and seen in winter), Cicadabird (spring—summer), White's Thrush, Rose (spring—summer), Flame and Eastern Yellow Robin, Crested Shrike-tit, Olive Whistler, Satin Flycatcher (spring—summer), Rufous Fantail (spring—summer), Pilotbird, Red-browed Treecreeper, Crescent Honeyeater, and Satin Bowerbird (commonly seen near the carpark).

Apart from wet sclerophyll forest Tidbinbilla has stands of dry eucalypt forest and open woodland, as well as areas of grassland. These habitats hold a variety of interesting birds, among them Stubble Quail, Painted Button-quail, Hooded Robin, Restless Flycatcher, Spotted Quail-thrush, Speckled Warbler and Diamond Firetail (the firetails can sometimes be found in quite large numbers in the grassland between the park entrance and the visitors centre).

With its fine network of walking tracks and varied birdlife, Tidbinbilla is undoubtedly one of the best places in the ACT to go bird-watching. Clearly you could spend a very full and enjoyable day in the reserve.

Lake George

If you cannot find many waterbirds around Canberra, try Lake George, just over the border in New South Wales. Situated about 35 km north-east of the city centre, the lake's western shores can be approached from the Federal Highway while its southern shores are accessible via the road to Bungendore.

Lake George is generally rather shallow and occasionally dries up completely. When full it covers a very large area (at times it may be as much as 25 km long and 10 km wide), and even during periods of prolonged drought there is usually some water at its southern end. The lake is therefore an important waterbird refuge and most of the species already mentioned have been recorded there. Over the years a large number of rare and interesting birds have turned up, including Great Crested Grebe, Darter, Pacific Heron, Little and Intermediate Egret, Australasian Bittern, Freckled, Pink-eared and Blue-billed Duck, Australasian Shoveler, Baillon's, Australian and Spotless Crake, Painted Snipe, Lesser Golden and Double-banded Plover, Red-necked Avocet and Marsh Sandpiper.

The country surrounding the lake holds a variety of interesting passerines – Speckled Warbler and Diamond Firetail for example – as well as raptors such as Whistling Kite, Peregrine Falcon and Australian Hobby. White-bellied Sea-Eagles visit the area occasionally.

NAMADGI NATIONAL PARK

Protecting an extensive tract of mountainous country between the Naas and Cotter Rivers, south of Canberra, Namadgi National Park covers an area of about 94 000 ha – more than a third of the ACT. Much of the park is an undisturbed wilderness characterised by steep-sided ranges, high open valleys and rocky barren ridges. Established in 1984, it is becoming increasingly popular with bushwalkers and is an excellent place to go bird-watching, particularly during the summer months.

The varied terrain within the reserve supports a wide range of plant communities: wet and dry eucalypt forests, alpine woodlands, grasslands, heaths, swamps and sphagnum bogs. The lofty peaks – Mt Clear (1603 m), Mt Gudgenby (1739 m), Mt Kelly (1829 m), Mt Bimberi (1911 m) and many others – are usually buried beneath a deep blanket of snow during winter, while in summer the meadow-like floors of the highland valleys are richly decorated with all kinds of colourful wildflowers.

The park headquarters are located at Glendale Crossing, some 60 km from Canberra via Tharwa and Naas. The unsealed road leading through the reserve (Boboyan Road) is narrow in places, and may be blocked by snow during the winter months. Petrol and food supplies can be obtained from the general store at Tharwa. There are small camping grounds at Orroral Crossing, about 10 km north of the park headquarters, and at Mt Clear about 24 km to the south. Toilets and fireplaces are provided at both

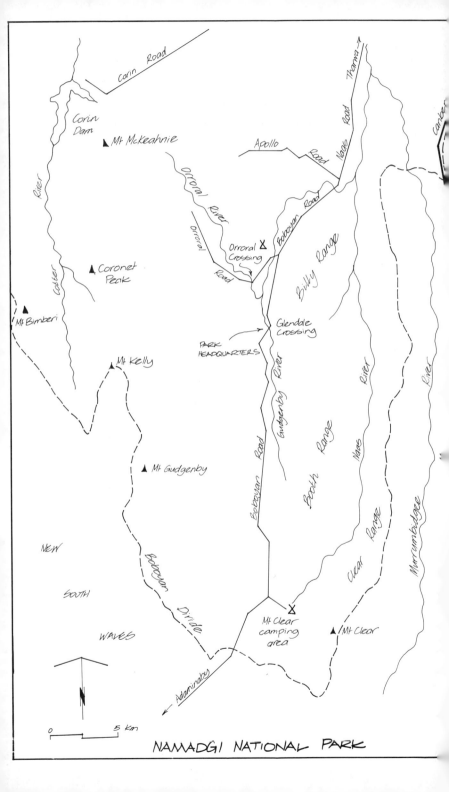

NAMADGI NATIONAL PARK

places, but there are no showers or powered sites. Other facilities include picnic areas and shelter huts.

Namadgi National Park encompasses some of the finest bush-walking country in the ACT, and indeed in south-eastern Australia. For experienced, hardy walkers there are numerous challenging treks across the high plains, and through the foothills to the park's towering peaks. For the less adventurous, many kilometres of fire trails provide ready access to the rugged ranges east of Boboyan Road. Bush camping is permitted at a number of sites, but you should seek advice from the ranger before setting out.

More than 130 species of birds have been recorded in the reserve, of which the following are perhaps the most notable: Grey Goshawk, Peregrine Falcon, Brown Quail, Brush Bronzewing, Wonga Pigeon, Gang-gang Cockatoo, Australian King-Parrot, White-throated Needletail (summer, especially during unsettled weather), Superb Lyrebird, White's Thrush, Rose (summer) and Hooded Robin, Olive Whistler, Satin Flycatcher (summer), Spotted Quail-thrush, Speckled Warbler, Red-browed Tree-creeper, Regent, Fuscous and Crescent Honeyeater, Diamond Firetail and Satin Bowerbird. A comprehensive bird list can be obtained from the park headquarters.

Key to Maps

▨	Public land
▨	Areas of water
▲	Mountain peak
〜〜〜	Mountain range or plateau
COBAR ●	Place name
✕	Camping area
⚲	Lighthouse
⟂⟂⟂	Marsh
▬▬▬	Major road or highway
───	Minor road
------	Foot track
--·--	National park boundary
-───	State boundary
～⌒	River or creek

Queensland

Useful addresses

Queensland Ornithological Society
PO Box 97
St Lucia, Qld 4067

Toowoomba Bird Club
PO Box 67
Darling Heights, Qld 4350

North Queensland Naturalists Club
PO Box 991
Cairns, Qld 4870

Queensland National Parks and Wildlife Service
239 George Street
Brisbane, Qld 4000

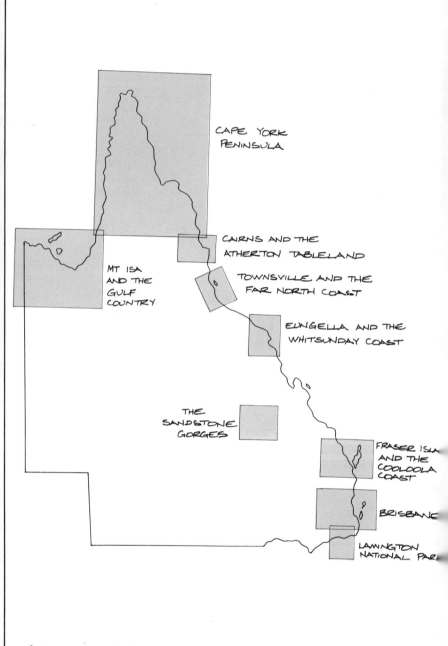

CAPE YORK
PENINSULA

CAIRNS AND THE
ATHERTON TABLELAND

TOWNSVILLE AND THE
FAR NORTH COAST

MT ISA
AND THE
GULF
COUNTRY

EUNGELLA AND THE
WHITSUNDAY COAST

THE
SANDSTONE
GORGES

FRASER ISLA
AND THE
COOLOOLA
COAST

BRISBANE

LAMINGTON
NATIONAL PAR

QUEENSLAND

BRISBANE

Twenty years ago visitors often remarked that Brisbane was more like a big country town than the capital of one of Australia's largest and most prosperous states. Since the late 1960s, however, the city has changed dramatically. Its centre, on the north bank of the Brisbane River, has been extensively redeveloped, and today a huge elevated freeway carries motorists to within a few hundred metres of the main business area, where high-rise office blocks and multi-storey carparks have replaced many fine old buildings.

Situated in the south-eastern corner of Queensland, about 100 km north of the New South Wales border and some 450 km south of the Tropic of Capricorn, Brisbane is Australia's third-largest city. Its suburbs are expansive, stretching more or less continuously from beyond Redcliffe in the north to Beenleigh in the south, and from the shores of Moreton Bay in the east to Ipswich in the west. As might be expected, much of the original vegetation in and around the city has been cleared, and many habitats altered or destroyed. Nevertheless the region supports an incredibly rich avifauna − 399 species of birds have been recorded in Brisbane and its environs. Rainforest species are of particular interest. Birds such as Rose-crowned and Wompoo Fruit-Dove, Topknot, White-headed and Wonga Pigeon, Sooty Owl, Noisy Pitta, Pale-yellow Robin, Black-faced and Spectacled Monarch, Logrunner, Yellow-throated Scrubwren, Satin and Regent Bowerbird, Green Catbird and Paradise Riflebird can be found in the D'Aguilar Range, less than 50 km from the city centre. Brisbane also has much to offer the wader enthusiast. Over forty species have been recorded, and in summer Moreton Bay holds an estimated 18 000 birds, which makes it one of the most important wader sites in the continent.

Brisbane has ample accommodation, including international-class hotels, motels and guest houses. There are youth hostels at 15 Mitchell Street, Kedron, and Hornibrook Esplanade, Woody Point; the Youth Hostels Association's head office is at 462 Queen Street, Brisbane. There are caravan parks at Tingalpa, Wynnum West, Capalaba, Upper Mt Gravatt, Sunnybank, Springwood, Eight Mile Plains and Aspley. The city has an international airport and numerous rental car outlets.

Brisbane has long enjoyed a reputation for being a friendly, informal city. Its historic buildings, now unfortunately somewhat overshadowed by modern towers of concrete and glass, are very beautiful: Old Government House, Parliament House, City Hall, Customs House and the Treasury Building are all well worth seeing. The Queensland Cultural Centre, a short distance from the city centre across Victoria Bridge, houses an art gallery, museum, library and performing arts complex.

Brisbane Botanic Gardens, Albert Park and Victoria Park

The Brisbane Botanic Gardens are situated about 1 km south-east of the city centre, between Alice Street and the north bank of the Brisbane River. Unlike those of most Australian capital cities, the gardens are not particularly good for birds, though a number of common species are usually present and can be observed readily enough. These include Great and Pied Cormorant, White-faced Heron, Pacific Black Duck, Grey Teal, Dusky Moorhen, Purple Swamphen, Silver Gull, Crested Tern, Rainbow and Scaly-breasted Lorikeet (chiefly winter−spring), Sacred Kingfisher (spring−summer), Welcome Swallow, Tree Martin, Willie Wagtail, Noisy Friarbird (winter−spring), Silvereye, Figbird and Australian Magpie-lark.

The gardens consist mainly of lawns dotted with trees and shrubs, but there is a small patch of lush rainforest vegetation in the southern section near Captain Cook Bridge. The gates are open daily between sunrise and sunset. Although many of the paths are wide and sealed, wheelchairs are not available.

Having visited the Botanic Gardens, you may care to walk about 1 km north-west of the city centre via Albert Street to Albert Park, then continue for another kilometre or so to Victoria Park via Wickham Terrace and Gregory Terrace. Victoria is the better of the two parks for birds; more than sixty species regularly occur there, including many of those already mentioned.

University of Queensland, Dutton Park and Long Pocket

University of Queensland: This might seem an unlikely place to go bird-watching, but quite a variety of species − Scaly-breasted Lorikeet, Pale-headed Rosella, Noisy Miner and Figbird, for example − can be seen in the university grounds, while the lake near College Road has waterbirds such as Australasian Grebe, Little Black and Little Pied Cormorant, Pacific Black Duck, Dusky Moorhen, Purple Swamphen and Eurasian Coot. The university is about 7 km south of the city centre via Coronation Drive and Sir Fred Schonell Drive.

Dutton Park: This small reserve on the banks of the Brisbane River is reputedly the only place near the city centre where Bush-

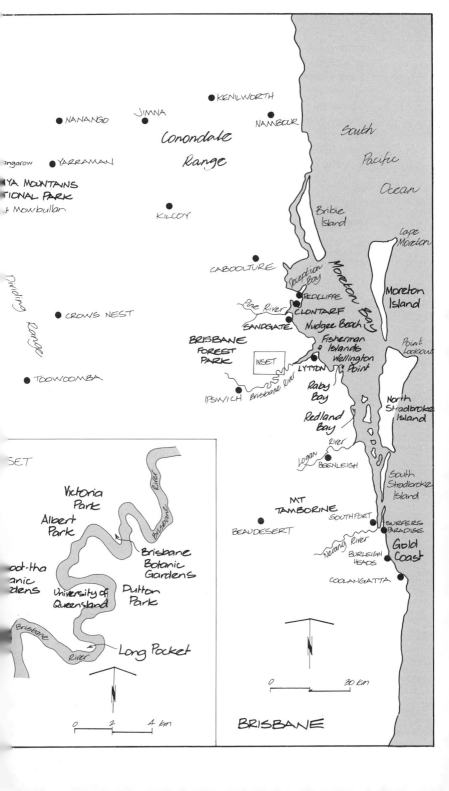

hens occur. The park can be reached via Victoria Bridge and Gladstone Road, or by ferry from the university.

Long Pocket: Situated 2 km or so south of the university, much of this area is a golf course and trees are rather few and far between. Despite this there are some remnants of native vegetation, and the banks of the Brisbane River are readily accessible and certainly worth exploring. There are picnic facilities in Sir John Chandler Park, adjacent to the Long Pocket Golf Club, and a public boat ramp near the end of Long Pocket Road.

Indooroopilly Island, just south of Long Pocket, is a roosting site for many thousands of flying foxes. On summer evenings they make a spectacular though eerie sight when they take to the air en masse and leave for their feeding grounds.

Mt Coot-tha Botanic Gardens and Mt Coot-tha Reserve

Mt Coot-tha Botanic Gardens: Were established by the Brisbane City Council in 1970 and are located some 5 km south-west of the city centre via Milton Road. The features of the gardens include an information centre, a planetarium, a tropical display dome with palms, ferns and epiphytes, a fragrance garden containing more than 150 different herbs and shrubs, a rainforest gully, a large collection of arid zone plants and a lagoon.

The gardens, which can be reached by public transport, are open daily between 9 a.m. and 5 p.m. They attract quite a large number of birds. Laughing Kookaburras, Noisy Miners, Striated Pardalotes and Torresian Crows are plentiful; Little Lorikeets and Noisy Friarbirds turn up when the eucalypts are in flower; and a variety of common waterbirds frequent the lagoon.

Mt Coot-tha Reserve (1377 ha): Forms part of the 25 000 ha Brisbane Forest Park and is situated just west of the Botanic Gardens via Mt Coot-tha Road and Sir Samuel Griffith Drive. The vegetation consists chiefly of open forest dominated by broad-leaved and grey ironbark, pink bloodwood, tallowwood, rose she-oak and brush box. Along watercourses and in sheltered gullies the vegetation is more luxuriant, and around the picnic areas there are many exotic trees and shrubs.

The reserve, a popular picnic spot, attracts large crowds at weekends and a visit during the week will be best for bird-watching. Sir Samuel Griffith Drive provides ready access to the main picnic grounds (Slaughter Falls and Simpson Falls) at the foot of the Taylor Range, and to the Mt Coot-tha Lookout (227 m) with its magnificent views of the city and Moreton Bay.

There are walking tracks from the Slaughter Falls picnic area to Constitution Hill (257 m), and from the Simpson Falls picnic ground to The Summit (290 m) − the highest point in the reserve. Although steep in places, both tracks offer excellent birding and visitors can look forward to seeing many of the following: Australian Brush-turkey, Wonga Pigeon, Pale-headed Rosella, Fantailed Cuckoo (mainly spring–summer), Shining Bronze-Cuckoo (mainly spring–summer), Forest Kingfisher, Dollarbird (summer), Black-faced Cuckoo-shrike, Cicadabird (summer), White's Thrush, Eastern Yellow Robin, Golden Whistler, Rufous Whistler, Grey Shrike-thrush, Grey Fantail, Eastern Whipbird, Spotted Quail-thrush, Superb Fairy-wren, White-browed Scrubwren, White-throated Gerygone, Brown and Striated Thornbill, White-throated Treecreeper, Bell Miner, Lewin's, Yellow-faced, White-throated and Scarlet Honeyeater, Mistletoebird, Spotted Pardalote, Red-browed Firetail, Olive-backed Oriole, Spangled Drongo, Grey and Pied Butcherbird, Australian Magpie and Pied Currawong.

Brisbane Forest Park

Brisbane Forest Park, stretching from the Mt Coot-tha Reserve in the south-east to the D'Aguilar State Forest in the north-west, encompasses Brisbane City Council reserves, national parks and state forests. It includes much of the D'Aguilar Range, a series of deeply dissected hills which provide a spectacular backdrop to Brisbane's north-western suburbs. Tall open eucalypt forest predominates, but there are large patches of subtropical rainforest in the vicinity of Mt Nebo and Mt Glorious townships. The highest point in the range, Mt D'Aguilar (745 m), is about 15 km north of Mt Nebo and about 50 km from the city centre.

The park is an outstanding place to go bird-watching and it would take some time to explore the area thoroughly. If you have only a day or two to spare, concentrate on the following spots, especially if you are eager to see rainforest species. Before setting out, call at the park headquarters in the Sir Douglas Tooth Centre (open daily between 9 a.m. and 5 p.m.) on Mt Nebo Road just west of The Gap. Here you can obtain information that includes a guide to the park and bird lists.

Samford State Forest: Is situated about 18 km north-west of the city centre via Samford Road. There are picnic facilities at Iron-bark Gully, in the south-eastern corner of the forest. From here several tracks provide ready access to an area of tall eucalypts where birds such as Laughing Kookaburra, Black-faced Cuckoo-shrike, Rufous Whistler, Grey Fantail, White-throated and Brown Honeyeater, Pied Butcherbird and Pied Currawong can be seen with ease. More interesting species – Rose Robin, Eastern Whipbird and Variegated Fairy-wren – are recorded from time to time.

Since Ironbark Gully is very popular you should go there during the week, preferably in the early morning or late afternoon. An illustrated leaflet describing some of the birds of the gully can be obtained from the park headquarters.

Camp Mountain State Forest: Lies to the north of Mt Nebo Road, about 17 km north-west of the city centre. The area is dominated by open eucalypt forest, while gullies and south-facing slopes support more luxuriant vegetation. Picnic facilities are provided at Camp Mountain and Bellbird Grove. From the Bellbird Grove picnic ground there is a short walking track along the banks of Cedar Creek.

Jollys Lookout (12 ha) and Boombana (38 ha) National Parks: Are located on Mt Nebo Road, some 30 km north-west of Brisbane. There are picnic facilities at both places (camping is not permitted), but Jollys Lookout attracts many people at weekends and a visit to Boombana is likely to be much more peaceful.

The Thylogale walking track (4 km), linking the Boombana picnic ground with Jollys Lookout, passes through tall, wet eucalypt forest and rainforest. Along the way you should see many birds, including Australian Brush-turkey, Topknot Pigeon, Brown Cuckoo-Dove, Emerald Dove, Yellow-tailed Black-Cockatoo, Australian King-Parrot, Crimson Rosella, Brush Cuckoo (summer), Yellow-eyed Cuckoo-shrike (mainly summer), Cicadabird (summer), Varied Triller, White's Thrush, Rose Robin (chiefly winter), Crested Shrike-tit, Little Shrike-thrush, Black-faced (summer) and (more rarely, and mainly in summer) Spectacled Monarch, Leaden Flycatcher (mostly summer), Rufous Fantail (chiefly summer), Logrunner, Large-billed and Yellow-throated Scrubwren, Brown Gerygone, White-throated and, more rarely, Red-browed Treecreeper, Lewin's and Scarlet Honeyeater, Eastern Spinebill and Red-browed Firetail.

From Jollys Lookout there are panoramic views of the Samford Valley and Moreton Bay. A short walking track — the Ergernia circuit (1.5 km) — commences at the lookout and takes you through a variety of vegetation types, including open grassy woodland and wet eucalypt forest.

Manorina National Park (139 ha): Some 37 km from Brisbane, just past Mt Nebo township, this reserve has a 3 km walking track leading from the roadside picnic area to the top of Mt Nebo (617 m). Overnight camping is allowed; permits can be obtained from the Brisbane Forest Park headquarters.

The vegetation ranges from open woodland to tall eucalypt forest dominated by flooded gum. White's Thrush, Pale-yellow Robin, Logrunner, Eastern Whipbird and a number of other interesting species occur in the park, and the clear bell-like calls of the Bell Miner can be heard ringing from the cool confines of the forest near the picnic area.

Maiala National Park (1140 ha): Lies approximately 46 km from Brisbane via Mt Nebo Road and Mt Glorious township, and is the best place to go if you want to see a wide variety of rainforest

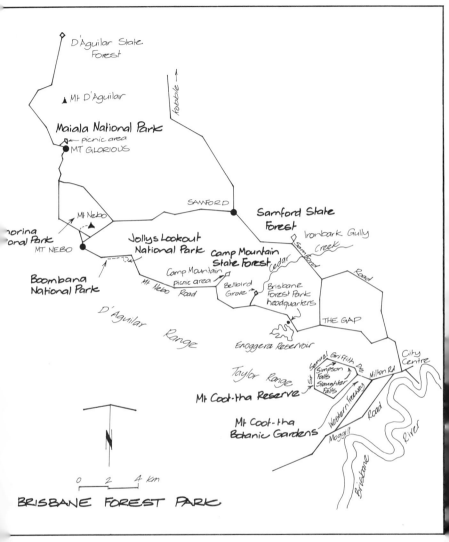

BRISBANE FOREST PARK

birds. The park's subtropical rainforests, the nearest of their type to Brisbane, are exceedingly beautiful. From the picnic ground walking tracks lead past the massive buttressed trunks of yellow carabeens and through groves of tall piccabeen palms into the cool, dark interior of the rainforest, where vines, ferns and strangler figs abound.

Visitors to Maiala can be assured of many hours of exciting birding. Pacific Baza, Grey Goshawk, Rose-crowned and Wompoo Fruit-Dove, Topknot and White-headed Pigeon, Brown Cuckoo-

Dove, Emerald Dove, Australian King-Parrot, Crimson Rosella, Common Koel (summer), Channel-billed Cuckoo (summer), Pheasant Coucal, Noisy Pitta, Varied Triller, Eastern Yellow and Pale-yellow Robin, Black-faced (summer) and (more rarely, and chiefly in summer) Spectacled Monarch, Rufous Fantail (mostly summer), Logrunner, Variegated Fairy-wren, Large-billed and Yellow-throated Scrubwren, Brown Gerygone, Bell Miner, Lewin's and Scarlet Honeyeater, Eastern Spinebill, Satin and Regent Bowerbird, Green Catbird and Paradise Riflebird are some of the many species that you can expect to see in and around the park. Three rare nocturnal birds — Powerful Owl, Sooty Owl and Marbled Frogmouth — are known to occur in the D'Aguilar Range and are well worth searching for.

You should try to arrange a trip to the national park during the week. It attracts masses of visitors at weekends and it is sometimes impossible to find a parking space near the picnic area. Camping is not permitted.

Moreton Bay

There are many places worth visiting for birds along the coast east of Brisbane. Migratory waders are perhaps the main attraction. For example, in summer Moreton Bay regularly supports about 1800 Mongolian Plovers and some 1100 Eastern Curlews, while rarities such as Grey Plover, Wood Sandpiper, Wandering Tattler, Redshank, Lesser Yellowlegs, Asian Dowitcher, Pectoral and Broad-billed Sandpiper and Ruff turn up from time to time. Other species of waterbirds — cormorants, herons, egrets, ibis, spoonbills, waterfowl, gulls and terns — occur in good numbers, and there are some extensive patches of mangroves where birds such as Collared Kingfisher and Mangrove Honeyeater can be found.

The following are generally regarded as the best birding spots. Most are readily accessible and easy to locate, though a Brisbane street directory will be helpful.

Redland Bay: Is situated a few kilometres north of the Logan River mouth, about 45 km south-east of the city centre via Cleveland. The entire area from Victoria Point south to the Logan River is worthy of thorough exploration. There are boat ramps at Victoria Point and Redland Bay, and picnic facilities in Victoria Point Reserve and Sel Outridge Park (off Broadwater Terrace, Redland Bay).

The Redland Bay to Beenleigh road follows the Logan River for 10 km or so, and there are many dams and lagoons close to the road where cormorants, herons, egrets and waterfowl can be seen with ease.

Raby Bay: Is one of the best known wader localities near Brisbane, and is situated about 30 km south-east of the city centre via

Capalaba or Birkdale. Access to the extensive mudflats along the southern shores of the bay can be gained via Cowley Street and Raby Esplanade. From here you can walk east around the edge of the mudflats towards Cleveland. Australian Pelican, Great, Pied, Little Black and Little Pied Cormorant, White-faced and Striated Heron, Great and Little Egret, Sacred Ibis, Royal Spoonbill, Black Swan, Pacific Black Duck, Osprey, White-bellied Sea-Eagle, Pied Oystercatcher, Masked Lapwing, Red-capped Plover and Caspian Tern are some of the species you can expect to see; and if you are fortunate, more interesting birds such as Beach Thick-knee, Red-kneed Dotterel, and Gull-billed, Sooty and Little Tern may be present.

In summer the area is favoured by many migratory waders, including Lesser Golden, Mongolian and Large Sand Plover, Ruddy Turnstone, Eastern Curlew, Whimbrel, Grey-tailed Tattler, Greenshank, Bar-tailed Godwit, Red and Great Knot, Red-necked Stint, and Terek, Sharp-tailed, Curlew and Broad-billed Sandpiper. In winter Double-banded Plover, a visitor from New Zealand, can be seen in fair numbers. The most productive time for waders is during high tide when the birds congregate in large flocks above the high-water mark. Remember to wear sandshoes and a hat, and carry something cool to drink.

At the end of Cowley Street there is a small patch of mangroves. This is a good spot for Collared Kingfisher, Mangrove Gerygone, and Mangrove and Brown Honeyeater, while Golden-headed Cisticola and Variegated Fairy-wren frequent the adjacent grassy areas.

There are picnic grounds just to the west of Raby Bay off Sturgeon Street, Ormiston, and to the east off North Street, Cleveland.

Wellington Point: Lies to the north-west of Raby Bay, about 30 km from Brisbane via Birkdale. At the tip of the point, just north of Erobin, there is a large picnic reserve and several boat ramps. The shores of Waterloo Bay to the west hold an assortment of waterbirds, mainly cormorants, waders, gulls and terns, and at low tide a variety of species can usually be seen feeding in the shallow pools. Wellington Point is best avoided at weekends since the reserve is often very crowded.

Collingwood Road, Birkdale: The small swamp behind the sewage pump on Collingwood Road is worth a brief visit. It is covered with emergent vegetation, but those prepared to get wet feet may well see something of interest. The surrounding paperbark woodland holds White-throated Gerygone and other bush birds.

Collingwood Road is just south of the Birkdale to Wellington Point road. The swamp is about 1 km east of the Birkdale Road − Collingwood Road turn-off.

Queens Esplanade, Thorneside: This would be an excellent place to take a disabled friend wader-watching. It runs for a kilometre or so along the shores of Waterloo Bay from Agnes Street, Birkdale, to Mooroondu Point, Thorneside. In summer, at high tide, a wealth of waders – Lesser Golden, Mongolian and Large Sand Plover, Ruddy Turnstone, Eastern Curlew, Whimbrel, Grey-tailed Tattler, Greenshank, Bar-tailed Godwit, Red and Great Knot, Red-necked Stint, and Terek, Sharp-tailed, Curlew and Broad-billed Sandpiper – can be viewed with ease from the roadside.

In winter a few Double-banded Plovers are usually present, while there is always a variety of waterbirds to be seen at any time of the year. These include cormorants, White-faced Heron, egrets, ibis, Pied Oystercatcher, Masked Lapwing, Red-capped Plover, Black-winged Stilt, and Gull-billed, Caspian, Little and Crested Tern. There are mangroves at Mooroondu Point where Collared Kingfisher, Mangrove Gerygone and Mangrove Honeyeater can be found.

Lytton and Fisherman Islands: Much frequented by Brisbane bird aficionados, the mudflats, swamps and mangroves near the mouth of the Brisbane River provide some of the best birding within 25 km or so of the city centre. In recent years the area has produced a string of interesting and rare species: Little Bittern, Wandering Whistling-Duck, Australasian Shoveler, Buff-banded Rail, Spotless Crake, Grey Plover, Red-necked Avocet, Little Curlew, Wood, Common, Marsh, Pectoral and Broad-billed Sandpiper, Lesser Yellowlegs (a bird seen at Lytton in early September 1984 was the first record of this species in Queensland and only the second for Australia), Asian Dowitcher (a rare though regular summer visitor), Black-tailed Godwit, White-winged Tern and Eastern Grass Owl. Other species recorded in and around Lytton include Australasian Grebe, cormorants, Cattle, Great, Little and Intermediate Egret, Striated Heron, ibis, Royal Spoonbill, Black Swan, Grey Teal, Chestnut Teal, Osprey, Black-shouldered, Brahminy and Whistling Kite, White-bellied Sea-Eagle, Australian Kestrel, Brown Quail, Dusky Moorhen, Purple Swamphen, Masked Lapwing, Red-capped and Black-fronted Plover, Black-winged Stilt, Ruddy Turnstone, Grey-tailed Tattler, Greenshank, Bar-tailed Godwit, Red and Great Knot, Red-necked Stint, Sharp-tailed and Curlew Sandpiper, Gull-billed, Caspian and Crested Tern, Bar-shouldered Dove, Pheasant Coucal, Forest, Sacred (mostly summer) and Collared Kingfisher, Rainbow Bee-eater (mainly summer), Fairy Martin (chiefly summer), Richard's Pipit, Clamorous Reed-Warbler (chiefly summer), Tawny Grass-bird, Golden-headed Cisticola, Red-backed Fairy-wren, Mangrove Gerygone, Mangrove Honeyeater, Chestnut-breasted

Mannikin and White-breasted Woodswallow.

Although a good deal of the area north of Lytton is in the process of being reclaimed (alas, it seems that many coastal swamps near our capital cities will soon disappear unless conservation groups can save them), there are still a number of excellent places for birds and most are readily accessible via Pritchard Street. Summer, of course, is the best time for migratory waders; a telescope would be a most useful addition to your equipment.

Nudgee Beach: Is one of a number of wader localities north of the Brisbane River and lies about 18 km north-east of the city centre via Nudgee Road. There are picnic facilities in Nudgee Beach Reserve, at the end of Fortitude Street. From here it is possible to walk west towards the mouth of Nudgee Creek, and east towards Cribb Island. High tide is the best time for waders; at low tide the birds disperse over a wide area and may be difficult to find. The mangroves just west of the picnic ground are worth visiting for mangrove species.

Sandgate: Is situated on the shores of Bramble Bay, about 20 km north-east of Brisbane via Sandgate Road and Deagon. There are three small lagoons in the area and one in particular, Dowse Lagoon between Southerden Street and Brighton Road, is an excellent place for waterbirds. Although the number of species present varies considerably, there is usually quite an assortment to be seen including at least a few of the following: Australasian Grebe, Australian Pelican, Darter, Great, Pied, Little Black and Little Pied Cormorant, Pacific and White-faced Heron, Cattle, Great, Little and Intermediate Egret, Sacred and Straw-necked Ibis, Magpie Goose, Wandering Whistling-Duck, Black Swan, Pacific Black and Pink-eared Duck, Grey Teal, Chestnut Teal, Hardhead, Dusky Moorhen, Purple Swamphen, Eurasian Coot, Comb-crested Jacana and Black-winged Stilt.

Adjacent to the lagoon there is an area of lightly timbered parkland where a number of bush birds — Peaceful Dove, Galah, Scaly-breasted Lorikeet, Laughing Kookaburra, Black-faced Cuckoo-shrike, Noisy and Little Friarbird, Brown Honeyeater and Figbird — can be found, while the overgrown margins of the lagoon hold Golden-headed Cisticola. There are picnic facilities nearby.

Einbunpin Lagoon, off Lagoon Street in the centre of Sandgate, has been made into an ornamental pond and attracts very few birds, but Third Lagoon between Bracken Ridge Road and Baskerville Street has some large patches of reeds and is virtually surrounded by an extensive melaleuca swamp. Those prepared to tramp through the swamp may be justly rewarded — it is one of the very few places near Brisbane where Australasian Bittern has been recorded.

Wyampa Road, Bald Hills: Providing ready access to the numerous swamps that lie between the Pine River and Bald Hills Creek, Wyampa Road can be reached from Sandgate via Bracken Ridge Road. The area is well known for its wealth of waterbirds and in recent years a number of interesting species have bred there, including Black-necked Storks in 1983 and 1984. Birds such as Darter, Cattle and Intermediate Egret, Glossy Ibis, Royal Spoonbill, Wandering Whistling-Duck, Hardhead, Marsh Harrier and Comb-crested Jacana can usually be found without difficulty.

There are picnic facilities in Deep Water Bend Reserve, on the banks of the Pine River.

Clontarf: Is situated 35 km or so north-east of the city centre via Sandgate Road and the Houghton Highway. The coast in the vicinity of Clontarf, particularly the eastern shores of Hays Inlet, Bramble Bay between Clontarf Point and Woody Point, and Deception Bay west of Reef Point, is excellent for cormorants, herons, egrets, ibis, waders, gulls, terns, coastal raptors and mangrove species.

There are many picnic grounds and boat ramps in the area (boats can be hired locally), and the mudflats at Deception Bay can be viewed with ease from Captain Cook Parade and the Esplanade.

North Stradbroke and Moreton Islands

Like Fraser Island, North Stradbroke and Moreton Islands consist almost entirely of sand carried by ocean currents from northern New South Wales and deposited over tens of thousands of years along Queensland's south-eastern coast. And like Fraser, North Stradbroke and Moreton are very beautiful. They are excellent places to go bird-watching away from the hustle and bustle of Brisbane, just 40 km or so to the west.

North Stradbroke Island: Can be reached readily enough by private boat, passenger ferry or vehicular ferry. If you intend taking a vehicle to the island − a four-wheel-drive, though desirable, is not essential − it would be wise to book in advance. There is a list of ferry operators in the Yellow Pages section of the Brisbane telephone directory. A wide range of accommodation, including a motel, hotel, guest house and holiday units, is available at Point Lookout, and there are caravan parks at Point Lookout, Myora and Dunwich. Accommodation can be booked at any branch of the Queensland Government Tourist Bureau.

North Stradbroke contains a wide diversity of habitats − melaleuca swamps, freshwater lakes, mangroves, beaches, sanddunes, heathlands, eucalypt forests and small pockets of rainforest − and as a result its birdlife is extremely rich. About 260 species have been recorded, including many that are highly sought-after:

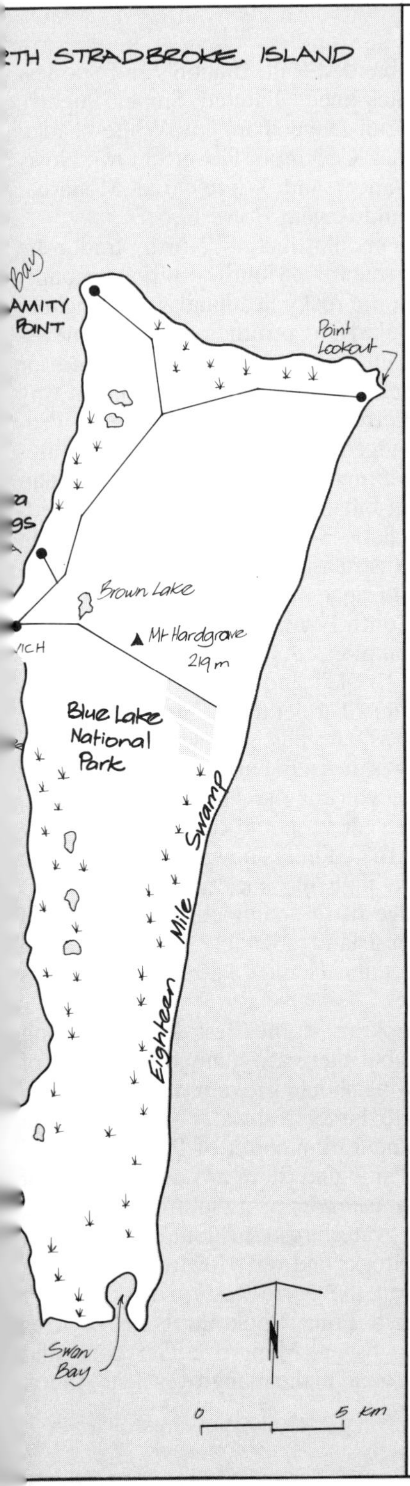

NORTH STRADBROKE ISLAND

MORETON ISLAND

(Bay)

AMITY
POINT

Point
Lookout

a
gs

Brown Lake

VICH

▲ Mt Hardgrave
219 m

Blue Lake
National
Park

Eighteen Mile Swamp

Swan
Bay

0   5 km

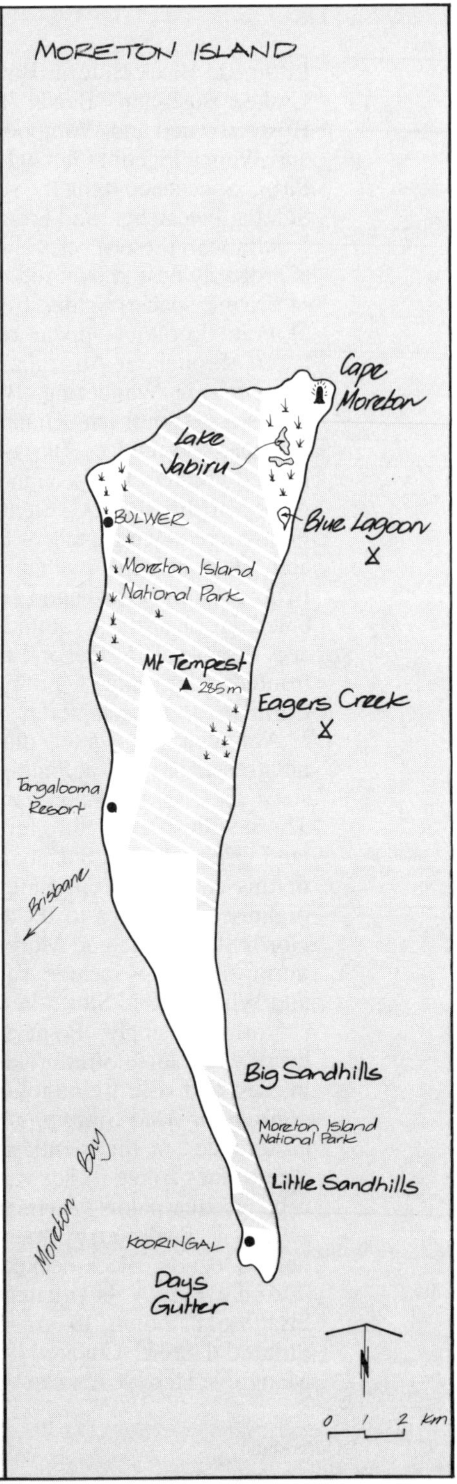

N

Cape
Moreton

Lake
Jabiru

BOLWER

Blue Lagoon
✗

Moreton Island
National Park

Mt Tempest
▲ 285 m

Eagers Creek
✗

Tangalooma
Resort

Brisbane

Big Sandhills

Moreton Island
National Park

Little Sandhills

KOORINGAL

Days
Gutter

Moreton Bay

0   1   2 km

N

Little and Black Bittern, Buff-banded Rail, Baillon's and Spotless Crake, Bush-hen, Beach Thick-knee, Painted Snipe, Superb, Rose-crowned and Wompoo Fruit-Dove, Topknot, White-headed and Wonga Pigeon, Glossy Black-Cockatoo, Powerful Owl, Noisy Pitta, Spectacled (chiefly summer) and White-eared Monarch, Shining Flycatcher, and Satin and Regent Bowerbird.

Although these species are a great attraction, North Stradbroke is probably best known for its seabirds. Mouth-watering accounts of oceanic species sighted from the rocky headlands in the vicinity of Point Lookout appear regularly in ornithological club news-letters throughout Australia. Among the many seabirds listed for the area are Wandering, Black-browed, Yellow-nosed and Shy Albatross, Southern Giant-Petrel, Cape, Great-winged, Pro-vidence, Kermadec, Black-winged and Cook's Petrel, White-necked Petrel (a bird seen in February 1983 was the first Australian record of this species), Slender-billed and Fairy Prion, Streaked, Flesh-footed, Wedge-tailed, Buller's, Sooty, Short-tailed, Fluttering and Hutton's Shearwater, Australasian Gannet, Masked and Brown Booby, Great and Least Frigatebird, Red-tailed and White-tailed Tropicbird, Great and South Polar Skua, Arctic, Pomarine and Long-tailed Jaeger, Common, Arctic, Roseate, White-fronted, Black-naped, Sooty, Bridled and Lesser Crested Tern, Common and Black Noddy, Grey Ternlet and White Tern.

Although the winter months are best for seabirds such as albatrosses, Point Lookout is worth visiting at any time of the year since there is always a chance you may see something unusual. Those wishing to venture further afield should contact the Queens-land Ornithological Society at the address shown at the beginning of this chapter. From time to time the society's seabird group organises boat trips to the edge of the continental shelf, east of North Stradbroke and Moreton Islands. Notable species recorded during such trips include Tahiti and Gould's Petrel, and Wilson's and White-bellied Storm-Petrel.

Not surprisingly, Point Lookout is the best known birding locality on North Stradbroke, but there are many other places of interest and visits to the following should prove rewarding.

Eighteen Mile Swamp: Is a large freshwater swamp on the eastern side of the island, some 15 km south of Point Lookout. Sand-dunes fringe its seaward side and there are dense stands of cabbage tree palms (*Livistona australis*) at its southern end. The swamp is favoured by many waterbirds, including cormorants, herons, egrets, Black-necked Storks and waterfowl.

Amity Point: Is situated on the north-western tip of North Stradbroke, about 10 km from Point Lookout. Birds such as Striated Heron, Collared Kingfisher, Mangrove Gerygone and Mangrove Honeyeater can be found in the mangroves near Amity, and there are a number of interesting swamps to the north of the road from Dunwich to Point Lookout.

Myora Springs: Lies on the western side of the island, a few kilometres north of Dunwich. The small patch of rainforest at Myora is one of the few places on North Stradbroke where the rare Superb Fruit-Dove has been seen.

Blue Lake National Park (501 ha):   Is situated about 12 km east of Dunwich and features an attractive freshwater lake fed from the island's vast underground water supply. The vegetation surrounding the lake consists chiefly of eucalypt forest where Bush Thick-knees and many of the island's eighteen species of honey-eater occur.

There are no facilities in the park, but bushwalkers are allowed to camp overnight. Permits should be obtained in advance from the Queensland National Parks and Wildlife Service, PO Box 42, Kenmore, Qld 4069. Remember to enclose a stamped, addressed envelope.

Moreton Island: Is accessible by private boat, passenger ferry or vehicular ferry, or by air from the light aircraft section at Brisbane Airport. All roads on the island are sandy, and therefore unsuitable for conventional vehicles. Accommodation can be obtained at the Tangalooma Resort, and there are houses available for rental at Kooringal and Bulwer. Bookings can be made at any branch of the Queensland Government Tourist Bureau. Petrol and food can be obtained in Kooringal and Bulwer.

Moreton Island is an ideal place for a camping and bushwalking holiday. Largely undeveloped, it has many massive sand-dunes, some 70 km of unspoilt beaches and numerous crystal-clear lakes. Moreton Island National Park (15 400 ha) protects many of the island's outstanding features, including Mt Tempest (285 m), which is reputed to be the highest coastal sand-dune in the world. There are camping grounds, with picnic facilities, toilets and showers, at Blue Lagoon and Eagers Creek. Permits should be obtained in advance from the Queensland National Parks and Wildlife Service, PO Box 42, Kenmore, Qld 4069 (enclose a stamped, addressed envelope when applying).

Moreton has fewer birds than North Stradbroke (about 190 species have been recorded), but because it is so peaceful birders will find it a delightful place to visit. The following areas in particular are worth exploring.

Cape Moreton: Lies on the north-eastern tip of the island and rises to over 100 m above sea level. In winter, especially during windy weather, it is a good spot to watch for pelagics such as albatrosses and petrels.

Lake Jabiru: As its name implies, this beautiful lake, accessible only by foot, is a favoured haunt of the Black-necked Stork. The lake is about 4 km south-west of Cape Moreton.

Blue Lagoon: Is the largest body of fresh water on the island and is situated some 8 km south of Cape Moreton. The extensive heathlands south-west of the lagoon are usually alive with honeyeaters during winter and spring.

Mt Tempest: In the centre of the island, about 15 km south-west of Cape Moreton, is well worth climbing for superb views of Moreton Bay. Eucalypt forest covers its lower slopes, while low, dense heath occurs higher up. Little Wattlebirds and Brown and White-cheeked Honeyeaters are a common sight in the heathlands when the banksias are in flower.

Eagers Creek: Is situated to the south-east of Mt Tempest, about 15 km south of Cape Moreton. The freshwater creek flows out across the ocean beach from Eagers Swamp − an excellent place for waterbirds.

The Big and Little Sandhills: Clearly visible from the mainland, these towering wind-blown dunes at the southern end of the island are largely bare and consequently hold few birds. Despite this they have a certain beauty, and there is always a chance that you will spot one of the Peregrine Falcons that breed in the area each year.

Days Gutter: Lying off the southern tip of Moreton Island, this wide expanse of intertidal seagrass flats is one of the richest oyster-producing areas in Moreton Bay. At low tide the flats attract large numbers of birds, including many migratory waders in summer.

Mt Tamborine

Situated some 70 km south of Brisbane, Mt Tamborine is truly a delightful place. During the humid summer months its cool, luxuriant rainforests, sparkling cascades and deep rock-pools provide welcome relief for those seeking to escape from the stifling heart of the city. And as you walk through the quiet forest, stopping now and then to focus on a Noisy Pitta or a Logrunner or, if you are very fortunate, an Albert's Lyrebird, it is difficult to believe that the Gold Coast, with all its commercialism and razzmatazz, is less than an hour's drive to the east.

Needless to say, Mt Tamborine is a splendid place to go birding. Even if you have only a few hours to spare you should see many interesting species: Pacific Baza, Grey Goshawk, Australian Brush-turkey, Rose-crowned and Wompoo Fruit-Dove, Topknot, White-headed and Wonga Pigeon, Brown Cuckoo-Dove, Emerald Dove, Australian King-Parrot, Brush Cuckoo (summer), Channel-billed Cuckoo (summer), Azure Kingfisher, Dollarbird (summer), Yellow-eyed Cuckoo-shrike (chiefly summer), Cicadabird (summer), Varied Triller, White's Thrush, Rose Robin (chiefly

The Macleay's Honeyeater is one of the most conspicuous birds at Paluma township, North Queensland

The largest island national park in Australia, Hinchinbrook Island lies off the coast between Townsville and Cairns, North Queensland

Red-necked Stint. The mudflats adjacent to the Esplanade at Cairns, North Queensland, offer excellent opportunities for observing migratory waders at close range

Grey-headed Robin − this unobtrusive rainforest-dweller can be found at The Crater (Mt Hypipamee) National Park on the Atherton Tableland, North Queensland

The Curtain Fig Tree, on the Atherton Tableland south-west of Cairns, North Queensland, is a popular tourist attraction and a good spot for birds

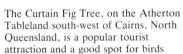

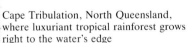

Termite mounds, grasslands and open eucalypt woodlands dominate the landscape north of Mt Isa in Queensland

Cape Tribulation, North Queensland, where luxuriant tropical rainforest grows right to the water's edge

Beautiful Wineglass Bay, just one of
many delightful spots in the Freycinet
National Park, eastern Tasmania

Looking south from Whitemark towards
Mt Strzelecki, Flinders Island, Bass Strait

Tree ferns and silvery water – Russell
Falls, Mt Field National Park, Tasmania

winter), Pale-yellow Robin, Little Shrike-thrush, Black-faced (summer) and (mostly summer) Spectacled Monarch, Eastern Whipbird, Variegated Fairy-wren, Large-billed and Yellow-throated Scrubwren, Brown Gerygone, Lewin's and Scarlet Honeyeater, Eastern Spinebill, Satin and Regent Bowerbird, Green Catbird and Paradise Riflebird. Nocturnal species are well represented with Southern Boobook and Tawny Frogmouth being reported regularly, while rarities such as Sooty Owl and Marbled Frogmouth breed in the area and are certainly worth searching for.

Mt Tamborine has plenty of accommodation, including two motels, a guest house and a caravan park. There are eight national parks and two environmental parks in the area; all are readily accessible and most have excellent facilities such as picnic grounds and well-graded walking tracks. Camping is not permitted in any of the parks.

Those wishing to see a wide variety of birds will find the following parks most rewarding. Before setting out pay a visit to the Mt Tamborine Natural History Association's information centre in Doughty Park. Here you can obtain a guide to the mountain's reserves and a bird list, and view displays covering the fauna and flora of the region.

Cedar Creek National Park (230 ha): Is about 6 km north of Doughty Park via Tamborine Mountain Road. The main feature of the reserve is Cedar Creek, along which there are cascades, waterfalls, and several deep rock-pools suitable for swimming. A 3.5 km walking track provides access to the creek and to the surrounding eucalypt forest.

The Knoll National Park (85 ha): Lies 2 km north-west of Doughty Park via Knoll Road. It has a 3.5 km walking track that passes through eucalypt forest into rainforest before forking to form a circuit. A short branch track leads to a lookout providing a view of Cameron Falls.

Joalah National Park (36 ha): Preserves an area of rich rainforest on Tamborine Mountain Road, a kilometre or so north of Doughty Park. From Curtis Falls, at the southern end of the reserve, a 2.5 km walking track follows Cedar Creek beneath a canopy of tall piccabeen palms and other rainforest trees. Joalah, an Aboriginal word meaning haunt of the lyrebird, is reputed to be one of the best places on Mt Tamborine for Albert's Lyrebird.

MacDonald National Park (12 ha): If you do not find the lyrebird at Joalah, try this reserve 3 km north-east of Doughty Park. Protecting a small but luxuriant patch of subtropical rainforest, it is an excellent place for a walk among strangler figs, piccabeen palms and tall trees festooned with vines and ferns. The park can be reached via Eagle Heights Road.

Palm Grove National Park (118 ha): Has an extensive walking track system through stands of mature rainforest with mighty, buttressed yellow carabeens, palms and strangler figs. From Burrawang Lookout, near the park's northern boundary, there are wonderful views over the coastal lowlands to the Gold Coast.

Palm Grove, 3 km east of Doughty Park, is accessible via Curtis Road or Eagle Heights Road.

Witches Falls National Park (131 ha): This reserve, declared in 1908, has the distinction of being the first national park in Queensland. It has a 3 km walking track, steep in places, that zigzags down the western side of the Tamborine Plateau through open eucalypt forest, then runs north through rainforest. Another 1.2 km track leads to the north-western corner of the park. From here you can walk along Beacon Road to Hendersons Knob (552 m), the best known lookout point on the mountain.

Witches Falls is 1.5 km south-west of Doughty Park via Tamborine Mountain Road.

Gold Coast

The Gold Coast is no ornithological paradise by any stretch of the imagination. Towering apartment blocks extend almost continuously for over 30 km along the beaches between Southport and Coolangatta, and the extensive mangroves lining many of the region's creeks and rivers have been largely destroyed by residential development. And in the hinterland vast tracts of heathland and open eucalypt forest, as well as numerous freshwater lagoons, tea-tree swamps and pockets of lowland rainforest, have long since disappeared.

You could be forgiven therefore for thinking that the Gold Coast is not worth visiting − at least, not if you are looking for birds. Yet surprisingly this is not the case, for even here there are national and environmental parks that provide refuges for both people and birds.

Pine Ridge Environmental Park (109 ha): Situated just south of Paradise Point, about 10 km north of Southport, this reserve is readily accessible via Pine Ridge Road. Protecting one of the few areas of lowland vegetation remaining on the Gold Coast, it consists of a series of parallel sand-dunes vegetated with banksia scrub and open eucalypt forest. Between the dunes there are a number of low-lying tea-tree swamps.

From the carpark on Pine Ridge Road a wide boardwalk − suitable for wheelchairs − leads into the reserve, passing through a variety of habitats including a swamp where birds such as Golden-headed Cisticola and Scarlet Honeyeater can be found. The park's taller trees provide homes for several different mammals; if you look closely you may catch sight of a koala.

Rosser Environmental Park (3.4 ha): Located some 10 km west of

Surfers Paradise, just north of the Broadbeach to Nerang road, this reserve features a freshwater lagoon that often supports a variety of birds — cormorants, herons, egrets, ibis, spoonbills and waterfowl. There are parklands with picnic facilities nearby.

Burleigh Head National Park (24 ha): Protects a rocky headland near the mouth of Tallebudgera Creek. The main entrance to the reserve can be reached via Goodwin Terrace, Burleigh Heads. From here sealed walking tracks lead to Tumgun Lookout, and along the park's rugged shoreline to Tallebudgera Creek. During spring and autumn whales on their seasonal migration can often be seen from the lookout; in winter it is a good place for seabirds. Near the southern entrance to the park, just east of the Gold Coast Highway, there is a specially constructed platform for disabled fishermen.

Within the reserve there is a surprising variety of vegetation types, including pandanus groves and small areas of rainforest. Birds are not plentiful, but there are a few to be seen. Australian Brush-turkeys, for example, are very tame and can be observed at close quarters.

For those wishing to spend more than a day or two on the Gold Coast there are several other reserves close by that are worth visiting. A comprehensive guide to the region's parks can be obtained from the Queensland National Parks and Wildlife Service, 6 Peggs Road, Burleigh Heads, or from the Gold Coast City Council administration centre in Bundall Road, Surfers Paradise. There is, of course, no shortage of accommodation in the area, including caravan parks at Southport, Burleigh Heads and Cool-angatta, and youth hostels at Surfers Paradise and Coolangatta.

Before leaving the Gold Coast you may care to visit the Currumbin Bird Sanctuary, about 7 km south of Burleigh Heads. World-famous for the thousands of Rainbow and Scaly-breasted Lorikeets that flock there daily to receive handouts from visitors, Currumbin is somewhat over-commercialised to say the least. It cannot be compared with Australia's best known avian tourist attraction — the nightly penguin parade at Summerland Beach on Phillip Island in Victoria.

Conondale Range

The Conondale Range, part of the coastal range system of south-eastern Queensland, lies about 100 km north of Brisbane via the Bruce Highway and Caboolture. Since the area is deeply dissected it contains a great diversity of landscapes, including numerous rocky gorges and steep-sided valleys. The vegetation is equally diverse, ranging from subtropical rainforest to open eucalypt forest, and as a result the region supports a wide variety of birds.

Much of the area is state forest, and there are many kilometres of forestry roads providing access to the numerous picnic grounds, walking tracks and lookouts between Kenilworth and Jimna. Camping grounds, with toilets and picnic facilities, are provided in Charlie Moreland and Booloumba Creek State Forest Parks near Kenilworth, and in Peach Trees State Forest Park near Jimna. It is not necessary to obtain a camping permit in advance, except during school holidays. A detailed guide to the region and camping information can be obtained from the Queensland Forestry Department in Kenilworth.

Conondale National Park (2126 ha), some 30 km north of Kilcoy and about 20 km south-east of Jimna, can be reached from the south via the D'Aguilar Highway. The park is largely undeveloped and it would be wise to contact the Queensland National Parks and Wildlife Service, 239 George Street, Brisbane, before going there.

The rainforests of the Conondale Range hold birds such as Wompoo Fruit-Dove, Topknot, White-headed and Wonga Pigeon, Australian King-Parrot, Pale-yellow Robin, Yellow-throated Scrubwren, Satin and Regent Bowerbird, Green Catbird and Paradise Riflebird, while a host of other interesting species occur in suitable habitat throughout the area. These include Crimson and Pale-headed Rosella, Common Koel (summer), Channel-billed Cuckoo (summer), Pheasant Coucal, Azure Kingfisher, Rose Robin (chiefly winter), Variegated and Red-backed Fairy-wren, White-throated Gerygone, Bell Miner, Blue-faced, Lewin's and Scarlet Honeyeater, Chestnut-breasted Mannikin, Olive-backed Oriole, Figbird and Spangled Drongo. No fewer than twenty-eight species of raptor have been recorded in the region, of which nineteen are resident. Of particular note are the Pacific Baza (occasionally present in large numbers − a flock of about thirty was seen near Jimna in May 1978), Grey Goshawk (regularly recorded in the Kenilworth area, sometimes along with Brown Goshawk and Collared Sparrowhawk), Red Goshawk (the Conondale Range is one of the few places in Australia where this very rare species is observed regularly) and Peregrine Falcon. Owls include Powerful, Masked and Sooty, all of which have been seen in the vicinity of Booloumba Creek. Another rare nocturnal species, the Marbled Frogmouth, breeds in the Conondale Range, and a thorough search of the rainforest bordering Booloumba Creek may bring results.

Clearly raptor buffs and nocturnal ramblers will find much of interest in the Conondale Range. There are, however, other noteworthy birds to be found in the area − Black-breasted Button-quail for example. During the past ten years or so this elusive ground-dweller has been reported on a number of occasions from Little Yabba Creek in Charlie Moreland State Forest Park,

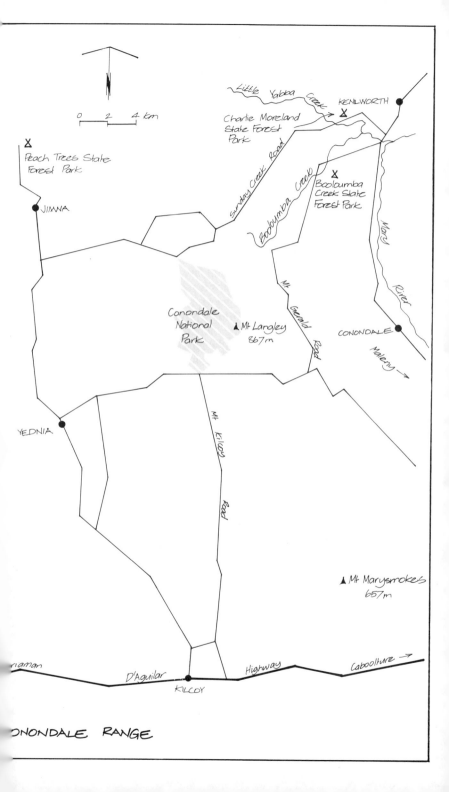

CONONDALE RANGE

and from the Nanango—Yarraman district to the west of the Conondale Range. The Button-quail's preferred habitat is dry rainforest with a dense litter layer, especially where there is thick overhead cover such as that provided by the introduced lantana. It is said that the easiest way to locate the bird is to look for the characteristic circular depressions that it scratches in the leaf litter while searching for food.

Bunya Mountains National Park

Situated some 270 km north-west of Brisbane via the Warrego Highway and Toowoomba, Bunya Mountains National Park covers an area of 11 700 ha and is Queensland's second-oldest reserve. Although the park is too far from Brisbane for a day trip, it has excellent facilities and is a splendid place to go bird-watching. The main camping area, at Dandabah just inside the reserve's south-eastern boundary, has picnic facilities, toilets and hot-water showers. Campsites should be booked in advance. Write to the ranger, Bunya Mountains National Park, MS 501, via Dalby, Qld 4405, enclosing a stamped, addressed envelope. For those not wishing to camp there is a guest house at Mt Mowbullan, near the turn-off to Dandabah. The road leading to the park is unsuitable for caravans; the nearest caravan park is at Dalby, about 55 km to the south-west.

Bunya Mountains is one of the most scenic parks in the state. Much of the area lies above 1000 m, and there are numerous lookouts offering fine views over the surrounding countryside. An extensive walking track system has been established, with tracks leading to waterfalls and viewing points through forests of bunya and hoop pine. Since most of these walks are less than 6 km, they can be enjoyed by people of all ages. However, if you are unable to walk you can still see a good deal of the reserve by driving the 10 km or so from Mt Mowbullan to Mt Kiangarow (1135 m), the highest point in the mountains.

As might be expected the park's birdlife is rich and varied, and includes many sought-after species: Pacific Baza, Grey Goshawk, Peregrine Falcon, Black-breasted Button-quail, Rose-crowned and Wompoo Fruit-Dove, Topknot, White-headed and Wonga Pigeon, Brown Cuckoo-Dove, Emerald Dove, Australian King-Parrot (large numbers of these colourful parrots frequent the camping area at Dandabah), Red-winged Parrot, Sooty Owl, Noisy Pitta, Black-faced (summer) and (mainly summer) Spectacled Monarch, Logrunner, Large-billed and Yellow-throated Scrubwren, Satin and Regent Bowerbird, Green Catbird and Paradise Riflebird. Many of these species are of special interest because they seldom occur further west in the region. A bird list and a walking track guide can be obtained from the ranger at Dandabah.

LAMINGTON NATIONAL PARK

There are probably few bird-watchers in Australia who have not heard of Lamington National Park. It is one of Queensland's best known reserves, protecting the most significant area of undisturbed subtropical rainforest remaining in the south-east of the state. With two comfortable lodges, camping and picnic areas, fine mountain scenery (there are said to be more than five hundred waterfalls in the park), and over 150 km of walking tracks, Lamington is the ideal place for a holiday.

This 20 200 ha reserve lies in the McPherson Range on the Queensland − New South Wales border, about 120 km south of Brisbane. At each of the park's two main entrances, O'Reilly's and Binna Burra, there are a guest house and a camping area; those with caravans should use the Binna Burra entrance because the narrow road leading from Canungra to O'Reilly's is steep and unsealed in places and therefore unsuitable for caravans.

Although Lamington's vegetation is largely subtropical, there are tracts of temperate rainforest dominated by Antarctic beech (*Nothofagus moorei*) on the higher ground, while the park's less fertile soils favour the growth of eucalypt woodland, heathland and surprisingly − mallee. The varied vegetation supports a rich avifauna and about 150 species of birds have been recorded in the reserve, including Albert's Lyrebird, Rufous Scrub-bird, Satin and Regent Bowerbird, and Paradise Riflebird.

O'Reilly's

O'Reilly's Guest House, in the north-western corner of Lamington National Park about 36 km south of Canungra, is well known to bird-watchers both within Australia and overseas. Accommodation should be booked well in advance: write to O'Reilly's Guest House, via Canungra, Qld 4275, or inquire at any branch of the Queensland Government Tourist Bureau. The national park camping area, about 500 m from the guest house, has toilets and cold-water showers but no powered sites. Since Lamington is a very popular park you should reserve a site: write to the ranger, Lamington National Park, via Canungra, Qld 4275, enclosing a stamped, addressed envelope.

Between the camping ground and the guest house there is a picnic area, together with a store and an information centre. A bird list and a walking track guide are available from the ranger. The store sells light refreshments and basic supplies; petrol and food should be purchased at Canungra. The nearest youth hostels are at Surfers Paradise and Coolangatta on the Gold Coast, but there are others in Warwick and Brisbane.

In almost every national park in Australia at least a few birds can be seen quite readily around the camping and picnic areas.

Indeed it is surprising how many species quickly accept the presence of man, especially if there is a free meal to be gained. At O'Reilly's, bird-watching begins the minute you set up camp. Flocks of Crimson Rosellas and Pied Currawongs appear from nowhere, noisily urging you to prepare a meal, while Australian Brush-turkeys strut silently around as if hoping to be noticed. The plump Wonga Pigeon is less conspicuous. This shy bird shuns the open spaces, preferring to linger on the edge of the forest and slipping quietly away if pressed too hard.

Many other species can be found near the camping area but the stars of the show are undoubtedly the Satin and Regent Bowerbirds. Male Regent Bowerbirds are unmistakable. The moment you begin breakfast, keeping a wary eye on the currawongs that are always ready to take advantage of your hospitality, these beautiful black and gold birds arrive unannounced. It is not unusual to find three or four fully plumaged male Regent Bowerbirds perched in the same tree. If you are patient they will take food from your hand, but it is best to feed them early in the morning because these gorgeous creatures are warmly welcomed at every campsite; by 8 a.m. they are almost invariably satiated. Satin Bowerbirds are also common at O'Reilly's, although they are not as confiding as the Regents, nor as photogenic. The glossy, blue-black male Satin Bowerbirds build their avenue bowers in the forest near the camping area, and these fascinating structures are often richly decorated with numerous bright blue objects such as plastic pegs, straws, and the tops of aerosol cans.

There are many walking tracks — short and long — commencing at O'Reilly's, including the famous Border Track (21.4 km) linking O'Reilly's with Binna Burra. A wide variety of birds can be seen along these walks — Topknot and White-headed Pigeon, Brown Cuckoo-Dove, Emerald Dove, Australian King-Parrot, Brush and Fan-tailed Cuckoo (both spring–summer), Shining Bronze-Cuckoo (spring–summer), Noisy Pitta, Varied Triller, White's Thrush, Rose (mainly winter), Eastern Yellow and Pale-yellow Robin, Golden Whistler, Little and Grey Shrike-thrush, Black-faced (summer) and (chiefly summer) Spectacled Monarch, Leaden Flycatcher (spring–summer), Rufous Fantail (spring–summer), Grey Fantail, Logrunner, Eastern Whipbird, Superb Fairy-wren, Large-billed, Yellow-throated and White-browed Scrubwren, Brown Gerygone, Brown Thornbill, White-throated Treecreeper, Lewin's and Scarlet Honeyeater, Eastern Spinebill, Spotted Pardalote, Red-browed Firetail, Figbird, Green Catbird and Paradise Riflebird.

Predators such as Pacific Baza, Brown Goshawk, Grey Goshawk, Wedge-tailed Eagle and Peregrine Falcon are quite common in the park, while nocturnal inhabitants include Southern Boobook

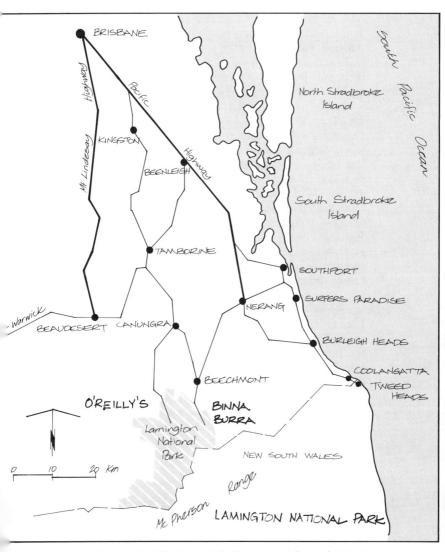

Powerful and Sooty Owl (both rarely), Tawny and (rarely) Marbled Frogmouth and Australian Owlet-nightjar.

Lamington boasts many special birds, but Albert's Lyrebird and Rufous Scrub-bird are the two species most bird-watchers would like to see there. Unfortunately both are more often heard than seen, although lyrebirds are quite plentiful in the vicinity of O'Reilly's and an early morning walk through the rainforest may bring results. The track to Morans Falls is reputed to be a good place to look for them. Those wishing to search for Rufous Scrub-bird — an exceedingly elusive species — should try the Border Track, especially where it passes through areas dominated by Antarctic beech. During the breeding season, October to December, male Scrub-birds will sometimes show themselves if you play back their calls from a tape recorder. This technique is often used by bird-watchers to attract shy species.

Once you have explored Lamington's rainforests, it is worth spending some time bird-watching along the road between Canungra and O'Reilly's. The relatively dry, open forest on the lower slopes of the range holds a number of species that are less likely to be found at higher elevations. These include Bar-shouldered Dove, Glossy Black-Cockatoo (especially where there are stands of casuarina), Rainbow and Scaly-breasted Lorikeet, Pale-headed Rosella, Common Koel (summer), Channel-billed Cuckoo (summer), Sacred Kingfisher, Dollarbird (summer), Rufous Whistler, Red-backed Fairy-wren, White-throated Gery-gone, Noisy and Little Friarbird, Noisy Miner, Blue-faced, Yellow-faced, White-throated and Brown Honeyeater, Olive-backed Oriole, Spangled Drongo and Grey Butcherbird.

Binna Burra

Like O'Reilly's, Binna Burra is famous for its wonderful network of walking tracks and its birdlife. Accommodation is available at the Binna Burra Lodge; for details write to Binna Burra Lodge, Beechmont, via Nerang, Qld 4211, or inquire at any branch of the Queensland Government Tourist Bureau. The lodge also has a small camping ground with powered sites and hot-water showers. Near the park entrance there is a picnic area, and also a kiosk which sells basic supplies. Park information can be obtained from the ranger's office on the Beechmont road about 500 m downhill from the lodge.

All the birds that occur at O'Reilly's can be seen in this section of the park, and Binna Burra's walking track system includes the specially constructed Senses Nature Trail, where a guide rope has been provided to assist blind walkers. Markers along the 400 m track have a braille text describing some of the features of the rainforest. Binna Burra is about 30 km south of Nerang and can be easily reached via a good sealed road.

Lamington can be pleasant at any time of the year, although rainfall is highest between November and March. And since much of the park lies above 800 m, winter nights can be very chilly: romantic for those sitting by a roaring log fire in one of the lodges, but no fun if you are camping and have forgotten to bring extra blankets — a wise precaution even in summer.

FRASER ISLAND AND THE COOLOOLA COAST

Fraser Island

With its long white beaches, patches of rainforest and numerous freshwater lakes, this exceedingly beautiful island attracts many thousands of visitors each year. About 120 km long and on average 15 km wide, it is the largest sand island in the world − in places its magnificent dunes rise more than 230 m above sea level.

In the early 1970s the island was the centre of a lengthy and sometimes bitter struggle between conservationists and sand-mining companies. The conflict was resolved in 1976 when the Commonwealth Government intervened and mining on the island was stopped. Today, however, much of Fraser Island remains unprotected. The Great Sandy National Park (52 400 ha) covers only the northern section, and unfortunately many of the island's outstanding features, including some of its most spectacular coloured sand formations, a large number of its unusual lakes perched in the dunes high above sea level, and the best of its forests, lie outside the park boundary. Much of the area south of the park (about 120 000 ha) is state forest, and large tracts are being logged by the Queensland Forestry Department.

Fraser Island is situated just off Queensland's south-east coast, about 270 km north of Brisbane. It has only a small permanent population, most of which lives on the east coast − at Eurong, Happy Valley and Orchid Beach. There are no sealed roads, and because the narrow forestry tracks are generally very sandy, conventional cars are not permitted on the island. Those with four-wheel-drive vehicles can reach the island by ferry. Vehicular ferries operate regularly between Inskip Point (north-east of Tin Can Bay) and Hook Point, between Mary River Heads (north-east of Maryborough) and Ungowa, and between Urangan (on the southern shores of Hervey Bay) and Sandy Point. You should book in advance − there is a list of ferry operators in the Yellow Pages section of the Maryborough telephone directory.

Before travelling to the island it would pay to call at the Forestry Department's office in Wharf Street, Maryborough. Here you can purchase a good set of maps (you will need them − there is a maze of tracks on Fraser Island and only a few are signposted), and obtain information about the island's geography, history, wildlife and state forests. While in Maryborough contact the Queensland National Parks and Wildlife Service, on the corner of Wharf and Richmond Streets, for information (including a bird list) about the Great Sandy National Park.

If you do not own a four-wheel-drive you can hire one in Maryborough − at a price! Alternatively several tour operators in the area offer day trips to Fraser Island (inquire at any local travel agent), or if you want to stay longer there is a comfortable resort at Orchid Beach as well as a number of holiday units at Eurong and Happy Valley. Bookings can be made at any branch of the Queensland Government Tourist Bureau.

Fraser Island has abundant fresh water, many kilometres of uninterrupted beaches and an extensive network of tracks and walking trails. It is an ideal place for a camping and walking holiday. The Forestry Department provides camping areas, with toilets, showers and picnic facilities, at Central Station, Lake Boomanjin and Lake McKenzie State Forest Parks, while the Queensland National Parks and Wildlife Service has constructed camping grounds at Dundubara and Wathumba Creek in the Great Sandy National Park. Sites should be booked well in advance, especially during school holidays. Permits to camp in state forests can be obtained from the District Forester, PO Box 219, Maryborough, Qld 4650. For a permit to camp in the national park write to the ranger, Great Sandy National Park, PO Box 101, Maryborough, Qld 4650. Remember to enclose a stamped, addressed envelope. Bush camping is permitted at many sites on the island, though not within 100 m of the lakes.

There is a wide range of habitats on Fraser Island, including woodlands, rainforests, mangroves, heaths, swamps and lakes. Its birdlife is rich and varied, and includes a large number of interesting species: Brown Booby, Great and Least Frigatebird, Striated Heron, Little and Black Bittern, Black-necked Stork, Brahminy Kite, Grey Goshawk, King Quail, Red-backed and Black-breasted Button-quail (Fraser Island is one of the few places in Australia where the latter species regularly occurs), Buff-banded Rail, Baillon's Crake, Brolga, Bush and Beach Thick-knee, White-winged (summer), Gull-billed, Common (summer), Roseate, Black-naped, Sooty, Little and Lesser Crested Tern, Common and Black Noddy, Rose-crowned and Wompoo Fruit-Dove, Topknot and White-headed Pigeon, Brown Cuckoo-Dove, Bar-shouldered and Emerald Dove, Glossy Black-Cockatoo, Scaly-breasted and Little Lorikeet, Ground Parrot (this is one of the region's special birds − it occurs in the Great Sandy National Park and on the mainland in Cooloola National Park), Pheasant Coucal, Powerful Owl, White-throated and Large-tailed Nightjar, Azure, Forest and Collared Kingfisher, Noisy Pitta, Cicadabird (summer), Varied Triller, White's Thrush, Rose Robin (winter), Little Shrike-thrush, Spectacled (chiefly summer) and White-eared Monarch, Eastern Whipbird, Tawny Grassbird, Large-billed Scrubwren, Brown, Mangrove and White-throated Gerygone, Mangrove, White-cheeked, Dusky and Scarlet Honeyeater, Figbird and Spangled Drongo.

While birds such as Little Bittern, Black-breasted Button-quail

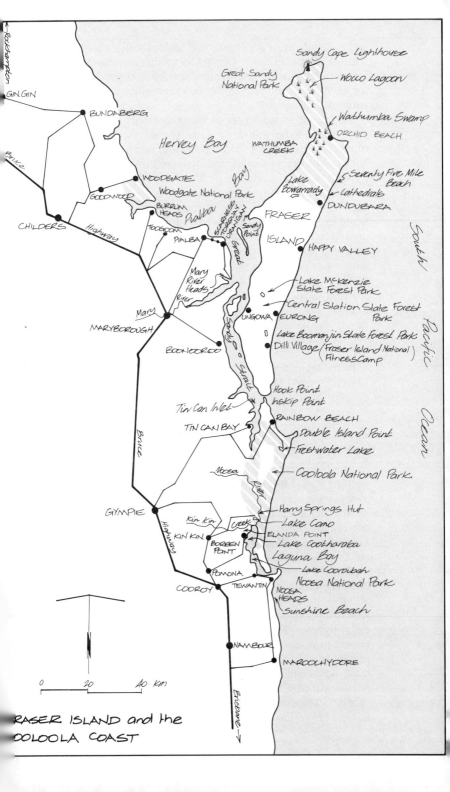

FRASER ISLAND and the
COOLOOLA COAST

and Ground Parrot are elusive and seldom seen, others — Brahminy Kite, Emerald Dove, Forest Kingfisher, Little Shrike-thrush, Large-billed Scrubwren, White-cheeked and Scarlet Honeyeater, for example — are reasonably common and can usually be found without difficulty.

You could spend a very pleasant week or two on Fraser Island and visits to the following spots should prove memorable and rewarding. Petrol and food can be obtained at Eurong and Happy Valley, but before leaving the mainland it would be wise to stock up with provisions because prices on the island are generally high.

Central Station State Forest Park: Situated approximately mid-way between Ungowa and Eurong, this is the best place to stay while exploring the southern half of the island. Near the camping area, which is located in a delightful setting among trees festooned with epiphytic ferns and orchids, there is an information centre where you can obtain many useful publications, including a guide to the walking trails of Fraser Island's central region.

From Central Station you can walk or drive to many places of interest — Pile Valley, and Lakes McKenzie, Wabby, Birrabeen, Benaroon and Boomanjin. Just north of the camping area is Woongoolbver Creek, a beautiful clear stream fringed with luxuriant vegetation. An early morning walk here will undoubtedly prove a highlight of your visit to Fraser Island. Wompoo Fruit-Dove, Emerald Dove, Azure Kingfisher, Noisy Pitta, Little Shrike-thrush, Spectacled Monarch, Eastern Whipbird, Large-billed Scrubwren, and Lewin's and Scarlet Honeyeater are some of the birds that frequent the creek and the surrounding rainforest.

Pile Valley: This superb patch of forest, with trees towering to over 60 m, lies about 2 km east of Central Station and can be reached via the track to Eurong or via the Woongoolbver Creek walking trail. Most of the giant trees are satinay (*Syncarpia hillii*), a species noted for its durable timber. Until recently it was harvested for marine piles — logs from areas near Pile Valley were used in the construction of the Suez Canal.

Lake McKenzie State Forest Park: One of the most visited lakes on the island, this popular swimming and canoeing spot is the ideal place for a picnic. For those wishing to stay longer there is a camping ground close to the lake's western shores. The lake is about 7 km north of Central Station and is readily accessible on foot or by four-wheel-drive.

Lake Wabby: From a lookout above this lake visitors can see clearly how the prevailing south-easterly winds continue to shape Fraser Island. The lake is slowly being filled by a massive sand-dune advancing steadily westwards. Lake Wabby, about 12 km north-east of Central Station, can be reached on foot or by vehicle. A walking trail leads from the lake to the ocean beach, some 3 km to the east.

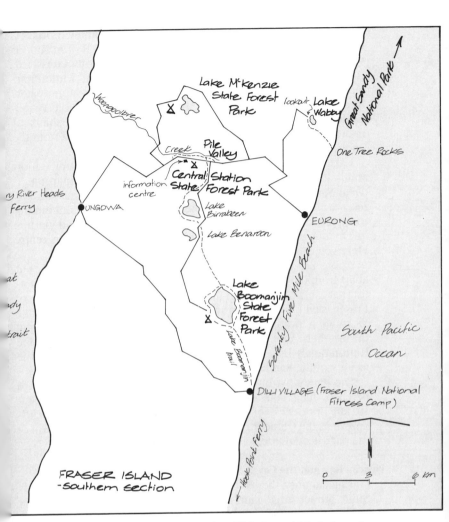

Lake M'Kenzie State Forest Park

lookout Lake Wabby

Great Sandy National Park →

Wanggoolbrer

Pile Valley

Creek

One Tree Rocks

Central Station State Forest Park

information centre

ry River Heads Ferry

UNGOWA

Lake Birrabeen

EURONG

Lake Benaroon

at ady trait

Lake Boomanjin State Forest Park

Lake Boomanjin trail

Seventy Five Mile Beach

South Pacific Ocean

DILLI VILLAGE (Fraser Island National Fitness Camp)

← Hook Point Ferry

FRASER ISLAND
-Southern section

0   3   6 km

Lake Boomanjin State Forest Park: This beautiful sheltered expanse of water covers an area of about 200 ha and is the largest perched dune lake on the island, and indeed in the world. From the camping ground, located in an attractive forested area near its shores, a 13 km walking trail leads around the lake then north-west to Central Station via Lakes Benaroon and Birrabeen.

Another walking track — the Lake Boomanjin trail — takes you in a south-easterly direction to the Fraser Island National Fitness Camp at Dilli Village. This route (about 7 km) passes through a wide range of habitats, including patches of blackbutt and scribbly gum forest, areas of banksia woodland, a paperbark swamp and sparsely vegetated dunes. Along the way you should see many of the following birds: Bar-shouldered Dove, Rainbow Lorikeet, Rainbow Bee-eater, Varied Triller, Eastern Yellow Robin, Rufous Whistler, Leaden Flycatcher (mostly summer), Tawny Grassbird, Red-backed Fairy-wren, Little Wattlebird, Noisy and Little Friarbird, White-throated, Brown and White-cheeked Honeyeater, Red-browed Firetail, Spangled Drongo, White-breasted Woodswallow and Pied Butcherbird. A leaflet describing points of interest along the Lake Boomanjin trail can be obtained from the information centre at Central Station.

Lake Boomanjin lies about 14 km south-east of Central Station and is accessible by vehicle via Lakes Birrabeen and Benaroon.

Great Sandy National Park: There are few vehicle tracks in this reserve and much of it is accessible only on foot. Before attempting to explore the area it would be best to call at the park headquarters at Dundubara, just inside the reserve's south-eastern boundary. Here you can obtain a map and camping information.

About 220 different birds have been recorded in the park, but apart from the Ground Parrot there are probably no species on its list that cannot be found in the more accessible southern section of Fraser Island. Localities worth visiting for Ground Parrots include Wathumba Swamp, west of Orchid Beach, and Wocco Lagoon at the northern end of the island. In recent years Black-breasted Button-quails have been seen on a number of occasions in the vicinity of the Sandy Cape lighthouse.

The park's two most popular features are Lake Bowarrady, a perched dune lake on the reserve's southern boundary about 10 km north-west of Dundubara, and the coloured sand cliffs known as the Cathedrals on Seventy Five Mile Beach just north of the park headquarters.

Hervey Bay and the Great Sandy Strait

During summer the shores of Hervey Bay and the Great Sandy Strait attract large numbers of migratory waders. In February 1983, for example, some 14 000 birds were counted during a national wader survey, including more than 1400 Mongolian Plovers and nearly 2000 Eastern Curlews. Other species recorded in the area were Grey, Lesser Golden and Large Sand Plover, Ruddy Turnstone, Whimbrel, Little Curlew, Grey-tailed Tattler, Greenshank, Common, Marsh, Sharp-tailed, Curlew, Broad-billed and Terek Sandpiper, Black-tailed and Bar-tailed Godwit, Red and Great Knot, Red-necked Stint and Sanderling.

Access to Hervey Bay can be gained via Woodgate, Burrum Heads, Toogoom, Pialba and Urangan, while the western shores of Great Sandy Strait can be reached via Urangan, Mary River Heads and Boonooroo. There are caravan parks at Woodgate, Burrum Heads and Toogoom, and motels, hotels, holiday units and caravan parks at Pialba, Scarness, Torquay and Urangan. There is a youth hostel in Boatharbour Drive, Torquay.

Woodgate National Park

Covering an area of 5498 ha, this reserve lies on the coast just south of the township of Woodgate. With its wide variety of habitats − sandy beaches, dunes, estuarine mangroves, swamps, lagoons, wallum heaths, and eucalypt and angophora forests − Woodgate is a splendid place to go birding. Almost two hundred species of birds occur in the park, including Darter, Great, Little and Intermediate Egret, Striated Heron, Black-necked Stork, Royal and Yellow-billed Spoonbill, Osprey, Pacific Baza, Brahminy Kite, White-bellied Sea-Eagle, Australian Brush-turkey, Brown Quail, Lewin's Rail, Pale-headed Rosella, Azure and Collared Kingfisher, White-bellied Cuckoo-shrike, Cicadabird (summer), Varied Triller, Spectacled Monarch (chiefly summer), Tawny Grassbird, Blue-faced, Mangrove and Scarlet Honeyeater, and Figbird.

This park is accessible on foot or by four-wheel-drive vehicle. It has walking tracks, picnic facilities and a camping ground. If you wish to book a campsite in advance (advisable during school holidays), write to the ranger, Woodgate National Park, c/- Post Office Woodgate, Qld 4660, enclosing a stamped, addressed envelope.

Tin Can Bay

Situated on the western shores of lovely Tin Can Inlet, this small township some 60 km north-east of Gympie has a motel, a hotel, holiday units and three caravan parks. It is much quieter than Rainbow Beach and Noosa Heads (these resort towns are extremely popular and therefore usually very crowded), and makes an excellent base for the bird-watcher.

With a small boat − you can hire one locally − you could explore the shallow waters of Tin Can Inlet north towards Inskip Point and south towards Cooloola National Park. The inlet is fringed by extensive sand and mud flats and is a well-known wader locality. In summer migratory species turn up in fair numbers − Grey, Lesser Golden, Mongolian and Large Sand Plover, Ruddy Turnstone, Eastern Curlew, Whimbrel, Grey-tailed Tattler, Greenshank, Black-tailed and Bar-tailed Godwit, Red Knot, Red-necked Stint, and Marsh, Sharp-tailed and Curlew Sandpiper. Resident waders such as Pied Oystercatcher, Masked Lapwing, Red-capped Plover and Black-winged Stilt are present throughout the year. Other birds regularly seen on the inlet include Black-necked Stork, Beach Thick-knee, and three coastal raptors − Osprey, Brahminy Kite and White-bellied Sea-Eagle.

Cooloola National Park

Protecting 39 400 ha of the coast between Tin Can Inlet and the Noosa River estuary, Cooloola is one of Australia's most valuable reserves, not least because it is a stronghold of the rare and endangered Ground Parrot. The park contains a wealth of natural features − massive dunes rising to 230 m; cliffs of coloured sands; long white beaches; heathlands alive with wildflowers during spring and early summer; woodlands of banksia and scribbly gum; blackbutt forests; rainforests; mangroves; and numerous peaceful lakes and waterways. This outstanding national park, with its rich and varied avifauna (some three hundred species have been recorded), has much to interest the bird-watcher.

The main camping area is situated near Freshwater Lake in the northern section of the park. To get there, turn off the Gympie to Rainbow Beach road about 4 km south-west of Rainbow Beach. About 16 km from the turn-off there are picnic facilities, and a camping ground with toilets and cold-water showers. The track leading into the park is narrow and sandy in places and unsuitable for caravans. The nearest caravan park is at Rainbow Beach, but you may prefer to stay at Tin Can Bay. Cooloola is a very popular park and it is advisable to book a campsite in advance. Write to the ranger, Cooloola National Park, PO Box 350, Gympie, Qld 4570, enclosing a stamped, addressed envelope. You can obtain information, including a walking track guide and a bird list, from the park headquarters adjacent to the camping area. An excellent map of the Cooloola Coast can be purchased at the Tourist Information Centre in Rainbow Beach.

Between the park entrance and Freshwater Lake there are a number of walking tracks − the Dundathu circuit (700 m), the Quandong to Bymien track (1 km), the Blackbutt−Quandong track (1.7 km), the Burwilla Lookout track (700 m) and the Qld Telegraph Line track (4.8 km). In addition, there are two walks commencing at Freshwater Lake − the Freshwater Lake circuit (2.6 km) and the Old Freshwater Road track (5.5 km). If you are reasonably fit the following route should prove highly rewarding. From the camping ground walk to Freshwater Lake (about 1 km), then continue along the Old Freshwater Road to the Bymien picnic area − a pleasant place to stop for lunch. From here you can return to the camping ground via the entrance road. You should allow a full day to complete this 16 km walk. A host of interesting birds can be seen in the rainforest between Freshwater Lake and the Bymien picnic area: Grey Goshawk, Australian Brush-turkey, Rose-crowned and Wompoo Fruit-Dove, Topknot and White-headed Pigeon, Brown Cuckoo-Dove, Emerald Dove, Australian King-Parrot, Brush Cuckoo (summer), Noisy Pitta (if you walk quietly you should have little difficulty finding this colourful

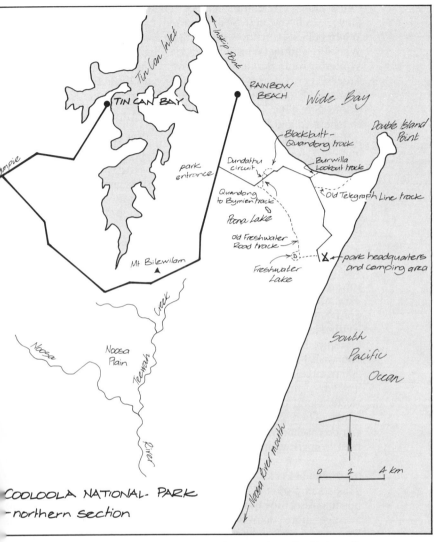

COOLOOLA NATIONAL PARK
- northern section

ground-dweller along the Old Freshwater Road), Pale-yellow
Robin, Little Shrike-thrush, Spectacled (mainly summer) and
White-eared Monarch, Eastern Whipbird, Large-billed Scrub-
wren, Lewin's and Scarlet Honeyeater, Figbird, Spangled Drongo,
Regent Bowerbird (winter) and Green Catbird.

If you do not want to venture far from the camping area you can
see at least some of the birds mentioned by walking around
Freshwater Lake; there is a small patch of rainforest near the
lake's edge. And many other species can be found in the open

forest along the entrance road. These include Bar-shouldered Dove, Rainbow and Scaly-breasted Lorikeet, Black-faced and White-bellied Cuckoo-shrike, Eastern Yellow Robin, Golden Whistler, Rufous Whistler, Leaden Flycatcher (chiefly summer), White-browed Scrubwren, Brown Thornbill, White-throated Treecreeper, Little Wattlebird, Noisy and Little Friarbird, White-throated, Brown and White-cheeked Honeyeater, Striated Pardalote, Silvereye, Red-browed Firetail, Olive-backed Oriole, Pied Butcherbird and Pied Currawong.

Those wishing to search for three of Cooloola's most notable birds — Ground Parrot, Eastern Grass Owl and Southern Emu-wren — should visit the northern part of the Noosa Plain, south-west of Freshwater Lake. Ground Parrots and Southern Emu-wrens are regularly reported from the vicinity of Teewah Creek; Emu-wrens have also been observed at the foot of Mt Bilewilam, just north of the Gympie to Rainbow Beach road.

Access to the southern section of Cooloola National Park is somewhat restricted. If you own a four-wheel-drive vehicle you can travel south along the ocean beach from Freshwater Lake towards the mouth of the Noosa River, then cross the river at Tewantin where there is a vehicular ferry. Lake Como (Harry Springs Hut) and Lake Cootharaba (Boreen Point), on the park's south-western boundary, are accessible via the road that links Gympie, Kin Kin and Pomona; a four-wheel-drive is desirable if you wish to visit Lake Como. There is an information centre, a 500 m circular walking track (which includes a boardwalk through a patch of mangroves) and a bird-observation hide at the north-western end of Lake Cootharaba, near the mouth of Kin Kin Creek. There is no road access to this area; the information centre can be reached via a 7 km walking track from Elanda Point, or by boat from Tewantin or Boreen Point.

Noosa National Park

This small park (432 ha), situated a kilometre or so east of the bustling resort town of Noosa Heads, is exceedingly popular — on average more than two thousand people visit the reserve on Saturdays and Sundays. Nevertheless it is a good place for birds (amazingly, more than 150 species have been recorded), although clearly you should go there during the week.

There is a picnic ground just inside the park entrance, and from the carpark several short walking tracks lead through rainforest to the centre of the reserve. Australian Brush-turkeys are a common sight, and with luck you may catch a glimpse of a White-eared Monarch. Much sought-after by bird-watchers, this delightful little flycatcher is one of Noosa's resident species. Unfortunately your chances of seeing one are rather slight — it is said that there are only about four pairs in the reserve.

Noosa National Park is well known for its splendid coastal scenery, and from the 2.7 km walking track that skirts its rugged shoreline there are lovely views northwards along the Cooloola Coast. The first kilometre or so of this walk is reasonably level − a fine place to take a disabled friend to watch the sun rise over the deep blue waters of Laguna Bay.

Camping is not permitted in the reserve, but there is of course no shortage of accommodation in Noosa Heads and elsewhere along the coast. There is a youth hostel in Douglas Street, Sunshine Beach, about 3 km south of Noosa.

THE SANDSTONE GORGES

In southern Queensland, on the eastern slopes of the Great Dividing Range, water pouring from the basalt-capped tablelands has eaten through the underlying sandstone, creating a series of spectacular gorges up to 200 m deep. In these protected places − luxuriant islands surrounded by a sea of dry woodland − grow a profusion of plants, including tree and ground ferns, mosses, figs, cabbage palms and cycads. Since the permanent rock-pools within the gorges attract a wealth of wildlife, the region was once of great significance to the Aboriginals; some outstanding examples of their rock art can be found throughout the area, and Carnarvon

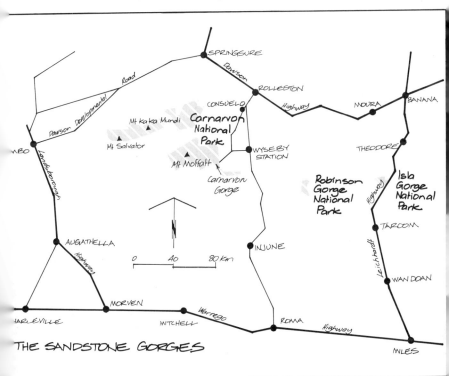

THE SANDSTONE GORGES

Gorge has one of the finest collections of stencil paintings in Australia. To protect the region's great natural beauty, the Queensland government has established a string of national parks between Springsure and Roma.

Carnarvon National Park

This massive, fragmented park covers an area of 217 000 ha and includes Carnarvon Gorge, Mt Moffatt, Mt Salvator and Mt Ka Ka Mundi. Much of the park is wilderness, and only Carnarvon Gorge has been developed. It lies about 250 km north of Roma via Injune, and about 160 km south of Springsure via Rolleston. Those approaching the gorge via Injune should turn west at Wyseby Station, about 110 km north of Injune. If you are travelling via Rolleston, turn off at Consuelo Road about 15 km south of the town. Both roads into the park are unsealed and may become impassable for weeks following heavy rain. It would be wise to check conditions in advance by contacting either the Queensland National Parks and Wildlife Service at Rockhampton, or the Carnarvon Gorge Oasis Lodge. In any case visitors are always advised to carry extra food.

Near the gorge entrance there is an information centre together with a very pleasant camping area offering shady sites among the ancient cycads. Cold-water showers are provided, but there is no power and generators are not permitted. The park is very popular and sites should be booked two or three months ahead; it is a long way to drive if you are going to find the camping area full. For a camping permit write to the ranger, Carnarvon National Park, via Rolleston, Qld 4702, enclosing a stamped, addressed envelope. For those wishing to bird-watch in comfort there is a privately owned lodge near the park entrance. The proprietors organise a special bird-watching week each year, usually in spring − for details write to the Carnarvon Gorge Oasis Lodge via Rolleston, or call at any branch of the Queensland Government Tourist Bureau. Petrol and basic food items can be purchased from the lodge.

The gorge is the main feature of the park. It extends for nearly 30 km between sandstone walls up to 200 m high and from 50 m to 400 m apart. There is a good walking track leading from the camping area along the floor of the gorge to Cathedral Cave, a distance of 10 km or so. The cave houses one of the park's most significant Aboriginal art sites and the return walk will occupy a full day, with excellent birding en route. Another of Carnarvon's main sites − aptly named the Art Gallery − features many beautiful rock stencils that are considered to be among the finest in Australia. The Art Gallery is about 6 km from the gorge entrance, but for those unable to walk far there is a third site −

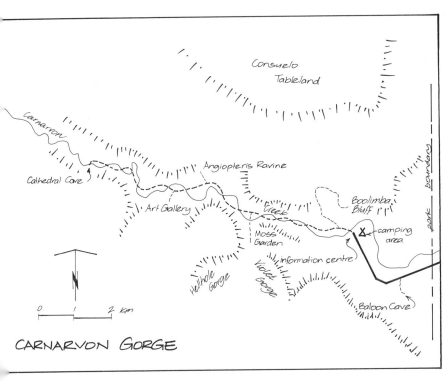

CARNARVON GORGE

Baloon Cave. Though only very small, it contains some interesting examples of stencil art and is only a few minutes stroll from the car-parking area, just inside the national park boundary. (An excellent information leaflet describing Carnarvon's Aboriginal rock art is available from the information centre.)

In addition to the main route through the gorge there are a number of short paths leading to side gullies, but elsewhere in the park there are no marked trails and only fit, experienced bush-walkers should leave the main track system. Most visitors will therefore be restricted to bird-watching around the camping area, in the gorge, and along the road in. About 170 bird species have been recorded at Carnarvon (bird lists and other publications are available from the information centre), but quite a number of these are waterbirds that only turn up occasionally.

Around the camping area the most conspicuous birds are the Laughing Kookaburras and Pied Currawongs. Like the pretty-face wallabies, they have become very tame and can be a real menace at mealtimes. Apostlebirds are also quite tame; these interesting birds are content to hop quietly around collecting scraps, whereas the kookaburras have the annoying habit of stealing the barbecued sausages from right under your nose!

Overhead, White-throated Gerygones pour out a continuous stream of silvery notes, but these small birds are very difficult to locate since they spend much of the time foraging high in the canopy above. Other frequent visitors to the camping area include Black-faced Cuckoo-shrike, Grey Shrike-thrush, White-throated Tree-creeper and Striated Pardalote, and the flowering eucalypts attract noisy flocks of Rainbow, Scaly-breasted and Little Lorikeet.

In the main gorge the vegetation is quite dense, with tall eucalypts (mainly spotted and flooded gums) growing alongside cabbage palms, she-oaks and callistemons, while cycads and grass trees form a shrub layer above an understorey of grass and bracken. In the narrow, moist side gullies the flora is more luxuriant: the Moss Garden is well known for its wealth of ferns and mosses, while Angiopteris Ravine is named after the king-fern *Angiopteris evecta*; some fine examples of this rare plant can be seen there.

The walking track through the gorge follows Carnarvon Creek for much of the time. The creek usually holds a few common waterbirds − Little Pied Cormorant, White-faced Heron, Grey Teal, Maned Duck and Dusky Moorhen − and the stealthy observer may catch a glimpse of the beautiful Azure Kingfisher. The rank vegetation along the margins of the creek holds Buff-banded Rail, Pheasant Coucal, Red-backed Fairy-wren and White-browed Scrubwren. Throughout the gorge small birds abound and honeyeaters are especially plentiful, with Noisy and Little Friarbird, Lewin's, Yellow-faced, White-throated, White-naped and Brown Honeyeater all occurring regularly. The de-lightful tiny Scarlet Honeyeater (a well-known nomad) turns up in good numbers at times, and another attractive species − the Yellow-tufted Honeyeater − is almost at the northern limit of its range here.

Many other birds can be seen in the gorge, including Fan-tailed Cuckoo, Eastern Yellow Robin, Jacky Winter, Golden Whistler, Leaden Flycatcher, Grey Fantail, Speckled Warbler, Weebill, Yellow Thornbill, Mistletoebird, Silvereye, Red-browed Firetail, Olive-backed Oriole and Figbird. Large birds are somewhat scarce, although the handsome Australian King-Parrot is quite plentiful and flocks of Yellow-tailed Black-Cockatoo sometimes visit the gorge where they feed in the she-oaks. The side gullies are worth exploring for Australian Brush-turkey and, perhaps, the fruit-eating Wonga Pigeon.

Away from the ranges the vegetation consists chiefly of open woodland with a grassy understorey. The avifauna here includes a number of species that are seldom seen in Carnarvon Gorge: Emu, Wedge-tailed Eagle, Brown Falcon, Australian Kestrel, Peaceful and Bar-shouldered Dove, Crested and, more rarely,

Squatter Pigeon (look for the latter along the road into the park), Red-winged Parrot, Pale-headed Rosella, Rainbow Bee-eater, Rufous Whistler, Grey-crowned Babbler, Varied Sittella, Brown Treecreeper, Noisy Miner, Striped, Blue-faced and White-eared Honeyeater, Double-barred and, more rarely, Plum-headed Finch, White-breasted, Black-faced and Little Woodswallow, Grey Butcherbird, Pied Butcherbird, Australian Magpie and Torresian Crow. Australian Bustards are sometimes plentiful − in 1984 about fifty were seen between the park boundary and Rolleston.

Carnarvon Gorge has spectacular scenery, many fascinating Aboriginal art sites and diverse flora and fauna. Clearly, several full and interesting days could be spent here. The best times to visit are winter and spring when the weather is cool enough for walking and the wildflowers are at their best.

Access to the more remote sections of Carnarvon National Park, including Mt Salvator, Mt Ka Ka Mundi and Mt Moffatt, is difficult. The Salvator − Ka Ka Mundi section can be reached via the Dawson Developmental Road linking Springsure with Tambo. There are no facilities, however, and if you are planning a visit you should write to the Queensland National Parks and Wildlife Service in Rockhampton for camping information.

Robinson Gorge National Park

This 8900 ha park lies about 120 km north-west of Taroom. It has many of the attractions of Carnarvon, which is not surprising since both parks have similar origins. However, Robinson Gorge has no facilities and access is difficult; only those with four-wheel-drive vehicles should contemplate a visit. From a bird-watcher's point of view there is probably nothing there that cannot be seen more easily at Carnarvon Gorge or Isla Gorge. Nevertheless, because of its inaccessibility Robinson Gorge receives few visitors, and it is therefore an ideal place to go bushwalking. Camping permits can be obtained from the Queensland National Parks and Wildlife Service in Rockhampton.

Isla Gorge National Park

This is the smallest (7800 ha) and most accessible park in the region. It is about 55 km north-east of Taroom and can be easily reached via the Leichhardt Highway, which is sealed. Although it is much smaller than Carnarvon, Isla Gorge has many similar features and a sizable bird list that includes many of the species mentioned earlier. Since the park is only 200 km or so from the coast, those travelling through Queensland via the Bruce Highway may care to spend a night or two here. Camping is allowed (again write to the Queensland National Parks and Wildlife Service in Rockhampton for a permit), but there are no facilities.

EUNGELLA AND THE WHITSUNDAY COAST

Along Queensland's central coast there are no rainforest-clad mountain ranges plunging dramatically right to the water's edge, as there are between Cairns and Cooktown. But the region does have its attractions, in particular Eungella National Park and the Whitsunday Coast.

Eungella National Park

This large reserve (49 654 ha) protects an isolated tract of rainforest in the Clarke Range, about 80 km west of Mackay. Most of the park is a rugged wilderness accessible only to experienced bushwalkers. The southern section, however, between the small township of Eungella and the Broken River, offers an extensive network of walking tracks and a short nature trail. Camping is permitted at a delightful spot on the banks of Broken River, 6 km south of Eungella township. Toilets and cold-water showers are provided (there is no power), and caravans are allowed. If you own a large caravan you may have difficulty getting to Eungella (the last section of the road leading to the township is very steep and narrow). If this is the case, you can make use of a caravan park in Finch Hatton, at the foot of the range. The national park headquarters are located near the camping ground; bird lists, a walking track guide and camping permits are available from the ranger. For those not wishing to camp in the reserve there is hotel accommodation at Eungella township. The nearest youth hostel is at Mackay.

Many of the birds that inhabit the rainforests north of Townsville — Southern Cassowary, Double-eyed Fig-Parrot, Grey-headed Robin, Bower's Shrike-thrush, Yellow-breasted Boatbill, Pied Monarch, Chowchilla, Macleay's Honeyeater, Golden Bowerbird, Tooth-billed Catbird and Victoria's Riflebird, for example — do not occur at Eungella. Indeed the park's avifauna is somewhat impoverished, possibly because of its isolation. Nevertheless serious students at least will find this an interesting region, for there is still much to be learnt about its birdlife. The Eungella Honeyeater, for instance, has only recently been described.

Although a few species can be seen quite readily around the camping and picnic areas — Australian Brush-turkey, Laughing Kookaburra, Pied Butcherbird, Pied Currawong — bird-watchers will find the park's two main walking tracks considerably more rewarding. Both tracks commence at the picnic ground near the Broken River bridge. One follows the Eungella to Broken River road in a northerly direction, while the other runs eastwards along the banks of the river. The track to Eungella township passes through a patch of superb rainforest, with tall groves of piccabeen palms and lofty tulip oaks festooned with epiphytic ferns and

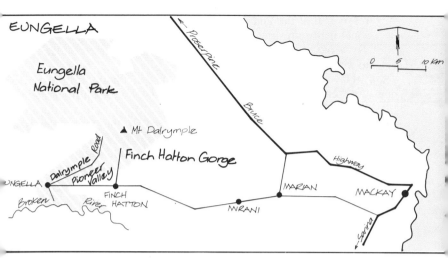

orchids. Along the way there are numerous lookouts offering fine views over Pioneer Valley, the floor of which lies some 1000 m below. This section of the park is quite good for birds, and visitors can expect to see many of the following: Superb and Wompoo Fruit-Dove, Topknot Pigeon, Brown Cuckoo-Dove (usually common along the road between Eungella township and Broken River), Australian King-Parrot, Crimson Rosella, Fan-tailed Cuckoo, Noisy Pitta, Eastern Yellow Robin, Little Shrike-thrush, Black-faced (summer) and Spectacled Monarch, Grey Fantail, Eastern Whipbird, Large-billed Scrubwren, White-browed Scrubwren, Brown Gerygone, Lewin's Honeyeater, Red-browed Firetail, Figbird and Regent Bowerbird. The striking black and gold male bowerbirds are surprisingly difficult to locate in the rainforest, but during the winter months they often visit gardens in Eungella township.

The Broken River track follows the river for about 8 km to Crediton Creek, providing access to several deep pools where the quiet observer has a good chance of seeing one of the curiosities of the animal world — the platypus. These odd creatures are quite plentiful at Eungella and are regularly seen in the early morning and late afternoon at Conical Pool, a short distance from the picnic area. A section of the track leading to the pool, although not sealed, is quite wide and level — a good place to take a disabled person for a walk through the rainforest. Azure Kingfishers frequent the river while four summer migrants, Common Koel, Channel-billed Cuckoo, Dollarbird and Cicadabird, favour the riverside vegetation.

Since there are about 20 km of walking tracks in Eungella National Park, several very full days could be spent exploring the reserve. If at the end of one of your walks you feel the need for some light refreshment, pay a visit to the kiosk at Broken River. Try a piece of Eungella mud cake − it tastes much better than its name suggests!

Having seen something of Eungella's southern section, bird-watchers may care to visit the following areas a little further afield. **Dalrymple Road:** This narrow, unsealed track runs northwards from Eungella township along the top of the range towards Mt Dalrymple (1280 m). It passes through dense forest − a good place to look for the Eungella Honeyeater and other rainforest species. About 5 km from Eungella there is a lookout with picnic facilities.

Pioneer Valley: Most of the original vegetation in this picturesque valley has been cleared for sugar cane, but it is still a pleasant place to go bird-watching. Pheasant Coucal, White-rumped Swift-let, Blue-winged Kookaburra, Forest Kingfisher, Rainbow Bee-eater, Chestnut-breasted Mannikin, Spangled Drongo and White-breasted Woodswallow can be seen along the roads, while the larger creeks hold waterbirds such as Wandering and Plumed Whistling-Duck, Buff-banded Rail and Azure Kingfisher. Pacific Bazas are said to be common in the valley.

Finch Hatton Gorge: Lies about 10 km north of the township of Finch Hatton, on the south-eastern boundary of the rugged northern section of Eungella National Park. The road leading to the gorge is very rough, and unsuitable for conventional vehicles. A small camping area with toilets and fireplaces, but no other facilities, is located near the entrance to the gorge. From the camping ground two short walking tracks provide access to some delightful creek and waterfall scenery, and for experienced bush-walkers there is a rough track to the top of Mt Dalrymple.

Although most people visit the region during the relatively dry winter months (May to September), the rainforest is undoubtedly at its best in the wet. However, since Eungella is an Aboriginal word meaning 'mountain of the mists', visitors can expect damp conditions (and plenty of leeches!) at any time of the year. If you are in the area between December and March keep an eye open for Buff-breasted Paradise-Kingfishers − this beautiful bird was sighted near the camping ground in Finch Hatton Gorge in 1981, and again in 1984.

The Whitsunday Coast

One of the delightful things about taking a holiday on the central coast of Queensland is that you can be standing soaking wet in the rainforest at Eungella one day, and basking in the tropical sun at Shute Harbour the next. The Whitsunday Coast, to the east of Proserpine, has all the attractions a travel agent could wish for −

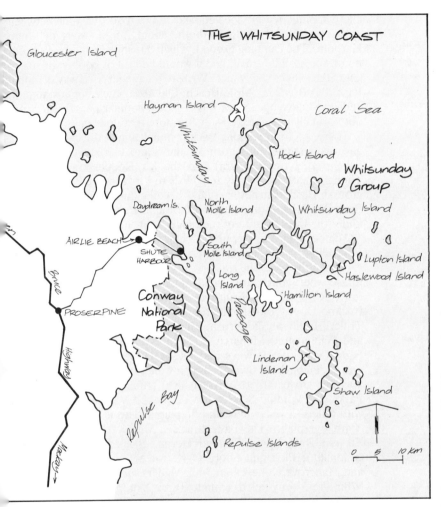

THE WHITSUNDAY COAST

Gloucester Island

Hayman Island

Coral Sea

Whitsunday

Hook Island

Whitsunday Group

North Molle Island

Daydream Is.

Whitsunday Island

AIRLIE BEACH

SHUTE HARBOUR

South Molle Island

Lupton Island

Haslewood Island

Long Island

Conway National Park

PROSERPINE

Hamilton Island

Bruce Highway

Passage

Lindeman Island

Shaw Island

Repulse Bay

Mackay Highway

Repulse Islands

0   5   10 km

emerald islands, clear blue coral seas, pure white silica beaches. Not surprisingly, the area draws thousands of visitors each year.

Airlie Beach, the main tourist centre, has a wealth of accommodation including motels, apartment blocks (fortunately there are no multi-storey monstrosities here, as there are along the Gold Coast), and numerous caravan parks. During the main tourist season (May to August) the caravan parks are usually crowded but, despite its popularity, the region has some very peaceful spots.

Conway National Park: Protects 23 800 ha of the mainland facing the Whitsunday Passage. Only the northern section between Airlie Beach and Shute Harbour is accessible. The ranger's office and camping area are located next to the road that runs between Airlie Beach and Shute Harbour, about 2.5 km west of Shute Harbour. The camping ground, which has showers and toilets but no power, is quite small, and it would be best to book your site at least eight weeks in advance. Write to the ranger, Conway National Park, PO Box 332, Airlie Beach, Qld 4802, enclosing a stamped, addressed envelope. Since this is such a popular park, visitors are not normally permitted to stay for more than four days.

There is a short walking track commencing at the camping area and two longer walks north of the Shute Harbour road — the Swamp Bay track (3 km) and the Mt Rooper track (4 km). Though there are usually few birds to be seen near the camping ground, Black Butcherbirds have become quite tame and a pair of Bush Thick-knees are often to be found roosting during the day under the trees in front of the ranger's office.

The best place to go bird-watching is along the track to Swamp Bay; allow two hours for the return walk, more if you intend exploring the bay. The track passes through an area of dense vine forest where birds are usually plentiful: Orange-footed Scrub-fowl, Rose-crowned Fruit-Dove, White-headed Pigeon, Brown Cuckoo-Dove, Bar-shouldered Dove, Emerald Dove, Varied Triller, Little Shrike-thrush, Black-faced (summer), Spectacled and White-eared Monarch, Leaden Flycatcher, Rufous Fantail, Fairy Gerygone, Lewin's and Dusky Honeyeater, Olive-backed Oriole, Figbird. At Swamp Bay, a wide expanse of tidal mudflats and mangroves (there is no beach), the Queensland National Parks and Wildlife Service has developed a small camping area with toilets, a water tank and fireplaces. This is an ideal place to camp overnight. The bay attracts a variety of birds including Eastern Reef Egret, Striated Heron, Black-necked Stork (occasionally), Pied and Sooty Oystercatcher, Collared Kingfisher and Mangrove Honeyeater, while waders such as Eastern Curlew, Whimbrel, Grey-tailed Tattler, Terek Sandpiper and Bar-tailed Godwit turn up regularly during summer.

The road between Airlie Beach and Shute Harbour (a distance of about 8 km) is also quite good for bird-watching, but you will need to be out early in the morning because at other times the traffic is very heavy. Rainbow and Scaly-breasted Lorikeet, Pale-headed Rosella, Laughing Kookaburra, Forest Kingfisher, Helmeted Friarbird, Spangled Drongo and White-breasted Woodswallow occur on the outskirts of Airlie Beach, while Blue-faced Honeyeaters and Yellow-bellied Sunbirds can often be seen in the town's busy main street.

Whitsunday Group: There are more than fifty islands in the Whitsunday Group. Daydream, South Molle, Hayman and a few others are internationally famous for their tourist resorts, but most of the islands are uninhabited and many are national parks. At least two of the national park islands — Whitsunday and North Molle — have bush-camping sites with toilets and water tanks. Here visitors have an opportunity to camp in splendid isolation. Several cruise boats will transport you to and from the islands; make inquiries at Shute Harbour jetty or at the ranger's office in Conway National Park. Camping permits must be obtained from the park ranger, and since you may be alone on an island for several days it is essential that you carry an adequate first-aid kit and check the availability of water before leaving the mainland.

For those with only a day or two to spare there are many cruise launches operating from Shute Harbour. Most of the day trips, however, involve a lengthy stay at one of the resorts, and if you are at all adventurous you will find a day's sailing much more fun. Several splendid ocean-going yachts, equipped with crew, visit the uninhabited islands, where you can swim, snorkel, fish, fossick for shells or simply lie in the sun. Prices are not unreasonable — about $30 for the day, including lunch.

Many of the mainland birds inhabit the larger islands, while seabirds, although not particularly numerous, include Brown Booby and Caspian, Crested and Lesser Crested Tern. Ospreys, Brahminy Kites and White-bellied Sea-Eagles breed throughout the Whitsunday Passage, and Beach Thick-knees favour the secluded bays and mudflats. Mangrove Golden Whistlers occur on Daydream and other islands in the group.

Although the Whitsunday Coast is commercialised, it is by no means a second Gold Coast. No doubt the mudflats and mangroves have discouraged the developers; even so, it is perhaps just as well that Airlie Beach is nearly 1100 km from Brisbane.

TOWNSVILLE AND THE FAR NORTH COAST

Australia, a predominantly flat, dry country, has relatively little tropical rainforest. This exceedingly complex and diverse plant community requires rich soil, constant moisture and a warm, even temperature for its development, and suitable conditions exist only in the north-eastern corner of the continent. Here the high mountains that lie to the north of Townsville trip moisture-laden clouds rolling in from the South Pacific Ocean, bringing annual rainfalls well in excess of 2500 mm to many places along the coast. Tully, the wettest town in Australia, regularly receives more than 4500 mm per annum.

This fascinating region, incredibly rich in animal and plant life, attracts bird-watchers from all over the world. On reaching Townsville, however, some visitors may be disappointed. Tropical rainforest does not form a continuous impenetrable belt along Queensland's far north coast as is sometimes thought. In fact, although Townsville is well within the tropics it has a relatively dry climate (its average annual rainfall is less than 1200 mm), and as a result the vegetation in the vicinity of the city differs little from the open eucalypt woodlands farther south.

The most accessible upland rainforest near Townsville occurs in the Paluma – Mt Spec area, while lowland rainforest can be found on the coastal plains north of Ingham – at Mission Beach for example. Sadly, however, much of the original vegetation in the region has been cleared, particularly on the lowlands between Tully and Cairns, and many of the remaining patches of forest are being logged by the timber industry.

The destruction of so much irreplaceable rainforest is heartbreaking to those who appreciate the value of this wonderfully luxuriant habitat. Nevertheless, despite gross over-exploitation of its natural resources, the far north coast still has a great deal to offer the bird-watcher.

Townsville

Situated some 1480 km north of Brisbane via the Bruce Highway, Townsville is the largest tropical city in Australia. It is an ideal place for a winter holiday (from May to September the average maximum temperature is a very comfortable 25 degrees C), and a convenient starting-point for an extended tour of Queensland's far north coast.

Townsville has an international airport, numerous rental car outlets and ample accommodation including motels, hotels, guest houses and at least seven caravan parks. The nearest youth hostel is on Magnetic Island, about 8 km from the city across Cleveland Bay.

The scenery around Townsville is somewhat unimpressive; indeed, apart from Magnetic Island there is little here to compare with the countryside farther north. There are nonetheless many excellent places to go birding near the city.

Townsville Town Common Environmental Park: Well known to bird-watchers throughout the world, this splendid 3248 ha environmental park has been likened to the Camargue in southern France and Slimbridge in England. It is one of the best places in Australia for waterbirds – a site of international importance.

During the wet season (December to March) a number of interesting species breed in the reserve – Black-necked Stork, Magpie Goose, Wandering Whistling-Duck, White-browed Crake, Bush-hen, Brolga and Comb-crested Jacana. At the end of the breeding season, when the swamp waters begin to recede, the Magpie Geese and Brolgas form dense flocks, providing visitors with magnificent opportunities for nature photography.

As the dry season progresses and swamps elsewhere in the

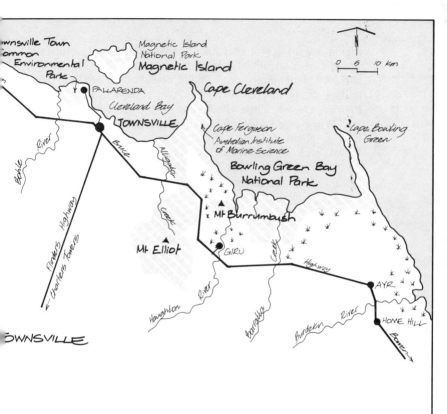

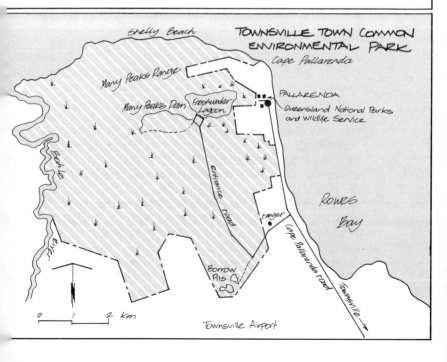

region dry up, a rich assortment of waterbirds seek refuge on the Town Common until finally it too becomes dry. Between April and July, depending on conditions, you should have little difficulty finding many of the following: Australasian Grebe, Australian Pelican, Darter, Little Black and Little Pied Cormorant, Pacific and White-faced Heron, Great, Little and Intermediate Egret, Rufous Night Heron, Glossy, Sacred and Straw-necked Ibis, Royal and Yellow-billed Spoonbill, Plumed Whistling-Duck, Black Swan, Pacific Black and Maned Duck, Grey Teal, Hard-head, Cotton and Green Pygmy-Goose, Buff-banded Rail, Masked Lapwing, Red-kneed Dotterel, Black-fronted Plover, Black-winged Stilt and Whiskered, Gull-billed and Caspian Tern.

The majority of these species occur in suitable habitat throughout the reserve, but several areas in particular are worth visiting.

Barramundi Pools: Ask the ranger for directions to this secluded spot, a favoured haunt of the rarely seen but much sought-after Little Kingfisher. Early morning is the best time of day to look for the kingfisher.

The Borrow Pits: Lie in the southern section of the park, adjacent to Townsville Airport. Cotton Pygmy-Goose and Comb-crested Jacana are two notable species that you will almost certainly find here, and a pair of Bush Thick-knees are known to frequent the shallow grassy depression to the right of the track leading to the pits.

Many Peaks Dam: Is in the northern part of the reserve, just west of Pallarenda. To get there, simply follow the entrance road towards Freshwater Lagoon and stop at the carpark near the dam wall.

A trip to the dam should prove a highlight during your visit to the Town Common. It is usually teeming with birdlife: pelicans, Darters, cormorants, herons, egrets, Black-necked Storks, ibis, spoonbills, waterfowl, Brolgas and terns can be seen with ease from the walking track running along the dam wall, west of the carpark. If possible get there early in the day, and remember to take your camera.

Although it is known chiefly for its wetlands, the Town Common also has some extensive patches of eucalypt woodland as well as remnants of rainforest and areas of mangrove. Indeed, one of the park's great attractions is its rich diversity of habitats. Many different bush birds have been recorded in the reserve and the woodlands in particular hold a wide variety of species including Peaceful Dove, Rainbow Lorikeet (especially when the eucalypts are in flower), Pale-headed Rosella, Brush Cuckoo (a common summer visitor), Common Koel (summer), Channel-billed Cuckoo (summer), Pheasant Coucal, Barking Owl, Large-tailed Nightjar, Blue-winged Kookaburra, Forest Kingfisher, Rainbow

Bee-eater, Dollarbird (summer), White-bellied Cuckoo-shrike, Varied Triller, Lemon-bellied and Leaden Flycatcher, Rufous Whistler, Red-backed Fairy-wren, Helmeted Friarbird, Blue-faced, Yellow, White-throated, Brown, Brown-backed and Dusky Honeyeater, Yellow-bellied Sunbird, Mistletoebird, Striated Pardalote, Double-barred Finch, Olive-backed Oriole, Figbird, Spangled Drongo, Great Bowerbird, White-breasted Woodswallow and Pied Butcherbird.

Having explored the woodlands, visitors may care to venture into the mangroves lining the Bohle River. Here you may find a number of species that occur nowhere else in the park — Great-billed Heron, Striated Heron, Collared Kingfisher, Shining Fly-catcher and Mangrove Gerygone. And in some of the more densely vegetated gullies of the Many Peaks Range, north-west of Pallarenda, you could see rainforest-dwellers such as Australian Brush-turkey, Rose-crowned Fruit-Dove, Brown Cuckoo-Dove, Emerald Dove, Little Shrike-thrush, White-eared Monarch (a regular winter visitor), Fairy Gerygone and Yellow-spotted Honeyeater.

Townsville Town Common is certainly an outstanding ornitho-logical site. Nearly two hundred and fifty species have been recorded in the reserve and in addition to those birds already listed visitors have a good chance of seeing at least a few of the following: Eastern Reef Egret (often at Shelly Beach), Black Bittern, Osprey (Shelly Beach is a good spot for this handsome raptor), Black and Brahminy Kite, Brown Goshawk, White-bellied Sea-Eagle, Peregrine Falcon, Brown Quail, Red-backed Button-quail, Sarus Crane (seen occasionally among the Brolgas), Aus-tralian Bustard (a regular winter visitor), Beach Thick-knee (an-other inhabitant of Shelly Beach), Pied Oystercatcher, Grey, Lesser Golden, Mongolian and Large Sand Plover (in small numbers during summer), Eastern Curlew (summer), Whimbrel (summer), Grey-tailed Tattler (summer), Greenshank (summer), Terek Sandpiper (a regular summer visitor to Shelly Beach), Bar-tailed Godwit (summer), Red and Great Knot (summer), Sharp-tailed Sandpiper (summer), Red-necked Stint (summer), Aus-tralian Pratincole, White-winged Tern (a regular summer visitor), Black-naped, Little, Crested and Lesser Crested Tern, Torresian Imperial-Pigeon (a breeding summer visitor), Bar-shouldered Dove, Red-tailed Black-Cockatoo (rare, although occasionally a few turn up late in the dry season), Sulphur-crested Cockatoo, Oriental Cuckoo (summer), Singing Bushlark (abundant in open grassy areas), Tawny Grassbird (a bird of the grasslands and swamp margins), Golden-headed Cisticola, Large-billed Gery-gone, Noisy and Little Friarbird (both species usually appear late in the dry season), Rufous-throated Honeyeater (an occasional visitor), Silvereye and Chestnut-breasted Mannikin.

The Town Common is about 3 km north-west of Townsville and is readily accessible via the Cape Pallarenda road. Park information can be obtained from the resident ranger, or from the Queensland National Parks and Wildlife Service in Marlow Street, Pallarenda. Camping is not permitted.

Magnetic Island: About half of this rugged, beautiful, 5000 ha continental island is a national park; the remainder is privately owned and extensively developed for tourism. The national park itself, although largely undeveloped, has about 22 km of walking tracks that make it an ideal place to go hiking. Camping is not permitted, but there is of course no shortage of accommodation outside the park boundary.

The island's vegetation, like that on the neighbouring mainland, consists chiefly of open eucalypt woodland while in some of the deeper gullies there are pockets of depauperate rainforest. On the rocky headlands hoop pines grow among the huge granite boulders, and graceful casuarinas fringe the island's many secluded beaches.

Although Magnetic Island boasts a rich avifauna (about 170 species have been recorded there), it probably has no birds that cannot be seen in and around Townsville. Nevertheless a trip to this delightful spot is highly recommended. There is a regular passenger ferry service from Townsville; there is also a vehicular ferry, but if you plan to go there for only a day or two it would be cheaper to hire a car on the island. Rental cars can be booked in advance at the ferry terminal in Townsville.

On the way over to the island keep a watch for seabirds such as Brown Boobies, frigatebirds and various species of tern.

Bowling Green Bay National Park: Covering almost 56 000 ha, this large reserve to the east of Townsville stretches from Cape Cleveland to Cape Bowling Green and includes the former Mt Elliot National Park. Much of the area is inaccessible, but the following spots can be reached quite readily from the Bruce Highway.

Cape Cleveland: Protecting an area of rugged granite hills, swamps and mangroves, this section of the park is accessible via the road to the Australian Institute of Marine Science at Cape Ferguson. To get there, turn off the Bruce Highway at the AIMS sign about 32 km south-east of Townsville. There are no facilities at Cape Cleveland and camping is not permitted.

This stretch of the coast contains much valuable waterbird habitat, but more importantly perhaps it is one of the best places in Australia for Zitting Cisticola. In Queensland, this somewhat elusive species is known only from a few isolated localities along the east coast and around the Gulf of Carpentaria. Visitors to Townsville, however, have a reasonable chance of seeing the bird since it is said to be common in the grassy country fringing the coastal saltmarshes between Ayr and Cape Cleveland. (Bear in mind that the Golden-headed Cisticola also occurs in the Cape Cleveland – Ayr district. The two species are very difficult to separate in the field, except during the breeding season – December to April – when with experience you can identify a male Zitting Cisticola by his call.)

Mt Elliot: Lies to the west of the Bruce Highway, between Townsville and Ayr. The vegetation on the slopes of the mountain consists mainly of open eucalypt forest, but in sheltered spots there are patches of tropical rainforest – the southernmost occurrence of this habitat in North Queensland. As might be expected, the birdlife is rich and varied.

To reach this section of the park, turn off the Bruce Highway about 25 km south-east of Townsville. There is a camping and picnic area on the banks of Alligator Creek some 7 km from the turn-off. The creek falls from the heights of Mt Elliot (1234 m) in a series of beautiful cascades, and its rock-pools provide excellent swimming during the humid summer months.

Mt Burrumbush: This massive granite outcrop, also known as the Feltham Cone, can be clearly seen from the Bruce Highway at a point some 40 km south-east of Townsville.

Although there are no facilities in this area of the park, and the mountain can only be reached on foot, it is worth a visit because the low-lying saltmarsh between .the highway and the reserve boundary is a favoured haunt of the Brolga. Large numbers of these lovely long-legged birds can usually be seen here. Have your camera ready – with luck you may see them performing their elaborate dancing displays.

Paluma, Mt Spec – Crystal Creek National Park and Jourama Falls National Park

As you drive along the Bruce Highway north of Townsville the countryside becomes increasingly luxuriant and mountainous. Some of the region's best birding areas lie ahead, including Hinchinbrook Island, Mission Beach and Dunk Island. Before reaching Ingham, however, it is well worth making short detours to several places just west of the highway.

Paluma: Is situated in dense rainforest at the northern end of the Paluma Range, more than 900 m above sea level. To reach this splendid area, turn off the Bruce Highway about 66 km north-west of Townsville and continue along the steep, winding Paluma road for 18 km or so. En route you will notice a distinct change in the vegetation as the elevation increases, and from the mountain road there are wonderful views over the coastal plains below.

Paluma consists of a collection of small cottages, most of which belong to Townsville residents who use them as weekend retreats during the oppressive summer months (the temperature on the mountain can be as much as 10 degrees C cooler than at sea level). Surprising as it may seem, for the bird-watcher one of the main attractions here is the tea-house. It is probably the only place in North Queensland where you can sit in a delightful tropical garden savouring delicious home-made scones and cream while enjoying (if that is the right word) the attentions of a host of normally elusive rainforest birds.

Pale-yellow Robin, Little Shrike-thrush, Lewin's and Dusky Honeyeater, Spotted Catbird and Victoria's Riflebird are just a few of the species that you can see without moving from your seat. Another is the Macleay's Honeyeater. Usually shy and unobtrusive, it is perhaps the most notable bird in the tea-house garden; certainly it is the most numerous. As a rule, before you've had time to pour your tea, the honeyeaters — masses of them — emerge from the surrounding forest and jostle with one another for a place at your table like sparrows squabbling over a piece of bread. Be warned — with so many birds about it would pay to keep the milk covered!

Having seen, fed and possibly photographed a Macleay's Honeyeater (and with luck some of the other species mentioned), you will find the rainforest around Paluma holds an abundance of sought-after birds, including many that are at or very near the southern limit of their range: Southern Cassowary, Grey-headed Robin, Grey Whistler, Bower's Shrike-thrush, Yellow-breasted Boatbill, Pied Monarch, Chowchilla, Australian Fernwren, Mountain Thornbill, Bridled Honeyeater, Golden Bowerbird and Tooth-billed Catbird.

At least a few of these species can be observed readily enough in and around the township, although if you have time a trip along the Paluma Dam road should prove more rewarding. Since this road is unsealed, it may become impassable after heavy rain; ask one of the local residents about its condition before setting out. Some of the birds you may see while driving to the dam include Pacific Baza, Grey Goshawk, Australian Brush-turkey, Superb, Rose-crowned and Wompoo Fruit-Dove, Topknot and White-headed Pigeon, Brown Cuckoo-Dove, Emerald Dove, Double-eyed Fig-Parrot (rather rare), Australian King-Parrot, Crimson Rosella, Brush Cuckoo (summer), Shining Bronze-Cuckoo, Lesser Sooty Owl (rather rare), Large-tailed Nightjar, Azure and Little Kingfisher, Noisy Pitta, Yellow-eyed Cuckoo-shrike, Varied Triller, White's Thrush, Eastern Yellow Robin, Golden Whistler, Black-faced Monarch (summer), Spectacled Monarch, Rufous Fantail (summer), Eastern Whipbird, Large-billed and Yellow-throated Scrubwren, Brown Gerygone, Little Tree-

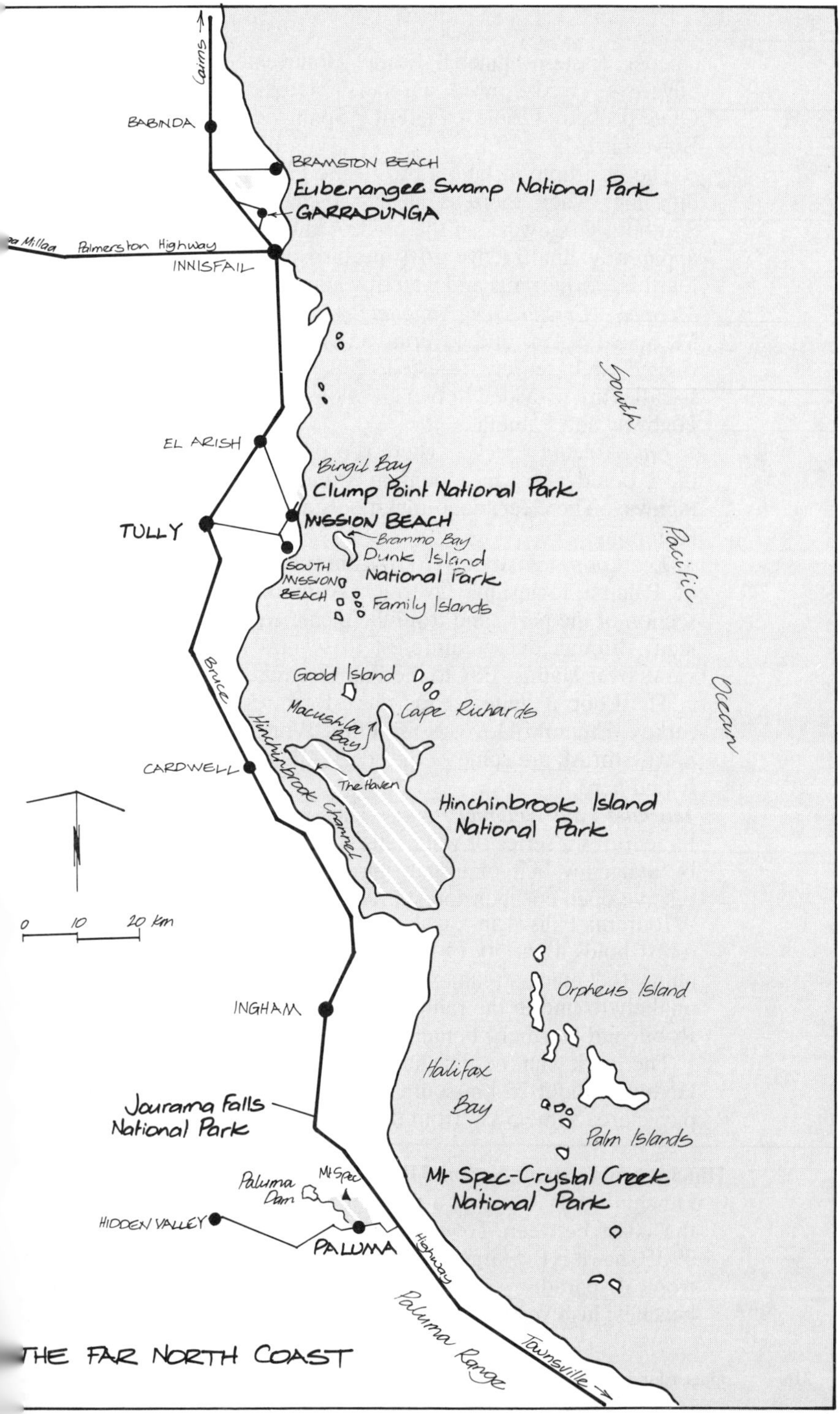
Cairns
BABINDA
BRAMSTON BEACH
Eubenangee Swamp National Park
GARRADUNGA
Palmerston Highway
INNISFAIL
South Pacific Ocean
EL ARISH
Bingil Bay
Clump Point National Park
MISSION BEACH
TULLY
Brammo Bay
Dunk Island National Park
SOUTH MISSION BEACH
Family Islands
Goold Island
Cape Richards
Macushla Bay
Bruce
Hinchinbrook Channel
The Haven
Hinchinbrook Island National Park
CARDWELL
N
0 10 20 km
INGHAM
Orpheus Island
Halifax Bay
Palm Islands
Jourama Falls National Park
Mt Spec-Crystal Creek National Park
Mt Spec
Paluma Dam
HIDDEN VALLEY
PALUMA
Highway
Paluma Range
Townsville
THE FAR NORTH COAST

creeper, Eastern Spinebill, Scarlet Honeyeater, Spotted Pardalote, Silvereye, Red-browed Firetail, Metallic Starling (summer), Olive-backed Oriole, Figbird, Spangled Drongo and Satin Bowerbird.

The best time to take a trip to the Paluma Dam is in the early morning, when there is always a chance that you will see a Southern Cassowary on the road. Although extensive, the dam is apparently unattractive to waterbirds, but occasionally grebes, Darters, cormorants and waterfowl are recorded there.

Mt Spec — Crystal Creek National Park: Stretching from Paluma to Mt Spec (991 m) and covering an area of 7224 ha, this reserve is rugged and densely forested. Much of it is inaccessible, but facilities are provided in two areas on the road between the Bruce Highway and Paluma.

Little Crystal Creek: There is a picnic area here on the banks of a boulder-strewn mountain stream, about 4 km from the highway. The clear, deep rock-pools along the creek are ideal for swimming.

The Loop: Is about 17 km from the highway, on the outskirts of Paluma township. Overnight camping is permitted in this section of the park, and from the picnic area a short walking track leads through dense rainforest to several lookouts offering fine views over Halifax Bay to the Palm Islands.

The Loop is quite a good place for birds — Australian Brush-turkey, Emerald Dove, Noisy Pitta, White's Thrush and Bower's Shrike-thrush are some of the species that you will almost certainly find here.

Jourama Falls National Park: This delightful small park of 1070 ha features a series of waterfalls, cascades and rock-pools fringed by a narrow belt of lush tropical vegetation. Elsewhere in the reserve open eucalypt forest predominates.

Jourama Falls is an excellent place to camp overnight. The open forest holds a variety of bush birds, and in the dense vegetation lining the main stream you may see two species that you are unlikely to find in the rainforest around Paluma — White-browed Robin and Northern Fantail.

The park can be reached by turning west from the Bruce Highway about 25 km south of Ingham. There is a camping and picnic area some 5 km from the turn-off.

Hinchinbrook Island National Park

Hinchinbrook is one of a number of continental islands lying off the coast between Townsville and Cairns. Covering an area of 39 350 ha, it is the largest island national park in Australia — a true tropical paradise with numerous secluded, casuarina-fringed beaches, lush vegetation, and waterfalls tumbling from mountains rising to over 1000 m. When seen from the mainland across the narrow, mangrove-choked Hinchinbrook Channel, this exceedingly beautiful reserve looks very inviting indeed, especially to bird-watchers eager to explore its rainforest-covered slopes. However, the island is mostly an undeveloped wilderness and only experienced bushwalkers should attempt to penetrate its rugged interior.

Nevertheless Hinchinbrook is a superb place for a birding holiday, although clearly the more time you can spend there the better. If you are adventurous and self-sufficient, stay for a week or so at one of the camping grounds provided. These are located at The Haven and Macushla Bay; park information and camping permits can be obtained from the Queensland National Parks and Wildlife Service in Pallarenda (Townsville), Cairns or Cardwell. Those not wishing to camp can obtain accommodation at the small, privately owned resort at Cape Richards, on the north-eastern tip of the island. Bookings can be made at any branch of the Queensland Government Tourist Bureau.

If you do not have time for an extended stay, you can see a little of what Hinchinbrook has to offer by taking a day trip from Cardwell to Cape Richards. This will at least give you a few hours to explore the area immediately south of the resort. Those planning to travel further north on the mainland, however, will find a day on Dunk Island much more rewarding. It too has rainforests, mangroves, beaches and a wide variety of birds, but because Dunk is small (730 ha) you can walk around it at a leisurely pace yet still have time to enjoy its many attractions.

Tully and beyond

Since European settlement, large tracts of beautiful rainforest on the lowlands north of Tully have been destroyed. Today the countryside is dominated by canefields and banana plantations, and the remaining isolated patches of forest are largely unprotected (there are only a few small national parks in the area) and threatened by residential development. At Mission Beach land sales are booming; everyone, it seems, wants a place in the sun, a plot of rainforest with a view of the sea.

In spite of this, the coastal strip between Tully and Cairns supports a remarkably rich avifauna. For example, over three hundred species of birds have been recorded in the Innisfail district, the most notable being Southern Cassowary, Great-billed Heron, Black Bittern, Grey Goshawk, Red Goshawk, Orange-footed Scrubfowl, King Quail, Red-necked and White-browed Crake, Bush-hen, Beach Thick-knee, Superb, Rose-crowned and Wompoo Fruit-Dove, Torresian Imperial-Pigeon, Topknot and White-headed Pigeon, Double-eyed Fig-Parrot, Rufous and Eastern Grass Owl, Papuan Frogmouth, Large-tailed Nightjar,

White-rumped Swiftlet, Little Kingfisher, Buff-breasted Paradise-Kingfisher, Noisy Pitta, Barn Swallow, Yellow-eyed Cuckoo-shrike, Mangrove Robin, Grey Whistler, Yellow-breasted Boat-bill, White-eared and Pied Monarch, Shining Flycatcher, Macleay's, Yellow-spotted, Graceful, Varied, Yellow and Brown-backed Honeyeater, Crimson Finch, Metallic Starling, Yellow Oriole, Victoria's Riflebird and Black Butcherbird.

There is a wealth of good birding spots along this stretch of the coast; indeed, it would be possible to spend a week or more exploring the area. The following in particular warrant a place on your itinerary.

Mission Beach: Is *the* place to go if you are looking for a Southern Cassowary. These large, flightless rainforest-dwellers are in fact something of a tourist attraction here. Road signs in the area warn motorists to beware of cassowaries crossing ahead, and the Beachcomber Caravan Park at South Mission Beach is often visited by a tame male bird, causing considerable consternation among the campers (especially the younger ones − a fully grown cassowary stands some 2 m tall).

If you are not fortunate enough to see one of these fine birds strolling past your caravan window, try the state forest on the road between South Mission Beach and Tully (ask one of the local residents for directions). Here, along the forestry tracks that cut through a superb patch of fan palms, you will find plenty of evidence of cassowaries − piles of droppings containing the undigested remains of rainforest fruits. The birds themselves are somewhat elusive. Considering their size, they are surprisingly nimble-footed, and on hearing an intruder they usually slip quietly away unnoticed. If possible, drive out to the forest early in the day and park along one of the access tracks. If you remain silent a cassowary will almost certainly appear.

Mission Beach has motels, holiday units and several caravan parks, and there is a youth hostel just north of the township on the Bingil Bay road.

Clump Point National Park: Is a small reserve (301 ha) about 3 km north of Mission Beach, overlooking Bingil Bay. There are no facilities here and camping is not permitted, but there is a walking track leading through rainforest to the top of Bicton Hill.

On a clear day the views from the top of the hill are magnificent, and the rainforest holds a variety of birds such as Emerald Dove, Little Shrike-thrush, Spectacled Monarch, Rufous Fantail (winter), Large-billed Scrubwren, Yellow-spotted and Graceful Honeyeater, Spotted Catbird, Victoria's Riflebird and Black Butcherbird.

Dunk Island National Park: Is one of the loveliest small islands off the North Queensland coast. The author E. J. Banfield lived on Dunk with his wife from 1897 until his death in 1923, and in his best-selling book *The Confessions of a Beachcomber* he gives a mouth-watering account of life on this tropical paradise. It makes fascinating reading since it contains a wealth of detail about the island's rich flora and fauna.

Unlike so much of the mainland, Dunk has changed little during the past hundred years or so and consequently it is a splendid place to go bird-watching. Although you cannot camp on the island, there is a regular launch service from the Clump Point jetty and a day on Dunk should prove highly rewarding. For those with the time (and money), accommodation is available at a small resort situated on the shores of beautiful Brammo Bay. Bookings can be made at any branch of the Queensland Government Tourist Bureau.

From the resort, a well-graded walking track leads to the summit of Mt Koo-tal-oo (264 m) then down through Palm Grove to Coconut Bay. From here it is an easy walk back to the resort along the western edge of the island. The round trip is about 7 km and along the way visitors should see numerous birds including Noisy Pittas on the slopes behind the resort, Beach Thick-knees near the mangroves at the eastern end of Coconut Bay, and Orange-footed Scrubfowls along the track between the bay and the airstrip.

Dunk offers some of the best rainforest walking in North Queensland. Palm Grove is especially interesting since here there are many giant cauliflorous trees (trees in which the flowers and fruits develop from the trunk − a phenomenon found only in tropical rainforest) growing right beside the main walking track.

Garradunga: This tiny township to the north of Innisfail might seem an unlikely place for birds; there is no rainforest here, only canefields stretching as far as the eye can see.

Garradunga, however, merits a mention because it is the best place in the region for Barn Swallow, a species that visits Australia during the summer months. At first glance you could easily confuse a Barn Swallow with the more common and widespread Welcome Swallow, but when perched the former can be readily identified by the narrow band of blue-black feathers separating its chestnut throat from its white underparts.

Over the past ten years or so small numbers of Barn Swallows have been regularly recorded at Garradunga. Usually they can be found sitting on power lines in the vicinity of the railway station, near the hotel. You may not of course be lucky enough to see them, but if you are in the area during summer (December and January are the best months to look for the swallows), it would certainly be worth making a short detour to the township.

Garradunga is about 10 km north of Innisfail and is readily accessible from the Bruce Highway.

Eubenangee Swamp National Park: Covers an area of 1520 ha and lies to the east of the Bruce Highway between Innisfail and Babinda. The reserve, an important waterbird refuge, protects a series of coastal swamps and lagoons fringed with melaleucas and rainforest. Some of the more interesting birds that have been recorded here include Great-billed Heron, Black Bittern, Wandering Whistling-Duck, King Quail, White-browed Crake, Bush-hen and White-winged Tern.

A boardwalk has been constructed, enabling visitors to observe the birdlife. However, since access is somewhat difficult it would be wise to contact the Queensland National Parks and Wildlife Service before visiting the reserve. Camping is not permitted.

CAIRNS AND THE ATHERTON TABLELAND

For the bird-watcher the Cairns − Atherton Tableland area is a very exciting region indeed; it is an avian paradise, one of the best places in Australia for an ornithological holiday. Here, within a relatively small area, there is a wide range of habitats − lowland and upland tropical rainforest, open forest, mangroves, mudflats, rivers, lakes, swamps, suburban parks and agricultural land.

The region's diverse and exceedingly rich avifauna includes a large number of species that are confined to the far north of Queensland: Southern Cassowary, Red-necked Crake, Papuan Frogmouth, Grey-headed Robin, Bower's Shrike-thrush, Yellow-breasted Boatbill, Pied Monarch, Chowchilla, Australian Fernwren, Atherton Scrubwren, Mountain Thornbill, Macleay's, Yellow-spotted, Graceful, Bridled, Varied and Brown-backed Honeyeater, Blue-faced Finch, Golden Bowerbird, Tooth-billed and Spotted Catbird, and Victoria's Riflebird. In addition, visitors have a good chance of seeing many highly sought-after species such as Great-billed Heron, White-browed Crake, Bush-hen, Sarus Crane, Superb, Rose-crowned and Wompoo Fruit-Dove, Double-eyed Fig-Parrot, Lesser Sooty Owl, Little Kingfisher, Buff-breasted Paradise-Kingfisher, Noisy Pitta, Mangrove and White-browed Robin, Crimson and Black-throated Finch, Metallic Starling and Yellow Oriole.

Cairns

This small but surprisingly cosmopolitan city, on the Coral Sea coast, is a convenient base for the bird-watcher. It has an international airport, good road and rail links with the south, rental car outlets, and a wide range of accommodation including an international-class hotel and numerous motels, hotels and guest houses. For those on a tight budget there are youth hostels at 67 The Esplanade, Cairns, and 28 Collins Avenue, Edge Hill, and another at Kuranda, about 23 km to the north-west. A number of

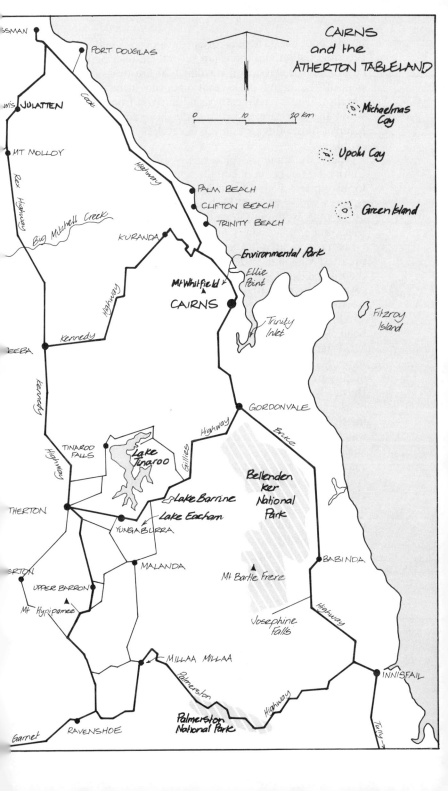

hotels and guest houses offer inexpensive bed and breakfast accommodation and there are several caravan parks close to the city, although it is worth travelling 20 km or so further north to one of the many parks that line the attractive palm-fringed beaches. The best time to visit Cairns is from May to October when the days are warm and the humidity is low; the region receives most of its rain during the cyclone season — December to April.

There are numerous places to go bird-watching in and around Cairns. If you stay in one of the northern suburbs — Clifton Beach for example — you will only have to go for an early morning stroll to see a wide variety of birds, including such sought-after species as Double-eyed Fig-Parrot. Many others — Black Kite, Bush Thick-knee, Pheasant Coucal, White-rumped Swiftlet, Tawny Grassbird, Golden-headed Cisticola, Crimson Finch, Chestnut-breasted Mannikin and White-breasted Woodswallow — frequent the canefields and can usually be found with little effort. The small swamp near the airport, beside the Captain Cook Highway, is worth a visit for waterbirds including Magpie Goose.

Although much of the original vegetation around Cairns has been cleared for sugar cane, there is a good patch of rainforest on Mt Whitfield. On the Atherton Tableland to the south-west, remnants of the dense upland rainforest that once covered much of the area are protected by a network of reserves. The Great Barrier Reef lies close to the mainland north of Cairns, and many of its sparsely vegetated coral cays are important breeding grounds for seabirds. The region warrants thorough exploration, but bird-watchers should visit the following spots before venturing further afield.

The Esplanade: Incredibly, about 170 species have been recorded along the Cairns foreshore, and there are probably few cities in the world where such a variety of birds can be seen within a few minutes walk of the main shopping centre. Waders are undoubtedly the main attraction; at least twenty-six different species regularly occur here. Although the mudflats do not support vast gatherings of waders (numbers peak at about three thousand in midsummer), compared with other sites in this country, the Cairns foreshore is readily accessible and consequently bird-watchers have an opportunity to observe many uncommon species at close range. Highlights include Grey, Lesser Golden, Mongolian, Large Sand and Oriental Plover, Ruddy Turnstone, Eastern Curlew, Whimbrel, Little Curlew, Grey-tailed and Wandering Tattler, Marsh, Terek, Pectoral and Broad-billed Sandpiper, Black-tailed and Bar-tailed Godwit, and Red and Great Knot. The best time for migratory waders is from September to March, but there are always a few to be seen at any time of the year; Double-banded Plovers visit the region in fair numbers between February and August. At high tide the birds gather at favoured roosting sites, often quite near the foreshore. During winter, when many waders leave for their breeding grounds, there is an influx of other waterbirds − cormorants, herons, egrets, ibis, spoonbills − and those prepared to walk the full length of the Esplanade should see many of the following: Australian Pelican, Great and Little Pied Cormorant, White-faced Heron, Great, Little, Intermediate and Eastern Reef Egret (several species of egrets are often seen together, providing a rare opportunity to compare their diagnostic features), Striated Heron, Black-necked Stork (more affectionately known as the Jabiru), Sacred and Straw-necked Ibis, Royal Spoonbill, Masked Lapwing, Red-capped Plover, Black-winged Stilt, Gull-billed, Caspian, Black-naped, Little, Crested and Lesser Crested Tern, and Sacred Kingfisher.

Apart from the waterbirds there are many other interesting species to be seen along the foreshore. Three coastal raptors − Osprey, Brahminy Kite and White-bellied Sea-Eagle − are often around the harbour, while the gardens adjacent to Marlin Parade and along the Esplanade are favoured by Peaceful Dove, Rainbow and Scaly-breasted Lorikeet (when the native trees are in flower), Helmeted Friarbird, Varied Honeyeater (this is one of the best places in Australia for the species), Yellow Honeyeater, Figbird, Spangled Drongo and White-breasted Woodswallow. Rufous Night Herons can sometimes be found roosting during the day in the large trees that line the Esplanade.

If you have time, the mangroves at Ellie Point to the north and around Trinity Inlet to the south are well worth visiting for Darter, Great-billed Heron, Black Bittern, Little and Collared Kingfisher, Mangrove Robin, Shining Flycatcher, Large-billed Gerygone, Brown-backed and Dusky Honeyeater, Yellow-bellied Sunbird, Yellow Oriole and Black Butcherbird. In summer large numbers of Torresian Imperial-Pigeons arrive from New Guinea to breed in the region; in the evening and early morning these conspicuous black and white birds can often be found roosting in mangroves around the harbour.

The Cairns foreshore is ornithologically so outstanding that even the most casual bird-watcher can expect to see many interesting species at close range. Two attractive posters featuring the birds of the Esplanade can be purchased from the City Council offices, and a comprehensive bird list is available from the Queensland National Parks and Wildlife Service at 41 Esplanade, Cairns. Unfortunately, as so often seems the case with mudflats, swamps and other 'useless' pieces of land, part of the area is to be reclaimed and used for a carpark. Worse still, there are plans to build a yachting marina, which would involve dredging a large section of the mudflats. Alas, by the time this book goes to press the foreshore may no longer be the bird-watchers' paradise it is now.

Flecker Botanic Gardens, Centenary Lakes and Mt Whitfield Environmental Park: The Botanic Gardens are situated on the lower slopes of Mt Whitfield in the suburb of Edge Hill, just a few minutes drive from the city. This is an excellent place for birds and well worth a day's visit, although even those with less time to spare should see something of interest. North of Collins Avenue the 6.5 ha of formal gardens include a fernery and orchid house. The gardens are open daily from sunrise to sunset, but the fernery and orchid house are closed at weekends.

Between Collins Avenue and Greenslopes Street lie a large open parkland, two lakes, a palm swamp and a patch of melaleuca wetland. The diversity of habitats makes this a very productive area. In the parklands and round the margins of the lakes look for cormorants, ibis, Dusky Moorhen, Purple Swamphen, Eurasian Coot, Masked Lapwing, Peaceful and Bar-shouldered Dove, Rainbow and Scaly-breasted Lorikeet, Forest Kingfisher, Rainbow Bee-eater, White-bellied Cuckoo-shrike, Varied Triller, Helmeted Friarbird, Yellow and Dusky Honeyeater, Yellow-bellied Sunbird, Mistletoebird, Red-browed Firetail and Spangled Drongo.

Centenary Lakes consist of a small freshwater lake and a larger one fed by Saltwater Creek. The freshwater lake is almost entirely covered with floating vegetation and at times holds quite a variety of birds, including herons, egrets, spoonbills and waterfowl. Comb-crested Jacana and Wandering Whistling-Duck have been seen here, and the diminutive Little Kingfisher turns up from time to time. As its name implies it is the smallest Australian kingfisher, measuring a mere 120 mm (about the size of a Silvereye) from head to toe. It is a truly delightful bird to watch, but you will definitely need binoculars to spot this tiny blue and white gem! Interestingly, the Azure and Little are the only true kingfishers found in Australia; both are exclusively aquatic, diving beneath the surface of the water in pursuit of prey. All the other Australian kingfishers, including the well-known Laughing Kookaburra, are terrestrial birds that usually hunt over dry land.

A boardwalk has been constructed through the otherwise impenetrable palm swamp that lies behind the lake. Although the vegetation is extremely dense, making bird-watching difficult, a walk here is highly recommended since it provides a rare glimpse of this complex and fascinating environment.

For the more energetic there is a walking track running northwards along the Mt Whitfield spur. It leaves from the corner of

Collins Avenue and MacDonnell Street and for the first kilometre or so climbs steeply to a lookout offering fine views over Cairns and Trinity Bay. From the lookout the track continues uphill, ending near the summit of Mt Whitfield. For much of the way it winds through relatively undisturbed rainforest with woody vines, epiphytes such as elkhorn, staghorn and bird's nest ferns, orchids, mosses and a wealth of tropical trees. Rainforest animals are rarely active during the day but the stealthy observer may see a musk rat-kangaroo, a small, primitive mammal that often appears on the track.

Birds abound, but since the dense canopy shuts out most of the sunlight they are extremely difficult to observe. However, Orange-footed Scrubfowl and Noisy Pitta are two ground-dwelling species that any diligent bird-watcher can expect to see. Both are quite common along the Mt Whitfield spur and in winter, when the forest floor is usually dry, they advertise their presence by noisily raking over the leaf litter in search of food. Other birds that may be seen along the track include Wompoo Fruit-Dove, White-headed Pigeon, Emerald Dove, Varied Triller, Pale-yellow Robin, Little Shrike-thrush, Black-faced (summer) and Spectacled Monarch, Leaden Flycatcher, Rufous Fantail (winter), Fairy Gerygone, Lewin's Honeyeater, Yellow Oriole and Figbird. Red-backed Fairy-wrens and Chestnut-breasted Mannikins inhabit the grassy areas on the margins, while White-rumped Swiftlets are commonly seen hawking over the treetops. In summer, those with a sharp eye may glimpse a flock of Metallic Starlings hurtling through the rainforest canopy. The birds roost in street trees around Cairns, and an evening visit to the dense vegetation opposite the entrance to the Botanic Gardens may prove rewarding.

The walk to the top of Mt Whitfield (about 7 km return) provides a true rainforest experience but needs a full day to do it justice. Along the way there are several log seats where you can sit and enjoy lunch while listening to a Noisy Pitta's cheerful 'walk-to-work' whistle. Wear sensible shoes and carry insect repellent to deter the mosquitoes from taking advantage of your frequent long stops.

Green Island, Michaelmas Cay and Upolu Cay: Many of the better known Great Barrier Reef islands are not coral cays but pieces of the mainland cut off thousands of years ago by the rising seas. There are, however, three true coral islands readily accessible from Cairns: Green Island and the Michaelmas and Upolu Cays. Green Island, the most famous cay in the region, is a tiny 7 ha national park attracting over 180 000 visitors annually. It has a small resort, an underwater observatory, a theatre and a marine-land. Each day glass-bottomed boats ferry hundreds of eager passengers out over the surrounding reef to peer down at fish flashing over the colourless coral. Many visitors are slightly disappointed; you need diving gear to see coral gardens as they appear in glossy magazines.

Walking tracks criss-cross the cay, passing through a small patch of rainforest where Emerald Dove, Spectacled Monarch, Yellow-bellied Sunbird and a few other birds can be found. Eastern Reef Egrets roost in the fringing casuarinas, while the reef attracts a sprinkling of seabirds and waders. Occasionally something really special turns up — Beach Thick-knee for example.

Because it receives so many visitors Green Island is not especially good for birds and a trip to Michaelmas Cay, just to the north, should prove more fruitful. The cay supports large breeding colonies of Common Noddy and Sooty, Crested and Lesser Crested Tern, while many seabirds can be seen on the island and during the boat trip out: Brown and, more rarely, Masked Booby, Great and Least Frigatebird, Roseate, Black-naped and Bridled Tern, and Black Noddy. Red-tailed and White-tailed Tropicbirds, both rare in the Cairns area, are certainly worth looking out for.

Cruise boat operators in Cairns offer day trips to Green Island, Michaelmas Cay and the outer reef. If you are with a group willing to share the cost, it might be best to charter a boat for a visit to Michaelmas because the commercial operators only stay there for a few hours. Remember to take snorkelling gear and, if you intend landing on Michaelmas, be careful not to disturb the nesting birds.

Kuranda tourist train: The 34 km train trip to Kuranda may not be the ornithological excursion of a lifetime, but no visitor should leave Cairns without experiencing this most enjoyable railway journey. From Cairns the line runs north through the canefields that crowd the Barron River delta, before veering west and climbing steeply to Kuranda, 330 m above sea level. Passengers are assured of an exciting ride since there are fifteen tunnels and the train passes close to several waterfalls. Unfortunately the once mighty Barron Falls are now harnessed for hydro-electricity, although during the wet season the 260 m falls are still a spectacular sight.

Kuranda Railway Station is a botanical delight, decorated with all kinds of tropical plants including epiphytic ferns and orchids. Bright green and yellow sunbirds dart about the platform, adding an extra splash of colour to the scene.

Having explored Cairns, bird-watchers should turn their attention to the small but widely known Atherton Tableland about 50 km to the south-west. Volcanic activity has endowed the region with rich red soil, and it is said to be the most fertile plateau in Australia. The early settlers, recognising its farming potential, soon set to work clearing and burning the dense tropical rainforest that covered much of the area. Today less than 10 per cent of the original vegetation remains.

The loss of so much beautiful rainforest − a priceless natural heritage − will undoubtedly sadden many visitors. With its great floral diversity and abundant animal life, tropical rainforest is the richest environment on earth. Incredibly, there are more than eight hundred different species of trees in the rainforests between Townsville and Cooktown, and as many as 160 species have been recorded in a single 2 ha plot. Bird-watchers accustomed to open eucalypt forests, where one can walk with comparative ease, will find the cool, cathedral-like confines of the rainforest a new and breathtaking experience. Massive buttressed trees tower above the lower levels of the forest; their dense crowns interlock, shutting out most of the sunlight and creating a humid environment in which orchids, ferns, mosses, lichens and fungi thrive. Epiphytes − elkhorn, staghorn and bird's nest ferns − cling to the trees, forming an aerial garden, while giant woody vines hang from the canopy like the torn rigging of a storm-ravaged sailing ship.

Many of the mammals that occur in north-eastern Queensland are nocturnal and seldom seen − green ring-tail and striped possums for example. Other rainforest inhabitants, including birds, have cryptic markings (nature's way of camouflaging them) or spend much of their time in the dense upper canopy. Bird-watching is therefore somewhat exasperating, though there are rewarding moments − a cassowary leading its three or four delightfully striped chicks along a forest track is a sight not easily forgotten.

Throughout the Atherton Tableland there are extensive dairy, tobacco, rice, maize and peanut farms, but despite the destruction of so much of its native vegetation this is one of the most attractive and ornithologically exciting areas in Australia. Remnants of rainforest are protected by a network of national parks; there are also substantial tracts of state forest, although the timber industry is logging many of the residual areas of rainforest and establishing hoop and caribbean pine plantations. The lakes, rivers and swamps attract a wealth of waterbirds.

From Cairns there are three routes to the tableland: the Kennedy Highway via Kuranda and Mareeba; the Gillies Highway via Gordonvale and Yungaburra; and the Palmerston Highway via Innisfail and Millaa Millaa. You can, of course, take day trips to the tableland from Cairns, but since many of the best birding spots are within 30 km or so of Atherton the best policy is to establish a base near the town and make excursions to the areas chosen. There is no shortage of accommodation, including motels and hotels at Atherton, Lake Tinaroo and Yungaburra, and caravan parks at Atherton, Lake Tinaroo, Lake Eacham and Malanda.

Lake Tinaroo

This huge man-made lake to the north-east of Atherton was formed in 1958 when the Tinaroo Dam was completed. The reservoir is used for irrigation and hydro-electricity, but boating, water-skiing, fishing and swimming are permitted and a small but flourishing tourist industry has developed around its shores. More importantly, for the bird-watcher at least, the lake provides ideal conditions for many waterbirds.

At Tinaroo Falls, on the lake's north-western shores, there are two motels and a pleasantly situated caravan park. The open forest behind the park is worth exploring for bush birds, while the lake attracts Great Crested and Australasian Grebe, Australian Pelican, Darter, cormorants, herons, egrets, Rufous Night Heron (especially along its wooded shores), Black-necked Stork (rarely), ibis, spoonbills, Wandering and Plumed Whistling-Duck, Black Swan, Pacific Black, Pink-eared and Maned Duck, Grey Teal, Hardhead, Cotton and Green Pygmy-Goose, Dusky Moorhen, Purple Swamphen, Eurasian Coot, Comb-crested Jacana and Caspian Tern. In spring and summer, when the water level is low, the lake's muddy margins hold a variety of waders including Red-kneed Dotterel, Black-fronted Plover and Black-winged Stilt. White-bellied Sea-Eagle and Osprey visit the area occasionally.

The country to the west of Lake Tinaroo has been extensively cleared for agriculture. There are generally few birds here, although between June and December Brolgas and Sarus Cranes can be seen in the paddocks. The irrigated pastures and lucerne fields are frequented by Red-backed Button-quail and Stubble, Brown and King Quail, while Red-chested Button-quail turns up infrequently during the monsoon season. The ranges to the north and east of the lake are considerably more interesting, since this area has rainforests, eucalypt forests and pine plantations. Access can be gained via the Danbulla Forest Drive, which begins at Tinaroo Dam and ends on the Gillies Highway near Lake Barrine. Along the 30 km forest drive there are many points of interest.

Platypus Rocks: Consist of a number of exposed granite tors about 3 km east of the dam. From the lookout there are fine views over Lake Tinaroo and the tableland.

Downfall Creek State Forest Park: Lies about 6 km from Tinaroo Dam. It has excellent picnic facilities and bush camping is permitted at a lovely site on the edge of the lake.

Kauri Creek State Forest Park: Is situated on the Kauri Creek inlet about 1 km further along the road. There are picnic and bush-camping facilities, and this would be a good spot to launch a canoe to explore the lake and the forested inlets.

Lake Euramoo State Forest Park: Features one of the tableland's famous crater lakes and is about 18 km from the dam. The lake is surrounded by dense tropical rainforest, and an early morning stroll along the short nature walk is highly recommended. There are picnic facilities in a beautiful setting on the rim of the crater, but camping is not permitted.

Mobo Creek Crater: Is a few kilometres on from Lake Euramoo; a walking track circles the small lake and provides access to the rainforest.

Fong-on Bay State Forest Park: This park, on Lake Tinaroo's eastern shores, is about 21 km from the dam. To get there, follow the forest drive for about 16 km and turn off at the side road leading to the bay. From the picnic and camping ground there are magnificent views across the lake to the rainforest-clad Tinaroo Ranges. The area is well known for the impressive gatherings of waterfowl and waders to be seen there in spring and summer.

The Cathedral Fig Tree: Is located in lush rainforest near the end of the forest drive, about 5 km from the Gillies Highway. Though not as impressive as the famous Curtain Fig Tree near Yungaburra, this remarkable strangler fig is well worth seeing. Orange-footed Scrubfowl, Pale-yellow and Grey-headed Robin, Little Shrike-thrush, Eastern Whipbird and Yellow-throated Scrubwren can be seen near the boardwalk that has been constructed through the rainforest.

Although you could travel along the Danbulla Forest Drive in an hour or so, plan to spend a full day here. Many birds can be seen along the way: Southern Cassowary (particularly in the early morning and late afternoon), Pacific Baza, Grey and, very rarely, Red Goshawk, Australian Brush-turkey, Bush-hen (near the water's edge), Superb, Rose-crowned and Wompoo Fruit-Dove, Topknot and White-headed Pigeon, Brown Cuckoo-Dove, Emerald Dove, Double-eyed Fig-Parrot, Australian King-Parrot, Brush (summer) and Fan-tailed Cuckoo, Gould's Bronze-Cuckoo, Common Koel (summer), Channel-billed Cuckoo (summer), Rufous Owl (rarely), Large-tailed Nightjar, Azure and Little Kingfisher, Dollarbird (summer), Noisy Pitta, Yellow-eyed Cuckoo-shrike, Cicadabird (summer), Eastern Yellow Robin, Golden Whistler, Bower's Shrike-thrush, Yellow-breasted Boat-bill, Black-faced (summer), Spectacled, White-eared and Pied Monarch, Rufous Fantail (summer), Chowchilla, Large-billed Scrubwren, Brown Gerygone, Little Treecreeper, Macleay's, Lewin's, Bridled and Scarlet Honeyeater, Metallic Starling (summer), Olive-backed Oriole, Satin Bowerbird, Tooth-billed and Spotted Catbird, and Victoria's Riflebird.

A leaflet describing aspects of the Danbulla Forest Drive can be obtained from the Forestry Department's offices in Cairns and

Atherton. If you plan to stay in any of the state forest parks, it would be wise to contact the Forestry Department for camping information.

Lake Barrine and Lake Eacham National Parks

These two small parks, about 20 km east of Atherton, are famous for their water-filled volcanic craters. Both are of considerable interest because the dense tropical rainforest surrounding the lakes abounds with birdlife.

Lake Barrine (491 ha): This is one of the most popular tourist destinations on the tableland, attracting coachloads of visitors. Most people head straight for the tea rooms or take an organised cruise on the lake's glassy waters. A few may venture along the walking track to the giant twin kauri trees, each with a circumference exceeding 6 m.

It is perhaps fortunate that the majority of visitors are content to remain near the picnic area, for the 6 km track around the lake is usually quiet − except for the birds. Australian Brush-turkey, Wompoo Fruit-Dove, Noisy Pitta, Chowchilla, Yellow-throated Scrubwren, Macleay's, Lewin's and Bridled Honeyeater, and Tooth-billed and Spotted Catbird are just a few of the many species that can be seen and heard here. At times the lake holds quite a variety of waterbirds, chiefly common species − grebes, Darter, cormorants, Hardhead, Dusky Moorhen, Eurasian Coot − although White-browed Crake has been recorded in the park. The narrow walking track may be blocked by fallen trees and some stretches are rather muddy. Leeches − those particularly unpleasant inhabitants of the rainforest − thrive in the damp conditions; as a precaution wear long trousers tucked securely into your socks and spray insect repellent liberally on your clothing and boots.

Lake Barrine has picnic facilities and toilets but camping is not permitted. The park is on the Gillies Highway, about 10 km east of Yungaburra.

Lake Eacham (485 ha): Similar in many respects to Lake Barrine, Lake Eacham has only 50 ha of water compared with Lake Barrine's 100 ha. A 6 km walking track circles the lake, passing through dense rainforest where you may see carpet pythons, forest and water dragons (two species of lizard), green-eyed tree frogs, red-legged pademelons and musk rat-kangaroos. Over one hundred bird species are on the park's list, including many that are highly sought-after: Superb and Rose-crowned Fruit-Dove, White-headed Pigeon, Double-eyed Fig-Parrot, Rufous Owl, Bower's Shrike-thrush, Yellow-breasted Boatbill, White-eared and Pied Monarch, Macleay's and Bridled Honeyeater, Metallic Starling, Tooth-billed Catbird and Victoria's Riflebird. To have the best

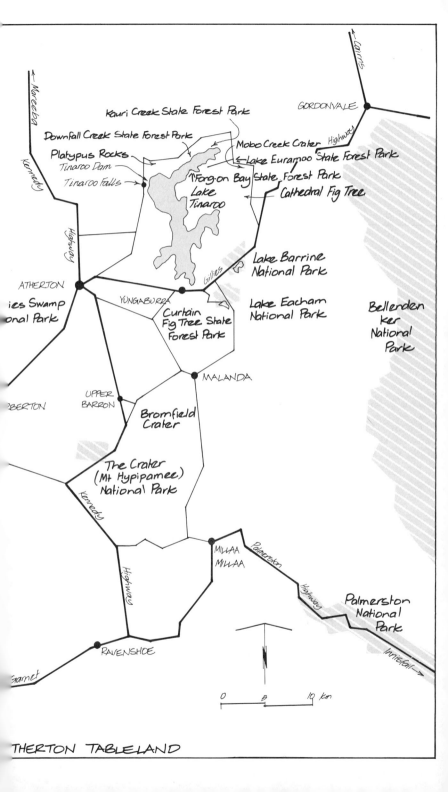

ATHERTON TABLELAND

chance of seeing these birds you should be out on the track early in the day.

If you are unable to walk far — or do not want to risk an encounter with a leech — try the margins of the forest near the picnic area and along the roads leading into the park. Australian Brush-turkey, Emerald Dove, Pale-yellow and Grey-headed Robin, Little Shrike-thrush, Large-billed Scrubwren, Little Tree-creeper, Lewin's Honeyeater and Spotted Catbird should be quite easy to find, but other species will require more time and patience — the Wompoo Fruit-Dove for example. This large, colourful pigeon spends much of its time feeding on succulent fruits high in the rainforest canopy and, although the bird is rarely seen, the sound of falling fruit and a guttural 'wollack-a-woo, wollack-a-woo' confirm its presence.

Lake Eacham is about 6 km from Lake Barrine and about 4 km from Yungaburra. It is undoubtedly one of the best places to go bird-watching on the tableland, but try to arrange a visit in the early morning when the roads running through the park are quiet. Since these roads are sealed, Lake Eacham would be a good place to take a disabled friend to see some rainforest birds. The park has a pleasant picnic area on the shores of the lake and, although camping at that spot is not allowed, there is a caravan park a short distance away on the road to Malanda.

Curtain Fig Tree State Forest Park

The Curtain Fig Tree is the most famous strangler fig in North Queensland and one of the tableland's best known natural features. The magnificent fig has developed from a seed deposited by a fruit-eating creature in the crown of a sloping tree, and its rope-like roots drop 15 m to the forest floor. A well-marked track leads to the tree and the surrounding forest is relatively open. Orange-footed Scrubfowl, Australian Brush-turkey, Pale-yellow Robin, Grey-headed Robin, Eastern Whipbird and a number of other rainforest species can be seen here quite readily. Across the road there is a patch of much denser rainforest where forestry tracks provide access.

Despite its popularity this small state forest abounds in birdlife; an early morning visit (before the coaches arrive) will be best. There are picnic facilities but camping is not permitted. The park is on the Malanda road, about 2 km from Yungaburra.

The Crater (Mt Hypipamee) National Park

This 364 ha reserve is about 24 km south of Atherton on the Ravenshoe road (Kennedy Highway). The Mt Hypipamee crater is something of a geological curiosity — its walls are granite, a rock not usually associated with volcanic activity, yet the surrounding material is solidified ash. In fact it is a diatreme, an explosion crater formed when volcanic activity blasted a hole through the surrounding granite. A walking track leads to a lookout some 60 m above the dark green waters of the crater lake.

For many visitors, however, the park's main attraction is not its crater but its birds. Mt Hypipamee rises nearly 1000 m above sea level and a number of species that typically occur at high altitudes can be seen there – Australian Fernwren, Atherton Scrubwren, Mountain Thornbill, Bridled Honeyeater and, outstandingly, the very beautiful Golden Bowerbird. Although bowerbirds are present at Mt Hypipamee throughout the year, the best time to look for them is during the breeding season. Between October and January male Golden Bowerbirds spend much of the day tending their bowers, and if you can find one of these magnificent structures the bird is sure to be in the vicinity. A thorough search of the rainforest at Mt Hypipamee may prove rewarding; fortunately the forest is relatively open in places and quite easy to walk through. If you cannot face the prospect of having to remove the inevitable leech, the park's picnic area is about 2.5 km off the Kennedy Highway, and bowerbirds are occasionally seen along the entrance road. Alternatively, try the narrow tracks that enter the forest at several points along the highway.

Even if you do not find a bowerbird the park has many other avian attractions, including the Bridled and Lewin's Honeyeaters that frequent the picnic area where they can be hand-fed. Other species – Orange-footed Scrubfowl, White's Thrush, Grey-headed Robin, Chowchilla, Australian Fernwren, Atherton Scrubwren – can usually be found near the walking tracks. The Crater is also a good place to go spotlighting for rainforest mammals and nocturnal birds such as Lesser Sooty Owl.

It is possible to camp in the park for one night only, but a permit should be obtained from the Queensland National Parks and Wildlife Service at Lake Eacham.

Bromfield Crater

This flat-floored depression, the largest crater on the tableland, has been partially drained, and the surrounding rainforest cleared for agriculture. Within the crater there is a huge swamp about a kilometre wide, with numerous open pools surrounded by grasses, sedges, reeds, rushes and paperbarks. Many waterbirds can be found here, including herons, egrets, ibis, spoonbills, Magpie Goose, Hardhead, Cotton and Green Pygmy-Goose, Buff-banded Rail, Spotless Crake, Comb-crested Jacana, Red-kneed Dotterel, Black-winged Stilt and Latham's Snipe (summer).

The swamp is on private property and you will need to seek permission from the owner if you wish to bird-watch there.

However, between June and December large numbers of Brolgas and Sarus Cranes roost in the swamp, and towards dusk they can usually be seen standing on the slopes of the crater. Both species are widely distributed in the region but this is the best place to see them; up to three hundred Sarus Cranes and more than seven hundred Brolgas have been recorded roosting in the swamp on a single evening.

The crater is about 6 km south-west of Malanda. It can be reached via the Upper Barron to Malanda road, which skirts the volcano's high northern rim.

Hasties Swamp National Park

Hasties Swamp is 3 km south of Atherton on the road to Herberton. The swamp is another good place for waterbirds and, depending on the season, it is possible to see over fifty species here within a few hours. Access can be gained via Hastie Road, but the surrounding area is privately owned and permission should be obtained before venturing too far. There are no facilities and camping is not permitted.

Palmerston National Park

This 2556 ha reserve was established in 1941 to protect the dense vegetation along the Palmerston Highway between Innisfail and Millaa Millaa. It is not a large park, yet significantly it has more upland rainforest than Lake Barrine, Lake Eacham and The Crater combined.

From the picnic areas along the highway, walking tracks cut through the lush greenery to a series of picturesque cascades and spectacular waterfalls. Platypus live in the beautiful crystal-clear streams and these endearing creatures are occasionally seen in the deeper pools, particularly early in the day. The park's flora is exceedingly rich (over five hundred tree species have been recorded), while the avifauna, not surprisingly, includes so many species it is impossible to list them all. Pacific Baza, Grey Goshawk, Topknot Pigeon, Double-eyed Fig-Parrot, Little Kingfisher, Yellow-eyed Cuckoo-shrike, Grey Whistler, Mountain Thornbill, Satin Bowerbird and Victoria's Riflebird are just a few.

With its extensive network of walking tracks, Palmerston National Park offers an opportunity to experience tropical rainforest at its very best. This is one of the wettest parts of Australia (the average annual rainfall is 3500 mm), and visitors should expect damp, muddy conditions even in the relatively dry winter months. The camping area at Henrietta Creek, about 5 km beyond the park entrance as you approach from Innisfail, has only a toilet and shelter hut. There are no showers, but drinking water can be obtained from the nearby creek. Camping permits are available six to twelve weeks in advance: write to the ranger, Palmerston National Park, PO Box 800, Innisfail, Qld 4860, or to the Queensland National Parks and Wildlife Service, PO Box 2066, Cairns, Qld 4870. Enclose a stamped, addressed envelope. Park information, including a bird list, is available from the ranger's office, which is located near the reserve entrance, 33 km from Innisfail.

Bellenden Ker National Park

A 32 000 ha wilderness on the coast between Cairns and Innisfail, Bellenden Ker is by far the largest national park in the region and one of the most valuable reserves in Queensland. It is undeveloped except for the small Josephine Falls area in the south-eastern corner of the park. The road to the falls (signposted) leaves the Bruce Highway about 20 km north of Innisfail. The park entrance is 8 km from the turn-off.

From the picnic area a short (700 m) walking track leads through dense rainforest to Josephine Falls. Birds are not particularly plentiful but the path is sealed and fairly level, making this one of the very few places where the disabled can be taken to enjoy Queensland's tropical rainforest.

There is also a track to the summit of Mt Bartle Frere — the state's highest peak (1622 m). The walk to the top of the mountain (about 8 km) should only be attempted by fit, experienced bushwalkers, since the slippery conditions and overhanging vegetation make this a hazardous and difficult ascent. Walkers should be self-sufficient and register with the park ranger at Josephine Falls before setting out. Bellenden Ker has no camping area but permits to stay overnight are issued to bushwalkers.

Julatten

Julatten is a loose collection of houses on the Rex Highway about 10 km north of Mt Molloy. There are no national parks in the immediate vicinity, and at first glance the tiny township does not appear to have anything to offer the bird-watcher. However, Julatten caravan park has earnt a considerable reputation for being one of the best places in the region for rainforest birds. Members of ornithological clubs throughout Australia, having read glowing accounts of its avifauna, travel to the park in the hope of seeing many species at close range, particularly the Red-necked Crake and the Buff-breasted Paradise-Kingfisher.

Crakes, especially those that inhabit rainforests, are exceedingly elusive creatures, and the Red-necked Crake seldom behaves so obligingly as it does at Julatten. During winter it usually appears just before dusk at a small pool in the rainforest not far from the park-owner's house. There, to the delight of onlookers, it can be seen at the water's edge along with Emerald Dove, Pale-yellow and Grey-headed Robin, Little Shrike-thrush, Spectacled Monarch, Rufous Fantail, Australian Fernwren, Large-billed Scrubwren, Yellow-throated Scrubwren and Mountain Thornbill. As a bonus, Australian Brush-turkey, Brown Cuckoo-Dove, Grey Whistler, Bower's Shrike-thrush, Yellow-breasted Boatbill, White-eared Monarch, Pied Monarch and Tooth-billed Catbird frequent the surrounds.

Near the well-worn track leading to the pool there is a small termite mound containing the nesting chamber of a Buff-breasted Paradise-Kingfisher. These beautiful long-tailed kingfishers breed in Australia during summer, then fly north to spend winter in New Guinea. They are usually seen at Julatten between December and March.

Within the grounds of the caravan park there is a small citrus orchard where Macleay's, Lewin's, Yellow-spotted and Graceful Honeyeaters can be readily observed attacking the over-ripe fruit. Other orchard-raiders include Satin Bowerbird, Spotted Catbird and Victoria's Riflebird.

It would be as well to spend several days at Julatten and to include on your itinerary a visit to Mt Lewis State Forest, a few kilometres to the west. Much of this area is above 1000 m, and high-altitude species such as Atherton Scrubwren, Bridled Honey-eater and Golden Bowerbird occur there. In addition, Mt Lewis has the distinction of being one of the few places in Australia where Blue-faced Finches have been recorded in recent years. A narrow track provides access to the forest but it is steep and unsuitable for conventional vehicles. In any case it is better to walk; there is more chance of seeing shy species such as Southern Cassowary, and you can listen for the high-pitched 'tseet tseet' calls of the Blue-faced Finches.

Julatten is about 80 km north of Atherton via Mareeba; over-night vans are available at the caravan park and many of the campsites are hidden away in the forest. Those travelling from Atherton should plan a stop at Big Mitchell Creek, about 20 km north of Mareeba. There are usually plenty of birds here, including White-browed Robin, Black-throated Finch and Great Bowerbird.

MT ISA AND THE GULF COUNTRY

Each year between May and September a growing number of bird-watchers head for northern Australia to find new birds and to escape the rigours of the southern winter. Many travel up the east coast via Brisbane to Townsville and Cairns, then west to the Northern Territory via Mt Isa. And while fellow birders shiver at home in the southern capitals, these intrepid travellers spend their days birding in the northern sunshine, pursuing Sarus Cranes,

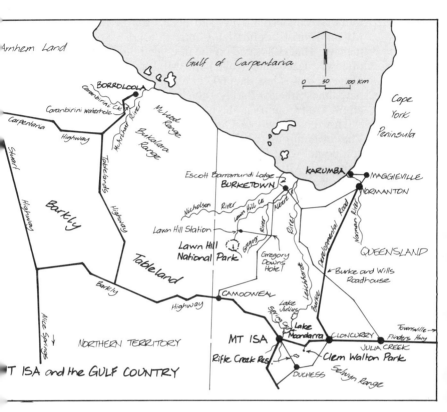

Flock Bronzewings, Northern Rosellas, White-browed Robins, White-breasted Whistlers, Northern Fantails, Spinifexbirds, Purple-crowned Fairy-wrens, Carpentarian Grasswrens, Painted Firetails, Crimson Finches, and a host of other highly sought-after species.

Mt Isa

At first glance Mt Isa, the copper capital of Australia, seems to have little to offer the bird-watcher. Situated on the Barkly Highway about 890 km west of Townsville and about 1650 km south-east of Darwin, the city is dominated by a giant mining complex and the surrounding stony hills are sparsely vegetated and somewhat inhospitable. Nevertheless Mt Isa does have its attractions, and with its motels, hotels, caravan parks and youth hostel it is a convenient place to rest for a few days when travelling from east to west or vice versa.

The Mt Isa mine is well worth seeing. It produces more lead than any other mine in the world and is one of the largest producers of copper, silver and zinc. Surface and underground tours are conducted daily, and details can be obtained from the Mt Isa Tourist Information Centre in Marian Street. Away from the city, which is located on the tree-lined Leichhardt River, a belt of low, rugged hills (called the Mt Isa Highlands, though the highest point is less than 600 m above sea level) gives way to the flat, almost treeless Barkly Tableland in the west, and to the vast, empty Gulf Country in the north.

This remote part of Queensland is forbidding yet fascinating. The adventurous traveller could spend many weeks here, but if you do not want to venture too far from civilisation the following spots near Mt Isa are reasonably accessible and should provide some excellent birding.

Lake Moondarra: This large (2376 ha) man-made lake, the main source of Mt Isa's water supply, lies to the north of the city and is a very good place indeed for waterbirds. A wide variety of species can be found here at any time of the year, and in the dry season (April to November) the lake is an important refuge in an otherwise arid region. To get there, drive along the Barkly Highway towards Camooweal and turn off about 5 km north of Mt Isa. The lake is about 15 km from the turn-off. Picnic facilities are provided at several sites along the entrance road, but camping is not permitted. There is, however, a caravan park in a pleasant setting on the banks of the Leichhardt River near the turn-off to the lake.

The deep northern section of Lake Moondarra is a popular swimming and boating spot and generally holds fewer birds than the shallow southern section. Much of the area is a bird sanctuary and, depending on conditions elsewhere in the region, visitors can expect to see many of the following: Great Crested, Hoary-headed and Australasian Grebe, Australian Pelican, Darter, Great, Pied, Little Black and Little Pied Cormorant, Pacific and White-faced Heron, Great, Little and Intermediate Egret, Rufous Night Heron, Black Bittern (rare, but should not be discounted), Black-necked Stork (usually present in ones or twos), Glossy, Sacred and Straw-necked Ibis (several hundred Glossy Ibis are sometimes present, particularly during the wet season), Royal and Yellow-billed Spoonbill, Plumed Whistling-Duck (flocks of several hundred are usually present late in the dry season and early in the wet), Grey Teal, Pacific Black, Pink-eared and Maned Duck, Hardhead, Green Pygmy-Goose (uncommon, but occasionally seen in small numbers), Black-tailed Native-hen, Dusky Moorhen, Purple Swamphen, Eurasian Coot, Brolga (one or two are usually present), Comb-crested Jacana (restricted to areas of floating vegetation at the southern end of the lake), Painted Snipe (rare, but certainly worth looking for), Masked Lapwing, Red-kneed Dotterel, Black-fronted Plover, Black-winged Stilt, and Whiskered, Gull-billed and Caspian Tern.

About seventeen species of migratory wader have been recorded in the Mt Isa area, and in summer there is usually a fair variety to be found in the vicinity of Lake Moondarra. These include Wood and Common Sandpiper, Greenshank, Marsh Sandpiper, Latham's Snipe, Sharp-tailed Sandpiper and, more rarely, Long-toed Stint. The north-western shore of the lake, especially near the mouth of Spring Creek, is one of the best places for waders.

Although waterbirds are undoubtedly the main attraction, the spinifex-covered hills surrounding Lake Moondarra hold a host of interesting bush birds. The aptly named Spinifexbird is perhaps the most notable. This sparrow-sized, somewhat drab species is reasonably common, especially along creek beds and at the bases of the rocky hills. It is, however, rather difficult to find since it usually slips quietly into the spinifex at the first sign of an intruder. To have the best chance of seeing the bird you should go to the lake early in the day and thoroughly search the area to the right of the entrance road. The tall, dense spinifex some 12 km from the turn-off is a good place to begin.

If you are not fortunate enough to find a Spinifexbird there are always many other species to be seen near the lake. These include Diamond Dove, Spinifex Pigeon, Red-backed Kingfisher, Rainbow Bee-eater, White-winged Triller, Rufous Whistler, Restless Flycatcher, Grey-crowned Babbler, Variegated and Red-backed Fairy-wren, Black-tailed Treecreeper, Silver-crowned and Little Friarbird (mainly in the wet season), Yellow-throated Miner, Singing, Grey-headed, Grey-fronted, Brown and Rufous-throated (mainly in the wet season) Honeyeater, Red-browed Pardalote, Painted Firetail, Zebra Finch, Pictorella Mannikin (an irregular wet-season visitor), and White-breasted, Black-faced and Little Woodswallow.

Lake Moondarra is a very pleasant place to go bird-watching and a most enjoyable day could be spent here. At the end of the entrance road, just beyond the dam wall, there is a delightful picnic area with lawns and tall, shady trees. This is a perfect place to eat lunch (or breakfast if you are an early riser) while keeping a watch for birds such as Peaceful Dove, Little Corella, Varied Lorikeet, Red-winged Parrot, Blue-winged Kookaburra and Pied Butcherbird.

Rifle Creek Reservoir: This small (186 ha) dam is situated in the Selwyn Range, some 40 km south-east of Mt Isa via the road to Duchess. Although it attracts fewer birds than Lake Moondarra and is rather less accessible, the reservoir is worth visiting, particularly in the early morning or late afternoon when there is often a variety of finches present. Painted Firetail, Zebra, Double-barred and Long-tailed Finch, Pictorella and, more rarely, Chestnut-breasted Mannikin are the species to look for.

Clem Walton Park: An oasis in the rugged ranges east of Mt Isa, this idyllic spot is a superb place to go birding. It is situated approximately 4 km south of the Barkly Highway, about 65 km east of Mt Isa and about 50 km west of Cloncurry. The park, a well-known local beauty spot, is not well signposted and it would be wise to seek precise directions before leaving Cloncurry or Mt Isa.

Just south of the highway, to the right of the track leading to the park, there is a large, shallow lake — an excellent place for waterbirds. Some 2 or 3 km further on there are picnic facilities and toilets on the banks of a permanent creek. In the dry season the creek and the surrounding area are usually alive with birds. Australasian Grebe, White-faced Heron, Rufous Night Heron, Black Bittern, Whistling Kite, Dusky Moorhen, Purple Swamphen, Peaceful and Diamond Dove, Little Corella, Varied Lorikeet, Red-winged Parrot, Cockatiel, Budgerigar, Mallee Ringneck (better known as the Cloncurry Parrot), Rainbow Bee-eater, Clamorous Reed-Warbler, Black-tailed Treecreeper, White-plumed and Brown Honeyeater, Painted Firetail, Double-barred Finch, Chestnut-breasted Mannikin, Spotted Bowerbird and Little Woodswallow are some of the species you will almost certainly find here.

Most of the birds mentioned can be observed with ease in and around the picnic area. The park is usually crowded at weekends, however, and it would be best to go there during the week if you want to see secretive species such as the Black Bittern. The surrounding hills, although stony and rather uninviting, have a certain beauty and are well worth exploring on foot.

The Gulf Country

It is probably fair to say that most people, having perhaps travelled thousands of kilometres to get there, are somewhat disappointed when they reach the Gulf Country. For at least eight months of the year this vast region, stretching from Cape York Peninsula in the east to Arnhem Land in the west, receives little or no rain. The flat, featureless countryside is parched and dusty, and rivers that flowed swiftly during the wet season are reduced to a string of dark, muddy pools. Grassland and open eucalypt woodland dominate the seemingly endless plains, and lush tropical vegetation is largely confined to the margins of permanent waterholes.

This remote part of the continent is sparsely populated even by Australian standards. Large areas are virtually inaccessible, but there are sealed roads leading to Karumba (about 70 km northwest of Normanton) on the Queensland side of the border, and to Borroloola in the Northern Territory. In addition there are a number of unsealed roads and tracks between the coast and the Barkly Highway. A four-wheel-drive vehicle, though desirable, is not essential since you can see a good deal of the country without leaving the main roads. You should, however, be well prepared — carry food, water, extra fuel, spare parts and a good map. It would be a good idea to fit a windscreen guard (if your windscreen is broken you may have to drive hundreds of kilometres on dusty roads before a replacement can be fitted), and when travelling on unsealed roads look out for 'bulldust' holes. These deep holes, full of powdery sediment, are very difficult to spot at a distance.

The following route (suitable for conventional cars — those with four-wheel-drive vehicles need not, of course, keep to the main roads) will take you through the heart of the Gulf Country and to many of the best birding localities. From Cloncurry, head north along the Burke Developmental Road (sealed, though narrow in places) to Normanton, continue on to Maggieville, then west to Karumba, about 450 km from Cloncurry. Petrol can be obtained in Cloncurry, at the Burke and Wills Roadhouse (shown as Dismal Crossing on some maps) and in Normanton. From Karumba, return to Normanton and travel south-west then north-west via the direct route to Burketown. The road from Normanton to Burketown is unsealed; petrol can be obtained in Burketown, which is about 235 km from Normanton. From Burketown travel south-west to Camooweal, a distance of 335 km or so. The road from Burketown to Camooweal is unsealed; petrol can be obtained at the Gregory Downs Hotel, about 120 km south-west of Burketown, and in Camooweal. From Camooweal, drive west along the Barkly Highway for about 270 km, then north along the Tablelands and Carpentaria Highways to Borroloola. The Barkly, Tablelands and Carpentaria Highways are sealed, but narrow in places. Borroloola is about 500 km from the Barkly Highway; petrol can be obtained at Camooweal and Borroloola, and there are several roadhouses in between. Allow at least a week to complete the trip, and avoid travelling in the wet season, when much of the region may be flooded.

Although generally speaking the landscape is rather dreary, the Gulf Country has a rich and varied birdlife and visitors can look forward to seeing a wide range of species. These include Square-tailed Kite, Black-breasted Buzzard, Little Eagle, Spotted Harrier, Brolga, Sarus Crane (this species was first recorded in Australia near Normanton in 1966), Australian Bustard, Australian Pratincole, Bar-shouldered Dove, Red-tailed Black-Cockatoo, Red-winged Parrot, Northern Rosella, Channel-billed Cuckoo (a wet-season visitor, though a few may be present at the beginning and end of the dry season), Pheasant Coucal, Barking Owl, Azure Kingfisher, Ground Cuckoo-shrike, Red-backed Fairy-wren,

White-throated Gerygone, Silver-crowned Friarbird, Blue-faced, White-gaped, Yellow-tinted, Black-chinned, Bar-breasted, Rufous-throated, Banded and Red-headed Honeyeater, Masked and Long-tailed Finch, Olive-backed Oriole, Figbird, Great Bowerbird, and White-breasted, Black-faced and Little Woodswallow.

Those wishing to search for the region's special birds − White-browed Robin, White-breasted Whistler, Purple-crowned Fairy-wren and Carpentarian Grasswren for example − will find the following spots highly rewarding.

Karumba: This small township at the mouth of the Norman River is the base for the gulf's prawn-fishing fleet. It has a hotel-motel and a caravan park. The wide mudflats and mangrove swamps in the vicinity of Karumba hold a host of sought-after birds − Striated Heron, Black-necked Stork, Mangrove Robin, Mangrove Golden Whistler, White-breasted Whistler, Broad-billed Flycatcher, Mangrove Gerygone, Red-headed Honeyeater and Yellow White-eye.

Burketown: Is situated about 40 km inland from the Gulf of Carpentaria, on the banks of the Albert River. Famous for its barramundi fishing, the township has a caravan park and accommodation is available at the Escott Barramundi Lodge, a cattle station and fishing resort on the Nicholson River about 10 km to the west. The mudflats and mangroves near the mouth of the Albert River, though less accessible than those at Karumba, are worth visiting for birds such as Mangrove Robin, Mangrove Golden Whistler, White-breasted Whistler and Broad-billed Flycatcher.

Lawn Hill National Park: Covering an area of 12 200 ha, this is the only national park in north-west Queensland. Situated on the ragged edge of the Barkly Tableland near the Northern Territory border, the reserve is about 220 km south-west of Burketown and about 320 km north-east of Camooweal. To get there, turn off the Burketown to Camooweal road at the Gregory Downs Hotel; the park entrance is about 100 km west of the hotel via Lawn Hill Station. The last 30 km or so of the road leading to the reserve is very rough; those with conventional vehicles should call at the hotel and inquire about conditions before setting out.

About 5 km inside the park boundary, on the banks of Lawn Hill Creek, there is a small camping area with toilets and showers. Sites should be booked in advance, for it is a long way to go to find the camping area full. Write to the ranger, Lawn Hill National Park, PMB 12 MS 1463, Mt Isa, Qld 4825, enclosing a stamped addressed envelope.

The park has many splendid features, including several kilometres of multicoloured sandstone walls plunging some 60 m to the deep, emerald-green pools along Lawn Hill Creek. Walking tracks provide access to many lookouts high above the water, and to several of the park's numerous important Aboriginal art sites. Other attractions include a waterfall, an island stack (a massive rock plug at the north-eastern end of the main gorge), and a natural spa bath set against a backdrop of dense tropical vegetation and rugged cliffs.

The lush vegetation within the gorge system contrasts sharply with that of the surrounding dry country. Plants such as cabbage palms, Leichhardt pines and figs thrive in the moist conditions, creating an oasis in the heart of a generally arid environment. Not surprisingly, Lawn Hill is a haven for birds and bird-watchers — Black Bittern, Peregrine Falcon, White-browed Robin (quite common around the camping area), Sandstone Shrike-thrush, Northern Fantail, Purple-crowned Fairy-wren (fairly plentiful along Lawn Hill Creek), Yellow-tinted, Rufous-throated and Banded Honeyeater, Crimson and Long-tailed Finch, and Great Bowerbird are some of the many species you can expect to see here. A comprehensive bird list can be obtained from the resident ranger.

In addition to its birds, the park has many interesting mammals and reptiles — agile wallabies, rock ringtail possums, solitary wallaroos, olivine pythons, tortoises, water monitors (a species of lizard) and freshwater crocodiles.

A visit to Lawn Hill should prove a highlight during your trip to the Gulf Country. Its clear pools are ideal for swimming (freshwater crocodiles are said to be harmless!), and the gorges can be explored by canoe — a most pleasant way to look for birds.

Barkly Tableland: Widely known for its astonishingly level landscape, this vast stretch of country is not the most attractive part of Australia. Nevertheless it is of considerable interest to birders because it is one of the few places in the continent where Flock Bronzewings are regularly sighted.

Because the tableland covers such a huge area (it stretches some 550 km from north to south and is about 250 km wide), it is impossible to say exactly where the bronzewings can be found. The best plan is to camp overnight near water — there are hundreds of boreholes in the area bounded by the Stuart, Carpentaria, Tablelands and Barkly Highways. With the aid of a good map (the *Reader's Digest Atlas of Australia* shows where many of the boreholes are located), you should be able to find a suitable spot quite close to one of the highways. Towards dusk, and less frequently at dawn, large numbers of Flock Bronzewings fly to water. They usually land some distance away, then walk in lines like toy soldiers to the water's edge. If you are not fortunate enough to find the birds, call at one of the properties on the tableland — the owner may know of a place where the bronze-wings come regularly to drink.

Borroloola: This tiny township at the end of the Carpentaria Highway is the place to go if you want to search for one of Australia's least known birds — the Carpentarian Grasswren. An attractive species, somewhat like a small White-throated Grasswren, it is confined to the craggy, spinifex-covered hills south-west of the Gulf of Carpentaria, and is most often reported from the McArthur River near Borroloola.

Since it is a rather elusive bird — when disturbed it takes flight more readily than the White-throated Grasswren, flying with rapid wing beats low over the spinifex before taking cover — you must be prepared for some hard work if you want to see one. The steep, rocky sandstone country in the vicinity of Caranbirini Waterhole is the best place to begin searching because the grass-wren has been seen here on a number of occasions. The water-hole, a lovely spot and an ideal place to camp, is situated about 40 km south-west of Borroloola and is readily accessible via the Carpentaria Highway.

CAPE YORK PENINSULA

At one time Cape York Peninsula was regarded as real frontier country. Like Arnhem Land in the Northern Territory and the Kimberley region of Western Australia it was a part of the continent where only the experienced, the fearless and, some would say, the foolhardy dared venture. It is still a place many people would think twice about visiting, but despite its inaccessibility, perhaps even because of it, Cape York is becoming increasingly popular as a holiday destination. The Peninsula Developmental Road, while not crowded by any means, is no longer the quiet bush track it was ten or fifteen years ago, and with more and more people buying four-wheel-drive vehicles, now every bit as luxurious and comfortable as conventional cars, it is likely that the road will become even busier in the near future.

Whether increased tourism is a good or bad thing is open to debate, for inevitably more visitors will result in more development. Already the region is beginning to feel the assault of civilisation. Cape Tribulation National Park, for example, at the south-eastern extremity of the peninsula between Cairns and Cooktown, is threatened by a proposal to build a road along the coast from Cape Tribulation to Bloomfield. Construction of the road, which will cut a swath through one of the few remaining examples of undisturbed coastal rainforest in the world, is being fiercely opposed by conservationists who see it as the first step in a plan to open up the area. Cape Tribulation is indescribably beautiful: the virgin rainforest forms a dark green mantle that sweeps down from the cloud-capped mountain tops and extends right to the edge of the cape's magnificent sandy beaches. If the road goes ahead the results could be disastrous, for it will provide access to areas of pristine rainforest outside the national park that might then be carved up by real estate developers.

Fortunately Cape York Peninsula is vast – it covers an area twice the size of Tasmania – and so far at least human activities have had little overall impact on the environment. Much of the peninsula is exceedingly remote, and it remains one of the most thinly populated parts of Australia. Long recognised as a wilderness of world importance, the region contains some of the country's largest national parks – Lakefield (537 000 ha), Staaten River (467 000 ha), Rokeby (291 000 ha), Jardine River (253 000 ha) and Archer Bend (166 000 ha).

The region's flora and fauna are immensely rich, but contrary to what one might expect, given its close proximity to New Guinea (Torres Strait is only about 150 km wide), Cape York Peninsula is not dominated by rugged highlands clothed in impenetrable jungle. Certainly it is mountainous in places, and there are substantial tracts of rainforest, particularly on the coast south of Cooktown and in the area between Princess Charlotte Bay and Temple Bay. For the most part, however, Cape York Peninsula is a region of comparatively low relief; of flat to undulating countryside with eucalypt woodlands and open grassy plains stretching monotonously to the horizon. It is also a region of great rivers and swamps – many of them well populated with crocodiles! – but while much of the area is lush and green in the wet season (usually December to March), it can be dry and dusty for months at a time. In the south-west rainfall is relatively low, averaging about 800 mm per annum. Elsewhere on the peninsula annual rainfall is higher (Cape York itself receives about 1800 mm), although still much less than in New Guinea, where more than half the island has an average annual rainfall exceeding 2500 mm.

For the bird-watcher Cape York Peninsula has a special attraction because its avifauna includes many species that occur nowhere else in Australia – Buff-breasted Button-quail, Palm Cockatoo, Eclectus, Red-cheeked and Golden-shouldered Parrot, Chestnut-breasted Cuckoo (this species may not in fact be confined to Cape York Peninsula since there have been a number of unconfirmed sightings well south of the region), Yellow-billed Kingfisher, Red-bellied Pitta, Northern Scrub-robin (isolated populations of this species may survive in the Roper River region of the Northern Territory, but the bird has not been recorded from there since the early 1900s and is possibly extinct), Yellow-legged Flycatcher, White-faced Robin, Frilled Monarch, Tropical Scrubwren, Tawny-breasted, Green-backed and White-streaked

Honeyeater, Pale White-eye (so far as is known this species is confined to islands in Torres Strait and off the east coast of Cape York Peninsula; sightings south of the region have never been confirmed), Fawn-breasted Bowerbird, Magnificent Riflebird, Trumpet Manucode and Black-backed Butcherbird.

While these species alone are enough to lure any bird-watcher, Cape York Peninsula has a great many more interesting birds of which the following are perhaps the most notable. The list is rather long, an indication of just how rich the region's birdlife is: Southern Cassowary (restricted to areas of rainforest along the peninsula's east coast), Brown Booby, Great and Least Frigatebird, Great-billed and Pied Heron, Black Bittern, Black-necked Stork, Magpie Goose, Wandering and Plumed Whistling-Duck, Radjah Shelduck, Cotton (most often recorded in the southeastern part of the region) and Green Pygmy-Goose, Pacific Baza, Square-tailed Kite, Black-breasted Buzzard, Grey Goshawk, Red Goshawk (very rare, but definitely worth looking for), Orange-footed Scrubfowl, King Quail, Red-backed and Red-chested Button-quail, Red-necked (mainly along the east coast) and White-browed Crake, Bush-hen, Brolga, Sarus Crane, Australian Bustard, Comb-crested Jacana, Bush and Beach Thick-knee, Roseate, Black-naped, Sooty, Bridled and Lesser Crested Tern, Common and Black Noddy, Superb, Rose-crowned and Wompoo Fruit-Dove, Torresian Imperial-Pigeon (a common spring–summer visitor), Squatter Pigeon (most numerous in the drier southern part of the region; often seen along the road between Mt Molloy and Cooktown), Red-tailed Black-Cockatoo, Double-eyed Fig-Parrot (most often recorded in areas of lowland rainforest along the east coast), Red-winged Parrot, Oriental Cuckoo (summer), Gould's Bronze-Cuckoo, Rufous, Barking and Eastern Grass Owl, Papuan and Marbled Frogmouth (the latter species is restricted to areas of rainforest; though rarely seen it probably occurs only along the east coast, north of Princess Charlotte Bay), Large-tailed Nightjar, White-rumped Swiftlet (it would pay to look very closely at any small swift-like birds you see on Cape York Peninsula since two other species of swiftlet, Glossy and Uniform, have been recorded in the area), Azure, Little and Collared Kingfisher, Buff-breasted Paradise-Kingfisher (a summer visitor; restricted to areas of rainforest, chiefly on the east coast), Noisy Pitta (mainly summer), Yellow-eyed Cuckoo-shrike (largely confined to the east coast), Varied Triller, Mangrove and White-browed Robin, Lemon-bellied Flycatcher, Mangrove Golden Whistler, Grey Whistler, White-breasted Whistler (to date this mangrove-dwelling species has only been recorded in the vicinity of the Edward River Mission on the shores of the Gulf of Carpentaria, but the bird may be more widespread than records

CAPE YORK PENINSULA

suggest because the coast between Weipa and Karumba is so remote it is seldom visited by bird-watchers), Yellow-breasted Boatbill (restricted to patches of rainforest), Black-winged (summer, and chiefly along the east coast), Spectacled and (confined to the east coast) White-eared Monarch, Broad-billed (mainly along the west coast) and Shining Flycatcher, Northern Fantail, Tawny Grassbird, Zitting Cisticola (recorded only in the vicinity of the Edward River Mission on the peninsula's west coast; there is, however, an unconfirmed record from Weipa) Large-billed, Mangrove (chiefly along the west coast) and Fairy Gerygone, Helmeted, Silver-crowned, Noisy and Little Friarbird Blue-faced, Yellow-spotted, Graceful, Varied (mainly along the east coast), Yellow, Brown-backed, Bar-breasted (mainly in the south), Rufous-banded, Rufous-throated (chiefly in the southwest), Banded, Dusky and Red-headed Honeyeater, Yellowbellied Sunbird, Red-browed Pardalote, Yellow White-eye (confined to the west coast of the peninsula, south of Weipa) Star, Crimson and Masked Finch (all three species occur mainly in the southern part of the region), Black-throated Finch, Pictorella Mannikin (recorded only from the Edward River Mission area on the west coast), Metallic Starling (mainly summer), Yellow Oriole Great Bowerbird, Spotted Catbird (restricted to rainforest on the east coast) and Black Butcherbird.

The best time to visit Cape York Peninsula is at the height of the dry season — June to September. During the wet season, and often for a month or more afterwards, much of the area is completely cut off by floodwaters. Even at the driest times there are numerous creeks and several large rivers to cross, including the Jardine, which is usually 1 m deep and some 200 m wide at the crossing point. Needless to say a four-wheel-drive vehicle is essential if you wish to travel much beyond Cooktown (the road to Cooktown, though rough in places, is quite suitable for conventional cars). Supplies and petrol can be obtained at Cooktown Coen and Weipa, but these places are separated by hundreds of kilometres of rough roads and you should be prepared for any eventuality. Carry an ample supply of food and water, extra fuel a wide range of spare parts (including tyres), a full set of up-to date maps and a compass. Before you set out it would be wise to call at the police station in Cairns to inquire about road condition on the peninsula.

If you do not own a four-wheel-drive you can hire one in Cairns, but unless you are travelling in a group the cost could prove prohibitive. Alternatively, several commercial tour operator based in Cairns offer a wide range of camping holidays on the peninsula. Further information can be obtained from any branch of the Queensland Government Tourist Bureau, or from travel agent in Cairns. ('Going Places', 26 Abbott Street, Cairns, specialises in adventure holidays – for a detailed brochure write to PO Box 2097, Cairns, Qld 4870.) If you do decide to take a safari to Cape York, bear in mind that the region is vast and that it can take many days to travel from place to place. The more time you can spare the better; an eight-day safari, for example, will leave you little time each day for birding since you will be travelling from dawn to dusk.

If you do not have a four-wheel-drive vehicle and cannot afford to hire one, or if you are short of time, you can fly from Cairns to the Iron Range airstrip, from where transport can be arranged to Iron Range National Park. Situated on the peninsula's east coast, south of Temple Bay, the Iron Range – Cape Weymouth district contains the largest remaining areas of lowland tropical rainforest in Australia. A bird-watcher's mecca, Iron Range attracts visitors from all over the world and is *the* place to go for birds such as Palm Cockatoo, Eclectus and Red-cheeked Parrot, Chestnut-breasted Cuckoo, Yellow-billed Kingfisher, Red-bellied Pitta, Northern Scrub-robin, Yellow-legged Flycatcher, White-faced Robin, Black-winged and Frilled Monarch, Tropical Scrubwren, Tawny-breasted, Green-backed and White-streaked Honeyeater, Fawn-breasted Bowerbird, Magnificent Riflebird, Trumpet Manucode and a host of other highly sought-after species. Provided you have some bushwalking experience and are self-sufficient you could spend a most memorable week or so exploring Iron Range on foot. Camping permits and information about Iron Range and other national parks on Cape York Peninsula can be obtained from the Queensland National Parks and Wildlife Service at 41 Esplanade, Cairns.

Cape Tribulation National Park
Cape Tribulation National Park covers an area of 17 000 ha and lies to the north of Mossman, between the Daintree and Bloomfield Rivers. The reserve, one of the most important in Queensland, contains a wealth of outstanding features – superb coastal scenery with mountains rising to more than 1000 m, numerous cool, fresh-water streams that flow throughout the year, long stretches of white sandy beaches, and exceptionally rich vegetation including fine stands of upland and lowland rainforest, and highly complex mangrove communities.

The park can be reached by conventional vehicle from Mossman via the Daintree River vehicular ferry. Cape Tribulation itself is about 40 km north of the river via a narrow, unsealed road that may become impassable to all traffic following heavy rain. Camping is permitted at two delightful spots, Cape Tribulation beach and Noahs Beach, where you can pitch your tent or park your caravan in the rainforest within a stone's throw of the ocean. At present there are no facilities, but the reserve has only recently been established and there are plans to provide amenities in the near future.

Just outside the reserve, close to Cape Tribulation, there are two privately owned caravan parks — Masons near the mouth of Myall Creek (inquire at Masons shop nearby), and Pilgrim Sands a kilometre or so north of the cape. There is also a youth hostel in beautiful surroundings at the foot of Mt Sorrow, just a few hundred metres from a secluded, palm-fringed beach. Petrol can be obtained at the Floravilla tea gardens, some 12 km north of the Daintree River, and basic provisions are available at Masons shop. For those without their own transport a regular bus service operates between Cairns and the Cape Tribulation youth hostel.

The coastal strip and highlands between the Daintree and Bloomfield Rivers support a wide variety of birds, including Southern Cassowary, Great-billed and Striated Heron, Eastern Reef Egret, Black Bittern, Pacific Baza, Brahminy Kite, Grey Goshawk, Red Goshawk, Orange-footed Scrubfowl, King Quail, Red-backed Button-quail, Red-necked Crake, Bush-hen, Beach Thick-knee, Superb, Rose-crowned and Wompoo Fruit-Dove, Torresian Imperial-Pigeon (spring—summer), Topknot and White-headed Pigeon, Brown Cuckoo-Dove, Emerald Dove, Double-eyed Fig-Parrot, Channel-billed Cuckoo (summer), Rufous and Lesser Sooty Owl, Papuan Frogmouth, Large-tailed Nightjar, White-rumped Swiftlet, Little Kingfisher, Buff-breasted Paradise-Kingfisher (summer), Noisy Pitta, Yellow-eyed Cuckoo-shrike, Cicadabird (summer), Varied Triller, Mangrove, Pale-yellow and Grey-headed Robin, Lemon-bellied Flycatcher, Grey Whistler, Little and Bower's Shrike-thrush, Yellow-breasted Boatbill, Black-faced (chiefly summer), Spectacled, White-eared and Pied Monarch, Shining Flycatcher, Northern Fantail, Chowchilla, Australian Fernwren, Large-billed and Yellow-throated Scrubwren, Large-billed and Fairy Gerygone, Mountain Thornbill, Little Treecreeper, Macleay's, Yellow-spotted, Graceful, Bridled, Varied, Yellow, Brown-backed, Dusky and Scarlet Honeyeater, Yellow-bellied Sunbird, Chestnut-breasted Mannikin, Metallic Starling (summer), Yellow Oriole, Golden Bowerbird (seldom found below 900 m), Tooth-billed and Spotted Catbird, Victoria's Riflebird and Black Butcherbird.

At least a few of the species mentioned, like the Red Goshawk, are of note because they are extremely rare, while others — White-headed Pigeon, Lesser Sooty Owl, Pale-yellow and Grey-headed Robin, Bower's Shrike-thrush, Pied Monarch, Chowchilla, Australian Fernwren, Mountain Thornbill, Macleay's Honeyeater, Golden Bowerbird and Tooth-billed Catbird for example — are of particular interest because they do not occur on Cape York Peninsula north of Cooktown.

The rainforests in the vicinity of Cape Tribulation, like those in

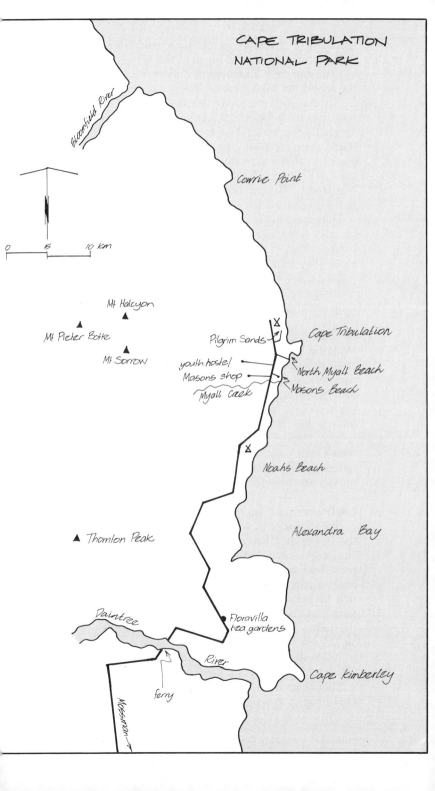

the Cairns − Atherton Tableland region to the south, are virtually impenetrable. Access to much of the area is somewhat restricted, but you can enjoy excellent birding by simply driving slowly along the road from the Daintree River to the cape, stopping wherever tracks lead into the forest. At Noahs Beach, a particularly good spot for Orange-footed Scrubfowl and Noisy Pitta, the vegetation is relatively open and quite easy to walk through, while further north there are plenty of tracks near the youth hostel, providing access to the lower slopes of Mt Sorrow. For mangrove species such as Collared Kingfisher and Shining Flycatcher pay a visit to North Myall Beach, just past the youth hostel, where a boardwalk has been constructed through a patch of mangroves.

Those wishing to see something of the region's famous marine life will find Cape Tribulation the perfect place from which to explore what is perhaps the finest section of the Great Barrier Reef. (South of the Daintree many coral reefs have been killed by pollution following land development.) You can hire diving gear, and obtain information about boat trips to the reef, from Masons shop and the youth hostel.

Cape York Peninsula, north of 16 degrees latitude

With the exception of Iron Range, Cape York Peninsula north of 16 degrees latitude has until recently been little explored by birdwatchers. As a result much remains to be discovered about the distribution and habits of many of the region's birds. For example, the nest of the Yellow-legged Flycatcher was not found in Australia until as late as 1977, yet the bird is not uncommon in suitable habitat throughout the northern part of the peninsula. Clearly then Cape York has a great deal to offer the keen observer; the following list of places, while by no means complete, will at least provide the basis for a stay of two, three, or even four weeks in the area.

Cooktown: Is a small, historic township some 330 km north of Cairns. Situated in very pleasant surroundings near the mouth of the Endeavour River, it is the most northerly settlement of any size on Australia's east coast. It has motels, hotels and a caravan park, and makes a good base from which to explore the southeastern part of the peninsula, including the splendid rainforests that lie between the township and the Bloomfield River. Cooktown has many fine old buildings; if you are interested in history the James Cook Memorial Museum on the corner of Furneaux and Helen Streets is well worth a visit, as are Cook's landing place in Adelaide Street and the cemetery in Charlotte Street. It is also worth taking a cruise on the Endeavour River.

There are four national parks in the area: Endeavour River (1840 ha), a reserve of great scientific and historic significance, situated some 5 km north-west of the township; Mt Cook (494 ha), another park of historical interest just 2 km south of Cooktown; Black Mountain (781 ha), an area almost devoid of vegetation, featuring huge black granite boulders and situated about 30 km from Cooktown, adjacent to the road to Mt Molloy; and Cedar Bay (5630 ha), an outstanding mountainous reserve — the best park near Cooktown for birds — located some 50 km south of the township on the coast near the Bloomfield River. For further information about these parks contact the Queensland National Parks and Wildlife Service in Cairns.

Lizard Island National Park: This 1012 ha continental island lies some 90 km north-east of Cooktown, close to the outer Great Barrier Reef. It can be reached by private boat, or by plane from Cooktown or Cairns. For those with money to spare (rooms start at $130 a day), accommodation is available at the Lizard Island Lodge, a small but exclusive resort on the western side of the island. You are permitted to camp in the national park, but only for a week; for a permit and further information about the reserve contact the Queensland National Parks and Wildlife Service in Cairns.

If you have the time — and cash! — to visit Lizard Island you will not be disappointed. It really does have everything — a marvellous climate, superb scenery, secluded beaches, varied vegetation and birdlife, and of course the Great Barrier Reef. Lizard is almost entirely surrounded by undisturbed coral gardens and has a reputation for being one of the best places in the world to go diving.

The national park is largely undeveloped. There are, however, basic facilities in the camping area, just north of the resort, and a walking track leading to Cooks Look (360 m), the highest point on the island and the place where Captain Cook stood in 1770 while searching for a safe passage through the reef for his ship the *Endeavour*.

Lakefield National Park: Established in late 1979, this 537 000 ha reserve is the second-largest national park in Queensland (Simpson Desert, 555 000 ha, is the largest). It encompasses a wide variety of habitats ranging from the mudflats and mangroves fringing Princess Charlotte Bay in the north to the open grasslands and woodlands in the south, and includes the Normanby, Laura and Kennedy River systems. Much of the area is flooded during the wet season.

Nearly two hundred species of birds have been recorded, including sought-after species such as Black-necked Stork, Cotton and Green Pygmy-Goose, Brolga, Sarus Crane and Comb-crested Jacana, and that outstanding rarity the Golden-shouldered Parrot. The park is undeveloped, but bush camping is allowed at a number of sites. You must obtain a permit in advance; for further information contact the Queensland National Parks and Wildlife Service in Cairns, or write to the ranger, Lakefield National Park, PMB 29, Cairns Mail Centre, Qld 4870, enclosing a stamped, addressed envelope. Access to the park can be gained during the dry season from Cooktown via Battle Camp Station, from Laura via Olive Vale Station, and from the Peninsula Developmental Road via Musgrave Station. (There are numerous termite mounds on the plains in the vicinity of Musgrave Station. Since this is a favoured haunt of the Golden-shouldered Parrot a thorough search of the area should prove rewarding.)

Weipa: Is the site of a giant bauxite mine on the shores of the Gulf of Carpentaria. Accessible by air from Cairns, and in the dry season via the Peninsula Developmental Road, the township has a motel-hotel called, perhaps inappropriately, the Albatross (Cape York is not a place where you would normally expect to find an albatross). Weipa makes a good base from which to explore the peninsula's west coast. Large numbers of Great and Least Frigate-birds are said to roost each evening in trees beside the road to the airport; Great-billed Herons are quite common along the shores of the gulf (particularly in the vicinity of Tent Pole Creek — ask locally for directions to this and other places of interest around Weipa); Pied Herons are often seen at the town's sewage works; Yellow-billed Kingfishers and Frilled Monarchs frequent the monsoon forest at Batavia Landing; and Mangrove Golden Whistlers and Shining Flycatchers occur in the mangroves along Beening Creek.

Iron Range National Park (34 600 ha): This famed bird-watching area is accessible during the dry season via the Peninsula Developmental Road and Wenlock. Up-to-date information about facilities, and further details about access, can be obtained from the Queensland National Parks and Wildlife Service in Cairns.

5

Tasmania

Useful addresses

Bird Observers Association of Tasmania
GPO Box 68A
Hobart, Tas. 7001

Tasmanian Field Naturalists Club
GPO Box 68A
Hobart, Tas. 7001

Launceston Field Naturalists Club
Secretary, 7 Carmen Court
Hadspen, Tas. 7257

Tasmanian National Parks and Wildlife Service
16 Magnet Court
Sandy Bay, Tas. 7005

Key to Maps

▨	Public land
▨	Areas of water
▲	Mountain peak
⏦	Mountain range or plateau
COBAR ●	Place name
⨯	Camping area
⚲	Lighthouse
⏧ ⏧ ⏧	Marsh
▬▬▬	Major road or highway
———	Minor road
- - - - -	Foot track
··—·—	National park boundary
-———	State boundary
⤳	River or creek

HOBART

Australia's most southerly capital nestles beneath Mt Wellington, near the mouth of the River Derwent. It has been said that Hobart is one of the world's most ideally situated cities, and from a bird-watcher's point of view there is much truth in the claim. Within 30 km or so of the city centre there is a wide variety of habitats that include alpine grasslands and marshlands, dry and wet sclerophyll forests, riverside marshes and reedbeds, and coastal lagoons and mudflats. About 150 bird species regularly occur in the region, including all the Tasmanian endemics – Tasmanian Native-hen, Green Rosella, Dusky Robin, Scrubtit, Tasmanian Thornbill, Yellow Wattlebird, Yellow-throated, Strong-

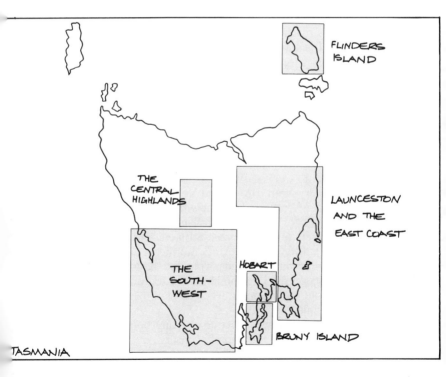

TASMANIA

FLINDERS ISLAND

THE CENTRAL HIGHLANDS

LAUNCESTON AND THE EAST COAST

THE SOUTH-WEST

HOBART

BRUNY ISLAND

billed and Black-headed Honeyeater, Forty-spotted Pardalote and Black Currawong.

By Australian standards Hobart is a historic city; more than ninety of its buildings have National Trust classification, and the harbour boasts the finest collection of old warehouses and stores in any Australian port. Constitution Dock, terminal point of the famous Sydney to Hobart yacht race, lies close to the city centre.

The city offers a wide choice of accommodation, including the international-class hotel-casino at Wrest Point, motels, hotels and guest houses. For those on a tight budget there are youth hostels at 52 King Street, Bellerive, and 7 Woodlands Avenue, New Town. The Youth Hostels Association's head office is at 28 Criterion Street, Hobart. The nearest caravan parks are at Sandy Bay, Berriedale and Goodwood. Hobart's airport is of international standard, and there are direct flights to most mainland capitals as well as weekly services to Christchurch and Auckland in New Zealand. Rental cars and campervans are readily available.

Royal Tasmanian Botanical Gardens

Botanical gardens are always pleasant places to visit, and Hobart's are no exception. Situated within Queens Domain, just 2 km north of the city centre, the gardens cover an area of 13.5 ha and are easily reached by car or public transport via Brooker Avenue or the Tasman Highway. They are open daily from 8 a.m., admission is free, there is a restaurant within the gardens, and a wheelchair is available on request.

Since many of the plants are exotic, this is not one of the best places near Hobart for native birds. Nevertheless quite a number of common species are usually present and readily observed. These include White-faced Heron, Pacific Black Duck, Silver Gull, Green and Eastern Rosella, Laughing Kookaburra, Welcome Swallow (spring−summer), Tree Martin (spring−summer), Black-faced Cuckoo-shrike (spring−summer), Grey Fantail, Superb Fairy-wren, Brown and Yellow-rumped Thornbill, Yellow and Little Wattlebird, Yellow-throated, Crescent (especially autumn−winter) and New Holland Honeyeater, Eastern Spinebill, Spotted and (summer) Striated Pardalote, and Silvereye (summer). More rarely, Musk Lorikeets and Swift Parrots turn up, usually when the eucalypts are flowering. The latter occasionally occur in large numbers in parks and gardens throughout the city, but not in winter, when most of their population migrates to the mainland.

The gardens have, of course, many botanical attractions. Be sure not to miss the superb conservatory; built in 1939, it is regarded as one of the best in the Commonwealth, and ten

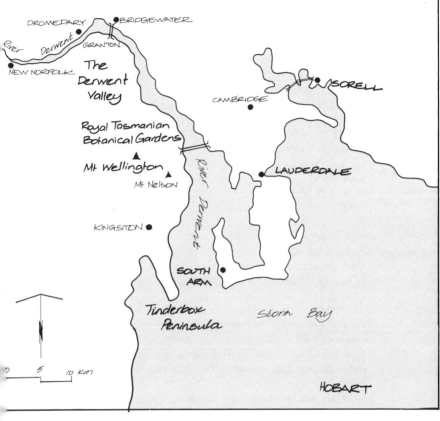

thousand plants are grown annually for inclusion in its colourful floral displays.

Mt Wellington

Hobart residents are very fortunate to have such an interesting and diverse bird-watching area right on their doorstep. At 1270 m the mountain dominates the entire region, providing an impressive backdrop to the city. A sealed road leads to the summit, which offers spectacular views over Hobart and the Derwent estuary to the Tasman Peninsula. Above 1100 m the alpine scenery is dominated by snow gums, with Austral-montane flora characterised by tough, low-growing vegetation on the summit plateau.

Although the effects of the disastrous 1967 fires can still be seen, most of the three hundred or so plant species found in the region survived; bird-watchers thus have a unique opportunity to visit many vegetational zones within a comparatively small area. The zones overlap to some extent, but for bird-watching purposes they can be broadly divided into four categories: cleared land and dry sclerophyll forest up to 500 m; wet sclerophyll forest and gully communities up to 800 m; woodlands dominated by urn gum up to 1100 m and by snow gum above that; and the treeless marshlands and grasslands of the upper regions.

About sixty bird species have been recorded in the area. Some are ubiquitous, namely Fan-tailed Cuckoo, Flame Robin and Forest Raven, but many show a preference for just one or two zones. Bird-watchers with limited time available will therefore find it more productive to visit a single site within each zone than to travel from place to place in search of birds. The picture is further complicated by summer−winter migration and altitudinal movement. Quite a large number of species leave Tasmania almost entirely in order to winter on the mainland. These include Swift Parrot, all the cuckoos, Welcome Swallow, Tree Martin, Black-faced Cuckoo-shrike, Satin Flycatcher, Striated Pardalote and Dusky Woodswallow. Altitudinal migrants include Flame Robin and Superb Fairy-wren; both are less widespread in winter than in summer. Conversely, Green Rosella, Yellow-tailed Black-Cockatoo, Pink Robin, Scarlet Robin and Eastern Spinebill all extend their ranges during winter.

Resident bird-watchers will find something of interest all year round and will undoubtedly want to explore the region fully. Access to Mt Wellington can be gained via the suburbs Fern Tree, Cascades and Lenah Valley. There are regular bus services to all these places. The visitor with only a day or two to spare will find the following spots easy to get to, and representative of the broad vegetational zones already outlined. Visits to Fern Tree, for ferns and birds, and to the summit, for alpine flora and wonderful views, are considered essential. Even in summer the weather is unpredictable, so that you should make the most of a sunny day; tomorrow it may be raining or perhaps snowing on top.

Halls Saddle: From the city centre take the Huon Highway to Fern Tree (9 km) and stop at the picnic area near the Chimney Pot Hill Road turn-off, about 1 km before Fern Tree. From here it is an easy downhill walk, via the well-graded Pipeline walking track, to the waterworks reserve. The vegetation is predominantly dry sclerophyll forest, but there are patches of open woodland and some cleared land. In summer look for Brown Goshawk, Swift Parrot, Pallid and Fan-tailed Cuckoo, Horsfield's Bronze-Cuckoo, Tawny Frogmouth, Tree Martin, Black-faced Cuckoo-shrike,

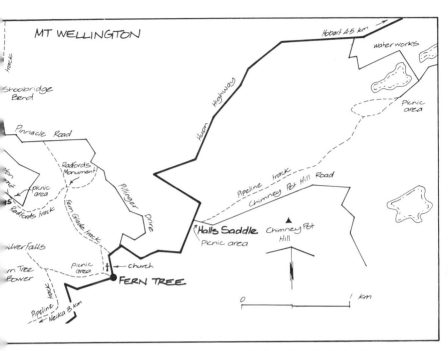

Scarlet Robin, Golden Whistler, Grey Shrike-thrush, Satin Fly-catcher, Grey Fantail, Superb Fairy-wren, Brown Thornbill, Yellow-throated and Black-headed Honeyeater, Eastern Spine-bill, Spotted and Striated Pardalote, Dusky Woodswallow and Grey Currawong. Marsh Harrier, Brown Falcon, Tasmanian Native-hen, Masked Lapwing, Common Bronzewing, Welcome Swallow, Richard's Pipit, Dusky Robin and Yellow-rumped Thornbill can be found in the cleared areas and along the forest margins.

There is a good network of walking tracks in the area and a full day of exploration is possible. However, a walk to the waterworks and back, a distance of 5 km or so, need only take a few hours.

Fern Tree: In contrast to the dry sclerophyll forest on the exposed lower slopes of Mt Wellington, wet forest occurs at higher elevations and in moist gullies. From the picnic area at Fern Tree, some good examples of this habitat are easily found via walking tracks to Fern Tree Bower and Silver Falls (suitable for wheelchairs), The Springs, Neika and elsewhere. Those with little time will find the Fern Glade track, just north of Fern Tree, highly rewarding. It follows Longhill Creek for about 1 km through a dense stand of tree ferns — a good place to look for Scrubtit. This small Tasmanian endemic looks rather like a White-browed Scrubwren, which is very common here, but the Scrubtit's white throat and treecreeper-like habits help to distinguish it from the duller, mostly ground-dwelling scrubwren. The attractive Pink Robin is also quite common and breeds in the gully — a quiet, diminutive bird easily overlooked. One species with a wide distribution in Tasmania and on the mainland, but which is usually difficult to locate, is White's Thrush. Along the Fern Glade track it is plentiful during summer and not at all shy. After about 1.5 km Radfords Monument is reached, and from here wide walking tracks lead in several directions. The dense, wet forest at this point holds Beautiful Firetail, which often appears briefly on the track ahead.

The Springs: Mt Wellington summit is easily accessible via Pillinger Drive and Pinnacle Road, and the 12 km trip is well worthwhile. En route the views are unsurpassed, and at 720 m there is a pleasant picnic area and a shelter hut at a spot known as The Springs. The vegetation above this point changes noticeably, with urn and snow gums starting to appear. About 500 m north of the picnic area, the Lenah Valley track leaves Pinnacle Road and connects with the Shoobridge track after about 1.5 km. These two paths are well constructed and a walk here is recommended. The middle-level forest holds a good variety of birds, including endemics such as Green Rosella, Tasmanian Thornbill, Yellow-throated and Strong-billed Honeyeater, and Black Currawong. Other birds include Shining Bronze-Cuckoo (summer), Grey Shrike-thrush, Grey Fantail, White-browed Scrubwren, Crescent Honeyeater, Striated Pardalote (summer) and Silvereye. Olive Whistlers are quite plentiful and usually easier to observe than in the densely vegetated gullies at lower elevations. Flocks of magnificent Yellow-tailed Black-Cockatoos frequently screech overhead, while predators such as Brown Goshawk, Wedge-tailed Eagle, Peregrine Falcon, Brown Falcon and Grey Goshawk are possibilities. The energetic observer may care to search for Spotted Quail-thrush in the woodlands above The Springs.

The Pinnacle: The treeless summit of Mt Wellington holds few birds, although Forest Ravens frequent the top (there are no identification problems here, as there are on the mainland, for this is the only corvid found in Tasmania), and the delightful Flame Robin breeds right up to the tree-line. In summer the robin can usually be found along the Collins Bonnet track, which leaves Pinnacle Road about 2 km downhill from the summit carpark. Here males can be seen perched in the snow gums, their brilliant orange-red breasts flashing in the sunlight. Another bird that occurs at high elevations is the Calamanthus; it is frequently found above 1000 m in woodlands dominated by snow gums.

The entire Mt Wellington region is worthy of thorough exploration. There are many fine walks ranging from an hour or so to a full day, but a good map is essential. The Mt Wellington Walk Map, which is particularly useful, can be purchased from the State Government Publications Centre in Hobart, or from the Tasmanian Wilderness Society. Since the weather may change rapidly at any time of the year, be prepared, especially when walking above 600 m.

Mt Nelson Signal Station and Truganini Reserves

These two adjoining reserves occupy about 60 ha on the slopes of Mt Nelson, 8 km south of the city centre. From the 340 m summit there are panoramic views over Hobart and the Derwent estuary. Picnic facilities, a tea-house (in the old Signal Station cottage), and walking tracks through the dry sclerophyll forest that covers much of the surrounding area make this the ideal spot for an early morning or afternoon visit. About fifty bird species have been recorded in the reserves, including at least five endemics − Green Rosella, Dusky Robin, Yellow-throated Honeyeater, Black-headed Honeyeater and Yellow Wattlebird. Other species include Black-faced Cuckoo-shrike (summer), Flame and Scarlet Robin, Grey Shrike-thrush, Satin Flycatcher (summer), Grey Fantail, Superb Fairy-wren, Brown Thornbill, Crescent and New Holland Honeyeater, Eastern Spinebill, Spotted and (summer) Striated Pardalote, and Silvereye. At least two cuckoos − Pallid and·Fan-tailed − are usually present during summer, and the noisy, gregarious Swift Parrot turns up (at times) in the spring and summer months. In winter the rare Forty-spotted Pardalote, which occurs nearby at Tinderbox, is a possibility.

From the Signal Station carpark, the Truganini walking track leads downhill through dry forest to the Channel Highway. Allow two hours for the return walk. For a time the track runs parallel to Cartwright Creek, where Beautiful Firetails and occasionally Masked Owls breed. Other nocturnal species seen in the reserves include Southern Boobook and Tawny Frogmouth.

The area is not famed for its birdlife but a pleasant few hours, particularly in the early morning, can be spent here. There are regular bus services from Hobart.

Tinderbox Peninsula

At first glance the lightly timbered Tinderbox Hills do not look very exciting, but the area is surprisingly good for birds; Tasmanian endemics are especially plentiful. Unfortunately there are few reserves and many of the most attractive areas are on private property where 'keep out' signs abound. However, Tinderbox Road is usually quiet, and good birding can be enjoyed simply by stopping at intervals.

The peninsula is approximately 14 km south of Hobart via

Kingston and Blackmans Bay. About 6 km south of Blackmans Bay, on the eastern side of the peninsula, there are some tennis courts and a lookout at Piersons Point. The slopes of Mt Louis, just across the road, are a known haunt of that elusive Forty-spotted Pardalote. This Tasmanian endemic was once quite widely distributed but is now confined to a few islands and peninsulas along the south-east coast. The total population is estimated at between 2500 and 3000, with about 75 birds inhabiting the Tinderbox Peninsula. Spotted Pardalotes also occur here; take care not to confuse the two. Many other species frequenting the area include Dusky Robin, Yellow Wattlebird, and Strong-billed and Black-headed Honeyeater. Indeed, mainland visitors with little time in Hobart will find this one of the best places for concentrated bird-watching. Tinderbox Road continues around the peninsula to Howden, and beyond Tinderbox Bay there is a good patch of scrub adjacent to a jetty. This area is not private property and several tracks provide easy access.

The Derwent Valley

Hobart's northern suburbs extend along the banks of the Derwent to beyond Glenorchy, but the river is still a good place to go bird-watching. The suburban parks hold hordes of Masked Lapwings, as well as Noisy Miners and a few other species. In summer Arctic Jaegers can be seen patrolling the lower reaches of the river near Hobart, while Marsh Harriers are plentiful throughout the area.

Along the southern banks of the river, especially between Granton and New Norfolk, there are many accessible spots worth visiting for grebes, cormorants, herons, egrets, waterfowl, rails and crakes. The area just west of the Bridgewater causeway is usually the best place for waterfowl. Black Swan, Australian Shelduck, Pacific Black Duck, Grey and Chestnut Teal (the latter sometimes in hundreds), Australasian Shoveler and Musk Duck are the most common species, but Hardhead and Blue-billed Duck turn up occasionally. Hoary-headed Grebe, Great, Little Black and Little Pied Cormorant, and Eurasian Coot, can also usually be seen here. Goulds Lagoon Wildlife Sanctuary, which lies next to the main road to Claremont, about 2 km south-east of Granton, is also worth a visit. This small, reed-fringed lagoon may be dry in summer but at times its muddy margins attract quite a variety of birds, particularly Tasmanian Native-hen, rails and crakes. (Interestingly, a Little Ringed Plover was seen at Goulds Lagoon in March 1982.) The lagoon is best viewed from behind on Hestercombe Road, as the main Claremont to Granton route is often very busy.

To the north of the river, the extensive marshes and reedbeds near Dromedary are worth looking over for White-faced Heron,

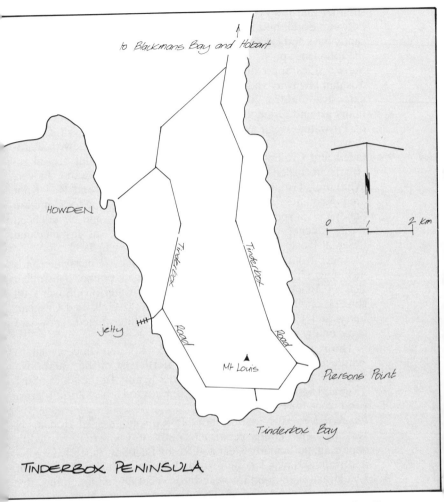

TINDERBOX PENINSULA

Great Egret (winter), Australasian Bittern (rarely), Swamp Quail, Lewin's Rail, Baillon's, Australian and Spotless Crake (the crakes are rather rare and most often recorded in summer), Purple Swamphen, Latham's Snipe (summer), Clamorous Reed-Warbler (summer), Little Grassbird and White-fronted Chat. Southern Emu-wren is a possibility. Green Point Nature Reserve, which lies just south of Bridgewater, is also worth exploring.

Sorell, Lauderdale and South Arm

Migratory waders rarely visit the Hobart region in large numbers because it lies at the southern limit of the range of many species. Nevertheless quite a variety of these birds can be seen during summer and the best wader localities lie to the east of the city, between Sorell and South Arm. Here the mudflats, saltmarshes, sandy bays and lagoons warrant thorough exploration, particularly the following spots.

Sorell: Lies approximately 25 km north-east of Hobart via the Tasman Highway and Midway Point. The mudflats there are very extensive, and from the Sorell causeway it is possible to walk for hours around Orielton Lagoon to the west, and along the shores of Pittwater as far as Iron Creek to the east. Lesser Golden Plover, Eastern Curlew, Greenshank, Bar-tailed Godwit, Sharp-tailed and Curlew Sandpiper, and Red-necked Stint are all regularly recorded, while Mongolian and Large Sand Plover, Whimbrel, Grey-tailed Tattler, Terek Sandpiper and Red Knot are possibilities. The causeway may be worth visiting for Common Sandpiper, a species that favours rocky habitat, and experienced wader-watchers may turn up something exciting — at least nineteen Oriental Plovers were seen on Orielton Lagoon in 1982.

Apart from waders, the area holds many other waterbirds including Great Crested and Hoary-headed Grebe, Australian Pelican, Black-faced Shag, herons, egrets, waterfowl, Silver Gull (breeds on the causeway), Pacific and Kelp Gull, and Caspian, Fairy and Crested Tern. In summer White-winged Terns are occasionally seen here.

Those travelling to Sorell from Hobart may find a visit to Barilla Bay worthwhile. It lies just north-east of the Cambridge Aerodrome and is a well-known wader haunt. To the south of the Tasman Highway, the grasslands adjacent to Hobart Airport are a good place for Banded Lapwing.

Lauderdale: This town is about 15 km south-east of Hobart via Rokeby. The entire peninsula south of Lauderdale is worth exploring, particularly Clear and Rushy Lagoons, Pipeclay Lagoon and Ralphs Bay. Clear and Rushy Lagoons, about 3 km south of Lauderdale, are good for waterbirds generally, although they dry up completely at times. They have produced some notable migratory species including Wood and Pectoral Sandpiper. Pipeclay Lagoon is about 6 km south of Lauderdale, between Cremorne and Clifton Beach. This extensive tidal lagoon is good for waders, including on occasions such rarities as Large Sand Plover, and in winter Double-banded Plovers arrive in substantial numbers from New Zealand.

Ralphs Bay, a wide expanse of mud and sand to the west of the peninsula, attracts a variety of waders including Pied and, more rarely, Sooty Oystercatcher, Lesser Golden (rarely), Double-banded (winter) and Red-capped Plover, Eastern Curlew (rarely), Grey-tailed Tattler (rarely), Greenshank, Bar-tailed Godwit, Red Knot (rarely), Red-necked Stint and Curlew Sandpiper. The

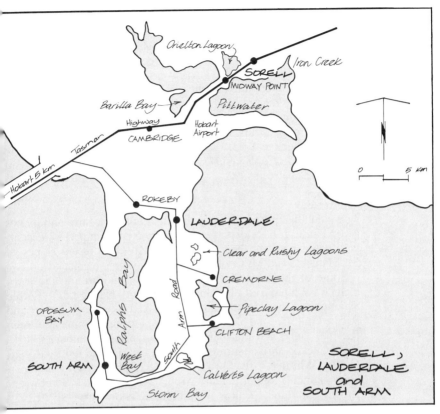

Map labels: Orielton Lagoon, Iron Creek, SORELL, MIDWAY POINT, Barilla Bay, Pittwater, Highway, Hobart Airport, Tasman, CAMBRIDGE, Hobart 5 km, 0 5 km, ROKEBY, LAUDERDALE, Ralphs Bay, Clear and Rushy Lagoons, CREMORNE, South Arm Road, OPOSSUM BAY, Pipeclay Lagoon, CLIFTON BEACH, SOUTH ARM, West Bay, Calverts Lagoon, Storm Bay, SORELL, LAUDERDALE and SOUTH ARM

whole of Ralphs Bay warrants attention, particularly the area known locally as West Bay.

South Arm State Recreation Area: About 30 km south-east of Hobart via South Arm Road, it covers an area of 122 ha and includes Calverts Lagoon. In summer, if it is not dry, the lagoon attracts quite a number of waders, and in winter Hooded Plovers can often be found there. The surrounding scrub holds a fair variety of bush birds. There are several picnic areas with fireplaces within the reserve and a fine beach, although strong rips make swimming dangerous. Goat Bluff, at the western end of the beach, offers fine views over Storm Bay and would be an excellent spot in winter for pelagics. Camping is not permitted; the nearest caravan parks are at Sorell and Hobart.

Some notable rarities have been recorded from the Lauderdale − South Arm area, including Little Curlew, Baird's Sandpiper (first Australian record) and Little Stint. Summer is the best time for migratory waders, although in winter there are still the resident species, Double-banded Plovers and seabirds to be seen.

BRUNY ISLAND

Bruny Island lies off the east coast of Tasmania, about 35 km south of Hobart. It is virtually two islands joined by a narrow isthmus. The northern section has been extensively cleared for agriculture, but the more attractive south island is still heavily forested and there are patches of temperate rainforest on Mt Mangana, the region's highest point (571 m). The island featured prominently in the early exploration of Australia, and Adventure Bay, on South Bruny, is named after Furneaux's ship, which anchored there in 1773. Other famous explorers who visited the region include Cook in 1777, Bligh in 1788, and the Frenchman D'Entrecasteaux in 1792.

Adventure Bay

This small historic township is the main holiday centre and makes a good base. It has stores, petrol, and two caravan parks pleasantly situated near the beach, with the densely forested slopes of Mt Mangana and Mt Cook providing an impressive backdrop.

Some of the birds that may be seen in and around the town include White-faced Heron, Tasmanian Native-hen, Purple Swamphen, Pied Oystercatcher, Masked Lapwing, Silver and Pacific Gull, Crested Tern, Swift Parrot (spring–summer), Green Rosella, Pallid and Fan-tailed Cuckoo (spring–summer), Black-faced Cuckoo-shrike (spring–summer), Scarlet and Dusky Robin, Golden Whistler, Grey Shrike-thrush, Satin Flycatcher (summer), Grey Fantail, Superb Fairy-wren, White-browed Scrubwren, Brown Thornbill, Yellow Wattlebird, Yellow-throated, Strong-billed, Black-headed, Crescent and New Holland Honeyeater, Eastern Spinebill, Spotted Pardalote, Silvereye, Beautiful Firetail, Dusky Woodswallow (summer), Black Currawong and Forest Raven. White-bellied Sea-Eagles sometimes soar majestically over Mt Cook, while Yellow-tailed Black-Cockatoos frequently screech overhead.

From East Cove, on the outskirts of Adventure Bay, there is a walking track along the lower slopes of Mt Cook to Fluted Cape. Little Penguins breed on an island off the cape, and there are usually Australasian Gannets fishing in the bay. Bruny Island is a stronghold of the Kelp Gull, which colonised Australia from New Zealand in the mid-1900s. It is now firmly established in the region and a few birds can generally be found at East Cove. The Kelp Gull's rollicking call, which will be instantly recognised by bird-watchers familiar with the 'seagulls' of Europe, helps to distinguish it from the similar Pacific Gull, which is common in the area. Indeed this is one of the few places in Australia where the two species can be seen side by side.

Mt Mangana lies to the south-west of Adventure Bay, via the

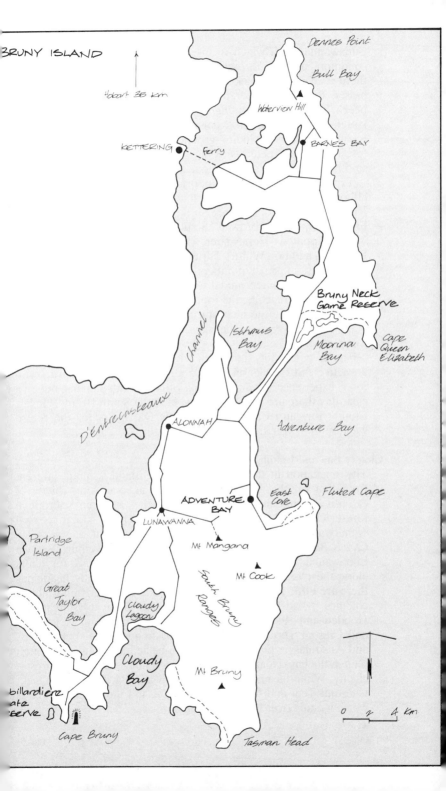

Lunawanna road, which is unsealed but normally in quite good condition. It winds through tall, wet forest and after about 4 km there is a walking track to the top of the mountain. The track passes through temperate rainforest characterised by myrtle beech (*Nothofagus cunninghamii*), sassafras, blackwood, native laurel, leatherwood, musk daisy-bush and celery-top pine. There is a feast of ferns including ground, epiphytic and tree ferns; the forest floor is carpeted with mosses; and the rocks and trees are smothered in lichen. The aroma, especially after rain, is superb.

Typically the rainforest supports only a small variety of birds, although there are the usual ubiquitous species such as Green Rosella, Dusky Robin, Grey Shrike-thrush, Grey Fantail, Superb Fairy-wren, White-browed Scrubwren, Tasmanian Thornbill, Yellow-throated Honeyeater, Black Currawong and Forest Raven. In addition White's Thrush, Pink Robin and Olive Whistler are present in small numbers along the track, and there are Crescent Honeyeaters and Eastern Spinebills near the summit. Shortly before reaching the top, the track drops into a moist, fern-filled gully where the inconspicuous Scrubtit occurs. This is probably the only place on the island where this Tasmanian endemic can be seen.

The ascent to the summit of Mt Mangana is one of the most attractive short walks on the island, offering visitors a true rainforest experience. The mountain is often shrouded in mist but on a clear day there are sweeping views over the South Bruny Ranges, Cloudy Bay and Cape Bruny. Allow two hours for the return walk, more if you are botanically minded.

Cloudy Bay and Labillardiere State Reserve

The vegetation in the south-west of the island is quite different from that on the slopes of Mt Mangana, consisting chiefly of extensive heathlands, swamps and patches of open sclerophyll forest. On the Labillardiere Peninsula there is superb coastal scenery and the beach at Cloudy Bay is magnificent.

Cloudy Bay: Lies about 18 km south-west of Adventure Bay via Lunawanna. From the carpark it is possible to walk for hours along the coast towards Tasman Head. In the sandy headlands there are Little Penguin and Short-tailed Shearwater (muttonbird) colonies, while the beach holds Pied and Sooty Oystercatcher, Hooded and Red-capped Plover, Silver, Pacific and Kelp Gull, and Crested Tern. Black-faced Shags frequent the rocky areas, and Australasian Gannets and White-bellied Sea-Eagles are often seen in the bay. Nearby, Cloudy Lagoon holds a few waterbirds – chiefly White-faced Heron, Black Swan, Pacific Black Duck, Chestnut Teal and Masked Lapwing – and the adjacent area is worth looking over for Swamp Quail.

Labillardiere State Reserve: Lies to the west of Cloudy Bay and is reached via the Lunawanna to Cape Bruny road. The reserve protects an extensive tract of coastal heath with patches of sclerophyll forest. Bush camping is permitted at a lovely site on the shores of Great Taylor Bay, about 6 km from the reserve entrance. From the camping ground there is a 15 km walking track around the peninsula, making this the ideal place for a most enjoyable day's hiking and bird-watching. The heathlands hold some interesting species — Calamanthus, Tawny-crowned Honeyeater, Beautiful Firetail and, perhaps, Ground Parrot — while the open forest supports a good variety of bush birds including Pallid and Fan-tailed Cuckoo (spring–summer), Scarlet and Dusky Robin, Golden Whistler, Grey Shrike-thrush, Grey Fantail, White-browed Scrubwren, Brown and Yellow-rumped Thornbill, Yellow and Little Wattlebird, Yellow-throated, Strong-billed, Black-headed, Crescent and New Holland Honeyeater, Eastern Spinebill, Spotted and (summer) Striated Pardalote, Silvereye, Dusky Woodswallow (summer), Grey Butcherbird, Grey Currawong and Forest Raven.

The lighthouse at Cape Bruny was built in 1836 and is the second-oldest manned lighthouse in Australia. It has been kept in good repair and is well worth a visit. The cape is very exposed, making this an ideal place to go seabird-watching during the winter months. Wandering, Royal (rarely), Black-browed, Yellow-nosed (rarely) and Shy Albatross, Southern and, more rarely, Northern Giant-Petrel, Cape, Great-winged and White-headed Petrel, prions and Fluttering Shearwater are some of the species you can expect to see.

Bruny Neck Game Reserve

To the west of the isthmus linking the north and south islands there is an extensive tidal bay worth looking over for waterbirds, while to the east, the long sweep of sandy beach holds Hooded Plover, gulls and terns. At the northern end Little Penguins and Short-tailed Shearwaters breed side by side in a well-known and clearly signposted colony. On a fine night this is a good spot to experience the joint spectacle of hundreds of shearwaters homing unerringly to their burrows and penguins popping — as if by magic — from the dark, cold waters of the Tasman Sea. Go at dusk and take a torch in order to avoid treading on a penguin or falling into a burrow.

About 2 km north of the isthmus a walking track leads to Moorina Bay and Cape Queen Elizabeth, passing a patch of woodland where Dusky Robins are usually plentiful. In the game reserve there are several lagoons that occasionally hold a few waterbirds, and the surrounding area is worth exploring for Marsh

Harrier, White-fronted Chat and a variety of other birds. Of particular interest is the small colony of Forty-spotted Pardalotes on a hill about 1.5 km north of Cape Queen Elizabeth. However, there are only a few pardalotes here and visitors wishing to see this rare Tasmanian endemic should search the northern slopes of Waterview Hill, about 3 km south of Dennes Point, where there is a much larger colony totalling a hundred birds or more. (Recent surveys indicate that Forty-spotted Pardalotes occur throughout much of North Bruny Island.)

Although Bruny Island is easily accessible by vehicular ferry from Kettering, it has remained relatively remote and unspoilt. The weather is rather unpredictable, but the generally cool climate at least deters the crowds. The Bligh Museum at Adventure Bay has a wealth of historical material and would be an excellent place to spend the inevitable wet day.

LAUNCESTON AND THE EAST COAST

Launceston

With a population of almost 65 000, Launceston is Tasmania's second-largest city. Founded in 1805, a year after Hobart, it is situated in a rich agricultural area at the head of the lovely Tamar River. Launceston has always been an important commercial centre and today, with tourism contributing significantly to its economy, the city offers the visitor a wide choice of accommodation including the international-class Country Club Casino. For those with fewer dollars to spare there are a number of inexpensive guest houses and a youth hostel in the city, though only one caravan park.

Launceston has many fine parks and gardens. City Park (12 ha), with its elegant fountain, Victorian bandstand and excellent conservatory, is perhaps the best known. Its lawns, flower-beds and exotic trees and shrubs do not, however, attract large numbers of native birds; a stroll through Cataract Gorge Reserve will prove more rewarding. Here you should have little difficulty finding common species such as White-faced Heron, Tasmanian Native-hen, Green Rosella, Fan-tailed Cuckoo (spring–summer), Black-faced Cuckoo-shrike (spring–summer), Grey Fantail, Superb Fairy-wren, Brown Thornbill, Striated Pardalote (spring–summer), Silvereye and Forest Raven. With luck, several Tasmanian endemic honeyeaters – Yellow Wattlebird, Yellow-throated and Black-headed Honeyeater – may be found in the reserve.

Cataract Gorge has quite a good network of walking tracks. One of the most popular walks, Cataract Walk, commences at Kings Bridge on Trevallyn Road. From here a well-formed path follows the northern edge of the gorge and terminates at the

Lake Pedder in the heart of Tasmania's wonderful south-west

Jagged mountain peaks and beautiful lakes are a feature of the Cradle Mountain − Lake St Clair National Park, Tasmania

Hooded Plover, a bird you can expect to see on Flinders Island, Bass Strait

Laughing Kookaburra, a common species throughout much of Tasmania

Towering sandhills and shallow lagoons: the Coorong, South Australia

Caspian (above), Fairy (above right) and Crested (right) Terns breed on islands in the Coorong

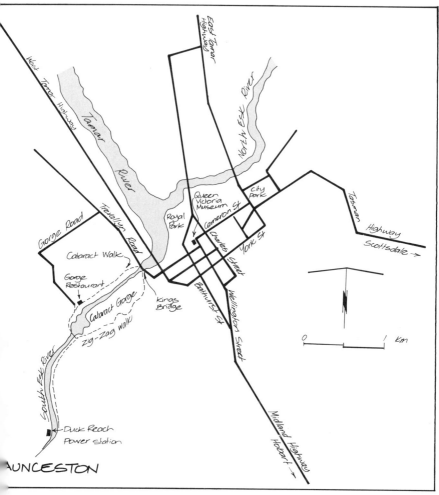

Gorge Restaurant, which is located in a delightful garden setting overlooking the South Esk River. Those wishing to continue upstream can cross the river via a suspension bridge, and follow the rough but well-defined track to the Duck Reach power station. Alternatively, after crossing the South Esk take the Zig-Zag Walk and return to Kings Bridge along the south side of the gorge.

Because the gorge is a popular picnic and swimming spot it is usually rather crowded at weekends, especially during summer. Nonetheless a very pleasant two or three hours could be spent here. Delicious Devonshire teas are served in the restaurant. A walking track guide can be obtained from the information centre,

Tasmania   273

which is housed in the old bandstand near the carpark at the end
of Gorge Road.

Perhaps more than any other part of the state, northern Tasmania
is a region of 'English' landscapes — winding rivers, deciduous
trees and narrow country lanes lined with hawthorn hedges. Some
of the early properties that dot the picturesque, rolling countryside surrounding Launceston have been extensively restored:
Entally House near Hadspen, 15 km south-west of Launceston,
and Clarendon House near Nile, 30 km south of the city, are both
open to the public and are well worth seeing. And before you
leave Launceston pay a visit to the Queen Victoria Museum in
Wellington Street. Open seven days a week, the museum has a
small but interesting bird section and admission is free.

From Launceston there are two routes south to Hobart — the
Midland Highway via Perth, Campbell Town, Ross and Oatlands
and the Tasman Highway via Scottsdale, St Helens, Bicheno,
Swansea, Orford and Sorell. From a bird-watcher's point of view
the latter route is the more rewarding because it provides ready
access to Tasmania's beautiful east coast, where there are two
outstanding national parks — Freycinet and Maria Island — and a
number of other good birding spots.

St Helens

St Helens, a small resort on the shores of Georges Bay about 170
km east of Launceston, is an excellent place to go bird-watching
particularly for those interested in waterbirds. Australian Pelican,
Australasian Gannet, Black-faced Shag, Great and Little Pied
Cormorant, Great (mainly in winter) and Little Egret (rather
rare, and mainly in winter), Black Swan, Australian Shelduck,
Pacific Black and Musk Duck, Chestnut Teal, White-bellied Sea-
Eagle, Pacific and (rather rare) Kelp Gull, Caspian and Crested
Tern are some of the species you can expect here. And look
closely at any small terns you encounter along this stretch of the
coast, because both Little and Fairy Terns have bred in the
St Helens area.

The extensive tidal mudflats and samphire flats lying between
the estuaries of the Golden Fleece and George Rivers, on the
northern shore of Georges Bay, attract a variety of waders. In
summer Lesser Golden Plover, Eastern Curlew, Greenshank,
Bar-tailed Godwit, Sharp-tailed Sandpiper and Red-necked Stint
can often be found here, while in winter Double-banded Plover
turn up in fair numbers. Non-migratory waders — Pied and Sooty
Oystercatcher, Masked Lapwing, Red-capped Plover — can be
found at St Helens (and at many other places along the coast)
throughout the year.

There are motels, guest houses, holiday units and two caravan

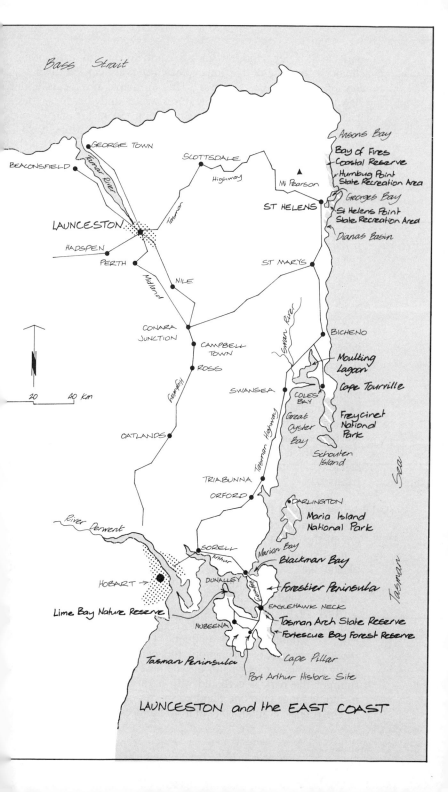

parks in St Helens; those wishing to camp in peaceful surroundings should stay in one of the three coastal reserves near the town.

Bay of Fires Coastal Reserve: This attractive reserve is about 10 km north of St Helens. It features white sandy beaches, rocky headlands and four lagoons − Big, Sloop, Swimcart and Grants Lagoons. To the west is Mt Pearson State Forest, while Ansons Bay, a well-known wader locality, lies to the north. Many of the wader species already mentioned can be seen in the bay; it is also a favoured haunt of the Ruddy Turnstone, and one of the few places in Tasmania where Sanderlings are regularly recorded.

Bay of Fires is an excellent place for swimming, boating and fishing, and there are at least seven sheltered camping areas within the reserve.

Humbug Point State Recreation Area: Is about 6 km north-east of St Helens. Its sandy beaches, low cliffs and rocky headlands are backed by open forest, heathland (likely habitat for Tawny-crowned Honeyeater) and grassland. Walking tracks and unsealed roads criss-cross the reserve, making it an ideal place for hiking. There is a boat ramp at Binalong Bay, and camping is permitted at several attractive sites.

St Helens Point State Recreation Area: This long, narrow reserve stretches from St Helens Point in the north to Dianas Basin in the south. Protecting a variety of habitats, including heathlands, wetlands and sand-dunes, the reserve is about 7 km east of St Helens. Maurouard Beach is a good place for Hooded Plover, while Dianas Basin is worth visiting for Hoary-headed and possibly Australasian and Great Crested Grebe.

Camping is permitted at Dianas Basin, Stieglitz Beach and St Helens Point. There are boat ramps at Stieglitz township and Burns Bay.

Freycinet National Park

Covering an area of almost 11 000 ha, Freycinet National Park − one of the oldest reserves in Tasmania − comprises the Freycinet Peninsula and Schouten Island. This beautiful, mountainous stretch of the east coast features spectacular red granite peaks (Mt Freycinet rises to 620 m), precipitous headlands, picturesque bays and broad sandy beaches.

Much of the park consists of coastal heathland, interspersed with areas of dry sclerophyll forest and patches of she-oak and banksia woodland. The endemic Oyster Bay pine *Callitris rhomboidea* occurs throughout the peninsula, and Freycinet is justly famous for its wealth of wildflowers − in spring and early summer the park is carpeted with a variety of colourful plants including more than one hundred species of orchids.

The reserve is about 300 km from Launceston via St Helens and

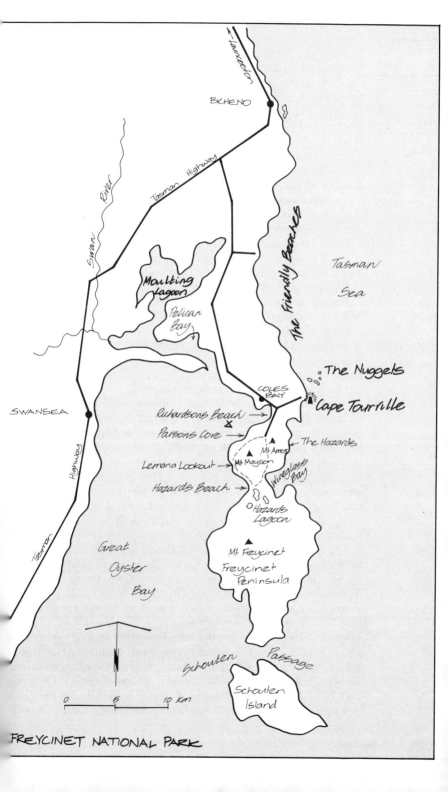

FREYCINET NATIONAL PARK

Bicheno. To get there, turn off the Tasman Highway about 11 km south-west of Bicheno and take the road to Coles Bay. The main camping area, at Richardsons Beach just south of Coles Bay township, has toilets and a few powered sites but no shower facilities. During the summer months Freycinet attracts crowds of visitors and it is necessary to book a campsite well in advance. Write to the ranger, Freycinet National Park, Coles Bay, Tas. 7215, enclosing a stamped, addressed envelope.

Away from Richardsons Beach, bush camping is permitted at a number of places on Freycinet Peninsula. In summer, however, fresh water is scarce; campers and walkers must therefore carry adequate supplies. You may also camp in splendid isolation on Schouten Island. Access to this beautiful, uninhabited island is by chartered boat from Coles Bay.

For those not wishing to camp, accommodation is available at The Chateau (a privately owned lodge a kilometre or so inside the park boundary) and at a small youth hostel in the reserve. In Coles Bay township there are holiday units, shops, a petrol station and a caravan park.

Freycinet National Park has much to offer the visitor. Fishing, swimming, sailing and canoeing are the chief attractions, but bird-watchers will find this an ideal place for a holiday since there are many kilometres of walking tracks in the reserve. (A detailed map can be purchased from the ranger's office.)

If you are reasonably fit, the following walk is highly recommended. From the carpark near Parsons Cove take the Wineglass Bay track, crossing The Hazards between Mt Mayson (400 m) and Mt Amos (420 m). At first the track is rather steep, but the climb is worth the effort since the view from the top of The Hazards is magnificent. On reaching Wineglass Bay − a long curve of pure white sand − head west to Hazards Beach via the Isthmus track, and return to the carpark via Lemana Lookout. Plan on an early start, and carry something to eat and drink (Wineglass Bay is the perfect place for a leisurely lunch).

The Wineglass Bay − Hazards Beach walk takes you through dry sclerophyll forest and there is usually an assortment of birds to be seen along the way: Brown Falcon, Common Bronzewing, Yellow-tailed Black-Cockatoo, Green Rosella, Pallid and Fan-tailed Cuckoo (spring−summer), Laughing Kookaburra, Black-faced Cuckoo-shrike (spring−summer), Scarlet Robin, Golden Whistler, Grey Shrike-thrush, Satin Flycatcher (spring−summer), Grey Fantail, Spotted Quail-thrush (not common, but worth searching for), Superb Fairy-wren, White-browed Scrubwren, Brown Thornbill, Yellow Wattlebird, Yellow-throated, Crescent and New Holland Honeyeater, Eastern Spinebill, Spotted and (spring−summer) Striated Pardalote, Silvereye, Dusky Woodswallow (spring—summer), Grey Butcherbird and Grey Currawong.

Australasian Gannets are often to be seen fishing in Wineglass Bay, while a few common coastal species — Pied Oystercatcher, Red-capped Plover, Silver Gull, Crested Tern — frequent the beach. On the isthmus linking The Hazards and Freycinet Peninsula there are a number of lagoons and swamps. Although it appears to be ideal for waterbirds, this area is rather disappointing — you should, however, find Swamp Quail here.

The walk from Hazards Beach to Parsons Cove is quite level, and considerably less strenuous than the trek to Wineglass Bay. In the vicinity of Lemana Lookout, where the track passes through dense, low vegetation, keep your eyes open for Beautiful Firetails. These small, dark finches are quite common around Coles Bay, but they usually remain well hidden; a bright red rump disappearing into the undergrowth is usually all that you will see of the bird.

The Wineglass Bay track is perhaps the most popular of Freycinet's many walks, but it is not necessary to venture far from Coles Bay in order to find birds; indeed, many species can be seen quite readily in the forest near Richardsons Beach. A family of Tasmanian Native-hens is usually to be found feeding in the main camping area (even at the height of the summer holiday season), while White's Thrush, a somewhat secretive species, occurs in a few of the deeper gullies near The Chateau. And should you feel the need for a nocturnal ramble, take a stroll along the Cape Tourville road. Here, with the aid of a torch, you could spot a Southern Boobook, a Tawny Frogmouth, or perhaps a Masked Owl.

Having spent several days exploring Freycinet National Park, birders may care to visit the following spots outside the reserve.

Cape Tourville: From the lighthouse, about 8 km east of Coles Bay, there are wonderful views along the rugged coast. In winter this would be an excellent place to watch for pelagics such as Wandering, Black-browed, Yellow-nosed and Shy Albatross.

The Nuggets: Are a group of four granite islets about 1 km north-east of Cape Tourville. Many seabirds breed on the islets: Little Penguin, Fairy Prion, Short-tailed Shearwater, White-faced Storm-Petrel, Black-faced Shag, Silver and Pacific Gull and Caspian Tern.

The Friendly Beaches: Lie to the north of Freycinet, between Cape Tourville and Bicheno. Access to this stretch of the coast (a good spot for Hooded Plover) can be gained via the Coles Bay to Bicheno road. The turn-off is signposted about 20 km north of Coles Bay.

Moulting Lagoon: This is a largely freshwater lagoon to the northwest of Coles Bay. It is the main breeding ground of the Black Swan in Tasmania, and at times thousands of swans congregate there. Other waterbirds include Australian Pelican, Great Cormorant, Little Pied Cormorant, White-faced Heron, Great Egret (mainly in winter), Australasian Bittern (rather rare), Australian Shelduck, Pacific Black Duck, Grey Teal, Musk Duck, Lewin's Rail, Purple Swamphen and Eurasian Coot.

The extensive mudflats at Pelican Bay, south-east of Moulting Lagoon, may be worth visiting for migratory waders such as Lesser Golden Plover, Eastern Curlew, Greenshank, Bar-tailed Godwit, Sharp-tailed Sandpiper, Red-necked Stint and Curlew Sandpiper.

Maria Island National Park

In 1825 Maria Island, 8 km off Tasmania's east coast, was chosen by Governor Arthur as the site for a second penal settlement to relieve the pressure on Macquarie Harbour. Named Darlington in honour of the Governor of New South Wales, the settlement was abandoned in 1832 in favour of Port Arthur. Since then European occupation has been almost continuous, and it was not until 1972 that Maria Island was proclaimed a national park.

Despite its chequered history — the island's industries have included sawmilling, grazing, wine-making, fruit-growing, and the manufacture of cement — much of Maria Island (9672 ha) is uncleared. As a result, its fauna and flora are exceedingly rich.

Like many of the islands off Tasmania's east coast, Maria consists of two well-defined parts joined by a narrow isthmus. The major habitats are open forest and woodland, dominated by eucalypts such as messmate stringybark, gum-topped stringybark, white gum, Tasmanian blue gum, white peppermint and black peppermint; wet and dry heaths; grassland (principally abandoned agricultural land); swamps and lagoons; and coastal sand-dunes and cliffs.

Not surprisingly, Maria Island supports a diverse avifauna. During an ornithological survey conducted in 1976−77, 127 species of birds were recorded, making this one of the best places in Tasmania to go bird-watching. Visitors should have little difficulty finding many of the following: White-faced Heron, Cape Barren Goose (introduced between 1968 and 1971, and now plentiful around Darlington), White-bellied Sea-Eagle, Swamp Quail, Tasmanian Native-hen (released at Darlington in 1967, it is now thriving on the island), Pied Oystercatcher, Masked Lapwing, Hooded and Red-capped Plover, Latham's Snipe (a regular summer visitor), Pacific Gull, Crested Tern, Brush Bronzewing (common in the wetter gullies), Yellow-tailed Black-Cockatoo, Green Rosella, Fan-tailed Cuckoo (spring−summer), Shining Bronze-Cuckoo (spring−summer), Laughing Kookaburra, Tree Martin (spring−summer), Richard's Pipit, White's Thrush (occurs in wet gullies), Pink Robin (also a bird of the wet gullies), Flame, Scarlet and Dusky Robin, Olive Whistler, Satin Flycatcher (spring—summer), Grey Fantail, Little Grassbird (on the margins of lagoons), White-browed Scrubwren, Tasmanian and Yellow-rumped Thornbill, Yellow Wattlebird, Yellow-throated, Strong-billed, Black-headed, Crescent and New Holland Honeyeater, Eastern Spinebill, White-fronted Chat, Spotted and (spring—summer) Striated Pardalote, Silvereye, Beautiful Firetail, Dusky Woodswallow (spring—summer), Australian Magpie, Black Currawong (sometimes in company with the Grey Currawong) and Forest Raven.

The Forty-spotted Pardalote, a Tasmanian endemic, is un-doubtedly the most sought-after species on Maria Island. It is one of Australia's rarest birds; during a recent survey fewer than 3000 pardalotes were found in Tasmania, and the Maria Island population is estimated at 500 individuals. Visitors have a reasonable chance of seeing the Forty-spotted Pardalote, but because this tiny, inconspicuous bird (it is smaller than a Silvereye) normally feeds high in the forest canopy, you will need powerful binoculars (preferably 10× or 12×) in order to distinguish it from the Spotted and Striated Pardalotes that also occur on the island. The best way of locating the bird is to listen for its call — a soft, nasal 'whit-whit', said by some observers to be characteristic. Having found your bird, lie on the ground and scan the foliage high above — this may seem a bit silly, but you will soon develop a stiff neck if you remain standing.

Maria Island is about 360 km from Launceston via Bicheno and Swansea, and about 90 km from Hobart via Sorell and Orford. Between October and April there is a daily passenger ferry to the island from the Louisville Resort jetty, near Orford (the service does not operate regularly during winter). Unfortunately it de-parts at 10.30 a.m. and returns at 2.30 p.m. (the crossing takes about fifty minutes), leaving day visitors little time to explore the island. If you are going to Maria Island just for the day, take a walk along Bernacchis Creek to the Darlington Reservoir (about 6 km return); the tall, wet forest surrounding the reservoir is rich in birdlife.

For those with more time to spare, the old penitentiary building at Darlington has been renovated, providing accommodation for a limited number of visitors. To book your 'cell', write to the ranger, Maria Island National Park, via Triabunna Post Office, Tas. 7190, enclosing a stamped, addressed envelope. Should you wish to camp, there are sites at Darlington and Chinamans Bay, but you must book in advance. And campers should carry adequate provisions because there are no shops on the island. Maria Island has many kilometres of walking tracks; an excellent map of the park can be purchased from the ranger's office at Darlington.

Tasman and Forestier Peninsulas

Port Arthur, on the Tasman Peninsula, is one of the best known tourist attractions in Australia. Founded in 1830, the penal settlement was sadly neglected after it closed in 1877; many of its fine stone buildings were demolished, others badly damaged by bushfires. Fortunately parts of important buildings such as the penitentiary (1844), church (1834), model prison (1848), guardhouse (1835), hospital (1842) and asylum (1867) are still standing, and smaller buildings including the commandant's house and the medical officer's house have been meticulously restored. Today Port Arthur Historic Site draws thousands of visitors annually.

To reach Port Arthur take the Tasman Highway to Sorell; from there the settlement is about 75 km via Dunalley and Eaglehawk Neck. The historic site covers an area of 115 ha and is administered by the Tasmanian National Parks and Wildlife Service. There is a visitors centre, and guided tours are available. Port Arthur township has motels, holiday units, a youth hostel and a caravan park.

Although the convict settlement is undoubtedly the region's main attraction, there are many other places of interest on the Tasman and Forestier Peninsulas.

Tasman Arch State Reserve: Near Eaglehawk Neck, about 20 km north of Port Arthur, this reserve protects several of the peninsula's well-known coastal features — the Blowhole, the Devils Kitchen and Tasman Arch itself. From the Devils Kitchen you can walk along the cliff-tops to Waterfall Bay, a distance of 3 km or so. The track passes through a small area of heath before entering a patch of tall, dense forest. When in bloom, the heathland holds a wealth of honeyeaters — Little Wattlebird, Yellow-throated, Crescent and New Holland Honeyeater — while Yellow Wattlebird, Strong-billed and Black-headed Honeyeater occur in the forest.

Fortescue Bay Forest Reserve: There is a tree-studded camping ground on the shores of this lovely, secluded bay. It has toilets but no showers, and caravans are not permitted since the road to the bay is narrow and winding. To get there leave the Arthur Highway about 4 km north of Port Arthur; Fortescue Bay is about 12 km from the turn-off. A walking track links the bay with Cape Pillar to the south, while another takes you northwards along the spectacular coast to Eaglehawk Neck.

Lime Bay Nature Reserve: Is about 30 km from Port Arthur via Nubeena and Saltwater River. This reserve (1310 ha), protecting the north-western tip of the Tasman Peninsula, features freshwater lagoons, beaches, open woodland and heathland. It is a good place to go bird-watching; the small population of Forty-spotted Pardalotes, estimated at between twenty and forty birds, is of particular interest. Camping is not permitted.

Blackman Bay: This is a well-known wader locality to the east of Dunalley. In summer Lesser Golden Plover, Ruddy Turnstone, Eastern Curlew, Greenshank, Bar-tailed Godwit, Sharp-tailed and Curlew Sandpiper, and Red-necked Stint can be found there. Double-banded Plovers turn up in winter. Most of the waders congregate on the mudflats at the northern end of the bay. This area can be reached quite easily via the Dunalley to Marion Bay road.

FLINDERS ISLAND

Flinders Island, off the north-east coast of Tasmania in Bass Strait, is the largest and most accessible of the fifty or so islands in the Furneaux Group. Whitemark on the west coast is the main centre, and it has accommodation, stores, a post office and petrol. The township is surrounded by farmland and it is necessary to hire a car (available locally) in order to get to the best bird-watching spots. Bicycles can also be hired, but hills and strong winds make this a rather tiresome mode of travel. Lady Barron, on the other hand, is situated on the shores of lovely Adelaide Bay, about 26 km south-east of Whitemark, and some of the best birding areas are within walking distance. It has a hotel with accommodation and would make a better base. Alternatively, several farmhouses on the island cater for a limited number of guests. Bookings for all types of accommodation can be made through any branch of the Tasmanian Government Tourist Bureau. The island is an ideal place to go hiking, and camping is permitted at Trousers Point (south of Whitemark near the Strzelecki National Park) and at beautiful Killiecrankie Bay to the north. Campers must be self-sufficient and should seek advice from the Tasmanian National Parks and Wildlife Service in Launceston or Hobart before visiting the island.

Flinders Island has a surprisingly mild climate but the incessant wind is troublesome; January to March is probably the best time to visit. There are daily flights from Launceston and three services a week from Essendon in Victoria. It is also possible to fly to Cape Barren Island, which lies just south of Flinders and is the only other island in the group with permanent habitation. Those wishing to visit the smaller islands can charter a boat at Whitemark or Lady Barron.

The region has an interesting, though not always admirable, history. In the late eighteenth and early nineteenth centuries the islands supported a flourishing sealing industry, but Flinders Island was not permanently settled until the 1830s, when the remnants of the Tasmanian Aboriginals were taken there in an attempt to save them from extinction. The Aboriginal settlement failed − the chapel at Wybalenna is all that remains of it — and the sealers exterminated two species of seal within a few decades. The famous Cape Barren Goose also came close to extinction. Fortunately measures to save it succeeded, and in 1977 numbers in the Tasmanian region were estimated at five thousand. Paradoxically culling now takes place on Flinders Island, where much to the annoyance of the local farmers the geese gather in summer to graze on pasture. Another well-known bird, the Short-tailed Shearwater or muttonbird, is harvested commercially and about half a million chicks are taken annually from islands in Bass Strait. It is thriving nonetheless and apparently expanding its range.

Today the thousand or so inhabitants derive their incomes chiefly from farming, fishing and muttonbirding, with tourism contributing increasingly to the coffers. Flinders Island is the ideal place for a relaxing holiday.

The vegetation varies from coastal heathland to dry sclerophyll forest, with patches of wet forest occurring in the protected gullies. She-oak, tea-tree, banksia and wattle are widespread, and over eighty species of orchids have been identified. Like so many other places in Australia the island has lost a good deal of its original vegetation, but there are still substantial areas of scrub along the east coast, in the north, and in the central ranges. In addition, Strzelecki National Park protects an area of 4215 ha, and there are numerous bays, inlets, swamps, lagoons and offshore islands worth exploring.

Since Flinders and the other islands in the group were once part of a land bridge linking Tasmania with the Australian mainland, the region's avifauna has affinities with that of both Tasmania and Victoria. Over 150 bird species have been recorded although, perhaps surprisingly, several Tasmanian endemics — Tasmanian Native-hen, Scrubtit and Yellow Wattlebird — do not occur on the island, and the Forty-spotted Pardalote has not been seen since it was recorded on the lower slopes of Mt Strzelecki in 1970. Nevertheless Flinders has a varied and interesting birdlife and warrants thorough exploration. Weather permitting, visits to other islands in the group should prove rewarding.

The inlets and lagoons on the east coast hold good numbers of waterbirds, including Great Crested, Hoary-headed and, more rarely, Australasian Grebe, Australian Pelican, cormorants, White-faced Heron, Great and, more rarely, Little Egret (winter), Australasian Bittern, Sacred Ibis (winter), Black Swan, Australian Shelduck, Pacific Black Duck, Grey Teal, Chestnut Teal, Australasian Shoveler, Hardhead (rarely), Blue-billed Duck (rare, but has been recorded breeding), Musk Duck, Lewin's Rail, Purple Swamphen, Eurasian Coot and Latham's Snipe (summer). Swamp Quail occur in suitable habitat throughout the island.

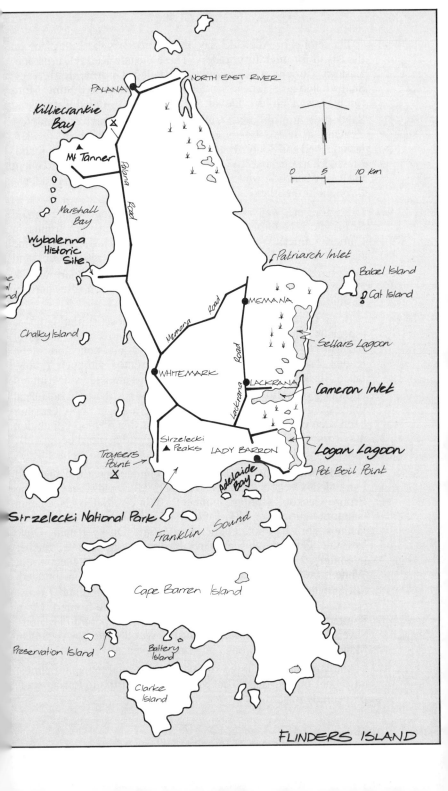

FLINDERS ISLAND

The shores of Adelaide Bay are regarded as the best place on the island for migratory waders. These include Ruddy Turnstone, Eastern Curlew, Greenshank, Bar-tailed Godwit, Red Knot, Sharp-tailed and Curlew Sandpiper, and Red-necked Stint. More rarely, Lesser Golden Plover, Whimbrel, Grey-tailed Tattler and Sanderling turn up, and Double-banded Plover arrives from New Zealand in fair numbers during winter. Non-migratory waders include Pied and Sooty Oystercatcher (often in quite large numbers), Masked Lapwing and Red-capped Plover. Hooded Plovers frequent the sandy beaches, while Banded Lapwings favour open paddocks throughout the island.

Raptors are well represented. The magnificent White-bellied Sea-Eagle breeds in several places and is often seen fishing in Cameron Inlet. Wedge-tailed Eagle, Marsh Harrier, Peregrine Falcon, Brown Falcon and Australian Kestrel also breed, and other birds of prey include Brown Goshawk, Collared Sparrowhawk and Australian Hobby (the hobby is seldom seen elsewhere in Tasmania).

Both Common and Brush Bronzewing occur; the latter is especially numerous and can usually be found on the slopes of Vinegar Hill, near Lady Barron, where it is quite tame and can be readily observed. Parrots are poorly represented, although Yellow-tailed Black-Cockatoos and Green Rosellas are widely distributed and quite plentiful. The Southern Boobook is the only nocturnal species regularly reported. (Interestingly, a single Sooty Owl has been seen on the island and it is believed that a small population may exist there; since the island's avifauna has not been greatly studied, the diligent observer could probably add to its bird list.)

Some of the other birds found on Flinders include Pallid and Fan-tailed Cuckoo (spring–summer), Horsfield's and Shining Bronze-Cuckoo (spring–summer), White-throated Needletail (summer–autumn), Black-faced Cuckoo-shrike (summer), White's Thrush, Pink, Flame, Scarlet and Dusky Robin, Olive Whistler, Golden Whistler, Grey Shrike-thrush, Satin Flycatcher (summer), Grey Fantail, Little Grassbird, Superb Fairy-wren, White-browed Scrubwren, Tasmanian Thornbill, Yellow-throated, Strong-billed, Black-headed, Crescent, New Holland and Tawny-crowned Honeyeater, Eastern Spinebill, White-fronted Chat, Spotted, Striated (summer) and possibly Forty-spotted Pardalote, Silvereye, Beautiful Firetail, Dusky Woodswallow, Australian Magpie, Black Currawong and Forest Raven.

Many of the birds listed can be seen in suitable habitat almost anywhere on the island, but visitors will find the following spots particularly rewarding.

Strzelecki National Park

This rugged reserve lies about 15 km south of Whitemark and includes the island's highest point, Mt Strzelecki (756 m). There is a walking track to the top of the mountain, but it is a steep and strenuous climb requiring three hours or more for the return trip. However, the views en route are superb, and sightings of Bennett's wallaby and two Tasmanian endemic bird species — Tasmanian Thornbill and Yellow-throated Honeyeater — are virtual certainties. Those planning to walk to the top should watch the weather; it can be fine and sunny to start with but may turn cloudy and cold near the summit. The track ascends through varied vegetation and after about one hour there is a patch of tall, wet forest along a creek fringed with tree ferns. This is a good spot for a rest and some bird-watching.

To reach the park, leave Whitemark on Lady Barron Road and after about 6 km turn off at Trousers Point Road. The walking track commences opposite a farmhouse about 6 km from the turn-off. At the end of Trousers Point Road there is a pleasant picnic and camping area near a fine beach. Access to the park from any other point is rather difficult although adjacent landowners may permit entry via their properties if asked. As has been mentioned, Forty-spotted Pardalotes were discovered in 1970 in a gully near Wallanippi, on the eastern slopes of Mt Strzelecki, but have not been seen since, despite organised searches.

Adelaide Bay

This attractive bay lies on the southern edge of Flinders Island, 26 km south-east of Whitemark. The shores favour waders and seabirds, and a walk from one end of the bay to the other should prove enjoyable and rewarding. Badger Corner Coastal Reserve, at the western end of the bay, has dense stands of tea-tree scrub where firebreaks provide easy access. It is a good spot for bush birds such as Brush Bronzewing, Green Rosella, Dusky Robin, Yellow-throated Honeyeater and Beautiful Firetail. The Vinegar Hill area is also worth visiting, particularly for Brush Bronzewing; from the lookout on the hill there are fine views across Franklin Sound to Cape Barren Island.

Logan Lagoon and Cameron Inlet

Along the east coast of Flinders Island, between Patriarch Inlet and Pot Boil Point, there are numerous lagoons and swamps. In many cases access is restricted by the lack of tracks, but Logan Lagoon can be reached from the south via Pot Boil Road, or from the north via Logan Lagoon Road (ask locally for precise directions). The lagoon covers an area of about 1000 ha and at times holds good numbers of waterfowl and waders, although it may dry up

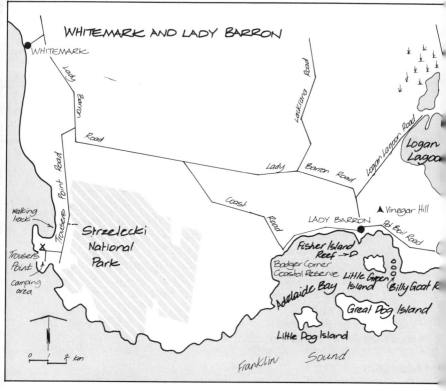

completely in summer. Another place worth visiting is Cameron Inlet, which is accessible via Lackrana Road and Cameron Inlet Road. This vast stretch of shallow water is good for all kinds of waterbirds, including grebes, pelicans, cormorants, herons, egrets, waterfowl, waders and terns, and it is a good spot to look for the White-bellied Sea-Eagle. In 1982 a fire devastated much of the surrounding area and it will be some time before the vegetation fully recovers.

Wybalenna Historic Site

This is the site of the ill-fated attempt to resettle the last of the Tasmanian Aboriginals. The chapel, reconstructed by the National Trust, is the only building still standing. Just to the north, at Marshall Bay, there is a Short-tailed Shearwater colony. Curiously it is the only one known on Flinders Island, although the shearwaters breed in vast numbers elsewhere in the region.

Mt Tanner and Killiecrankie Bay

Virtually the entire northern section of Flinders Island is unallotted crown land and therefore uncleared. Access is restricted by the lack of roads, but the Whitemark to Palana road runs right up the west coast and continues to North East River. En route a stop at Mt Tanner Lookout and beautiful Killiecrankie Bay will be worthwhile, if only for the superb coastal scenery. The fishing at North East River is said to be the best on the island.

The offshore islands
Many of the other islands in the group are wildlife sanctuaries supporting breeding colonies of seabirds. Most are under the care of the Tasmanian National Parks and Wildlife Service and permits to land should be obtained before visiting any of them. Species that breed regularly in the region include Little Penguin, Short-tailed Shearwater, White-faced Storm-Petrel, Black-faced Shag, Cape Barren Goose, Silver and Pacific Gull, and Caspian, Fairy and Crested Tern. Most of these nest on Chalky Island, which lies about 10 km north-west of Whitemark. Australian Pelicans breed on some of the more remote islets, and there is a small colony of Australasian Gannets on Cat Island, about 7 km east of Flinders Island. This colony was once quite large and between five thousand and ten thousand birds were present in the early 1900s. However, due to human interference it has diminished considerably and is now almost non-existent. According to local newspaper reports, only eighteen birds were present in 1984 and, inexplicably, a fire wiped out half the fledgelings.

Perhaps the most interesting seabird to breed in the region is the White-fronted Tern. This New Zealand species had not been positively recorded breeding in Australia until about six pairs were found nesting on Battery Island, just south of Cape Barren Island, in 1979. Since then the terns have bred on Fisher Island Reef and Billy Goat Reef in Adelaide Bay, but it remains to be seen whether or not they will become permanently established in the region.

Flinders Island is certainly a good place to get away from it all. The publicity brochures claim that the pace is slow, and it is − where else would the pilot who flies you over get off and help unload the baggage? A good map is essential; the 1:100 000 Flinders Island (special) map is excellent and can be purchased from the State Government Publications Centre in Hobart, the Lands Department in Launceston, or any good bookshop.

THE SOUTH-WEST
Tasmania's beautiful south-west is a wilderness of world significance, possessing some of the finest mountain and lake scenery in Australia. Until the 1960s, when the township of Strathgordon was constructed, virtually the entire region was uninhabited and

THE SOUTH-WEST

visited mainly by bushwalkers. Much of this remote corner of Tasmania is still accessible only on foot, but the building of roads by the Hydro-Electric Commission has opened up the area around Lake Gordon and Lake Pedder, enabling motorists to reach Scotts Peak Dam in the heart of the South West National Park. Here you can camp in incomparable surroundings between the Frankland and Arthur Ranges. In addition, Mt Field National Park and the historic harbour town of Strahan are both readily accessible from Hobart via the Lyell Highway. Mt Field in particular is well worth visiting since that reserve has an extensive network of walking tracks.

The region's man-made lakes are generally unattractive to

waterbirds, and its sedgelands, moorlands and temperate rain-forests somewhat poor in birdlife. The south-west has, however, one outstanding ornithological attraction — the Ground Parrot. These birds have become rare on the Australian mainland, but south-western Tasmania remains a stronghold for the species. Those prepared to tramp across the buttongrass plains will almost certainly be rewarded with a glimpse of one.

Mt Field National Park

This splendid 16 257 ha reserve is about 75 km west of Hobart via the Lyell Highway and Westerway. The well-appointed camping area, just inside the park entrance on the banks of the Tyenna River, has toilets, hot showers, laundry facilities and powered sites. During the summer months the camping ground is often full by nightfall, and it would be advisable to get there by mid-afternoon. The nearest alternative caravan park is at New Norfolk, 40 km to the east. At Lake Dobson, within the national park, there are three huts that provide basic accommodation for up to six people each. There is a youth hostel at New Norfolk, and another, together with a small private motel, near the reserve entrance.

Mt Field's avifauna is not especially rich (there are only about fifty species on its bird list) but Tasmanian endemics are well represented: Tasmanian Native-hen, Green Rosella, Dusky Robin, Scrubtit, Tasmanian Thornbill, Yellow-throated, Strong-billed and Black-headed Honeyeater, and Black Currawong all occur in the reserve. Quite a variety of birds can usually be seen near the camping area — Tasmanian Native-hen, Sulphur-crested Cockatoo, Green Rosella, Fan-tailed Cuckoo (spring—summer), Welcome Swallow (spring—summer), Tree Martin (spring—summer), Black-faced Cuckoo-shrike (spring—summer), Flame Robin, Golden Whistler, Grey Shrike-thrush, Satin Flycatcher (spring—summer), Grey Fantail, Superb Fairy-wren, Black-headed Honeyeater, Eastern Spinebill, Spotted and (spring—summer) Striated Pardalote, Silvereye, Black Currawong and Forest Raven.

For the more energetic there is a variety of short, medium and long walks at Mt Field; a detailed map showing most of the walking tracks can be purchased from the visitors centre near the park entrance. Even the unadventurous will find the park's three nature trails worth the effort, since they are well constructed and introduce visitors to the various vegetation communities that occur in the reserve.

Russell Falls Nature Walk: This is undoubtedly one of the most attractive short walks in Tasmania. The wide path leading to the beautiful falls, 12 m in breadth, has been sealed to allow access for the disabled; the staff of the Tasmanian National Parks and

Wildlife Service are to be congratulated on their thoughtfulness. The track to Russell Falls is about a kilometre long and the forest scenery is superb. Mighty buttressed swamp gums (*Eucalyptus regnans*, known as mountain ash in Victoria) tower above massed stands of tree ferns, while a rich assortment of ground ferns sprout from every available niche and cranny. Birds are not numerous here, although Scrubtits favour the tree ferns and Pink Robins can usually be found near the waterfall − a male robin glimpsed against a backdrop of silvery water is indeed a lovely sight.

From Russell Falls you can either return to the camping area via the nature trail, or continue along an unsealed track to Horseshoe and Lady Barron Falls. From Lady Barron Falls there is another path leading back to the camping area. The tracks linking the three sets of falls form a 5.5 km circuit through wet sclerophyll forest and rainforest where birds are quite plentiful. Those that can be seen en route include Grey Goshawk, Brush Bronzewing, Yellow-tailed Black-Cockatoo, Shining Bronze-Cuckoo (spring−summer), White's Thrush, Dusky Robin, Olive Whistler, White-browed Scrubwren, Tasmanian Thornbill, Yellow-throated and Strong-billed Honeyeater, and Beautiful Firetail.

Lyrebird Nature Walk: In 1934 Superb Lyrebirds were brought to Tasmania from Victoria and introduced at Mt Field. A shy species, the lyrebird spends much of its time raking over the forest floor in search of food. It has become firmly established in the park and you can find its scratchings − and with luck the bird itself − along the Lyrebird Nature Walk which commences about 7 km west of the park entrance on the Lake Dobson road. The nature trail passes through a patch of temperate rainforest characterised by myrtle beech, sassafras, celery-top pine and cheesewood; name plates have been placed near many of the trees, enabling you to identify them.

Pandani Grove Nature Walk: Follows the western shore of Lake Dobson, a picturesque tarn some 1031 m above sea level. Here the hardy vegetation is dominated by snow gum, King William pine and pencil pine. It is, however, the pandani grove that most people come to see. This palm-like plant, a member of the heath family, is a Tasmanian endemic. Heaths are typically low-growing plants but the pandani frequently reaches heights of 6 m or more, which makes it something of a botanical oddity.

The 1.5 km nature walk commences at the Lake Dobson carpark, about 16 km from the park entrance, and emerges on a four-wheel-drive track near Eagle Tarn. From here you can either return to the carpark along the eastern shore of the lake, or continue uphill and walk for hours through the superb alpine countryside. In summer Flame Robins, Crescent Honeyeaters and Black Currawongs can usually be found near the lake.

Mt Field National Park contains some of the highest country in Tasmania, including Mt Field West (1439 m). During the summer months visitors can enjoy unlimited bushwalking in glorious surroundings, while in winter the park's snow-capped peaks and frozen tarns provide magnificent opportunities for ski-touring.

South West National Park

The 442 240 ha South West National Park, one of the largest reserves in Australia, stretches from Lake Pedder in the north to the rugged, inhospitable coast between Nye and Surprise Bays. This is a true wilderness park; its features include the Eastern and Western Arthur Ranges, the Frankland Range, Federation Peak (1225 m) and Mt Anne (1425 m). The scenery is breathtaking, and not surprisingly it is a bushwalkers' mecca. Much of the park is, of course, inaccessible, but there is a good sealed road to Strathgordon, on the northern shore of Lake Pedder, and an unsealed road terminating at Scotts Peak Dam to the south of the lake.

Strathgordon is a rather soulless construction town. It consists mainly of prefabricated buildings that once housed Hydro-Electric Commission employees but are now largely abandoned. The town has a motel, a shopping centre, petrol (the only other petrol station in the area is at Maydena, about 70 km east of Strathgordon), and a caravan park. The caravan park is unattractive, to say the least; if you can do without the luxury of power and hot water the three bush-camping areas near Scotts Peak Dam are considerably more pleasant. To reach this section of the park turn off the Maydena to Strathgordon road at Scotts Peak Road, about 30 km south-west of Maydena. Scotts Peak Dam is about 40 km from the turn-off. Camping is permitted at Edgar Dam, Scotts Peak Dam and Huon River. All three areas have toilets and tank water but only the Huon River camping ground has sheltered sites hidden in a patch of rainforest — an important consideration in this part of Tasmania since gales are common even in midsummer. Lake Pedder is a very popular fishing spot and during the trout season (August to April) the camping areas are often crowded.

Ground Parrots are undoubtedly the park's main avian attraction. The parrots are relatively common in the wet south-west of Tasmania and a systematic search of the buttongrass plains near Lake Pedder should prove rewarding. And it is not always necessary to hike for hours in order to find them; in 1984 Ground Parrots were flushed from an area of swampy buttongrass right beside Scotts Peak Road. Nonetheless these elusive birds are usually difficult to locate. The best method is to drive to a spot with suitable habitat and listen for the bird's high-pitched, bell-like calls. Ground Parrots occasionally call during the day but they are most vocal at dusk. (Take care not to confuse the notes of the parrot with those of the Little Grassbird and Tawny-crowned Honeyeater; all three species may occur in the same area.)

Having located your parrot, walk directly to the spot and with luck the bird will emerge from the dense cover. You will need to be quick, for the parrots usually fly swiftly for a short distance then drop back into the undergrowth. They seldom flush a second time. If this method fails, try walking quickly and noisily through the buttongrass — it helps if there are several people walking in line. Needless to say, binoculars are often useless because the birds soon disappear from view. Wear waterproof clothing and stout boots, and take along a flask of hot coffee (or something stronger perhaps) for the post-parrot celebrations.

If the parrots prove too elusive there are at least two other interesting species that inhabit the buttongrass plains — Southern Emu-wren and Calamanthus. The secretive emu-wren, although quite common, may be difficult to find because its thin, almost inaudible trill is usually carried away by the wind. But the Calamanthus is more obliging. This small brown bird can often be seen perched on a tussock, tail cocked, calling exuberantly 'whirr-whirr-chick-chick-whirr-ree-ree'.

Tasmania's south-west is certainly a very peaceful place — and long may it remain that way. The best time for a visit is during the summer months (December to March), although the weather can be appalling at any time of the year. Make sure your tent is waterproof and remember to take along plenty of reading material.

Strahan

Strahan is an attractive port town on the northern shores of Macquarie Harbour, about 300 km from Hobart. It is the only settlement of any size on Tasmania's west coast, and since it has several motels and two caravan parks the town makes a good base for the bird-watcher. Cruise launches operate from here, carrying passengers across the harbour to the famous Gordon River.

The ocean beach, 6 km west of the town, holds Pied Oyster-catcher, Hooded Plover and a few other species, while Azure Kingfishers occur around Macquarie Harbour and along many of the rivers in the region. Those wishing to search for Ground Parrots should visit Strahan Aerodrome. During a census conducted in December 1978, forty-three parrots were recorded calling at dusk in the sedgeland surrounding the aerodrome. Botanical Creek Park, just to the east of the town on the road to Regatta Point, includes a small patch of rainforest where birds are quite plentiful.

THE CENTRAL HIGHLANDS

Like the south-west, the central highlands are remote and spec-

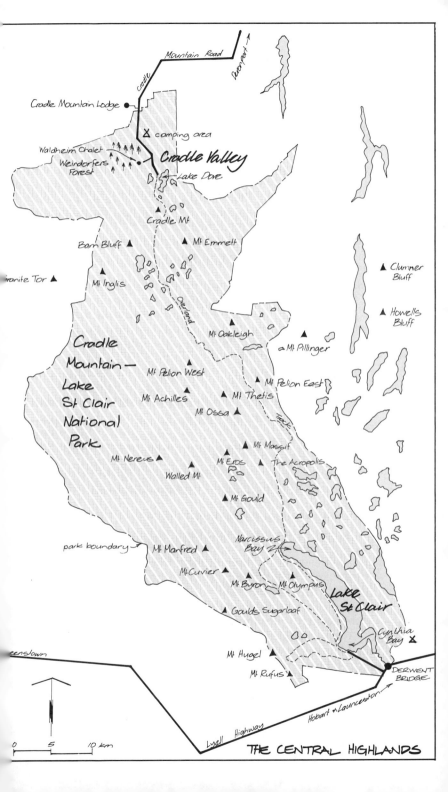

tacular. Here many of Tasmania's highest peaks, including the highest, Mt Ossa (1617 m), rise abruptly from vast empty moorlands. Innumerable glacial lakes fringed with bright green cushion plants and dark groves of pencil pine dot the enchanting landscape, while in summer the alpine meadows are ablaze with red, yellow and purple wildflowers. In winter much of the region may be buried for months beneath a deep blanket of snow.

The Cradle Mountain – Lake St Clair National Park is the region's, indeed Tasmania's, most famous reserve. It covers 131 915 ha and stretches from Cradle Valley in the north to Lake St Clair in the south. These two popular areas are linked by one of Australia's best known walks – the 80 km Overland Track. Although there are no roads running through the park, it is worth making the effort to visit both the northern and southern sections since each possesses a magic of its own.

Cradle Valley

Cradle Valley, about 85 km south-west of Devonport, is readily accessible via Sheffield or Wilmot. In winter, and occasionally at other times, the last section of the road leading to the park (about 30 km) may be blocked by snow for several days. The camping ground, just inside the park boundary, has good facilities including powered sites. For those not wishing to camp, private accommodation is available at the Cradle Mountain Lodge near the park entrance, while within the reserve there are a number of well-appointed cabins in a picturesque setting on the edge of Weindorfers Forest. The cabins are very popular and bookings are essential: for further details write to the ranger, Cradle Valley, PO Box 20, Sheffield, Tas. 7306, enclosing a stamped, addressed envelope. There are youth hostels at Devonport and Sheffield. Petrol and basic food supplies can be purchased from Cradle Mountain Lodge, but there are no other shops in the area.

For many visitors Cradle Valley's main attraction is its wonderful network of walking tracks. These vary in length from a fifteen-minute nature walk through a section of Weindorfers Forest, to half-day and full-day walks leading to Lake Dove, Crater Lake, Cradle Mountain summit (1545 m) and many other places of interest. An excellent map – the Cradle Mountain Day Walk Map – can be purchased from the ranger's office; a more detailed publication covering the entire national park is also available.

The Weindorfer Nature Walk commences at Waldheim Chalet and introduces visitors to the ancient forest of the Cradle Valley. Incredibly, some of the trees here are over a thousand years old. King William pine, celery-top pine and myrtle beech dominate the dense, dark lower section of the forest, while Tasmania's only native deciduous species – the tanglefoot or deciduous beech

(*Nothofagus gunnii*) — can be found at higher elevations. The forest holds a number of interesting bird species including White's Thrush, Pink Robin, Olive Whistler and Scrubtit, while Richard's Pipit, Flame Robin, Calamanthus and Crescent Honeyeater inhabit the exposed alpine moors. Wedge-tailed Eagles are sometimes seen soaring above the ranges, and Blue-winged Parrots visit the area occasionally during summer.

Although many of the park's mammals are nocturnal, Bennett's wallabies and red-legged pademelons are commonly seen grazing during the day in the open grassy areas, and wombats can be found in the forest near Waldheim Chalet. Those wishing to see one of the state's best known animals — the Tasmanian devil — should visit Cradle Mountain Lodge, where these carnivorous marsupials gather at dusk to feed on kitchen scraps. The proprietors of the lodge have installed spotlights, enabling visitors to observe the ferocious devils at close range.

Lake St Clair

This huge glacial lake, almost 200 m deep, is the most widely known feature of the southern section of the Cradle Mountain — Lake St Clair National Park. The lake is about 180 km north-west of Hobart via the Lyell Highway, and about the same distance south-west of Launceston via Deloraine and the Lake Highway. The park headquarters, a kiosk, picnic facilities and a well-appointed camping ground are located at Cynthia Bay, on the lake's southern shores. The camping area has a limited number of powered sites and there are several cabins, but you should book well in advance. Write to the ranger, Lake St Clair, via Derwent Bridge, Tas. 7140, enclosing a stamped, addressed envelope. Petrol and food can be purchased from Derwent Bridge on the Lyell Highway about 6 km south-east of Cynthia Bay, and several useful publications, including a detailed walk map, are available from the ranger's office.

In addition to rainforest, the southern section of Cradle Mountain — Lake St Clair National Park contains a small area of open eucalypt forest, and consequently it has a more diverse avifauna than Cradle Valley. Tasmanian Native-hens and Black Currawongs are common around the camping area, while Common Bronzewing, Yellow-tailed Black-Cockatoo, Green Rosella, Pallid and Fantailed Cuckoo (spring—summer), Shining Bronze-Cuckoo (spring—summer), Southern Boobook, Tawny Frogmouth, Black-faced Cuckoo-shrike (spring—summer), Scarlet and Dusky Robin, Golden Whistler, Grey Shrike-thrush, Satin Flycatcher (spring—summer), Grey Fantail, Superb Fairy-wren, White-browed Scrubwren, Tasmanian Thornbill, Striated Pardalote (spring—summer) and Silvereye inhabit the adjacent eucalypt forest. Along the road between Cynthia Bay and Derwent Bridge there are many banksias that flower for much of the year, attracting a wealth of honeyeaters — Yellow and Little Wattlebird, Yellow-throated, Strong-billed, Black-headed, Crescent and New Holland Honeyeater, and Eastern Spinebill.

Many of the birds mentioned can be found along the Watersmeet Nature Walk. This walk commences just west of the park headquarters and passes through several vegetation communities — eucalypt forest, buttongrass sedgeland and a small tea-tree swamp. The 1.7 km track, which is unsealed but well constructed, terminates in a patch of rainforest on the western shores of Lake St Clair. From here there are tracks leading to Mt Hugel, Mt Byron (Cuvier Valley track) and Narcissus Bay (Overland Track). The Overland Track skirts the shores of the lake for about 10 km; it is worth walking at least part of the way towards Narcissus Bay since this route takes you through dense rainforest where Pink Robins are usually plentiful. Lake St Clair itself is not especially good for birds because it has little emergent vegetation.

Summer is the best time to visit Cradle Mountain — Lake St Clair National Park, although sleet and snow can occur at any time of the year. Even in February the temperature may fall to below zero at night, but then the weather is part of the beauty of this wild region.

Chapter
6

South Australia

Useful addresses

South Australian Ornithological Association
c/- South Australian Museum
North Terrace
Adelaide, SA 5000

Adelaide Ornithologists Club
Secretary, 31 Wood Street
Millswood, SA 5034

Field Naturalists Society of South Australia
GPO Box 1594
Adelaide, SA 5001

South Australian National Parks and Wildlife Service
55 Grenfell Street
Adelaide, SA 5000

Key to Maps

▨	Public land
▨	Areas of water
▲	Mountain peak
ᛉᛘᛘᛘ	Mountain range or plateau
COBAR ●	Place name
✕	Camping area
⚐	Lighthouse
ⳬ ⳬ ⳬ	Marsh
▬▬▬	Major road or highway
———	Minor road
------	Foot track
··—··	National park boundary
·———	State boundary
∿	River or creek

ADELAIDE

South Australia's spacious and pleasant capital lies at the southern end of a long coastal plain, between the Mt Lofty Ranges and Gulf St Vincent. To the north and south of the city there are market gardens and vineyards, while in the Mt Lofty Ranges, to the east, large areas of forest have been cleared for housing and agriculture. Remnants of the original hills vegetation are protected by a network of reserves. The extensive saltworks to the north of the city provide ideal conditions for waders and other waterbirds, but various drainage and reclamation schemes have destroyed many wetlands elsewhere in the region.

In spite of the many changes since European settlement, Adelaide still offers the bird-watcher a wide choice of habitats; a good variety of birds can be found within 80 km or so of the city centre. During fieldwork for *A Bird Atlas of the Adelaide Region*, published in 1977 by the South Australian Ornithological Association, 295 species were recorded in the area.

Adelaide's population is less than a million and it is not a large city by world standards, although it is becoming increasingly cosmopolitan with the biennial Festival of Arts and, in recent years, the Australian Formula One Grand Prix, attracting visitors from all over the world. The city has an international airport with direct flights to London, Singapore and elsewhere, as well as frequent services linking Adelaide with all the other Australian capitals. A wide choice of accommodation is available: international-class hotels, various motels and guest houses, and caravan parks at Walkerville, Windsor Gardens, Brownhill Creek, West Beach, Reynella, Semaphore, Bolivar and Kingston Park. The city offers a variety of low-budget accommodation, including a youth hostel at 290 Gilles Street; the Youth Hostels Association's head office is at 1 Sturt Street. There are plenty of rental car outlets. Use an Adelaide street guide for precise directions to the following localities.

Adelaide parklands and the Botanic Garden

The city is well known for its parks and gardens. These consist mainly of open grasslands with scattered eucalypts, but there are also formal areas with many exotic plants. Although virtually none of the original vegetation remains, the parklands are surprisingly good for birds and many common species can be readily observed. These include Crested Pigeon, Galah, Rainbow Lorikeet, Adelaide Rosella, Red-rumped Parrot, Willie Wagtail, Red Wattlebird, Noisy Miner, White-plumed Honeyeater, Australian Magpie-lark and Little Raven.

The parklands adjacent to the River Torrens provide the best bird-watching close to the city centre. Over one hundred species (including introductions) are listed for the area, although many are only occasional visitors. A very enjoyable few hours may be spent here and the following walk is suggested. Enter the Botanic Garden (open from 7 a.m. weekdays and from 9 a.m. weekends and public holidays) via the main gate in Botanic Road. Walk east to the mallee section, a good spot for lorikeets and honeyeaters when the eucalypts are in flower, then north towards the zoo. Leave via the north gate, walk west across Frome Road and follow the river as far as the weir. Turn north across the weir and War Memorial Drive to the municipal golf course. In addition to the birds already listed, species seen en route should include at least some of the following: Hoary-headed and Australasian Grebe, Little Black and Little Pied Cormorant, White-faced Heron, Great Egret, Black Swan, Pacific Black and Maned Duck, Grey Teal, Dusky Moorhen (very common – it breeds on the main lake in the Botanic Garden), Purple Swamphen, Masked Lapwing, Silver Gull, Musk Lorikeet (visits the golf course in good numbers, along with Rainbow Lorikeets, when the eucalypts are flowering), Eastern Rosella, Welcome Swallow, Clamorous Reed-Warbler (summer), Little Grassbird, Little Wattlebird (winter) and Silvereye. Many of the paths in the Botanic Garden are suitable for wheelchairs and an information leaflet (with a map) is available from the main gate.

The lovely Red-rumped Parrot is common in the city and can often be found feeding in the grass between the Torrens Parade Ground and King William Road, opposite the Festival Centre. Both the Adelaide Zoo and the South Australian Museum have good bird collections and are worth a visit.

Belair Recreation Park

This 811 ha park lies in the Mt Lofty Ranges, about 13 km southeast of the city centre, and is accessible via Belair Road and Upper Sturt Road or by train from Adelaide. It is probably the most frequently visited park in the state, with city-dwellers flocking there at weekends for barbecues, tennis, horse-riding and other

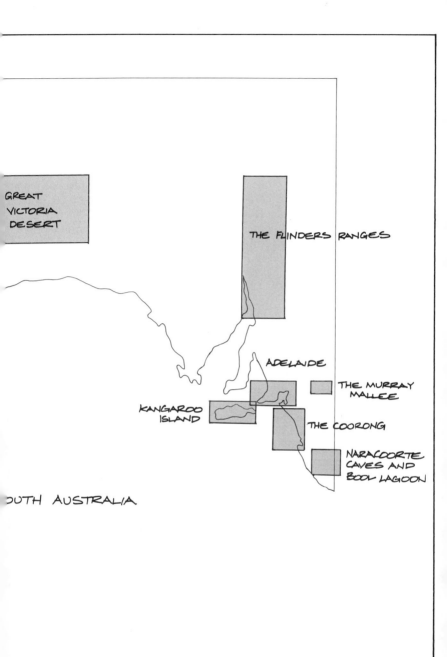

GREAT
VICTORIA
DESERT

THE FLINDERS RANGES

ADELAIDE

THE MURRAY
MALLEE

KANGAROO
ISLAND

THE COORONG

NARACOORTE
CAVES AND
BOOL LAGOON

SOUTH AUSTRALIA

activities. Since in summer it can be crowded and noisy, an early morning visit on a weekday will be best for bird-watching.

On the lower western slopes the vegetation is predominantly savannah woodland with peppermint box and South Australian blue gum (*Eucalyptus leucoxylon*, called yellow gum in Victoria), while the dry sclerophyll forest at higher elevations is dominated by messmate stringybark. Along the watercourses river red gums flourish and around the many recreation areas there is a profusion of introduced trees and shrubs.

In spite of its popularity, Belair is an excellent place to go bird-watching. Over one hundred species have been recorded and many birds are common and can be readily observed. These include Adelaide Rosella, Laughing Kookaburra, Sacred Kingfisher (spring–summer), Welcome Swallow, Tree Martin (spring–summer), Scarlet Robin (rarely in winter), Golden Whistler, Grey Shrike-thrush, Grey Fantail, Willie Wagtail, Superb Fairy-wren, White-browed Scrubwren, Weebill, Brown and Buff-rumped Thornbill, Red Wattlebird, Noisy Miner, White-plumed and New Holland Honeyeater, Mistletoebird, Striated Pardalote, Silvereye, Red-browed Firetail, Australian Magpie-lark, Dusky Wood-swallow (rarely in winter), Australian Magpie, Grey Currawong and Little Raven.

Playford Lake and Railway Dam usually hold a few waterbirds. Little Pied Cormorant, White-faced Heron, Black Swan, Pacific Black Duck, Grey Teal, Black-tailed Native-hen, Dusky Moorhen and Eurasian Coot can usually be seen, with rarer species such as Darter turning up occasionally. The golf course within the park is a good place to look for Maned Duck, Masked Lapwing, Crested Pigeon, Galah and Red-rumped Parrot. Rainbow, Musk and Purple-crowned Lorikeets occur throughout the park when the eucalypts are in flower, chiefly August to March. The lorikeets' raucous screeching may not be the most beautiful sound in the bush, but a cluster of these green gems hanging from the branch of a flowering eucalypt is certainly a lovely sight.

Emus have been introduced and can usually be found in the open woodland on the lower slopes, while Eastern Rosellas are common in the vicinity of Long Gully, Willows and Karka Ovals. On summer evenings the mournful cry of the Yellow-tailed Black-Cockatoo is often heard as flocks of these magnificent birds, occasionally numbering a hundred or more, drift lazily over the park. Raptors are rather poorly represented, although both Brown Goshawk and Australian Hobby are frequently recorded. Two nocturnal species, the Southern Boobook and Tawny Frogmouth, are breeding residents, most often reported from the Melville Gully area.

Many of the other species occurring in the park are less common

Bool Lagoon, one of the few wetlands of any size remaining in the south-east of South Australia

Majestic river red gums line many of the watercourses that criss-cross the Flinders Ranges, South Australia ▼

Arguably the most attractive part of South Australia, the Flinders Ranges provide an endless source of inspiration for artists and photographers

Inland Dotterel, an inhabitant of the arid, stony plains west of the Flinders Ranges, South Australia

Believe it or not this is a desert – the Great Victoria Desert, South Australia

Built by the World Wildlife Fund, the Herdsman Lake wildlife study centre is just a few kilometres from the heart of Perth, Western Australia

Three waterbirds you may see at Herdsman Lake are Australasian Grebe (above). Black-winged Stilt (below left) and Red-necked Avocet (below)

and favour stringybark habitat on the higher slopes. A walk along Jubilee Drive, east of the Woods and Forests plant nursery (opposite Old Government House), should produce many of the following: Common and occasionally Brush Bronzewing, Fantailed Cuckoo (spring and early summer), Black-faced Cuckooshrike (spring—summer), Crested Shrike-tit, Rufous Whistler (spring—summer), White-browed Scrubwren, Striated Thornbill, Varied Sittella, White-throated Treecreeper, Yellow-faced, White-naped and Crescent Honeyeater, Eastern Spinebill, and Spotted and Yellow-rumped Pardalote. Honeyeaters are most numerous during the spring and summer months when the forest is alive with wildflowers and flowering shrubs. Jubilee Drive, although rather steep in places, is sealed for some distance beyond the plant nursery and would be a good place to take a disabled friend.

Belair is undoubtedly the best bird-watching area close to Adelaide. Information, including a map showing the walking tracks, is available from the park headquarters just inside the main western entrance on Upper Sturt Road. Old Government House, built in 1859 as a summer residence for the state's governor, is open between 12.30 and 4 p.m. Fridays, weekends and public holidays and is well worth a visit. There is a caravan park adjacent to the golf course.

Para Wirra Recreation Park

This popular park lies about 40 km north-east of the city centre and is accessible via the Main North Road and One Tree Hill. The vegetation is similar to that found at Belair, with dry sclerophyll forest, consisting mainly of long-leaved box and pink gum, covering much of the area. On the flats there are patches of savannah woodland dominated by South Australian blue gum, while river red gums occur along several creeks and the South Para River.

At 1409 ha Para Wirra is somewhat larger than Belair. Even so the park supports about the same number of bird species — around one hundred. However, partly because of its location near drier country, it holds a number of birds that occur much less often at Belair. These include Wedge-tailed Eagle, Peaceful Dove, Horsfield's Bronze-Cuckoo (spring—summer), Australian Owlet-nightjar, Rainbow Bee-eater (late summer—autumn), Hooded Robin, Jacky Winter, Restless Flycatcher, White-browed Babbler, Southern Whiteface (South Oval), Brown Treecreeper, Brown-headed and Tawny-crowned Honeyeater, Diamond Firetail (especially savannah woodland), and White-winged Chough.

Other species include Emu (reintroduced to the park in 196

and now very common), Brush Bronzewing (especially South Oval), Purple-crowned Lorikeet (except December–January), Sacred Kingfisher (summer), Scarlet Robin, Rufous Whistler (summer), Crested Shrike-tit, Weebill, Buff-rumped, Yellow-rumped and Striated Thornbill, Varied Sittella, Red Wattlebird, Yellow-faced (winter), White-plumed, White-naped (winter), Crescent and New Holland Honeyeater, Eastern Spinebill, Mistle-toebird (especially May to December), Dusky Woodswallow and Grey Currawong. The Black-chinned Honeyeater, once wide-spread in the Mt Lofty Ranges but now rather rare, is still fairly common in the park and is known to breed. It can be distinguished from the similar White-naped Honeyeater by its larger size, its blue eye-crescent (the White-naped has a red crescent) and its high-pitched grating call. A good place to look for this bird is along the South Para River.

Wild Dog Creek dam and a number of smaller earth dams usually hold a few common waterbirds, while predators – although not commonly recorded – include Brown Goshawk, Collared Sparrowhawk, Australian Hobby, Brown Falcon and Australian Kestrel. Peregrine Falcon is a possibility.

The park has an information centre, barbecue sites and toilets, and there are many excellent walking tracks including The Knob (3 km), Devils Nose (5 km) and the South Para River walk (10 km). In spring the park is alive with wildflowers such as flame heath and a variety of native orchids. Camping is not permitted in the reserve but there is a caravan park nearby at Williamstown, a youth hostel at Kersbrook, and plenty of accommodation in Adelaide.

Cleland Conservation Park

Unfortunately this valuable and interesting reserve of 949 ha was burnt out during the disastrous 1983 fires. The park lies just 12 km east of Adelaide and extends from the summit of Mt Lofty (727 m) to the steep-sided gorge of Waterfall Gully. Numerous walking tracks wind through the stringybark forest and along the cool creeks, and before the fires this was one of the best places to go bird-watching close to the city. Although it will be some years before the park is restored to its former condition, the native fauna reserve within it miraculously escaped fire damage and is well worth a visit. Within the fauna reserve kangaroos and Emus roam freely. There are lakes for waterbirds, walk-through aviaries, and enclosures for smaller animals.

The park headquarters and native fauna reserve are accessible via Greenhill Road or the South Eastern Freeway, and Summit Road. The park is well signposted. Waterfall Gully is reached via

Greenhill Road, Glynburn Road and Waterfall Gully Road. Camping is not permitted.

Outer Harbour, Garden Island, St Kilda and Port Gawler

The mudflats, beaches and mangroves between Outer Harbour and Port Gawler hold good numbers of waders and other water-birds and are well worth exploring. The mangroves are rather difficult to get to and are best reached by boat. Elsewhere access is relatively easy and the following spots are recommended.

Outer Harbour: Lies about 18 km north-west of the city centre via Port Road. From Port Adelaide take Victoria Road, turn off at Pelican Point Road and follow the unsealed track alongside Port River. The muddy banks of the river and adjacent area support fair numbers of waders, with Pied and Sooty Oyster-catcher, Masked Lapwing, Red-capped Plover and Black-winged Stilt quite common throughout the year. Migratory waders (usually present only in summer) include Lesser Golden Plover, Eastern Curlew, Whimbrel (rarely), Common, Marsh (rarely), Sharp-tailed and Curlew Sandpiper, Greenshank and Red-necked Stint. The area is also good for other waterbirds such as Hoary-headed Grebe, Australian Pelican, cormorants, herons, Great and Little Egret, ibis, Royal and Yellow-billed Spoonbill, Black Swan, Australian Shelduck, Pacific Black Duck, Grey Teal, Chestnut Teal, Silver and Pacific Gull, Caspian, Fairy and Crested Tern.

Black-faced Shags breed on the Outer Harbour breakwater and Mutton Cove is a known summer—autumn haunt of the Rock Parrot, which is near the south-eastern limit of its range here. The more common Elegant Parrot also occurs in the area, therefore take care not to confuse the two.

Garden Island: Lies a little to the east of Outer Harbour and is accessible via the Grand Trunkway. After crossing North Arm, turn right before Torrens Island (a prohibited area). There are generally few birds here but a boat could be launched from the public boat ramp to explore the adjacent mangroves and mudflats.

St Kilda: This is by far the best part of the coast for bird-watching. It lies about 25 km north of the city centre via Port Wakefield Road and Waterloo Corner. Two of the best spots, Bolivar Sewage Works and ICI Saltworks, are fenced off and not open to the public, but it is still possible to see many waders and other species by walking around the edges of the saltworks and exploring neighbouring areas. The only sure way of gaining entry to ICI is to join a recognised group such as the South Australian Ornithological Association (the address is at the beginning of this chapter). The SAOA runs regular excursions to the saltworks and those unfamiliar with waders will benefit from joining such a group.

At low tide many waders leave ICI to feed on the exposed mudflats just north of St Kilda. Those prepared to get wet feet should see some interesting birds, including Grey and Lesser Golden Plover, Eastern Curlew, Whimbrel, Grey-tailed Tattler, Black-tailed and Bar-tailed Godwit, and Red and Great Knot. In summer the pans on either side of the road into St Kilda hold good numbers of Banded Stilt and, more rarely, a few Red-necked Avocet, as well as Red-capped Plover, Black-winged Stilt, Green-shank, Sharp-tailed and Curlew Sandpiper, and Red-necked Stint. In addition to waders the area supports a wide variety of other waterbirds: Great Crested and Hoary-headed Grebe, Australian Pelican, cormorants, White-faced Heron, Great and Little Egret, Rufous Night Heron (mangroves), ibis, Royal and Yellow-billed Spoonbill, Black Swan, Australian Shelduck, Pacific Black, Pink-eared, Blue-billed and Musk Duck, Grey Teal, Chestnut Teal, Australasian Shoveler and Hardhead. Terns include Whiskered (usually plentiful in summer), Caspian, Fairy and Crested, with White-winged occasionally being recorded in summer. Black-tailed Native-hens sometimes occur in huge numbers, as in 1975 when thousands were seen at Bolivar.

Apart from waterbirds, St Kilda is good for a number of species including the delightful White-winged Fairy-wren, which is close to the southern limit of its range (on the Adelaide Plain) here. The Fairy-wrens are usually to be found, sometimes in company with Zebra Finches, along the eastern boundary of the saltworks. This area is accessible via either Plain Road, off St Kilda Road, or Thompson Road, off Port Wakefield Road. In summer the flat bare fields to the east of ICI often hold a few pairs of Australian Pratincole, which sometimes breeds here.

There is a boat ramp at St Kilda and the breakwater may be worth a visit for waders, particularly at low tide. December to February is generally the best time for migratory species, but the area is rich in birdlife at any time of year.

Port Gawler: ICI Saltworks extend from St Kilda north towards the Port Gawler road. The northern section, between Buckland Park and the coast, is frequently inundated during the winter months and is generally less saline than the St Kilda area. To get there, drive north along Port Wakefield Road and turn off just before Two Wells. The Port Gawler road ends in mangroves near the mouth of the Gawler River and it would be possible to launch a small boat there to explore the surrounding area, including the Port Gawler Conservation Park (434 ha). When flooded, the shallow lagoons to the south of the road are quite good for waders, mainly common species, but also on occasions Red-kneed Dotterel and Wood, Common and Marsh Sandpiper. Much of the area can be dry in late summer. Port Gawler is also a good spot for other waterbirds including cormorants, egrets, waterfowl, rails and crakes. Land birds are rather few, although raptors such as Black-shouldered and Whistling Kite, Marsh Harrier, Brown Falcon and Australian Kestrel turn up at times. Other species include Elegant and, more rarely, Rock Parrot, Sacred Kingfisher, Little Grassbird, Brown Songlark (mainly summer), Slender-billed Thornbill (this is one of the very few places near Adelaide where this uncommon species can be seen), Spiny-cheeked and Singing Honeyeater, and White-fronted Chat.

The entire region is ornithologically outstanding and some notable rarities have turned up including Little Curlew, Red-shank, Little and Long-toed Stint, Terek, Cox's and Broad-billed Sandpiper, Ruff and Red-necked Phalarope. Obviously such species are not everyday occurrences, but wader-watchers will find thorough exploration here highly rewarding.

Aldinga Scrub and Aldinga Reef Aquatic Reserve

Aldinga Scrub lies about 50 km south of the city, at the southern extremity of the Adelaide Plain. It is accessible via the Main South Road, Noarlunga and Aldinga, and is situated east of the Esplanade between Aldinga Beach and Sellicks Beach. The reserve consists of 200 ha of dry sclerophyll woodland dominated by pink gum, she-oak and golden wattle, with scattered banksias and a few grass trees. At first glance it does not look particularly impressive, but the area holds a wide variety of birds (about 150 species) and is one of the few remaining patches of vegetation south of the city, as the adjacent bare hills testify.

Some of the birds that regularly occur here are Common Bronzewing, Musk and Purple-crowned Lorikeet (when the eucalypts are in flower), Adelaide Rosella, Red-rumped and Elegant Parrot, Pallid and Fan-tailed Cuckoo, Horsfield's Bronze-Cuckoo (spring-summer), Southern Boobook, Barn Owl, Tawny Frogmouth, Laughing Kookaburra, Sacred Kingfisher (chiefly summer), Black-faced Cuckoo-shrike, White-winged Triller (summer), Scarlet and Hooded Robin, Golden Whistler, Rufous Whistler (summer), Grey Fantail, White-browed Babbler, Rufous Songlark (summer), Superb Fairy-wren, Weebill, Yellow-rumped, Yellow and Striated Thornbill, Red Wattlebird, Singing, White-plumed, New Holland and Tawny-crowned Honeyeater, Mistle-toebird (seldom seen January–March), Yellow-rumped (October–November) and Striated Pardalote, Silvereye, Red-browed Fire-tail, Dusky Woodswallow (summer) and Little Raven. Probably the most interesting species found at Aldinga is the White-throated Gerygone. This bird is rather rare in South Australia but it regularly visits the scrub and is usually present between October and February.

The best time to visit the scrub is late winter and early spring, when the flowering shrubs provide a showy display and the birds are most active. A firebreak gives ready access and there are a number of walking tracks. There are no facilities, however, and camping is not permitted.

The surrounding agricultural land holds common species such as Brown Falcon, Australian Kestrel, Crested Pigeon, Galah, Richard's Pipit, Brown Songlark (chiefly spring−summer) and White-fronted Chat. Stubble Quail, Banded Lapwing, Australian Pratincole (summer) and Rainbow Bee-eater (summer) are also worth searching for.

Aldinga Reef Aquatic Reserve lies a few kilometres north of Aldinga Scrub and is quite good for waders, particularly common residents such as Red-capped Plover. On occasions some interesting migratory species may be seen, including Lesser Golden Plover, Ruddy Turnstone and Grey-tailed Tattler. Double-banded Plover visits the area in winter, and other birds include cormorants, herons, egrets, gulls and terns.

Victor Harbor and Waitpinga Beach

Victor Harbor: This small, pleasant holiday town is located about 84 km south of Adelaide, on the shores of Encounter Bay. It makes a good base for the bird-watcher, with the Fleurieu Peninsula and Lake Alexandrina both within easy reach. Victor Harbor itself has at least two ornithological attractions − the sewage works and Granite Island. To reach the sewage works, drive to the end of Crozier Road, turn left at Canterbury Road and take the first road on your right: the ponds lie directly ahead. The main ponds are fenced off but can be seen quite easily, and it is possible to walk around the perimeter of the works. At times they hold quite a selection of waterfowl including Pacific Black Duck, Grey Teal, Australasian Shoveler and Hardhead. Common Sandpiper is often present in summer, and to one side of the works there is a swamp that is good for rails and crakes. Lewin's Rail and Baillon's, Australian and Spotless Crake have all been seen here. The extensive reeds at the rear of the ponds are worth searching for Australasian Bittern.

Granite Island, a popular tourist attraction, is connected to the mainland by a causeway. Although no ornithological paradise, it does have a Little Penguin colony on its seaward side. During the spring and summer months the birds can be observed in their burrows right beside the main walking track. In winter, especially during gales, the island is a good place to watch for seabirds.

There are hotels, motels and three caravan parks at Victor Harbor.

Waitpinga Beach: This beautiful and popular fishing beach, on the south coast of the Fleurieu Peninsula, is about 15 km south-west of Victor Harbor. For the bird-watcher the main attraction is Newland Head at the eastern end of the beach. Its exposed position makes it an excellent bird-watching spot in winter when gales drive seabirds close to the shore. During bad weather almost anything can turn up — Black-browed, Yellow-nosed and Shy Albatross, Southern and Northern Giant-Petrel, Southern Fulmar, Cape, Great-winged and White-headed Petrel, prions, Fluttering Shearwater and Australasian Gannet, for example. Experienced seabird observers will find this one of the best places in the state for pelagics. Royal, Grey-headed and Sooty Albatross are just some of the notable rarities that have been seen here.

From the carpark at Waitpinga Beach it is about a thirty-minute walk to Newland Head, followed by a short but steep climb. Go when the weather is at its worst and take warm clothing, a hot flask and food. The area is well worth visiting at other times of the year and the beach is one of the few places close to Adelaide where Hooded Plover can be found. A pair is often to be seen near Newland Head.

Waitpinga Creek, just west of the carpark, at times holds a variety of waterbirds including Hoary-headed Grebe, cormorants, White-faced Heron, Great Egret, Yellow-billed Spoonbill, Black Swan, Pacific Black and Maned Duck, Grey Teal, Chestnut Teal, Buff-banded Rail, Australian Crake, Dusky Moorhen, Purple Swamphen, Masked Lapwing, Red-capped and Black-fronted Plover. Little Grassbird can be found along the edge of the creek, and the adjacent hills are worth looking over for interesting species such as Elegant Parrot, White's Thrush, Chestnut-rumped Hylacolä, Tawny-crowned Honeyeater and Beautiful Firetail.

Lake Alexandrina

This huge, shallow lake, on average less than 3 m deep, lies to the south-east of Adelaide and is fed by the Murray River. Not ninety minutes drive from the city, the lake's western shores are popular for water-skiing, fishing, yachting and other such activities. There are many holiday homes and shacks and much of the lake frontage is privately owned, making access rather difficult. Nevertheless the lake is very good for waterbirds and the adjacent countryside holds some interesting land species. Bird-watchers will undoubtedly want to explore the area fully, but particular attention should be paid to the following spots.

Goolwa: This small but popular resort is about 90 km from Adelaide. It lies on the lake's south-western shores, near the Murray Mouth, and has plenty of accommodation including motels, hotels and caravan parks. In spite of being crowded during

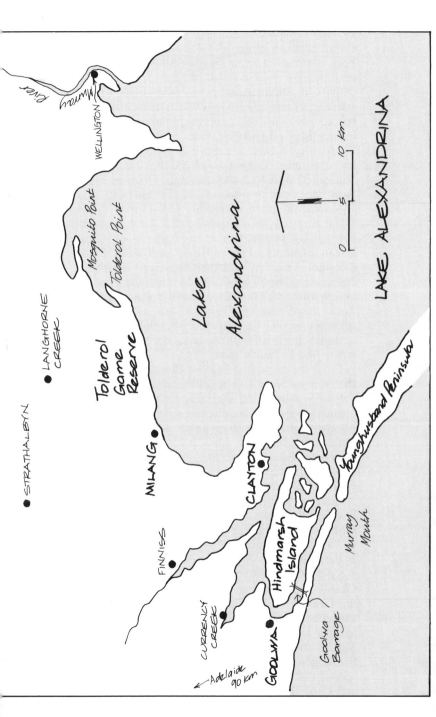

summer, Goolwa is probably the best base for the bird-watcher. From the town centre a sealed road leads to a barrage that has been constructed a few kilometres from the Murray Mouth. This road follows the shore of the lake, and beyond the barrage carpark it continues as an unsealed track to a boat ramp. In summer, at low tide, the muddy margins of the lake between the barrage and the boat ramp are usually alive with waders. These include Masked Lapwing, Grey (rarely) and Red-capped Plover, Black-winged Stilt, Eastern Curlew, Greenshank, Black-tailed and Bar-tailed Godwit (both rarely), Sharp-tailed and Curlew Sandpiper, and Red-necked Stint. There is usually a Common Sandpiper on or near the rocks at the barrage.

Masses of other waterbirds are normally present, including Great Crested and Hoary-headed Grebe, Australian Pelican, cormorants, herons, egrets, ibis, spoonbills, Black Swan, Australian Shelduck, Pacific Black and Musk Duck, Grey Teal, Chestnut Teal, Australasian Shoveler, Hardhead, Black-tailed Native-hen, Dusky Moorhen, Purple Swamphen, Eurasian Coot, and Whiskered, Gull-billed (rarely), Caspian, Fairy and Crested Tern. Marsh Harrier, Brown Falcon and Australian Kestrel are often seen along the barrage road, while the margins of the lake opposite Bristow-Smith Avenue are worth exploring for rails, crakes and Latham's Snipe.

From the carpark at Goolwa Beach it is about a 10 km walk to the Murray Mouth. The wide, windswept beach is backed by extensive dunes and Pied Oystercatchers − attracted by the abundant cockles − can often be seen there. In summer Sanderlings sometimes occur in large numbers, while Caspian and Crested Terns patrol the shore.

Hindmarsh Island: Is situated just east of Goolwa and is accessible by vehicular ferry (there is no charge). Although the island has been extensively cleared and much of it is private property, the southern section (opposite the Murray Mouth) repays a visit. At low tide the exposed mudflats support good numbers of waterbirds, while the adjacent marshland holds Golden-headed Cisticola and a few other species. To get there, simply drive from the ferry to the centre of the island: the Murray Mouth is signposted. There is a pleasantly situated caravan park on the island.

Clayton and Milang: Are north-east of Goolwa, accessible via the Goolwa to Strathalbyn road. The entire area bounded by Currency Creek and Finniss to the west, and by Clayton and Milang to the east, is excellent for birds. The Clayton to Milang road runs along the edge of Lake Alexandrina, and this is generally the best place for bird-watching. Many of the species occurring at Goolwa can be seen here, and Cattle Egrets and Cape Barren Geese frequently visit nearby pasture-land. (In summer Cape Barren Geese, together with Glossy Ibis and a host of waders, can usually be found at a shallow lagoon on the edge of Lake Alexandrina, a few kilometres south of Milang. The lagoon is on private property, but it can be easily viewed from the Clayton to Milang road.) The extensive reedbeds may hold Australasian Bittern, while Clamorous Reed-Warbler (summer) and Little Grassbird are quite common throughout the area. Buff-banded and Lewin's Rail, and Baillon's, Australian and Spotless Crake occur in suitable habitat beside the road. There are caravan parks at Milang and Clayton Bay.

Tolderol Game Reserve: Lies to the north-east of Milang, near Mosquito Point. Established by the South Australian National Parks and Wildlife Service as a drought refuge for waterfowl, the reserve was formed by flooding low-lying areas between embankments; the shallow water is attractive to all kinds of waterbirds, especially waders. With the addition of a few hides, Tolderol would be an excellent place to observe many species at close range. Depending on conditions, there is usually a good selection of waterfowl including Australian Shelduck, Pacific Black, Pink-eared, Maned, Blue-billed and Musk Duck, Grey Teal, Australasian Shoveler and Hardhead. In summer waders include Lesser Golden and Red-capped Plover, Black-winged Stilt, Wood, Marsh, Sharp-tailed and Curlew Sandpiper, Greenshank, Latham's Snipe, Black-tailed Godwit and Red-necked Stint. Interesting rarities such as Little Curlew and Ruff have been seen here, and both Pectoral Sandpiper and Long-toed Stint turn up regularly. Apart from waterfowl and waders, the reserve holds an interesting array of birds including Marsh Harrier, Sacred Kingfisher (summer), Clamorous Reed-Warbler (summer), Little Grassbird and Golden-headed Cisticola. Whiskered Terns are numerous and White-winged, Gull-billed and Common Terns are seen in summer. In winter the surrounding area is a good place to look for both Blue-winged and Elegant Parrot.

The reserve can be reached from Milang, but the easiest route is via Langhorne Creek. From here take the Wellington road and turn off after 5 km on to Dog Lake Road (signposted Tolderol Game Reserve). The country around Langhorne Creek is very pleasant and there are a number of wineries in the area.

In the summer of 1985–86 Tolderol was completely dry. It would pay to contact the South Australian National Parks and Wildlife Service in Adelaide before visiting the reserve, because it is a long way to drive only to find there are no birds present.

Swan Reach and Brookfield Conservation Parks

At one time mallee covered much of southern South Australia but over the years this habitat has been severely reduced, especially in the more closely settled Murraylands east of Adelaide. These two parks were privately owned by graziers until quite recently. They were acquired by the South Australian National Parks and Wildlife Service to conserve the southern hairy-nosed wombat, which occurs in fair numbers throughout the region. The parks are also good bird-watching areas, holding a number of mallee-frequenting species such as Southern Scrub-robin, Gilbert's Whistler, Chestnut Quail-thrush, Chestnut-crowned Babbler, Splendid Fairy-wren and Shy Hylacola, as well as many other dry-country birds.

Swan Reach Conservation Park: This 2017 ha park consists chiefly of open scrub dominated by mallee box, red mallee and yorrell, with patches of low woodland consisting mainly of false sandalwood and bullock bush. Along the park's northern boundary, and in the south-western corner, the vegetation has been completely cleared (by former owners), leaving small areas of open grassland. The varied habitat supports a good selection of birds and about sixty species have been recorded. Among these are Common Bronzewing, Purple-crowned Lorikeet, Cockatiel (summer), Budgerigar (summer), Mallee Ringneck, Mulga Parrot, Blue Bonnet, Australian Owlet-nightjar, Spotted Nightjar, Red-capped and Hooded Robin, Jacky Winter, Gilbert's and Rufous Whistler, Crested Bellbird, Restless Flycatcher, Chestnut Quail-thrush, White-browed and Chestnut-crowned Babbler, Splendid Fairy-wren, Weebill, Inland, Chestnut-rumped and Yellow-rumped Thornbill, Southern Whiteface, Varied Sittella, Brown Treecreeper, Spiny-cheeked, Striped, Singing, White-eared, Yellow-plumed, Brown-headed and White-fronted Honeyeater, Yellow-throated Miner, Yellow-rumped and Striated Pardalote, Zebra Finch, White-winged Chough and Grey Butcherbird.

A good place to look for the Chestnut Quail-thrush is in the mallee on either side of the track running down the park's western boundary, or along the unsealed road which runs parallel with the southern fence. This elusive and wary ground-frequenting species will not be easily found, but it is more likely to be located by quiet walking along tracks than by noisy searching through the mallee. Watch for it running ahead and listen for its characteristic high-pitched call. An early morning or late afternoon expedition will be best. Splendid Fairy-wren, sometimes together with Gilbert's Whistler and Chestnut-crowned Babbler, is often seen around the edges of the cleared area in the northern section of the park.

The reserve is about 120 km north-east of Adelaide via the Sedan to Swan Reach road. There are no facilities in the park and camping is not permitted, but there are picnic facilities and a caravan park on the River Murray nearby at Swan Reach. The river is quite good for waterbirds, and the adjacent cliffs hold Sulphur-crested Cockatoo and Peregrine Falcon.

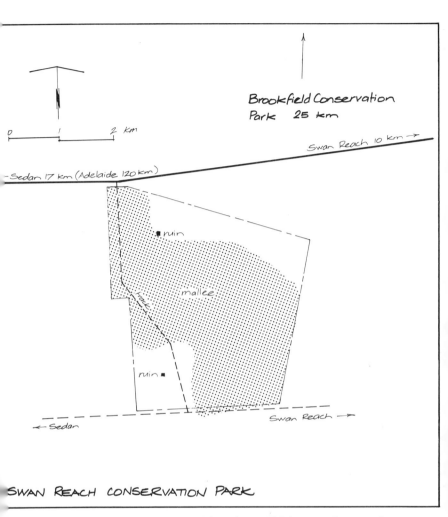

SWAN REACH CONSERVATION PARK

Within the map:

Brookfield Conservation Park   25 km

Swan Reach 10 km →

← Sedan 17 km (Adelaide 120 km)

0   1   2 km

ruin

mallee

track

ruin

← Sedan

Swan Reach →

Brookfield Conservation Park: Lies about 126 km north-east of Adelaide via the Truro to Blanchetown road (Sturt Highway). The vegetation is similar to that found at Swan Reach, with open scrub covering about half the reserve and low woodland elsewhere. At 6333 ha it is by far the larger reserve, and there are nearly one hundred species on its bird list, including many that occur at Swan Reach. Emu, Little Button-quail, Black-eared Cuckoo (spring–summer), Red-backed Kingfisher, Ground Cuckoo-shrike (regularly breeds), White-winged Triller (summer), Southern Scrub-robin, Variegated Fairy-wren, Shy Hylacola, Redthroat and, in summer, Masked, White-browed and Black-faced Woodswallow, are just some of the many interesting birds that can be found there. Visitors should call at the park head-quarters on arrival. This is located at the end of the main track into the park, which leaves the Sturt Highway about 11 km west of Blanchetown. Picnic facilities are provided and there is a short nature walk. Camping is not permitted, but Blanchetown has two caravan parks.

The Barossa Valley

This picturesque and famous wine-making area, about 60 km north-east of Adelaide, is one of the state's most popular tourist attractions. Most of the original vegetation has been cleared for agriculture and consequently it is not one of the best places for birds. Nevertheless there are two small reserves in the region − Kaiserstuhl and Sandy Creek Conservation Parks − and a visit to the latter in particular will be well worthwhile.

Kaiserstuhl Conservation Park: Is located in the heart of the valley, a few kilometres south-east of Tanunda, and is accessible via Menglers Hill Road and Tanunda Creek Road. It consists of 392 ha of brown stringybark woodland with occasional she-oaks and grass trees. The park holds mostly those birds that can be seen almost anywhere further south in the Mt Lofty Ranges. As it is virtually the only patch of scrub remaining in the region, its conservation value is quite considerable.

Sandy Creek Conservation Park: Lies about 50 km north-east of Adelaide via the Gawler to Lyndoch road. It is situated roughly midway between the Sandy Creek hotel and Lyndoch, about 1 km south of the main road. Sandy Creek is a small park, just 104 ha, yet its bird list contains an amazing 108 species, an indication of the park's great worth.

The varied vegetation is dominated by pink gum, she-oak, banksia and native pine, and the wonderful array of birds includes Whistling Kite, Brown Goshawk, Little Eagle, Brown Falcon, Australian Kestrel, Peaceful Dove, Common Bronzewing, Crested Pigeon, Musk and Purple-crowned Lorikeet, Galah, Adelaide Rosella, Red-rumped and Elegant Parrot, Pallid and Fan-tailed Cuckoo (winter−spring), Horsfield's Bronze-Cuckoo (spring−summer), Rainbow Bee-eater (spring−summer), Black-faced Cuckoo-shrike (spring), White-winged Triller (spring−summer), Scarlet, Red-capped and Hooded Robin, Jacky Winter, Crested Shrike-tit, Golden Whistler, Rufous Whistler (spring−summer), Grey Shrike-thrush, Restless Flycatcher, Grey Fantail, White-browed Babbler, Rufous Songlark (spring), Superb Fairy-wren, Weebill, Chestnut-rumped, Buff-rumped, Yellow-rumped and Yellow Thornbill, Varied Sittella, Brown Treecreeper, Red and Little Wattlebird, Noisy Miner, White-plumed, Black-chinned, Brown-headed and New Holland Honeyeater, Eastern Spinebill,

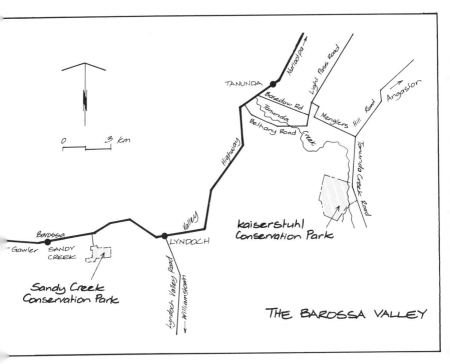

THE BAROSSA VALLEY

Mistletoebird, Yellow-rumped and Striated Pardalote, Silvereye, Red-browed and Diamond Firetail, Zebra Finch, Dusky Woodswallow, Australian Magpie, Grey Currawong and Little Raven.

This superb spot deserves more than just a brief visit and those with the time will find a full day here very rewarding. Camping is not permitted but there are hotels and motels throughout the Barossa Valley and caravan parks at Tanunda, Lyndoch and Nuriootpa. The Barossa Valley Vintage Festival is held every second year (odd years) in April.

KANGAROO ISLAND

Kangaroo Island is only a thirty-minute flight from Adelaide, yet despite a growing tourist trade it remains refreshingly free from commercialism. There are no neon signs flashing a welcome as you step off the plane at Kingscote Airport, no high-rise buildings to detract from the beauty of the island's many splendid beaches. Development has proceeded at a snail's pace since the island was discovered by Matthew Flinders in 1802, and although it is by far the largest off the South Australian coast it has fewer than four thousand inhabitants and no major industries.

It is a peaceful place; a place where people clearly value their natural heritage. Indeed, wildlife features prominently throughout the island's tourist publications. Certainly there are those who would like to see a greater effort being made to attract visitors, but it seems likely that the island will remain something of a backwater for many years to come. And for bird-watchers at least that is good news.

You can get to Kangaroo Island by air or by sea. Those planning to travel by air should call at their local travel agent, or at any South Australian Government Travel Centre, and compare ticket prices. Several light aircraft operators, including Emu Airways and Albatross Airlines, provide a regular service to and from the island and they charge considerably less than the larger airlines. If you are planning to go by sea — with or without a vehicle — you can travel on the *Troubridge* from Port Adelaide (or from Port Lincoln on Eyre Peninsula if approaching from the west) to Kingscote, or on the *Philanderer III* from Cape Jervis (at the tip of the Fleurieu Peninsula, about 110 km south of Adelaide) to Penneshaw. The journey from Port Adelaide to Kingscote takes about seven hours, from Cape Jervis to Penneshaw about one hour. You should of course book in advance.

There is no shortage of accommodation on the island, but most of the motels, hotels, holiday units and caravan parks are located at the eastern end — in Kingscote, American River and Penneshaw. There are, however, many beach houses and farm properties available for rental throughout the island. Bookings for all types of accommodation can be made at any South Australian Government Travel Centre. Those travelling on a shoestring will find a youth hostel in Penneshaw.

Kangaroo Island is large — about 160 km from its most easterly to its most westerly point, and on average about 45 km wide. It has no public transport, therefore if you do not have a vehicle you will need to hire one. Rental cars and campervans are readily available, but it would be wise to compare rates. At least one outlet in Kingscote offers a fixed rate per day (unlimited kilometres), an important consideration since you could easily clock up several hundred kilometres over a period of three or four days. Bicycles can be hired in Kingscote, American River and Penneshaw. However, while there are few hills, rough roads and long distances make cycling rather exhausting.

Although a good deal of the island has been cleared for agriculture, especially during the past forty years or so, a substantial amount of the original vegetation remains and large areas are protected by an extensive network of reserves. These comprise Flinders Chase National Park (73 662 ha), the largest reserve on Kangaroo Island and one of the most important in the state, and fifteen conservation parks ranging in size from 21 254 ha (Cape Gantheaume) to 10 ha (Busby and Beatrice Islets). Flinders

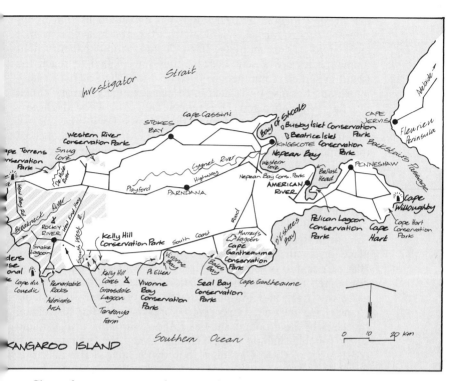

Kangaroo Island map showing: Investigator Strait, Cape Cassini, Stokes Bay, Western River Conservation Park, Cape Torrens Conservation Park, Snug Cove, Cygnet River, Ravine Highway, Playford, Parndana, Breaknack River, Rocky River, West End Hwy, South West Rd, Kelly Hill Conservation Park, South Coast Rd, Snake Lagoon, Flinders Chase National Park, Cape du Couedic, Remarkable Rocks, Admirals Arch, Kelly Hill Caves, Grassdale Lagoon, Tandonya Farm, Pt Ellen, Vivonne Bay Conservation Park, Vivonne Bay, Murray's Lagoon, Cape Gantheaume Conservation Park, Bales Bay, Seal Bay Conservation Park, Cape Gantheaume, D'Estrees Bay, Bay of Shoals, Busby Islet Conservation Park, Beatrice Islet, Kingscote, Nepean Bay Conservation Park, Nepean Bay, Western Cove, Nepean Bay Cons. Park, American River, Ballast Head, Penneshaw, Pelican Lagoon Conservation Park, Cape Willoughby, Cape Hart Conservation Park, Cape Hart, Backstairs Passage, Cape Jervis, Fleurieu Peninsula, Adelaide, Southern Ocean, KANGAROO ISLAND. Scale bar: 0 10 20 km.

Chase features spectacular coastal scenery, and conserves vast
tracts of dense mallee scrub and coastal heathland, as well as tall
stands of eucalypt forest containing sugar, pink and swamp gums.
The island's conservation parks protect a wide variety of habitats,
including offshore islands, coastal cliffs, sandy beaches and freshwater lagoons.

Kangaroo Island's birdlife shows the greatest affinity with that
of the Fleurieu Peninsula, just 14 km to the east, yet curiously the
island lacks many land birds that occur regularly on the nearby
mainland — birds such as Crested Pigeon, Red-rumped Parrot,
Hooded Robin, Jacky Winter, Crested Shrike-tit, Rufous Whistler,
White-browed Babbler, Weebill, Buff-rumped and Yellow
Thornbill, Varied Sittella, White-throated Treecreeper, Noisy
Miner, Yellow-faced and White-plumed Honeyeater, Mistletoebird and Diamond Firetail.

Much has been written about the island's avifauna, but there
are differing views as to the causes of its impoverishment. Some
ornithologists believe that many species do not occur on the island
because suitable habitat is lacking. They point out, for example,
that until recently there was relatively little open country on
Kangaroo Island. If this explanation is correct, one would expect

the Crested Pigeon, a species that has expanded its range considerably since European settlement, to establish itself now that large areas of bushland have been cleared. Another theory, that many species are absent because they have failed to reach the island in sufficient numbers to become established, is particularly interesting because birds such as the Red-rumped Parrot, Varied Sittella, White-throated Treecreeper and Yellow-faced Honeyeater occur on the extreme tip of the Fleurieu Peninsula. Lack of suitable habitat does not appear to account for the absence of these species, yet it is hard to believe they are unable to cross the narrow stretch of water separating the island from the mainland. The island's absent species continue to be the subject of much debate, but it is unlikely that the controversy will ever be satisfactorily resolved.

Despite its somewhat depauperate land bird fauna, however, Kangaroo Island has much to offer the bird-watcher. It is the only place in South Australia where the much sought-after Glossy Black-Cockatoo occurs, and although these magnificent birds are not numerous (in 1980 the population on the island was estimated at between 115 and 150 individuals), visitors have a reasonable chance of seeing one. The cockatoos appear to feed exclusively on the seeds of the drooping she-oak (*Allocasuarina verticillata*), and since suitable habitat exists chiefly along the island's north coast, west of Cape Cassini, a thorough search of the casuarina woodlands between the cape and the Breakneck River should bring results. Yellow-tailed Black-Cockatoos also occur on the island and are much more plentiful. However, the two species are not difficult to separate in the field. The Glossy (460−500 mm) is smaller than the Yellow-tailed (630−690 mm), has red panels in its tail, and calls rather feebly 'tarr-red', 'tarr-red'. The Yellow-tailed Black-Cockatoo's characteristic call is a loud, drawn-out wail, 'whee-la'.

The Western Whipbird is another of the island's sought-after species. Unlike the Glossy Black-Cockatoo, the whipbird has a wide though broken range in South Australia. It occurs on the tips of Eyre and Yorke Peninsulas, and in a few places in the mallee country near the Victorian border. It is fairly common on Kangaroo Island, but its preference for areas of dense mallee-heath makes it a difficult bird to find. Flinders Chase National Park is perhaps the best place to look for this secretive species − Cape du Couedic and West Bay are two likely spots.

In addition to the cockatoo and whipbird, the island has a number of notable land birds, including Osprey, White-bellied Sea-Eagle (both of these handsome raptors are common throughout the island), Australian Brush-turkey (introduced in 1936 and now recorded quite regularly in Flinders Chase National Park and

Kelly Hill Conservation Park), Bush Thick-knee (although rare on the mainland, this ground-dwelling species thrives on Kangaroo Island, possibly because foxes have never been introduced), Brush Bronzewing, Crimson Rosella, Rock Parrot, White's Thrush (quite common in densely vegetated gullies, particularly at the western end of the island), Southern Emu-wren (fairly plentiful in coastal heaths — for example at D'Estrees Bay), Shy Hylacola, Purple-gaped, Crescent and Tawny-crowned Honeyeater, and Beautiful Firetail (Kangaroo Island is possibly the stronghold of the species in South Australia).

About one hundred of the 220 or so species recorded on Kangaroo Island are waterbirds. The island has almost 500 km of coastline, and there are many headlands suitable for sea-watching. A variety of oceanic birds have been sighted in the waters around the island, including Black-browed, Yellow-nosed and Shy Albatross, Southern and, more rarely, Northern Giant-Petrel, Southern Fulmar, Cape Petrel, Fairy Prion, Flesh-footed, Short-tailed and Fluttering Shearwater, Wilson's and White-faced Storm-Petrel and Australasian Gannet. Winter is the best time for albatrosses; Cape du Couedic on the island's rugged south-west coast is a good place to look for them. Those travelling to Kangaroo Island by sea, especially on the *Troubridge*, should keep an eye open for seabirds at any time of the year — Great Skua, and Arctic and Pomarine Jaeger are species to look for.

In addition to the birds already mentioned, visitors can expect to see at least a few of the following: Little Penguin, Australian Pelican, Black-faced Shag, Pied Cormorant, Eastern Reef Egret, Cape Barren Goose (at one time thought to be endangered, this species was introduced to the island between 1923 and 1936 and is now a common sight in some parts of Flinders Chase National Park), Pied and Sooty Oystercatcher, Hooded and Red-capped Plover, Silver and Pacific Gull, and Caspian, Fairy and Crested Tern. Migratory waders — Grey and Lesser Golden Plover, Ruddy Turnstone, Eastern Curlew, Whimbrel, Common, Marsh, Sharp-tailed and Curlew Sandpiper, Greenshank, Latham's Snipe, Bar-tailed Godwit, Red Knot and Red-necked Stint — visit the island in summer, and occasionally some of the rarer species turn up in fair numbers. For instance, in January 1981, ninety-five Grey and seventeen Lesser Golden Plovers were seen at the mouth of the Cygnet River in Nepean Bay.

There are over 1600 km of roads on Kangaroo Island and a very full and enjoyable week could be spent visiting the following spots. Most of the localities mentioned are readily accessible, but you should take great care while driving on the island. Even those used to travelling on unsealed roads will find the loose gravel surfaces extremely hazardous, especially at speeds greater than 60 km per hour.

Bay of Shoals, and Beatrice Islet and Busby Islet Conservation Parks

The Bay of Shoals, a beautiful sheltered stretch of water some 3 km north of Kingscote, is an excellent place for waterbirds. Its southern shores in particular are readily accessible, and some of the species you can expect to see here are Hoary-headed Grebe, Australian Pelican, Little Black and Little Pied Cormorant, White-faced Heron, Great Egret, Eastern Reef Egret, Sacred Ibis, Black Swan, Australian Shelduck, Chestnut Teal, Musk Duck, Pied and Sooty Oystercatcher, Masked Lapwing, Red-capped Plover, Black-winged Stilt, Silver and Pacific Gull, and Caspian, Fairy and Crested Tern.

Beatrice Islet and Busby Islet are part of a chain of low, sandy islands situated about 3.5 km north-east of Kingscote. Beatrice Islet, visible only at low tide, is an important feeding and roosting site for many birds, while Busby Islet provides breeding habitat for a number of species, including Black-faced Shag (more than two thousand were present in June 1983), Pied Cormorant, Pied and Sooty Oystercatcher, and Silver and Pacific Gull.

Those wishing to visit the islets should contact the South Australian National Parks and Wildlife Service, Dauncy Street, Kingscote. Camping is not permitted.

Nepean Bay

Nepean Bay lies to the south of Kingscote and can be reached via the American River road. The entire area, particularly the Cygnet River estuary, Western Cove and the tidal flats adjacent to the Nepean Bay Conservation Park (30 ha), is a favoured feeding ground for waterbirds. In summer a variety of waders usually frequent the shores of the bay: Grey and Lesser Golden Plover, Ruddy Turnstone, Eastern Curlew, Whimbrel, Grey-tailed Tattler, Common, Marsh, Sharp-tailed and Curlew Sandpiper, Green-shank, Bar-tailed Godwit and Red-necked Stint.

Although there are no facilities for visitors in Nepean Bay Conservation Park, bush camping is permitted − contact the ranger at Kingscote for details.

American River, and Pelican Lagoon Conservation Park

The small township of American River is located in delightful surroundings about 37 km south-east of Kingscote. The area to the south of the township, including Pelican Lagoon Conservation Park (366 ha), is an important waterbird refuge and worthy of thorough exploration on foot or by boat (there is a boat ramp at American River). Bush camping is permitted in the conservation park, but you should contact the ranger in Kingscote before visiting the reserve.

To the north of American River township, in the vicinity of

Ballast Head, there are some small stands of casuarina where Glossy Black-Cockatoos are occasionally found. Raptors regularly sighted in this part of the island include Osprey, White-bellied Sea-Eagle, Wedge-tailed Eagle and Marsh Harrier.

Cape Willoughby and Cape Hart

The lighthouse at Cape Willoughby is the oldest in South Australia. Situated at the eastern end of Kangaroo Island, some 27 km south-east of Penneshaw, it was built in 1852 and is open to the public between 1 p.m. and 3.30 p.m., Monday to Friday.

The coast between Cape Willoughby and Cape Hart is magnificent, and the heathlands here are usually alive with Tawny-crowned Honeyeaters. Along the Cape Hart road you may hear the call of the Western Whipbird — a variety of harsh, grating sounds not unlike the creaking of an unoiled cartwheel.

Access to Cape Hart Conservation Park (311 ha), which lies approximately midway between Cape Willoughby and Cape Hart, is somewhat difficult since you must cross private property to reach it. If you wish to visit the reserve seek directions from the ranger at Kingscote. There are no facilities for visitors, but bush camping is permitted.

Cape Gantheaume, Seal Bay and Vivonne Bay Conservation Parks

Cape Gantheaume Conservation Park: Situated on the rugged south coast between Seal Bay and D'Estrees Bay, this is the largest conservation park on the island. Much of it is a wilderness, with vegetation ranging from low, stunted heath near the coast to dense, almost impenetrable mallee scrub inland.

The park's eastern boundary can be reached via the D'Estrees Bay road, while the western boundary is accessible via the road to Seal Bay. Bush camping is permitted, but there are no facilities for visitors. Bushwalkers should be fit and well prepared. Contact the ranger in Kingscote if you intend to camp or walk in the reserve.

Murray's Lagoon, the largest body of fresh water on Kangaroo Island, lies just inside the northern boundary of Cape Gantheaume Conservation Park, about 35 km south-west of Kingscote. It is readily accessible via the South Coast Road and is a superb place to go birding. Some of the many species of waterbirds that have been recorded on the lagoon are Hoary-headed and Australasian Grebe, Australian Shelduck, Pacific Black and Pink-eared Duck, Grey Teal, Chestnut Teal, Australasian Shoveler, Hardhead, Australian Crake, Black-tailed Native-hen, Eurasian Coot, Red-kneed Dotterel, Black-fronted Plover, Black-winged and Banded Stilt, and Greenshank. The rare and endangered Freckled Duck turns up occasionally, sometimes in quite large numbers — fifty-four were present in April 1980.

Seal Bay Conservation Park: This well-known reserve with its breeding colony of Australian sea lions attracts visitors from all over the world. The colony, the second-largest in Australia, contains several hundred sea lions — about 10 per cent of the world population. A wide boardwalk (suitable for wheelchairs) leads to a platform overlooking the bay, and visitors are permitted to walk along the beach where the sea lions can be observed at close quarters. To stand among these beautiful creatures as they bask in the sun is truly a memorable experience.

Seal Bay Conservation Park (700 ha) is about 60 km south-west of Kingscote and is readily accessible via the South Coast Road. The park is well signposted. Camping is not allowed, but there are picnic facilities and toilets at Bales Bay (about 2 km east of Seal Bay).

Vivonne Bay Conservation Park: Covering an area of 887 ha, this reserve lies to the west of Seal Bay and is about 65 km from Kingscote via the South Coast Road.

The park contains some of the finest coastal scenery on Kangaroo Island, and the views from Point Ellen, on its south-eastern boundary, are superb. The reserve is not one of the best places to go birding; it has no facilities and camping is not permitted. However, the long sandy beaches along this stretch of the coast are a favoured haunt of the Hooded Plover.

Kelly Hill Conservation Park

With its extensive limestone cave system and varied flora and fauna, Kelly Hill Conservation Park (6307 ha) is one of the most interesting reserves on Kangaroo Island. Some of the caves contain fascinating formations — stalactites, stalagmites and helictites — and are open to the public. Ranger-guided tours are available daily between 10 a.m. and 3.30 p.m. throughout the year. The park headquarters, an information centre, picnic facilities and a camping ground (tents only) are located near the caves.

The park's north-western corner is perhaps the best place to go bird-watching. Here several tracks provide ready access to the area west of the park headquarters, and from the camping ground a good walking track leads past the caves to the South West River, then south along its banks to the coast. This is a long walk (18 km return), but well worth the effort. En route a stop at Grassdale Lagoon should prove rewarding. It is one of only two places on Kangaroo Island where the Great Crested Grebe has been recorded, and Freckled Ducks have been seen there on at least two occasions.

Kelly Hill Conservation Park is about 90 km from Kingscote via the South Coast Road.

Flinders Chase National Park

One of Australia's outstanding national parks, Flinders Chase comprises almost the entire western end of Kangaroo Island. It contains a wide diversity of habitats, and supports a rich flora and fauna — nearly 450 species of native plants (including more than fifty different orchids), and over two hundred species of birds have been recorded.

The park headquarters are situated at Rocky River, about 100 km from Kingscote via the Playford Highway, the West End Highway, and the South Coast Road. At Rocky River there are picnic facilities, together with a camping area and a caravan park. Hot-water showers are provided, but there are no powered sites. Bush camping is permitted at a number of places, including Snake Lagoon, Breakneck River and West Bay. Those requiring a little home comfort can rent one of the two stone cottages in the reserve. Advance bookings are essential — contact the South Australian National Parks and Wildlife Service in Kingscote for further details. If the cottages are already booked, you may care to stay at a farm property (Tandanya) just outside the park boundary.

Although much of Flinders Chase is an undisturbed wilderness and accessible only to experienced bushwalkers, two of the park's better known natural features — Remarkable Rocks and Admirals Arch in the Cape du Couedic area — can be reached readily enough by car. In addition, many kilometres of walking tracks lead from the West Bay Road to places of interest along the coast. For the less adventurous, there are always Emus, Cape Barren Geese, kangaroos and koalas to be seen near the park headquarters at Rocky River.

Western River and Cape Torrens Conservation Parks

Western River Conservation Park (2364 ha): Lies to the north of the Playford Highway, about 90 km west of Kingscote. It can be reached via the road to Snug Cove. Within the reserve there are fine stands of sugar gum and drooping she-oak — habitat of the Glossy Black-Cockatoo, a species that is regularly recorded in the park. Other more common birds seen here include Scarlet Robin, Golden Whistler, Grey Shrike-thrush, Grey Fantail, Superb Fairy-wren, White-browed Scrubwren, Brown Thornbill, Red Wattle-bird, Brown-headed, Crescent and New Holland Honeyeater, Eastern Spinebill, Dusky Woodswallow and Grey Currawong.

There are no facilities in the park and camping is not allowed. You should contact the ranger at Kelly Hill Conservation Park before visiting the reserve.

Cape Torrens Conservation Park (916 ha): The main feature of this reserve is its spectacular 200 m coastal cliffs — among the highest in South Australia. The vegetation ranges from low open scrub, with coastal white mallee, brown stringybark and messmate, to woodlands of sugar gum and drooping she-oak. Both the Glossy Black-Cockatoo and Western Whipbird have been recorded.

The park is about 100 km west of Kingscote via the Playford Highway. If you intend visiting the reserve, seek directions from the ranger at Flinders Chase National Park because there are no public roads leading to it. Camping is not permitted.

THE COORONG

Most accounts of this well-known stretch of coast paint a picture of towering white sandhills, mirror-like lagoons and isolated islands; a place of peace and solitude where squadrons of pelicans fly into the setting sun. But the Coorong has another side. In winter it is often cold, windy and bleak. In summer the mudflats give off a powerful odour and the air is alive with insects. However, bird-watchers accustomed to such 'disadvantages' will find the Coorong a place of great natural beauty, an unspoilt wilderness free from the intrusion of modern development.

Birds abound: 214 000 waders, comprising at least twenty-seven species, were recorded during a detailed survey in February 1982, making this one of the most important wader sites in Australia. It is also an important drought refuge and at times supports huge numbers of waterfowl, as in 1964—65 when an estimated two million ducks were present. Pelicans breed off Policemans Point, and Caspian, Fairy and Crested Terns breed on islands elsewhere in the Coorong.

For bird-watching the region can be broadly divided into four areas: Lakes Alexandrina and Albert to the north, huge but shallow freshwater lakes fed by the River Murray; the Younghusband Peninsula to the west, a long, narrow strip of barrier sand-dunes densely vegetated in places but out of the reach of most bird-watchers; the lagoons and islands of the Coorong itself, stretching from the Murray Mouth in the north to just south of Salt Creek; and the hinterland to the east, where remnants of the original vegetation are protected by several reserves, notably Mt Boothby and Messent Conservation Parks.

Lake Alexandrina and Lake Albert

From Meningie, on the shores of Lake Albert, it is possible to explore the surrounding district including the southern shores of Lake Alexandrina and the northern section of the Coorong. The town makes a convenient base and has stores, petrol, accommodation and a pleasantly situated caravan park. Both lakes are easy to get to via the Princes Highway, but for those wishing to see as much of the area as possible in a short time, the following route

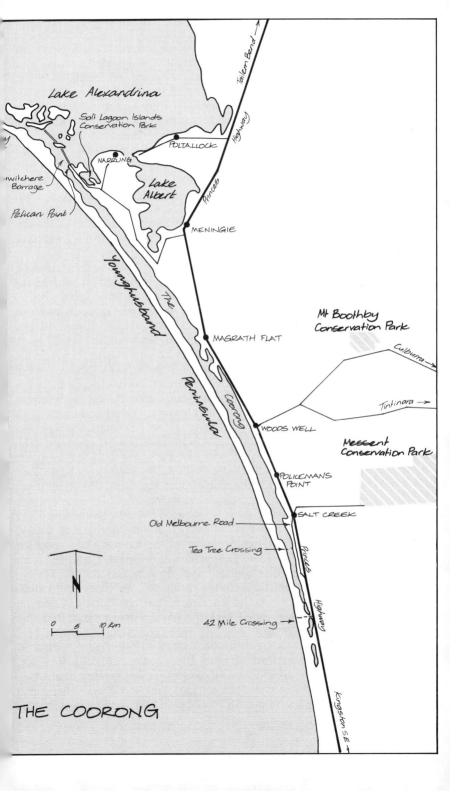

is suggested. Take the highway north towards Tailem Bend and turn off after about 23 km to Narrung. The unsealed Narrung road skirts the southern shores of Lake Alexandrina for about 15 km. Although much of the adjacent area is privately owned there are good views over the lake, especially in the vicinity of Poltallock, a picturesque property about 10 km from the turn-off. This spot is usually good for waterbirds including Australian Pelican, cormorants, White-faced and, occasionally, Pacific Heron, Great and Little Egret, Sacred, Straw-necked and, more rarely, Glossy Ibis, Royal and Yellow-billed Spoonbill, Black Swan, Cape Barren Goose, Australian Shelduck, Pacific Black and Musk Duck, Grey Teal, Purple Swamphen, Masked Lapwing, Black-winged Stilt and Whiskered Tern. Opposite Poltallock there is a shallow lagoon that holds a few waders in summer. It is also a good place for rails and crakes.

A little further along the road, near the Narrung ferry crossing, is a ramp from which a boat could be launched to explore the extensive reedbeds. Royal Spoonbill and all three species of ibis breed nearby in the Narrung Narrows. Marsh Harrier is common and Clamorous Reed-Warbler (summer), Little Grassbird and Golden-headed Cisticola frequent the margins of the lake.

From Narrung it is possible to drive to Pelican Point at the northern end of the Coorong (use the 1:50 000 Narrung map, available from Mapland, 12 Pirie Street, Adelaide). From here a series of barrages stretch northwards and one can walk across them to Tauwitchere Island and beyond. The adjacent area holds numerous waterbirds, including grebes, pelicans, cormorants, herons, egrets, ibis, spoonbills, waterfowl, waders and terns. The islands in Salt Lagoon Conservation Park, just to the east, support breeding colonies of Great, Pied, Little Black and Little Pied Cormorant, Great and possibly Little and Cattle Egret, all three species of ibis, both spoonbills and Rufous Night Heron. A permit to land on the islands must be obtained from the South Australian National Parks and Wildlife Service in Adelaide or Salt Creek. The sand-bars and rocky shores of the Coorong are good for waders such as Pied Oystercatcher, Masked Lapwing, Red-capped Plover, Black-winged Stilt, Red-necked Avocet, Greenshank, Sharp-tailed and Curlew Sandpiper, and Red-necked Stint. Occasionally Lesser Golden Plover, Eastern Curlew, Common Sandpiper, Black-tailed and Bar-tailed Godwit, and Red and Great Knot turn up.

In times of drought the backwaters of both lakes hold good numbers of waterfowl, including Black Swan, Australian Shelduck, Pacific Black and Musk Duck, Grey Teal, Chestnut Teal, Australasian Shoveler and Hardhead. Pink-eared and Blue-billed Duck occur less frequently, and the endangered Freckled Duck is a possibility. Many of the best spots are on private property and permission should be obtained before venturing too far.

From Pelican Point the road back to Meningie follows the shores of Lake Albert for much of the way. The surrounding countryside has been extensively cleared and land birds are rather few, although raptors such as Black-shouldered and Whistling Kite, Wedge-tailed Eagle, Marsh Harrier, Brown Falcon and Australian Kestrel are reasonably plentiful.

Younghusband Peninsula

The towering white sandhills that look so inviting from the mainland are accessible only to owners of four-wheel-drive vehicles. However, the ocean beach, although certainly a place of great beauty and isolation, holds few birds except Pied Oystercatcher, Hooded Plover and gulls and terns. The dense scrub on the landward side does have some interesting species — Rufous Bristlebird, Beautiful Firetail and possibly Southern Emu-wren (at the northern end) — but these can be seen more easily elsewhere in the region.

The peninsula may be reached at any time of year via 42 Mile Crossing, about 18 km south of Salt Creek. Tea Tree Crossing, about 8 km from Salt Creek, is an alternative route that is usually under water during winter and spring. A permit to travel on the beach must be obtained in advance from the ranger at Salt Creek.

The Coorong

The Coorong National Park and Game Reserve extends from the Murray Mouth in the north to about 40 km south of Salt Creek, a distance of 130 km or so. Almost 40 000 ha are protected in the national park, and a further 6841 ha in the game reserve which lies between Policemans Point and Salt Creek. The Coorong lagoons rarely exceed 3 km in width and are shallow, with an average winter depth of only 2.5 m. The salinity varies from season to season and from north to south; in the southern lagoons it can rise to between two and three times that of seawater.

It is probably fair to say that the Coorong is to Australian bird-watchers what the Camargue in France is to the Europeans — only in place of flamingoes we have pelicans. It can be wild and desolate in winter, when huge black storm clouds roll in from the Southern Ocean, and calm and tranquil in summer when the bobbing bodies of thousands of Banded Stilts appear like flotsam on the glassy waters. Pelicans are certainly the most conspicuous and probably the best known birds in the region. They breed on islands off Policemans Point, but since their young are extremely vulnerable to disturbance, the colonies are prohibited areas. In good years between three thousand and four thousand birds breed here, making it one of the most important permanent nesting sites in south-eastern Australia. As well as pelicans, Caspian, Fairy and Crested Terns all breed regularly in the region. In summer, non-breeding terns include large numbers of Whiskered Terns, with Gull-billed, White-winged and Common Tern being seen occasionally.

Waterfowl may occur in huge numbers, chiefly in late spring and summer when alternative areas have dried up. The most common species are Black Swan, Australian Shelduck, Pacific Black and Musk Duck, Grey Teal and Chestnut Teal, but fair numbers of Australasian Shoveler, Pink-eared and Blue-billed Duck, and Hardhead also occur regularly. Great Crested Grebes are sometimes present in hundreds, while Hoary-headed Grebes are usually plentiful throughout the year.

Apart from being a haven for pelicans, terns and waterfowl, the Coorong is probably the most important wader area in the state and one of the most significant sites in Australia. It should be noted, however, that unlike estuaries where the birds are normally forced into a compact group at high tide, much of the Coorong is affected only minimally by tidal action. As a result, waders are usually spread thinly over a wide area. Bird-watchers who visit the Coorong expecting to see mudflats teeming with birds are therefore likely to be disappointed. Nevertheless the patient and thorough observer will find many of the following: Pied and (rarely) Sooty Oystercatcher, Masked Lapwing, Grey (rarely), Lesser Golden, Hooded and Red-capped Plover, Black-winged and Banded Stilt, Red-necked Avocet, Ruddy Turnstone, Eastern Curlew, Common, Marsh (rarely), Sharp-tailed and Curlew Sandpiper, Greenshank, Black-tailed and Bar-tailed Godwit (rarely), Red and Great Knot (rarely), Red-necked Stint and Sanderling (rarely). The Oriental Plover, a notable rarity, has also been recorded and is well worth searching for. Banded Stilts are usually very numerous in summer, with about sixty thousand present in 1982. The lovely Red-necked Avocet is also quite common, although it usually occurs in smaller numbers than the stilts. Double-banded Plovers visit the region from New Zealand during the winter months. Between Magrath Flat and Policemans Point, the Princes Highway follows the shores of the Coorong and, depending on the water level, this is usually the best area for waders. Tea Tree Crossing is another good spot. The best time for migratory waders is January to March, although it can be very hot then.

Salt Creek is a good place to look for Buff-banded Rail, and Baillon's, Australian and Spotless Crake. A walk along the banks of the creek in the early morning or late afternoon should prove rewarding.

Although waterbirds are certainly its chief attraction, the Coorong is also a good place to see many land birds, especially Rufous Bristlebird and Beautiful Firetail. Both are quite plentiful in suitable habitat south of Salt Creek, but the bristlebird, with its loud 'chip, chip, chip, chew, chewee' call is more often heard than seen. A good spot to look for this elusive species is along the Old Melbourne Road, which leaves the Princes Highway just south of the bridge at Salt Creek. In the early morning or late afternoon bristlebirds often appear briefly on the track as they scuttle from one side to the other.

About 2 km from the park entrance at Salt Creek the South Australian National Parks and Wildlife Service has constructed a 3 km circular nature trail. It follows the shoreline of a carbonate lake for about a kilometre before crossing a densely vegetated sanddune. In early summer the lake often holds Banded Stilt and a few waterfowl. The adjacent paperbark flats and mallee are good for a variety of bush birds including Common and Brush Bronzewing, Eastern Rosella, Pallid and Fan-tailed Cuckoo (spring–summer), Horsfield's Bronze-Cuckoo (spring–summer), Black-faced Cuckooshrike, Grey Shrike-thrush, Grey Fantail, White-browed Babbler, Superb Fairy-wren, Rufous Bristlebird, White-browed Scrubwren, Yellow-rumped and Striated Thornbill, Red and Little Wattlebird, Spiny-cheeked, Singing, Purple-gaped and New Holland Honeyeater, White-fronted Chat, Striated Pardalote, Silvereye, Beautiful Firetail, Dusky Woodswallow, Grey Butcherbird and Grey Currawong. One species that probably few people expect to find at Salt Creek is the Malleefowl. Along the nature trail, especially just before dusk, they can occasionally be seen feeding around the edges of the sand-dunes. Another bird which surprisingly occurs here is the delightful Eastern Yellow Robin.

As well as supporting many interesting resident land birds the Coorong acts as a corridor for a number of species migrating north during the autumn and winter months. One of these is the rare and endangered Orange-bellied Parrot, which breeds in Tasmania and migrates to the mainland in winter. The Flame Robin is another bird that is only seen in winter. Summer migrants include Masked and White-browed Woodswallows, with Fork-tailed Swifts often turning up ahead of a storm.

The park has several campsites with basic facilities, and bush camping is permitted throughout the reserve, including the islands. A permit should be obtained first from the ranger. For those requiring a little more luxury, there are caravan parks at Policemans Point and Woods Well. The park headquarters are located at Salt Creek and information, including a leaflet describing aspects of the nature trail, can be obtained from the ranger's office.

Messent and Mt Boothby Conservation Parks

Much of the original vegetation to the east of the Coorong has been cleared for agriculture and there are few accessible areas worth exploring. The best place is Messent Conservation Park, which is about 7 km north-east of Salt Creek. At 12 245 ha, it is one of the largest conservation parks in south-eastern South Australia and could almost be called a wilderness. The firebreaks around the perimeter and the narrow track running through it are rough and sandy in places and subject to inundation during winter. Inquiries about conditions should be made of the ranger at Salt Creek before visiting the area. With a four-wheel-drive vehicle it is possible to experience fully its many attractions, but those with conventional cars can drive from Salt Creek to the gate at the south-western corner and walk the remaining 1.5 km to the narrow track running through the reserve from east to west. For the first one or two kilometres the track crosses a patch of mallee heathland where Southern Emu-wrens can be found. This elusive species is often difficult to locate, although an early morning or late afternoon search on a still day (the wind carries away the bird's timorous trill) is likely to bring results. Emu-wrens also occur elsewhere in the park in suitable habitat.

Much of the area consists of low-lying swampy ground and sedge flats, with dense vegetation dominated by yellow and narrow-leaved red mallee on the higher ground and stabilised dunes. In winter and early spring the swamps attract waterbirds and the park supports an interesting array of other species. Just a few of these are Malleefowl, Mallee Ringneck, White-winged Triller (summer), Southern Scrub-robin, Hooded Robin, Crested Bellbird, Rufous Bristlebird, Shy Hylacola and Calamanthus. Purple-gaped, Brown-headed and Tawny-crowned Honeyeaters are common, the latter being especially numerous when the flowering shrubs are in bloom. Along the southern boundary of the park there are patches of quite tall timber which hold a few birds not found in the mallee. Eastern Yellow Robin occurs here at the northern limit of its range in South Australia.

The park has not been burnt for a number of years and is in pristine condition. Visit the area on a cool day and be sure to see the ranger beforehand: remember that there are few landmarks here and that the park is large enough to get well and truly lost in; stay on the tracks at all times. There are no facilities.

Mt Boothby is a small (4045 ha) but attractive park with interesting granite formations and surprisingly varied vegetation. Much of the park is covered by low, spindly mallee with patches of open pink gum forest and some heathland. It is particularly pleasant in spring and early summer when the flowering shrubs attract a wealth of honeyeaters, including Tawny-crowned. Mallee-fowls occur here also.

To reach the park, turn off the Princes Highway just south of Woods Well and head east on the Culburra road. The park lies to the left of the road about 24 km from the turn-off. It has no sign but is easily recognised by its granite outcrops. There are no facilities.

NARACOORTE CAVES AND BOOL LAGOON

The south-east of South Australia once supported dense stands of forest and there were numerous lakes, lagoons and swamps. Today, less than 10 per cent of the original vegetation remains and many of the wetlands have been drained. Nevertheless the region still boasts a rich and varied avifauna (over three hundred species have been recorded), and there is a wide range of places for bird-watching. A very full and interesting week could be spent exploring the Naracoorte area, using the Naracoorte Caves Conservation Park as a base.

Naracoorte Caves Conservation Park

This important reserve of 304 ha lies 12 km south-east of Naracoorte and protects seventeen of the region's sixty or so known caves. Three are open to the public: Blanche Cave, a dry or dormant cave featuring huge caverns and columns; Alexandra Cave, a wet or live cave, which has some of the most beautiful and delicate decorations at Naracoorte; and the Victoria Fossil Cave, which assumed world-wide significance in 1969 following the discovery of a fossil bed containing the bones of many extinct and present-day animals. It is rated as one of the top three such deposits in the world.

Bat Cave is perhaps the most interesting of the remaining fourteen caves that are not open for inspection. It holds a massive colony of bent-wing bats and each year in spring hundreds of thousands of these animals arrive from all over south-eastern Australia to breed there.

The park has an informal, tree-studded camping area with powered sites for caravans. Within the excellent information centre there are reconstructed caves and a laboratory where visitors can see scientists working on fossils. The park is also a good place for bush birds: around the camping ground Eastern Yellow Robin, White-browed Babbler and Superb Fairy-wren have become very tame and can be readily observed. The White-throated Treecreeper often visits picnic tables, at which it can be viewed feeding horizontally, in contrast to its more usual vertical position.

South of the camping area, and adjacent to Victoria Cave, there is an extensive patch of brown stringybark forest and heathland. Mosquito Creek flows through the forest and river red gums grow along the creek banks. This is the best spot for birds, of which the following may be seen: Common Bronzewing, Crimson and Eastern Rosella, Red-rumped and (especially in winter) Blue-winged Parrot, Fan-tailed Cuckoo (spring—summer), Horsfield's Bronze-Cuckoo (spring—summer), Southern Boobook, Tawny Frogmouth, Laughing Kookaburra, Sacred Kingfisher (summer), Black-faced Cuckoo-shrike, Flame Robin (winter), Scarlet Robin, Jacky Winter, Crested Shrike-tit, Golden Whistler, Rufous Whistler (spring—summer), Grey Shrike-thrush, Restless Flycatcher, Grey Fantail, Rufous Songlark (spring—summer), White-browed Scrubwren, Chestnut-rumped Hylacola, Brown, Buff-rumped, Yellow-rumped and Striated Thornbill, Varied Sittella, Brown Treecreeper, Red and Little Wattlebird, Noisy Miner, Yellow-faced, White-eared, White-plumed, Black-chinned, White-naped and New Holland Honeyeater, Eastern Spinebill, Mistletoebird, Spotted, Yellow-rumped and Striated Pardalote, Silvereye, Red-browed Firetail, Dusky Woodswallow and Grey Currawong. In spring and summer the flowering eucalypts attract Rainbow, Musk, Purple-crowned and occasionally Little Lorikeets, while the White-throated Gerygone is a rare but regular summer visitor. Three species of raven — Australian, Little and Forest (the latter is close to the north-western limit of its range here) — occur in and around the park, making life even more difficult for those who have problems with this frustrating group.

The surrounding countryside consists mainly of cleared agricultural land with a few small patches of brown stringybark forest and some extensive plantations of introduced pine. The pines attract large numbers of Yellow-tailed Black-Cockatoos, which feed on the cones, and elsewhere Sulphur-crested Cockatoos and Long-billed Corellas are quite common. The rare Red-tailed Black-Cockatoo maintains a tenuous foothold in the region and is most likely to be found along the Victorian border between Penola and Bangham.

There are some good swamps in the Naracoorte area but most are on private property and permission should be obtained before venturing too far. There are also a number of other conservation parks worth visiting, especially Bangham, Mullinger Swamp and Glen Roy. Bangham Conservation Park lies to the north-east of Naracoorte, about 13 km north of Frances. It covers an area of 738 ha and consists chiefly of an open forest of South Australian blue gum and brown stringybark, with an understorey dominated by banksias, hakeas and grass trees. It is a haunt of the Red-tailed Black-Cockatoo and probably the last place in south-eastern South Australia where the Grey-crowned Babbler still occurs.

Mullinger Swamp Conservation Park, a small reserve of 15 ha, is good for waterbirds. It is 25 km north-east of Naracoorte via

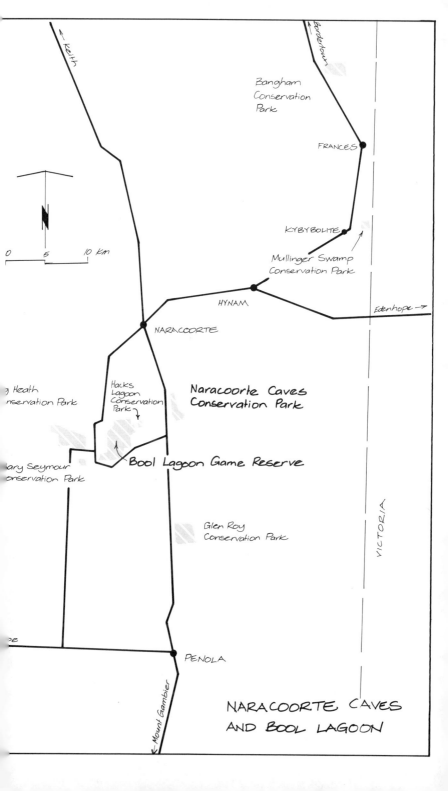

Kybybolite, but is only accessible in dry weather. Glen Roy Conservation Park (540 ha) lies 24 km south of Naracoorte, just east of the Naracoorte to Penola road. Most of the park supports an open forest of brown stringybark and it is one of the few places in South Australia where the White-bellied Cuckoo-shrike is regularly seen during spring and summer. Contact the South Australian National Parks and Wildlife Service at Naracoorte Caves before visiting any of these parks.

Bool Lagoon Game Reserve

This splendid wetland lies about 20 km south-west of Naracoorte and consists of a large central lagoon, fed by Mosquito Creek, and a number of smaller ones including the important Hacks Lagoon Conservation Park. The reserve covers an area of 2883 ha and is undoubtedly the best place for waterbirds in South Australia; it is in fact one of the most significant wetlands in southern Australia. When full, the main lagoon covers much of the total area. It is only about 1 m deep, with a large area of tea-tree, extensive reedbeds, and other emergent vegetation. Forty-seven species of waterbirds breed there, among them Great, Little Black and Little Pied Cormorant, Great Egret, Rufous Night Heron, Royal Spoonbill, and many species of waterfowl including Black Swan, Pacific Black, Pink-eared, Blue-billed and Musk Duck, Grey Teal, Australasian Shoveler and Hardhead. In good years up to ten thousand Sacred and Straw-necked Ibis breed in the main lagoon. There is also a small but important Glossy Ibis colony, and this bird is quite common in the reserve.

An important refuge in times of drought, the lagoons attract many interesting waterbirds such as the endangered Freckled Duck and Plumed Whistling-Duck. The latter is seldom seen elsewhere in the state. Other more common species include Great Crested, Hoary-headed and Australasian Grebe, Australian Pelican, Australian Shelduck, Chestnut Teal, Maned Duck, Dusky Moorhen, Purple Swamphen and Eurasian Coot. Bool Lagoon is one of the very few places in South Australia (or anywhere else) where visitors are virtually guaranteed at least a glimpse of an Australasian Bittern. This secretive species is quite common, breeding throughout the reserve, and up to ten birds have been seen in a single day. The diminutive Little Bittern also nests here but, unlike its larger relative, is very rarely seen. Cattle Egrets, dressed in their glorious orange breeding plumage, frequently occur, but they are not known to nest locally. The rare Intermediate Egret has also been recorded. Rails and crakes are well represented, with Australian Crake plentiful at times and Buff-banded and Lewin's Rail, Baillon's and Spotless Crake turning up regularly.

The region has many special birds but the Brolgas are perhaps the most spectacular. They never occur in really large numbers – usually between 150 and 200 are present – and late summer to winter is the best time for them. During the day many of the Brolgas move out to the surrounding farmland and the park ranger may be able to suggest the place to look. The ranger may also be prepared to show interested visitors the Magpie Geese that are being bred at the lagoon for possible reintroduction to the area. The geese were formerly quite widespread in the south-east but became extinct following extensive draining of the wetlands.

The reserve is a good place for waders, and some notable rarities including Painted Snipe (thirty-one were present in autumn 1980), Little Ringed Plover, Wood and Pectoral Sandpiper, Long-toed Stint and Ruff have turned up. More usually Masked Lapwing, Red-capped Plover, Black-winged Stilt, Greenshank, Latham's Snipe, Sharp-tailed and Curlew Sandpiper, and Red-necked Stint are present. In winter Double-banded Plovers arrive in fair numbers from New Zealand, but the best time for other migratory waders is from December to February. The main wader localities are Hacks Lagoon, the Mosquito Creek channel and Little Bool Lagoon, which lies just to the north-west and is accessible via Moyhall Road.

As yet there are no facilities in the park, but the area can be easily covered from Naracoorte, only 20 km to the north-east. Bush camping may be allowed, but see the ranger first. The lagoons are worth visiting any time, although the birdlife is at its best during the breeding season, September to January, and in times of drought. The area may dry up completely as often as one year in three, and it would be wise to contact the ranger before planning a long trip. In any case it is always good policy to approach the ranger for up-to-date information on the park's birds. In summer tiger snakes are often plentiful, so take care and wear stout boots or waders.

Mary Seymour and Big Heath Conservation Parks lie just to the west of Bool Lagoon and are also well worth a visit. Mary Seymour (339 ha) has areas of dense tea-tree and banksia, forests of brown stringybark and pink gum, and a small area of river red gum woodland. The park is an important breeding area for waterbirds (twenty-two species have been recorded breeding there) and is a good place to look for the Brolgas. Big Heath (2351 ha) also supports a diverse flora and is frequently inundated during the winter months. It holds a varied bird population (115 species), including many waterbirds that breed when the park is flooded. It is also a good spot for Brolgas. There are no facilities in either park and access may be difficult in winter. Contact the ranger at Bool Lagoon before visiting the reserves.

The Bool Lagoon region is ornithologically very rich and worthy of thorough exploration. Apart from waterbirds the area supports many interesting land birds such as predators. Marsh Harrier is very common and Black-shouldered Kite, Whistling Kite, Wedge-tailed Eagle, Black Falcon, Australian Hobby, Brown Falcon and Australian Kestrel are all sighted regularly. Quails too are well represented, although often overlooked. Stubble Quail is quite common and Painted Button-quail can be found in Big Heath and Mary Seymour Conservation Parks. Little Button-quail is a frequent spring—summer visitor to the region and the rare Red-chested Button-quail has also been seen in summer.

THE MURRAY MALLEE

At first glance the mallee country between Loxton and Lameroo does not look very exciting — much of the original vegetation has been cleared and there is little or no surface water. As is often the case, however, first impressions can be misleading. The region's avifauna, which is by no means impoverished, includes many highly sought-after species: Malleefowl, Red-lored Whistler, Western Whipbird, Chestnut Quail-thrush, Rufous-crowned Emu-wren, Striated Grasswren, Shy Hylacola. To have the best chance of seeing these birds, especially elusive species such as Western Whipbird and Rufous-crowned Emu-wren, you will need to visit the region's three conservation parks — Billiatt, Peebinga and Karte. Unlike Wyperfeld and Little Desert National Parks in north-western Victoria, these conservation parks have no visitor facilities, but there are motels and caravan parks at Pinnaroo on the Ouyen Highway, and at Berri, Loxton and Renmark on the River Murray.

Billiatt Conservation Park

This 59 143 ha reserve, consisting mainly of low, irregular sand-dunes densely vegetated with mallee and broom-bush, is about 40 km north of Lameroo. Access can be gained via the Lameroo to Alawoona road, which bisects the park. It is possible to walk through much of the reserve using firebreaks and four-wheel-drive tracks, but take great care not to get lost because the vegetation is very thick in places and there are few landmarks. The park holds Malleefowl, Red-lored Whistler, Gilbert's Whistler, Rufous-crowned Emu-wren, Striated Grasswren and Shy Hylacola. The exceedingly secretive Western Whipbird has been recorded at Billiatt and may be quite common there.

Peebinga Conservation Park

At 3370 ha this reserve is significantly smaller than Billiatt. Nonetheless Peebinga is an important park in an area where so

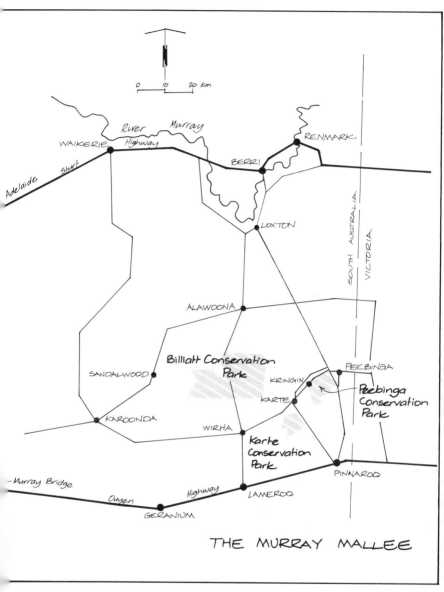

THE MURRAY MALLEE

much of the vegetation has been cleared for agriculture. It is a good place to go bird-watching, especially if you are inexperienced, because the mallee in the northern section of the reserve (adjacent to the Kringin to Peebinga railway line) is relatively open and there is little danger of getting lost providing you are careful. Spotted Nightjars and Chestnut Quail-thrushes are quite common here, while in the early morning and late afternoon Malleefowls can often be seen in the surrounding farmland. At harvest time Malleefowls are said to gather in large numbers along the railway track, where they feed on the grain spilled from passing trains.

Peebinga township is about 40 km north of Pinnaroo on the road to Loxton. The reserve is south of the railway line and west of the township.

Karte Conservation Park

Another small mallee park (3564 ha), Karte is about 30 km north-west of Pinnaroo and about 25 km south-west of Peebinga township. The reserve protects an area of steep sand-dunes and dense mallee. Needless to say access is difficult, but there are probably no birds in the park that cannot be seen more readily at Peebinga.

The region's birdlife is not, of course, restricted to the conservation parks. Many species can be seen by simply driving through the area and stopping at intervals; indeed, in places where the roadside vegetation remains intact there is often a surprising variety of birds. Species regularly recorded from the Murray Mallee include Emu, Black-shouldered Kite, Brown Goshawk, Collared Sparrowhawk, Wedge-tailed and Little Eagle, Brown Falcon, Australian Kestrel, Stubble Quail, Little Button-quail, Banded Lapwing, Black-fronted Plover (on farm dams and along the River Murray), Common Bronzewing, Crested Pigeon, Pink Cockatoo, Purple-crowned Lorikeet, Regent Parrot (often occurs along roads, feeding on spilled grain), Yellow Rosella (along the River Murray), Mallee Ringneck, Mulga Parrot, Blue Bonnet, Pallid Cuckoo, Horsfield's Bronze-Cuckoo, Southern Boobook, Barn Owl, Tawny Frogmouth, Australian Owlet-nightjar, Red-backed Kingfisher, Rainbow Bee-eater (summer), White-backed Swallow, Southern Scrub-robin, Red-capped and Hooded Robin, Jacky Winter, Rufous Whistler, Crested Bellbird, Restless Flycatcher, White-browed and Chestnut-crowned Babbler, Splendid and Variegated Fairy-wren, Weebill, Inland, Chestnut-rumped and Yellow-rumped Thornbill, Southern Whiteface, Varied Sittella, Brown Treecreeper, Spiny-cheeked, Striped, Singing, White-eared, Yellow-plumed, Brown-headed and White-fronted Honeyeater, Yellow-throated Miner, Mistletoebird, Yellow-rumped and Striated Pardalote, White-winged Chough, Masked, White-browed and Dusky Woodswallow, Grey Butcherbird and Grey Currawong.

Late winter, spring and early summer are the best seasons to visit the mallee. At these times many eucalypts are in flower and, if winter rains have been good, there is a wealth of wildflowers.

THE FLINDERS RANGES

Rising dramatically from the vast, empty plains north of Leigh Creek, the Flinders Ranges extend southwards some 400 km to just beyond Port Pirie. Arguably the most attractive part of South Australia, the rugged ranges are cut by deep gorges, the wide valleys criss-crossed by watercourses lined with towering river red gums. The uniquely Australian landscapes, so skilfully recreated on canvas by Sir Hans Heysen, provide an endless source of inspiration to artists and photographers. Magnificent panoramas abound, and the ever-changing colours of the countryside are a delight to the eye.

Rainfall in this semi-arid to arid region is extremely variable. It averages between 250 mm and 350 mm per annum but many areas, particularly in the north, receive less than 250 mm. In the south, annual rainfall may be as high as 600 mm. Climatic and other factors have produced a complex mosaic of vegetation throughout the Flinders Ranges; many plant communities can be identified, including dry sclerophyll forest, savannah woodland, mallee, shrubland, heathland, herbland and grassland.

In the southern Flinders, at Mt Remarkable National Park for example, the flora resembles that of the Mt Lofty Ranges with its tracts of dry sclerophyll forest and savannah woodland. As you travel north, the vegetation becomes more sparse; apart from river red gums, large trees are scarce. There are, however, areas of mallee, many small groves of casuarina, and some fine stands of cypress pines, particularly in the vicinity of Wilpena Pound. North of Blinman, the eucalypts are gradually replaced by species of acacia, cassia and eremophila.

Over 220 species of birds have been recorded from the region, but more than thirty of these are confined to the ranges south of about Quorn, while another fifty or so are waterbirds that only turn up occasionally. The density of birdlife is somewhat low, but there is much to interest the bird-watcher and quite a variety of species can be observed readily enough: Emu, Black Kite, Collared Sparrowhawk, Wedge-tailed Eagle, Brown Falcon, Australian Kestrel, Banded Lapwing, Peaceful Dove, Crested Pigeon, Galah, Little Corella, Mallee/Port Lincoln Ringneck (these two closely related parrots interbreed in the Flinders Ranges), Red-rumped, Mulga and Elegant Parrot, Pallid Cuckoo, Horsfield's Bronze-Cuckoo, Red-backed Kingfisher, White-backed Swallow, Tree Martin, Richard's Pipit, Black-faced Cuckoo-shrike, White-winged Triller (spring−summer), Red-capped Robin, Rufous Whistler, Chirruping Wedgebill, White-browed Babbler, Brown Songlark (spring−summer), Variegated Fairy-wren, Redthroat, Weebill, Inland, Chestnut-rumped and Yellow-rumped Thornbill, Southern Whiteface, Brown Treecreeper, Yellow-throated Miner,

Spiny-cheeked, Singing, Grey-fronted, White-plumed and White-fronted Honeyeater, Mistletoebird, Striated Pardalote, Zebra Finch, Black-faced Woodswallow and Grey Butcherbird.

Although the majority of the birds listed can be found in suitable habitat throughout the Flinders, three of the region's most interesting species − Cinnamon Quail-thrush, Thick-billed Grasswren and Gibberbird − inhabit the arid plains adjacent to the ranges, and those wishing to search for them should visit the area between Lyndhurst and Marree.

Because the Flinders Ranges cover such a vast area, you could easily spend a three-week holiday here. If you have sufficient time, the following route will take you to all the main places of interest. Commence the tour at Mt Remarkable National Park, then travel north via Pichi Richi Pass, Quorn and Hawker to Wilpena Pound. From Wilpena continue northwards to Blinman, exploring the Flinders Ranges National Park en route. From Blinman there are two roads north. One takes you westwards at first through the very attractive Parachilna Gorge to the main Hawker to Leigh Creek road. From here drive north to Copley, then east through Italowie Gorge to Balcanoona Homestead. A second, more lonely route takes you east from Blinman to Wirrealpa Homestead, then north via Wertaloona Homestead to Balcanoona. Those travelling this way will find the short detour to Mt Chambers Gorge worth the effort. From Balcanoona continue north to Arkaroola in the Gammon Ranges. Even those with conventional cars can undertake this tour; a four-wheel-drive vehicle, while certainly an advantage, is not essential. It seldom rains, but if it does you will have no option but to stay where you are until the creeks subside and the roads dry out (whether you have a four-wheel-drive vehicle or not!).

Mt Remarkable National Park

Mt Remarkable, the smallest (8648 ha) and most southerly of the region's national parks, consists of three main areas − Alligator Gorge, Mambray Creek and Mt Remarkable itself.

One of the state's most scenic reserves, it is noted for its varied flora and fauna. Over forty species of orchid occur here, red kangaroos and euros are plentiful, and several small colonies of rare yellow-footed rock wallabies inhabit its rocky slopes. The park's avifauna, totalling about 120 species, has affinities with that of both the more arid ranges to the north and the wetter Mt Lofty Ranges to the south.

In 1984 fire destroyed much of the area around Alligator Gorge, but fortunately the Mambray Creek and Mt Remarkable sections were not affected. Because the park is normally closed to the public when the fire danger is high, you should telephone the

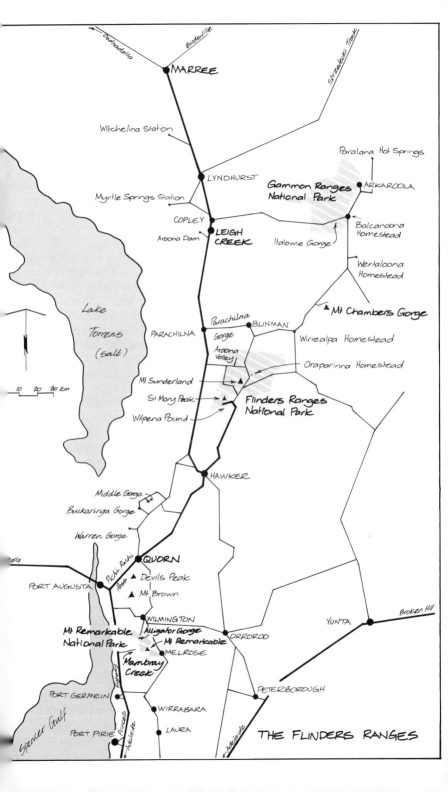

THE FLINDERS RANGES

ranger if you intend visiting Mt Remarkable between November and March.

Alligator Gorge: This section of the park is reached via a picturesque 10 km drive south from Wilmington (the access road is unsuitable for caravans). There is a picnic area with toilets at Blue Gum Flat, some 4 km from the park entrance. Several walking tracks provide access to the small but attractive red-walled gorge, while for the more energetic there are longer walks south to Mambray Creek (about 13 km). Bushwalkers are allowed to camp overnight (a permit must be obtained from the park ranger), but there is no formal camping ground at Alligator Gorge.

Mambray Creek: Lies to the east of the Port Pirie to Port Augusta road (the Princes Highway). To get there turn off about 45 km north of Port Pirie; the park entrance is 5 km from the highway. About 2 km inside the reserve there is a picnic area and camping ground. The park is very popular — you should book a site during school holidays and at long weekends: write to the ranger, Mt Remarkable National Park, PMB 7, Port Germein, SA 5495, enclosing a stamped, addressed envelope.

There is a good network of walking tracks at Mambray Creek, and information (including a walking track guide) can be obtained from the park headquarters near the camping area.

Mt Remarkable: The small Mt Remarkable section is accessible via Melrose, an attractive township about 24 km south of Wilmington. The mountain (960 m) dominates the landscape; it can be climbed, with care, but there is no marked track to the summit and you should contact the park ranger before attempting the ascent.

There are no facilities in this part of the reserve. However, Melrose has motel accommodation and a caravan park, while about 30 km south of the township there is a youth hostel in a delightful setting on the edge of the Wirrabara State Forest.

Quorn

Gateway to the central Flinders Ranges, Quorn is some 70 km north of Wilmington via the Pichi Richi Pass. This old railway town has many historic buildings, hotel and motel accommodation, a caravan park and a tourist information centre. The surrounding ranges, though not as rugged as those to the north, are nonetheless beautiful and there are many places worth visiting for birds — Middle Gorge, Buckaringa Gorge (the area between Middle and Buckaringa Gorges is a haunt of the elusive Striated Grasswren), Warren Gorge, Devils Peak and Mt Brown.

Visitors to Quorn will find a trip on the Pichi Richi Railway a memorable experience. Built in 1879, the line was closed in 1957 but it has recently been restored and today a magnificent old steam train carries passengers through the picturesque Pichi Richi Pass.

Flinders Ranges National Park

One of Australia's best known national parks, this outstanding reserve covers 80 578 ha of the central Flinders Ranges. It stretches from Wilpena Pound north towards Blinman, encompassing some of the finest scenery in South Australia – Edeowie Gorge, Bunyeroo Gorge, Brachina Gorge, Wilkawillana Gorge, the Aroona Valley and Mt Sunderland.

The park headquarters are located at Oraparinna Homestead, about 30 km beyond Wilpena on the road to Blinman. The main camping area at Wilpena Pound makes an excellent base and is readily accessible from Quorn via a good sealed road. There are over 400 campsites hidden in trees near Wilpena Creek, and although the pound is very popular, especially during school holidays, there is usually no shortage of space. The facilities, however, are rather inadequate and at peak periods you may have to queue for a shower.

Accommodation is available at the Wilpena Motel; bookings can be made through any branch of the South Australian Government Tourist Bureau. Food and petrol can be purchased from the store, while park information (including a bird list) is available from the ranger's office near the camping ground.

Wilpena Pound, with its extensive network of walking tracks, is one of the best places to go bushwalking in South Australia. Some of the walks can be easily completed in two or three hours, but others are strenuous since they involve rock-climbing. These longer treks are, however, more rewarding. If you are fit, the climb (this is no walk!) to St Mary Peak, 1165 m, is not to be missed. From this, the highest point in the Flinders, the grandeur of the surrounding countryside can be fully appreciated.

Wilpena is a good place to go bird-watching and many species can be observed quite readily. Of particular interest are the birds that inhabit areas of mallee within the pound; these include Shy Hylacola, Redthroat, and Grey-fronted and White-fronted Honeyeater. If you wish to search for these birds try the track to Glenora Falls on the north-western edge of the pound. This is a full day's walk, but the track is quite level and therefore not too strenuous.

Having explored the area around Wilpena, visitors will find the following spots also have much to offer.

Bunyeroo Gorge: This is one of three main gorges cutting through the Heysen Range, which forms the western boundary of the park. To reach it drive north towards Blinman and turn west about 10 km from Wilpena. The gorge is about 18 km from the turn-off.

Brachina Gorge: Lies about 12 km north of Bunyeroo Gorge and is readily accessible via the Bunyeroo Valley road. Perhaps the most attractive gorge in the park, it is very popular and there are several delightful camping areas on the banks of Brachina Creek (none of these campsites have facilities).

Aroona Valley: This is an excellent place for bushwalking. A section of the famous Heysen Trail commences just west of the Aroona Ruins, while to the east there is a four-wheel-drive track through Bulls Gap to Red Hill lookout in the ABC Range. Many interesting birds occur here. Redthroats are quite plentiful in the scrub between the Aroona Valley road and Aroona Creek, while Peaceful Doves, Variegated Fairy-wrens and a host of other species can be found along the creek itself. There is a camping area with toilets near the ruins.

Mt Sunderland: Lies between Wilpena and Oraparinna, just west of the main road. Its rocky slopes are well vegetated with spinifex and those prepared to search the Mt Sunderland to Appealinna Hill area may be rewarded with the sighting of a Striated Grasswren.

Wilkawillana Gorge: Is in the north-eastern corner of the park. To get there turn off the Blinman road about 25 km north of Wilpena; the gorge is some 20 km from the turn-off. From the carpark at the end of the access road there is a walking track along Mt Billy Creek.

Camping is allowed at many localities within the national park but a permit must be obtained beforehand. Camping permits and a guide to bushwalking in the reserve are available from the ranger at Wilpena or Oraparinna.

Mt Chambers Gorge

This gorge, to the east of the Flinders Ranges, is not a reserve but it is an excellent place to camp overnight. Because Mt Chambers Creek usually flows all year, bird-watchers will find the area very rewarding. Australasian Grebe, White-faced Heron, Black-fronted Plover and a few common waterfowl are often present, while more unusual waterbirds − Rufous Night Heron for example − turn up occasionally.

Unfortunately a few thoughtless campers have removed all the firewood and left a good deal of litter. Nevertheless it is a very pleasant spot; Aboriginal paintings can be found on the walls of the gorge and the climb to the summit of Mt Chambers is well worth the effort.

Mt Chambers Gorge is signposted from the Wirrealpa Homestead to Balcanoona road. The rough track leading to the gorge (a distance of 10 km or so) follows the creek bed for a short distance and those with conventional vehicles should take care not to get

FLINDERS RANGES
NATIONAL PARK

bogged. If it should rain, keep an eye on the water level — and be prepared to stay in the gorge a few extra days.

Gammon Ranges National Park

The 128 228 ha Gammon Ranges National Park, in the far north of the region, includes some of the most rugged and inaccessible country in Australia. In this magnificent wilderness, a stronghold of the rare yellow-footed rock wallaby, properly equipped bush-walkers have an opportunity to explore areas seldom visited by Europeans.

The national park headquarters are located at Balcanoona Homestead; information and camping permits (there is no formal camping ground) can be obtained from the ranger. Although this is not a place for the inexperienced, visitors can safely see a little of the park by driving west from Balcanoona to Italowie Gorge (Splendid Fairy-wrens occur in the gorge) or north to Arkaroola on the north-eastern boundary of the reserve.

At Arkaroola there is a motel together with a surprisingly well-appointed caravan park that has a limited number of powered sites, and hot-water showers. If you do not require power, camp among the river red gums on the banks of Arkaroola Creek; the main caravan area is rather open and dusty. Petrol and food can be purchased at Arkaroola, and the motel proprietors offer a variety of aerial and four-wheel-drive tours of the Gammon Ranges.

Although many of the tracks in the ranges are steep and rough, those with conventional vehicles should have no difficulty reaching Paralana Hot Springs, about 30 km north-east of Arkaroola. You should allow a full day for this trip since there are numerous narrow gorges, tree-lined creeks and permanent waterholes worth visiting en route. For the first 15 km or so the track to the springs winds through rugged ranges. In this area keep a watch for Painted Firetail and Little Woodswallow; both are rather rare in South Australia but they have been recorded on a number of occasions near Arkaroola.

After about 20 km the track leaves the ranges, crossing an open plain where Chirruping Wedgebills are common. As you approach the springs you may have the good fortune to find South Australia's beautiful floral emblem, Sturt's desert pea, growing along the sandy edges of the track. The lush vegetation surrounding Paralana Hot Springs is quite rich in birdlife and you could easily spend two or three hours here.

Leigh Creek to Marree

To the north-west of the Gammon Ranges, arid plains stretch to the shimmering horizon. So much open space is a little daunting, even if you are an experienced outback traveller. But this sparsely populated part of the country is becoming more accessible every year and today there is a good sealed road between Hawker and Lyndhurst, some 40 km north of Leigh Creek. The road from Lyndhurst to Marree is unsealed, but in dry weather you should have no trouble getting through in a conventional vehicle. Although the country does not look very exciting, there is much here to interest the bird-watcher.

Thick-billed Grasswrens occur west of the Leigh Creek to Marree road. A secretive species, the grasswren is notoriously difficult to flush and is easily overlooked. To have the best chance of finding the bird you should stop at intervals and thoroughly search the saltbush-bluebush plains. If you are unsuccessful, there are many other interesting species to be seen — Cinnamon Quail-thrush, White-winged Fairy-wren, Calamanthus, Crimson Chat, Orange Chat and, if you are very fortunate, Chestnut-breasted Whiteface. The whiteface, one of Australia's least known birds (its nest and eggs remained undescribed until 1968), is confined to South Australia. Though seldom seen, it has been recorded on Myrtle Springs Station, south-west of Lyndhurst, and on Witchelina Station to the north.

Beyond Marree the landscape becomes increasingly desolate; those with conventional vehicles should not venture too far from the township. If you own a four-wheel-drive, however, the Marree to Oodnadatta track is worth exploring. The stony plains west of Marree are virtually devoid of vegetation, yet even here birds such as Inland Dotterel and Gibberbird have adapted to the harsh conditions.

It is about 120 km from Leigh Creek to Marree. Petrol, food and water can be obtained at both ends of the journey, and for those not wishing to camp in the bush there are hotels at Copley, Lyndhurst and Marree. Before leaving Leigh Creek, pay a visit to the Aroona Dam, about 10 km west of the town.

GREAT VICTORIA DESERT

A desert may seem an unlikely place for a holiday but the Great Victoria Desert, though vast and uninhabited, is no sandy waste-land. On the contrary, despite an average rainfall of less than 200 mm per annum, much of it is surprisingly well vegetated. And because this part of South Australia has never been developed for pastoral use, unlike the north-east of the state, its flora and fauna have remained virtually untouched.

The Great Victoria Desert lies to the north of the Nullarbor Plain and stretches from about Lake Minigwal in Western Australia to just east of Lake Dey-Dey in South Australia. It consists of a series of long, regular sand-ridges interspersed with salt lakes, claypans and watercourses marking former drainage systems. There are four major vegetation communities: mallee with an understorey consisting chiefly of spinifex (*Triodia*); myall woodland with a shrub layer dominated by saltbush and bluebush; open marble gum woodland; and mulga scrub. There are also groves of graceful casuarinas, stands of cypress pines and scattered desert poplars, while majestic river red gums line some of the larger watercourses.

Although there is usually little or no surface water, the desert supports quite a rich avifauna. Some one hundred species of birds have been recorded, including Wedge-tailed Eagle, Spotted Harrier, Little Button-quail, Australian Bustard, Pink Cockatoo, Alexandra's Parrot (this highly nomadic parrot is probably rare, although since few bird-watchers visit the desert it may be more plentiful than records suggest), Port Lincoln Ringneck, Mulga Parrot, Blue Bonnet (the distinctive subspecies *narethae*, known as the Naretha Parrot, occurs in southern parts of the region), Bourke's Parrot, Scarlet-chested Parrot (the status of this very beautiful parrot is uncertain but it is regularly reported and is quite common at times), Black-eared Cuckoo, Tawny Frogmouth, Australian Owlet-nightjar, Spotted Nightjar, Red-backed Kingfisher, White-backed Swallow, Ground Cuckoo-shrike, White-winged Triller, Red-capped and Hooded Robin, Gilbert's and Rufous Whistler, Crested Bellbird, Chiming Wedgebill, Chestnut Quail-thrush, Splendid, Variegated and White-winged Fairy-wren, Redthroat, Inland, Chestnut-rumped and Slaty-backed Thornbill (the last apparently confined to the northern parts of the desert), Southern Whiteface, White-browed and Rufous Treecreeper, Yellow-throated Miner, Spiny-cheeked, Singing, Greyfronted, White-fronted, Black (a highly nomadic species) and (also a nomad) Pied Honeyeater, Crimson Chat, Orange Chat, Red-browed and Striated Pardalote, and Masked, White-browed and Black-faced Woodswallow.

Although the Eyre Highway is the only sealed road in the region, there is a network of tracks to the north of the trans-Australian railway line. These tracks have not been maintained for many years, but most are in reasonable condition. There is also a rough road running parallel to the railway line. The following route will take you through the heart of the desert: leave the Eyre Highway about 300 km west of Ceduna and travel northwards to Cook; from Cook continue north to Vokes Hill ·(about 250 km), then travel west across the border to Neale Junction (about 500 km); from Neale Junction drive south to Rawlinna (about 350 km), and continue southwards to Cocklebiddy on the Eyre Highway. Clearly this is not a trip for the fainthearted and you will, of course, need a four-wheel-drive

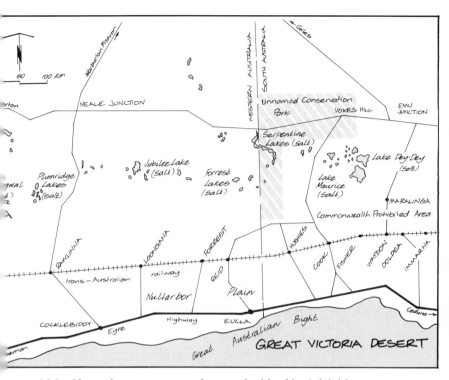

vehicle. If you do not own one, they can be hired in Adelaide – at a price! It would be wise to team up with several like-minded people and travel in convoy; driving alone in the desert is not recommended, even if you are experienced. Indeed, it is as well to remember that although the vegetation may look deceptively lush following good rains, this is an exceedingly remote and arid part of Australia.

If you are thinking of travelling to the Great Victoria Desert you should plan your trip very carefully and be prepared for any eventuality – sudden illness, an accident, a mechanical break-down or becoming lost. A set of accurate, up-to-date maps is absolutely essential. The South Australian Department of Lands map sales outlet (Mapland) at 12 Pirie Street, Adelaide, will advise you which ones to buy. Every member of your party should possess a good compass (and know how to use it) and a whistle. At least one driver should have the mechanical knowledge neces-sary to carry out major repairs; even a new vehicle can break down when you least expect it. If an emergency does arise a transceiver will enable you to summon help. They are expensive to buy and unless you regularly travel in remote areas it would be better to hire one (see the radio communication equipment section in the Adelaide Yellow Pages). Needless to say you should carry adequate food, water and fuel, including extra supplies in case of mishap.

Part of the Great Victoria Desert in South Australia is protected by the huge Unnamed Conservation Park (2 132 600 ha), and you should contact the South Australian National Parks and Wildlife Service in Adelaide, or the park ranger at Streaky Bay on Eyre Peninsula, if you intend travelling through the park. You should also seek advice from the Department of Aboriginal Affairs concerning Aboriginal reserves, and contact the Department of Defence because a large section of the desert to the east of the Cook to Vokes Hill track is a prohibited area.

A holiday in the Great Victoria Desert will require a great deal of preparation; those who do not have the necessary equipment (or confidence) to undertake such a trip should contact Rex Ellis, a four-wheel-drive safari tour operator who includes the desert on his itinerary. He can be contacted at Transcontinental Safaris Pty Ltd, PMB 251, Kingscote, SA 5223; otherwise inquire at any branch of the South Australian Government Tourist Bureau.

Winter and early spring are the best seasons to visit the desert. At these times the days are pleasantly warm and there is often a colourful display of wildflowers and flowering shrubs. Although rain can occur at any time of the year it falls mainly during the winter months, and some parts of the desert may receive more than others. In August 1979, for example, the area to the north of Cook was dry, there were few flowers, and the birdlife was rather disappointing. But the eastern margins of the desert were covered with millions of white everlastings; the unforgettable scene resembled a snowfield. And there were birds everywhere − Port Lincoln Ringnecks, Mulga Parrots, White-winged Trillers, Red-capped Robins, Splendid Fairy-wrens, Pied Honeyeaters, Crimson Chats and Orange Chats.

Western Australia

Useful addresses

Royal Australasian Ornithologists Union (Western Australian Group)
Suite 30 Rowleys Centre
15 Ogilvie Road (South)
Canning Bridge, WA 6153

Western Australian Naturalists Club
Naturalists Hall
63−65 Meriwa Street
Nedlands, WA 6009

Western Australian Department of Conservation and Land Management
50 Hayman Road
Como, WA 6152

Key to Maps

▭	Public land	♰ ♰ ♰ Marsh	
▦	Areas of water	▬▬	Major road or highway
▲	Mountain peak	───	Minor road
⌇⌇⌇	Mountain range or plateau	-----	Foot track
COBAR ●	Place name	··—··—	National park boundary
⚔	Camping area	·───	State boundary
🕯	Lighthouse	∿	River or creek

 CHRISTMAS ISLAND

 COCOS (KEELING) ISLANDS

THE KIMBERLEY

THE PILBARA

GERALDTON
AND
CARNARVON

THE NULLARBO

PERTH

THE SOUTH-WEST CORNER

WESTERN AUSTRALIA

PERTH

Perth, capital of Australia's largest state, is situated in the south-western corner of the continent, some 2700 km from Adelaide via the Eyre Highway and more than 4000 km from Darwin via the Great Northern Highway. The city is built on a narrow coastal plain between the Darling Range and the Indian Ocean. Its centre, on the north bank of the beautiful Swan River, is 19 km from the historic port of Fremantle. Like Adelaide, Perth is a well-planned, spacious city with many fine parks and gardens. It enjoys a marvellous climate, receiving on average eight hours' sunshine a day – more than any other capital except Darwin.

For many overseas visitors Perth is the gateway to Australia. It has ample accommodation, including at least four international-class hotels and numerous motels and guest houses. There are youth hostels at 60 Newcastle Street and 44 Francis Street, Perth, and others – away from the city – at Fremantle, Piesse Brook and Mundaring Weir. The Youth Hostels Association's head office is at 257 Adelaide Terrace, Perth. The nearest caravan parks are located at Como, Queens Park and Redcliffe, all within 10 km of the city centre, but there are many others along the coast to the north and south of Perth, and in the Darling Range to the east. From Perth Airport there are frequent flights to many parts of the world, as well as daily services to most major cities within Australia. Rental cars are readily available.

Western Australia covers almost a third of the continent and has vast tracts of barren, inhospitable country – the Nullarbor Plain, and the Great Sandy and Gibson Deserts for example – yet paradoxically the south-western part of the state contains some of Australia's most valuable wetlands. Near Perth many wetlands have been reclaimed or polluted, but the city still has a great deal to offer the waterbird enthusiast. In fact it is one of the best places in Australia for waterbirds: there are more than fifty lakes in the metropolitan area, including at least twenty within 15 km or so of the GPO. Even those unable to venture far afield can therefore expect to see a wide range of species within a day or two – grebes, Australian Pelican, Darter, cormorants, herons, egrets, ibis, spoonbills, waterfowl, Dusky Moorhen, Purple Swamphen, Eurasian Coot, waders, gulls and terns.

Although waterbirds are undoubtedly the chief attraction, the capital also has some interesting bush birds. Among these are endemics such as the large, colourful Red-capped Parrot and the small but equally attractive Western Spinebill. Both species can usually be found within a short distance of the city centre. Other land birds of note include Port Lincoln Ringneck, Rainbow Bee-eater, Western Gerygone, and Brown and White-cheeked Honeyeater, all of which occur in Kings Park, less than a kilometre from the heart of Perth.

The following are some of the best birding spots near the capital. Many can be reached by public transport, and most should be easy to find with the aid of a Perth street directory.

Kings Park

Situated just west of the city centre, overlooking the Swan River, this popular park covers an area of approximately 400 ha and is open twenty-four hours a day throughout the year. It is readily accessible on foot, by bus or by car.

About two-thirds of the park is natural bushland (mostly low open forest or woodland dominated by she-oaks and banksias), and as a result the area supports quite a variety of birds — about sixty species. Honeyeaters are well represented, with Red and Little Wattlebird, Singing, Brown, New Holland and White-cheeked Honeyeater and Western Spinebill occurring regularly. Other species include Port Lincoln Ringneck, Pallid Cuckoo (winter—spring), Shining Bronze-Cuckoo (mainly spring), Laughing Kookaburra, Sacred Kingfisher (spring—summer), Rainbow Bee-eater (spring—summer), Welcome Swallow, Black-faced Cuckoo-shrike, Golden Whistler, Rufous Whistler, Grey Fantail, Willie Wagtail, Western Gerygone (chiefly spring—summer), Yellow-rumped Thornbill, Striated Pardalote, Silvereye, Australian Magpie-lark, Grey Butcherbird, Australian Magpie and Australian Raven.

In addition to areas of undeveloped bush, Kings Park has wide expanses of lawn fringed with formal gardens, several artificial lakes, and a 17 ha botanic garden featuring more than 1200 species of native Western Australian plants. Picnic facilities are provided at several sites along May Drive, one of three roads running through the park, and there are a restaurant and a kiosk off Fraser Avenue, just south of the main Kings Park Road entrance. Numerous walking tracks provide easy access for those wishing to explore the area on foot; a guide map, together with other useful publications, can be obtained from the administration centre near the restaurant.

You could spend many enjoyable hours in Kings Park, especially

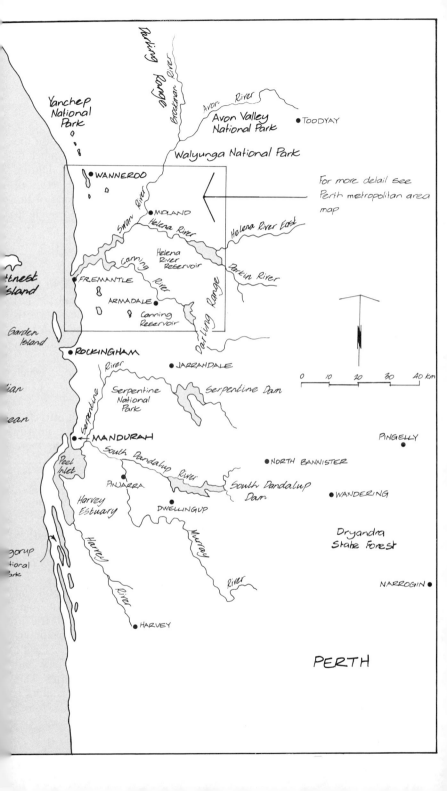

in spring when the wildflowers are in full bloom, but if you are short of time the botanic garden is probably the best place for concentrated bird-watching. Here you should have little difficulty finding a number of honeyeaters (the botanic garden is one of the few places close to Perth where White-cheeked Honeyeaters can usually be found throughout the year), as well as the tiny, unobtrusive Western Gerygone. Outside the breeding season the gerygone is somewhat difficult to locate because it spends much of its time feeding quietly in the outer foliage of tall trees. During spring, however, the male's far-carrying whistle − a series of sweet silvery notes, first rising then falling away − is one of the most familiar bush-sounds in Kings Park, and indeed throughout much of the south-west of the state.

Pelican Point and Matilda Bay Reserve

One of the best known wader localities near Perth, Pelican Point lies a little to the east of Matilda Bay Reserve, a small (25 ha) recreation area on the banks of the Swan River. The reserve is situated south of Kings Park, about 5 km from the city centre via Mounts Bay Road and Hackett Drive. Access can be gained via the road that runs eastwards from Hackett Drive past the Royal Perth Yacht Club. This road leads to a carpark, beyond which there is a raised bird-observation area overlooking the river and Pelican Point.

Despite its close proximity to the city, Pelican Point attracts a wide variety of waders and other waterbirds. If you are primarily interested in migratory waders you should of course go there during summer, preferably late in the day when many birds fly in from neighbouring areas to roost on the point and around the adjacent shallow lagoon. Species to look for include Grey and, more rarely, Lesser Golden and Large Sand Plover, Whimbrel (rarely), Bar-tailed Godwit, Red and Great Knot, Red-necked Stint, and Common, Terek (rarely), Sharp-tailed and Curlew Sandpiper. Every so often something really special turns up − a lone Red-necked Phalarope was seen swimming in the lagoon at the point in April 1981.

Resident waders − Red-capped Plover, Black-winged Stilt and Red-necked Avocet − may be present at any time of the year, while other waterbirds frequenting the area include Australian Pelican, Great, Pied, Little Black and Little Pied Cormorant, White-faced Heron, Black Swan, Australian Shelduck, Pacific Black Duck, Grey Teal, Silver Gull, and Caspian, Fairy and Crested Tern. Another species to look out for is the Darter. This distinctive bird, with its characteristic snake-like neck, is quite a common sight around Perth; small numbers can usually be found

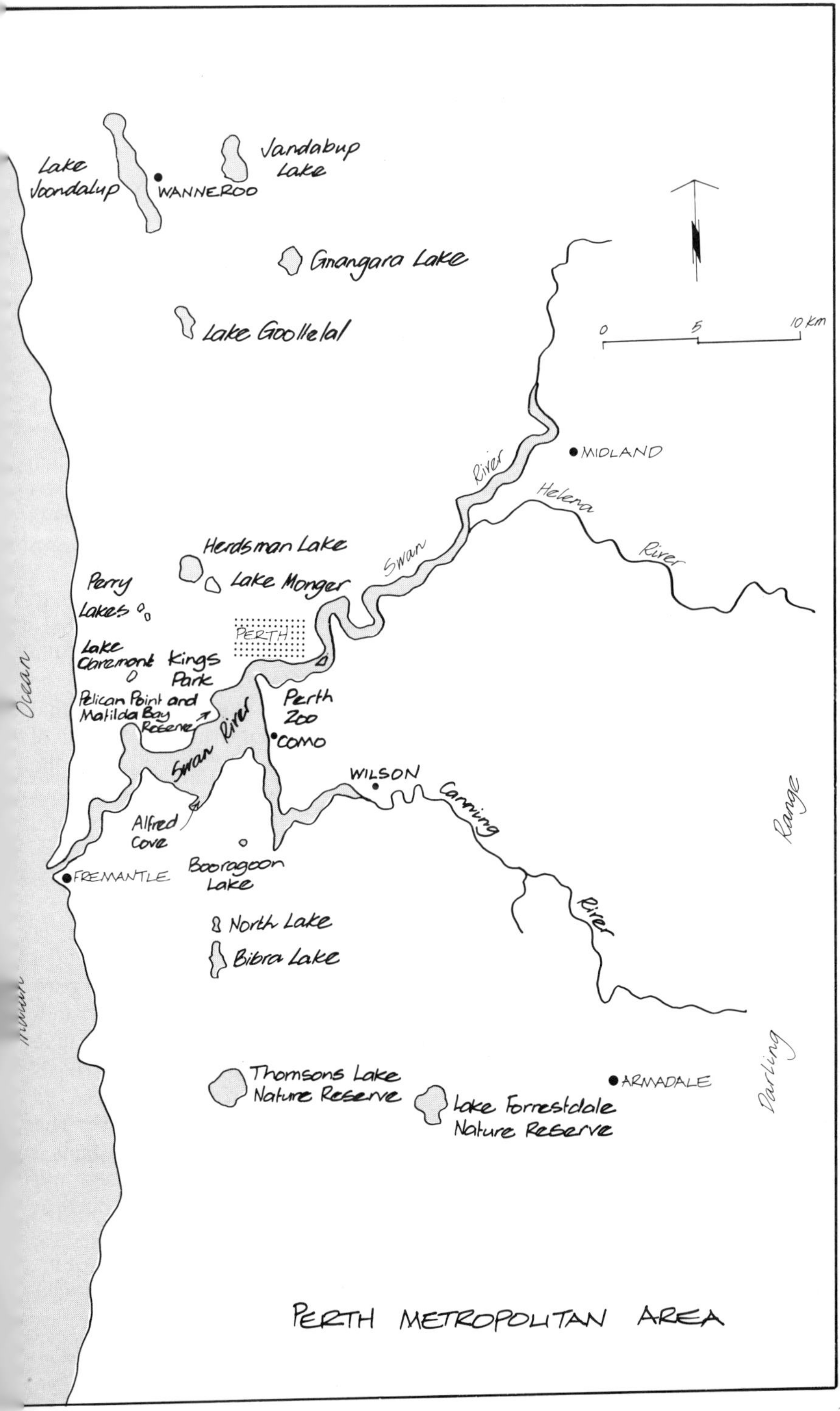
Lake Joondalup
WANNEROO
Jandabup Lake
Gnangara Lake
Lake Goollelal
0
5
10 km
MIDLAND
Swan River
Helena River
Herdsman Lake
Lake Monger
Perry Lakes
PERTH
Lake Claremont
Kings Park
Pelican Point and Matilda Bay Reserve
Perth Zoo
COMO
Swan River
Ocean
Indian
WILSON
Canning River
Alfred Cove
Booragoon Lake
FREMANTLE
North Lake
Bibra Lake
Thomsons Lake Nature Reserve
Lake Forrestdale Nature Reserve
ARMADALE
Darling
Range
PERTH METROPOLITAN AREA

sitting on jetties just north of Pelican Point, particularly during the winter months.

Before leaving Pelican Point it may be worth your while searching for Variegated Fairy-wrens in the dense vegetation lining the Swan River. Perth lies at the southern extremity of the Fairy-wren's range in Western Australia, and Pelican Point is one of the few places in the metropolitan area where the bird is regularly recorded. It may also be worth walking a kilometre or so northwards along Hackett Drive to the University of Western Australia. Rainbow Lorikeets, an uncommon species in Perth, can often be found feeding in flowering eucalypts in the university grounds.

Swan River, Como

The Swan River foreshore at Como, and indeed the entire area between the Narrows Bridge and the Canning Bridge, is worth exploring for waterbirds such as Hoary-headed Grebe, Australian Pelican, Darter, cormorants and Caspian Tern. To get to this part of the river simply drive south from Perth along the Kwinana Freeway – the Narrows Bridge is about 1 km from the city centre, Canning Bridge 5 km or so further south.

Since you cannot stop on the freeway the best plan is to drive to Mill Point (at the southern end of the Narrows Bridge) where there is a carpark. From here you can walk along the banks of the river to Canning Bridge via the cycle track that runs alongside the Kwinana Freeway. In summer most of the migratory waders that occur nearby at Pelican Point can be found in the vicinity of Como, while in winter Ospreys can often be seen patrolling the foreshore or resting on the jetty at Como Beach. If you do not want to walk far there are usually a few pelicans, cormorants and terns on the breakwater near Mill Point.

Perth Zoo

This attractively laid out zoo, with numerous animal enclosures set among lakes and tree-studded gardens, is an ideal place to spend a relaxing morning or afternoon. Its features include a wildlife park where kangaroos and wallabies can be observed in natural surroundings, a large nocturnal enclosure housing a collection of native Australian animals, and several lakes where you can see waterbirds such as penguins, pelicans, cormorants, herons, egrets, ibis (Sacred Ibis breed in the zoo grounds), spoonbills and waterfowl. The walk-through aviary is of particular interest because it contains a variety of terns – Whiskered, Gull-billed, Roseate, Bridled and Crested. If you have problems identifying these graceful birds in the field you will find a visit to the aviary very helpful.

The zoo is open every day of the year from 10 a.m. until 5 p.m. It is situated a few kilometres south of the city centre, between

Mill Point Road and Labouchere Road, South Perth. (The main entrance is in Labouchere Road.) If you do not have your own transport you can get to the zoo by ferry from the Barrack Street jetty, or by bus via route 36. There is a restaurant within the zoo grounds, and wheelchairs are available on request.

Alfred Cove, Attadale

Alfred Cove is one of only three significant wading bird localities remaining on the Swan River (the others are Pelican Point and the Como foreshore), and as such it is a site of considerable ornithological importance. More than seventy bird species have been recorded from the area, including at least twenty-five species of wader. Resident waders such as Red-capped Plover, Black-winged Stilt and Red-necked Avocet are usually present most months of the year, while regular summer migrants include Grey and, more rarely, Lesser Golden Plover, Ruddy Turnstone, Grey-tailed Tattler (rarely), Greenshank, Bar-tailed Godwit, Red and Great Knot, Red-necked Stint, and Common, Sharp-tailed and Curlew Sandpiper.

Some of the other waterbirds listed for the cove are Hoary-headed Grebe, Great Egret, Rufous Night Heron, Australian Shelduck, Chestnut Teal, Hardhead, Buff-banded Rail (this secretive species breeds in the area — though quite common, it is rarely seen except early in the day and towards dusk), Australian and Spotless Crake, Black-tailed Native-hen, and Caspian, Fairy and Crested Tern.

Alfred Cove is well patronised by Perth bird-watchers and as might be expected an impressive number of rare and interesting species have been seen there in recent years — Hooded Plover, Banded Stilt, Wood, Marsh, Terek, Pectoral and Broad-billed Sandpiper, Black-tailed Godwit, Long-toed Stint, Sanderling, and Whiskered, White-winged, Gull-billed, Common and Arctic Tern.

The cove lies about 12 km south-west of the city centre via the Kwinana Freeway and the Canning Highway. Access to the best wader area — Point Waylen, on the northern shores of the cove — can be gained on foot from Burke Drive, Attadale. Those wishing to look for bush birds such as Western Thornbill, Varied Sittella, and Singing and Brown Honeyeater, should search the densely vegetated margins of Alfred Cove, east of Burke Drive.

Canning River, Wilson

Over the years most of the swampy ground adjacent to the Swan River and Canning River has been reclaimed, resulting in the loss of much valuable wetland habitat. Parks, gardens, sports fields and golf courses now occupy many areas that were once important feeding and breeding grounds for waders and other waterbirds, but some sections of the Canning River have escaped 'improvement' — notably the area between Riverton Bridge, Wilson, and the Nicholson Road bridge, Ferndale.

To reach this part of the Canning River drive south from Perth along the Kwinana Freeway, then east along the Leach Highway towards the suburb of Wilson. Riverton Bridge lies just south of the Leach Highway, about 15 km from the city centre; the Nicholson Road bridge is a few kilometres further east via Manning Road, the Albany Highway and Nicholson Road. Toilets and picnic facilities are provided at several sites on the north bank of the river — off Fern Road, adjacent to Riverton Bridge; off Marriamup Street, near the Nicholson Road bridge; and in Wilson Park (this small reserve, situated approximately midway between the two bridges, can be reached via Kent Street and Queens Park Road).

More than eighty species of birds have been observed in the area, including Hoary-headed and Australasian Grebe, Australian Pelican, Darter, cormorants (especially Little Black and Little Pied), Pacific and White-faced Heron, Great Egret, Rufous Night Heron, Sacred and Straw-necked Ibis, Yellow-billed Spoonbill, Black Swan, Australian Shelduck, Pacific Black, Maned and Musk Duck, Grey Teal, Australasian Shoveler, Hardhead, Dusky Moorhen, Purple Swamphen and Eurasian Coot. At least a few of the species mentioned can usually be found without difficulty in the vicinity of Riverton Bridge, but to have the best chance of seeing a wide variety of birds (including more elusive inhabitants such as Buff-banded Rail and Spotless Crake) you will need to explore this section of the Canning River thoroughly. Access to some parts of the river will not be easy because the waterside vegetation is very dense in places; however, with a small boat or canoe you could travel for some distance upstream from Riverton Bridge towards Nicholson Road and visit the backwaters that provide refuge for large numbers of waterbirds during summer.

Booragoon Lake

Though not as rich in birdlife as some of the other lakes near Perth, Booragoon Lake is well worth a brief visit because it supports large breeding colonies of Great, Little Black and Little Pied Cormorant. In addition Darter and Sacred Ibis breed in small numbers and, since the surrounding area is well covered with native vegetation, the lake is a good place for bush birds such as Grey Fantail, Western Gerygone, Singing and Brown Honeyeater, Striated Pardalote and Silvereye.

Booragoon Lake is situated immediately north of the Leach Highway, about 12 km south-west of the city centre via the Kwinana Freeway. Good views of the cormorant colonies can be obtained from Aldridge Road, which runs right around the lake. The best time to visit the area is late winter through to early spring, when nesting activity reaches a peak.

North Lake and Bibra Lake

Situated a few kilometres south-west of Booragoon Lake, these freshwater wetlands are readily accessible via the Leach Highway and North Lake Road. Both are good for waterbirds though Bibra Lake, with its larger area and greater variety of habitats, is the more important of the two. At times the lakes hold large numbers of waterfowl, including Australian Shelduck, Grey Teal, Australasian Shoveler, Hardhead, and Pink-eared, Blue-billed and Musk Duck. The rare Freckled Duck turns up occasionally, chiefly during the winter months. In summer, when the water level is low, the muddy margins of Bibra Lake attract an assortment of wading birds, notably Yellow-billed Spoonbill and migratory species such as Black-tailed Godwit. If you are very fortunate you may find something really special − in June 1978 a lone Ruff was observed at Bibra Lake among a group of Black-winged Stilts and Red-necked Avocets.

Access to the western shores of both lakes can be gained via Progress Drive. There are picnic facilities and toilets near Bibra Lake, as well as a walking track leading to a bird-observation hide situated at the water's edge. While in the area it would pay to keep an eye open for Masked Lapwings. Perhaps surprisingly the lapwing, so common throughout much of northern and eastern Australia, is seldom recorded near Perth, the North Lake and Bibra Lake area being one of the very few places where it has been observed in recent years.

Thomsons Lake Nature Reserve

Thomsons Lake, one of the largest and least developed freshwater wetlands in the Perth metropolitan area, is located about 34 km south-west of the city centre via the Kwinana Freeway, the Canning Highway, Stock Road and Russell Road. Consisting of a large (about 172 ha) shallow lake surrounded by some 300 ha of woodland and open forest, the reserve is readily accessible on foot from Russell Road, Lorimer Road, Wedge Road or Hammond Road. The south-western corner of the centrally placed lake can be reached by car via Pearse Road.

Although the amount of water varies considerably depending on season and rainfall (the area may be completely dry in late summer), Thomsons Lake usually supports quite a variety of waterbirds. Most of the species previously mentioned have been recorded at one time or another. Some of the more interesting birds that have turned up at the lake during the past fifteen years or so are Great Crested Grebe, Pacific Heron, Rufous Night Heron, Little and Australasian Bittern (the low, booming call of the latter is often heard during winter and early spring), Glossy Ibis, Royal and Yellow-billed Spoonbill, Australasian Shoveler (sometimes present in hundreds, even thousands), Blue-billed Duck, and Baillon's, Australian and Spotless Crake (crakes are plentiful at times – for instance, twenty-two Spotless Crakes have been recorded during a single visit). Other notable species include Black-tailed Native-hen, Red-kneed Dotterel, Double-banded Plover, Banded Stilt, Wood and Marsh Sandpiper, Black-tailed Godwit, Long-toed Stint, Oriental Pratincole (though rather rare, this graceful long-winged wader is seen from time to time, particularly in autumn), White-winged Tern (a summer visitor, sometimes present in quite large numbers – between sixty and eighty were recorded in April 1985) and Barn Swallow (a single swallow was seen at the lake in early 1986, the first record of this species in the south-west of Western Australia).

Given the number of rarities on the reserve's list, it is hardly surprising that Thomsons Lake is one of the most popular birding spots near Perth. Waterbirds are not all the reserve has to offer, however. There is a wide diversity of plant associations dominated by flooded gum, jarrah, pricklybark, swamp paperbark and banksia, and as a result the area supports a host of land birds. These include Black-shouldered and Whistling Kite, Brown Goshawk, Marsh Harrier, Australian Hobby, Brown Falcon, Australian Kestrel, Common Bronzewing, Red-capped Parrot (Thomsons Lake is probably the best place near the capital for this species – look for it around the south-western edge of the lake and listen for its harsh, distinctive 'curr-uk, curr-uk' call), Pallid and Fan-tailed Cuckoo (mainly winter–spring), and Horsfield's and Shining Bronze-Cuckoo (chiefly winter–spring). Among the other species to look for are Sacred Kingfisher (summer), Rainbow Bee-eater (summer), White-backed Swallow, Black-faced Cuckoo-shrike, Scarlet Robin, Golden Whistler, Rufous Whistler, Grey Fantail, Splendid Fairy-wren, Weebill, Western Gerygone (spring–summer), Western Thornbill, Red and Little Wattlebird, Singing, Brown and New Holland Honeyeater, Western Spinebill, White-fronted Chat, Mistletoebird, Striated Pardalote, Silvereye and Grey Butcherbird.

Thomsons Lake Nature Reserve is a superb spot, well worth thorough exploration. Pack a picnic lunch and spend a full day there. Camping is not permitted and there are no facilities for visitors.

Lake Forrestdale Nature Reserve
Another prime birding locality on the Swan Coastal Plain south of

Perth, Lake Forrestdale is about 30 km from the city centre via the Albany Highway, Nicholson Road and Forrest Road. The lake's northern shores can be reached via either Weld Street or Moore Street, Forrestdale, while its western shores are accessible via Weld Street and Commercial Road.

Like nearby Thomsons Lake, Forrestdale is a large but shallow expanse of water (it too may be dry in late summer) fringed with extensive reedbeds and surrounded by low, open forest. It is a wetland of national, indeed international importance, as yet the only place in Western Australia where the Little Stint and White-rumped Sandpiper have been recorded. Among the other notable species on the reserve's list are Little Bittern (breeds locally), Glossy Ibis, Freckled Duck, Baillon's and Spotless Crake, and a wealth of migratory waders including such sought-after birds as Little Ringed Plover (first recorded in 1981 – seen again in 1982 and 1984), Black-tailed Godwit, Long-toed Stint (occasionally in large numbers – more than ninety have been seen at the lake during a single visit), Ruff, and Wood, Marsh, Pectoral and Broad-billed Sandpiper. The lake regularly supports large numbers of waterfowl (more than 10 000 at times), while 2000+ Black-winged Stilts may be present in summer. Marsh Harriers are usually quite plentiful, and the surrounding forest is worth looking over for bush birds, including many of the species listed for Thomsons Lake.

The best time to visit Lake Forrestdale is late spring through to late summer; remember to wear sandshoes and a hat. There are no facilities and camping is not permitted.

Lake Monger

If you want to obtain good views (and photographs) of waterbirds such as Hoary-headed Grebe, Black Swan, Pacific Black Duck, Purple Swamphen, Eurasian Coot and Black-winged Stilt, you should visit Lake Monger, a popular picnic spot less than 5 km north-west of Perth's central business district. And if you are fortunate you may see something more unusual. Australian Shelducks, Australasian Shovelers, and Pink-eared, Blue-billed and Musk Ducks are sometimes present in small numbers, while Great Crested Grebes and Little Bitterns have been known to breed on the lake.

To get to Lake Monger simply drive north-west from Perth along the Mitchell Freeway; there are carparks, picnic facilities and toilets just west of the freeway, between the water's edge and Lake Monger Drive. Most waterbirds congregate on and around the small, densely vegetated island that is situated in the south-western corner of the lake. Though the surrounding area has been largely cleared, the tall trees along the lake's southern shores are favoured by Little Corellas, as well as a few other bush birds.

Herdsman Lake

This important freshwater wetland, so close to the centre of Perth yet so rich in birdlife, lies a little to the north-west of Lake Monger via Grantham Street, Selby Street and Flynn Street. The lake is of outstanding interest not only for the variety of birds it supports (well over a hundred species have been recorded), but also because it is the site of a most impressive wildlife study centre featuring displays covering the flora and fauna of the area. Built by the World Wildlife Fund, the centre is one of the few of its type in Australia. It is situated at the southern end of the lake, off Flynn Street, and is open daily from 9 a.m. until 4.30 p.m. In addition to natural history displays it houses a lecture room, a book shop and an information centre, while on the mezzanine floor there are viewing areas equipped with binoculars.

Visitors and residents alike will find that Herdsman Lake has much to offer. Most, if not all, of the waterbirds mentioned so far have been recorded there. Great Crested, Hoary-headed and Australasian Grebe, Australian Pelican, Darter, cormorants, Black Swan, Australian Shelduck, Pacific Black, Pink-eared, Maned, Blue-billed and Musk Duck, Grey Teal, Australasian Shoveler, Hardhead and Eurasian Coot favour areas of open water; Little and Australasian Bittern, Buff-banded Rail, Baillon's, Australian and Spotless Crake, Black-tailed Native-hen, Dusky Moorhen, Purple Swamphen, Clamorous Reed-Warbler and Little Grassbird inhabit the extensive reedbeds; and Pacific and White-faced Heron, Great and Little Egret, Rufous Night Heron, Glossy, Sacred and Straw-necked Ibis, Royal and Yellow-billed Spoonbill, Red-kneed Dotterel, Red-capped and Black-fronted Plover, Black-winged and Banded Stilt, Red-necked Avocet and a variety of migratory waders can often be seen feeding in the shallows or at the water's edge. Many of the reed-dwelling species listed are secretive and usually difficult to observe, but watch for Little Bitterns flying past the study centre — they are often seen from the observation area, especially in November.

As might be expected Herdsman Lake has produced a good crop of rarities, among them Wandering Whistling-Duck, Freckled Duck, Long-toed Stint, Oriental Pratincole, White-winged Tern and Yellow Wagtail. And although the lake is best known for its waterbirds, the paperbarks, flooded gums and native shrubs surrounding the wetland attract a number of bush birds — thornbills, honeyeaters and pardalotes for example — while species such as Richard's Pipit and White-fronted Chat frequent open grassy areas. Some eleven species of raptor have been observed at the lake, including Black-shouldered and Whistling Kite, Little Eagle,

Australian Pelican, commonly seen around the shores of Peel Inlet, Western Australia

Looking north towards the Stirling Range from Porongurup National Park, south-western Western Australia

Even inexperienced observers should have little difficulty finding the Rufous Treecreeper at Porongurup National Park, south-western Western Australia

Rolling white sandhills near Eucla, Western Australia

Lined with river red gums and coolabahs, the Murchison River winds through Kalbarri National Park, Western Australia

Cambridge Gulf from Five Rivers Lookout, Wyndham, Western Australia

Brolgas taking flight, Kimberley, Western Australia

Marsh Harrier, Australian Hobby and Australian Kestrel. A comprehensive bird list, together with a number of other useful publications, can be obtained from the study centre.

Perry Lakes and Lake Claremont

In the unlikely event that you do not find many birds at either Lake Monger or Herdsman Lake, it may be worth travelling a few kilometres south-west to Perry Lakes and Lake Claremont. In fact, if time permits you should include all four spots on your itinerary — a few hours spent at each locality should provide a most enjoyable day's birding.

Perry Lakes: These two small freshwater lakes are situated some 2 or 3 km south-west of Herdsman Lake via Selby Street, Cambridge Street and Oceanic Drive. There are picnic grounds and toilets off Perry Lakes Drive, which runs from Oceanic Drive southwards to Underwood Avenue. The lakes lie just east of Perry Lakes Drive, while to the west there are pine plantations (a good place to look for White-tailed Black-Cockatoos) and patches of bushland.

Lake Claremont: Is located about 3 km south of Perry Lakes via Underwood Avenue, Stephenson Avenue, Rochdale Road and Alfred Road. Access can be gained on foot from Alfred Road via the Lake Claremont golf course. The normally permanent lake provides a summer refuge for a wide variety of waterbirds, including the engaging Pink-eared Duck, which sometimes breeds there.

Rottnest Island

One of the most popular tourist destinations in Western Australia, attracting up to 250 000 visitors annually, Rottnest Island lies in the Indian Ocean about 20 km west of Fremantle. You can get there by ferry or by plane. If you are going to the island just for the day it would be best to fly, since then you will have more time to explore the area. Air fares are not unreasonable, and at least one local airline offers a cheap day trip to Rottnest. Those travelling by ferry during winter have some chance of seeing seabirds such as Wandering, Black-browed, Yellow-nosed and Shy Albatross, Southern and, more rarely, Northern Giant-Petrel, Cape Petrel and possibly other petrels, prions, shearwaters, Wilson's Storm-Petrel, Australasian Gannet and Great Skua, while in summer Arctic and, more rarely, Pomarine Jaeger are possibilities. There are two hotels, numerous holiday units and a camping ground if you wish to stay on Rottnest for more than a day; for further information contact your nearest travel agent or call at any Western Australian Government Travel Centre.

Despite its popularity Rottnest is a splendid place to go birding, not so much because of the number of birds it supports (there are more than a hundred species on the island's list, but fewer than fifty regularly occur there) as because it is small and reasonably flat and therefore easy to explore. Furthermore, the 1900 ha island contains a remarkable diversity of habitats — sandy beaches, rocky headlands and cliffs, salt lakes, brackish swamps, freshwater soaks, and patches of melaleuca woodland, acacia scrub and heath — thus visitors have an excellent chance of seeing an interesting range of birds within a relatively short time.

The following are among the best bird-watching spots on Rottnest. Using a bicycle (they are the chief form of transport and are readily available and inexpensive to hire) you could travel around much of the island in a day, yet still have time to spend thirty minutes or so at most of the places mentioned. If you are not feeling particularly energetic, at least some of the localities listed can be easily reached on foot from Thomson Bay, the site of the island's main tourist resort.

Serpentine Lake and Government House Lake: Are situated just west of Thomson Bay, near the airstrip. Both are salt lakes, much favoured by waterbirds such as Australian Shelduck (one of the island's more common resident species), Red-capped Plover, Banded Stilt and Red-necked Avocet. In summer the lakes attract a sprinkling of migratory waders, including Grey and, more rarely, Lesser Golden, Mongolian and Large Sand Plover, Ruddy Turnstone, Grey-tailed Tattler, Red-necked Stint, and Sharp-tailed and Curlew Sandpiper. Government House Lake has the considerable distinction of being one of the very few places in Western Australia where the Red-necked Phalarope has been recorded — two were seen in the north-west corner of the lake in February 1980.

Before leaving this part of the island take a look around for Banded Lapwings; the lapwings favour areas of short grass and can usually be found in the vicinity of the airstrip.

Bickley Swamp: Lies a little to the east of the airstrip and may be worth a brief visit for Pacific Black Duck, Grey Teal and possibly other waterfowl. The large patch of melaleuca woodland adjacent to the swamp is, however, of greater interest since it holds an assortment of bush birds. These include Fan-tailed Cuckoo (winter—spring), Shining Bronze-Cuckoo (winter—spring), Black-faced Cuckoo-shrike (winter), Red-capped Robin (an isolated population of this delightful species occurs on Rottnest; interestingly, it is absent from the adjacent mainland, though occasionally a few birds visit the Swan Coastal Plain during winter), Golden Whistler, White-browed Scrubwren, Western Gerygone (most often heard during the breeding season — September to December), Singing Honeyeater (the Rottnest Island Singing Honeyeater is an endemic form; the birds on the island are noticeably larger and darker than

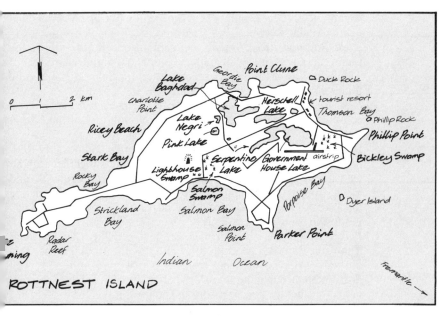

those on the neighbouring mainland), and Silvereye.

Phillip Point: Is at the extreme eastern end of the island and would be a good place to look for seabirds in winter. Phillip Rock, just north of the point, is a favoured haunt of the Pied Cormorant and Bridled Tern (the latter being a common breeding summer visitor).

Parker Point: Situated on the south coast, about 5 km from Thomson Bay tourist resort, Parker Point is another good place for pelagics during winter. Ospreys breed regularly nearby at Salmon Point (this coastal raptor is quite a common sight on Rottnest – several pairs breed on the island), and a walk along the shores of Salmon Bay, a little to the west of Parker Point, should produce a fair variety of birds – Eastern Reef Egret, Pied Oystercatcher, Whimbrel (rather rare, and mainly in summer), Bar-tailed Godwit (summer), Sanderling (summer) and Crested Tern.

Lighthouse Swamp and Salmon Swamp: Lie just to the north of Salmon Bay, some 8 km from Thomson Bay via the coast. A stop here might produce a few waterbirds – White-faced Heron, Pacific Black Duck and Grey Teal for example.

Cape Vlaming: Is at the far western end of Rottnest, about 12 km from Thomson Bay. The cape is probably the best place on the island for seabirds – Black-browed and Yellow-nosed Albatross, Southern Giant-Petrel and Australasian Gannet are among the species to look for in winter. During summer Wedge-tailed Shearwaters breed in large numbers in the vicinity of Cape Vlaming and nearby Radar Reef.

Stark Bay and Ricey Beach: Are on the northern side of the island, about 5 km east of Cape Vlaming and about 7 km west of Thomson Bay. Most of the species listed for Salmon Bay can be found along this stretch of the coast.

Lake Baghdad, Lake Negri, Pink Lake and Herschell Lake: You could easily spend an hour or more exploring the salt lakes that dominate the north-eastern part of Rottnest. Red-capped Plovers, Silver Gulls, Caspian, Fairy and Crested Terns, and possibly Red-necked Avocets, breed in the area; Banded Stilts together with an assortment of migratory waders visit the lakes regularly; and White-fronted Chats commonly occur in the open country bordering the lakes. Several roads provide ready access to the area, which lies to the south of Geordie Bay.

Point Clune: On the north coast, between Geordie Bay and Thomson Bay, is a good place to look for the Rock Parrot. This attractive species, the only resident parrot on Rottnest, is well distributed throughout the eastern half of the island, even occurring in and around the tourist resort at Thomson Bay.

Needless to say the longer you spend on Rottnest the better. However, if you have only a day to spare and decide to travel by ferry, you should still be able to find a few birds in the vicinity of the resort. These include at least some of the species already mentioned — Banded Lapwing, Rock Parrot and Singing Honey-eater for example — as well as Sacred Kingfisher (unlike that of the nearby mainland, the kingfisher population on Rottnest is apparently sedentary), Rainbow Bee-eater (spring—summer), Welcome Swallow and Tree Martin (summer). And keep an eye open for Roseate Terns — these beautiful birds are occasionally seen in Thomson Bay and at other sites around the island during winter. (Roseate Terns bred on Rottnest for the first time in late winter 1985.)

Summer is probably the best season to visit Rottnest, although the island may be rather crowded at this time. If you go there during the warmer months remember to carry something to eat and drink while on your travels; there are few shops away from the main settlement and fresh water is scarce. And remember to look out for the quokka. This small member of the wallaby family is quite plentiful; in fact the island was given the name Rottnest because the Dutch seamen who discovered it in the late 1600s mistook the quokka for an oversized species of rat, a mistake that led to them calling the island 'rat nest'.

Darling Range

Rising less than 30 km to the east of Perth, the heavily forested

Darling Range runs from north to south, forming a pleasing natural backdrop to the capital and providing panoramic views over the Swan Coastal Plain to the Indian Ocean. In some areas large tracts of forest are being destroyed by bauxite mining, but much of the region is reserved as either water catchment area or state forest. In addition, there are eight national parks scattered along the western escarpment of the Darling Range close to Perth. Unfortunately most of these parks are small — only one, Avon Valley, is larger than 2000 ha, and three are smaller than 100 ha.

Some of the Darling Range parks, John Forrest and Gooseberry Hill for instance, are renowned for their spectacular wildflower displays — the showy pink Swan River myrtle, the brilliant blue lechenaultia and the beautiful red and green Mangles kangaroo paw (Western Australia's floral emblem) are just a few of the more conspicuous flowering plants. The best displays are seen between August and October, but there are always some blooms at any time of the year. Other attractions include picturesque waterfalls and tall forests of jarrah, marri and wandoo, and many of the region's reserves have picnic grounds and well-established walking tracks.

From north to south, the national parks and other places of interest in the Darling Range are as follows. Most of the localities mentioned are less than an hour's drive from Perth.

Avon Valley National Park (4368 ha): Is the largest but least accessible park in the region. Situated to the north of the Midland to Toodyay road, about 80 km from Perth, the reserve protects an extensive tract of steep, hilly country — an undulating plateau deeply dissected by the Avon River and its tributaries. Forests of jarrah and marri occur on the uplands, open wandoo woodlands cover the lower slopes and the floors of the valleys, and flooded gums grow along the river banks.

Vehicular access to much of Avon Valley National Park is limited. There are, however, several picnic grounds in the vicinity of Bald Hill, just south of the Avon River. This section of the reserve can be reached via Morangup Road, which leaves the Midland to Toodyay road about 40 km north-east of Midland. Avon Valley is a popular hiking and canoeing spot; bush camping is permitted at a number of sites, but you should contact the ranger at Bald Hill before setting out.

Walyunga National Park (1811 ha): Is situated a little to the south-west of Avon Valley National Park, some 40 km from Perth via the Great Northern Highway. The reserve lies along the attractive upper reaches of the Swan River; there are a number of large pools suitable for swimming, while in winter several sets of rapids provide ideal conditions for canoeing. Picnic facilities are provided adjacent to Walyunga Pool and Long Pool, and there are two walking tracks — the Creek Trail (1 km return) commencing at the Walyunga Pool carpark and leading northwards to the Long Pool carpark, and the Hills Trail (2.7 km) beginning at Long Pool and leading southwards to the park entrance road. Camping is not permitted.

John Forrest National Park (1580 ha): Was established in 1900 and is the oldest national park in Western Australia. It lies about 25 km east of Perth and is readily accessible via the Great Eastern Highway, which forms the reserve's southern boundary. From the highway a scenic drive (Park Road) winds through the tall open forests of jarrah and marri that cover much of the area — lookouts at the edge of the road provide outstanding views over Perth and the Swan Coastal Plain, while in late winter and early spring the forests are alive with a profusion of colourful wildflowers. Bush birds are abundant: some of the species you can expect to see are White-tailed Black-Cockatoo, Red-capped Parrot, Port Lincoln Ringneck, Laughing Kookaburra, Black-faced Cuckoo-shrike, Scarlet Robin, Golden Whistler, Rufous Whistler, Grey Fantail, Splendid Fairy-wren, Western Gerygone (spring–summer), Red Wattlebird, New Holland Honeyeater, Western Spinebill, Striated Pardalote, Silvereye, Dusky Woodswallow and Grey Butcherbird.

Camping is not permitted in the reserve, but there are picnic grounds, toilets, tea rooms and a tavern just to the north of the Great Eastern Highway, between Glen Brook Dam and Mahogany Creek Dam. The park has many fine walking tracks, and swimming is allowed in the natural pool adjacent to the tea rooms.

Greenmount National Park (57 ha): Situated a little to the south of the Great Eastern Highway, close to the south-western boundary of John Forrest National Park, this small reserve offers extensive views over Perth and is noted for its spring wildflower displays. There are no facilities for visitors and camping is not permitted.

Helena Valley: This popular bird-watching area, between Greenmount National Park and Gooseberry Hill National Park, can be reached from the Great Eastern Highway via Scott Street, or from the Roe Highway via Helena Valley Road. From the junction of Scott Street and Helena Valley Road you can walk (or drive) for several kilometres eastwards along the banks of the Helena River to Pipehead Dam, birding en route. Among the species to look for are Square-tailed Kite (this somewhat elusive raptor is rather rare throughout much of its range, but is regularly recorded from the Helena Valley area, particularly during the summer months), Painted Button-quail, Red-capped Parrot, Horsfield's and Shining Bronze-Cuckoo (chiefly winter–spring), Splendid Fairy-wren, and White-cheeked and Tawny-crowned Honeyeater. Other honey-eaters — Yellow-plumed, Brown-headed and White-naped for

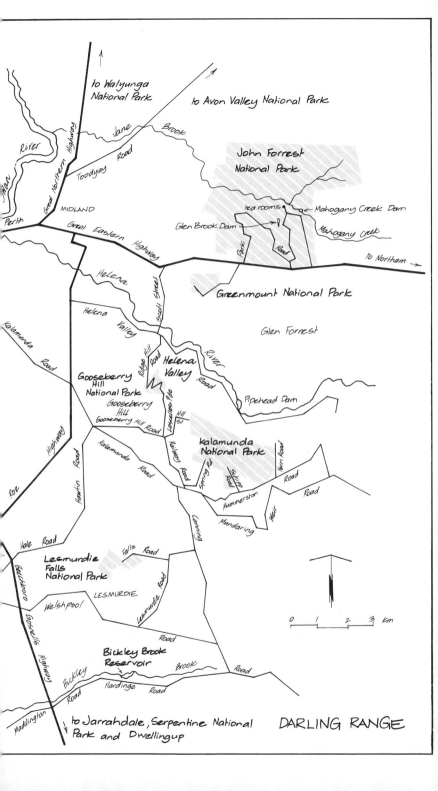

example – are possibilities, while those with the time to explore the area east of Pipehead Dam may be rewarded with a sighting of a Red-eared Firetail. During the past five years the firetail has been known to breed in the vicinity of Glen Forrest, this locality being close to the northern limit of the bird's range.

Gooseberry Hill National Park (33 ha):   Like Greenmount National Park, this small reserve is noted for its spring wildflowers and scenic views. There are no facilities for visitors and camping is not permitted; you can, however, drive through the park via a steep, one-way scenic road that follows the route of an old narrow gauge railway. (The railway was built in 1891 to transport timber from Canning Mills to Midland Junction. It was closed in 1949.) The scenic drive zigzags down the western edge of the Darling Range, providing ready access to areas of heathland and eucalypt woodland where wildflowers and birds are plentiful during late winter and early spring.

Gooseberry Hill National Park is about 24 km east of Perth via the Great Eastern Highway and Kalamunda Road. The scenic drive commences at the end of Lascelles Parade, Gooseberry Hill.

Kalamunda National Park (375 ha):   Situated a couple of kilometres south-east of Gooseberry Hill, this reserve protects a relatively undisturbed patch of dry eucalypt forest and is a good place for bush birds. Walking tracks criss-cross the park, but there are no facilities for visitors and camping is not allowed. Access to the area can be gained from Hill Street, Spring Road, Schipp Road, Hummerston Road or Fern Road.

Lesmurdie Falls National Park (56 ha):   Possesses most of the features typical of the parks of the Darling Range, including spring wildflowers and open forests of jarrah, marri and wandoo. The main attraction is the small waterfall, which can be reached on foot from Falls Road, Lesmurdie. The reserve has toilets, picnic facilities and walking tracks, but no camping area. It is located about 25 km from Perth via the Albany Highway and Welshpool Road.

Bickley Brook Reservoir: Lies a little to the south of Lesmurdie Falls via the Beechboro Gosnells Highway, Maddington Road and Hardinge Road. The chief attraction is not the reservoir itself (it seldom holds more than a few common waterbirds) but the surrounding countryside – the Bickley Brook area is one of the few places in the Darling Range where Southern Emu-wrens can be found. A diminutive species, the Emu-wren is seen quite frequently in the heathlands immediately east of the reservoir. Other birds of note recorded from time to time include Square-tailed Kite, Elegant Parrot and White-breasted Robin.

There are picnic facilities and toilets adjacent to Bickley Brook Reservoir. Hardinge Road continues as a track beyond the reservoir and provides ready access to the western slopes of the Darling Range.

Jarrahdale: Is a small township in the Darling Range some 55 km south-east of Perth via Armadale and the South Western Highway. Much of the surrounding area is state forest, and picnic grounds are provided at a number of sites close to the township — Langford Park to the north, Blue Rock to the east, Gooralong Brook to the west, and Serpentine Dam to the south. Most of these sites have toilets, and there are walking tracks leading from several of the picnic areas into the adjacent forest.

Jarrahdale would be an excellent place for a day excursion. Those able to explore the area thoroughly have a good chance of seeing one of the state's most attractive and sought-after endemics — the Red-eared Firetail. Further information about walking tracks and other facilities in the state forests around Jarrahdale can be obtained from the Department of Conservation and Land Management, 50 Hayman Road, Como, WA 6152.

Serpentine National Park (635 ha): With its 15 m high waterfall, deep natural swimming pools, walking tracks and picnic grounds, Serpentine is one of the most popular national parks near Perth. The reserve is important not only for recreation, but also because it contains fine stands of jarrah and marri, as well as two rare species of trees — the salmon white gum, which occurs at the foot of the Darling Range escarpment, and the butter gum, which is found on the slopes. The park is about 56 km south-east of Perth via the South Western Highway. Camping is not permitted.

Dwellingup: Lies to the south of Serpentine National Park, some 110 km from Perth via the South Western Highway and Pinjarra. Like Jarrahdale, Dwellingup is a small forestry township — an ideal spot to spend the day birding. Species to look out for include three Western Australian endemics — White-breasted Robin, Red-winged Fairy-wren and Red-eared Firetail. There are numerous picnic and camping grounds in the area, most of which are situated in delightful surroundings on the banks of the Murray River. A detailed guide to the state forests of the Dwellingup district can be obtained from the Department of Conservation and Land Management.

Yanchep National Park

Yanchep is Western Australia's best known national park. Though not particularly large (it covers an area of 2799 ha), it contains a wealth of interesting features and has much to offer the visitor. Its natural attractions include an ancient underground limestone cave system (two caves, Crystal and Yonderup, are open to the public and guided tours are available), extensive forests of tuart, jarrah and marri, large areas of banksia scrub where masses of colourful wildflowers can be seen during late winter and spring, and a chain of coastal lakes and swamps that stretches almost the entire length of the reserve. In addition the park has numerous facilities for visitors — a swimming pool, several sports fields, tennis courts, a golf course, kiosks, many picnic grounds, and a walk-through flora and fauna complex where koalas can be observed in natural surroundings. Accommodation is available within the reserve at the Yanchep Inn, but camping is not permitted (there is a caravan park on the coast a short distance west of the national park).

Given the diversity of habitats within the park it is hardly surprising that Yanchep supports a wide variety of birds. About 130 species have been recorded and, while many are seen only occasionally, you should have little difficulty finding at least a few of the following: Australasian Grebe, Little Pied Cormorant, White-faced Heron, Black Swan, Pacific Black and Musk Duck, Brown Goshawk, Wedge-tailed Eagle, Marsh Harrier, Australian Kestrel, Dusky Moorhen, Purple Swamphen, Eurasian Coot, Black-winged Stilt, Common Bronzewing, White-tailed Black-Cockatoo, Galah, Red-capped Parrot, Port Lincoln Ringneck, Pallid Cuckoo (winter—spring), Horsfield's Bronze-Cuckoo (winter—spring), Sacred Kingfisher (spring—summer), Rainbow Bee-eater (spring—summer), White-backed Swallow, Scarlet Robin, Rufous Whistler, Grey Shrike-thrush, Grey Fantail, Little Grassbird, Splendid and White-winged Fairy-wren, Western Gerygone (spring—summer), Inland, Western and Yellow-rumped Thornbill, Red and Little Wattlebird, Singing, Brown, New Holland, White-cheeked and Tawny-crowned Honeyeater, Western Spinebill, Striated Pardalote, Silvereye, Black-faced and Dusky Woodswallow, and Grey Butcherbird. A comprehensive bird list can be obtained from the park ranger. Among the more notable species on the list are Rufous Night Heron, Little Bittern, Freckled Duck and Garganey (two birds, a male and female, were seen on Loch McNess in March 1971; this was the first time the Garganey had been recorded in Western Australia).

Yanchep National Park has quite a number of walking tracks. These include the Yanjidi Trail, an easy 2 km walk around the densely vegetated margins of Loch McNess, and the Boomerang Gorge Nature Trail, a wide, level track specially designed to enable disabled visitors to explore picturesque Boomerang Gorge — the result of a collapsed underground cave system.

Yanchep is about 52 km north-west of Perth via Wanneroo Road. A visit during the week, when the reserve is relatively quiet, will be best for bird-watching.

Wanneroo wetlands

There are a number of lakes in the vicinity of Wanneroo, north of

Perth. From a bird-watcher's point of view the four most important are as follows.

Lake Goollelal: Lies just to the west of Wanneroo Road, about 17 km north of the city centre. The lake's western shores can be reached on foot from Goollelal Drive, Kingsley.

Lake Joondalup: Is a large freshwater lake fringed with emergent vegetation and, in places, by forests and woodlands of tuart, jarrah, marri, banksia and paperbark. The lake is an important summer refuge for a wide variety of waterbirds, including Great Crested Grebe and other grebes, pelicans, cormorants, herons, Great Egret, Glossy, Sacred and Straw-necked Ibis, waterfowl (Australasian Shovelers and Blue-billed Ducks occur in good numbers at times) and Black-winged Stilt. Areas of native vegetation, particularly those along the lake's western shores, attract an assortment of bush birds.

Lake Joondalup is about 20 km from Perth. To get there head north along Wanneroo Road, turn left at Ocean Reef Road, then right into Edgewater Drive. There is a picnic ground between Edgewater Drive and the lake, and another at Neil Hawkins Park, which is situated at the end of Boas Avenue, Joondalup. A walking track has been constructed along the western edge of the lake.

Jandabup Lake: This extensive shallow wetland, some 2 or 3 km east of Lake Joondalup, can be reached from Wanneroo Road via Elliott Road, Lenore Road, Trichet Road and Hawkins Road. It is almost entirely surrounded by private property, making thorough exploration somewhat difficult, but the lake's southern shores are accessible on foot from Hawkins Road (there is a rough track leading to the lake about 500 m north of the junction of Trichet Road and Hawkins Road). Jandabup is a haunt of the elusive Little Bittern, and in summer is visited by interesting waders such as Wood Sandpiper and Oriental Pratincole.

Gnangara Lake: Situated about 10 km south-east of Jandabup Lake, this wetland is readily accessible via Badgerup Road and Gnangara Road. There are picnic facilities and toilets near the south-eastern corner of the lake, at the end of Alexander Drive.

Rockingham and Mandurah

Rockingham and Mandurah are resort towns on the coast south of Perth. Rockingham is about 46 km from the city centre, Mandurah another 30 km or so further south. Both places have ample accommodation, including hotels, motels, holiday units and caravan parks, and both make excellent bases from which to explore the numerous birding spots that lie along this stretch of the coast. The following are some of the better known localities.

Lake Cooloongup: Is less than 10 km east of Rockingham via

Dixon Road. During summer the lake supports large numbers of waterbirds, particularly ducks, and the tall, open tuart forests that surround it are home to a wide variety of bush birds. Notable among these are Regent Parrot and Yellow-plumed Honeyeater, both of which may be found along the lake's western and northern shores. Raptors such as Little Eagle are also well worth looking for. There is a picnic ground to the north of the lake, off Dixon Road.

Lake Walyungup: Lies a little to the south of Lake Cooloongup, some 10 km from Rockingham, and is best approached from Safety Bay Road, which skirts its northern shores. Though perhaps not as good for water and bush birds as Lake Cooloongup, Lake Walyungup is well worth a visit nonetheless, especially in summer when interesting waders such as Pectoral Sandpiper and Long-toed Stint may be present.

Lake Richmond: This small, permanent freshwater lake is situated near the centre of Rockingham and can be reached from Safety Bay Road or from Lake Street. Though surrounded by urbanisation the lake is relatively unspoilt and supports a good range of birds – grebes, cormorants, herons, egrets, waterfowl, and waders such as Black-winged Stilt.

Point Peron: Just 4 or 5 km north-west of Rockingham town centre, Point Peron is a good spot for seabirds such as Australasian Gannet (winter), Bridled Tern (summer) and Roseate Tern (late autumn). It is also a haunt of the Eastern Reef Egret and Rock Parrot.

Bird Island, a kilometre or so south of the point, holds a breeding colony of Pied Cormorants, while Penguin Island, some 3 km south again, supports colonies of Little Penguins and Crested Terns. (Interestingly, a pair of Little Shearwaters were found nesting on Penguin Island in August 1985.) You can reach Penguin Island by ferry from the Mersey Point jetty – late August through to early December is the best time for the penguins (the island is closed to the public between May and August).

Mandurah: Although this extremely popular beach resort is starting to look a little like Queensland's Gold Coast, it is still a splendid place to go birding. Peel Inlet and the Harvey Estuary, south of the town, are worth a full day of exploration, but before leaving Mandurah you should pay a visit to the coast just west of the town centre. The rocky breakwaters between Town Beach and Robert Point are favoured by terns, notably Common (summer–autumn), Roseate (late summer–autumn) and Arctic (rarely, and mostly September to May), while the muddy margins of the channel that extends from Peel Inlet to the Indian Ocean are worth looking over for migratory waders such as Lesser Golden Plover, Eastern Curlew and Whimbrel. Other waterbirds, Aus-

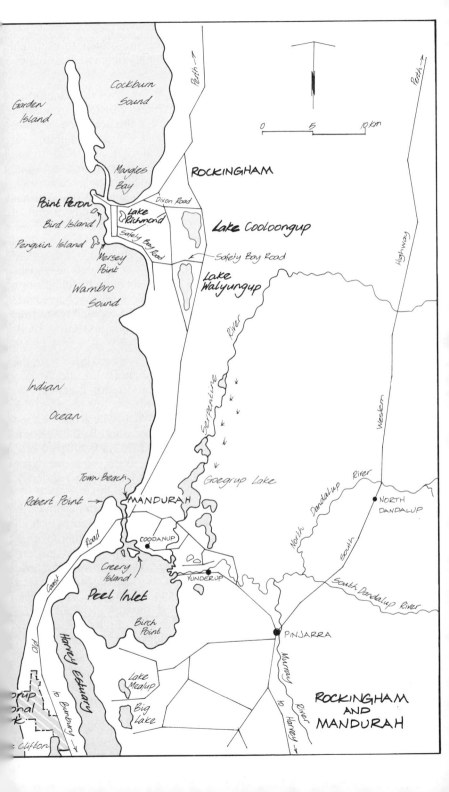

tralian Pelican and Darter for example, are usually to be found resting on jetties throughout the area, providing excellent opportunities for bird photography.

Peel Inlet and the Harvey Estuary: Are the two most important waterbird sites in the south-west of Western Australia. In summer as many as twenty thousand waders visit the area, and at times Peel Inlet and the Harvey Estuary hold impressive numbers of waterfowl. Black-winged Stilt, Banded Stilt and Red-necked Avocet are among the most common resident waders, while migratory species include Greenshank and Sharp-tailed Sandpiper, with Bar-tailed Godwit being particularly abundant on occasions — 537 were recorded near Birch Point, at the southern end of Peel Inlet, in November 1985. Other waterbirds include grebes, Australian Pelican (pelicans breed on several islands in Peel Inlet), Darter, cormorants (Great, Little Black and Little Pied Cormorants breed locally), herons, egrets (Great Egrets are usually plentiful during winter, and Little Egrets can often be found along the northern and eastern shores of Peel Inlet), Glossy, Sacred and Straw-necked Ibis, Royal and Yellow-billed Spoonbill, waterfowl (particularly Black Swan, Australian Shelduck and Grey Teal), rails, crakes, gulls and terns.

Many rare and interesting species have been recorded from the area, among them Freckled Duck, Chestnut Teal, Little Curlew, Redshank (a single Redshank, seen on Creery Island at the northern end of Peel Inlet in July 1985, was the first record of this species for southern Western Australia), Wood, Marsh and Pectoral Sandpiper, Black-tailed Godwit, Long-toed Stint, Ruff (five Ruffs were observed on Yunderup Island, Peel Inlet, in February 1982), Whiskered, White-winged and Gull-billed Tern (this is one of the few places in the south-west where these terns occur regularly), and White-bellied Sea-Eagle (which breeds locally).

The Old Coast Road, which runs from Mandurah southwards to Bunbury, provides ready access to the western shores of both Peel Inlet and the Harvey Estuary. Peel Inlet's northern shores can be reached from Mandurah via Coodanup, while its eastern and southern shores are accessible via Yunderup and Pinjarra. There are a number of roads and tracks leading to the eastern section of the Harvey Estuary, south of Pinjarra. November, December and January are the best months for waders; the northern, eastern and southern shores of Peel Inlet are generally regarded as the most rewarding areas for bird-watching.

Yalgorup National Park (11 466 ha): Lies on the coast some 25 km south of Mandurah via the Old Coast Road. A long narrow reserve, it possesses delightful heath and woodland scenery, and contains a number of lakes and swamps that are noted for their birdlife. There is a resident ranger and the park has picnic facilities and toilets, but no camping area.

Dryandra State Forest

This superb spot is rather a long way from Perth, about 165 km, but a trip to the forest should prove most enjoyable. It is an area of extensive undisturbed wandoo woodlands, well known for its flourishing numbat population (Dryandra is one of the last strongholds of this attractive, squirrel-like marsupial) and rich and varied birdlife. To get there take the Albany Highway to North Bannister, head east to Wandering, and continue on towards Pingelly. Dryandra State Forest is situated about 25 km south of the Wandering to Pingelly road, just west of the road to Narrogin. The forest is clearly signposted. Picnic grounds are provided at several sites, and conservation and other groups can make use of the Dryandra Forest Village, a former forestry settlement that is now leased to the Lions Club of Western Australia. The village provides accommodation for over a hundred people; for further information write to Lions Dryandra Forest Village, c/− Post Office, Cuballing, WA 6311.

Even if you are unable to stay at Dryandra for more than a day you should see a great many interesting birds. Some of the more noteworthy species that occur there are Malleefowl, Painted and Little Button-quail, Purple-crowned Lorikeet, Red-capped and Elegant Parrot, Western Rosella, Red-capped, Hooded and Western Yellow Robin, Crested Shrike-tit, Restless Flycatcher, White-browed Babbler, Blue-breasted Fairy-wren, Varied Sittella, Rufous Treecreeper, Yellow-plumed and White-naped Honeyeater, Dusky Woodswallow and Grey Currawong. Many of these species are of interest because they seldom occur in the forests near Perth.

There are plenty of tracks running through the area; even though most are well signposted you should take care not to get lost. Those wishing to look for numbats should try Gura Road. The numbat, also known as the banded anteater, is a small (about 20 cm in length), delightful creature. Though normally shy, they are curious animals − if you spot one while driving through the forest it will probably take cover in a log, but if you remain sitting quietly in your car it may re-emerge and begin feeding again. Unlike most Australian mammals numbats are diurnal − that is, they search for food during the day rather than at night.

THE SOUTH-WEST CORNER

The south-west corner of Western Australia is truly a magnificent region; indeed it is one of the most attractive parts of the continent. Virtually the entire coast between Cape Naturaliste in the west and Israelite Bay in the east is wild and dramatic, with long, wide sandy beaches separating massive granite headlands and densely forested inlets. And in places the extensive coastal dunes and adjacent sand plains support heathlands that are incredibly rich in flowering plants. In late winter and spring the bewildering diversity of wildflowers that occurs in Fitzgerald River National Park, between Albany and Esperance, has to be seen to be believed. No fewer than fourteen varieties of banksia can be found in the reserve, while other plants of interest include the oak-leaved dryandra, the beautiful yellow-flowered bell-fruited mallee, the four-winged mallee, with its large, red, angular gumnuts, the pincushion hakea and, perhaps most outstanding of all, the fantastic royal hakea, a large shrub with vertical stems bearing masses of multicoloured, shell-like leaves.

Away from the coast the scenery is just as attractive, the habitats every bit as diverse and interesting. The small but impressive Porongurup Range rises from rolling agricultural land a little to the north of Albany, while some 30 or 40 km further north is the Stirling Range, where a series of jagged peaks, extending more than 65 km in an east−west line, tower above the surrounding countryside. To the north-east of Albany, near Esperance, lie numerous lakes and patches of mallee, and to the north-west, in the Pemberton district, fast-flowing permanent rivers cut through luxuriant forests of karri, a tree that rivals the mountain ash of south-eastern Australia as the world's tallest hardwood.

You could easily spend three or four weeks touring the region, and Red-tailed Tropicbird, Black Bittern, Malleefowl, Red-tailed and White-tailed Black-Cockatoo, Western Rosella, Regent, Ground, Red-capped and Rock Parrot, Noisy Scrub-bird, White-breasted and Western Yellow Robin, Western Whipbird, Blue-breasted and Red-winged Fairy-wren, Southern Emu-wren, Western Bristlebird, Shy Hylacola, Calamanthus, Rufous Tree-creeper, Purple-gaped, White-cheeked, White-fronted and Tawny-crowned Honeyeater and Red-eared Firetail are some of the more noteworthy birds you could look forward to seeing.

From west to east the main places of interest are as follows. All offer excellent opportunities for bird-watching, bushwalking, camping or sightseeing, thus all warrant a place on your itinerary.

Benger Swamp

Benger is a small township on the South Western Highway about 12 km south of Harvey. Benger Swamp covers an area of approximately 320 ha, and is situated less than 2 km west of the township's railway station. The swamp is a well-known waterbird spot − some sixty species have been recorded there, including Great Crested, Hoary-headed and Australasian Grebe, Australian Pelican, Darter, cormorants, herons (the Pacific Heron is a regular visitor),

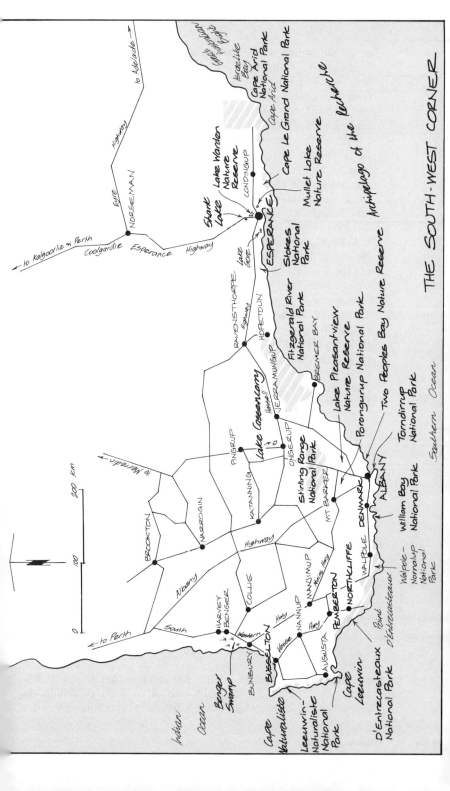

THE SOUTH-WEST CORNER

egrets (including the occasional Cattle and Little Egret), Rufous Night Heron, Little and Australasian Bittern, Glossy, Sacred and Straw-necked Ibis, Royal and Yellow-billed Spoonbill, Freckled (rare, but one to watch out for), Pacific Black, Maned, Blue-billed and Musk Duck, Australian Shelduck, Grey Teal, Australasian Shoveler, Hardhead, Buff-banded Rail, Australian and Spotless Crake, Purple Swamphen, Eurasian Coot, Black-fronted Plover, Black-winged Stilt, Red-necked Avocet, and Whiskered Tern (an occasional visitor). In summer Wood Sandpipers are usually present in fair numbers (thirteen have been observed during a single visit), while other migratory waders of note include Common and Marsh Sandpiper, Greenshank, Black-tailed Godwit and Oriental Pratincole.

Winter, spring and early summer are the best times to go to the swamp, although there are usually some birds to be seen throughout the year.

Busselton

This popular holiday resort, situated in very pleasant surroundings on the shores of Geographe Bay, has a wealth of accommodation that includes motels, hotels, guest houses, holiday cottages and caravan parks. There is a youth hostel at Quindalup, about 20 km west of the town on the road to Yallingup, and another at Noggerup, which lies some 100 km to the east of Busselton via Donnybrook.

New River, just south of Busselton town centre, and the Vasse Estuary, a little to the east, are two of the most favourable birding localities in the district, the latter being one of the most important wetlands in the south-west of Western Australia. Both are excellent places for waterbirds such as Great Egret, Yellow-billed Spoonbill, Grey Teal, Australasian Shoveler, Dusky Moorhen, Eurasian Coot and waders. January, February and March are the best months for migratory waders: Black-tailed Godwit, Wood and Pectoral Sandpiper and Long-toed Stint are among the more notable species to look for. Resident waders — Black-winged Stilt and Red-necked Avocet for example — may be present at any time of the year. (Interestingly, in February 1986 a female Painted Snipe — a rare bird indeed in Western Australia — was found entangled in a barbed-wire fence on the edge of the Vasse Estuary near Busselton. Fortunately it was released unharmed.)

Laymans Road, which leaves the Bussell Highway about 10 km east of Busselton, provides ready access to the north-eastern shores of the Vasse Estuary, as well as to the south-western section of the adjacent Wonnerup Estuary (another good waterbird spot). White-bellied Sea-Eagles are often seen patrolling this stretch of the coast, while Forrest Beach, at the northern end of the Wonnerup Estuary, is an important breeding ground for Black Swans. Mature forests of tuart, a magnificent grey-barked eucalypt that grows to a height of 40 m or more, occur in the vicinity of the Vasse and Wonnerup estuaries and are well worth looking over for bush birds.

Cape Naturaliste to Cape Leeuwin

Spectacular limestone caves, beautiful beaches ideal for surfing and swimming, historic properties, and some of the state's finest wineries are just a few of the attractions that draw many thousands of visitors annually to the coast south-west of Busselton. There is also an abundance of good bird-watching spots, the following being some of the most rewarding.

Leeuwin-Naturaliste National Park: Covers an area of 15 515 ha and consists of a number of separate reserves that extend along the coast from Cape Naturaliste in the north to Cape Leeuwin in the south. Access to all but a few sections of the park can be gained from Caves Road, which runs from Dunsborough south-wards towards Augusta. The reserve has quite good facilities for visitors, including picnic grounds and many kilometres of walking tracks. A map of the park, together with other useful publications, can be obtained from the ranger; his office is situated on the road to Yallingup Cave, about 8 km south-west of Dunsborough. There are caravan parks at Dunsborough, Yallingup, Margaret River, Prevelly Park, Hamelin Bay and Augusta, and motels, hotels and holiday units throughout the area.

Although Leeuwin-Naturaliste National Park is best known for its caves and coastal scenery, some sections of the reserve contain fine stands of jarrah and marri, while others protect patches of banksia scrub, melaleuca woodland or heath. Consequently the entire area warrants attention, but if you are short of time, or merely wish to search for some of the park's more interesting birds, visits to the following localities should prove particularly fruitful.

Cape Naturaliste: Is situated about 13 km north-west of Dunsborough. Readily accessible via a good sealed road, the cape would be an ideal place to look for seabirds in winter: Yellow-nosed Albatross and Australasian Gannet are just two of the species you can expect to see. During the summer months some twenty to thirty pairs of Red-tailed Tropicbirds breed on Sugarloaf Rock, which lies about 3 km south of Cape Naturaliste. Since the rock is little more than 50 m offshore the tropicbirds can be observed quite easily from the mainland – numbers reach a peak between December and February, but there are usually a few birds present throughout the year.

Yallingup, Canal Rocks and Wyadup Beach: Lie to the west of Caves Road, some 10 to 15 km from Dunsborough. The coast here is very attractive — Western Rosella, Red-winged Fairy-wren and Red-eared Firetail are three south-western endemics that you will almost certainly find in the area. Yallingup Cave is open to the public and guided tours are available.

Moses Rock: Can be reached via Moses Rock Road, which leaves Caves Road about 20 km south-west of Dunsborough. This locality is said to be good for Painted Button-quail.

Cowaramup Bay and Prevelly Park: Are situated near Margaret River township, some 35 to 45 km south-west of Dunsborough. Both places hold a variety of birds — Brush Bronzewing and Red-eared Firetail are among the species to watch for. Mammoth Cave and Lake Cave, 10 to 15 km south-east of Prevelly Park via Caves Road, are open for inspection and are well worth a visit.

Hamelin Bay: Hooded Plovers can often be found on the beach at this popular fishing spot, while in summer Bridled Tern and Sanderling are distinct possibilities. The bay is about 80 km from Dunsborough, and approximately 20 km from Augusta. While you are in the area pay a visit to Jewel Cave, just off Caves Road, a little to the north-west of Augusta. One of the region's most famous caves, it features a vast cavern almost 100 m high and 91 m long, a beautiful underground lake, and a wealth of delicate limestone formations including a 6 m stalactite said to be one of the longest in the world.

Cape Leeuwin: Like Cape Naturaliste, this is an excellent place to go seabirding in winter. Black-browed, Yellow-nosed and Shy Albatross, Southern and Northern Giant-Petrel, Cape and Great-winged Petrel, Wilson's Storm-Petrel and Australasian Gannet are some of the species that have been sighted from the cape in recent years. The area is also a favoured haunt of the Rock Parrot. A sealed road provides ready access to this part of the coast; the cape itself is about 8 km south-west of Augusta.

Margaret River: This thriving agricultural and tourist centre, surrounded by lush green hills and jarrah forests, has plenty of accommodation and would make an ideal base from which to explore the region's wineries. There are at least seven wineries in and around the town, and a further fourteen or so just to the north, between the Bussell Highway and the coast. Margaret River is about 45 km south of Dunsborough via Caves Road.

Boranup State Forest: Lies between Caves Road and the boundary of Leeuwin-Naturaliste National Park, some 30 km south-west of Margaret River township. The forest is dominated by tall karri trees; a walk along one of the many tracks running through the area should produce birds such as Purple-crowned Lorikeet, White-breasted Robin, Crested Shrike-tit and Golden Whistler.

Augusta: Has ample accommodation, including a youth hostel,

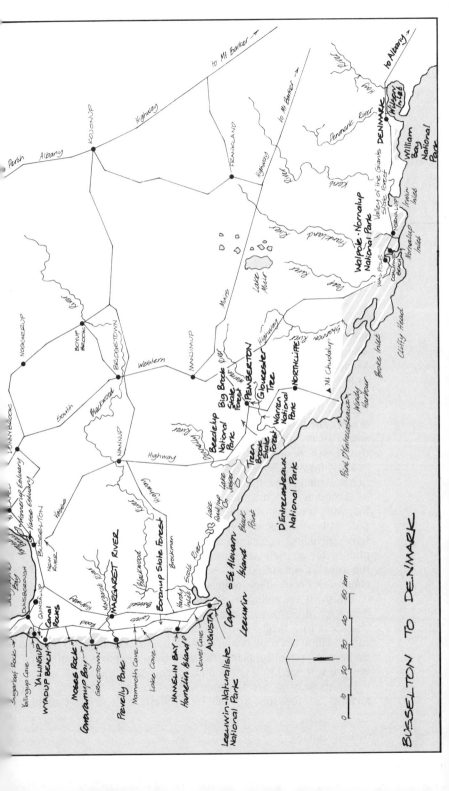

BUSSELTON TO DENMARK

and could be used as a base for exploring Hardy Inlet and the Blackwood River, which lie a short distance north-east of the town. Sheltered and peaceful, Hardy Inlet is the perfect place to go boating, while the Blackwood River provides excellent opportunities for canoeing. Birds to look out for include the Black Bittern; though by no means a certainty, the bittern has been recorded along the Blackwood River on several occasions during the past five years or so.

Hamelin Island and St Alouarn Island: Situated just off the coast to the north-west and south-east of Augusta, these small islands support colonies of seabirds — Bridled and Crested Terns breed on Hamelin, while Little Penguins, Flesh-footed and Little Shearwaters and Bridled Terns nest on St Alouarn. Both islands are reserves, and strictly speaking you should obtain permission from the Western Australian Department of Conservation and Land Management if you wish to visit them. Hamelin Island is quite easy to get to (it is only 700 m from the shore); St Alouarn Island on the other hand is difficult to reach, except in very calm conditions.

Pemberton

The small timber town of Pemberton, about 30 km south-west of Manjimup, can be reached via either the South Western Highway or the Vasse Highway. Located deep in the heart of karri country, amidst rolling farmland and towering forests, it has several attractive guest houses as well as motels, hotels, caravan parks and a youth hostel. The huge timber mill that dominates the town is well worth seeing (it is open weekdays from 8 a.m. until 4 p.m.), as are the trout hatchery and pioneer museum.

Karri forests, though certainly very beautiful, are not especially rich in birdlife. Nevertheless the countryside surrounding Pemberton is exceedingly picturesque, and a trip to one or more of the following localities should prove most enjoyable and should produce at least a few interesting birds. A number of useful publications, including a guide to the state forests of the district, can be obtained from the Pemberton Tourist Bureau, which is situated in the town's main street.

Gloucester Tree: This famous landmark is about 3 km south-east of the town via Johnston Street and Burma Road. Named after the Duke of Gloucester, the giant karri is three hundred years old and soars to a height of 61 m. If you have a cool head you may care to climb the rope ladder that leads to a lookout cabin perched in the tree's upper branches; the view from the top is breathtaking, but you will need to be fit — and surefooted!

For those who prefer more sedate activities there are picnic facilities at the foot of the tree. Western Rosella, Laughing

Kookaburra, White-breasted Robin and Rufous Treecreeper are common around the picnic area, while a stroll through the adjacent forest may result in the sighting of a Red-tailed Black-Cockatoo, Crested Shrike-tit or Red-winged Fairy-wren.

Big Brook State Forest: Lies a few kilometres north-west of Pemberton via Pumphill Road and Stirling Road. A number of scenic forest drives, notably the Rainbow Trail and the Tramway Trail, permit easy access to the area, and picnic grounds and walking tracks are provided at several sites — near the Big Brook Arboretum for instance. Dominated by tall karri trees, Big Brook is home to a variety of bird species, among them White-breasted Robin, Golden Whistler, Red-winged Fairy-wren, White-browed Scrubwren, White-naped Honeyeater and Red-eared Firetail.

Treen Brook State Forest: Situated some 6 km west of Pemberton, and readily accessible via the Vasse Highway, Treen Brook is another good place to go picnicking and birding. All the species listed for Big Brook State Forest can be found there.

Warren National Park (1356 ha):   Protecting an area of magnificent virgin karri forest, with many trees rising more than 70 m above the forest floor, Warren National Park lies between Old Vasse Road and the Warren River, about 10 km south-west of Pemberton. A narrow, unsealed road (the Maidenbush Trail) runs through the reserve and leads to a number of picnic and camping grounds along the banks of the Warren River. An overnight stay in this peaceful, beautiful park is highly recommended.

Beedelup National Park (1531 ha):   Is some 20 km or so west of Pemberton, on the road to Nannup. It has few facilities for visitors, but is worth a brief visit because Red-tailed Black-Cockatoos are often seen there. Beedelup Falls lie within the reserve and can be reached on foot; featuring two cascades with a total drop of 106 m, the falls are considered to be among the most beautiful in the state.

Northcliffe: There are numerous scenic spots in the vicinity of Northcliffe, a small township about 30 km south-east of Pemberton on the road to Point D'Entrecasteaux. Superb views of the coast can be obtained from Mt Chudalup, which lies about 20 km to the south of the township.

D'Entrecasteaux National Park (36 599 ha):   This important reserve, containing wetlands, forests and heathlands, stretches along the coast from Black Point in the west towards Walpole in the east. Since it encompasses a wide range of habitats it is rich in birdlife; however, apart from Point D'Entrecasteaux and Windy Harbour, much of the park is virtually inaccessible. In winter, Point D'Entrecasteaux is a good spot for seabirds such as Yellow-nosed Albatross and Australasian Gannet, and Rock Parrots can usually be found in the vicinity of the point and at nearby Windy

Harbour. Other species to look for along this stretch of the coast include Splendid Fairy-wren and Southern Emu-wren – the latter is said to be plentiful in areas of low heath.

For information about access to other sections of D'Entrecasteaux National Park you should contact the ranger at Pemberton; his office is situated near the junction of the Vasse Highway and Old Vasse Road, between Warren and Beedelup National Parks.

Walpole-Nornalup National Park

Walpole-Nornalup National Park, the first portion of which was set aside in 1910, is one of the oldest reserves in Western Australia. It was greatly enlarged in 1924 and since then various parcels of land have been added, bringing the park to its present size of 18 789 ha. Situated some 120 km south-east of Pemberton via the South Western Highway, the reserve is noted for its scenic beauty and for its rich and varied flora and fauna. It protects almost 50 km of coastline, extending from Cliffy Head in the west to Irwin Inlet in the east, and contains some fine stands of karri as well as areas of red tingle (*Eucalyptus jacksonii*) and yellow tingle (*E. guilfoylei*). In addition there are patches of heath where colourful wildflowers grow in profusion during late winter and spring; peaty swamps where the scented boronia (a plant much used by perfume manufacturers) and the fascinating insect-catching pitcher plant may be found; and a large sandy area, known appropriately as the Ficifolia Block, where the beautiful red-flowering gum (*Eucalyptus ficifolia*) occurs in abundance. Though a common ornamental tree in Perth and other cities, the red-flowering gum has a very restricted natural distribution, being confined to a small area along Western Australia's south coast.

Some of the more interesting birds that you may find in the park are Great Crested Grebe (seen occasionally on Walpole and Nornalup Inlets within the reserve, and on Broke Inlet a little to the west), Black Bittern (rare, but possibly occurs along some of the larger rivers), Osprey, White-bellied Sea-Eagle, Brown Quail, Spotless Crake, Brush Bronzewing, White-tailed Black-Cockatoo, Purple-crowned Lorikeet (especially when the eucalypts are in flower), Red-capped Parrot, Western Rosella, White-breasted Robin, Crested Shrike-tit, Splendid and Red-winged Fairy-wren, Southern Emu-wren (quite common in areas of swampy heath), Rufous Treecreeper, White-naped and Tawny-crowned Honeyeater (the former prefers karri forest, the latter areas of coastal heath), and Red-eared Firetail.

The park's main camping ground is located at Coalmine Beach, about 3 km south of Walpole township. There are twenty powered sites suitable for caravans; demand for space is often very heavy, however, and it may be necessary to look elsewhere for accommodation, especially during peak holiday periods such as Christmas and Easter. The nearest alternative caravan parks are at Rest Point, on the western shore of Walpole Inlet some 8 km from Coalmine Beach, and at Peaceful Bay, which lies about 35 km to the east. For those not wishing to camp there are two guest houses (Tinglewood Lodge and Jesmond Dene Lodge) just outside the national park boundary, a motel-hotel in Walpole township, and a youth hostel near Tingledale, about 20 km to the north-east.

Much of Walpole-Nornalup National Park can be seen from a car, but for the more adventurous there are long walks from several roads to various points along the coast. A detailed guide to the reserve can be obtained from the ranger's office at Coalmine Beach. If you have only an hour or two to spare pay a visit to Knoll Drive, south of Walpole Inlet, where you will find several shady picnic grounds adjacent to a karri-covered hill. Besides being most attractive, this area is easy to explore since there are a number of short walking tracks leading through the tall forest that at this point grows right to the water's edge. Rufous Treecreepers are common in the timber bordering Knoll Drive and can usually be found in the vicinity of the picnic sites.

If you have access to a small boat or canoe you could spend many enjoyable hours exploring the park's protected waterways; boat ramps are provided at Rest Point, Coalmine Beach, Nornalup and Peaceful Bay. And before you leave the Walpole district be sure to take a trip to the Valley of the Giants State Forest, which lies some 15 km or so east of the township. Massive buttressed karri and tingle trees line the well-signposted route through the forest − the birdlife is not outstanding, but the scenery certainly is.

Denmark

Denmark, on the northern shores of Wilson Inlet about 70 km east of Walpole, has plenty of accommodation − motels, hotels, holiday cottages, caravan parks and a youth hostel − as well as an abundance of good birding spots. The following are some of the best places to visit.

Wilson Inlet: Holds a wide variety of waterbirds, with some species occurring in quite large numbers. Since it is one of the most extensive inlets on the south coast it is best covered by boat; there is a launching ramp at Poddyshot − ask locally for directions. If you do not have a boat available there are usually at least some birds to be seen around the edge of the inlet, which can be easily reached by car from Denmark.

Hay River Bridge: Is about 10 km east of the town via the South Coast Highway. In summer this spot is said to be much favoured by waders.

Ocean Beach: Lies 8 km south of Denmark via Ocean Beach

Road, and is the site of a very pleasant caravan park. The fishing here is excellent and, as a bonus, Hooded Plovers may be seen on the beach.

William Bay National Park (1902 ha): Encompassing a beautiful stretch of coast with heath-covered dunes and rocky headlands, this small reserve is approximately 15 km south-west of Denmark via the South Coast Highway. Picnic facilities are provided at the end of the entrance road, but camping is not permitted. Birds to look out for include Pied and Sooty Oystercatcher and Rock Parrot – all three species are plentiful in the area and should be easy to find.

Albany

Founded in 1826, some two and a half years before the Swan River Colony was established, Albany is Western Australia's oldest settlement and the largest town on the state's south coast. Apart from its historical interest Albany has much to offer the visitor, for within 40 or 50 km of the town there is a wide variety of natural attractions ranging from lakes, rivers and estuaries to mountains, forests and heathlands. It is an important administrative, agricultural and tourist centre and has ample accommodation, including motels, hotels, guest houses, holiday cottages, caravan parks and a youth hostel.

Some of Albany's more notable historic properties are the Old Gaol, built in 1851 and now a folk museum; the Albany Residency, built in the 1850s and occupied by magistrates and government officials between 1873 and 1953 (it too is now a museum); Patrick Taylor Cottage, which dates from the early 1830s – recently restored, it houses more than two thousand historic items including period costumes, clocks, silverware and kitchenware; the Old Farm at Strawberry Hill, a two-storey stone house built in 1836; and the Whaling Station at Frenchman Bay where an extensive collection of relics and lithographs dating from the old hand-whaling days are on show. Information about these and other places of historic interest in the district can be obtained from the Albany Tourist Bureau in York Street.

Birders eager to see something of Albany's rich and varied avifauna will find the following spots most rewarding. A map of the area showing most of the places mentioned is available from the tourist bureau.

Lake Seppings: This large expanse of open water, fringed with rushes and thickets, lies just a few kilometres north-east of Albany town centre. It is best approached from Golf Links Road, which skirts the lake's eastern shores. Parking is easy, and there is a well-defined walking track leading to a pumphouse off Golf Links Road. Rock Parrots can almost always be found in the area, while

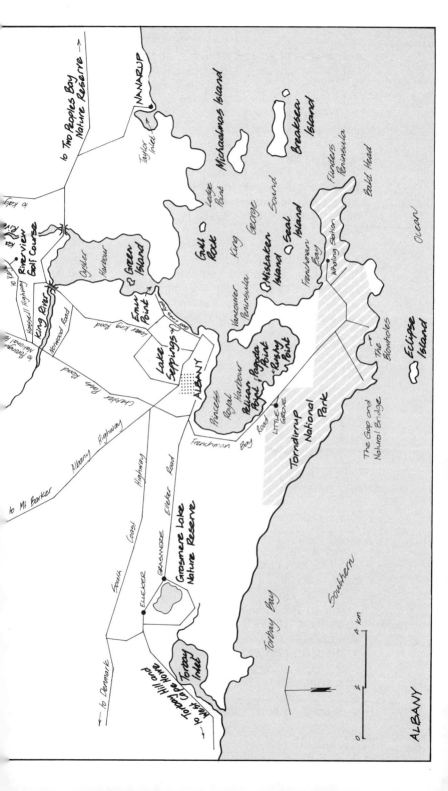

other species of interest include Australasian Bittern (often seen near the pumphouse), Buff-banded Rail and Red-eared Firetail.

Emu Point: Is 3 or 4 km north-east of Lake Seppings via Golf Links Road and Mermaid Avenue. Situated at the mouth of Oyster Harbour, the point is a good place for migratory waders (notably Large Sand Plover and Bar-tailed Godwit) as well as other waterbirds such as terns.

Lower King River and Lower Kalgan River: The King and Kalgan Rivers enter Oyster Harbour some 10 to 12 km north-east of Albany, and in summer the lower reaches of both rivers are worth looking over for waders such as Large Sand Plover, Grey-tailed Tattler, Bar-tailed Godwit, and Red and Great Knot. Among the other waterbirds usually present are pelicans, cormorants and ducks. Access to the northern shores of Oyster Harbour, and to the banks of both the Lower King River and the Lower Kalgan River, can be gained with ease from the road to Nanarup.

Nanarup: This tiny fishing township, on the coast about 20 km east of Albany, is an excellent place for Red-eared Firetails − look for them around the shacks adjacent to the carpark. A visit in the early morning or late afternoon will be best, since at these times a variety of other birds may be present − Western Rosella, Rock Parrot and White-breasted Robin for example.

Riverview Golf Course: Is worth a brief visit for bush birds such as Western Rosella, Western Yellow Robin and, perhaps, Red-capped Parrot. The golf course is about 12 km north-east of Albany via the road to Kalgan. Ask at the clubhouse for permission to enter the area.

Torndirrup National Park (3864 ha): Protecting a particularly rugged and very beautiful section of the coast south of Albany, where white-capped waves rolling in from the Southern Ocean thunder incessantly against immense cliffs of grey granite, this reserve contains three of the region's best known natural features − The Gap, a deep crevice in the cliffs where waves beat and surge; Natural Bridge, a massive arch beneath which the foaming waters of the ocean rush in and out over shelving granite slopes; and The Blowholes, spouts in the granite through which spray bursts violently from the boiling sea below.

Birds of the area include Osprey, Rock Parrot and Tawny-crowned Honeyeater (quite common in the coastal heathlands). In winter a visit to the lookout at The Gap should produce an assortment of seabirds, among them Yellow-nosed Albatross and Australasian Gannet. (The Gap is one of the best places in the state to go seabird-watching, especially if you have problems identifying often elusive species such as albatrosses. The Yellow-nosed Albatross frequently comes to within a hundred metres or so of the shore here, close enough for you to get a good long look at this, one of the smallest members of a group of celebrated oceanic travellers.)

Torndirrup National Park is about 13 km from Albany via the road to Frenchman Bay. The reserve has scenic drives, picnic areas and walking tracks, but no camping ground.

Rushy Point, Pelican Point and Pagoda Point: Lie along the south-western shores of Princess Royal Harbour, near Little Grove, and can be reached on foot from the road to Frenchman Bay. The area is reputed to be good for a variety of waders − in summer Red and Great Knots can often be found there, while Mongolian Plovers turn up from time to time.

Grasmere Lake Nature Reserve: Is situated alongside the road to Elleker, about 10 km west of Albany. A shallow lake, fringed with rushes and thickets, Grasmere is an excellent waterbird spot and nearly fifty species have been recorded there. Some of the more notable birds on its list are Little and Australasian Bittern, Yellow-billed Spoonbill, Blue-billed Duck, Marsh Harrier, Buff-banded Rail, Baillon's, Australian and Spotless Crake (crakes are most plentiful when the water level is low − no fewer than twenty-five Spotless Crakes were recorded during a single visit in March 1985), Black-tailed Native-hen, Red-kneed Dotterel, Black-fronted Plover, Red-necked Avocet and Wood Sandpiper.

Torbay Inlet, Torbay Hill and West Cape Howe: The Torbay area, a few kilometres to the south-west of Elleker, is well worth visiting for raptors (Ospreys breed regularly in the vicinity of Torbay Inlet), bush birds such as Crested Shrike-tit, Red-winged Fairy-wren and Red-eared Firetail, and seabirds. (Like The Gap, West Cape Howe provides excellent opportunities for seabirding during winter.)

Two Peoples Bay Nature Reserve (4639 ha): It is unthinkable that any birder should leave Albany without taking a trip to this world-renowned wildlife area. The reserve, which embraces a wide diversity of habitats ranging from low woodland and heathland to shallow lakes and rush-filled swamps, is of outstanding interest because a host of rare and sought-after birds occur in the area. There are nearly 150 species on the reserve's list, among them such ornithological gems as Little and Australasian Bittern, Square-tailed Kite, Peregrine Falcon, Noisy Scrub-bird (so far as is known, Two Peoples Bay is the only place in Australia where this species occurs), Western Whipbird (exceedingly shy but fairly plentiful − it has been estimated that there are about one hundred pairs within the reserve), Red-winged Fairy-wren, Southern Emu-wren, Western Bristlebird (another of the reserve's special birds − in 1983 the population was estimated at about one hundred pairs), Calamanthus and Red-eared Firetail.

To have the best chance of seeing the star attractions − Noisy

Scrub-bird, Western Whipbird and Western Bristlebird − you should visit Two Peoples Bay early in the morning. Areas where the three species occur are not difficult to reach on foot (the resident ranger will tell you where to begin searching), but even so you may have great difficulty sighting any of them because all favour areas of dense vegetation and are therefore more often heard than seen. Before visiting the reserve it would be best to familiarise yourself with the birds' distinctive calls (consult your field guide for descriptions of their voices), and even then only hard work and persistence will bring results. (Note that at times the calls of both the male Noisy Scrub-bird and male Western Whipbird may seem ventriloquial − you will think that the caller is just in front of you, when in fact it is some distance away.) Looking on the bright side, if the scrub-bird, whipbird and bristlebird prove too elusive, there is a good chance that you will find at least a few of the reserve's less secretive birds − White-breasted Robin, Red-winged Fairy-wren and Western Spinebill for example − while occasionally even the shy Southern Emu-wren can be quite obliging.

Camping is not permitted at Two Peoples Bay; there is, however, a pleasant tree-studded picnic ground near the park office, as well as many kilometres of walking tracks, including a short, self-guiding nature trail. The reserve is about 30 km east of Albany via the road to Nanarup.

Lake Pleasantview Nature Reserve: Situated just north of the road to Jerramungup, some 40 km north-east of Albany, this reserve is another of the area's prime waterbird spots − both Little and Australasian Bittern have been recorded there. The reserve has no facilities for visitors and camping is not allowed.

Albany seabird islands: There are many islands lying off the coast in the vicinity of Albany; some are difficult to reach, but if you have a seaworthy boat visits to the following could be contemplated. Before going to any of the islands mentioned you should contact the Western Australian Department of Conservation and Land Management, 44 Serpentine Road, Albany, for information about access and permits.

Michaelmas Island: Is situated in King George Sound, some 10 km east of Albany. It holds a breeding colony of Flesh-footed Shearwaters, estimated at between a hundred and a thousand pairs.

Seal Island: Also in King George Sound, this island lies about 8 km south-east of Albany and 2 km north of Flinders Peninsula. It supports a few pairs of Little Penguin and Crested Tern, as well as Sooty Oystercatcher and, on occasion, Caspian Tern.

Gull Rock: Is just 600 m or so west of Ledge Point, in the northern part of King George Sound. The rock is most notable for its small colony of Great-winged Petrels — about twenty pairs breed there between late January and October. Many hundreds of Crested Tern, together with a few Caspian, nest on the rock during summer.

Mistaken Island: One of the easiest islands to get to, lying only 100 m or so off the Vancouver Peninsula south-east of Albany, Mistaken Island holds fifty to a hundred pairs of Little Penguin (most plentiful between August and December), as well as a pair or two of Sooty Oystercatcher.

Eclipse Island: Lies 14 km south-west of Bald Head, and supports Little Penguin (about 100 pairs), Great-winged Petrel (10 000 to 15 000 pairs), Flesh-footed Shearwater (6000 to 8000 pairs) and Little Shearwater (up to 2000 pairs).

Breaksea Island: Situated 12 km south-east of Albany and 5 km north-east of Bald Head, Breaksea Island has colonies of Little Penguin, Great-winged Petrel and Flesh-footed Shearwater, and is visited by other seabirds such as Sooty Oystercatcher, Pacific Gull, and Caspian and Crested Tern.

Green Island: In Oyster Harbour, little more than 800 m offshore from Emu Point, it holds a few pairs of Pied Oystercatcher and Caspian Tern, as well as large numbers of Silver Gull.

Coffin Island: Forms part of Two Peoples Bay Nature Reserve, lies 250 m from the mainland, and supports Little Penguin, Great-winged Petrel, Flesh-footed Shearwater and White-faced Storm-Petrel.

Porongurup National Park

The Porongurup Range consists of a number of steep-sided, round-topped granite peaks that extend about 12 km from east to west and rise to a height of between 390 and 670 m above sea level. Much of the range is covered by a luxuriant forest of tall karri, which is of considerable botanical and ornithological significance because the nearest similar habitat is at least 50 km away. The Porongurups receive about 100 mm more rainfall a year than the surrounding plains, thus the karri, together with a variety of understorey plants such as the blue hovea (*Hovea elliptica*), climbing native wisteria (*Hardenbergia comptoniana*) and yellow water bush (*Bossiaea aquifolium*), has survived in isolation, though interestingly some of the other plants typical of the forests of the Pemberton district, notably the karri oak and karri wattle, are absent from the Porongurups. Altogether nearly four hundred species of plants have been recorded from the range.

Given its isolation it is perhaps not surprising that Porongurup National Park (2401 ha) has a somewhat impoverished avifauna. There are only about fifty species on the park's bird list; nevertheless it is a beautiful reserve, ideal for walking and picnicking, and some of the birds that occur there are common and readily observed. These include White-tailed Black-Cockatoo, Western Rosella, Scarlet, White-breasted and Western Yellow Robin (all three robins should be easy to locate – the White-breasted frequently visits the main picnic area), Golden Whistler, Grey Shrike-thrush, Restless Flycatcher, Grey Fantail, Red-winged Fairy-wren, White-browed Scrubwren, Western Thornbill, Varied Sittella, Rufous Treecreeper, White-naped and New Holland Honeyeater, Striated Pardalote, Silvereye and Grey Currawong.

Many of the species listed can be found along the walk to Nancy Peak via Hayward Peak. Though steep in places, this is an excellent walk for bird-watching because it takes you through a range of vegetation types, including patches of jarrah, marri and karri forest. Commencing at the main picnic ground, which is situated at a spot known as Tree in the Rock, the Hayward Peak to Nancy Peak walk is about 4 to 5 km long and takes about three to four hours to complete at a leisurely pace. If you do not find a Rufous Treecreeper (one of the park's special birds) along this walk, try the picnic area adjacent to Bolganup Dam, some 800 m or so back along the entrance road. Usually less crowded than Tree in the Rock, the Bolganup Dam picnic ground is much favoured by the treecreepers – it is not unusual for four or five birds to be present in the area at the one time. You can obtain good views (and photographs) of the birds while they forage on the forest floor, or creep mouse-like up the trunks of the tall trees.

The national park lies about 45 km north of Albany via Chester Pass Road. The main entrance is on Bolganup Road, a kilometre or so south of the road to Mt Barker. Information can be obtained from the resident ranger (his office is on Bolganup Road, near the park entrance), and accommodation is available at a guest house just outside the reserve boundary. Camping is not permitted within the park.

Stirling Range National Park

Situated approximately 40 km north of Porongurup National Park along Chester Pass Road, this reserve of 115 671 ha is one of the most important in the state. It encompasses the entire Stirling Range mountain system, includes five peaks exceeding 1000 m (Bluff Knoll, the highest point in the park, is 1073 m above sea level), and is a mecca for bushwalkers and rock climbers.

Being a large reserve, Stirling Range National Park contains a wide variety of habitats – jarrah and marri forests, yate and wandoo woodlands, extensive tracts of mallee and heath, large swampy areas dominated by sedges, and a number of shallow, saline lakes – and consequently the avifauna is considerably richer than that of the nearby Porongurups. Of the 120 or so bird

A Great Egret waits for a meal, Kakadu National Park, Northern Territory

Fogg Dam, in the Northern Territory south-east of Darwin, is a haven for birds and bird-watchers

Kakadu National Park, though best known for its waterbirds, is also very good for bush birds — this is a Peaceful Dove

Katherine Gorge, one of the Northern Territory's major tourist attractions

During the dry season the Victoria River, in the Northern Territory west of Katherine, is reduced to a series of tranquil waterholes

Situated in the MacDonnell Ranges west of Alice Springs, Standley Chasm is a very good spot for Dusky Grasswrens

Palm Valley in the Northern Territory is famous for its cabbage palms *(Livistona mariae)* and cycads

The Spinifex Pigeon should be easy to find at Ormiston Gorge, west of Alice Springs, Northern Territory

The Olgas, Uluru National Park, Northern Territory

species recorded from the park, the following are among the more notable: Emu, Square-tailed Kite, Wedge-tailed Eagle (one of the more conspicuous birds of prey), Peregrine Falcon (moderately common about the higher parts of the range), Malleefowl, Brown Quail, White-tailed Black-Cockatoo (reasonably plentiful), Purple-crowned Lorikeet (especially when the eucalypts are in flower), Red-capped Parrot (usually found in patches of marri), Western Yellow Robin, Crested Bellbird, Western Whipbird (this elusive ground-dweller may be quite common in the park; during a survey carried out in 1985 it was recorded on the north side of Bluff Knoll, and along Stirling Range Drive in the vicinity of Mt Hassell), Southern Emu-wren (quite common in the sandplain heath), Shy Hylacola, Calamanthus, White-cheeked and Tawny-crowned Honeyeater, and Red-eared Firetail (largely confined to patches of damp heath).

The reserve has good facilities for visitors. Picnic grounds are provided at numerous sites along Stirling Range Drive, which runs from Chester Pass Road westwards through the central section of the park; there is also a picnic ground along Red Gum Pass Road, and another at the end of Bluff Knoll Road. Walking tracks lead from these roads to many of the park's higher peaks, including The Abbey (732 m), Mt Magog (856 m), Talyuberlup Peak (783 m), and the highest − Bluff Knoll. Camping is permitted at one locality only − on Chester Pass Road, just south of the Toolbrunup Road turn-off. The camping area has toilets and fireplaces, but there are no showers or powered sites. Those requiring a little more luxury should continue for another 15 km or so north along Chester Pass Road to the privately owned Stirling Range Caravan Park. This park has full facilities, including hot-water showers, a laundry and forty powered sites.

The best seasons to visit the Stirling Range are winter and spring. The reserve is one of Australia's most outstanding wild-flower areas − nearly a hundred plant species are confined to the range and some, like the mountain bells (*Darwinia* sp.), may be restricted to individual mountain tops. Other botanical highlights include many species of spider and greenhood orchid, red kangaroo paws, scarlet banksias, mountain banksias, and numerous varieties of dryandra, acacia, hakea and grevillea. A detailed brochure describing the park's flora and fauna, and a comprehensive bird list, can be obtained from the ranger's office adjacent to the camping area.

Lake Cassencarry

While you are in the Stirling Range area it might be worth your while taking a trip to Lake Cassencarry, which lies some 80 km to the north-east via the road to Ongerup. A large lake, about 230 ha, it only fills about once every seven years, but when it does it attracts a wide range of waterbirds. Between July 1978 and February 1979, when the lake was full, a total of thirty species was recorded there, including Hoary-headed Grebe, Pacific Heron, Sacred Ibis, Yellow-billed Spoonbill, Pacific Black, Pink-eared and Maned Duck, Grey Teal, Black-fronted Plover, Black-winged and Banded Stilt, Red-necked Avocet, Red-necked and Long-toed Stint, and Whiskered Tern.

The lake is approximately 10 km north of Ongerup, just east of the road to Pingrup. It is surrounded by farmland and you should seek permission from the owner before entering the area. (If permission is refused, there are numerous lakes in the vicinity of Pingrup that might be worth exploring. And keep your eyes open for Regent Parrots while travelling through this area.)

Fitzgerald River National Park

This magnificent reserve embraces one of the loveliest sections of the state's south coast. Covering an area of 242 803 ha, it stretches from Hopetoun in the east to Bremer Bay in the west, and extends inland for many kilometres towards the main Albany to Esperance road. Much of the park consists of an undulating sand plain cut by wide, flat valleys and narrow, deep gorges, but the reserve also contains a series of jagged peaks known collectively as the Barrens.

Fitzgerald River has a well-deserved reputation for being one of Australia's most outstanding botanical reserves. The flora is indeed immensely rich, and approximately sixty of the six hundred or more plant species that occur there are restricted to the area. Among the genera particularly well represented in the reserve are hakea (sixteen species), banksia (fourteen), acacia (twenty-five), eucalyptus (twenty-five) and boronia (twelve). Needless to say the park's avifauna is exceedingly rich (there are about 180 species on its bird list); bear in mind, however, that the reserve is very large and many sections are accessible only on foot or by four-wheel-drive vehicle. In addition three of the special birds – Ground Parrot, Western Whipbird and Western Bristlebird – are notoriously difficult to locate and could take a great deal of tracking down. It would therefore be best to stay at least several days in the area.

The park is most easily reached from Hopetoun, which lies a few kilometres from the reserve's eastern boundary, about 50 km south of Ravensthorpe. You can also get to the park from the main Jerramungup to Ravensthorpe road, or from Bremer Bay, but many of the tracks running through the northern and western sections of the reserve are extremely rough and may become impassable after heavy rain. At Hopetoun there is a caravan park with powered sites and full facilities, while at Mylies Beach, some

15 km west of Hopetoun and 7 km within the park boundary, there is a small camping area with toilets and fireplaces. Bush camping is permitted throughout the reserve; for further information you should call at the park office, which is situated off Hamersley Drive, about 10 km west of Hopetoun. Though unsealed, Hamersley Drive is suitable for conventional vehicles and provides ready access to the extensive heathlands that dominate the eastern section of the reserve. From Hamersley Drive there are four-wheel-drive tracks leading to West Beach, Edwards Point, Hamersley Inlet and many other places along the coast.

Those with the time to explore the area thoroughly can expect to see a wide range of birds, among them such interesting species as Eastern Reef Egret (quite common along rocky parts of the coast), Square-tailed Kite (not especially plentiful, but certainly one to look out for), Malleefowl (a breeding resident, found mainly in areas of mallee and low woodland), Painted Button-quail, Australian Bustard (moderately common in the heathlands), Bush Thick-knee (a rather rare inhabitant of the woodlands), Hooded Plover (favours sandy beaches − often seen outside the park at Hopetoun and Bremer Bay), Brush Bronzewing, Ground Parrot (though much sought-after, this species is seldom seen; there has, however, been at least one recent sighting in the area − in February 1983 a single parrot was recorded in low heathland along the Drummond Track, about 8 km south of Old Ongerup Road), Elegant and Rock Parrot (the former prefers mallee and low woodland, the latter coastal heath), and Spotted Nightjar.

Other noteworthy birds include White-winged Triller (spring−summer), Southern Scrub-robin (common in areas of mallee), Western Yellow Robin, Crested Bellbird, Western Whipbird (probably quite well distributed throughout much of the park − it has been recorded in recent years from the area where Old Telegraph Road crosses the Hamersley River, and along the main Ravensthorpe to Hopetoun road outside the park), Blue-breasted Fairy-wren (common in the mallee), Southern Emu-wren (common in the heathlands), Western Bristlebird (most records of this species come from the more remote, western section of the park − if you can get there, try the area bounded by the Fitzgerald Track, the Twertup Track and the park's north-western boundary; bristlebirds are apparently quite plentiful in this area), Shy Hylacola (moderately common in areas of mallee), Calamanthus (a common inhabitant of the heathlands), Purple-gaped (common in mallee areas), White-cheeked and Tawny-crowned Honeyeater, Western Spinebill, and Yellow-rumped Pardalote (a bird of the mallee).

Fitzgerald River is an interesting park not only because of the large number of sought-after birds it supports, but also because many different types of habitat occur within a comparatively short distance of each other. Thus, for example, honeyeaters such as White-cheeked and Tawny-crowned can be seen in the heathlands, while Purple-gaped and Brown-headed occur in the mallee. And you may find White-naped Honeyeater and Western Spinebill in the well-timbered gullies. An up-to-date bird list, complete with habitat notes, can be obtained from the park office.

Esperance

Esperance, the only settlement of any size on the coast between Albany and the South Australian border, has motels, hotels, caravan parks and a youth hostel, making it an ideal place to stay while exploring the eastern part of the south-west region. The town is virtually surrounded by good birding spots, and visits to the following localities should prove most productive.

Esperance Bay: Romantically dubbed the 'bay of isles', Esperance Bay is almost tropical in appearance − its aquamarine waters are dotted with numerous small islands, its shores fringed with white sandy beaches with names like Lovers Beach, Twilight Beach and Blue Haven Beach. It is a delightful place to go swimming, boating and fishing, as well as bird-watching − Pacific Gulls frequent the foreshore (keep an eye open for Kelp Gulls as well), and Arctic Terns are seen on rare occasions, usually in summer.

Lake Warden Nature Reserve: Is situated a little to the north of the town and consists of a chain of wetlands − Lake Warden, Lake Wheatfield, Lake Windabout and Woody Lake. The Lake Warden area is considered to be the best spot for birds, the lake itself being much favoured by waders such as Hooded Plover (240 were present in February 1985, which to date is the second-highest number recorded at any one site in Australia), Banded Stilt (10 000+ may be present at times), Sharp-tailed Sandpiper (1000+ on occasions), Pectoral Sandpiper (up to six have been recorded during a single visit − this species is rarely seen elsewhere along the south coast), and Broad-billed Sandpiper (like the Pectoral Sandpiper, this wader is rare throughout much of the region). Some of the other waterbirds attracted to the lake in large numbers are Australian Shelduck (5000+ may be present in early summer), Chestnut Teal and Whiskered Tern. Bush birds include Calamanthus − often seen near Lake Warden.

Lake Windabout is also worth a visit. It lies just east of Lake Warden and can be reached on foot via the Esperance golf course. Cape Barren Geese occasionally turn up on the golf course, while the lake is good for Great Crested Grebe and Blue-billed Duck. A search of the surrounding area might produce some noteworthy bush birds − Red-capped Parrot for example.

Shark Lake: This small lake is located alongside the main Esperance to Norseman road, some 10 km north of the town. In

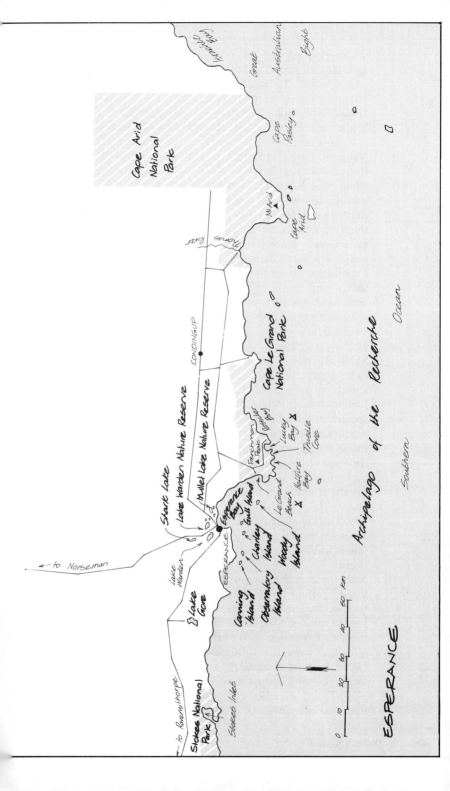

summer, when the water level is low, it is an excellent spot for Buff-banded Rail and three species of crake — Baillon's, Australian and Spotless. It is also a haunt of the Blue-billed Duck, and attracts a variety of other waterbirds.

Mullet Lake Nature Reserve: Consisting of three lakes — Station, Mullet and Ewans — this reserve is situated about 10 km northeast of Esperance, just south of the road to Cape Le Grand National Park. The entire area is good for waders; Hooded Plovers are regularly recorded in the vicinity of Station Lake, while Red Knots and, more rarely, Black-tailed Godwits occur around Ewans Lake. Summer, of course, is the best time for migratory birds, though Ewans Lake, which has a bird list totalling thirty-seven species, is worth visiting at any time of the year.

Lake Gore: Known locally as Lake Gage, this extensive shallow wetland, 3 km in diameter, is situated near the coast to the west of Esperance. To get there take the road from Esperance to Ravensthorpe and turn left (south) after about 35 km at McCalls Road. This road will take you to the lake's northern shores.

Lake Gore is interesting for a variety of reasons. In February 1983 it held about 390 Hooded Plovers, to date the largest number ever recorded at a single site in Australia. In addition Banded Stilts, Australian Shelducks and Chestnut Teals are often present in very large numbers; in summer the lake is favoured by a wide variety of migratory waders, including notable species such as Lesser Golden Plover, Black-tailed Godwit and Sanderling; many species of waterbird, particularly Black-winged Stilt, breed in the swamps along the lake's north-western and eastern shores; and Fairy Terns nest occasionally in one of the smaller lakes that lie to the west of Lake Gore.

Autumn is the best time of year for Hooded Plovers; the birds usually congregate along the lake's north-eastern shores, near the end of McCalls Road. And if you want to see masses of Australian Shelducks at close range, go to the lake in early summer when the birds are moulting. They can usually be found roosting at various points around the edge of the lake, particularly along its northern shores.

Stokes National Park (9493 ha): Centred on Stokes Inlet, and situated about 90 km west of Esperance via the road to Ravensthorpe, this reserve is an excellent place for White-bellied Sea-Eagles, as well as for waders and Fairy Terns. It has only limited facilities for visitors, but bush camping is permitted at certain sites — contact the resident ranger for details.

Cape Le Grand National Park (31 390 ha): Lies some 40 km or so south-east of Esperance and is readily accessible via a well-sign-posted road (unsealed but normally in quite good condition). It is the most popular park in the district — a bird list, together with several other useful publications, can be obtained from the ranger's office on Cape Le Grand Road, about 1 km inside the reserve's northern boundary. Camping is allowed at Le Grand Beach, some 12 km from the park entrance, and at Lucky Bay, about 17 km from the park entrance. Both areas have toilets and fireplaces, but there are no showers or powered sites. The camping grounds are small, and if you visit the park during the school holidays you may have difficulty finding a space.

Cape Le Grand Road and Lucky Bay Road provide ready access to much of the park (both are unsealed, but suitable for conventional vehicles), and there are two main walking tracks − a short (1 km or so) climb to the 262 m summit of Frenchman Peak, and a much longer (15 km) coastal walk from Le Grand Beach to Rossiter Bay. If you are reasonably fit and have a full day to spare, the coastal trail is highly recommended. It winds through heath-lands where a wealth of colourful wildflowers can be seen from September to November, crosses several rocky headlands, and passes close to three of the park's most attractive beaches − Hellfire Bay, Thistle Cove and Lucky Bay.

Although Cape Le Grand is a much smaller park than Fitzgerald River, it contains a similar range of habitats − sandplain heaths, areas of mallee and coastal swamps, for example − and as a result the avifaunas of the two parks have much in common, except that Cape Le Grand has fewer species − about 120. Among the birds you can expect to see are Emu, Australasian Bittern, Square-tailed Kite, White-bellied Sea-Eagle, Painted Button-quail, Australian Bustard, Common and Brush Bronzewing, White-tailed Black-Cockatoo, Purple-crowned Lorikeet, Elegant and Rock Parrot, Hooded Robin, Crested Bellbird, Southern Emu-wren, Calamanthus, White-naped, Brown and Tawny-crowned Honey-eater, Western Spinebill, and Red-eared Firetail (an isolated population).

Cape Arid National Park (279 415 ha): Encompassing a huge tract of country to the east of Esperance, Cape Arid National Park is of great botanical significance because Robert Brown, the botanist who accompanied Matthew Flinders on his voyage of exploration in 1801, collected many specimens from the area. Thus Cape Arid is the type locality for a large number of Western Australian plant species.

The reserve lies about 140 km from Esperance via the road to Condingup. This route is sealed for a hundred kilometres or so, but the last stretch leading to the reserve is not, nor are any of the tracks within the park. However, if you do not own a four-wheel-drive vehicle it is not essential that you visit Cape Arid − equally spectacular wildflower displays can be seen in some of the region's more accessible reserves (Fitzgerald River, Stirling Range and

Cape Le Grand), and Cape Arid probably has no birds that cannot be found more readily elsewhere in the south-west.

There are a number of bush-camping sites within the park; details can be obtained from the ranger's office, which is situated near the mouth of the Thomas River. If you do decide to take a trip to Cape Arid you may care to spend some time searching for one of the reserve's special birds – the Ground Parrot. In recent years this elusive inhabitant of the park's coastal heaths has been sighted in the vicinity of Mt Arid, some 20 or 30 km south-east of the Thomas River mouth.

Archipelago of the Recherche: Stretching from about 25 km west of Esperance to the western end of the Great Australian Bight, the Archipelago of the Recherche consists of about a hundred named islands, many unnamed ones, and numerous rocks and reefs. Most of the outlying islands are difficult to reach, but those in the vicinity of Esperance are comparatively easy to get to and some, like Woody Island, are visited by tourist boat operators based in the town. Information about day trips to Woody Island can be obtained from the Esperance Tourist Bureau in Dempster Street. If you wish to visit any of the other islands in the group you must first obtain a permit from the Western Australian Department of Conservation and Land Management in Perth or Albany.

Woody Island: Lies 15 km south-east of Esperance and is a good place for Osprey and White-bellied Sea-Eagle, as well as Black-faced Shag, Cape Barren Goose, Sooty Oystercatcher and Caspian Tern. Breeding seabirds include Little Penguin, Flesh-footed Shearwater and White-faced Storm-Petrel.

Charley Island: Is about 6 km south of Esperance and supports a few pairs of Little Penguin, as well as an estimated five hundred to a thousand pairs of Flesh-footed Shearwater (the latter is most numerous from September to April). Cape Barren Geese, Sooty Oystercatchers and Caspian Terns also breed in small numbers.

Canning Island: Holds a large colony (estimated at between two thousand and three thousand pairs) of White-faced Storm-Petrels, and is situated a short distance off the coast, about 20 km south-west of Esperance. Other species recorded from the island include Eastern Reef Egret, Cape Barren Goose, Sooty Oystercatcher and Crested Tern.

Observatory Island: Lies 11 km south-west of Esperance, about a kilometre offshore from Observatory Point. It supports a small (twenty to thirty pairs) Little Penguin colony, as well as a few pairs of Caspian Tern.

Gull Island: Little Penguins, Cape Barren Geese and Pacific Gulls breed on this island, which is situated 6 km south of Esperance.

THE NULLARBOR

Stretching some 800 km from just west of Rawlinna in Western Australia to beyond Ooldea in South Australia, and in places extending more than 200 km from the coast to the Great Victoria Desert, the legendary Nullarbor Plain is for the most part flat, sparsely vegetated and uninhabited. The region has a formidable reputation for being desolate and inhospitable, and most people try to complete the 1200 km journey from Norseman to Ceduna as quickly as possible, pausing only to photograph the magnificent white sandhills that are steadily engulfing the old telegraph station near Eucla, or to view the spectacular limestone cliffs south of Koonalda Homestead.

The Nullarbor is certainly not the ideal place for an extended holiday, but if you hurry through the region you may miss some exciting birds. And it is not necessary to venture far off the beaten track in order to enjoy good birding; there are a number of spots close to the Eyre Highway where interesting species can be found, and stops at the following localities should produce birds such as Australian Bustard, Pink Cockatoo, Blue Bonnet (the distinctive subspecies *narethae* — the Naretha Parrot — occurs in the region), Southern Scrub-robin, Crested Bellbird, Chestnut and Nullarbor Quail-thrush (as its name implies, the latter is confined to the region), Blue-breasted Fairy-wren, Shy Hylacola, Redthroat, Calamanthus, Slender-billed Thornbill, Purple-gaped and White-

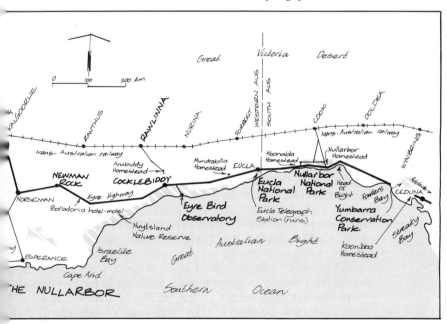

fronted Honeyeater, Crimson Chat, Orange Chat, Yellow-rumped Pardalote and Masked Woodswallow.

Newman Rock

Newman Rock is situated a kilometre or so north of the Eyre Highway, about 50 km north-west of the Balladonia hotel-motel. A good all-weather track leads from the highway to the rock where a small, permanent freshwater pool attracts many birds, including on occasion such gems as Orange Chat. The surrounding bush is usually alive with birds, especially in the early morning and late afternoon, and a few hours spent walking through the area should prove very rewarding. Among the species to look for are Purple-crowned Lorikeet, Port Lincoln Ringneck, Black-eared Cuckoo, Australian Owlet-nightjar, Red-capped Robin, Gilbert's Whistler, Chestnut Quail-thrush (quite common in the open woodland between the rock and the Eyre Highway), White-browed Babbler, Redthroat, Rufous Treecreeper, Yellow-throated Miner and White-eared, Brown-headed, Brown and White-fronted Honeyeater. Two outstanding rarities, Grey Falcon and Scarlet-chested Parrot, have been recorded from the Newman Rock area and are well worth keeping an eye open for.

An overnight stay at this delightful spot is highly recommended. There are no facilities for visitors, but there is plenty of level, open ground where you can pitch a tent or park a caravan.

Cocklebiddy to Rawlinna

Many bird-watchers travel to the Nullarbor in the hope of finding a Nullarbor Quail-thrush, but most come away without getting so much as a glimpse of one. This is hardly surprising, for the bird lives on the plain proper where the country is exceedingly flat and open. The chances are that long before you can get close enough to spot the cryptically coloured Quail-thrush it will see you approaching and will seek refuge under a bush or down a rabbit burrow. And because the plain is so vast, searching for the bird is rather like looking for the proverbial needle in a haystack. It helps, however, if you begin searching in an area where the Quail-thrush is seen regularly, and Arubiddy Station, some 30 km north-west of Cocklebiddy, is such a place.

You can get to Arubiddy Station from the Eyre Highway via the track to Rawlinna. Normally the section of the track leading from Cocklebiddy to the homestead on Arubiddy Station is graded; even so, if you do not own a four-wheel-drive vehicle it would be wise to inquire about its condition at the Cocklebiddy motel. You should also seek precise directions to the homestead; there are numerous tracks in the vicinity of Cocklebiddy, and since only a few are signposted you could easily become lost.

The Nullarbor Quail-thrush has been seen on Arubiddy Station on a number of occasions during the past ten years or so; if you ask at the homestead the manager may direct you to the place where the bird was last sighted. Then it is simply a matter of scouring the countryside — but keep within sight of your vehicle at all times. Should you wander too far afield (easily done when you are looking at the ground) the results could prove disastrous. If the Quail-thrush eludes you there are compensations — you will almost certainly come across other interesting species such as Australian Bustard, Crested Bellbird, White-winged Fairy-wren, Redthroat, Calamanthus and Masked Woodswallow, and the Blue Bonnet or Naretha Parrot is seen regularly in at least one part of the area (again, inquire at the homestead for details).

Eyre Bird Observatory

In 1977 the Royal Australasian Ornithologists Union established Australia's first bird observatory in the old telegraph station at Eyre, some 50 km south-east of Cocklebiddy. Situated within the Nuytsland Nature Reserve, a magnificent 650 000 ha wilderness stretching from Israelite Bay in the west to Mundrabilla in the east, the observatory is set among sand-dunes just a kilometre or so from the Southern Ocean. To the north, between the observatory and the Eyre Highway, is a large area of undisturbed mallee.

Being on the coast yet close to the bush, Eyre is an ideal place for observing a wide range of birds, including seabirds, migratory waders, nomadic honeyeaters, and resident species such as Mallee-fowl and Pink Cockatoo. No fewer than 215 different birds have been recorded from the area, among them such notable rarities as Baird's and Buff-breasted Sandpiper, Little Stint, Red-necked Phalarope, Arctic Tern, Scarlet-chested Parrot and Yellow Wagtail. You have little hope of seeing birds such as these, of course, but there is a good chance you will find at least a few of the following: Emu, Little Penguin, Australasian Gannet (especially autumn— winter), Pied Cormorant, Black Kite (nomadic, but very common at times), Brown Goshawk, Collared Sparrowhawk, Wedge-tailed Eagle, Spotted Harrier (an irregular spring—summer visitor in years of good rainfall), Australian Hobby, Malleefowl (frequently seen on the track leading from the Eyre Highway to the observatory), Pied and Sooty Oystercatcher, Double-banded Plover (winter), Ruddy Turnstone (spring), Common and Sharp-tailed Sandpiper (spring), Greenshank (spring), Bar-tailed Godwit (spring), Red and Great Knot (spring), Red-necked Stint (spring and autumn), Sanderling (spring and autumn), Pacific Gull, and Caspian and Crested Tern. There may also be Brush Bronzewing (often drinks at water points near the observatory), Pink Cockatoo (one of the special birds — flocks of twenty-five or more regularly occur in the vicinity of the observatory), Port Lincoln Ringneck, Fan-tailed Cuckoo (spring—summer), Tawny Frogmouth, Australian Owlet-nightjar, Fork-tailed Swift (sometimes seen between November and April flying over the observatory in large numbers) and Rainbow Bee-eater (spring—summer).

Among the other species to look for are White-winged Triller (spring—summer), Southern Scrub-robin (a common breeding resident), Golden Whistler, Chestnut Quail-thrush (common in the mallee — may be seen crossing the track between the observatory and the Eyre Highway), White-browed Babbler, Blue-breasted Fairy-wren (another common breeding resident), White-browed Scrubwren, Shy Hylacola (resident, but sparsely distributed in areas of mallee), Weebill, Inland Thornbill, Red Wattlebird, Yellow-throated Miner, Spiny-cheeked, Singing, White-eared, Purple-gaped, Brown-headed, Brown, New Holland and White-fronted Honeyeater, Crimson and White-fronted Chat (the former is highly nomadic, but occasionally turns up in large numbers), Yellow-rumped Pardalote (sparsely distributed throughout the mallee), Silvereye, Grey Butcherbird and Grey Currawong.

To get to the bird observatory, turn off the Eyre Highway about 16 km east of Cocklebiddy. The track leading to the observatory is extremely rough in places and you should not attempt to get through in a conventional vehicle; however, if you make arrangements in advance the warden will collect you from Cocklebiddy. You can stay just for the night if you wish; better still, why not go for a week and attend one of the many courses run by the RAOU? These include bird-watching for beginners, field ornithology (bird-banding, censusing and behaviour), and bird drawing and painting. Full details can be obtained from the RAOU in Perth or Melbourne. You do not have to be a member of the RAOU to attend, but you should of course book well in advance.

Eucla National Park

Covering an area of 3342 ha, this reserve is situated on the coast between Eucla and the South Australian border. It features massive sandhills and tracts of mallee, and contains the ruins of the Eucla Telegraph Station, which can be reached by turning off the Eyre Highway about 15 km west of Eucla. The track to the telegraph station is well signposted and suitable for conventional vehicles.

There are no facilities for visitors within the national park, but there are motels and caravan parks nearby at Eucla, and at the Western Australia — South Australia border a little to the east. The park's birdlife, though not especially rich, includes at least some of the species previously mentioned — Pink Cockatoos can sometimes be found near the old telegraph station, while Blue-breasted Fairy-wrens inhabit areas of mallee.

Nullarbor National Park

A large reserve (231 900 ha), Nullarbor National Park lies some 110 km east of Eucla and extends from the Great Australian Bight inland for 30 km or so towards the trans-Australian railway line. The Eyre Highway runs the entire length of the reserve; otherwise access is very limited, although there are a few unsealed roads leading northwards from the highway to Cook. Lookouts to the south of the Eyre Highway provide outstanding views over the ocean, but there are no facilities for visitors in the park.

The vegetation on this part of the Nullarbor is sparse and birds are not plentiful. However, the Nullarbor Quail-thrush and Slender-billed Thornbill have been recorded from the general area (both species have been observed in recent years in the vicinity of the Western Australia − South Australia border), therefore it might be worth your while stopping at intervals along the Eyre Highway and searching the extensive bluebush-saltbush plains that lie between Eucla and Nullarbor Homestead.

Yumbarra Conservation Park

Although it is the least accessible reserve in the region, Yumbarra warrants a mention because with an area of 106 189 ha it is one of the largest and most important conservation parks in South Australia. Among the many interesting birds recorded from the reserve are Chestnut Quail-thrush, Variegated Fairy-wren, Shy Hylacola and Purple-gaped Honeyeater. The park is situated about 50 km north-west of Ceduna and about 15 km north of the Eyre Highway. It can only be reached by four-wheel-drive vehicle via the road to Koonibba Homestead. There are no facilities for visitors at the park, but there are several motels and caravan parks at Ceduna.

GERALDTON AND CARNARVON

Geraldton

With a population of almost 21 000, Geraldton is the largest town on the Western Australian coast north of Perth. It is the state's premier winter holiday resort and there is ample accommodation, including motels, hotels, guest houses, holiday units and caravan parks. The Youth Hostels Association has a hostel at 80 Francis Street. Apart from an ideal climate (the tourist brochures claim that on average the sun shines eight hours a day, all year round), Geraldton had plenty to offer the visitor − many kilometres of safe swimming beaches, numerous excellent fishing spots, two championship-standard golf courses, several superb seafood restaurants (the town is the home of Western Australia's lobster-fishing industry), and a wealth of museums and historic properties.

Much of the country around the town has been cleared for agriculture and good bird-watching areas are rather few and far between. However, Kalbarri National Park is well worth a visit, as are the islands of the Houtman Abrolhos — if you can get to them.

Kalbarri National Park: Every year thousands of people travel to Western Australia to see the state's magnificent wildflowers, and nowhere are the displays more impressive than in this splendid 186 076 ha reserve. During the wildflower season (August to November), blooms every colour of the rainbow can be seen in the heathlands that stretch from the park's roadsides to the far horizon. Among the more decorative flowering plants are bright yellow and orange banksias, some with flower heads fully 200 mm long; many varieties of grevillea, including *Grevillea leucopteris* with its white, scented flowers borne on the ends of long leafless canes; two species of native hibiscus, the blue-flowered *Hibiscus drummondii* and *Alyogyne hakeifolia*, which bears a yellow-centred blue flower; beautiful white, red and yellow featherflowers, *Verticordia*; pussytails, or mulla mullas — *Ptilotus* — with their delicate feathery heads; and a number of typical south-western species, notably Mangles kangaroo paw and the pink-flowered form of milkmaids, *Burchardia umbellata*, that are of particular interest because they do not occur north of Kalbarri.

Even though Kalbarri is a large reserve it does not support a particularly wide range of birds because most of the area consists of low, sandplain heath. As might be expected, honeyeaters feature prominently among the bush birds. Spiny-cheeked, Singing, Brown, White-fronted and Tawny-crowned are the most common species, but it is also worth keeping an eye open for Black and Pied Honeyeaters. Both are resident and breed in the park and, although usually somewhat scarce, are sometimes plentiful, especially in spring when the emu-bushes, *Eremophila*, are in flower. Other bush birds of note include Peaceful and Diamond Dove, Red-tailed Black-Cockatoo, Black-eared Cuckoo, Rainbow Bee-eater (spring–summer), White-backed Swallow, White-winged Triller (spring–summer), Southern Scrub-robin, Red-capped and Hooded Robin, Golden Whistler, Rufous Whistler, Crested Bellbird, Splendid, Variegated, Blue-breasted and White-winged Fairywren, Redthroat, Calamanthus (quite common along the coast south of Kalbarri township), Crimson Chat (in some years this species may be present in very large numbers), Zebra Finch, Black-faced and Little Woodswallow (the latter is quite common around the gorges), and Pied Butcherbird.

Apart from those mentioned, many of the birds on Kalbarri's

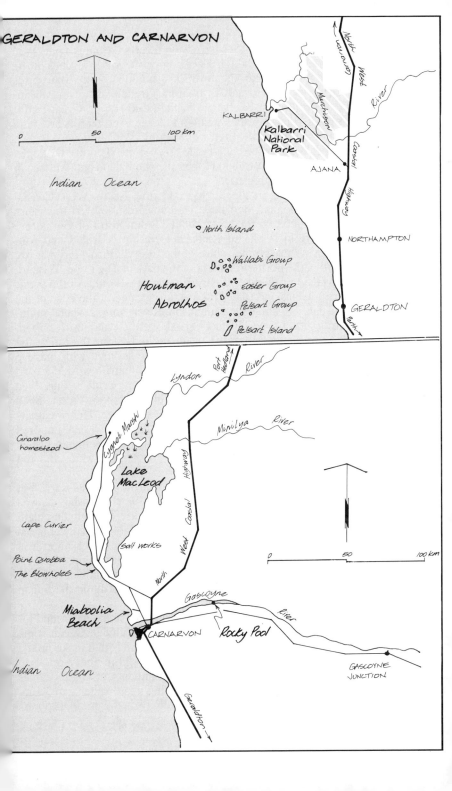

GERALDTON AND CARNARVON

Indian Ocean

50   100 km

KALBARRI

Kalbarri National Park

Murchison

North West Coastal Highway

River

AJANA

NORTHAMPTON

GERALDTON

North

○ North Island

Wallabi Group

Houtman Abrolhos

Easter Group

Pelsart Group

Pelsart Island

Lyndon

Port Hedland River

Minilya River

Gnaraloo homestead

Cygnet Marsh

Lake MacLeod

Cape Cuvier

Salt works

West Coastal Highway

Point Quobba

The Blowholes

North

Miaboolia Beach

Gascoyne

CARNARVON

Rocky Pool

River

GASCOYNE JUNCTION

Indian Ocean

Geraldton

0   50   100 km

list (in all about 170 species have been recorded from the park) are seen rather rarely, although a walk along the lower reaches of the Murchison River near the township should produce waterbirds such as Hoary-headed and Australasian Grebe, Australian Pelican, Darter, cormorants, Pacific and White-faced Heron, Great Egret, Black Swan, ducks, waders, gulls and terns. And raptors are quite plentiful throughout the area with Osprey, Whistling Kite, Brown Goshawk, White-bellied Sea-Eagle, Wedge-tailed and Little Eagle, Spotted Harrier, Australian Hobby, Brown Falcon and Australian Kestrel occurring regularly.

To get to the national park take the North West Coastal Highway to Ajana, then head west towards Kalbarri township, which is situated on the coast about 170 km north of Geraldton. The road from Ajana to Kalbarri township is sealed and runs more or less through the centre of the reserve. Picnic facilities are provided in the northern section of the park at The Loop, Z Bend, Hawks Head Lookout and Ross Graham Lookout. All the picnic sites have tables and toilets, and all are located at the edge of the spectacular, 80 km long Murchison River gorge, where multi-coloured cliffs tower 150 m or so above the winding river bed. Walking tracks lead from the picnic grounds along the top of the cliffs and, in places, down to tranquil pools lined with massive river red gums and coolabahs. South of Kalbarri township a road runs along the coast to Natural Bridge, passing richly coloured sea cliffs and coastal gorges with names like Rainbow Valley, Shell House, Grandstand Rock and Layer Cake Gorge. Here weathering of the limestone and sandstone cliffs that rise a hundred metres or more from the jade-green waters of the Indian Ocean has exposed layer after layer of brown, yellow, white and red rock.

There is no formal camping ground in the national park, but there are at least five caravan parks at Kalbarri township, as well as two motels and numerous holiday units. Though unsealed, most of the tracks within the reserve are suitable for conventional vehicles. A map of the park, a bird list and other publications can be obtained from the ranger's office near the township. The best seasons to visit the area are winter and spring; in summer it can be very hot and dry, though you can always take a dip in the Indian Ocean to cool off at the end of the day.

Houtman Abrolhos: Long famous as a major breeding ground for seabirds, the Houtman Abrolhos lies in the Indian Ocean some 60 km west of Geraldton. The numerous islands that make up the Abrolhos are low — none rises higher than 14 m above sea level — and of two origins: some are the remnants of coastal dunes separated from the mainland by rising seas, others are coral platforms. Pelsart Island, the most southerly in the group, supports

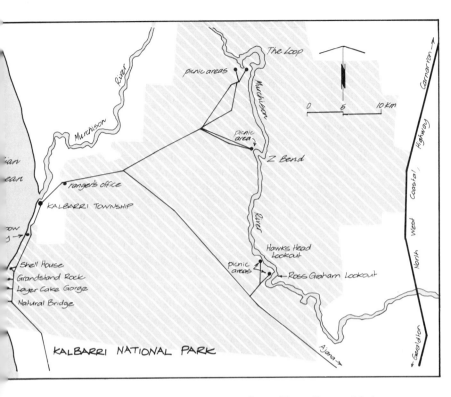

both the greatest variety and largest number of breeding seabirds, among them Wedge-tailed Shearwater, White-faced Storm-Petrel, Pacific Gull, Caspian, Roseate, Sooty, Bridled, Fairy and Crested Tern, and Common and Lesser Noddy. All of these species are abundant and some occur in their tens of thousands — in November 1982 there were at least a hundred thousand pairs each of Sooty Tern, and Common and Lesser Noddy (the Houtman Abrolhos is the only locality in Australia where the latter breeds and it is seldom seen away from the area).

Other species regularly recorded from Pelsart Island include Pied Cormorant, Red-tailed Tropicbird, Eastern Reef Egret, Osprey, White-bellied Sea-Eagle, Buff-banded Rail, Spotless Crake, Pied and Sooty Oystercatcher, Grey (summer) and Red-capped Plover, Ruddy Turnstone (summer), Grey-tailed Tattler (summer), Greenshank (summer), Bar-tailed Godwit (summer), Great Knot (summer) and Curlew Sandpiper (summer).

The entire Houtman Abrolhos is a wildlife sanctuary to which entry is strictly controlled. Even so, if you live in the Perth area it would be worth contacting the Royal Australasian Ornithologists Union (the address is at the beginning of this chapter) because its seabird group occasionally runs boat trips to Pelsart. Alternatively, if you are a visitor to Western Australia it might pay to call at the Geraldton Tourist Bureau on the corner of Chapman Road and Durlacher Street. The town's lobster fishermen sometimes organise charter fishing trips to the waters around the islands where there is a good chance you will see at least a few of the seabirds listed.

Carnarvon

Carnarvon, a town of some five thousand inhabitants, is located at the mouth of the Gascoyne River, approximately 480 km north of Geraldton. It is an important commercial centre, acclaimed for its prawning industry and for its luxuriant plantations of bananas and other tropical fruits. There is a wide range of accommodation that includes motels, hotels, holiday units and at least seven caravan parks.

Carnarvon is an excellent place to stay for a few days — it is virtually surrounded by good birding spots and, since it is the western gateway to tropical Australia, it offers those travelling from the south an opportunity to see many new and exciting birds. Some of the species that you are likely to find in the area are Striated Heron, Brahminy Kite, Lesser Crested Tern, Blue-winged Kookaburra, Yellow White-eye and Star Finch. Visits to the following localities should produce most of the birds listed — and a lot more.

Babbage Island: Situated just west of Carnarvon town centre and reached via a causeway, this island consists of sandy beaches, low samphire scrub and mangroves. It is a good spot for Little Egret, Striated Heron, White-winged Fairy-wren, Calamanthus, Singing Honeyeater and Yellow White-eye; Pelican Point, at the southern end of the island, is worth visiting in summer for migratory waders such as Grey, Lesser Golden, Mongolian and Large Sand Plover, Ruddy Turnstone, Bar-tailed Godwit, and Red and Great Knot, while nearby Oyster Creek is a favoured haunt of the Brahminy Kite.

Fishing Boat Harbour and Pickles Point: Lie only a couple of kilometres south-west of the town centre. At low tide both places offer wader enthusiasts the chance to see a wide variety of migratory species, including all those listed for Pelican Point as well as Eastern Curlew, Whimbrel, Grey-tailed Tattler, Red-necked Stint, and Terek and Curlew Sandpiper. Fishing Boat Harbour is also good for terns — Gull-billed, Roseate and Lesser Crested are the ones to look out for.

Gascoyne River mouth: The tidal mudflats at the mouth of the Gascoyne River, a little to the north-west of Carnarvon town centre, are said to be excellent for waders, especially in September and April when large numbers pass through on migration. At

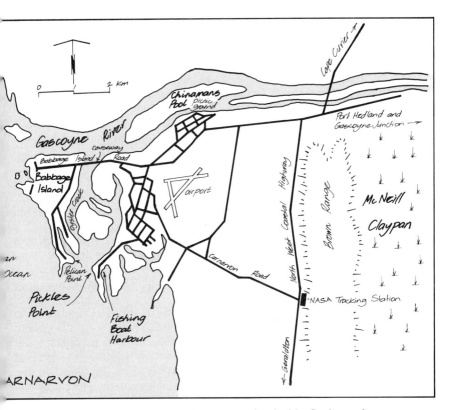

other times some species may be present in sizable flocks — for instance, in February 1981 more than ninety Long-toed Stints were observed in the area. You can get to the river mouth on foot from Babbage Island Road.

McNeill Claypan: Situated 8 km or so to the east of the town, just behind the NASA Tracking Station, this extensive seasonal swamp can be reached with ease from the North West Coastal Highway, which skirts its northern edge. At times the claypan supports a wide range of waterbirds, including Pacific Heron, Straw-necked Ibis, a variety of ducks, Buff-banded Rail, Baillon's, Australian and Spotless Crake, Black-tailed Native-hen, waders such as Red-kneed Dotterel and Little Curlew, and Whiskered Tern.

Chinamans Pool: Although it is one of the longest rivers in Western Australia, the Gascoyne is reduced to a series of pools during the dry season and Chinamans Pool, being permanent, has become a very popular picnic spot. Situated some 5 km north-east of Carnarvon town centre, it is usually a good place for waterbirds such as Hoary-headed and Australasian Grebe, Pied and Little Pied Cormorant, White-faced Heron, Glossy Ibis (rather rare),

Pacific Black and, more rarely, Pink-eared Duck, Grey Teal, Eurasian Coot, Red-kneed Dotterel, Black-fronted Plover, Black-winged Stilt, Common Sandpiper (summer), Greenshank (summer) and Whiskered Tern.

Miaboolia Beach: Is a sandy beach backed by dunes, situated approximately 20 km north of Carnarvon via the road to Cape Cuvier. The beach itself is favoured by Pied Oystercatcher, Large Sand (summer) and Red-capped Plover and Pacific Gull, while the open country bordering the road leading to the beach is worth looking over for bush birds such as Red-capped Robin, Crested Bellbird, Chiming Wedgebill, White-browed Babbler, White-winged Fairy-wren, Redthroat, Pied Honeyeater, Crimson Chat and Zebra Finch.

Lake MacLeod: This huge salt lake lies on the coast about 80 km north of Carnarvon via the road to Cape Cuvier. The lake, which is several metres below sea level, is usually predominantly dry, but in times of very high rainfall it may be flooded to a depth of about 1 m. The area is of considerable interest to naturalists because it is one of only two places in Western Australia where inland mangrove communities occur.

The most accessible part of the lake is the section adjacent to the salt works that have been established along its south-western shores, east of the Cape Cuvier road. If you inquire at the salt works office the manager may allow you to enter the area. If permission is refused, or if the salt works prove unproductive (the ponds at Lake MacLeod are high in salinity and therefore unattractive to waders and other waterbirds), there are two more places along the coast worth visiting: The Blowholes, just south of Point Quobba, which is a good spot for migratory waders such as Grey, Lesser Golden and Large Sand Plover, Ruddy Turnstone, Eastern Curlew, Whimbrel and Common Sandpiper, as well as for White-winged, Gull-billed, Caspian, Common, Roseate, Fairy, Crested and Lesser Crested Tern; and Cape Cuvier, about 30 km north of The Blowholes, which is a favoured breeding haunt of the White-bellied Sea-Eagle.

If you own a four-wheel-drive vehicle you may care to continue along the coast from Cape Cuvier to Cygnet Marsh. Situated on the edge of Lake MacLeod, 20 km or so east of Gnaraloo homestead, the marsh consists of a number of shallow lagoons fringed with mangroves, and with a small boat or canoe you could spend many hours exploring the area. Great Crested Grebe, Darter, Little Egret, Striated and Rufous Night Heron, Dusky Gerygone and Yellow White-eye are among the more unusual birds you can expect to see.

Rocky Pool: Lined with massive river red gums, and surrounded by mulga scrub, this deep, permanent freshwater pool is on the

Gascoyne River about 55 km east of Carnarvon. A popular picnicking spot, the pool itself is frequented by waterbirds such as grebes, Australian Pelican, Darter, cormorants, herons, egrets, Black Swan, ducks, Eurasian Coot and Black-fronted Plover, while the surrounding countryside holds a wide assortment of birds, including Whistling Kite, Brown Goshawk, Wedge-tailed and Little Eagle, Brown Falcon, Australian Kestrel, Little Button-quail, Australian Bustard, Banded Lapwing, Peaceful and Diamond Dove, Little Corella, Cockatiel, Budgerigar, Port Lincoln Ringneck, Mulga Parrot, Black-eared Cuckoo, Blue-winged Kookaburra, Crested Bellbird, Chiming Wedgebill, White-plumed Honeyeater, Zebra Finch, White-breasted, Masked and Black-faced Woodswallow, and Pied Butcherbird.

Rocky Pool can be reached via the road to Gascoyne Junction, which is unsealed but quite suitable for conventional cars except after heavy rain.

THE PILBARA

Covering an area considerably larger than the state of Victoria, the Pilbara is situated to the north of the Tropic of Capricorn and extends from the coast inland to the edge of the Great Sandy and Gibson Deserts. The region lies entirely within the arid zone, and most of it is regarded as desert or semi-desert; not surprisingly, it is a part of Western Australia sometimes given little attention by birdwatchers eager to get from Perth to the Kimberley and beyond. A few weeks spent touring the area should prove very rewarding, however, for contrary to what you might expect the Pilbara has a good deal to offer — two large and interesting national parks, Millstream-Chichester and Hamersley Range, some spectacular gorge and range scenery, and a rich and diverse avifauna.

Among the many birds that you can expect to find in the region are Spinifex Pigeon, Bourke's Parrot, Mangrove Robin, Mangrove Golden and White-breasted Whistler, Chiming Wedgebill, Cinnamon Quail-thrush, Spinifexbird, Rufous-crowned Emu-wren, Striated Grasswren, Redthroat, Dusky Gerygone, Slaty-backed Thornbill, Banded Whiteface, Black-tailed Treecreeper, Grey-headed, Grey, Black and Pied Honeyeater, Painted Firetail, Star Finch and Spotted Bowerbird. And who knows, while on your travels you may come across a Night Parrot! This celebrated nocturnal ground-dweller, perhaps Australia's most sought-after bird, has been reliably reported from only a handful of sites throughout the interior of the continent during the past fifty years or so. In 1979–80, however, a single parrot was seen near Meetheena homestead, about 130 km north-east of Nullagine, while some years earlier, in 1970, an observer found what could have been a Night Parrot's nest 16 km north-east of Balfour Downs homestead, which is situated about 180 km south-east of Nullagine. The day after the freshly built nest was discovered, four birds, thought to be Night Parrots, were flushed from spinifex some 110 km north-east of the homestead, near the Throssell Range. The chances of finding the parrot are extremely slim to say the least, but since the country to the east of Nullagine contains large areas of habitat that are apparently suitable for the bird, those prepared to search this part of the region thoroughly may be richly rewarded for their efforts. Be sure to have your camera ready, otherwise it is likely that nobody will believe you.

The Pilbara is famous for its immense deposits of iron ore, vast quantities of which are being mined at Shay Gap, Mt Goldsworthy, Mt Newman, Paraburdoo and Tom Price, transported to the coast by rail, then shipped overseas from Port Hedland and Dampier. The region is also noted for its intense summer heat. Marble Bar, south-east of Port Hedland, has the dubious distinction of being the hottest town in Australia: during one particularly blistering hot spell, which began on 31 October 1923, the temperature in the town reached the old century mark on 160 days in succession. As you might expect, average annual rainfall throughout the Pilbara is low, ranging from just 230 mm in the lower Ashburton River valley to little more than 400 mm on the highest parts of the Hamersley Range. Over much of the area rain falls mostly during the summer months, December to March.

Apart from spinifex, which forms dense, prickly hummocks that in places stretch for kilometre upon kilometre in every direction, the vegetation is generally sparse, although there are extensive tracts of mulga and eucalypt woodland south of the Fortescue River, as well as large stands of mangroves along the coast. In addition, many of the larger watercourses are lined with majestic river red gums, beautiful white-barked coolabahs and massive cadjeputs (tropical paperbarks), while at Millstream, on the Fortescue River, there is a shady green oasis where the graceful endemic Millstream palm (*Livistona alfredii*) grows alongside a chain of permanent crystal-clear pools connected by small streams and waterfalls.

Starting with Port Hedland in the north-east, the following are some of the best bird-watching sites in the Pilbara.

Port Hedland

Since the early 1960s, when the Pilbara's huge mineral reserves were first developed, Port Hedland has grown from a sleepy coastal township into a flourishing modern centre with a population of almost 13 000. Situated about 880 km north-east of Carnarvon via the North West Coastal Highway, it has a number of hotels and

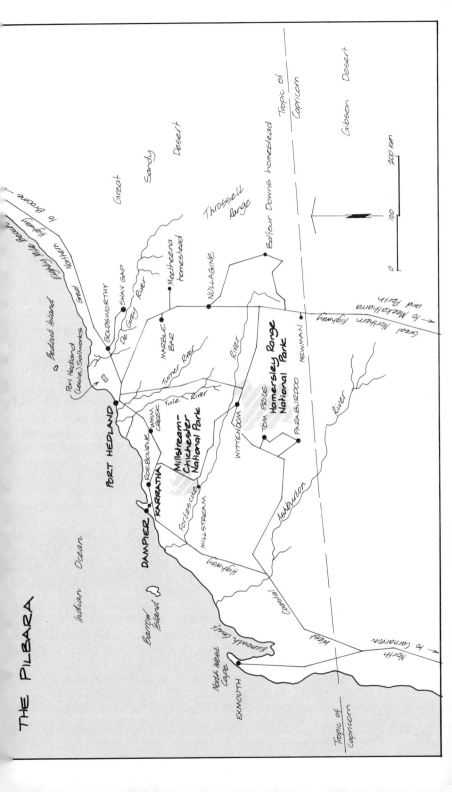

THE PILBARA

motels as well as several caravan parks. A few hours spent at one or more of the following localities, most of which are easy to reach, should produce at least a few exciting birds.

Port Hedland Sewage Works: Like most sewage ponds, especially those located in arid areas, the Port Hedland Sewage Works attract many waterbirds, notably migratory waders such as Ruddy Turnstone, Wood Sandpiper, Grey-tailed Tattler, Pin-tailed Snipe and Long-toed Stint, and waterfowl such as Grey Teal, Hardhead, and Pacific Black and Pink-eared Duck. Other species to look out for include Barn Swallow and Yellow Wagtail — both can often be found at the sewage ponds between November and March. The works are situated just off Cooke Point Road, about 1.5 km north of Wilson Street.

Port Hedland Racecourse and Sports Complex: This might seem an unlikely place to look for birds, but at high tide a fair assortment of waders can usually be seen roosting on the racecourse and the adjacent sports grounds. Oriental Plover and Little Curlew are two species that you can expect to find here, particularly at the beginning and end of summer. The racecourse and sports complex lie a little to the west of the sewage works, immediately north of Wilson Street.

Cemetery Beach: Migratory waders such as Mongolian and Large Sand Plover, Grey-tailed Tattler and Terek Sandpiper, along with Pied and Sooty Oystercatcher and terns like Gull-billed, Fairy and Lesser Crested, can frequently be found at Cemetery Beach, and indeed at many other coastal sites in the vicinity of the town centre. The beach is readily accessible from Wilson Street via McGregor Street or Cooke Point Road.

Finucane Island: Situated approximately 20 km west of Port Hedland town centre, and easily reached via a causeway, Finucane Island is another good place for migratory waders, including Grey and Lesser Golden Plover, Eastern Curlew, Whimbrel, Greenshank, Common, Terek, Sharp-tailed and Curlew Sandpiper, Bartailed Godwit, Red and Great Knot, and Red-necked Stint. The reef on the ocean side of the island is said to be one of the best areas for waders (it is also a haunt of the Eastern Reef Egret), while the island's sports ground is favoured by Little Curlews, which may be numerous in early and late summer.

En route to Finucane Island it is well worth stopping to explore the area adjacent to the causeway. At high tide waders such as Terek Sandpiper and Bar-tailed Godwit often congregate near the causeway, and Striated Heron, Bar-shouldered Dove, Collared Kingfisher, Mangrove Golden and White-breasted Whistler, Dusky Gerygone and Yellow White-eye occur in the mangroves nearby.

Port Hedland (Leslie) Saltworks: Not only are the Port Hedland Saltworks important to the prosperity of the town (the Leslie Salt

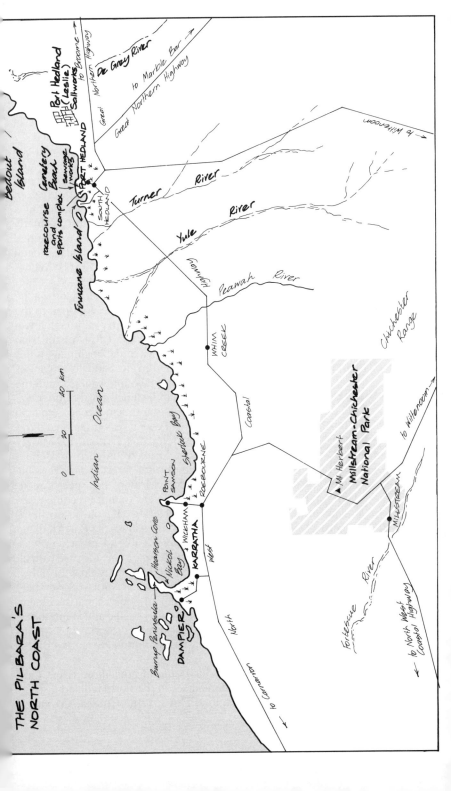

THE PILBARA'S
NORTH COAST

Indian Ocean

Bedout Island

Port Hedland
(Leslie) Saltworks
to Marble Bar
to Broome
Great Northern Highway

De Grey River

to Wittenoom

Cemetery Beach
Sewage Works
Racecourse and Sports complex
PORT HEDLAND
SOUTH HEDLAND

Finucane Island

Turner River

Yule River

Peawah River

Highway

Chichester Range

WHIM CREEK

Millstream-Chichester National Park

Coastal

▲ Mt Herbert

to Wittenoom

Sholdock Bay
POINT SAMSON
ROEBOURNE
WICKHAM

Hearson Cove
Nickol Bay
KARRATHA

Burrup Peninsula
DAMPIER

West

North

MILLSTREAM

Fortescue River

to North West Coastal Highway

to Carnarvon

0   20   40 km

Company exports something like two million tonnes of salt each year), they also provide ideal conditions for large numbers of waders and other waterbirds. Some idea of the importance of this area can be gained from the following figures. In November 1982 the saltworks held an estimated 60 000 waders, and surveys in recent years have revealed that some species congregate there in exceptionally large numbers. For instance, in March–April 1982 there were 500 Mongolian Plover, 130 Asian Dowitcher and 500 Broad-billed Sandpiper present; in November 1982 an estimated 1050 Oriental Plover and 500 Marsh Sandpiper were recorded; and in January 1986 no fewer than 24 Red-necked Phalarope were seen at the saltworks, to date the largest number ever recorded at a single location in Australia. Other waders of interest regularly sighted in the area include Grey and Lesser Golden Plover, Banded Stilt, Red-necked Avocet, Whimbrel, Redshank and Oriental Pratincole, while in March–April 1982 an estimated 15 000 White-winged Terns were present.

The saltworks lie some 35 km north-east of Port Hedland via the Great Northern Highway. Unfortunately they are not open to the public and visitors have little hope of gaining entry, although if you live in the Perth area it might pay to contact the Royal Australasian Ornithologists Union at the address shown at the beginning of this chapter. The union's wader studies group occasionally organises expeditions to the north-west coast to count waders, and the saltworks at Port Hedland are usually included on the itinerary.

Bedout Island: Is a small sandy cay in the Indian Ocean, about 90 km north-east of Port Hedland. If you own a seaworthy boat a trip to the island should prove most rewarding, for it is home to a variety of breeding seabirds, among them Masked and Brown Booby, Least Frigatebird, Sooty, Crested, Lesser Crested and possibly Roseate Tern, and Common Noddy. Most of the species mentioned can be seen about the island all year round; breeding takes place mainly between March and October. (If you do not have access to a boat and wish to go to Bedout Island, the Port Hedland Tourist Bureau in Wedge Street may be able to assist you.)

Yule River, Turner River and De Grey River: As is the case with all the region's rivers, the Yule, Turner and De Grey flow for only a short period each year. During the dry season (April to November) they are reduced to a string of permanent pools that attract many waterbirds, including Darter, cormorants, Pacific and White-faced Heron, Great and Little Egret, Black-necked Stork, ibis, spoonbills, ducks, Red-kneed Dotterel, Black-fronted Plover and Black-winged Stilt.

In the woodlands and forests bordering the three rivers (and some of the other large watercourses in the Port Hedland district) look for Peaceful and Diamond Dove, Little Corella, Cockatiel,

Budgerigar, Port Lincoln Ringneck, Pheasant Coucal, Blue-winged Kookaburra, Sacred Kingfisher, Rainbow Bee-eater, Black-tailed Treecreeper, Yellow-throated Miner, White-plumed and Brown Honeyeater, Red-browed Pardalote, Star Finch (especially where thickets of dragon trees and paperbarks occur) and White-breasted Woodswallow.

All three rivers are less than an hour's drive from Port Hedland. The North West Coastal Highway crosses the Turner River at a point some 35 km south-west of the town, while the Yule River crossing is about 30 km further on. To get to the De Grey River, which is said to be the best of the three for birds, simply head east from Port Hedland along the Great Northern Highway towards Broome; the highway crosses the river at a point some 90 km from the town. Though somewhat monotonous and rather uninviting, the wide, spinifex-covered plains in the vicinity of Port Hedland hold a number of interesting birds — Emu, Australian Bustard, Spotted Nightjar and White-winged Fairy-wren for example. And in summer, particularly during thunderstorms or ahead of tropical cyclones, Oriental Pratincoles sometimes turn up in flocks of thousands — the area between Whim Creek and the Peawah River is a good place to look for them.

Karratha and Dampier

Generally speaking the Karratha and Dampier districts are not as favourable for bird-watching as the Port Hedland area. Nonetheless the coast here is lined with extensive stands of mangroves where species such as Striated Heron, Bar-shouldered Dove, Collared Kingfisher, Mangrove Robin, Mangrove Golden and White-breasted Whistler, Dusky Gerygone and Yellow White-eye can be found, while in summer the wide tidal mudflats offer wader enthusiasts the chance to see a good variety of migratory birds, among them Eastern Curlew and Whimbrel. The rather rare Beach Thick-knee is a possibility at any time of the year.

Karratha, with two hotels and three caravan parks, is the best place to stay; Dampier has little by way of accommodation — just one hotel. Spots to visit while in the area include Hearson Cove on the Burrup Peninsula, some 10 km north-east of Dampier; the shores of Nickol Bay, a kilometre or so to the north of Karratha; and Point Samson, which lies about 60 km from Karratha and about 20 km north of Roebourne.

Millstream-Chichester National Park

Situated some 130 km south-east of Karratha, on the road leading from Roebourne to Wittenoom, this 199 710 ha reserve embraces an area of exceedingly rough country — a section of the Chichester Range where the rocky, spinifex-covered hills are cut by a number of large watercourses lined with tall gums. Mt Herbert, south of Roebourne, offers panoramic views over the virtually treeless red and brown ridges that dominate the western end of the park; from a bird-watcher's point of view, however, the most interesting part of the reserve is undoubtedly the area known as Millstream, which lies about 40 km south-west of Mt Herbert. Here the pockets of lush vegetation fringing the permanent, lily-clad pools along the Fortescue River attract many birds, among them the Black Bittern, a species seldom recorded elsewhere in the Pilbara.

Millstream can be reached readily enough by conventional vehicle from the Roebourne to Wittenoom road, but vehicular access to other sections of the national park is very limited. Camping is permitted at certain sites, some of which have toilets and barbecues; for further information about access to the reserve, and its facilities, contact the Western Australian Department of Conservation and Land Management, SGIO Building, Welcome Road, Karratha.

Hamersley Range National Park

Even more spectacular than Millstream-Chichester, and the better of the two reserves for bird-watching, the 617 606 ha Hamersley Range National Park is the second largest in Western Australia. It encompasses a vast tract of wild, dramatic countryside and is set deep in the rugged heart of the Pilbara. Within the reserve's boundaries are many of the state's highest peaks — Mt King (1035 m), Mt Bennett (1084 m), Mt Frederick (1176 m) and Mt Bruce (1235 m), to name just a few — as well as a maze of deep, sheer-sided canyons, some with walls more than 100 m high. The landscape is exceedingly harsh but incredibly beautiful — and the colours are truly magnificent, with the rich earthy browns, reds and oranges of the stony hills and ridges standing out vividly beneath a brilliant blue tropical sky, the golden-yellow spinifex of the hot, exposed hilltops providing a sharp contrast to the lush greenery of the cool, sheltered gorges.

Although a good deal of the Hamersley Range south of Mt Bruce is inaccessible, most of the area's more colourful and spectacular gorges can be reached from Wittenoom, a small township located just outside the national park's northern boundary. If you wish you can make your base at Wittenoom, which has a motel, hotel and caravan park as well as petrol stations and shops, and visit the gorges from there, or you can stay at one of the two main camping grounds within the national park. These are situated at Weano Gorge and Dales Gorge; both sites are accessible by conventional vehicle, and both have picnic tables, fireplaces and toilets. A detailed map covering the northern section of the reserve, together with a comprehensive bird list, can be obtained from the ranger's

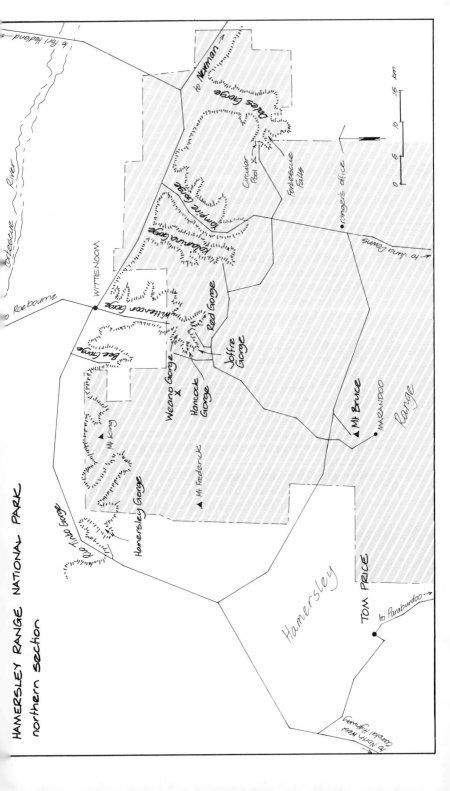

HAMERSLEY RANGE NATIONAL PARK
northern section

office, which is on the road to Juna Downs about 60 km south-east of Wittenoom.

More than 150 species of birds have been recorded from the Wittenoom area, and about 135 from the national park itself. Visits to the following localities, for sightseeing and walking as well as bird-watching, are highly recommended. (Some of the places mentioned lie outside the reserve, but are close enough to Wittenoom and the two main camping grounds for a day trip.)

Wittenoom Gorge: Probably the best known scenic attraction in the Pilbara, the mighty Wittenoom Gorge extends for 15 km or more into the Hamersley Range, south of Wittenoom township. A good road runs from the township nearly to the end of the gorge, providing ready access to Pyramid Pool, Cathedral Pool, Garden Pool, Magazine Pool, Club Pool and many other picturesque picnic spots. Birds that you are likely to see along the way include Pacific Heron, Rufous Night Heron, Whistling Kite, Wedge-tailed Eagle, Australian Hobby, Black-fronted Plover, Peaceful and Diamond Dove, Common Bronzewing, Spinifex Pigeon, Little Corella, Cockatiel, Budgerigar, Port Lincoln Ringneck, Blue-winged Kookaburra, Sacred Kingfisher, Rainbow Bee-eater, Black-faced Cuckoo-shrike, Grey Shrike-thrush, Variegated Fairy-wren, Weebill, Yellow-throated Miner, Grey-headed, White-plumed and Brown Honeyeater, Mistletoebird, Red-browed and Striated Pardalote, Painted Firetail, Zebra and possibly Star Finch, Spotted Bowerbird, Black-faced and Little Woodswallow, and Pied Butcherbird.

The best time of day to visit Wittenoom Gorge (and the other places listed) is early morning when the area is quiet and the birds are most active.

Yampire Gorge and Dales Gorge: Lie to the south-east of Wittenoom township and can be reached via the road to Newman. A visit to either place should produce most of the species listed for Wittenoom Gorge; to get to Yampire Gorge turn off the Newman road after about 24 km and head south into the Hamersley Range. Dales Gorge is also accessible via this route – it is situated about 60 km from Wittenoom township, some 20 km beyond Yampire Gorge. From the carpark at the head of Dales Gorge, walking tracks lead to Fortescue Falls and nearby Circular Pool.

Kalamina Gorge: Although picturesque, this gorge is not especially deep and is therefore a good place to go walking. It is located about 78 km from Wittenoom township via Yampire Gorge.

Red Gorge, Joffre Gorge, Hancock Gorge and Weano Gorge: From the parking area near the junction of these four tremendous canyons, a walking track runs along the narrow, rocky spine that separates Hancock Gorge from Weano Gorge to a lookout with frightening vertical drops on three sides. The view from the lookout is breathtaking, to put it mildly — if you have a head for heights a trip to the Red Gorge area should certainly find a place on your itinerary. To get there take the road from Wittenoom through Yampire Gorge; the lookout is approximately 100 km from the township.

Mt Bruce: Slightly lower than Mt Meharry (1245 m), which lies a little to the east of the national park and is the highest point in Western Australia, Mt Bruce is about 45 km south-west of the Red Gorge area. If you are feeling energetic you can follow the path that leads to the 1235 m summit of the mountain — the climb is not too strenuous, for Mt Bruce rises only a few hundred metres above the surrounding plateau, which itself is 700—1000 m above sea level.

Bee Gorge: Situated about 15 km west of Wittenoom township, south of the road to Tom Price, Bee Gorge is reputed to be one of the best spots in the area for Spinifexbird, Rufous-crowned Emu-wren and Striated Grasswren. All three species are elusive and usually difficult to detect, even when present in relatively large numbers, but a thorough search of the rocky, spinifex-covered slopes bordering the road leading into the gorge may produce at least one of the group.

Rio Tinto Gorge and Hamersley Gorge: Are located on the north-western boundary of the national park, some 40 to 50 km west of Wittenoom along the road to Tom Price. Both are good places to go walking and birding — most of the species listed for Wittenoom Gorge can be found in the area.

Hot and dry for much of the year, Hamersley Range National Park and the Wittenoom district are best explored in winter and early spring when the days are pleasantly warm, the nights cold but clear. The national park is situated about 290 km south of Port Hedland, and about 320 km south-east of Karratha.

Tom Price

The modern mining town of Tom Price, in the Hamersley Range some 130 km south-west of Wittenoom, warrants a mention not because the town itself is particularly inspiring, but because it is the best place in the region — perhaps even in Australia — for Grey Honeyeater. A somewhat drab though much sought-after species, the honeyeater can usually be found foraging in the foliage of river red gums around the town; you may, of course, be unlucky and not see the bird, but since Tom Price has a motel and caravan park it could be worthwhile staying there for a night while travelling from the coast to Wittenoom or vice versa.

Newman

One of the region's largest mining towns, with a population close to 5500, Newman is situated about 280 km south-east of Wittenoom, just off the Great Northern Highway. It has a motel and two caravan parks and could be used as a base for exploring the Night Parrot country to the east of the highway; more realistically, perhaps, some of the birds that you are likely to see in this part of the Pilbara are Spotted Harrier, Little Button-quail, Australian Bustard, Mulga and Bourke's Parrot, Spotted Nightjar, Red-backed Kingfisher, White-winged Triller, Red-capped and Hooded Robin, Rufous Whistler, Cinnamon Quail-thrush, Grey-crowned Babbler, Spinifexbird, Variegated and White-winged Fairy-wren, Striated Grasswren, Chestnut-rumped and Slaty-backed Thornbill, Banded Whiteface, Grey-headed, Black and Pied Honeyeater, Crimson and possibly Orange Chat, Painted Firetail, Zebra Finch, Spotted Bowerbird, Masked, Black-faced and Little Woodswallow, and Pied Butcherbird. Before you leave Newman, pay a visit to the town's sewage works where you could find something of interest — Wood, Common and Pectoral Sandpiper, and Long-toed Stint, are possibilities during the summer months.

THE KIMBERLEY

If you were to ask a group of bird-watchers to name the parts of Australia that they would most like to visit, the Kimberley would almost certainly be on all their lists. It is easy to see why, for this remote corner of the continent, regarded by many as Australia's last true frontier, has an alluring quality all its own. It is a region of great contrasts, an area where short wet summers give way to long dry winters, raging wet-season rivers become tranquil dry-season waterholes, towering coastal cliffs separate wide, mangrove-fringed mudflats, silvery waterfalls drop from rough, spinifex-covered plateaux into crystal-clear rock-pools lined with luxuriant tropical vegetation, and vertical-sided, flat-topped mountains rise abruptly from grassy plains dotted with huge, bottle-shaped baobab trees and termite mounds.

Then there are the birds, among them a host of sought-after species: Great-billed Heron, Black Bittern, Chestnut Rail, White-browed Crake, Partridge Pigeon, White-quilled Rock-Pigeon, Northern Rosella, Rainbow Pitta, Mangrove and White-browed Robin, Kimberley Flycatcher, White-breasted Whistler, Sandstone Shrike-thrush, Northern Fantail, Zitting Cisticola, Purple-crowned Fairy-wren, Black Grasswren, Dusky and Green-backed Gerygone, White-lined, Yellow-tinted, Bar-breasted, Rufous-throated, Banded and Red-headed Honeyeater, Yellow Chat, Yellow White-eye, Star, Crimson, Masked, Long-tailed and Gouldian Finch, Pictorella and Yellow-rumped Mannikin, Yellow Oriole and Great Bowerbird.

The Kimberley proper lies approximately north of a line drawn between Wyndham and Derby, but since most people travel to the

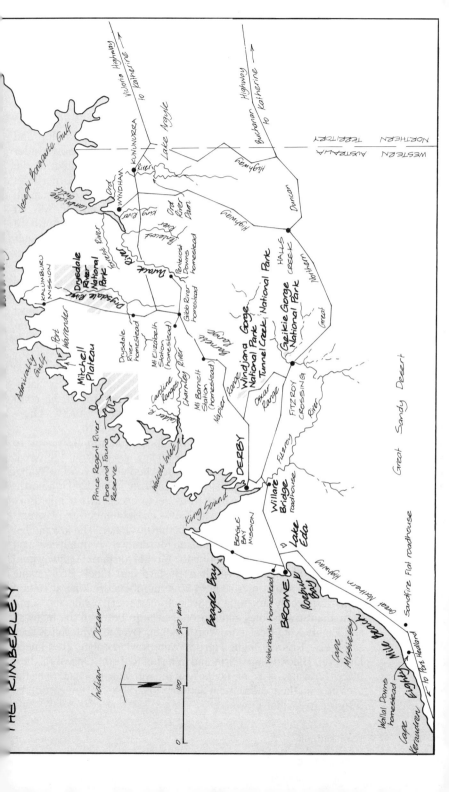

THE KIMBERLEY

region via either Broome or Kununurra this account includes some places to the south-west and some to the south-east. Our tour begins in the south-west, at Eighty Mile Beach.

Eighty Mile Beach

Until quite recently little was known about the distribution and numbers of waders in northern Australia because most wader surveys took place in the southern states — for example, at the Coorong in South Australia and Port Phillip Bay and Corner Inlet in Victoria. In the early 1980s, however, the Royal Australasian Ornithologists Union began a programme of aerial surveys and special expeditions to count waders along Australia's northern coastline, and during the past few years the importance of sites such as Eighty Mile Beach has become fully apparent. The figures speak for themselves. Surveys have revealed that the coast between Broome and Port Hedland regularly supports between half a million and a million waders during the summer months, making it the most important wader area in Australia and one of the most significant in the world. Many species occur in considerable numbers: in August–September 1981 the Eighty Mile Beach area alone held an estimated 2785 Large Sand Plover, 853 Oriental Plover, 371 Terek Sandpiper, 7300 Bar-tailed Godwit, 15 200 Red Knot, 21 800 Great Knot, 27 600 Red-necked Stint and 22 150 Curlew Sandpiper. Other species that regularly visit this section of the coast include Grey Plover, Ruddy Turnstone, Eastern Curlew, Grey-tailed Tattler, Greenshank and Black-tailed Godwit.

Eighty Mile Beach extends from Cape Keraudren in the west to Cape Missiessy in the east, and is well signposted from the Great Northern Highway. It is most easily reached via the road to Wallal Downs homestead, which leaves the highway about 250 km north-east of Port Hedland. Apart from being excellent for migratory waders — numbers reach a peak between September and November — the area has much to offer the bird-watcher. The low pindan woodlands (pindan is the local name for scrubby savannah country) and open grassy plains bordering the Great Northern Highway hold interesting birds like Australian Bustard and Flock Bronzewing (the latter is sometimes seen in large numbers drinking at station dams, especially an hour or so before sunset), while the semi-permanent waterholes and seasonal swamps between the highway and Eighty Mile Beach are worth looking over for waterbirds such as egrets, Rufous Night Heron, waterfowl, Brolga, Red-kneed Dotterel, Black-winged Stilt and Whiskered Tern. One of the best places for waterbirds, particularly in the wet season, is said to be the area around the roadhouse at Sandfire Flat, about 50 km east of the turn-off to Wallal Downs.

Broome

Broome, a thriving tropical centre of some four thousand inhabitants and once the home of the largest pearling-lugger fleet in the world, is situated on the coast about 620 km north-east of Port Hedland. It makes a handy base, being located in the heart of good birding country and having a wide range of accommodation that includes motels, hotels and caravan parks. And the town may soon become the site of Australia's first tropical bird observatory – the Royal Australasian Ornithologists Union has plans to build one at Fall Point, on the shores of Roebuck Bay. For further information about the proposed observatory contact the RAOU in Perth or Melbourne.

Even if you can only manage a stay of about a day or so in Broome, you should be able to find a wide variety of interesting birds within a short distance of the town. Red-winged Parrots, Red-backed Fairy-wrens, White-throated Gerygones, Black-chinned Honeyeaters and a host of other bush birds occur in the extensive pindan woodlands nearby; during the wet season masses of Brolgas and Little Curlews can usually be seen on the Roebuck Plains, a little to the east of Broome, while large numbers of Australian Pratincoles turn up in winter; Mangrove Robins, Mangrove Golden and White-breasted Whistlers, Broad-billed Flycatchers, Dusky and Mangrove Gerygones, and Red-headed Honeyeaters can be found in patches of mangroves and paperbark thickets along the coast; and raptors such as Ospreys, Brahminy Kites and White-bellied Sea-Eagles, together with Brown Boobies, Least Frigate-birds, and White-winged (autumn), Gull-billed and Lesser Crested Terns, can often be observed patrolling the shoreline.

For those with more time to spare, visits to the following spots are highly recommended. Most of the places mentioned can be reached by conventional vehicle, except of course during the wet season; nevertheless it would be wise to inquire about road conditions at the police station in Broome before setting out.

Roebuck Bay: Like Eighty Mile Beach, Roebuck Bay is one of the most significant wader sites in Australia. In recent years surveys have shown that the area regularly supports more than 50 000 waders (for example, in March 1985 an estimated 87 000 birds were present), with some species occurring in large numbers: 2300 Large Sand Plover, 300 Oriental Plover, 850 Eastern Curlew, 850 Grey-tailed Tattler, 1000 Black-tailed Godwit, 10 000 Bar-tailed Godwit, 4200 Red Knot and 17 000 Great Knot were recorded in August–September 1981. Among the other species regularly making use of the bay are Grey Plover, Ruddy Turnstone, Whimbrel, Green-shank, Terek Sandpiper and Sanderling, while much sought-after waders such as Redshank and Asian Dowitcher visit the area from time to time.

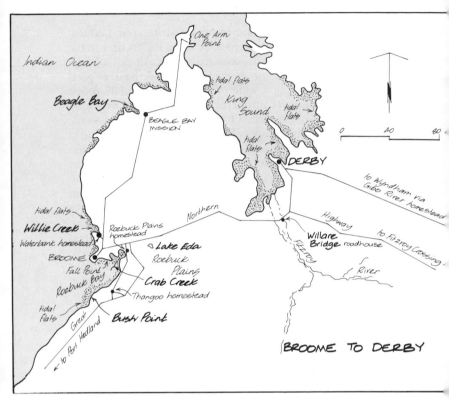

Roebuck Bay lies just to the south of Broome and is accessible via several tracks, one of which leads from Roebuck Plains homestead southwards to Thangoo homestead. The waders are most readily observed at high tide, September to April being the best time of year for migratory species.

Crab Creek: Is situated about 20 km south-east of Broome, between Roebuck Plains homestead and the shores of Roebuck Bay (ask locally for precise directions). The creek is reputed to be a very good place for waders, especially at high tide, while a trek across the adjacent grassy plains may produce something special – an Eastern Grass Owl was flushed from grassland near Crab Creek in September 1981.

Bush Point: Another excellent wader spot, at times supporting concentrations of more than fifty thousand birds, Bush Point is situated about 60 km south of Broome via Thangoo homestead. If you wish to go there you should call at the homestead and ask the station manager for permission to enter the area.

Lake Eda: Lies some 60 km east of Broome, approximately 10 km south of the Great Northern Highway (again, seek precise directions locally). Depending on conditions, a trip to the lake could prove very fruitful; some interesting birds have been recorded from the area over the past few years, among them Little and Intermediate Egret, Glossy Ibis, Garganey, Black Falcon and Yellow Chat.

Willie Creek: Is situated on the coast about 30 km north of Broome via the track to Waterbank homestead, and is a favoured haunt of the Beach Thick-knee.

Beagle Bay: If you do not find a Beach Thick-knee at Willie Creek, it may be worth travelling a further 100 km or so along the coast to Beagle Bay. Among the other noteworthy birds to look for here are Striated Heron and Black Bittern — and keep an eye open for Gouldian Finches along the track between Waterbank homestead and Beagle Bay Mission.

Willare Bridge

Situated on the Great Northern Highway about 170 km east of Broome, the roadhouse at Willare Bridge has a small caravan park conveniently located close to a patch of monsoon forest. The forest and adjacent floodplain provide good birding — Brush Cuckoo (a wet-season visitor), Barking Owl, Blue-winged Kookaburra, Dollarbird (quite plentiful in the wet season), Leaden Flycatcher, Grey-crowned Babbler, Silver-crowned Friarbird, Black-chinned Honeyeater and Great Bowerbird are among the species that you can expect to see.

Derby

Gateway to the western Kimberley, Derby has a population of almost three thousand and is situated on the shores of King Sound, approximately 230 km north-east of Broome via the Great Northern Highway. It has several hotels and a caravan park, making it an ideal place to stay while exploring the surrounding countryside.

Birds to look out for around the town include two interesting migrants, Barn Swallow and Yellow Wagtail, both of which visit the area regularly during the summer months (November to March). And a trip to the mangroves in the vicinity of Derby wharf should result in a few notable sightings — Collared Kingfisher, Mangrove Robin, White-breasted Whistler, Dusky and Mangrove Gerygone, Red-headed Honeyeater and Yellow White-eye for example. One of the region's really special birds, the Yellow Chat, is frequently seen on the tidal flats near the town and is certainly worth pursuing.

Windjana Gorge, Tunnel Creek and Geikie Gorge National Parks

Well known for their spectacular, rugged scenery, these three small reserves lie to the south-east of Derby, between the Great Northern Highway and the Gibb River road.

Windjana Gorge National Park (2134 ha):   Encompassing a section of the Napier Range, where the Lennard River has cut a narrow, exceedingly picturesque canyon some 4 km long and up to 100 m deep, Windjana Gorge National Park is of great geological significance because it contains an ancient fossilised reef complex regarded as one of the best of its type in the world. Weathering of what was once a living coral reef, formed hundreds of millions of years ago when a shallow tropical sea covered much of the area, has produced the fantastically sculptured limestone walls for which Windjana Gorge is justly famous, and created countless tunnels and caves, some richly decorated with Aboriginal rock paintings.

The national park is also noted for its abundant wildlife. Noisy, gregarious flying foxes leave their colonies just before dusk, filling the still evening air with their eerie shrieks, while during the day freshwater crocodiles can be seen gliding effortlessly — and a little menacingly, though they are said to be harmless! — through the placid, dry-season pools within the gorge. There are birds too, of course — among them Rufous Night Heron, Black Bittern, Black-necked Stork, Black-breasted Buzzard, Red-tailed Black-Cockatoo, Little Corella, Barking Owl, Azure Kingfisher, Blue-winged Kookaburra, Sandstone Shrike-thrush, Green-backed Gerygone (Windjana Gorge is one of the few readily accessible places in the Kimberley where this species can be found), Black-tailed Treecreeper, White-gaped, Yellow-tinted, Brown and Rufous-throated Honeyeater, Double-barred and Long-tailed Finch, Pictorella Mannikin, Figbird, Great Bowerbird and White-breasted Woodswallow.

Windjana Gorge is about 150 km from Derby via the Gibb River road. There is a small camping ground, with toilets and cold-water showers, just inside the reserve's western boundary; the camping area is closed during the wet season, however, because the park may be cut off by floodwaters for weeks at a time.

Tunnel Creek National Park (91 ha):   Situated about 180 km southeast of Derby, between Windjana Gorge and Geikie Gorge, this reserve features a remarkable geological formation — a 750 m long cave-like tunnel cut by Tunnel Creek as it flows through the limestone Napier Range. With the aid of a powerful torch you can walk from one end of the tunnel to the other; but be prepared — the permanent pools within it are inhabited by freshwater crocodiles, and its walls are home to large numbers of bats. Near the centre of the tunnel the roof has collapsed, exposing a long shaft that extends right through to the top of the range. Aboriginal paintings can be seen near one of the tunnel entrances, and in places the roof is festooned with stalactites.

The park is inaccessible during the wet season, and there are no facilities for visitors.

Geikie Gorge National Park (3136 ha): Without doubt the most popular reserve in the region, Geikie Gorge lies some 320 km south-east of Derby via the Gibb River road and Tunnel Creek, or about 285 km from the town via the Great Northern Highway and Fitzroy Crossing. Like Windjana Gorge and Tunnel Creek, the reserve is not accessible during the wet season.

Geikie Gorge is a beautiful park featuring a wide, 14 km long canyon where, during the winter months, the Fitzroy River flows placidly between multicoloured cliffs up to 30 m high. The long, dark pools of the dry season are fringed with dense vegetation, including cadjeputs (tropical paperbarks), river red gums, native figs, pandanus, Leichhardt trees and freshwater mangroves. Among the more notable birds to watch out for are Darter, Black Bittern, Bar-shouldered Dove, Red-winged Parrot, Pheasant Coucal, Azure Kingfisher, White-browed Robin, Sandstone Shrike-thrush, Northern Fantail, Purple-crowned Fairy-wren (though now rarely recorded along the Fitzroy River, where it was once quite plentiful, this species is still seen on occasions at Geikie Gorge — a party of four was sighted there in July 1986), White-gaped, Yellow-tinted, White-throated and Rufous-throated Honeyeater, Red-browed Pardalote, Crimson and Double-barred Finch, and Great Bowerbird.

A cool, shady oasis that provides refuge for both people and birds, Geikie Gorge is a very pleasant place to rest for a few days while travelling through the Kimberley. There is an attractive camping ground, with toilets, showers and fireplaces, near the entrance to the gorge; those not wishing to stay in the national park will find motel accommodation, as well as two caravan parks, at Fitzroy Crossing, some 20 km to the south-west. At least part of the reserve can be readily explored on foot (there is a walking track leading from the camping area along the west bank of the Fitzroy River) but the magnificent scenery is best appreciated from the water. Ranger-guided boat tours are available daily throughout the dry season — a most relaxing way to view the gorge and many of its inhabitants, notably the freshwater crocodiles that bask in the warm winter sunshine at the river's edge.

The Kimberley proper

The Kimberley proper — that is, the area to the north of the Gibb River road linking Derby with Wyndham — is exceedingly rugged and remote. There are few vehicle tracks and only a handful of settlements in the northern Kimberley ranges; despite this it is well worth making the effort to get to this part of the region for it is the home of a wide assortment of sought-after birds, among them the very handsome Black Grasswren, a species found nowhere else in Australia.

Although a four-wheel-drive vehicle would be a distinct advantage, particularly if you want to search for the Black Grasswren, those with conventional vehicles should be able to get from Derby to Wyndham via the Gibb River road since this route, though mostly unsealed, is usually in quite good condition during the dry season (April to November), except for the 280 km section between Gibb River homestead and the Great Northern Highway, south of Wyndham. (This section may be extremely rough in places unless maintenance has just been carried out.) If you are contemplating the trip, with or without a four-wheel-drive, remember that it is a long way from Derby to Wyndham — about 720 km. Petrol and basic food supplies can usually be obtained at Mt Barnett Station, approximately 310 km north-east of Derby, but you should of course carry ample fuel, food and water, as well as an up-to-date map and a range of spare parts (including tyres).

If the foregoing comments haven't dampened your enthusiasm, you can look forward to an exciting journey along the Gibb River road — stops at the following localities should prove enjoyable and ornithologically rewarding. One last piece of advice — before setting out call at the police station in Derby, or Wyndham if approaching from the east, and glean what information you can about the state of the road.

Lennard River Gorge: Is located a few kilometres south of the Gibb River road, about 190 km from Derby. The 5 km long gorge makes an ideal overnight camping spot — a waterfall, just north of the entrance, feeds a small pool where you can enjoy a refreshing dip at the end of the day. The track leading to the gorge is rather rough, however, and those with conventional vehicles may not be able to reach it.

Adcock Gorge: Is another pleasant place to camp, being the site of a small waterfall and freshwater pool. The gorge lies some 270 km north-east of Derby, just south of the Gibb River road, and although not quite so attractive as Lennard River Gorge, it has the advantage of being readily accessible by conventional vehicle.

Mt Barnett Station: An area of cool, deep waterholes, sparkling cascades, and small but very scenic river gorges, Mt Barnett Station is situated on the Gibb River road about 40 km north-east of Adcock Gorge. There are numerous places to camp along this section of the road — Galvans Gorge, Manning Gorge and Barnett River Gorge being among the more accessible.

Since it is relatively easy to reach, the Mt Barnett area attracts bird-watchers from all over Australia, and glowing accounts of its avifauna appear regularly in ornithological club newsletters throughout the country. Diamond Dove, White-quilled Rock-Pigeon, Red-tailed Black-Cockatoo, Red-collared and Varied Lorikeet, Northern Rosella, White-bellied Cuckoo-shrike, White-winged Triller, Sandstone Shrike-thrush, Variegated Fairy-wren, Black-tailed Treecreeper, Silver-crowned and Little Friarbird, Blue-faced, White-gaped, Yellow-tinted, Bar-breasted, Rufous-throated and Banded Honeyeater, Crimson, Masked and Long-tailed Finch, Olive-backed Oriole, Figbird and Pied Butcherbird are just some of the many species that you can expect to see.

The Munja Track: Strictly for four-wheel-drives only, this narrow track runs from Mt Elizabeth Station westwards through the Caroline Ranges to Walcott Inlet. The 170 km trip is definitely not for the fainthearted — en route there are numerous steep-sided creeks to negotiate, and in places the winding track is extremely rough. But for the well-equipped, adventurous traveller the rewards are great indeed: the countryside is spectacular, the views magnificent, and the birdlife rich and diverse. If the idea of passing through territory seldom visited by Europeans appeals to you, then the Munja Track is what you are looking for. Before undertaking the journey, however, be sure to call at the homestead on Mt Elizabeth Station and seek precise directions to Walcott Inlet — this part of the Kimberley is lonely in the extreme.

Between Mt Elizabeth Station and the coast there is much to see — lily-covered lagoons, colourful gorges harbouring Aboriginal rock paintings, and a wealth of unusual plants — as well as plenty of birds to look out for: Pacific Baza, Black-breasted Buzzard, Spotted Harrier, Black and Peregrine Falcon, Red-backed and Chestnut-backed Button-quail, Australian Bustard, Bush Thick-knee, Partridge Pigeon, White-quilled Rock-Pigeon, Northern Rosella, Varied Triller, White-browed Robin, Northern Fantail, Variegated Fairy-wren, Black-tailed Treecreeper, Silver-crowned and Little Friarbird, Grey-fronted, Bar-breasted and Banded Honeyeater, Masked, Long-tailed and Gouldian Finch, and White-breasted and Little Woodswallow.

Those wishing to search for the northern Kimberley's star attraction, the Black Grasswren, should stay a night or two at Bachsten Gorge in the Caroline Ranges, on the southern edge of the Prince Regent River Flora and Fauna Reserve. The grasswren has been recorded in the vicinity of the gorge on a number of occasions in recent years; you will, however, need to ask at Mt Elizabeth homestead for directions to this spot because it is not shown on most maps.

From the Caroline Ranges the Munja Track leads down to the shores of Walcott Inlet, where the Calder and Charnley Rivers meet the waters of the Indian Ocean. Here, in the shallow, reed-fringed swamps bordering the inlet, you should have little difficulty finding a wide variety of birds — herons, egrets, Black-necked Storks, ibis, spoonbills, Magpie Geese, Wandering and Plumed Whistling-Ducks, Brolgas and waders, as well as Yellow Chats,

Star Finches and Pictorella Mannikins.

The Mitchell Plateau: Situated in the far north of the region, overlooking Port Warrender and Admiralty Gulf, the Mitchell Plateau offers some of the best bird-watching in the Kimberley. And unlike Walcott Inlet, the plateau is not too difficult to reach — providing, that is, you have a four-wheel-drive vehicle and a good map to guide you. To get there head north from Gibb River homestead to Drysdale River homestead, a distance of 120 km or so, then continue northwards along the track towards Kalumburu Mission. About 120 km from Drysdale River homestead there is a well-used route leading west then north-west to the mining camp that has been established near the airstrip on the Mitchell Plateau. There is no shortage of camping spots in the area, as well as plenty of places worth exploring for birds. Visits to the following, all of which are reasonably easy to reach by vehicle or on foot, are highly recommended.

Airfield Swamp: Covering an area of about 80 ha, this large swamp lies some 5 km north of the mining camp. It is surrounded by tall, dense vegetation, and usually holds water through to about the middle of the dry season. Among the more noteworthy birds that have been recorded there are Pacific Heron, Green Pygmy-Goose, Brolga, Swinhoe's Snipe, Tawny Grassbird, Golden-headed Cisticola and Chestnut-breasted Mannikin.

Surveyors Pool: Set in an area of heavily dissected sandstone clothed with low woodland and dense spinifex, Surveyors Pool is located about 25 to 30 km north-west of the mining camp. It is *the* place for Black Grasswrens — if you can't find them here it's time to hang up your binoculars!

Crystal Creek: Lies 15 to 20 km north-east of Surveyors Pool, on the western side of Port Warrender. Over much of its length the creek is fringed with tall melaleucas interspersed with dense stands of pandanus, while extensive areas of mangroves occur at its mouth. Birds to look for along the creek edge include Brown Quail, Pheasant Coucal, Azure Kingfisher, White-bellied Cuckoo-shrike, Varied Triller, White-browed Robin, Red-backed Fairy-wren, White-lined, White-gaped, Yellow-tinted, Bar-breasted and Banded Honeyeater, Crimson and Long-tailed Finch, and Great Bowerbird. Mangrove-dwellers such as Mangrove Robin, Shining Flycatcher, Large-billed Gerygone, Red-headed Honeyeater and Yellow White-eye can be found at the creek mouth, south-west of Crystal Head.

Walsh Point: Situated on the western shores of Port Warrender, between the mining camp and Crystal Head, Walsh Point and the coast south to the Lawley River estuary are excellent for mangrove birds, notably Great-billed and Striated Heron, Chest-

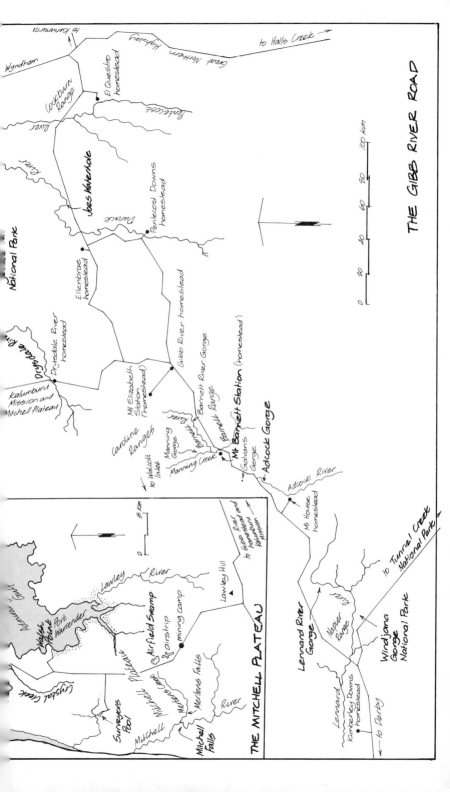

THE GIBB RIVER ROAD

THE MITCHELL PLATEAU

nut Rail, Mangrove Robin, Little Shrike-thrush, Kimberley, Broad-billed and Shining Flycatcher, Mangrove Golden Whistler, Red-headed Honeyeater and Yellow White-eye.

Mitchell Falls: Located on the western edge of the plateau, 15 km or so from the mining camp, these beautiful falls are considered to be among the finest in Australia. The marvellous scenery alone makes a trip to this spot worthwhile. As a bonus the surrounding precipitous hills, strewn with rocks and boulders, hold a host of interesting birds, including Black Grasswren and White-lined Honeyeater, while the pockets of dense vegetation in the vicinity of the falls (and at nearby Mertens Falls) support species like Yellow Oriole, Figbird and Spangled Drongo.

While excursions to the places mentioned are essential if you want to see a wide range of species, it is not necessary to travel more than a few kilometres from the mining camp in order to enjoy good birding. The open grassy woodlands that cover much of the central plateau provide habitat for a large number of birds, among them Chestnut-backed Button-quail, Australian Bustard, Part-ridge Pigeon, Northern Rosella, Spotted Nightjar and a variety of honeyeaters and finches, while the patches of luxuriant vine forest around the edge of the plateau are favoured by Orange-footed Scrubfowl, Torresian Imperial-Pigeon, Bar-shouldered and Em-erald Dove, Rufous Owl, Rainbow Pitta, Cicadabird, Rufous and Northern Fantail, Green-backed Gerygone and Yellow Oriole. And raptor buffs should have a field day – some twenty species have been recorded from the area, including such gems as Pacific Baza, Square-tailed Kite, Black-breasted Buzzard, Grey Goshawk and Peregrine Falcon. The very rare Red Goshawk is a remote possibility.

Drysdale River National Park (435 591 ha): Centred on the Drys-dale River, this huge, remote, virtually inaccessible reserve pro-tects a vast tract of rugged sandstone country some 120 km or so to the east of the Mitchell Plateau. It contains spectacular gorges and waterfalls, and is dominated by savannah woodland interspersed with small areas of lush vine forest. The Carson Escarpment, which lies along the reserve's western boundary, can be reached by four-wheel-drive vehicle from the Gibb River homestead to Kalumburu Mission track; however, if you wish to enter the reserve you must obtain a permit from the Western Australian Department of Conservation and Land Management in Kununurra, Karratha or Perth. As you might expect, there are no facilities for visitors.

Drysdale River crossing: This most attractive camping spot offers excellent birding, particularly for those unable – or unwilling – to venture too far from the Gibb River road. The banks of the river are lined with dense stands of pandanus, a habitat much favoured by the gorgeous Purple-crowned Fairy-wren (the main avian attraction here). To get to this section of the Drysdale River, head north along the track from Gibb River homestead towards Kalumburu Mission; the track crosses the river just a few kilometres beyond Drysdale River homestead.

Durack River crossing: Another good place to stay for the night, the Durack River crossing is on the Gibb River road some 130 km north-east of Gibb River homestead. In the evening, listen for the distinctive, dog-like 'wook-wook' calls of Barking Owls as you sit by the campfire.

Joes Waterhole: Though somewhat spoilt as a result of receiving too many visitors, this large, permanent pool on the Durack River offers good fishing and birding. Among the many species that can usually be found in the vicinity of the waterhole are Darter, White-bellied Sea-Eagle, Masked Lapwing, Black-fronted Plover, Peaceful and Diamond Dove, White-quilled Rock-Pigeon, Spinifex Pigeon, Cockatiel, Budgerigar, White-winged Triller, Restless Flycatcher, Little Friarbird, Grey-fronted, Yellow-tinted and Rufous-throated Honeyeater, Crimson, Double-barred, Masked, Long-tailed and Gouldian Finch, Pictorella and Chestnut-breasted Mannikin, and Black-faced Woodswallow.

Joes Waterhole is about a kilometre north of the Gibb River road, some 160 km north-east of Gibb River homestead.

Pentecost River crossing: Situated a little to the west of the incredibly lovely Cockburn Range, about 220 km along the road from Gibb River homestead and less than 60 km from the sealed Great Northern Highway, the Pentecost River crossing would make a good alternative camping spot if Joes Waterhole is too crowded.

Wyndham

Wyndham is not one of the far north's more colourful centres, but its petrol stations, shopping centre, hotel and caravan park certainly make a welcome sight if you arrive from Derby via the Gibb River road. The town is situated on the eastern edge of the Kimberley, where five great rivers — the Ord, King, Pentecost, Durack and Forrest — enter Cambridge Gulf. Although there are no national parks nearby, there are a number of rewarding birding areas in the district as well as several well-known tourist spots.

Five Rivers Lookout: As its name suggests this lookout, in the Bastion Range just a few kilometres from the town centre via Dulverton Street, provides panoramic views over Cambridge Gulf and the ruggedly beautiful countryside surrounding Wyndham. Take your camera and go there at sunset when the wide waters of the gulf are tinged with gold — an unforgettable sight. Barbecue facilities are provided at the lookout; the road leading to it passes through an area of rough red rocks where Spinifex Pigeons are common.

Three Mile Valley: Is the site of a pleasant picnic ground, reached via a track that branches off the road to Five Rivers Lookout. Two walking trials, the Jump Up Trail and Upland Trail, lead from the picnic area uphill towards the lookout, while a third, the Valley Trail, runs eastwards into a small gorge containing several clear freshwater pools.

Blood Drain: So called because it carries offal from the Wyndham meatworks to the sea, Blood Drain has become a popular tourist attraction on account of the large number of saltwater crocodiles that congregate near its mouth to feed on the easy pickings. If you felt a little intimidated when you first encountered the freshwater variety, wait until you meet one of these 5 m specimens for the first time!

On a lighter note, the shores of Cambridge Gulf adjacent to the meatworks support large stands of mangroves where birds such as Mangrove Robin, Rufous Fantail, Mangrove Gerygone and Yellow White-eye can be found; Black Kites are plentiful in the area; and White-bellied Sea-Eagles are often to be seen in the vicinity of Wyndham wharf, where at least one pair has built a nest.

The meatworks and wharf are about 5 km north-west of the town centre.

Moochalabra Dam: Constructed in 1971 to provide Wyndham with an assured water supply, this dam lies to the west of the Erskine Range, some 25 km south of the town centre via the King River road. Readily accessible by conventional vehicle, it is a particularly good place for birds — Peaceful and Bar-shouldered Doves, Pheasant Coucals, Blue-winged Kookaburras, White-bellied Cuckoo-shrikes, Yellow-tinted and Brown Honeyeaters, together with a number of other species, can be found around the margins of the dam; White-quilled Rock-Pigeons inhabit the rocky slopes of the nearby Erskine Range; and Brolgas, Australian Bustards and Zebra, Double-barred, Masked and Long-tailed Finches occur in the open country bordering the King River road.

Marlgu Billabong: The swamps and lily-clad lagoons to the east of the Great Northern Highway leading into Wyndham, especially those in the vicinity of Marlgu Billabong, offer waterbird devotees the chance to see enormous flocks of birds, including Australian Pelicans, Darters, cormorants, herons, egrets, Black-necked Storks, ibis, spoonbills, Brolgas, and waterfowl such as Magpie Geese, Wandering and Plumed Whistling-Ducks, Radjah Shelducks and Green Pygmy-Geese. And wader-watchers should wipe the Kimberley dust off their binoculars — at the beginning and end of the wet season Little Curlew and Oriental Pratincole turn up in tens of thousands along with smaller numbers of other species,

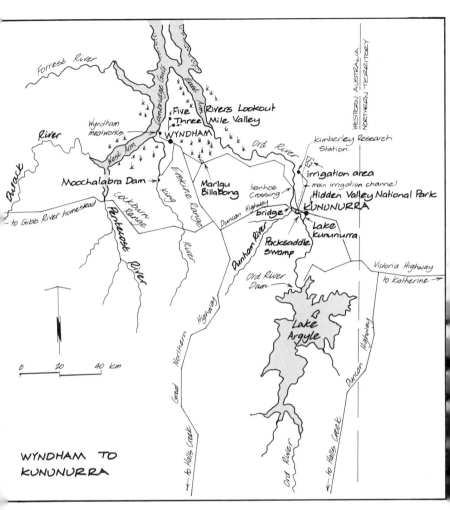

Map labels:
Forrest River
Cambridge Gulf
West Arm
East Arm
Five Rivers Lookout
Three Mile Valley
WYNDHAM
Wyndham meatworks
River
Durack River
Moochalabra Dam
— to Gibb River homestead
Cockburn Range
Pentecost River
King River
Erskine Range
Marlgu Billabong
Ord River
Ivanhoe Crossing
Duncan Highway
bridge
Kimberley Research Station
irrigation area
main irrigation channel
Hidden Valley National Park
KUNUNURRA
Lake Kununurra
Packsaddle Swamp
Dunham River
Ord River Dam
Victoria Highway
to Katherine
Lake Argyle
Great Northern Highway
Duncan Highway
Ord River
to Halls Creek
to Halls Creek
WESTERN AUSTRALIA / NORTHERN TERRITORY
0   20   40 km

WYNDHAM TO KUNUNURRA

notably Swinhoe's Snipe, Wood and Pectoral Sandpiper, and Black-tailed Godwit. The secretive Painted Snipe, a species rarely seen in Western Australia, has been recorded in the area on at least one occasion during the past few years and could be a regular visitor.

Marlgu Billabong lies some 15 to 20 km south-east of Wyndham and can be easily reached from the Great Northern Highway. (Note that you should take great care when driving on tracks away from the highway; if wet, the blacksoil plains surrounding the billabong are extremely treacherous, and should you become bogged you will have considerable difficulty getting out.) Though at its best from December through to about May or June, when

Western Australia 447

waterbirds are usually present in vast numbers, the area is worth visiting even late in the dry season since there is always a chance of finding something special – Flock Bronzewings, Zitting Cisticolas or Yellow Chats perhaps.

Kununurra

Situated in the heart of the Ord River irrigation district, about 100 km south-east of Wyndham, Kununurra is the last town before the Northern Territory border and, with petrol stations, shops, motels, hotels and four caravan parks, makes a convenient base from which to conduct sorties into the surrounding countryside. Trips to the following localities should provide many enjoyable hours of birding, and should result in at least a few new sightings.

Hidden Valley National Park (1817 ha): Located on the north-eastern outskirts of Kununurra, 3 km or so from the town centre, this small reserve offers birders approaching the Kimberley from the east a taste of what is to come. The rough red sandstone hills and valleys encompassed by the park are home to a variety of northern specialities, among them White-quilled Rock-Pigeon and Sandstone Shrike-thrush. Camping is not permitted and there are no facilities for visitors, although there are a few unmarked walking tracks leading from the access road into the adjacent hills.

Lake Kununurra: There are two caravan parks on the shores of this lake, which is situated a short distance from the town centre, just south of the Duncan Highway. An hour or two spent walking around the edge of the lake, or along the banks of the main irrigation channel that runs northwards towards the coast (the channel can be reached via the road to Ivanhoe Crossing), should produce a wide assortment of waterbirds, including Darter, cormorants, Pacific, White-faced and Pied Heron, Cattle, Great, Little and Intermediate Egret, Rufous Night Heron, Black Bittern, Black-necked Stork, Glossy, Sacred and Straw-necked Ibis, Royal and Yellow-billed Spoonbill, Magpie Goose, Radjah Shelduck, Pink-eared Duck, Hardhead, Green Pygmy-Goose, White-browed Crake (often seen in the vicinity of Kona Caravan Park), Brolga, Comb-crested Jacana (Lake Kununurra is the best place in Western Australia for this species – Kona Caravan Park is a good spot to look for it), Black-winged Stilt, Wood and Marsh Sandpiper (chiefly summer), and Gull-billed Tern.

Kununurra golf course, not far from the lake, is notable for two reasons – the rank vegetation surrounding it is favoured by Red-backed and Red-chested Button-quails (March is said to be the best month to look for them), while the large waterbird colony directly opposite holds Cattle, Great and Intermediate Egrets, as well as Darters and Pied Herons (most birds are present December–January).

Kununurra irrigation area: Accessible via the road to the Kimberley Research Station, the rich blacksoil plains to the north of Kununurra have been irrigated with water drawn from the Ord River to produce rice, sugar cane, peanuts, sorghum and other crops. Needless to say the presence of such lush vegetation has attracted many birds to the area, among them a wealth of finches: Star, Crimson, Double-barred, Masked, Long-tailed and Gouldian Finch, and Pictorella, Chestnut-breasted and Yellow-rumped Mannikin. And if you are visiting Kununurra between November and March, it would pay to keep an eye open for Yellow Wagtails − a flock of about fifty was seen near the town in February 1980.

Dunham River bridge: Less than 10 km west of Kununurra, where the Duncan Highway crosses the Dunham River, there is a patch of lush monsoon forest worth looking over for Pacific Baza, White-browed Robin, Shining Flycatcher, Northern Fantail and Yellow Oriole.

Packsaddle Swamp: Lies a few kilometres from the centre of Kununurra, west of the lake and south of the Duncan Highway. It is reputed to be an excellent spot for Little Bittern and Great Reed-Warbler (the latter is a rare summer migrant to Australia), but should you miss these two gems − both are denizens of the swamp's dense, reedy margins − you should be rewarded with sightings of Pied Herons, Magpie Geese, Wandering and Plumed Whistling-Ducks, Radjah Shelducks, Green Pygmy-Geese, White-browed Crakes, Comb-crested Jacanas, and many other sought-after birds.

Lake Argyle

Completed in 1972, the main Ord River Dam holds back the waters of the Ord and several other rivers to form Lake Argyle, the largest body of fresh water in tropical Australia. Since its formation the lake has become one of the north's best known tourist attractions; swimming, fishing and boating are popular activities, and boat tours and scenic flights are available. There is a large caravan park, together with a motel, near the main Ord River Dam, some 70 km south of Kununurra via the Duncan Highway and Lake Argyle Road.

Lake Argyle's northern and western edges are generally steep-sided and therefore unattractive to waterbirds, but its eastern and southern margins, being shallow, provide ideal feeding habitat for a wide range of species. During a survey carried out by the Royal Australasian Ornithologists Union in August 1986, more than 180 000 waterbirds made up of fifty-nine species were recorded, including large numbers of Pied Cormorants, Magpie Geese, Wandering Whistling-Ducks, Radjah Shelducks, Grey Teals, Hardheads, Green Pygmy-Geese, Eurasian Coots and Comb-crested Jacanas. The lake is also an important feeding ground for migratory waders — September to November is the best time of year for them, and Wood Sandpiper and Long-toed Stint are two of the more notable species to look for. Other noteworthy birds that visit the area include Flock Bronzewing and Yellow Chat.

The eastern shores of Lake Argyle can be reached from the Duncan Highway, which runs from Kununurra south-east into the Northern Territory, then south-west to Halls Creek, while its southern shores are accessible from the Great Northern Highway, between Halls Creek and the Kununurra turn-off. Those not wishing to venture far from the main Ord River Dam will find a visit to the Argyle Homestead Museum well worthwhile, not least because Red-winged Parrots, Great Bowerbirds, and a variety of honeyeaters and finches can be readily observed in the homestead's grounds.

CHRISTMAS ISLAND

Christmas Island is the coral-encrusted tip of an extinct volcano, the highest point of which reaches 361 m above sea level. One of Australia's more isolated external territories, it lies in the Indian Ocean some 360 km south of Java and approximately 1400 km north-west of Port Hedland. The island is small, a little over 20 km from east to west and on average less than 10 km wide, and dominated by a gently undulating plateau. Surrounding the plateau is an almost continuous shore terrace, varying in width from 50 m to 250 m, and between the plateau and the shore terrace is a series of steep cliffs and heavily vegetated slopes, giving the island its characteristic stepped appearance.

Christmas Island is rich in phosphate and the majority of its three thousand or so inhabitants are employed in the phosphate mining industry, which has been operating almost without interruption since the late 1800s. Despite the mining operations the island is relatively unspoilt, and only about a quarter of its unusual tropical rainforest has been cleared.

Although a few ocean-going yachts call at the island from time to time, most people go there by plane. At present there are two flights a week, both chartered by the local administration. One leaves Perth Airport on Tuesdays and flies via the Cocos (Keeling) Islands, while the other departs from Kuala Lumpur in West Malaysia each Sunday. The return airfare from Perth in late 1986 was about $760; the return trip from Kuala Lumpur would have cost you around $580 at that time. All bookings should be made through the Government Services Officer, Administration for the Territory of Christmas Island, Government Offices, Christmas Island, Indian Ocean, WA 6798.

Once you arrive on the island you will, of course, require accommodation and, since the terrain is very rugged, it would be

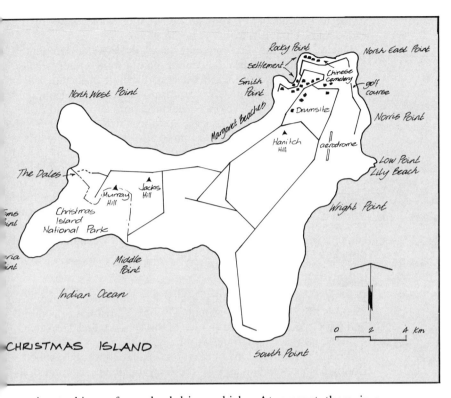

CHRISTMAS ISLAND

wise to hire a four-wheel-drive vehicle. At present there is a limited range of accommodation — just a few basic flats and an ex-mining company mess where visitors are housed and fed. Prices are fairly high ($466 weekly for one person or $794 weekly for two people in 1986, meals included), but you can cut costs considerably by staying at a flat where meals are not provided and eating at one of the four or five cheap restaurants on the island. Alternatively you could stay in Christmas Island National Park, where camping is permitted at certain sites. Bookings for accommodation should be made through the Hospitality Services Clerk, Christmas Island Services Corporation, Christmas Island, Indian Ocean, WA 6798. For further information about the national park write to the Australian National Parks and Wildlife Service, PO Box 636, Canberra City, ACT 2601, or PO Box 1260, Darwin, NT 5794. If you wish to camp in the park you must obtain a permit in advance. Four-wheel-drive vehicles can be hired from the Christmas Island Services Corporation, or from Mustapha Sahari, c/— Post Office, Christmas Island. The hire rate in 1986 was about $215 a week, including fuel, but you may be able to obtain a vehicle more cheaply from one of the local residents. (It would also be worth trying to hire a boat − you can obtain spectacular views of the island and its seabirds from the ocean.)

Having read this far you may have already decided that a holiday on Christmas Island is out of the question, either because of the expense involved, or because of the lack of facilities. But don't give up the idea just yet. Tourism is now being encouraged and there are many developers seeking approval to build hotels and chalets on the island. In fact, work on a five-star hotel-casino has already begun. Even if you cannot afford to stay at any of the proposed developments it is more than likely that increased tourism will lead to a wider range of facilities being provided, possibly making a visit a little less expensive. And a holiday on Christmas Island will certainly prove exciting, for no fewer than ten of its nineteen resident breeding birds are endemic forms (species or subspecies), and most are very tame. If you are still not convinced, the following account of the island's avifauna should dispel any lingering doubts.

Seabirds

Due to its isolation Christmas Island has long been a haven for seabirds, three of which − Abbott's Booby, Christmas Frigatebird and the Golden Bosunbird (a race of the White-tailed Tropicbird) − breed nowhere else in the world.

Abbott's Booby: One of the rarest of all seabirds, the Abbott's Booby has its breeding area on the central plateau, where it nests high in the rainforest trees. It is seldom seen around the settled, north-eastern part of the island, but is frequently encountered along the road leading from Drumsite to Murray Hill. The number of breeding pairs is estimated to be fewer than 1200.

Red-footed Booby: This is the island's most abundant seabird, with a population of approximately 12000 pairs. Like Abbott's Booby it nests in trees − colonies can be found on many parts of the shore terrace, and on the slopes between the terrace and the inland plateau. It is commonly seen over the settled area and breeds at several sites nearby − for example, behind the Chinese cemetery and in the vicinity of the golf course.

Brown Booby: Another of the island's more numerous seabirds, with a population estimated at about 5000 pairs, the Brown Booby does not nest in trees but on the ground near the edge of the sea cliff. Tame and easy to photograph, it can be found breeding in quite large numbers along the coast between North East Point and Lily Beach.

Christmas Frigatebird: With a total population of about 1600 pairs, the Christmas Frigatebird is considered an endangered species. It nests in trees on the shore terrace and is confined to four localities close to the settlement − there is a colony behind the Chinese cemetery and another behind the golf course, while the other two breeding grounds are situated along the island's north coast, just west of Smith Point.

Great Frigatebird: The more numerous of the island's two frigatebirds, numbering approximately 3000 pairs, the Great Frigatebird nests in trees along much of the shore terrace, with one colony being situated close to the golf course and another near Lily Beach.

Red-tailed Tropicbird: Also known as the Silver Bosunbird, this species nests in crannies high on the inland cliff and under bushes at the edge of the sea cliff. It is relatively abundant (about 1400 pairs breed on the island), and is often seen in display over the settled area.

Golden Bosunbird: Throughout much of its range the White-tailed Tropicbird is mostly white, but on Christmas Island many adults have a rich golden-apricot plumage — hence the bird's local name. It is probably the island's least numerous seabird, having a population of only about 600 pairs, and although it is regularly seen over the settled area it is most abundant within Christmas Island National Park, where it nests in hollows in trees and cliffs.

Common Noddy: On Christmas Island this species is very tame — so tame, in fact, that there are reports of birds being killed with sticks and barbecued during beach parties. The noddy nests on small ledges along the sea cliff and in trees at the edge of the shore terrace; the birds can often be found roosting in the vicinity of the wharf, and at Lily Beach.

Land birds

As previously mentioned, approximately 75 per cent of the vegetation on Christmas Island remains intact. Vine forest or tall rainforest covers much of the island, but because of its isolation and small size it supports only a limited number of land birds. Nevertheless seven of the nine land birds that occur there are of great interest because they are endemic, and at least five are very tame.

Christmas Island Goshawk: One of only three predators on the island, this bird is an endemic subspecies of the Brown Goshawk found throughout much of the Australian mainland. At one time severely persecuted by the island's poultry-owners, the goshawk is now fully protected. It is fairly plentiful and should be quite easy to find.

Australian Kestrel: Self-introduced from Australia, this species is common on the island and can be found along roads and around clearings in the rainforest.

Christmas Island Imperial-Pigeon: A close relative of the Torresian Imperial-Pigeon, which occurs in northern Australia, this endemic species is quite common on the plateau where it feeds on the fruits of the rainforest trees. During the dry season (May to November) it travels to the shore terrace in search of water — The Dales, at the western end of the island, is said to be one of its favoured haunts.

Christmas Island Emerald Dove: This attractive small dove, a subspecies of the Emerald Dove found on the Australian mainland, spends most of its time searching for fruits and berries on the forest floor. It is quite plentiful and can be found virtually throughout the island.

Christmas Island Hawk Owl: An endemic subspecies of the Oriental Hawk Owl, the Christmas Island Hawk Owl is considered endangered and, being nocturnal, is seldom seen.

Christmas Island Glossy Swiftlet: This small swiftlet can be seen hawking for insects all over the island. Nesting in caves and other dark places, the bird is an endemic subspecies of the Glossy Swiftlet that occurs on many islands between the Indian Ocean and the Pacific Ocean, but which only rarely reaches the Australian mainland.

Christmas Island Thrush: Abundant and easy to approach, this thrush can be seen at dusk feeding on lawns and in clearings throughout the settled area. The bird is an endemic subspecies of the Island Thrush, which is widely distributed on islands between the Indian Ocean and the Pacific Ocean.

Christmas Island White-eye: Closely related to the Silvereye of Australia, this confiding endemic species can be found all over the island.

Java Sparrow: Introduced in the early 1900s, the Java Sparrow is present in large numbers around the settlement, but is seldom seen elsewhere on the island.

Apart from those listed, the only other birds that breed on Christmas Island are the White-faced Heron, which has established itself during the past twenty years or so, and the Eastern Reef Egret, which is present in small numbers. A wide variety of migratory waders, as well as other waterbirds such as cormorants, herons, egrets and ducks, visit the island from time to time, as do land birds such as the Barn Swallow and Yellow Wagtail. In all about twenty-five waders and thirty vagrants have been recorded from the island.

Although for many visitors the breeding seabirds are the main attraction, the most striking feature of Christmas Island's fauna is undoubtedly the profusion of land crabs. Some sixteen species occur on the island, the most prolific being the red crab. At the start of the wet season red crabs can be seen in their millions migrating from the plateau to the shoreline to breed. The island's flora is also rich — there are about 385 species of flowering plants, twenty of which are endemic.

The best months to visit Christmas Island are May through to November (breeding activity among the seabirds reaches a peak during May and June). Because of oceanic influences humidity and temperature vary little from season to season (even in summer the temperature rarely exceeds 28 degrees C), but between December and April the island is subject to monsoons, and heavy rain may fall for several days at a time. If you do decide to go to the island you should contact the Christmas Island Services Corporation for up-to-date information about flights and accommodation.

COCOS (KEELING) ISLANDS

Situated in the Indian Ocean some 900 km south-west of Christmas Island, the Cocos (Keeling) Islands consist of twenty-six small, low-lying tropical islets surrounding a central lagoon, and North Keeling Island, which lies about 24 km north of the main atoll.

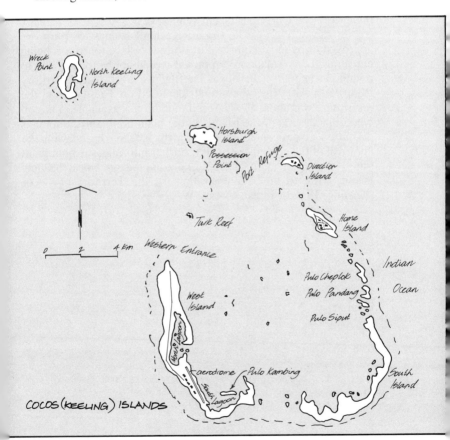

First settled in 1825, the islands are an Australian external territory.

The original vegetation on all but one of the islands in the main atoll has been cleared to make way for coconut plantations, and as a result they are virtually barren of birds. North Keeling Island, on the other hand, being relatively isolated and difficult to reach, retains much of its indigenous flora and fauna and is home to a wide variety of seabirds. These include Wedge-tailed Shearwater, Red-footed, Masked and Brown Booby, Great and Least Frigatebird, White-tailed Tropicbird, Sooty and White Tern, and Common Noddy. Other species of interest are the Eastern Reef Egret and Rufous Night Heron (both are abundant and can be found on islands in the main atoll as well as on North Keeling), and the Cocos Buff-banded Rail, which is the only endemic bird in the territory. Though apparently rare on the southern islands, the rail is plentiful on North Keeling where it can be found in all habitats. Land birds are very poorly represented, even on North Keeling Island, and the only resident species that you are likely to see is the introduced Christmas Island White-eye.

You can only go to the Cocos (Keeling) Islands for purposes approved of by the administrator; however, since tourism is being encouraged on a small scale approval should not be too difficult to obtain. In late 1986 there was one flight a week to the territory from Perth Airport — the aircraft departed on Tuesdays and the return fare was about $760. Accommodation is available in motel-type units on one of the islands in the main atoll, and camping is permitted at designated sites on North Keeling Island with the approval of the administrator. For further information about flight times, accommodation charges and camping on North Keeling Island, write to the Administration for the Territory of Cocos (Keeling) Islands, Indian Ocean, WA 6799.

Chapter

8

Northern Territory

Useful addresses

Australian Birding Association
24 Milkwood Circuit
Sanderson, NT 5793

Northern Territory Field Naturalists Club
PO Box 39565
Winnellie, NT 5789

Alice Springs Field Naturalists Club
PO Box 2483
Alice Springs, NT 5750

Australian National Parks and Wildlife Service
84 Smith Street
Darwin, NT 5790

Conservation Commission of the Northern Territory
Berrimah Research Farm Complex
Berrimah, NT 5788

Key to Maps

▨	Public land
▨	Areas of water
▲	Mountain peak
⌇	Mountain range or plateau
COBAR ●	Place name
✕	Camping area
⚱	Lighthouse
⚘ ⚘ ⚘	Marsh
▬▬▬	Major road or highway
────	Minor road
------	Foot track
--·--·--	National park boundary
-─────	State boundary
∾	River or creek

DARWIN

On Christmas Eve of 1974, tropical Cyclone Tracy swept in from the Arafura Sea and devastated Darwin, the only city on Australia's north coast. Many of its inhabitants were evacuated and the population, which stood at 48 000 at the time of the cyclone, fell to around 18 000. Yet Darwin recovered, and is now a modern, thriving centre with a population of about 55 000.

Darwin has always had a large Asian community – in 1900 more than three-quarters of the population were Chinese – and today it is probably the most cosmopolitan city in Australia. It is certainly the most tropical. During the wet season, December to March, the humidity can be stifling; in the dry season the days are pleasant although the temperature invariably exceeds 30 degrees C.

Visitors can choose from a wide range of accommodation, including the international-class hotel-casino at Mindil Beach, hotels, motels, guest houses and holiday flats. The YMCA has a hostel in Doctors Gully, at the northern end of The Esplanade, while the YWCA hostel is located at 119 Mitchell Street. There is a youth hostel in Beaton Road, Berrimah, some 12 km east of the city centre, and caravan parks at Winnellie, Berrimah, Wanguri, Malak and Howard Springs.

Darwin has a modern shopping centre, many excellent restaurants, an international airport and a wealth of rental car outlets. The city's commercial tour operators regularly visit many of the top end's better known wildlife areas – Howard Springs, Fogg Dam and Kakadu National Park for example. Details can be obtained from any branch of the Northern Territory Government Tourist Bureau.

Bird-watchers will find Darwin a very exciting place because its avifauna is quite different from that of southern capitals. And it could be said that Darwin is the 'rarity capital' of Australia – an amazing number of uncommon and vagrant species have turned up there: Christmas Frigatebird, Garganey, Little Ringed, Ringed and Caspian Plover, Spotted Greenshank, Redshank, Stilt and Green Sandpiper, Pin-tailed and Swinhoe's Snipe, Asian Do-witcher, Little Stint, Ruff, Red-necked Phalarope, Black-tailed

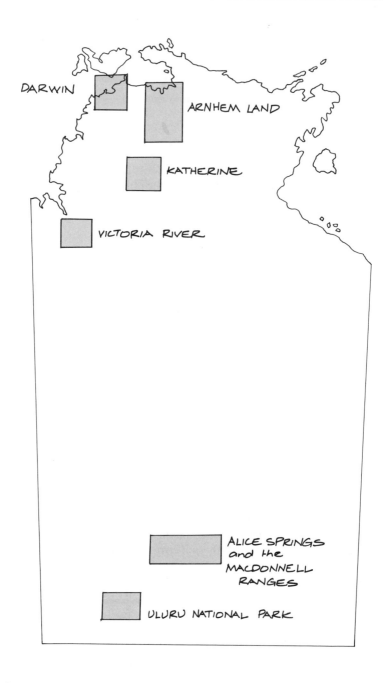

DARWIN

ARNHEM LAND

KATHERINE

VICTORIA RIVER

ALICE SPRINGS
and the
MACDONNELL
RANGES

ULURU NATIONAL PARK

NORTHERN TERRITORY

and Sabine's Gull, Yellow Wagtail, Grey Wagtail, Gray's Grass-hopper Warbler and Great Reed-Warbler.

While the majority of these birds are vagrants (Australia lies outside the normal range of many of them), others may be regular visitors to the top end, overlooked simply because there are few bird-watchers living in the region. Birders visiting Darwin, especially between September and March, should therefore look closely at anything unusual — that strange gull or wader may be a new record for Australia.

Something of Darwin's rich and varied birdlife can be seen along The Esplanade, a few minutes walk from the city centre. And a visit to the wharf area may prove fruitful; a Sabine's Gull (the first recorded in Australia) was seen near Stokes Hill Wharf in 1982.

Darwin Botanical Gardens

Like the rest of the city, the botanical gardens were flattened by Cyclone Tracy in 1974. Many plants were destroyed, but the wounds have healed and today the gardens are lush and green. An ideal place for a quiet stroll, it is full of fragrant frangipani and colourful bougainvilleas. Surprisingly, birds are somewhat scarce, although Brown Honeyeater, Figbird, Spangled Drongo and White-breasted Woodswallow are common enough. A patch of rainforest has recently been planted in a gully near the restaurant; in time this area should prove attractive to birds.

The gardens are open daily from sunrise to sunset. They are about 1.5 km north of the city centre and access can be gained via either Gardens Road or Geranium Street.

East Point Recreation Reserve

Situated to the north of Fannie Bay, this reserve is about 6 km from the city centre via Gilruth Avenue and East Point Road. It is one of the best birding spots close to Darwin; from the War Museum (at the end of East Point Road) you can walk along the coast to Ludmilla Creek.

East Point is an excellent place for waders. Migratory species are most numerous in summer, but there is usually a fair assortment to be seen at any time of the year: Grey, Lesser Golden, Mongolian, Large Sand and Oriental Plover, Ruddy Turnstone, Eastern Curlew, Whimbrel, Little Curlew (very common October–November, when it can be found on almost any area of short grass including lawns, sports grounds and roadsides in suburban Darwin), Grey-tailed Tattler, Common, Terek, Sharp-tailed, Curlew and Broad-billed Sandpiper, Greenshank, Black-tailed and Bar-tailed Godwit, Red and Great Knot, and Red-necked Stint. Masked Lapwing and Australian Pratincole (chiefly in winter) can be found in the grassy areas near the War Museum.

When the mudflats are exposed at low tide, it is possible to explore the extensive mangroves at the mouth of Ludmilla Creek (sandshoes and insect repellent are essential). Here you should have little difficulty finding a number of interesting species, including Collared Kingfisher (Sacred Kingfisher is quite common in the mangroves — take care not to confuse the two), Rainbow Bee-eater, Lemon-bellied Flycatcher, Large-billed and Mangrove Gerygone, and White-gaped, Brown and Red-headed Honey-eater. The Chestnut Rail, a very shy and seldom-observed species, has been recorded breeding along Ludmilla Creek and may be worth searching for.

Other birds in the East Point — Ludmilla Creek area include Little Egret, Eastern Reef Egret, Striated Heron, Osprey (breeds locally), Brahminy Kite, and Gull-billed, Caspian, Crested and Lesser Crested Tern. Golden-headed Cisticolas are plentiful in the tall grass behind the beach at East Point.

Lee Point, Buffalo Creek and Leanyer Swamp

Like the East Point — Ludmilla Creek area, this stretch of coast is attractive to waders; many of the species already mentioned can be found between Lee Point and Buffalo Creek. To get there, turn off the Stuart Highway at Bagot Road, then right at McMillans Road and left at Lee Point Road. Near Lee Point, about 18 km north-east of the city centre, there is a carpark, together with toilets and picnic facilities. Casuarina Beach, just to the south-west, may be worth a visit for Sanderling and perhaps Beach Thick-knee.

Buffalo Creek is fringed with dense mangroves, making thorough exploration somewhat difficult. There is, however, a boat ramp near its mouth, and with a dinghy (you can hire them in Darwin) you could travel upstream towards Leanyer Swamp, a favoured haunt of the Zitting Cisticola. Great-billed Heron, Striated Heron and Chestnut Rail are possibilities here; on the creek's muddy margins you will see large numbers of fiddler crabs standing guard at the entrances of their burrows, waving their enlarged claws to attract females and warn off other males.

To reach Buffalo Creek, turn off Lee Point Road about 1 km south of the point. At the mouth of the creek, near the boat ramp, there is a carpark, and nearby a patch of monsoon forest where you should find Orange-footed Scrubfowl, Rose-crowned Fruit-Dove, Torresian Imperial-Pigeon (a summer visitor), Cicadabird, Varied Triller, Leaden Flycatcher, Large-billed Gerygone, White-gaped, Brown and Red-headed Honeyeater, and Spangled Drongo. Look for Pheasant Coucals in areas with an understorey of long grass.

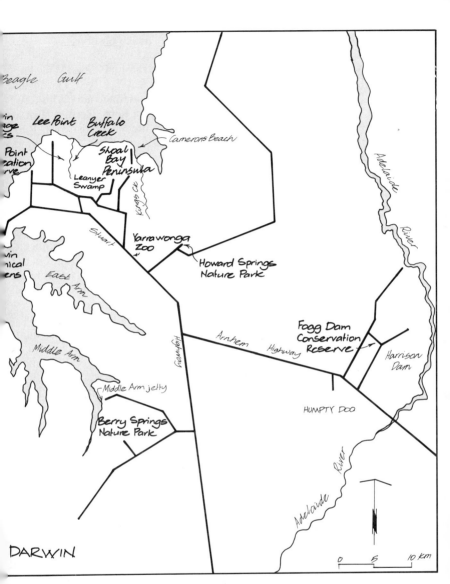

Darwin Sewage Works

Sewage farms are always good for birds, and the Darwin Sewage Works are no exception. As is usually the case, however, the ponds are surrounded by a high fence and permission must be obtained before entering the works. If you are refused entry, or if the gates are locked, the main ponds can be viewed quite well through the fence and many of the larger waterbirds – Pied Heron (sometimes present in their hundreds), egrets, Glossy Ibis, Magpie

Goose, Radjah Shelduck — should be easy to observe.

Those fortunate enough to be allowed into the works will be richly rewarded — Wandering and, more rarely, Plumed Whistling-Duck, Pacific Black and Pink-eared Duck, Grey Teal, Hardhead, Black-winged Stilt, Wood and Marsh Sandpiper, and Whiskered Tern are some of the birds you can expect here. Rarities such as Garganey, Little Ringed Plover, Spotted Greenshank, Red-necked Phalarope and Grey Wagtail turn up from time to time, while the delightful Yellow Wagtail is a regular summer visitor.

The sewage works are about 15 km north-east of the city centre; access is via Lee Point Road and Fitzmaurice Drive.

Shoal Bay Peninsula

The Shoal Bay Peninsula lies to the north-east of Darwin, between Buffalo Creek and Kings Creek. Access is rather difficult, especially during the wet season, because most of the roads in the area are unsealed and there are few signposts. Nevertheless visiting bird-watchers will find a trip to this part of the coast well worthwhile (ask locally for precise directions).

The peninsula is ornithologically rewarding because it has a variety of habitats, including sedgelands, mixed forests, mangroves, beaches and mudflats. The Camerons Beach area is particularly interesting. Notable species reported on the Shoal Bay Peninsula include Black Bittern, Pacific Baza, King Quail, Brolga, Eastern Grass Owl, Large-tailed Nightjar, Little Kingfisher, Mangrove Robin, Mangrove Golden Whistler, White-breasted Whistler, Zitting Cisticola and Yellow White-eye.

Yarrawonga Zoo

This small but interesting zoo is administered by the Northern Territory Conservation Commission and features wildlife from the top end — crocodiles, dingoes, wallabies, snakes and birds. It has several aviaries housing birds of prey, parrots and cockatoos, and a small swamp that is usually packed with waterbirds. If you do not find Pied Herons at the sewage works, you are sure to see them here.

The zoo, open seven days a week, is about 20 km south-east of Darwin via the Stuart Highway. Admission is free.

Howard Springs Nature Park

This popular picnic and swimming spot, 30 km east of Darwin, is readily accessible via the Stuart Highway. Within the 1880 ha reserve there are shady picnic areas, a swimming pool fed by a natural spring, and a kiosk. The small patch of monsoon forest surrounding the pool holds quite a variety of birds: Rose-crowned Fruit-Dove, Torresian Imperial-Pigeon (summer), Oriental

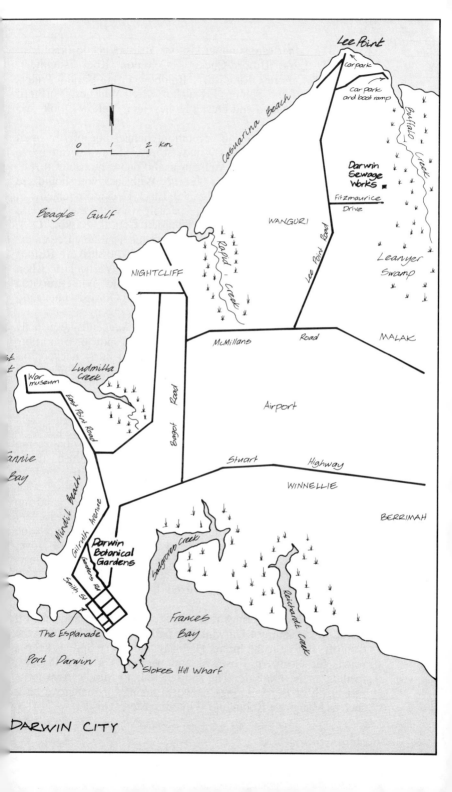

Cuckoo (a rather rare summer visitor), Brush Cuckoo (mainly in summer), Little Bronze-Cuckoo, Common Koel (summer), Rufous Owl, Forest Kingfisher, Rainbow Pitta, Varied Triller, Lemon-bellied and Shining Flycatcher, Grey Whistler, Northern Fantail, White-gaped and Dusky Honeyeater, Yellow Oriole and Spangled Drongo.

Away from the pool the vegetation changes abruptly to open eucalypt forest with a grassy understorey. Here you can move around more readily than you can in the dense monsoon forest, and birds are much easier to observe. With luck you should see many of the following: Red-tailed Black-Cockatoo (chiefly in winter), Red-collared Lorikeet (especially when the eucalypts are in flower), Red-winged Parrot, Pheasant Coucal, Barking Owl, Blue-winged Kookaburra, Sacred Kingfisher, Rainbow Bee-eater, Dollarbird (summer), White-bellied Cuckoo-shrike, Rufous Whistler, Silver-crowned and Little Friarbird (particularly when the eucalypts are flowering), Blue-faced and White-throated Honeyeater, Striated Pardalote, Olive-backed Oriole (winter) and Figbird.

Howard Springs is usually crowded at weekends, especially during summer. Nevertheless it is a pleasant spot for a morning walk followed by a picnic lunch (Sacred and Straw-necked Ibis patrol the picnic areas, willingly accepting handouts). Camping is not permitted in the park.

Berry Springs Nature Park

Situated about 60 km south-east of Darwin, Berry Springs is another well-known picnic and swimming spot. The 247 ha reserve features several large natural pools fringed with lush, dense tropical vegetation. There are toilets, picnic facilities and an information centre in the park, but camping is not permitted.

Much of the reserve consists of open eucalypt forest, and the presence of both open and closed habitat makes this an excellent place for birds. Visitors should have little difficulty finding a wide variety of species including Peaceful and Bar-shouldered Dove, Azure Kingfisher, Blue-winged Kookaburra, Large-billed Gerygone, Silver-crowned Friarbird, White-throated, Dusky and Red-headed Honeyeater, Double-barred Finch, Yellow Oriole and Figbird.

To reach Berry Springs take the Stuart Highway and turn off about 50 km south of Darwin. The park is about 10 km from the turn-off. Between the Stuart Highway and Berry Springs keep a watch for Northern Rosellas, and perhaps Partridge Pigeons, feeding at the roadside. The short detour to Middle Arm jetty, just north of Berry Springs, is worth taking for mangrove birds such as Mangrove Robin and White-breasted Whistler.

Fogg Dam Conservation Reserve

Fogg Dam was built to provide water for a rice-growing scheme. The project failed, however − partly because waterfowl persisted in eating the crops. Perhaps ironically, the dam is now a haven for birds and bird-watchers; indeed it has become one of the top end's best known wildlife attractions.

During the dry season a large number of species congregate there: Darter, cormorants, Pacific, White-faced and Pied Heron, Cattle, Great, Little and Intermediate Egret, Rufous Night Heron, Black-necked Stork, Glossy, Sacred and Straw-necked Ibis, Royal Spoonbill, Magpie Goose, Wandering and, more rarely, Plumed Whistling-Duck, Radjah Shelduck, Green Pygmy-Goose and Black-winged Stilt.

Most of these birds frequent the shallow, marshy area below the dam wall. The wall is made of earth and you can drive across it, thus obtaining excellent views of the birds. Not surprisingly, the dam is very popular with nature photographers.

The deep water north of the wall is usually covered with masses of gorgeous waterlilies, home to large numbers of Comb-crested Jacanas. These handsome birds have incredibly long toes that enable them to walk with ease on the floating vegetation. The White-browed Crake − another species equipped with long toes − can also be seen at Fogg Dam, particularly in the early morning and late afternoon.

Fogg Dam is at its best in the dry season, when the absence of water elsewhere in the region forces many birds to seek refuge there. Those visiting the dam in the wet season, however, have a chance of seeing something notable − for example Garganey, Pin-tailed and Swinhoe's Snipe, and Yellow Wagtail.

In addition to waterbirds, the reserve holds an interesting array of passerines including Broad-billed Flycatcher, Green-backed Gerygone, Bar-breasted, Rufous-banded and Dusky Honeyeater, and Crimson Finch.

The reserve (1500 ha) is about 70 km south-east of Darwin via the Stuart and Arnhem Highways. There are no facilities and camping is not allowed. Since mosquitoes outnumber birds by about a thousand to one, be prepared!

Fogg Dam is certainly one of the region's premier birding localities, but if you can spare the time there are at least two more spots nearby that are worth visiting: Humpty Doo, just south of the Arnhem Highway, and Harrison Dam to the north.

ARNHEM LAND

With its mighty river systems and vast coastal floodplains, western Arnhem Land fits the popular conception of a wildlife paradise more readily than any other region in our generally dry continent.

And it is easy to see why this narrow belt of monsoon country at the top of the Northern Territory attracts bird-watchers from all over the world; more than a third of Australia's birds, some 270 species, can be found there. Not surprisingly, waterbirds are especially numerous. With the onset of the wet season countless thousands of Magpie Geese, and smaller numbers of Darters, cormorants, herons, egrets, bitterns, storks, ibis, spoonbills and ducks, gather to breed in the coastal wetlands and along the mangrove-fringed rivers. At the end of the breeding season, as the floodwaters recede, these birds congregate in huge numbers around permanent billabongs and lagoons.

Arnhem Land, a remote and rugged wilderness to the east of Darwin, is not an easy place to explore. Much of it is an Aboriginal reserve and there are few roads. However, a significant section of this fascinating region is protected by the incomparable Kakadu National Park, which is readily accessible from Darwin via the sealed Arnhem Highway.

Kakadu National Park

One of the world's great national parks, Kakadu covers an area of almost 13 000 sq km between the Wildman and East Alligator Rivers and stretches from Van Diemen Gulf to the edge of the Arnhem Land Plateau. It contains a wide range of habitats: sedgelands; grasslands; dense monsoon forests; open eucalypt woodlands; paperbark swamps; freshwater and saltwater mangroves; billabongs; rivers; and, importantly, the western Arnhem Land escarpment. This fractured sandstone wall extends from Oenpelli in the north to beyond El Sherana in the south, and in places rises 240 m above the wooded plains.

Although waterbirds are undoubtedly Kakadu's chief ornithological attraction (nearly a hundred species have been recorded in the park), the birds of the Arnhem Land Plateau, especially its western escarpment, are of outstanding interest. Three of these — the rare Banded Fruit-Dove, the Chestnut-quilled Rock-Pigeon and the White-throated Grasswren — occur nowhere else in Australia, while the White-lined Honeyeater is known only from the sandstone country at the top of the Northern Territory and from the Kimberley in Western Australia.

For many of its visitors, however, Kakadu's fascination extends beyond the rugged beauty of its landscape and its wealth of wildlife. The park is of major anthropological significance, and the immensely rich Aboriginal art sites decorating large sections of the escarpment are considered equal to those found in some of Western Europe's prehistoric art galleries. Indeed there is evidence to suggest that some of the paintings at Obiri Rock may be more than twenty thousand years old — among the most ancient artistic works in the world.

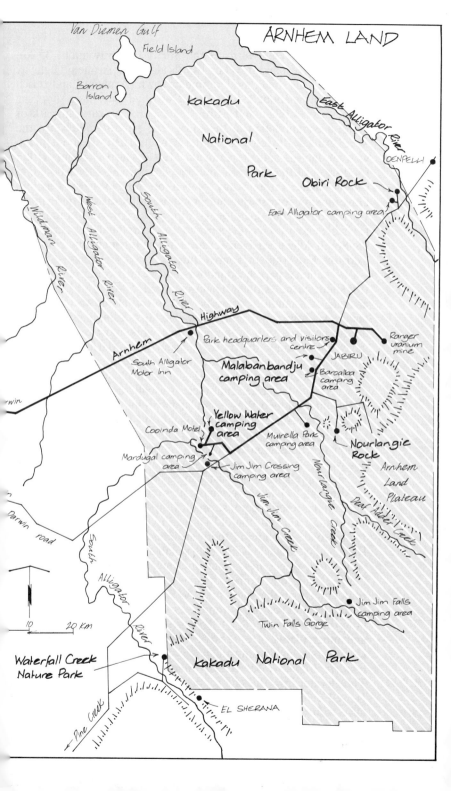

To reach Kakadu turn off the Stuart Highway about 35 km south of Darwin and travel eastwards along the Arnhem Highway to Jabiru. This small, modern mining town (Arnhem Land is rich in uranium) is about 255 km from Darwin. Jabiru has a shopping centre, a post office and petrol, but there is no caravan park or motel accommodation in the town. The nearest motels are the South Alligator Motor Inn, on the Arnhem Highway about 40 km west of Jabiru, and the Cooinda Motel, which is about 60 km south-west of the town via the Pine Creek road. Motel bookings can be made through any branch of the Northern Territory Government Tourist Bureau. For those without transport, many Darwin-based tour operators visit the park. A variety of tours are available and most include a trip to the escarpment and a cruise on the South Alligator River; for further details contact the Northern Territory Government Tourist Bureau.

The national park headquarters and visitors centre are located just south of the Arnhem Highway, about 5 km from Jabiru. On arriving at Kakadu it would be best to call at the visitors centre and seek advice concerning the availability of camping sites. There are no powered sites in the park and, while most camping areas have toilets, only the East Alligator and Mardugal camping grounds have showers. In the dry season, especially during the school holidays, both East Alligator and Mardugal are often crowded with fishermen, but there is usually no shortage of space in the undeveloped sites — Malabanbandju, Baroalba, Muirella Park, Yellow Water, Jim Jim Crossing and Jim Jim Falls.

Displays covering the fauna, flora and Aboriginal history of the region are housed in the visitors centre. Informative brochures describing aspects of the park's landscape, rock art and wildlife, and a comprehensive bird list, can be obtained from the ranger.

Although Kakadu is very large, it is relatively easy to plan a trip through the reserve because apart from the Arnhem Highway the only main roads are the old Darwin road and the Pine Creek — Jabiru road. In addition there are minor roads leading to Obiri Rock and Nourlangie Rock, both suitable for conventional vehicles, and a four-wheel-drive track to Jim Jim Falls and Twin Falls Gorge. Since the Arnhem Highway is the region's only sealed route much of the park may be inaccessible for long periods during the wet season, but in the dry months visitors should have little difficulty reaching all the park's major Aboriginal art sites and other places of interest. Bird-watchers should find the following areas highly rewarding.

Arnhem Highway, between the South Alligator River and Jabiru: The floodplains adjacent to the South Alligator River can be viewed quite readily from the Arnhem Highway and are usually alive with waterbirds, even in the dry season. Large numbers of herons, egrets, Black-necked Stork, ibis, spoonbills, waterfowl and Brolga can be seen here, while those prepared to search the extensive wetlands bordering the river may be rewarded with a sighting of a Yellow Chat, a rarely observed and little-known species.

As you approach Jabiru look for Partridge Pigeons in the open woodlands, particularly in areas where the grassy understorey has been recently burnt. Although difficult to locate in the bush, the ground-dwelling pigeons are quite easy to see on the edge of the highway, where they often feed late in the day.

East Alligator River and Obiri Rock: The East Alligator camping area, about 40 km north of Jabiru, makes an excellent base for the bird-watcher because it is conveniently located close to the river and the escarpment at Obiri Rock. The eucalypt woodland between the camping ground and the river holds a wide variety of birds: Chestnut-backed Button-quail, Bush Thick-knee, Peaceful and Bar-shouldered Dove, Red-tailed Black-Cockatoo, Little Corella, Sulphur-crested Cockatoo, Red-collared and Varied Lorikeet (especially when the eucalypts are flowering), Red-winged Parrot, Northern Rosella, Oriental Cuckoo (a wet-season visitor), Pallid Cuckoo, Pheasant Coucal, Southern Boobook, Barking Owl, Tawny Frogmouth, Australian Owlet-nightjar, Spotted Nightjar, Blue-winged Kookaburra, Forest Kingfisher, Rainbow Bee-eater, Black-faced and White-bellied Cuckoo-shrike, White-winged Triller, Rufous Whistler, Leaden Flycatcher, Northern Fantail, Grey-crowned Babbler, Red-backed Fairy-wren, Varied Sittella, Black-tailed Treecreeper, Silver-crowned and Little Friarbird (especially when the eucalypts are flowering), Blue-faced, White-gaped, White-throated and Brown Honeyeater, Mistletoebird, Striated Pardalote, Double-barred, Masked and Long-tailed Finch, Olive-backed Oriole, Black-faced Woodswallow and Pied Butcherbird.

About 3 km south-east of the camping area you will find a public boat ramp and a picnic ground. From here it is possible to walk along the west bank of the East Alligator River via a rough but well-defined track. White-bellied Sea-Eagles and the occasional Osprey can be seen patrolling the river, while a number of interesting species frequent the waterside forest. These include Orange-footed Scrubfowl and Rainbow Pitta; both favour patches of the forest where the interlocking canopies of the taller trees shut out much of the sunlight. They are ground-living birds, and you should look for them in areas where the forest floor is well covered with leaf litter − a loud rustling of leaves often betrays their presence.

Obiri Rock is 3 km north of the East Alligator camping area. Adorning the rock's sandstone walls are some of the finest examples of Aboriginal art in Australia, including many beautiful 'X-ray paintings' showing the internal organs and skeletons of barramundi and other animals that featured prominently in the lives of Arnhem Land's Aboriginal people. From a lookout at the top of Obiri Rock there are wonderful views over the lush green floodplains to the north.

Malabanbandju camping area: Although this small campsite has no facilities other than toilets, it is splendidly situated on the banks of a permanent billabong where many waterbirds can be readily observed. Darter, cormorants, herons, egrets, Rufous Night Heron, Black-necked Stork, ibis, spoonbills, and waterfowl such as Radjah Shelduck and Green Pygmy-Goose are usually present, while the waterside vegetation holds a good variety of passerines, especially honeyeaters and finches. A 4 km walking track commencing at the camping ground provides access to the adjacent floodplain.

The Malabanbandju camping area is about 18 km south-west of Jabiru via the Pine Creek road. Some 2 km further south there is another campsite on Baroalba Creek; caravans are not permitted here but those with tents will find it a very peaceful spot.

Nourlangie Rock: Another of Kakadu's well-known Aboriginal art sites, Nourlangie Rock is about 40 km south of Jabiru via the Pine Creek road. The area is well worth visiting for its paintings, but the rock is also of outstanding ornithological interest since it is a haunt of Australia's rarest pigeon — the Banded Fruit-Dove. So far as is known this large, handsome bird is virtually confined to the western escarpment of the Arnhem Land Plateau. Quiet and unobtrusive, especially during the heat of the day, the fruit-dove favours patches of forest growing at the foot of the escarpment and in deep gullies, particularly areas where fruit-bearing trees such as figs occur. The Banded Fruit-Dove can be found in suitable habitat elsewhere in Kakadu, but since it is readily accessible, Nourlangie Rock is probably the best place to look for it. In 1984 two birds were seen within 500 m of the walking track leading to the main art site.

If you are not fortunate enough to find a Banded Fruit-Dove, four other escarpment-dwellers can be seen at Nourlangie — Chestnut-quilled Rock-Pigeon, Sandstone Shrike-thrush, Helmeted Friarbird and White-lined Honeyeater.

There are picnic facilities at the rock but camping is not permitted.

Yellow Water camping area: Yellow Water Lagoon is one of the most famous waterbird localities in the top end. At this marvellous spot — a bird photographer's paradise — a wide variety of species can be observed with little effort: Hoary-headed and Australasian Grebe, Australian Pelican, Darter, Little Black and Little Pied

Cormorant, Pacific, White-faced and Pied Heron, Cattle, Great, Intermediate and Little Egret, Rufous Night Heron, Black-necked Stork, Glossy, Sacred and Straw-necked Ibis, Royal and Yellow-billed Spoonbill, Magpie Goose, Wandering and Plumed Whistling-Duck, Radjah Shelduck, Pacific Black and Pink-eared Duck, Grey Teal, Hardhead, Green Pygmy-Goose, Osprey, Brahminy Kite, White-bellied Sea-Eagle, Brolga, Comb-crested Jacana, Masked Lapwing, Red-kneed Dotterel, Black-fronted Plover, Black-winged Stilt, and Whiskered, Gull-billed and Caspian Tern. More rarely Great-billed Heron, Black Bittern, Buff-banded Rail, and Baillon's and White-browed Crake are recorded.

The Yellow Water camping area, about 60 km south-west of Jabiru, has no facilities other than toilets, but the Mardugal campsite is only about 8 km to the south. Accommodation is available at the Cooinda Motel nearby, and boat tours of Yellow Water Lagoon can be booked there. The proprietors of the motel also operate a small caravan park.

In addition to birds, Yellow Water Lagoon is well known for its wealth of waterlilies, and for its buffaloes, crocodiles and barramundi. There are also mosquitoes − millions of them! Pack a good supply of insect repellent.

Waterfall Creek Nature Park

Having explored Kakadu, no visitor should leave Arnhem Land without staying at least one night at Waterfall Creek Nature Park. The reserve is just outside the south-western boundary of Kakadu, about 180 km from Jabiru and about 110 km from Pine Creek. During the dry season Waterfall Creek can be reached via the Pine Creek to Jabiru road, but those approaching from Jabiru will have to ford the South Alligator River. Normally the water is not very deep, and those with conventional vehicles should have no trouble getting through. Nevertheless before setting out it would be wise to call at Kakadu's visitors centre and inquire about the level of the river.

The park protects a section of the western Arnhem Land escarpment some 10 km north-west of the El Sherana mine site. At the foot of the escarpment there is a huge, deep swimming hole (there are no crocodiles here) and a patch of luxuriant monsoon forest. Waterfall Creek is a small park, 236 ha, and despite being crowded at times it is one of the best places to go bird-watching in the top end.

Because of its accessibility, bird-watchers from throughout Australia travel to the reserve in the hope of finding a White-throated Grasswren. The grasswren, undoubtedly the most outstanding species on the park's list, inhabits the sparsely vegetated plateau; you will have little chance of seeing one unless you climb the 100 m escarpment. The ascent, while somewhat strenuous, is not difficult if you are nimble-footed — simply follow the well-worn route to the top.

Like other species of *Amytornis*, the White-throated Grasswren is an elusive bird. But you can be lucky. In June 1984, late one afternoon, a party of five grasswrens were the first birds seen on top of the escarpment. The following morning, however, they could not be found despite a thorough search of the boulder-strewn plateau. The White-throated, perhaps the most beautifully marked grasswren, is large — not much smaller than a Grey-crowned Babbler. Outside the breeding season the grasswrens form small flocks of up to six or seven birds; when disturbed they move with astonishing speed, running rapidly over rocks and seeking shelter in deep crevices. If you remain still they may show themselves, peering at you from a safe distance.

Many other interesting species inhabit the rocky, spinifex-covered plateau, and while searching for the grasswrens you may see Chestnut-quilled Rock-Pigeon, Sandstone Shrike-thrush, Variegated Fairy-wren, Helmeted Friarbird, White-lined Honey-eater and Little Woodswallow.

For those unwilling (or unable) to scramble up the escarpment, a wide variety of birds can be found in the monsoon forest adjacent to the camping area: Emerald Dove, Azure Kingfisher, Rainbow Pitta, Lemon-bellied, Leaden and Shining Flycatcher, White-browed Robin, Little Shrike-thrush, Northern Fantail, Red-backed Fairy-wren, White-gaped, Brown and Dusky Honey-eater, and Crimson and Double-barred Finch.

Waterfall Creek Nature Park is certainly delightful. The shady camping area has toilets and fireplaces, and a refreshing dip in the waterhole more than compensates for the lack of shower facilities. If you are travelling south via Pine Creek you can look forward to finding many exciting birds in the open woodlands along the way — Partridge Pigeons, Red-tailed Black-Cockatoos and Hooded Parrots, to name a few.

KATHERINE

You could be forgiven for breathing a sigh of relief on arriving at Katherine. After all, the town is 1200 km from Alice Springs, 1300 km from Mt Isa and 1600 km from Broome. Fortunately Katherine has more to offer the weary traveller than just a main street and a pub. It is, in fact, the Northern Territory's third-largest settlement, a thriving tourist centre with shops, banks, at least seven motels, four caravan parks and a youth hostel. There is also a youth hostel at Pine Creek, some 90 km to the north-west, and another at Mataranka, about 115 km to the south-east.

Katherine Gorge National Park is undoubtedly the best place to

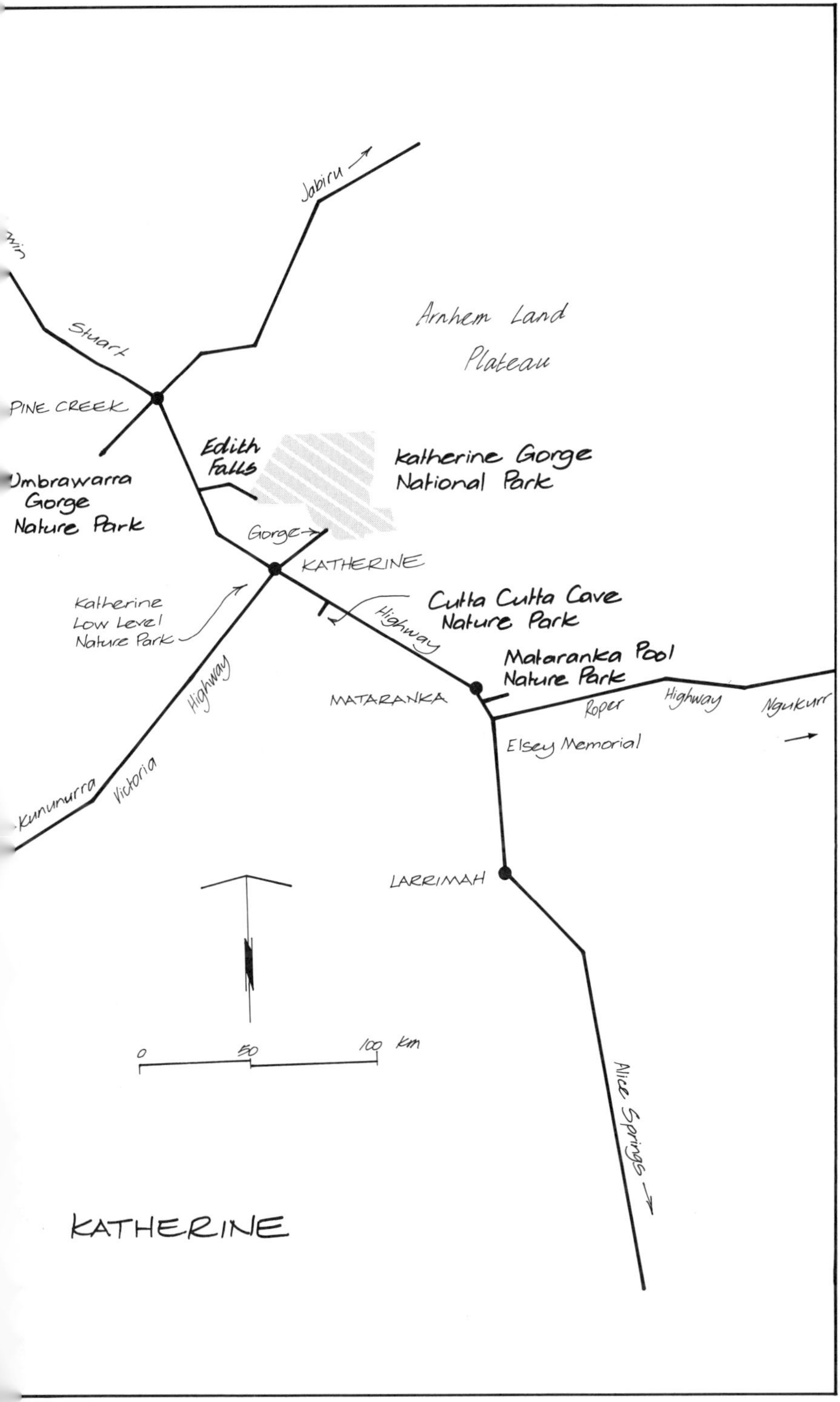

Jabiru
Stuart
Arnhem Land Plateau
PINE CREEK
Edith Falls
Katherine Gorge National Park
Umbrawarra Gorge Nature Park
Gorge
KATHERINE
Katherine Low Level Nature Park
Cutta Cutta Cave Nature Park
Highway
Mataranka Pool Nature Park
MATARANKA
Roper
Highway
Ngukurr
Elsey Memorial
Highway
Victoria
Kununurra
LARRIMAH
0
50
100 km
Alice Springs
KATHERINE

go bird-watching. There are, however, many other places of interest within 100 km or so of the town — Edith Falls, and the Umbrawarra Gorge, Cutta Cutta Cave and Mataranka Pool Nature Parks for example. And bird-watchers should not overlook Katherine Low Level Nature Park, 5 km south-west of Katherine on the road to Kununurra. A 3 km stretch of the Katherine River is included in this 105 ha reserve and well over a hundred species of birds have been recorded there. Picnic facilities are provided but camping is not allowed.

Katherine Gorge National Park

This 180 190 ha reserve protects the south-western corner of the rugged Arnhem Land Plateau to the north-east of Katherine. The best known feature of the park is Katherine Gorge; one of the most spectacular river canyons in Australia, it attracts many thousands of visitors each year. During the wet season (December to March) the Katherine River becomes a raging torrent, thundering through the narrow gorge and flooding much of the surrounding area. But in the dry season, when the river is quiet, cruise launches ferry tourists far upstream to where the canyon's richly coloured sandstone walls rise vertically from the water's edge.

The main entrance to the park is about 30 km from Katherine, via a sealed road which may be closed periodically during the wet season. Near the mouth of the gorge, close to the river, there is a privately operated caravan park with good facilities and powered sites. Petrol and food supplies can be purchased from the kiosk. An excellent visitors centre housing displays covering the fauna, flora and Aboriginal history of the region is located just inside the national park boundary. A comprehensive walking track guide, a bird list and several other useful publications are available from the ranger. About 1 km from the visitors centre are a picnic area and public boat ramp. This section of the Katherine River is a popular fishing spot, and boats with motors under 10 h.p. are permitted in the reserve. For the more adventurous, canoes can be hired in Katherine — an exhilarating way of exploring the upper reaches of the river.

Those travelling to the Northern Territory's top end for the first time will find the region's avifauna very exciting. More than 160 species of birds have been recorded in Katherine Gorge National Park, including many that are highly sought-after. Of outstanding interest are Red Goshawk, Hooded Parrot and Gouldian Finch, which occur in the reserve, while other land birds of note include Partridge Pigeon, Chestnut-quilled Rock-Pigeon, Lemon-bellied and Shining Flycatcher, White-browed Robin, Sandstone Shrikethrush, Green-backed Gerygone, Bar-breasted and Banded Honeyeater, Star, Crimson, Masked and Long-tailed Finch, Yellow-

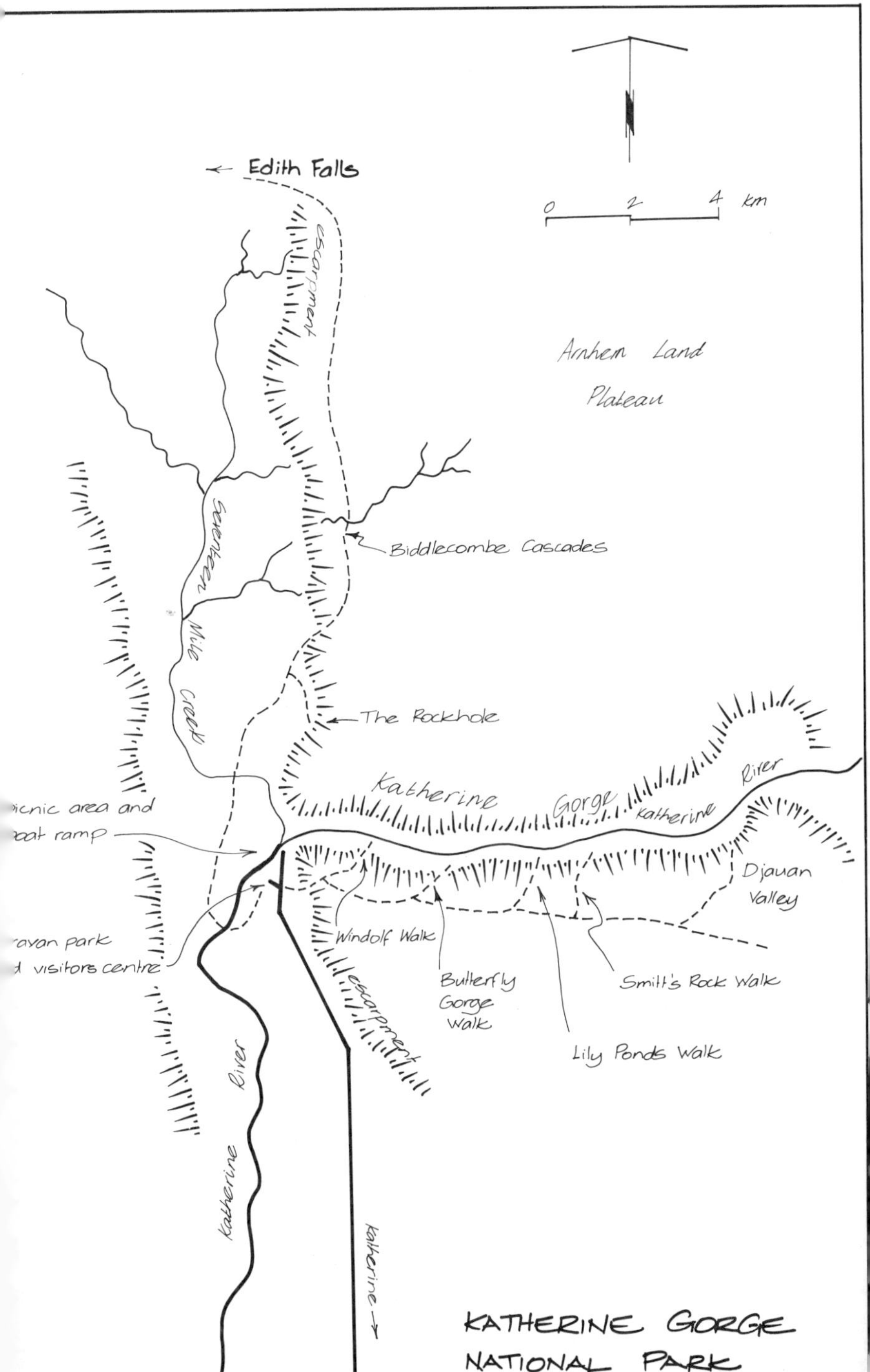

Edith Falls
0 2 4 km
Arnhem Land Plateau
escarpment
Seventeen Mile Creek
Biddlecombe Cascades
The Rockhole
Katherine Gorge
Katherine River
icnic area and
oat ramp
ravan park
d visitors centre
Windolf Walk
Butterfly Gorge Walk
Lily Ponds Walk
Smitt's Rock Walk
Djauan Valley
escarpment
Katherine River
Katherine
KATHERINE GORGE NATIONAL PARK

rumped Mannikin and Yellow Oriole. The White-throated Grasswren is also on the park's list, but you are more likely to find this elusive bird if you search the western Arnhem Land escarpment between the East and South Alligator Rivers (see the Arnhem Land section of this book).

Quite a variety of cormorants, herons, egrets, ibis and waterfowl can usually be seen around Katherine, although these birds rarely occur in large numbers, especially in the dry season, and if you wish to see vast gatherings of waterbirds you should drive further north and visit the coastal floodplains between Darwin and the East Alligator River.

Although Katherine Gorge National Park has over 100 km of walking tracks, visitors can enjoy excellent birding without venturing far from the camping area. Here, within a radius of 2 km or so, you can explore three different types of habitat − the densely vegetated margins of the Katherine River; the harsh, rocky sandstone plateau and escarpment; and the open eucalypt woodland between the river and the plateau.

The most conspicuous bird around the park's camping area is the Great Bowerbird. This large, noisy, somewhat drab species visits picnic tables and willingly accepts anything edible. The bird's bower is not difficult to find; indeed one enterprising male regularly constructs his avenue of thin twigs near the carpark adjacent to the boat ramp, decorating it with litter left behind by picnickers − his bower glistens with hundreds of metal rings from the tops of drink cans. In addition to Great Bowerbirds, a number of species frequent the camping ground: Black Kite, Peaceful and Bar-shouldered Dove, Sulphur-crested Cockatoo, Red-winged Parrot, White-bellied Cuckoo-shrike, Blue-faced and White-throated Honeyeater, and Double-barred Finch. In the dry season, when many of the eucalypts produce masses of bright orange flowers, Red-collared and Varied Lorikeets, and Silver-crowned and Little Friarbirds invade the park. The din these birds make is incredible; if you camp beneath a flowering eucalypt you will not need an alarm clock!

River pandanus and freshwater mangroves line the banks of the Katherine River, just west of the camping area, and an early morning walk here should produce interesting birds such as Darter, Rufous Night Heron, Black Bittern, Azure Kingfisher and Crimson Finch. In the gorge itself there is very little vegetation and consequently it is ornithologically rather unexciting. Nevertheless it is certainly worth seeing. In the early morning, with the river's mirror surface reflecting a cloudless tropical sky, tour boats carry visitors into the cool, red-walled canyon where the stillness is broken only by the drone of the boats' engines. Here and there freshwater crocodiles lie motionless on the banks of the river, waiting for the first rays of the sun to warm their fascinating yet fearsome bodies. It is comforting to know that unlike the larger saltwater crocodiles these timid reptiles are not considered dangerous to man because their diet consists mainly of fish. Even so, it would be quite a shock to meet a fully grown 3 m male while walking along the banks of the river.

The park's ten main walking tracks commence at the visitors centre. Some, like the Edith Falls Wilderness Walk, are long and rather strenuous. Only the well-equipped, experienced bush-walker should attempt this route since it takes about five days to complete the 76 km from Katherine Gorge to Edith Falls. But there are less demanding treks, including the 4 km Windolf Walk, the 7 km Butterfly Gorge Walk (so called because hundreds of black and white common crow butterflies cluster in the dark corners of the gorge), and the 10 km Lily Ponds Walk. These walks involve a short but steep climb up the escarpment (a haunt of the Sandstone Shrike-thrush) to the sparsely vegetated plateau where Chestnut-quilled Rock-Pigeon is a possibility.

From a bird-watcher's point of view, the Biddlecombe Cascades Walk is perhaps the most rewarding track in the park. This is quite a long walk, 14.5 km, but those not wishing to go all the way to the cascades may care to stop after about 10 km at The Rockhole, a picturesque waterhole at the foot of the escarpment. You could take a well-earned lunch break here, enjoy a refreshing swim, and return to the camping area at a leisurely pace during the afternoon.

For the first 3—4 km, the Biddlecombe Cascades track passes through open eucalypt woodland with a grassy understorey. A wide variety of birds can be seen along the way: Square-tailed (rarely) and Whistling Kite, Black-breasted Buzzard, Brown Goshawk, Red Goshawk (rarely), Wedge-tailed Eagle, Brown Falcon, Australian Bustard, Peaceful and Diamond Dove, Partridge Pigeon, Red-tailed Black-Cockatoo, Northern Rosella, Hooded Parrot, Blue-winged Kookaburra, Red-backed King-fisher, Rainbow Bee-eater, Dollarbird (a wet-season visitor), White-winged Triller, Rufous Whistler, Restless Flycatcher, Grey-crowned Babbler, Red-backed Fairy-wren, Varied Sittella, Black-tailed Treecreeper, White-gaped, Black-chinned, Brown and Banded Honeyeater, Mistletoebird, Striated Pardalote, Olive-backed Oriole, White-breasted and Black-faced Woodswallow, and Pied Butcherbird.

Finches are a feature of the region's avifauna, and en route to the cascades you should have little difficulty finding Masked and Long-tailed Finch, while Chestnut-breasted and Yellow-rumped Mannikin are possibilities. The Gouldian Finch — one of Australia's most beautiful birds — is regularly sighted in the park, although it is more plentiful in some years than in others. Like other finches,

Gouldians feed on grass seeds; they usually occur in flocks of twenty or more and are frequently active during the heat of the day. The finches are difficult to spot in the long grass, but when disturbed they often fly only a short distance before perching in a nearby tree where, with luck, the gorgeous males will reveal their brilliant colours.

About halfway to The Rockhole, the Biddlecombe Cascades track crosses Seventeen Mile Creek. You could easily spend an hour or so at this delightful spot, bird-watching in the luxuriant tropical vegetation that grows along the banks of the creek. Common Koel (a frequent wet-season visitor), Channel-billed Cuckoo (an uncommon wet-season visitor), Azure Kingfisher, Lemon-bellied, Leaden and Shining Flycatcher, White-browed Robin, Little Shrike-thrush, Northern Fantail, Bar-breasted and Rufous-throated Honeyeater, and Yellow Oriole are just a few of the many species that can be found here.

Beyond Seventeen Mile Creek there is another stretch of open woodland; after 4 km or so you can either take a side track to The Rockhole, or continue along the main path to Biddlecombe Cascades.

The walk to the cascades and back will take a full day. Plan on an early start, when the birds are most active, and wear sturdy shoes because the track is quite rough in places, especially the last section leading up the escarpment and across the plateau to the cascades. And remember that even in the dry season the temperature frequently exceeds 30 degrees C — take along a hat and something cool to drink.

Edith Falls

Edith Falls, a series of small waterfalls where the Edith River drops over the western edge of the Arnhem Land Plateau, lie on the boundary of Katherine Gorge National Park, about 70 km north of Katherine. To get there take the Stuart Highway, turn east after about 50 km and follow the sealed road to the falls. This well-known swimming spot is very popular; you should therefore not arrive too late in the day because the camping ground (which has toilets and fireplaces but no other facilities) may be full.

From the base of the falls a walking track provides access to the plateau, following the Edith River through a picturesque gorge where the clear, deep rock-pools are fringed with pandanus. Most visitors, however, do not come to walk but to swim in the huge waterhole that has formed at the foot of the escarpment; it usually remains full throughout the dry season. Of course there are birds here too — an early morning walk along the banks of the river, downstream from the camping area, should prove most rewarding.

Umbrawarra Gorge Nature Park

This narrow, small gorge is not spectacular, but during the dry season the permanent pools within it attract many birds, especially honeyeaters and finches. A rough walking track winds through the gorge where White-gaped, White-throated, Brown, Bar-breasted, Rufous-throated and Banded Honeyeater, and Crimson, Double-barred, Masked and Long-tailed Finch can usually be found quite readily.

The park is about 120 km north-west of Katherine, and about 25 km south-west of Pine Creek. The 972 ha reserve has a camping area with toilets and fireplaces; it is not a particularly attractive site, but quite adequate for an overnight stay. The road from Pine Creek to the park entrance, although unsealed and rather rough, is suitable for conventional vehicles. En route the diligent observer will almost certainly see Hooded Parrots, especially in the vicinity of Pine Creek where there are numerous termite mounds (the parrots breed in these mounds), and it is worth keeping a watch for Partridge Pigeons in areas where the grass has been recently burnt.

Cutta Cutta Cave Nature Park

This 1500 ha reserve is about 27 km south-east of Katherine via the Stuart Highway. The park protects an area of limestone country and features a number of caves, some of which harbour an interesting array of rare fauna including blind shrimps, ghost bats and golden horseshoe bats.

Ranger-guided tours of the main Cutta Cutta Cave are conducted twice daily throughout the dry season (April–October), and coach tour operators in Katherine include the park on their itineraries. The park is for day use only and there are no facilities other than toilets.

Mataranka Pool Nature Park

A thermal pool surrounded by lush tropical vegetation is the main feature of this tiny 4 ha reserve. The underground spring feeding the pool flows at the incredible rate of five million gallons a day and maintains a steady temperature of 34 degrees C.

The park is about 5 km east of Mataranka township and about 115 km south-east of Katherine. Accommodation is available at the Mataranka Homestead, just outside the park boundary; the proprietors of the homestead also operate a caravan park adjacent to the thermal pool. The reserve is very popular, hence it is not one of the best places to go bird-watching. Nevertheless there are always a few species to be seen along the walking tracks leading through the monsoon forest, and Great Bowerbirds frequent the caravan park.

Pioneering life in this fascinating part of the Northern Territory was vividly portrayed by Mrs Aeneas Gunn, the most famous of the region's early settlers, in her book *We of the Never-Never*. The Elsey Memorial, on the Stuart Highway about 10 km south of Mataranka, contains the grave of the author's husband — the much-loved 'Maluka'.

VICTORIA RIVER

The Victoria River, which has its origins in the plateau country near the border between Western Australia and the Northern Territory, reaches the sea in Joseph Bonaparte Gulf some 300 km south-west of Darwin. Because of its very large catchment, the river is most impressive when in full flood at the height of the wet season. During the dry it is reduced to a series of tranquil billabongs that reflect the red sandstone cliffs, in places rising 200 m above the water.

This is one of the most sparsely populated and remote parts of Australia. Since it shares a common origin with the Arnhem Land Plateau to the north-east and the Kimberley to the west, its vegetation and avifauna have affinities with both regions. The rich and varied birdlife includes many top end specialities — White-quilled Rock-Pigeon, Sandstone Shrike-thrush, Green-backed Gerygone, Long-tailed Finch and Yellow-rumped Mannikin are just a few. Nearly two hundred species have been recorded in the region and bird-watchers will undoubtedly want to spend many days exploring the river and the adjacent area. Unfortunately it will be difficult to plan a long holiday here, since the only road is the narrow (though sealed) Victoria Highway linking Katherine and Kununurra. If you do not wish to leave the highway, plan an overnight stop at the Victoria River Crossing, about 195 km south-west of Katherine. There is a caravan park here, pleasantly situated on the banks of the river. It has powered sites, and petrol, stores and accommodation are available at the Wayside Inn nearby.

Those planning an extended stay can see a good deal of the region by travelling south on Delamere Road (it leaves the Victoria Highway about 125 km south-west of Katherine) as far as Top Springs. From here, take the unsealed Timber Creek road via Victoria River Downs and beautiful Jasper Gorge. If you intend travelling this way, remember to carry extra petrol, spares and supplies, and be prepared to camp out overnight.

The Purple-crowned Fairy-wren, a much sought-after species, is one of the region's special birds. There are two subspecies — an eastern race and a western race — and both are patchily distributed throughout their ranges. The western subspecies occurs in isolated pockets of suitable habitat in the Victoria River region, but these

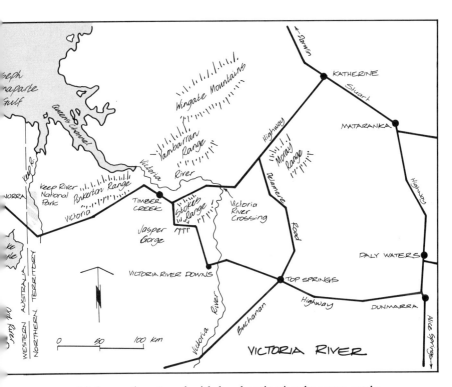

VICTORIA RIVER

gorgeous birds are threatened with local extinction because cattle trample the riverside vegetation in which they live. Fortunately a patch of canegrass has survived at the western end of the Victoria River bridge, opposite the caravan park at Victoria River Crossing. The fairy-wrens can often be found here, but the vegetation is very dense and virtually impenetrable. The best policy is to stand on the road in the early morning, making the well-known squeaking noises (achieved by sucking air through pursed lips) that bird-watchers use to call up small birds. With luck the fairy-wrens will be drawn out of the dense cover, the normally shy male climbing to the top of the canegrass to investigate the intrusion into his territory.

Even if you are not lucky enough to find the fairy-wren, there are many other birds to be seen. Tame Brolgas often visit the camping area, while a variety of interesting species frequent the surrounds: Peaceful and Bar-shouldered Dove, Little Corella, Sulphur-crested Cockatoo, Red-collared and Varied Lorikeet (particularly when the eucalypts are flowering), Channel-billed Cuckoo (an uncommon wet-season visitor), Pheasant Coucal, Blue-winged Kookaburra, Rainbow Bee-eater, Dollarbird (a frequent wet-season visitor), White-bellied Cuckoo-shrike, Restless Flycatcher, Varied Sittella, a host of honeyeaters including Silver-crowned and Little Friarbird, Blue-faced, White-gaped, Yellow-tinted, White-throated, Brown, Bar-breasted, Rufous-throated and Banded Honeyeater, Red-browed and Striated Pardalote, Great Bowerbird, White-breasted, Black-faced and Little Woodswallow, and Pied Butcherbird.

From the eastern end of the bridge it is possible to walk for some distance north or south along the banks of the river. Although the vegetation has been decimated by cattle, birds are quite plentiful, and there is a chance of White-browed Robin and Northern Fantail, as well as a variety of finches – Star, Crimson and Double-barred Finch, and Pictorella, Chestnut-breasted and Yellow-rumped Mannikin. The permanent waterholes and billabongs attract an assortment of waterbirds, chiefly Australasian Grebe, cormorants, herons, egrets, ibis and spoonbills, but also on occasions more unusual species such as Darter, Black-necked Stork, Wandering and Plumed Whistling-Duck, and Green Pygmy-Goose. Black-fronted Plover frequents the bare margins, while Rufous Night Heron, Black Bittern, Brown Quail and White-browed Crake (a rare but regular wet-season visitor) inhabit the dense waterside vegetation.

Away from the river the vegetation consists mainly of open woodland with a grassy understorey, and here too birds are plentiful. Australian Bustards are relatively common (they are often seen along the Victoria Highway, especially early in the day), and other species include Bush Thick-knee, Oriental Pratincole (sometimes in large numbers during the wet season), Australian Pratincole (chiefly during the dry season), Diamond Dove, Red-tailed Black-Cockatoo (in large flocks during the dry season), Red-winged Parrot, Cockatiel, Budgerigar (particularly in the dry season), Red-backed Kingfisher, Grey-crowned Babbler, Red-backed Fairy-wren, Black-tailed Treecreeper, and a variety of finches – Zebra, Masked, Long-tailed and, more rarely, the very beautiful Gouldian. Raptors are well represented, with Black Kite, Black-breasted Buzzard, Spotted Harrier and Australian Hobby all commonly recorded.

The surrounding rich red countryside is exceedingly beautiful; towards evening, when the sandstone cliffs glow like embers in the setting sun, the view from the Victoria River bridge provides a fitting end to the day. For those with the time, boat tours of the river can be booked at the inn. A visit (by road) to Jasper Gorge, which lies about 90 km to the south-west, should prove worthwhile, for the gorge's vertical walls are a haunt of the White-quilled Rock-Pigeon and Sandstone Shrike-thrush (the rock-pigeon is close to the south-eastern limit of its range here), and other interesting species occurring in the area include Northern

Rosella, Leaden Flycatcher and Green-backed Gerygone.

The Victoria Highway is the main route from the top end of the Northern Territory into Western Australia. Those travelling this way will find the river crossing an ideal place for an overnight stop, or perhaps a stay of a few days. The best time to visit the region is during the dry winter season (usually April to November).

ALICE SPRINGS AND THE MACDONNELL RANGES

The MacDonnell Ranges consist of many parallel ridges, sweeping from east to west in a great 300 km arc. They form part of The Centre, a vast, fascinating region often referred to as the 'dead heart' of Australia. Yet even during periods of prolonged drought the interior is by no means dead, for the central Australian ranges are something of an oasis. Here run-off from the rocks creates vegetation communities that are much richer than one might expect, considering the climatic characteristics of the region. And in the deep gorges, protected from the burning summer sun by high cliffs, permanent pools attract and sustain a wealth of wildlife, including many species of birds.

The region has much to offer the visitor. In the ranges near Alice Springs there are numerous reserves, and while a four-wheel-drive vehicle would be an advantage, many of the better known places of interest — Simpsons Gap, Standley Chasm and Ormiston Gorge, for example — are readily accessible by conventional vehicle. And now that the South Australian section of the Stuart Highway is completely sealed, the journey from Port Augusta to Alice Springs is no longer a motorist's nightmare.

Alice Springs

Many visitors to Alice Springs, especially those from overseas, are somewhat surprised by what they see. Originally the name of a repeater station on the overland telegraph line linking Adelaide with Darwin, Alice Springs became a town that was home to many thousands of Australian soldiers when it was used as a garrison during World War II. Since then it has grown considerably and today, with tourism the main industry, it has numerous hotels and motels, a casino, at least seven caravan parks, a modern shopping centre and a mall. For those travelling on a shoestring there is a youth hostel on the corner of Todd Street and Stott Terrace.

Whether you arrive by air, rail or road, 'the Alice' makes an ideal base for the bird-watcher. It is located on the banks of the Todd River — dry for much of the time — near Heavitree Gap in the MacDonnell Ranges. For many visitors the spectacular gorges and canyons to the east and west of Alice Springs are the region's main attraction. Before leaving the town, however, pay a visit to the following spots.

Alice Springs Telegraph Station Historical Reserve: Lies on the Todd River some 5 km north of the town and is easily reached via the Stuart Highway. Within the 445 ha reserve there are a collection of interesting historic buildings, a small native fauna sanctuary, many shaded picnic areas, and a network of walking tracks. During winter the reserve is open daily between 8 a.m. and 7 p.m., and in summer (1 October to 30 April) between 8 a.m. and 9 p.m. Camping is not permitted.

From the old telegraph station, which has been extensively restored, walking tracks follow the Todd River and lead into the surrounding boulder-strewn hills. Here you should have little difficulty finding at least some of the following birds: Wedge-tailed Eagle, Crested Pigeon, Red-tailed Black-Cockatoo (occasionally in flocks of fifty or more), Galah, Cockatiel, Port Lincoln Ringneck, Red-backed Kingfisher, Rainbow Bee-eater, Rufous Whistler, Grey-crowned Babbler, Splendid Fairy-wren, Weebill, Yellow-rumped Thornbill, Yellow-throated Miner, White-plumed and Brown Honeyeater, Mistletoebird, Red-browed Pardalote (frequents the tall gums near the telegraph station), Zebra Finch, Australian Magpie-lark, Black-faced Woodswallow, Pied Butcherbird, Australian Magpie and Little Crow.

Two sought-after species, Redthroat and Spotted Bowerbird, may not be easy to locate but are well worth searching for.

Alice Springs Sewage Ponds: Well known to birders throughout Australia, the sewage works are about 3 km south of the town centre. To get there, drive south (towards the airport) on the Stuart Highway and turn right at Commonage Road. The ponds are on the left, opposite the rubbish dump (an excellent spot for Whistling and Black Kites).

The sewage farm is one of the few places close to Alice Springs where permanent water exists. Not surprisingly, it attracts a wide variety of waterbirds — Hoary-headed and Australasian Grebe, Darter (rather rare), Little Black and Little Pied Cormorant, Pacific and White-faced Heron, Great and (rather rare) Intermediate Egret, Black-necked Stork (very rare), Glossy, Sacred and Straw-necked Ibis, Royal and Yellow-billed Spoonbill, Plumed Whistling-Duck (rather rare), Black Swan, Freckled (very rare), Pacific Black, Pink-eared and Maned Duck, Grey Teal, Hardhead, Australian Crake, Black-tailed Native-hen, Eurasian Coot, Silver Gull, and Whiskered and Gull-billed Tern.

Wader-watchers should not discount Alice Springs simply because it is a long way from the coast. In addition to the resident species — Masked Lapwing, Red-kneed Dotterel, Black-fronted Plover, Black-winged Stilt and Red-necked Avocet — a string of

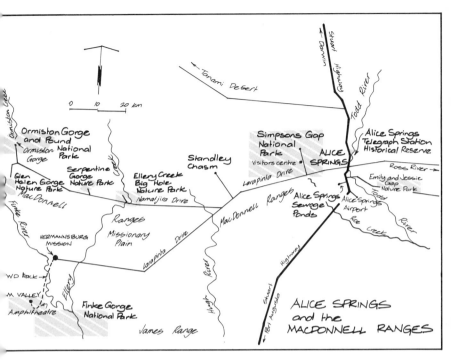

interesting migratory waders have turned up at the ponds. These include Little Curlew, Wood, Common, Marsh and Pectoral Sandpiper, and Red-necked Phalarope.

Although not as spectacular as the Flinders Ranges in South Australia, the MacDonnell Ranges are nonetheless very beautiful. Many of the more famous tourist spots, featuring picturesque waterholes, steep-sided ravines and mighty gorges, lie to the west of Alice Springs. Simpsons Gap, Standley Chasm, Ellery Creek Gorge, Serpentine Gorge, Ormiston Gorge and Glen Helen Gorge are all readily accessible via a good sealed road, but those wishing to visit Palm Valley, in Finke Gorge National Park, will need a four-wheel-drive because the rough track into the park follows the sandy bed of the Finke River. If you do not own a four-wheel-drive vehicle, you can still get to Palm Valley because several commercial tour operators in Alice Springs regularly visit the park. Details can be obtained from any branch of the Northern Territory Government Tourist Bureau.

Simpsons Gap National Park
Much of this 30 950 ha reserve is a wilderness, accessible only to hardy bushwalkers. To reach the park, turn off the Alice Springs to Glen Helen Gorge road (Larapinta Drive) about 15 km west of

Alice Springs. From the visitors centre, 3 km along the entrance road, it is possible to walk to Rocky Gap (7 km), Bond Gap (10.5 km), Spring Gap (19.5 km), Fairy Spring (8 km), Wallaby Gap (11.5 km), Kangaroo Flat (14 km), and to many other places of interest within the reserve. There is no formal camping area, but bushwalkers are permitted to camp overnight. You must, however, be adequately prepared and leave details of your itinerary with the park ranger. A detailed walk map is available from the visitors centre, but many of the tracks are not well defined and you should carry a compass.

For those not wishing to walk far there are toilets and picnic areas at the end of the entrance road, some 5 km north of the visitors centre, and from the carpark it is an easy stroll along the bed of Roe Creek (normally dry) to Simpsons Gap. There are generally only a few species of birds to be seen here, although Grey-headed Honeyeaters are plentiful in the trees bordering Roe Creek, and raptor buffs should scan the adjacent cliff-face for Peregrine Falcon — splashes of white show clearly where the falcons roost. Away from the gap, Little Woodswallows can be seen hawking over the ridges, while White-browed Treecreepers occur on the plains.

Black-flanked rock wallabies are common in the park; look for them on the rocky slopes near Simpsons Gap.

Standley Chasm

This well-known cut in the ranges is about 50 km west of Alice Springs. In places its walls rise to over 100 m, yet the average distance between them is less than 5 m. As a result the gorge receives sunlight for only a short period at midday, and it is then that tourists arrive by the coachload.

Standley Chasm is Aboriginal land, and a small entrance fee is charged. Near the carpark there are toilets, a cafe, and picnic facilities. The chasm is undeniably spectacular; the rich red rocks, the cycads and the ghost gums make a memorable sight.

If you are fit, scramble up the boulder-strewn slope beyond the main gorge and listen for the high-pitched reeling trill of the Dusky Grasswren. The chasm holds a small number of these normally elusive grasswrens and they are not difficult to find. You should, however, get there early in the day, before the crowds arrive. To obtain good views of the grasswrens purse your lips and suck hard, producing a high-pitched squeak similar to the birds' contact calls. More often than not they will come bouncing over the rocks to investigate.

Ellery Creek Big Hole Nature Park

Situated about 93 km west of Alice Springs, this 1776 ha reserve features a delightful waterhole fringed with massive river red gums. Cycads can be found in the narrow moist gorge beyond the waterhole, while native figs grow at the foot of the cliffs. Away from the creek the vegetation is sparse, consisting mainly of spinifex (*Triodia*) with scattered trees and shrubs. From the tops of the ridges there are superb views south to the James Range.

Ellery Creek is an excellent spot for birds. Grey-crowned Babblers are common, and their bulky domed nests can be seen in the river red gums near the waterhole. Other species include Whistling Kite, Wedge-tailed Eagle, Australian Hobby, Port Lincoln Ringneck, Black-eared Cuckoo, Red-backed Kingfisher, Splendid Fairy-wren, Weebill, Inland and Yellow-rumped Thornbill, Yellow-throated Miner, Spiny-cheeked, Grey-headed, White-plumed and Brown Honeyeater, Crimson Chat (a nomadic species), Mistletoebird, Red-browed Pardalote, Painted Firetail, Zebra Finch, Black-faced Woodswallow and Pied Butcherbird.

The Rufous-crowned Emu-wren is one of the most interesting birds at Ellery Creek. The habitat here is ideal for them − spinifex on rocky ridges − but it is an exceedingly difficult species to find. Like its close relative the Southern Emu-wren, the Rufous-crowned is best located by its call − a high-pitched, silvery trill. When disturbed the bird runs mouse-like between clumps of spinifex, but if you walk quietly you may catch a glimpse of one clinging to a seed-stem or flying feebly ahead of you.

Visitors are permitted to camp in the park; there are toilets and picnic facilities near the waterhole.

Serpentine Gorge Nature Park

Covering an area of 518 ha, Serpentine Gorge Nature Park is about 104 km west of Alice Springs. It features a small but picturesque gorge and a permanent waterhole. Over much of the area the vegetation consists of spinifex with scattered trees and shrubs; in the gorge and along the watercourses there are river red gums, ironwoods and corkwoods.

Like Ellery Creek, this is a good place to go bird-watching since the presence of water attracts a wide variety of species. The Spinifexbird has been recorded at Serpentine Gorge. A somewhat elusive species, it shows a distinct preference for tall spinifex, especially that growing along creek beds and at the bases of hills.

The park has toilets and picnic facilities; camping is not permitted.

Ormiston Gorge and Pound National Park

No visitor to central Australia should miss Ormiston Gorge. It is outstandingly beautiful − on a cloudless winter's day the combination of orange rocks, white-trunked gums and vivid blue sky is truly breathtaking. Artists and photographers will find it a magical spot, and bird-watchers will be equally enraptured.

Spinifex Pigeons are arguably the most attractive birds at Ormiston — they are certainly the most confiding. In the early morning and late afternoon coveys of these cryptically coloured, plump little birds emerge from the spinifex-covered hills behind the camping area. If you are quiet they will come within a metre or so of where you are standing; a handful of rice will keep them busy long enough for you to admire their rich rusty plumage.

Other species occurring in the park include Whistling Kite, Budgerigar (highly nomadic), Port Lincoln Ringneck, Rainbow Bee-eater, Red-capped and Hooded Robin, Grey-crowned Babbler, Yellow-throated Miner, Grey-headed, Brown, Black and Pied Honeyeater (like the Budgerigar, the last two birds are highly nomadic), Mistletoebird, Painted Firetail, Spotted Bower-bird (usually common around the camping area), Black-faced and Little Woodswallow, and Pied Butcherbird. Pacific Heron and Black-fronted Plover can be found at many of the larger waterholes along Ormiston Creek, and the surrounding rugged countryside is worth exploring for Dusky Grasswren and, perhaps, Spinifexbird.

Despite its isolation, Ormiston Gorge has excellent facilities including solar-heated showers and a laundry (visitors should bring their own drinking water). Since it is one of the most popular parks in the MacDonnell Ranges, it would pay to get there by mid-afternoon at the latest because the camping area is quite small. There are no marked tracks in the reserve; neverthe-less it is possible to walk for hours along Ormiston Creek through the gorge to Ormiston Pound.

The national park is 4655 ha in area and about 132 km west of Alice Springs via Larapinta and Namatjira Drives. Both these roads are sealed, but there is an 8 km stretch of unsealed road leading to the reserve.

Glen Helen Gorge Nature Park

This gorge, to the south of Ormiston, has been created by the cutting of the Finke River through the MacDonnell Ranges. It boasts many of the features found at other reserves in the region, and is a good spot for Peregrine Falcon.

There is a motel (the Mt Sonder Safari Lodge), with a caravan park near the park boundary. Petrol and food supplies can be obtained there. The 386 ha park is about 135 km west of Alice Springs.

Finke Gorge National Park

Lying to the south of Hermannsburg Mission, this 45 856 ha park comprises a section of the Finke River and the surrounding rugged countryside. The best known feature of the reserve is Palm

Valley, famous for its cabbage palms (*Livistona mariae*) and cycads.

The reserve is about 150 km south-west of Alice Springs. To get there take Larapinta Drive and turn south at Hermannsburg; the park is signposted from the mission (the track into the park is very sandy, making it unsuitable for conventional vehicles). Some 20 km south of Hermannsburg there is a shady camping area with grassed sites, toilets and showers.

From the camping ground it is a short walk to The Amphitheatre, a great natural basin featuring towering columns of red sandstone encircled by spectacular cliffs. There are no marked walking tracks here; however, since The Amphitheatre is sparsely vegetated and there are many landmarks, you are unlikely to become lost. Birds are not especially numerous, but there is a chance that you will see something notable — Bourke's Parrot, Black-eared Cuckoo, Chiming Wedgebill, Redthroat, Slaty-backed Thornbill, Banded Whiteface or Grey Honeyeater for example.

Finke Gorge National Park is of considerable interest to botanists because over four hundred plant species, nearly a third of the known central Australian flora, have been recorded there. Of greatest significance are the three thousand or so cabbage palms in Palm Valley, some 5 km west of the camping area. Although you can drive to the valley, the walk is well worthwhile since you can then appreciate the full majesty of the scenery — scramble up the spinifex-covered slopes near the entrance to the valley and look for Spinifex Pigeons and Dusky Grasswrens.

Far from being dead, central Australia is tremendously exciting; there are enough places of interest near Alice Springs to keep even the most energetic bird-watcher occupied for a week or more. In addition to the reserves already mentioned, there are another five to the east of 'the Alice' — Emily and Jessie Gap Nature Park, Corroboree Rock Conservation Reserve, Trephina Gorge Nature Park, N'Dhala Gorge Nature Park and Arltunga Historical Reserve.

ULURU NATIONAL PARK

This well-known national park in the arid heart of the continent protects two of Australia's most famous natural features — Ayers Rock and the Olgas. Ayers Rock, or Uluru as it is known to the Aboriginal people, is one of our greatest tourist attractions. Indeed there can surely be few people in this country who have not seen a photograph of that remarkable red monolith, and for many it symbolises not just the outback, but Australia itself. Ayers Rock is truly an amazing sight. When first glimpsed it is nothing more than a purple spot on the distant, shimmering horizon; as you approach, its colour gradually changes until at last the massive orange-red sandstone dome stands before you. Like a huge beach-washed whale it rises 342 m above the surrounding desert; it has a perimeter of approximately 8.8 km. In the evening, when the last of the sun's rays touch its surface, the rock glows in the remarkable way so often portrayed in photographs. Then, for a few moments, the surrealistic scene is captured by hundreds of tourists eagerly clicking their cameras in unison.

Uluru National Park covers an area of 126 132 ha and lies 470 km south-west of Alice Springs. From Erldunda, on the Stuart Highway, there is an excellent sealed road all the way to Ayers Rock and the recently completed Yulara tourist resort. This multi-million dollar development has been designed to cater for the 300 000 people expected to visit the park each year. An impressive complex — painted a subdued pink so as to blend with the desert sand — it houses an international-class hotel, a shopping and community centre, medical facilities, and a well-designed park information centre with displays covering the flora, fauna and Aboriginal history of the region. Away from the main complex, holiday cabins provide inexpensive accommodation, and there is a large camping ground with powered sites and on-site caravans.

Many visitors express surprise when they see such luxury in what is, after all, one of the most arid and remote parts of Australia. Indeed, some Swiss tourists were heard to remark rather ruefully, 'This is not the outback we came to see.' Nevertheless most people will welcome the splendid facilities, not least the solar-heated showers!

Ayers Rock dominates the landscape, and for many it is the sole reason for visiting the park. Ranger-guided tours are arranged for those wishing to learn more about the rock, especially its ritual and mythological significance to the Aboriginals. There are also natural history walks introducing visitors to the flora and fauna of the region. If you wish to see Ayers Rock and the Olgas from a totally different perspective, try one of the scenic flights that leave daily from the resort's airport.

Having seen and perhaps climbed the rock, the bird-watcher will find the park has a lot more to offer. While the region is a desert, it is by no means devoid of vegetation; in fact, the flora is remarkably rich — over three hundred plant species occur in the park. The vegetation can be grouped into three major components — sand plain and dune communities, run-off communities and upland communities. On the plains and dunes the vegetation is dominated by spinifex (*Triodia*), with scattered trees and shrubs, including witchetty bush, desert grevillea, honey grevillea, rattle-pod grevillea, desert poplar, desert oak and mulga. Around Ayers Rock and the Olgas there are run-off communities comprising relatively dense stands of mulga, while the third main

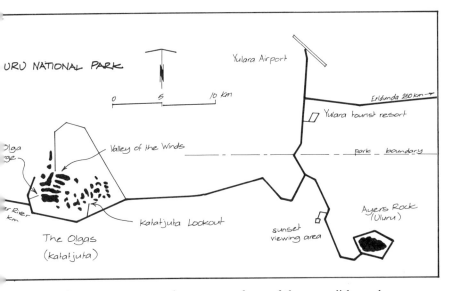

vegetation type occurs on the upper surfaces of the monoliths and on the adjacent foothills. Here there is only a sparse covering of hardy spinifex.

Rainfall in the region is extremely variable, averaging less than 200 mm per annum. It can rain at any time of the year; when it does, the desert sands disappear beneath a carpet of colourful wildflowers. In summer the daytime temperature may reach 44 degrees C, while in winter the thermometer frequently drops to minus 4 degrees C at night. The region's fauna has adapted to the harsh conditions, and many desert animals are nocturnal and rarely seen. However, dingoes and red kangaroos are reasonably plentiful and are often active during the day; those planning a trip to the Olgas may see a euro, or hill kangaroo.

There are over 150 bird species on the park's list (about forty of these are waterbirds that only turn up occasionally), and while none are confined to the park, many have ranges that are largely within the arid zone: Grey Falcon, Inland Dotterel, Spinifex Pigeon, Pink Cockatoo, Alexandra's, Bourke's and Scarlet-chested Parrot, Chiming Wedgebill, Cinnamon Quail-thrush, Rufous-crowned Emu-wren, Striated and Dusky Grasswren, Redthroat, Slaty-backed Thornbill, Banded Whiteface, White-browed Tree-creeper, Grey-headed, Grey-fronted, Grey, Black and Pied Honeyeater, Crimson Chat, Orange Chat and Painted Firetail. Other interesting species occurring in the park include Black-breasted Buzzard, Spotted Harrier, Black and Peregrine Falcon, Australian Bustard, Diamond Dove, Port Lincoln Ringneck, Mulga Parrot, Black-eared Cuckoo, Spotted Nightjar, Ground Cuckoo-shrike, Red-capped Robin, Crested Bellbird, Splendid, Variegated and White-winged Fairy-wren, White-fronted Honeyeater, Spotted Bowerbird, and Masked, Black-faced and Little Woodswallow.

Thorough exploration of the park will be difficult as there are few walking tracks and road access is only provided in the Ayers Rock — Mt Olga section. Furthermore, it is unwise to walk for any distance away from the roads — you could become lost or wander unknowingly onto an Aboriginal sacred site. (The national park is surrounded by Aboriginal land, which you will require a permit to enter.) Despite these restrictions, Uluru provides an opportunity to experience an arid and seemingly inhospitable environment in relative safety.

Visitors will spend much of their time in the vicinity of the resort. The Yulara camping area is surrounded by sand-dunes that are well vegetated with shrubs and spinifex, and many birds are attracted by the resort's permanent water supply. Zebra Finches are certainly the most numerous, while Little Crows are unquestionably the noisiest — these gregarious scavengers have the irritating habit of perching on campers' tents, greeting the sunrise with incessant 'nark, nark, nark' calls. Other more welcome visitors include Crested Pigeon, White-backed Swallow, Richard's Pipit, Black-faced Cuckoo-shrike, Willie Wagtail, Yellow-throated Miner, Singing Honeyeater, Crimson Chat, Black-faced Woodswallow and Australian Magpie. Black Kites continually soar overhead, twisting their long forked tails characteristically, and small groups of Budgerigars speed over the sandhills on their way to favoured feeding grounds. These small parrots are highly nomadic, but since Yulara provides them with a year-round source of water they may become permanent residents in the area.

Away from the resort there are roads leading to Ayers Rock, the Olgas and the airport. A walk along any of these should prove rewarding. Remember that bush birds are always most active in the early morning, especially in a desert environment; a dawn sortie is therefore advisable.

The Olgas lie about 30 km west of Ayers Rock and are readily accessible via a well-signposted road. Known to the Aboriginals as Katatjuta — meaning many heads — the Olgas are unlike any other range in Australia. From a distance the rounded domes are merely a jumble of purple-hued boulders; as you approach, the sheer-sided hills tower above you, rising to nearly 550 m at Mt Olga itself. Broad valleys separate some of the domes while others are bunched closed together, divided only by narrow ravines.

Since there are a number of walking tracks in this section of the park it is perhaps the best place to go bird-watching. There are tracks leading to Mt Olga Gorge and Katatjuta Lookout, and another through the Valley of the Winds. All of these walks are suitable for families, and none is longer than 4 km. There are also a number of unmarked routes, but only experienced bushwalkers should attempt the longer treks because some involve difficult climbs. Always advise a ranger if you intend leaving the marked tracks.

The desert is a fascinating and delicate environment, full of beauty and surprisingly rich in animal life. At night the stars have to be seen to be believed, and the howls of distant dingoes confirm that this really is the outback. Coach tour operators regularly visit the park from Alice Springs, and there are frequent air services. The road from Erldunda runs for nearly 250 km across the desert; there are usually plenty of Pink Cockatoos and many other birds to be seen en route. A stop at the salt lakes just east of Curtin Springs may produce something of interest, such as Red-necked Avocets, Banded Whitefaces or Orange Chats.

Further Reading

General

Blakers, M., Davies, S. J. J. F. and Reilly, P. N. *The Atlas of Australian Birds.* Melbourne University Press, Melbourne, 1984.

Pizzey, G. *A Field Guide to the Birds of Australia.* Collins, Sydney, 1980.

Reader's Digest Complete Book of Australian Birds. 2nd edn. Reader's Digest Services, Sydney, 1986.

Slater, P., Slater, P. and Slater, R. *The Slater Field Guide to Australian Birds.* Rigby, Sydney, 1986.

The Birds of Australia. A Book of Identification. 2nd edn. Ed. K. Simpson. Lloyd O'Neil, Melbourne, 1986.

Victoria

Aston, H. I. and Balmford, R. A. *A Bird Atlas of the Melbourne Region.* Victorian Ornithological Research Group, Melbourne, 1978.

Bardwell, S. *National Parks of Victoria and State, Coastal and Historic Parks.* Gregory's Publishing, Sydney, 1980.

Bedggood, G. W. 'Bird notes from East Gippsland'. *Aust. Bird Watcher,* 3, 1970, pp. 252−65.

——. 'Birdlife between Lake Tyers and Marlo, Victoria'. *Aust. Bird Watcher,* 8, 1980, pp. 147−62.

Beumer, J. P., Burbury, M. E. and Harrington, D. J. 'Birds at Macleods Morass, Bairnsdale, Victoria'. *Aust. Bird Watcher,* 8, 1980, pp. 232−6.

Birds of Heidelberg and the Yarra Valley. Warringal Conservation Society, Melbourne, 1981.

Conole, L. 'Birds of the Steiglitz area, Brisbane Ranges, Victoria, 1978−1980'. *Aust. Bird Watcher,* 9, 1981, pp. 14−23.

Cooper, R. P. 'Additional records of birds from Wilson's Promontory'. *Aust. Bird Watcher,* 3, 1970, pp. 239−45.

——. 'The avifauna of Wilson's Promontory'. *Aust. Bird Watcher,* 5, 1974, pp. 137−74, 205−33, 253−76; 6, 1975, pp. 17−34, 47−60, 87−102, 103−16.

Fleming, A. M. 'Birds of the Yarra Valley, Ivanhoe, Victoria'. *Aust. Bird Watcher,* 6, 1976, pp. 151−60.

Garnett, S., Lane, B. A., Schulz, M. and Wood, K. L. *Birds of Port Phillip Bay.* Ministry for Planning and Environment, Melbourne, 1986.

Humphreys, J. S. 'Birds of Cherry Lake, Altona, Victoria − Annotated comments on species and seasonal movements'. *Aust. Bird Watcher,* 11, 1986, pp. 153−66.

Jones, J. 'The Hattah Lakes camp-out, October 1951, with general notes on the birds of the Kulkyne State Forest'. *Emu,* 52, 1952, pp. 225−54.

Loyn, R. H. 'A survey of birds in Westernport Bay, Victoria, 1973−74'. *Emu,* 78, 1978, pp. 11−19.

McCann, I. R. *Grampians Birds − An Illustrated Checklist.* Halls Gap Tourist Information Centre, Halls Gap, 1982.

——. *Little Desert Wildlife − An Illustrated Checklist.* Little Desert Tours Pty Ltd, Nhill, 1983.

Morgan, D. G. 'Seasonal changes in populations of Anatidae at the Laverton Saltworks, Victoria, 1950–1953'. *Emu*, 54, 1954, pp. 263–78.

Norris, K. C., Mansergh, I. M., Ahern, L. D., Belcher, C. A., Temby, I. D. and Walsh, N. G. *Vertebrate Fauna of the Gippsland Lakes Catchment Victoria* (Occasional Paper Series Number 1). Ministry for Conservation, Melbourne, 1983.

Pascoe, B. *The Birds of Mallacoota*. Mallacoota School, Mallacoota, 1979.

Pescott, T. *Birds of Geelong*. Neptune Press, Geelong, 1983.

Robinson, L. N. *Birds of the Mallacoota area, Victoria*. Bird Observers Club, Melbourne, 1965.

Rotamah Island Bird Observatory Report 1980–81. Royal Australasian Ornithologists Union, Melbourne, 1982.

Victorian Bird Report, 1981. Ed. D. Robinson. Bird Observers Club, Melbourne, 1982.

Victorian Bird Report, 1982. Ed. D. Robinson. Bird Observers Club, Melbourne, 1983.

Victorian Bird Report, 1983. Ed. D. Robinson. Bird Observers Club, Melbourne, 1984.

Victorian Bird Report, 1984. Ed. R. Drummond. Bird Observers Club, Melbourne, 1985.

Victorian Bird Report, 1985. Ed. R. Drummond. Bird Observers Club, Melbourne, 1986.

Watson, I. M. 'Some species seen at the Laverton Saltworks, Victoria, 1950–1953, with notes on seasonal changes'. *Emu*, 55, 1955, pp. 224–48.

Wheeler, W. R. 'Charadriiformes at the Laverton Saltworks, Victoria, 1950–1953'. *Emu*, 55, 1955, pp. 279–95.

——. 'Field outing 1965 at Mt. Beauty, north-east Victoria'. *Emu*, 66, 1966, pp. 163–85.

——. *A Handlist of the Birds of Victoria*. Victorian Ornithological Research Group, Melbourne, 1967.

——. *The Birds of Phillip Island*. Western Port Bird Observers Club, Melbourne, 1981.

New South Wales

Brown, I. 'Birds of Ball's Pyramid, Lord Howe Island'. *Aust. Birds*, 13, 1979, pp. 41–2.

Disney, H. J. de S. 'Royal Australasian Ornithologists Union Pilot Atlas Scheme'. *Corella*, 2, 1979, pp. 97–163.

Environmental Survey of Lord Howe Island. Ed. H. F. Recher and S. S. Clark. Australian Museum, Sydney, 1974. (A report to the Lord Howe Island Board.)

Fairley, A. *A complete guide to Warrumbungle National Park*. Revised edn. Child & Henry, Sydney, 1983.

Fullagar, P. J. 'Cabbage Tree Island, New South Wales'. *Aust. Bird Bander*, 14, 1976, pp. 94–7.

Gall, B. C. and Longmore, N. W. 'Avifauna of the Thredbo Valley, Kosciusko National Park'. *Emu*, 78, 1978, pp. 189–96.

Gibson, J. D. 'The birds of the County of Camden (including the Illawarra district)'. *Aust. Birds*, 11, 1977, pp. 41–80.

Gregory's National Parks of New South Wales. 2nd edn. Gregory's Publishing, Sydney, 1984.

Hindwood, K. A. and Hoskin, E. S. 'The waders of Sydney (County of Cumberland), New South Wales'. *Emu*, 54, 1954, pp. 217–55.

Hindwood, K. A. and McGill, A. R. *The Birds of Sydney*. Royal Zoological Society of NSW, Sydney, 1958.

Howe, R. W., Howe, T. D. and Ford, H. A. 'Bird distributions on small rainforest remnants in New South Wales'. *Aust. Wildlife Research*, 8, 1981, pp. 637–51.

Jacobs, B. *Birds in the Gardens*. Royal Botanic Gardens, Sydney, 1976.

Kikkawa, J., Hore-Lacy, I. and Le Gay Brereton, J. 'A preliminary report on the birds of the New England National Park'. *Emu*, 65, 1965, pp. 139−43.

Lane Cove River State Recreation Area. Lane Cove River State Recreation Area Trust, Sydney, 1983.

Lane, S. G. 'Lion Island, New South Wales'. *Aust. Bird Bander*, 13, 1975, pp. 34−7.

―――. 'Broughton Island, New South Wales'. *Aust. Bird Bander*, 14, 1976, pp. 10−13.

―――. 'Little Broughton Island, New South Wales'. *Aust. Bird Bander*, 14, 1976, pp. 14−15.

―――. 'North Rock, Broughton Island, New South Wales'. *Aust. Bird Bander*, 14, 1976, pp. 16−17.

―――. 'Inner Rock, Broughton Island, New South Wales'. *Aust. Bird Bander*, 14, 1976, pp. 18−19.

Lindsey, T. 'N.S.W. Bird Report for 1978'. *Aust. Birds*, 14, 1979, pp. 1−22.

―――. 'NSW Bird Report for 1979'. *Aust. Birds*, 15, 1980, pp. 17−26.

―――. 'NSW Bird Report for 1980'. *Aust. Birds*, 16, 1981, pp. 1−23.

―――. 'NSW Bird Report for 1982 [1981]'. *Aust. Birds*, 17, 1982, pp. 1−26.

―――. 'NSW Bird Report for 1982'. *Aust. Birds*, 18, 1984, pp. 37−69.

―――. 'New South Wales Bird Report for 1983'. *Aust. Birds*, 19, 1985, pp. 65−100.

―――. 'New South Wales Bird Report for 1984'. *Aust. Birds*, 20, 1986, pp. 97−132.

Longmore, W. 'Birds of the alpine region, Kosciusko National Park'. *Birds*, 8, 1973, pp. 33−5.

McFarland, D. 'Seasonal changes in the avifauna of New England National Park'. *Aust. Bird Watcher*, 10, 1984, pp. 255−63.

McKean, J. L. and Hindwood, K. A. 'Additional notes on the birds of Lord Howe Island'. *Emu*, 64, 1965, pp. 79−97.

Milledge, D. 'One year's observations of seabirds in continental shelf waters off Sydney, N.S.W.'. *Corella*, 1, 1977, pp. 1−12.

Morris, A. K. 'The birds of Gosford, Wyong and Newcastle (County of Northumberland)'. *Aust. Birds*, 9, 1975, pp. 37−76.

―――. 'The status and distribution of the Turquoise Parrot in New South Wales'. *Aust. Birds*, 14, 1980, pp. 57−67.

Morris, A. K., McGill, A. R. and Holmes, G. *Handlist of Birds in New South Wales*. New South Wales Field Ornithologists Club, Sydney, 1981.

The Natural History of Sydney. 2nd edn. Trustees of the Australian Museum, Sydney, 1972.

Pegler, J. 'A wader survey of the northern shores of Port Stephens and the lower Myall River'. *Aust. Birds*, 14, 1980, pp. 68−72.

Recher, H. F. 'Survey of the avifauna of Myall Lakes, NSW: Report of the 1972 RAOU field-outing'. *Emu*, 75, 1975, pp. 213−25.

Rogers, A. 'N.S.W. Bird Report for 1976'. *Aust. Birds*, 11, 1977, pp. 81−104.

Rogers, A. and Lindsey, T. 'N.S.W. Bird Report for 1977'. *Aust. Birds*, 13, 1978, pp. 1−21.

Truran, J. 'Birds near Smith's Lake'. *Hunter Natural History*, 6, 1974, pp. 98−100.

Australian Capital Territory

Balfour, D. 'Birds of Mount Ainslie'. *Canberra Bird Notes*, 5(4), 1980, pp. 11−16.

Bell, H. L. 'Composition and seasonality of mixed-species feeding flocks of insectivorous birds in the Australian Capital Territory'. *Emu*, 80, 1980, pp. 227−32. (A survey of the Black Mountain area.)

Clark, G. S. and Lenz, M. 'Bird Report, 1 July 1977 to 30 June 1978'. *Canberra Bird Notes*, 4(4), 1978, pp. 2−13.

Davey, C. 'Some observations on the common waterbirds of Lake Ginninderra: 1978−79'. *Canberra Bird Notes*, 5(2), 1980, pp. 3−12.

A Field List of the Birds of Canberra and District. 3rd edn. Canberra Ornithologists Group, Canberra, 1985.

Hermes, N. 'Mixed species flocks in a dry sclerophyll forest in autumn and winter'. *Corella*, 5, 1981, pp. 41–5. (A survey of the Black Mountain area.)

Lamm, D. W. 'Seasonal counts of birds at Lake George, New South Wales'. *Emu*, 64, 1965, pp. 114–28.

Lamm, D. W. and Wilson, S. J. 'Seasonal fluctuations of birds in the Brindabella Range, Australian Capital Territory'. *Emu*, 65, 1966, pp. 183–207.

Lenz, M. 'Bird Report, 1 July 1978 to 30 June 1979'. *Canberra Bird Notes*, 5(1), 1980, pp. 2–21.

———. 'Bird Report 1 July 1979 to 30 June 1980'. *Canberra Bird Notes*, 6, 1981, pp. 3–42.

———. 'Bird Report 1 July 1980 to 30 June 1981'. *Canberra Bird Notes*, 7, 1982, pp. 2–33.

National Botanic Gardens. Australian Government Publishing Service, Canberra, 1980.

Prendergast, H. 'Bibliography of birds of the Canberra region'. *Canberra Bird Notes*, 9, 1984, pp. 31–7. (An extensive review of the ornithological literature relating to the Canberra region.)

Ross, A. D. 'Observations of birds at Jerrabomberra Wetlands and eastern Lake Burley Griffin: July 1982–June 1983'. *Canberra Bird Notes*, 9, 1984, pp. 2–23.

Taylor, I. 'Annual Bird Report: 1 July 1981 to 30 June 1982'. *Canberra Bird Notes*, 8, 1983, pp. 5–52.

———. 'Annual Bird Report: 1 July 1982 to 30 June 1983'. *Canberra Bird Notes*, 9, 1984, pp. 50–139.

Taylor, I. and Davey, C. 'Annual Bird Report: 1 July 1983 to 30 June 1984'. *Canberra Bird Notes*, 10, 1985, pp. 26–85.

Taylor, I., Davey, C. and Gibson, J. 'Annual Bird Report: 1 July 1984 to 30 June 1985'. *Canberra Bird Notes*, 11, 1986, pp. 26–88.

Taylor, I., Lenz, M. and Lepschi, B. J. 'Annual Bird Report: 1 July 1985 to 30 June 1986'. *Canberra Bird Notes*, 12, 1987, pp. 30–83.

Williams, J. *Nature Guide*. Australian Government Publishing Service, Canberra, 1976. (A guide to Black Mountain Nature Reserve and the Ainslie-Majura Reserve.)

Queensland

Austin, C. N. 'Further notes on the birds of Dunk Island, Queensland'. *Emu*, 49, 1950, pp. 225–31.

Banfield, E. J. *The Confessions of a Beachcomber*. Angus & Robertson, Sydney, 1933.

Beruldsen, G. R. 'Ten days at Weipa, Cape York Peninsula'. *Aust. Bird Watcher*, 8, 1979, pp. 128–32.

Bravery, J. A. 'Waders of Tinaroo Dam, North Queensland'. *Emu*, 64, 1964, pp. 61–4.

———. 'The birds of Atherton Shire, Queensland'. *Emu*, 70, 1970, pp. 49–63.

Breeden, S. and K. *Tropical Queensland*. Collins, Sydney, 1970.

Brown, A. G. 'Notes on some birds of the Whitsunday Group, Queensland'. *Emu*, 49, 1949, pp. 44–9.

Czechura, G. V. 'The raptors of the Blackall–Conondale Ranges and adjoining lowlands, south-eastern Queensland'. *Corella*, 9, 1985, pp. 49–54.

Domm, S. 'Sea birds and waders of the Lizard Island area'. *Sunbird*, 8, 1977, pp. 1–8.

Durbidge, E. and Covacevich, J. *North Stradbroke Island*. Stradbroke Island Management Organisation, Brisbane, 1981.

Finlayson, C. M. 'Water birds recorded from five artificial lakes in north-western Queensland'. *Sunbird*, 11, 1980, pp. 49–57.

Forshaw, J. M. and Muller, K. A. 'Annotated list of birds observed at Iron Range, Cape York Peninsula, Queensland, during October 1974'. *Aust. Bird Watcher*, 7, 1978, pp. 171–94.

Garnett, S. and Bredl, R. 'Birds in the vicinity of Edward River Settlement'. *Sunbird*, 15, 1985, pp. 6−23, 25−40.

Garnett, S. and Cox, J. *Birds of the Townsville Town Common*. Authors, Townsville, 1983.

Gill, H. B. 'Birds of Innisfail and hinterland'. *Emu*, 70, 1970, pp. 105−16.

Griffin, A. C. M. 'Birds of Mount Spec'. *Sunbird*, 5, 1974, pp. 29−39.

Groom, W. A. *National Parks of Queensland*. Cassell Australia, Sydney, 1980.

Horton, W. 'The birds of Mount Isa'. *Sunbird*, 6, 1975, pp. 49−69.

Jahnke, B. R. 'Notes on the birds of Isla Gorge National Park, August 1973'. *Qld Naturalist*, 21, 1976, pp. 100−3.

_____. 'Notes on birds seen on Hinchinbrook Island, August 1975'. *Qld Naturalist*, 22, 1978, pp. 44−9.

Johnson, H. R. and Hooper, N. 'The birds of the Iron Range area of Cape York Peninsula'. *Aust. Bird Watcher*, 5, 1973, pp. 80−95.

Kikkawa, J. 'Birds of Weipa, Cape York Peninsula'. *Sunbird*, 6, 1975, pp. 43−7.

_____. 'The birds of Cape York Peninsula'. *Sunbird*, 7, 1976, pp. 25−41, 81−106.

King, B. R. 'Michaelmas Cay, Great Barrier Reef, Queensland'. *Corella*, 9, 1985, pp. 94−6.

Lavery, H. J. and Hopkins, N. 'Birds of the Townsville district of North Queensland'. *Emu*, 63, 1963, pp. 242−52.

Liddy, J. 'Waders at Mount Isa, Queensland'. *Emu*, 55, 1955, pp. 297−302.

Niland, D. C. 'The Queensland Ornithological Society Bird Report, 1985'. *Sunbird*, 16, 1986, pp. 49−67.

Palliser, T. 'The Queensland Ornithological Society Bird Report, 1984'. *Sunbird*, 15, 1985, pp. 45−70.

Popple, W. 'Birds seen at Hinchinbrook Island in 1979'. *Qld Naturalist*, 24, 1983, pp. 61−3.

Rainforests of Australia. Ed. P. Figgis. Weldons, Sydney, 1985.

Roberts, G. J. *The Birds of South-East Queensland*. Queensland Conservation Council, Brisbane, 1979.

Roberts, G. J. and Ingram, G. J. 'An annotated list of the land birds of Cooloola'. *Sunbird*, 7, 1976, pp. 1−20.

Sinclair, J. *Discovering Cooloola*. Pacific Maps, Sydney, 1978.

Stewart, D. A. 'Queensland Bird Report, 1983'. *Sunbird*, 14, 1984, pp. 45−65.

Storr, G. M. 'Birds of the Cooktown and Laura districts, North Queensland'. *Emu*, 53, 1953, pp. 225−48.

_____. *List of Queensland Birds* (Western Australian Museum Special Publication No. 5). WA Museum, Perth, 1973.

_____. *Revised List of Queensland Birds* (Records of the Western Australian Museum, Supplement Number 19). WA Museum, Perth, 1984.

Tarr, H. E. 'Birds of Dunk Island, North Queensland'. *Emu*, 48, 1948, pp. 8−13.

Vernon, D. P. *Birds of Brisbane and environs* (Queensland Museum Booklet No. 5). Qld Museum, Brisbane, 1968.

Vernon, D. P. and Barry, D. H. 'Birds of Fraser Island and adjacent waters'. *Mem. Queensland Museum*, 16, 1972, pp. 223−32.

_____. 'Further notes on the birds of Fraser Island and adjacent waters'. *Sunbird*, 7, 1976, pp. 107−11.

Warham, J. 'Bird notes from the Carnarvon Ranges, Queensland'. *Emu*, 60, 1960, pp. 1−7.

Watson, R. 'Bird list − Victoria Park, Brisbane − 1970−74'. *Qld Naturalist*, 21, 1976, pp. 140−1.

Wheeler, W. R. 'The birds of Cairns, Cooktown and the Atherton Tablelands'. *Aust. Bird Watcher*, 3, 1967, pp. 55−76.

_____. 'The birds of Green Mountains'. *Aust. Bird Watcher*, 4, 1973, pp. 257−69.

Wildlife of the Brisbane area. Ed. W. Davies. The Jacaranda Press, Brisbane, 1983.

Tasmania

Bird Observers' Association of Tasmania. 'Birds of Queen's Domain, Hobart'. *Tas. Naturalist*, 33, 1973, pp. 7–8. (Results of a survey carried out by members of BOAT, 1969–71.)

Bulman, C., Rounsevell, D. E. and Woinarski, J. C. Z. *The Forty-Spotted Pardalote* (An RAOU Conservation Statement). Royal Australasian Ornithologists Union, Melbourne, 1986.

Green, R. H. *The Birds of Flinders Island* (Records of the Queen Victoria Museum No. 34). Queen Victoria Museum, Launceston, 1969.

Green, R. H. and Mollison, B. C. 'Birds of Port Davey and south coast of Tasmania'. *Emu*, 61, 1961, pp. 223–36.

Napier, J. R. 'Birds of the Break O'Day Valley, Tasmania'. *Aust. Bird Watcher*, 3, 1969, pp. 179–92.

Ratkowsky, A. V. and D. A. 'The birds of the Mt Wellington Range, Tasmania'. *Emu*, 77, 1977, pp. 19–22.

———. 'A survey of the birds of the Mt Wellington Range, Tasmania, during the non-breeding months'. *Emu*, 78, 1978, pp. 223–6.

Rounsevell, D. E., Blackhall, S. A. and Thomas, D. G. *Birds of Maria Island* (Wildlife Division Technical Report 77/3). Tas. National Parks and Wildlife Service, Hobart, 1977.

Rounsevell, D. E. and Woinarski, J. C. Z. 'Status and conservation of the Forty-spotted Pardalote, *Pardalotus quadragintus*'. *Aust. Wildlife Research*, 10, 1983, pp. 343–9.

Sharland, M. *A Guide to the Birds of Tasmania*. Drinkwater Publishing, Hobart, 1981.

Tasmanian Bird Report No. 7 (1977). Ed. D. G. Thomas. Bird Observers' Association of Tasmania, Hobart, 1979.

Tasmanian Bird Report No. 8 (1978). Ed. D. G. Thomas. Bird Observers' Association of Tasmania, Hobart, 1980.

Tasmanian Bird Report No. 9 (1979). Ed. W. G. Jones. Bird Observers' Association of Tasmania, Hobart, 1980.

Tasmanian Bird Report No. 10 (1980). Ed. W. G. Jones. Bird Observers' Association of Tasmania, Hobart, 1981.

Tasmanian Bird Report No. 11 (1981). Ed. W. G. Jones. Bird Observers' Association of Tasmania, Hobart, 1982.

Tasmanian Bird Report No. 12 (1983). Ed. W. G. Jones. Bird Observers' Association of Tasmania, Hobart, 1983.

Tasmanian Bird Report No. 13 (1984). Ed. W. G. Jones. Bird Observers' Association of Tasmania, Hobart, 1984.

Tasmanian Bird Report No. 14 (1985). Ed. W. G. Jones. Bird Observers' Association of Tasmania, Hobart, 1985.

Tasmanian Bird Report No. 15 (1986). Ed. I. Wilson. Bird Observers' Association of Tasmania, Hobart, 1986.

Thomas, D. G. 'Birds of the R.A.O.U. 1964 field outing, Bicheno district, Tasmania'. *Emu*, 64, 1965, pp. 220–8.

———. 'Waders of Hobart'. *Emu*, 68, 1968, pp. 95–125.

———. *Tasmanian Bird Atlas* (Fauna of Tasmania Handbook No. 2). University of Tasmania, Hobart, 1979.

Wall, L. E. and Thomas, D. G. 'Recent visits to wader grounds on the east coast of Tasmania'. *Aust. Bird Watcher*, 2, 1965, pp. 182–7.

South Australia

Abbott, I. 'The avifauna of Kangaroo Island and causes of its impoverishment'. *Emu*, 74, 1974, pp. 124–34.

——.. 'Is the avifauna of Kangaroo Island impoverished because of unsuitable habitat?'. *Emu*, 76, 1976, pp. 43–4.

Ashton, C. B. 'The birds of the Aldinga–Sellicks Beach Scrub'. *S.A. Ornithologist*, 29, 1985, pp. 169–79.

Attiwill, A. R. 'Birds breeding in Naracoorte district, 1941–1971'. *S.A. Ornithologist*, 26, 1972, pp. 59–64.

_____. 'A list of the birds of Big Heath'. *S.A. Naturalist*, 47, 1972, pp. 38–40.

Badman, F. J. 'Birds of the southern and western Lake Eyre drainage'. *S.A. Ornithologist*, 28, 1979, pp. 29–81.

_____. 'Birds of the Willouran Ranges and adjacent plains'. *S.A. Ornithologist*, 28, 1981, pp. 141–53.

Barritt, M. K. *Observations on Birds and Mallee Islands in the Murray Mallee*. Nature Conservation Society of South Australia, Adelaide, 1985.

Baxter, C. I. 'Birds of Belair Recreation Park'. *S.A. Ornithologist*, 28, 1980, pp. 90–8.

_____. 'Some remarks on the birds of Kangaroo Island'. *S.A. Ornithologist*, 28, 1981, pp. 172–4.

A Bird Atlas of the Adelaide Region. South Australian Ornithological Association, Adelaide, 1977. (Information for the 1977 Bird Atlas was collected between 1 April 1974 and 31 December 1975. A Bird Atlas covering the period 1 January 1984 to 31 December 1985 will be published in 1987 or 1988.)

Bransbury, J. 'Bird Report, 1977–1981'. *S.A. Ornithologist*, 29, 1984, pp. 121–68.

_____. 'Waders of littoral habitats in south-eastern South Australia'. *S.A. Ornithologist*, 29, 1985, pp. 180–7.

Carpenter, G. and Matthew, J. 'The Birds of Billiatt Conservation Park'. *S.A. Ornithologist*, 30, 1986, pp. 29–37.

Close, D. H., Bonnin, J. M., Waterman, M. H. and Connell, D. J. 'Breeding waterbirds on the Salt Lagoon Islands, South Australia'. *Corella*, 6, 1982, pp. 25–36.

Close, D. H. and Jaensch, R. P. 'Birds of the north-west of South Australia'. *S.A. Ornithologist*, 29, 1984, pp. 81–99.

Condon, H. T. *A Handlist of the Birds of South Australia*. 3rd edn. South Australian Ornithological Association, Adelaide, 1969.

Cox, J. B. 'A review of the Procellariiformes occurring in South Australian waters.' *S.A. Ornithologist*, 27, 1976, pp. 28–82.

_____. 'Bird Report, 1973–74'. *S.A. Ornithologist*, 27, 1976, pp. 102–9.

Cox, J. B. and Pedler, L. P. 'Birds recorded during three visits to the far north-east of South Australia'. *S.A. Ornithologist*, 27, 1977, pp. 231–50.

A Field Guide to the Flinders Ranges. Ed. D. Corbett. Rigby, Adelaide, 1980.

A Field List of the Birds of South Australia. 3rd edn. South Australian Ornithological Association, Adelaide, 1985.

Ford, H. A. and Paton, D. C. 'Impoverishment of the avifauna of Kangaroo Island'. *Emu*, 75, 1975, pp. 155–6.

_____. 'Birds of Para Wirra Recreation Park: changes in status over 10 years'. *S.A. Ornithologist*, 27, 1976, pp. 88–95.

Ford, J. 'Distribution and taxonomy of southern birds in the Great Victoria Desert'. *Emu*, 71, 1971, pp. 27–36.

Glover, B. 'Bird Report, 1971–72'. *S.A. Ornithologist*, 26, 1973, pp. 121–5.

_____. 'Bird Report, 1972–73'. *S.A. Ornithologist*, 26, 1975, pp. 175–80.

The Great Victoria Desert. Ed. P. Greenslade, L. Joseph and R. Barley. Nature Conservation Society of South Australia, Adelaide, 1986.

Hatch, J. H. 'The birds of Comet Bore (Ninety-mile Plain)'. *S.A. Ornithologist*, 27, 1977, pp. 163–72.

_____. 'Further notes on the birds of Kangaroo Island'. *S.A. Ornithologist*, 27, 1977, pp. 193–4.

Natural History of Kangaroo Island. Ed. M. J. Tyler, C. R. Twidale and J. K. Ling. Royal Society of South Australia, Adelaide, 1979.

Natural History of the South East. Ed. M. J. Tyler, C. R. Twidale, J. K. Ling and

J. W. Holmes. Royal Society of South Australia, Adelaide, 1983.

Parker, S. A., Eckert, H. J., Ragless, G. B., Cox, J. B. and Reid, N. C. H. *An Annotated Checklist of the Birds of South Australia. Part one: Emus to Spoonbills.* South Australian Ornithological Association, Adelaide, 1979.

Parker, S. A., Eckert, H. J. and Ragless, G. B. *An Annotated Checklist of the Birds of South Australia. Part 2A: Waterfowl.* South Australian Ornithological Association, Adelaide, 1985.

Parker, S. A. and Lashmar, A. F. C. 'Some notes on the birds of Kangaroo Island'. *S.A. Ornithologist*, 27, 1976, pp. 123−4.

Parker, S. A. and May, I. A. 'Additional notes on seabirds recorded in South Australia'. *S.A. Ornithologist*, 28, 1982, pp. 213−16.

Paton, P. A. 'A survey of the Adelaide Botanic Park and Gardens'. *S.A. Ornithologist*, 27, 1976, pp. 131−4.

‗‗‗‗. *Biota of the Coorong.* Department of Environment and Planning, Adelaide, 1982. (A study for the Cardwell Buckingham Committee.)

Pedler, L. P. and Ragless, G. B. 'Birds observed near Lakes Frome and Callabonna'. *S.A. Ornithologist*, 27, 1978, pp. 274−6.

Reid, J. 'Bird Report, 1976'. *S.A. Ornithologist*, 28, 1980, pp. 127−37.

‗‗‗‗. *Survey of Birds of the Bangham district.* Nature Conservation Society of South Australia, Adelaide, 1984.

Reid, J., Barritt, M. K. and Houston, C. *Birds and Habitats of the Bangham district.* Nature Conservation Society of South Australia, Adelaide, 1985.

Reid, N. 'Bird Report, 1975'. *S.A. Ornithologist*, 27, 1976, pp. 147−58.

Rix, C. E. 'The birds of Sandy Creek Conservation Park'. *Aust. Bird Watcher*, 6, 1976, pp. 209−22, 255−88, 330−54.

Whatmough, R. J. 'Birds of the Torrens River, Adelaide'. *S.A. Ornithologist*, 28, 1978, pp. 1−15.

Wheeler, J. R. 'The R.A.O.U. camp-out at Kangaroo Island, South Australia, 1959'. *Emu*, 60, 1960, pp. 265−80.

The Wildlife of some existing and proposed nature reserves in the Gibson, Little Sandy and Great Victoria Deserts, Western Australia (W.A. Wildlife Research Bulletin Number 8). Ed. N. L. McKenzie and A. A. Burbidge. Department of Fisheries and Wildlife, Perth, 1979.

Western Australia

Abbott, I. 'Avifauna of Black Point − Cape Beaufort area, S.W. Australia'. *W.A. Naturalist*, 13, 1976, pp. 158−9.

‗‗‗‗. 'Observations on the distribution of bird species on small islands near Perth'. *W.A. Naturalist*, 13, 1977, pp. 196−9.

‗‗‗‗. 'Breaksea Island, King George Sound, Western Australia'. *Corella*, 2, 1978, pp. 24−5.

‗‗‗‗. 'Michaelmas Island, King George Sound, Western Australia'. *Corella*, 2, 1978, pp. 26−7.

‗‗‗‗. 'Seal Island, King George Sound, Western Australia'. *Corella*, 2, 1978, pp. 30−1.

‗‗‗‗. 'Mistaken Island, King George Sound, Western Australia'. *Corella*, 2, 1978, pp. 32−3.

‗‗‗‗. 'Green Island, Oyster Harbour, Western Australia'. *Corella*, 2, 1978, pp. 34−5.

‗‗‗‗. 'Hamelin Island, Western Australia'. *Corella*, 2, 1978, pp. 38−9.

‗‗‗‗. 'Woody Island, Archipelago of the Recherche, Western Australia'. *Corella*, 5, 1981, pp. 62−3.

‗‗‗‗. 'The avifauna of the Porongurup Range, an isolated habitat in south-western Australia'. *Emu*, 81, 1981, pp. 91−6.

A Biological Survey of the Drysdale River National Park North Kimberley, Western Australia (W.A. Wildlife Research Bulletin Number 6). Ed. E.D. Kabay and

A. A. Burbidge. Department of Fisheries and Wildlife, Perth, 1977.

A Biological Survey of the Prince Regent River Reserve North-West Kimberley, Western Australia (W.A. Wildlife Research Bulletin Number 3). Ed. J. M. Miles and A. A. Burbidge. Department of Fisheries and Wildlife, Perth, 1975.

Breeden, S. and K. *Australia's North*. Collins, Sydney, 1975.

Bristowe, E. K., Laybourne-Smith, H. and Lendon, A. 'Further notes on Northern Territory and Kimberley birds'. *Aust. Bird Watcher*, 4, 1971, pp. 84−95.

Brooker, M. G., Ridpath, M. G., Estbergs, A. J., Bywater, J., Hart, D. S. and Jones, M. S. 'Bird observations on the north-western Nullarbor Plain and neighbouring regions, 1967−1978'. *Emu*, 79, 1979, pp. 176−90.

Christmas Island National Park Plan of Management. Australian National Parks and Wildlife Service, Canberra, 1985.

Crook, I. G. and Evans, T. *Thomsons Lake Nature Reserve* (Western Australian Nature Reserve Management Plan No. 2). Department of Fisheries and Wildlife, Perth, 1981.

Curry, P. *A survey of the birds of Herdsman Lake 1980−81* (Bulletin 105). Department of Conservation and Environment, Perth, 1981.

Daw, A. K. 'Canning Island, Archipelago of the Recherche, Western Australia'. *Corella*, 6, 1982, pp. 73−4.

Emory, K., Lantzke, I. R., Lambert, G. L. and Osborne, F. 'Waterfowl seen at Lake Claremont (Butler's Swamp) in the springs of 1972 and 1974'. *W.A. Naturalist*, 13, 1975, pp. 34−7.

Eyre Bird Observatory Report 1977−1979. Royal Australasian Ornithologists Union, Perth, 1980.

Eyre Bird Observatory Report 1979−1981. Royal Australasian Ornithologists Union, Perth, 1982.

Eyre Bird Observatory Report No. 3 1981−1983. Royal Australasian Ornithologists Union, Perth, 1985.

Fletcher, T. 'Birds of the Pilbara Region, Western Australia, 1967−1972'. *Aust. Bird Watcher*, 8, 1980, pp. 220−31.

Ford, J. 'Distribution and taxonomy of southern birds in the Great Victoria Desert'. *Emu*, 71, 1971, pp. 27−36.

Ford, J. and Sedgwick, E. H. 'Bird distribution in the Nullarbor Plain and Great Victoria Desert region, Western Australia'. *Emu*, 67, 1967, pp. 99−124.

Fullagar, P. J. 'Eclipse Island, Western Australia'. *Corella*, 2, 1978, pp. 21−3.

Fullagar, P. J. and van Tets, G. F. 'Bird notes from a winter visit to Eclipse Island, Western Australia'. *W.A. Naturalist*, 13, 1976, pp. 136−44.

Fuller, P. J. and Burbidge, A. A. *The Birds of Pelsart Island, Western Australia* (W.A. Department of Fisheries and Wildlife Report No. 44). Department of Fisheries and Wildlife, Perth, 1981.

Garstone, R. 'Notes on the birds of Pelsart Island, Abrolhos'. *W.A. Naturalist*, 14, 1978, pp. 62−4.

Gray, H. S. *Christmas Island Naturally*. Author, Perth, 1981.

Heron, S. J. 'The birds of Middle Swan, Western Australia'. *Emu*, 70, 1970, pp. 155−8.

Hnatiuk, S. H. 'Utilization of a Perth metropolitan wetland by water birds'. *W.A. Naturalist*, 16, 1985, pp. 75−8.

Howard, M. J. 'A Gascoyne Junction bird list'. *W.A. Naturalist*, 14, 1980, pp. 205−7.

——. 'Birds of the Carnarvon Region, Western Australia'. *Aust. Bird Watcher*, 10, 1983, pp. 86−97.

——. 'Notes on Birds of the Wittenoom area, Western Australia'. *Aust. Bird Watcher*, 11, 1986, pp. 247−57.

Jaensch, R. *Waterbirds in Nature Reserves of south-western Australia*. Department of Conservation and Land Management, Perth, 1987.

Jenkins, C. F. H. *The National Parks of Western Australia*. National Parks

Authority of Western Australia, Perth, 1980.

Job, R. 'A bird list from the Dryandra Forest'. *W.A. Naturalist*, 11, 1969, pp. 90−7.
_____. 'Birds seen at Pelican Point, 1966−1968'. *W.A. Naturalist*, 12, 1972, pp. 56−9.

Kitchener, D. J., Chapman, A. and Dell, J. *A Biological Survey of Cape Le Grand National Park* (Records of the Western Australian Museum, Supplement No. 1). WA Museum, Perth, 1975.

Kolichis, N. and Abbott, I. 'Gull Rock, King George Sound, Western Australia'. *Corella*, 2, 1978, pp. 28−9.

Lane, J. A. K. 'Saint Alouarn Island, Western Australia'. *Corella*, 2, 1978, pp. 36−7.

Lane, S. G. 'Avifauna of islands off Esperance, Western Australia'. *Corella*, 6, 1982, pp. 37−9.
_____. 'Cull Island, Archipelago of the Recherche, Western Australia'. *Corella*, 6, 1982, pp. 69−70.
_____. 'Observatory Island, Archipelago of the Recherche, Western Australia'. *Corella*, 6, 1982, pp. 71−2.

Lane, S. G. and Daw, A. K. 'Charley Island, Archipelago of the Recherche, Western Australia'. *Corella*, 8, 1985, pp. 119−20.

McNee, S. *Surveys of the Western Whipbird and Western Bristlebird in Western Australia, 1985* (RAOU Report No. 18). Royal Australasian Ornithologists Union, Melbourne, 1986.

Morris, K. D. and Knott, B. 'Waterfowl utilization of Lake Claremont during 1977'. *W.A. Naturalist*, 14, 1979, pp. 145−9.

Newbey, B. J. and K. R. 'Birds of Lake Cassencarry'. *W.A. Naturalist*, 16, 1985, pp. 45−8.

Reilly, P. N., Brooker, M. G. and Johnstone, G. W. 'Birds of the south-western Nullarbor Plain'. *Emu*, 75, 1975, pp. 73−6.

Saunders, D. A. and de Rebeira, C. P. *The Birdlife of Rottnest Island*. Authors, Perth, 1985.
_____. 'Seasonal occurrence of members of the suborder Charadrii (waders or shorebirds) on Rottnest Island, Western Australia'. *Aust. Wildlife Research*, 13, 1986, pp. 225−44.

Saunders, D. A., Smith, G. T. and de Rebeira, C. P. *Birds of Rottnest Island – a checklist*. Authors, Perth, 1981.

Sedgwick, E. H. 'Birds of the Harvey district'. *W.A. Naturalist*, 12, 1973, pp. 131−9.
_____. 'Birds of the Benger Swamp'. *W.A. Naturalist*, 12, 1973, pp. 147−55.
_____. 'Further notes on birds of Benger Swamp'. *W.A. Naturalist*, 14, 1977, pp. 22−4.
_____. 'Relative frequency of bird species in the Harvey irrigation area, Western Australia'. *Aust. Bird Watcher*, 11, 1986, pp. 146−9.

Sedgwick, E. H. and L. E. 'An Esperance bird list'. *W.A. Naturalist*, 2, 1950, pp. 111−18.

Sedgwick, L. E. 'Birds of the Stirling Ranges, Western Australia'. *Emu*, 64, 1964, pp. 7−19.

Serventy, D. L. and Whittell, H. M. *Birds of Western Australia*. 5th edn. University of Western Australia Press, Perth, 1976.

Smith, G. T. and Kolichis, N. 'Coffin Island, Western Australia'. *Corella*, 5, 1981, pp. 66−8.

Smith, L. A. and Johnstone, R. E. 'The birds of Lake MacLeod, upper west coast, Western Australia'. *W.A. Naturalist*, 16, 1985, pp. 83−7.

Stokes, T., Sheils, W. and Dunn, K. 'Birds of the Cocos (Keeling) Islands, Indian Ocean'. *Emu*, 84, 1984, pp. 23−8.

Storr, G. M. 'The avifauna of Rottnest Island, Western Australia'. *Emu*, 64, 1964−65, pp. 48−60, 105−13, 172−80.
_____. 'Rottnest Island, Western Australia'. *Aust. Bird Bander*, 14, 1976, pp. 35−8.

_____. _Birds of the Kimberley Division, Western Australia_ (Western Australian Museum Special Publication No. 11). WA Museum, Perth, 1980.

_____. _Birds of the Pilbara Region, Western Australia_ (Records of the Western Australian Museum Supplement No. 16). WA Museum, Perth, 1984.

_____. _Birds of the Gascoyne Region, Western Australia_ (Records of the Western Australian Museum Supplement No. 21). WA Museum, Perth, 1985.

Storr, G.M. and Johnstone, R. E. _Field Guide to the Birds of Western Australia._ WA Museum, Perth, 1979.

Tingay, A. and S. _Common animals in Kings Park and Perth gardens._ Kings Park Board, Perth, 1982.

van Tets, G. F. and P. A. 'A report on the resident birds of the Territory of Christmas Island'. _Emu_, 66, 1967, pp. 309–17.

Western Australian Bird Report 1982 (RAOU Report No. 6). Ed. T. G. D. Shannon. Royal Australasian Ornithologists Union, Melbourne, 1984.

Wildlife of the Dampier Peninsula, South-West Kimberley, Western Australia (W.A. Wildlife Research Bulletin Number 11). Ed. N. L. McKenzie. Department of Fisheries and Wildlife, Perth, 1983.

Woehler, E. J. _Breeding seabirds on the shore terraces Christmas Island, Indian Ocean_ (RAOU Report No. 12). Royal Australasian Ornithologists Union, Melbourne, 1984.

Northern Territory

Barnett, L. _A Checklist of the Birds of Kakadu National Park and the Alligator Rivers Region of the Northern Territory._ Australian National Parks and Wildlife Service, Darwin, 1980.

Boekel, C. 'Birds of Victoria River Downs Station and of Yarralin, Northern Territory'. _Aust. Bird Watcher_, 8, 1980, pp. 171–93, 205–11.

Breeden, S. and K. _Australia's North._ Collins, Sydney, 1975.

Bristowe, E. K., Laybourne-Smith, H. and Lendon, A. 'Further notes on Northern Territory and Kimberley birds'. _Aust. Bird Watcher_, 4, 1971, pp. 84–95.

Crawford, D. N. 'Birds of Darwin area, with some records from other parts of Northern Territory'. _Emu_, 72, 1972, pp. 131–48.

Estbergs, E. 'Bibliography on Northern Territory Ornithology'. _N.T. Naturalist_, 3, 1980, pp. 20–36. (An extensive review of the ornithological literature relating to the Northern Territory.)

Fisher, K. and L. 'Some observations of Jasper Gorge, Victoria River Downs, N.T.'. _N.T. Naturalist_, 8, 1985, pp. 13–16.

Klapste, J. 'Bird observations at Alice Springs sewage farm, N.T.'. _Aust. Bird Watcher_, 7, 1978, pp. 148–51.

Lendon, A. 'Notes on Northern Territory birds'. _Aust. Bird Watcher_, 2, 1966, pp. 191–206.

McKean, J. L. 'Birds of the Keep River National Park (Northern Territory), including the Night Parrot _Geopsittacus occidentalis_'. _Aust. Bird Watcher_, 11, 1985, pp. 114–30.

McKean, J. L., Bartlett, M. C. and Perrins, C. M. 'New records from the Northern Territory'. _Aust. Bird Watcher_, 6, 1975, pp. 45–6.

McKean, J. L. and Hertog, A. L. 'Some further records of uncommon migrant waders near Darwin, N.T.'. _N.T. Naturalist_, 4, 1981, pp. 10–12.

McKean, J. L., Thompson, H. A. F. and Estbergs, J. A. 'Records of uncommon migrant waders near Darwin, N.T.'. _Aust. Bird Watcher_, 6, 1976, pp. 143–8.

Parker, S. A. 'New and interesting distribution records of central Australian birds'. _S.A. Ornithologist_, 25, 1969, pp. 59–71.

Roberts, G. J. 'Records of interest from the Alice Springs region'. _S.A. Ornithologist_, 28, 1980, pp. 99–102.

_____. 'Observations of water-birds at the Alice Springs sewage ponds'. _S.A. Ornithologist_, 28, 1981, pp. 175–7.

Storr, G. M. *List of Northern Territory Birds* (Western Australian Museum Special Publication No. 4). WA Museum, Perth, 1967.

———. *Birds of the Northern Territory* (Western Australian Museum Special Publication No. 7). WA Museum, Perth, 1977.

Thompson, H. A. F. 'Notes on birds in the Darwin and northern areas of the Northern Territory'. *Sunbird*, 8, 1977, pp. 83–91.

———. 'Common birds of the Darwin suburbs'. *N.T. Naturalist*, 1, 1978, pp. 7–12.

———. 'The status of cuckoos *Cuculidae* in the Darwin area, Northern Territory, 1974–1980'. *N.T. Naturalist*, 5, 1982, pp. 13–19.

———. 'The status of kingfishers and their allies (*Coraciiformes*) in the Darwin area, N.T., 1974 to 1982'. *N.T. Naturalist*, 7, 1984, pp. 18–29.

Index